JOHN XXIII

Born into a simple family on the northern edge of Italy, Angelo Giuseppe Roncalli spent much of his working life in unfashionable diplomatic postings in Sofia and Istanbul until his surprise appointment as Papal Representative in Paris in the difficult years immediately after the Second World War. In 1953 he became Patriarch of Venice in what was assumed to be the last appointment of a man whom many considered worthy but naïve. When at the age of 77 he was elected to succeed the austere and aristocratic Pope Pius XII they called him the stop-gap pope, not expected to reign long or to do much.

Yet in a mere four and a half years Pope John XXIII transformed the Roman Catholic Church and gave a new image to the Papacy. He called the Second Vatican Council and gave it a vision for the future. People saw in him the Good Shepherd of the Gospels. When he died on June 3, 1963 the whole world mourned. No pope has been so loved.

What formed this man whose faith and hope illuminated the world? What did he believe? Would he have been horrified to see the long-term effects of his policies?

In this definitive biography Peter Hebblethwaite addresses such questions with important new evidence and insights from ecclesiastic and diplomatic sources, from the personal archives of Mgr Loris Capovilla, Pope John's secretary, and from private sources. He provides an outstanding contribution to the history of the Church in the twentieth century together with a moving account of a man with human failings and doubts who became a pope 'in whom the Church and the world were prodigiously blessed'.

Peter Hebblethwaite was born near Manchester in 1930. He joined the Society of Jesus at the age of seventeen. He studied philosophy in France, took a first in French and German at Oxford and read theology in Heythrop College. While assistant editor of *The Month* in 1965 he went to Rome to report on the final session of the Council. Early in 1974 he parted amicably with the Jesuits and began to write free-lance, including books on *The Runaway Church* and *Christian-Marxist Dialogue and Beyond*. His notable book *The Year of Three Popes* resulted in an invitation to become Vatican correspondent for an American paper, the *National Catholic Reporter*. This led him to Rome and allowed him to work on John XXIII. He has become well known for his television and radio broadcasts, articles, and reviews.

He is married to the Catholic writer Margaret Hebblethwaite. They have three children and live most of the year in Oxford.

'*Il passato non torna più. Dunque circonstanze nuove, provvidenze nuove*'
'The past will never return. New situations require new dispositions'

Angelo Giuseppe Roncalli, December 2, 1933

'*Defunctus adhuc loquitur*'
'He died, but is still speaking to us'

Hebrews 11.4, quoted by Roncalli in February 1921

JOHN XXIII

Pope of the Council

PETER HEBBLETHWAITE

GEOFFREY CHAPMAN
LONDON

A Geoffrey Chapman book published by
Cassell Ltd
1 Vincent Square, London SW1P 2PN

Paperback edition
first published 1985

ISBN 0 225 66477 1

British Library Cataloguing in Publication Data

Hebblethwaite, Peter
 John XXIII: Pope of the Council.
 1. John, XXIII *Pope*   2. Popes—Biography
 I. Title
 282' .092' 4   BX1378.2

Set in 10 point Bembo by Bookform, Formby, Merseyside
Printed and bound in Great Britain by Biddles Limited, Guildford

Contents

Acknowledgements

The author and publisher wish to acknowledge especially Mgr Loris Capovilla for his help and support without which this book would not have been possible. We are grateful to him for permission to quote from the many documents and publications listed in *Bibliography and Sources*. We wish to thank also the Italian publishers of his books especially Storia e Letteratura, Rome; Messagero, Padua; Grafica e Arte, Bergamo, and Istituto Paolo VI, Brescia. Thanks are also due to all those indicated in the sources to extracts quoted especially Libreria Editrice Vaticana (Actes et documents); Queriniana, Brescia (Alberigo); Vatican Polyglot Press (DMC); Cittadella Editrice, Assisi (Utopia).

Many of the photographs appearing in this book are from the personal archive of Mgr Capovilla and are reproduced with his permission. The author and publisher thank him for making the photographs available and also acknowledge the collaboration of Grafica e Arte, Bergamo.

Thanks are also due to Tony Spina for permission to reproduce the photographs credited to him.

Preface

Why another book about Pope John XXIII? Because in the words of Mgr Gianbattista Busetti who edited over a hundred new letters in 1982, 'the rich personality of Pope John has not yet been discovered' (*Pastore*, p. 30). Apart from over ten thousand printed pages, there are diaries, letters, sermons, memoranda, diplomatic reports, telegrams, *pensées*. This mass of material has scarcely been gone through, let alone digested and translated. We thought we knew Pope John well enough, but we didn't. It was high time for a biography.

The danger of biography was well put by John Henry Newman in a letter to his sister, Jemina: 'Biographers varnish; they assign motives; they conjecture feelings; they interpret Lord Burleigh's nods; they palliate or defend' (Martin, Brian, p. 152). Except in the Prologue, I have tried not to interpret 'Pope John's nods'. It would, however, be a bloodless biography that offered no interpretation. The worst effects of subjectivity can be mitigated by letting Pope John speak for himself. Hence the copious quotations from his letters, diaries and reported conversations.

To avoid cumbersome footnotes, references have been simplified as far as possible. A quotation is usually 'sourced' by the name of its author. Since the numerous works edited by Pope John's literary executor, Mgr Loris F. Capovilla, could not be usefully listed under his name, they have been given abbreviated titles. Capovilla's version of texts of sermons and addresses has been followed where available: in AAS and DMC Pope John was zealously over-edited.

In a not very distant future, Pope John will be known as 'Blessed Pope John'. We cannot pre-empt the event. In any case, he has already been canonised in the hearts of so many believers and unbelievers. The Sacred Congregation for the Causes of Saints has trawled through this same biographical material, but with a different set of questions and different criteria. The historian can only judge holiness by its effects. Pope John passes this test. As Cardinal Suenens put it: 'He made the supernatural seem natural' (Novak, p. 20).

Pope John developed throughout his eighty-two years. His name changes with him. He is successively Angelino, Angelo, Don Angelo, Canon Roncalli, Mgr

Roncalli, Archbishop Roncalli, his excellency, his eminence, Patriarch Roncalli, Pope John. I have not thought it disrespectful to call him plain Roncalli sometimes and plain John when he becomes pope. He never had much use for titles. Other dignitaries are treated in the same ruthlessly democratic way.

Though many people have been extremely helpful, the usual litany of thanks can be cut down to one name. This book could not have been written without the unfailing help of Mgr Capovilla, who was Pope John's secretary in Venice and in the Vatican and is now guardian of the Loreto Shrine. He has borne patiently with my questions and unearthed some vital documents. He is, however, not responsible for anything I have written, and will perhaps not like some of it.

I have done most of the translations myself, and revised existing translations to make John less wooden-sounding in English.

In the relationship between life and history there is a law of compression. Pope John lived for nearly eighty-two years. I have been working on his life for seven years. Depending on your habits or motives, you may take a week or a month to read it. Now that it is over, I feel rather sad: there will be a gap. Now read on.

Oxford, Whitsunday, June 10, 1984

Prologue

Introducing
Angelo Roncalli

I picture you, Pope John, in your vast bedroom on the top floor of the Apostolic Palace, not long before your eightieth birthday on November 25, 1961. Don't ask how I got in here. Let's just say your secretary, Don Loris Capovilla, fixed it (*Letture*, pp. 138–40, where John's room is described). He also tells me that your eyes are 'autumn-brown'.

You are standing at your window, overlooking St Peter's Square. Mgr Loris claims you never made that remark about 'opening the windows of the Vatican' that every journalist in the world has felt obliged to repeat. You didn't like draughts. Still, it was spiritually true, which is why they will go on saying it.

There goes the clock, chiming the hours with the Lourdes hymn – *Ave, ave, Maria*, part of the furniture left behind by Pius XII. Your light goes on at four a.m., sometimes three. You said to Cardinal Antonio Bacci: 'I always get up at four in the morning: it's my time'. 'That's too early', he said timidly, 'even your holiness needs sleep'. And you replied: 'Yes, yes, sleep. But I also need to work ... Anyway, one prays so well at first light, when everything is silent' (Bacci, p. 93). In your eightieth year you don't need so much sleep. But you like a nap in the afternoon, always in an armchair, never in bed.

You keep your diaries and personal notes in this drawer over here, carefully catalogued. You started keeping a diary in 1895 as a record of graces received and to check if you were keeping your resolutions. Leo XIII was Pope then and much older than you are now. He was still Pope when you arrived in Rome, a raw provincial from Bergamo, in 1901.

Only the other day you dug out your retreat notes for that year, and underlined the passage which said that you had been 'led to Rome by the hand of Christ so that I may live under the protection of his Vicar, alongside the fountain of Catholic truth and the tomb of his apostles, where the very soil is stained with the blood of his martyrs, and the air is alive with the odour of sanctity of his confessors' (*Journal*, p. 95). So you needed your intercessors in the Communion of Saints then.

There's not much of the 'odour of sanctity' in Rome today as the cars cross and

1

criss-cross out there in . . . Italy. Padre Pio, the famous Franciscan stigmatic, is said to emit 'the odour of roses'. You've never met him. You've nothing against him. But you prefer more ordinary and workaday virtues.

Mgr Loris tells me you have given him permission to publish your diaries after your death, because you believe they will help people. They will, no doubt, but it's a terrible risk, exposing yourself to the derision of the sophisticated, revealing your vulnerability, your naïveté. Some will fail to see that it is a record of growth in which the end crowns and explains the beginning. You want it to be known as the *Journal of a Soul* on the model of St Theresa of Lisieux's *Story of a Soul*. I hope people will realise it is the *journey* of a soul, and that it is only a tiny selection from what you called 'sixty years spent with pen in hand'.

You never throw anything away, do you? You have your Mass intentions for every day of your life, and all the dog-eared passports and visas you ever collected. Is this the peasant in you, squirrel-like hanging on to everything 'in case it might come in handy some day'. Or is it rather your historian's instinct for the *document*, however apparently insignificant? It's the latter, obviously. You said that every diocese should keep its archives in a professional way.

Then there are all these statues which make your room look like a shop for religious *bric-à-brac*, if you'll forgive me. But they all have a meaning for you. Opposite the crucifix is St Mark, patron of Venice and *interpres Petri* (some translate this as Peter's secretary or amanuensis). Mark is flanked by the two Johns, the Baptist and the Evangelist. It was to honour them, and your father, that when for the first time in your life you could give yourself a name, you chose John. At least that was what you said. I suspect there were other motives.

Madonnas abound, icons picked up in Turkey and Greece, mediaeval paintings from France. There's your favourite Madonna of Covadonga. 'Through Mary to Jesus': how many times have you preached on that theme? You had it inscribed above the door of your chapel in Istanbul.

We've still not finished with statuary. Sts Peter and Paul: obvious why they are here, the pastor and the missionary. St Joseph: that is your middle name, and very soon you are going to surprise the Council by including his name in the canon of the Mass. St Charles Borromeo: your whole life was bound up with him: he was archbishop of Milan, he visited your diocese of Bergamo, you were ordained in his church on the Corso here in Rome where his heart is still kept, and your five volume edition of his episcopal visitations – over there on the shelf, proudly displayed, was the main literary work of your life. Unless, of course, you have something else up your sleeve, like a letter about peace to the whole world.

Here is St Francis de Sales, whose quality of gentle self-acceptance and unforced naturalness you always liked. Leigh Hunt, an English writer you won't have read called him 'the gentleman saint'. One of your problems in France was that you imagined all Frenchmen were going to be like St Francis de Sales. Now St

Gregory Barbarigo is something of a poser. You knew all about him but I had to look him up. He started adult life as a Venetian diplomat, then became bishop of Bergamo, and emulated Charles Borromeo in implementing the Council of Trent. He was beatified in 1761. He then had to wait until 1960, last year, for you to canonise him. Yet another Italian saint, complained the foreign leader writers, but for you he was an old and familiar friend.

Then, of course, the obligatory busts of your immediate predecessors. Pius X and Pius XI both died in this very room. Benedict XV died next door. Pius XII died at Castelgandolfo. So much for statues.

The photographs are less daunting and more intimate. Your parents: Giovanni Battista Roncalli and Marianna Mazzola; the three deceased sisters, Teresa, Ancilla, and Maria, to whom you were so close; your three surviving brothers, Zaverio, Alfredo and Giuseppe who came to Rome for your coronation and fidgeted with their Sunday hats, solid peasants astonished to find themselves brothers of a pope. There's Giovanni, who died on September 18, 1956.

Now some clerics you'll have to explain for the uninitiated. Don Francesco Rebuzzini was the parish priest of Sotto il Monte. He baptised you the day you were born, taught you better than most of your teachers, and left you his copy of *The Imitation of Christ*. To be more accurate, you just took it as a memento. Canon Giovanni Morlani who helped pay for your studies. Mgr Vincenzo Bugarini, rector of the Roman seminary, who died in your flat in 1922. Fr Francesco Pitocchi C.SS.R., invalid and spiritual director at the seminary. Then a group photograph of your class looking earnest and puddingy. The layman with long flowing beard is Count Giovanni Grosoli, advocate of 'Catholic social doctrine', and owner at the start of the century of a newspaper chain.

But pride of place goes to Giacomo Radini Tedeschi, *your* bishop, whose secretary and biographer you were. You still describe him, with capital letters as '*il Mio Vescovo*'.

This lot of photographs show people you met in the East, beginning with the tragic King Boris and his Italian queen, Giovanna. These are all the bishops you ordained in Istanbul with their amazing variety of headgear. Here are pictures of the French bishops on your arrival as Nuncio in 1945 and on your departure in 1953: this would remind you how many had survived de Gaulle's 'purge'. Finally, two paintings: the cemetery at Sotto il Monte where most of your family is buried, but you will not be; and Cardinal Andrea Carlo Ferrari, archbishop of Milan, who died in 1921. A thesis has just rehabilitated him. He was your spiritual guide and friend.

So much of Pope John was gathered in what Capovilla calls his 'gallery'. His love for the saints of the Gospel, and the saints of the Counter-Reformation. His loyalty to his modest family. His fidelity to the past and Bergamo. The sheer length of his life and diversity of his experience – he had lived for long periods in five different countries. His neglect of his own achievements – none of the photographs are of himself – and his attentiveness to others. His need for 'models' of the priestly and episcopal ministry. His sense of continuity in the office he now held. But this collection was in the room of the man who happened to be pope. Anywhere else one might have been tempted to regard it as the dusty débris of a lifetime or the self-indulgence of a very old man who could not let go of the past. But he had already called an Ecumenical Council that would launch the Church on an adventure of hope. Far from being buried in the past, the old man had a keen eye for the contemporary world. He was always looking to the future, right up to the end. He was open to the Holy Spirit, whom he believed to be at work, burrowing away in the modern world. That was why he could surprise people.

His 'gallery' was like the iconostasis of an Orthodox church: the bond between earth and heaven in the communion of saints. People were always more important to him than ideas – or rather, he saw ideas as embodied in people: he was less interested in the decrees of the Council of Trent than in St Charles Borromeo who lived them as a reforming bishop. So here he was in the room where he will die, surrounded by saints, relatives, friends, and spiritual guides who were all involved in the onward rolling story of salvation.

Dates, anniversaries, birthdays were important to him. John entered salvation history in 1881. Also born in that year were four boys whose lives were to intersect with his own: Pierre Teilhard de Chardin, Jesuit, paleontologist, mystic; Ernesto Buonaiuti, his fellow-seminarian who was driven out of the Church as a 'Modernist'; Alcide De Gasperi, who spent the Second World War in the Vatican Library and emerged to lead the Christian Democrats; and Augustin Bea, another Jesuit, who became the founder-president of the Secretariat for Christian Unity. Angelo Giuseppe Roncalli came last in this vintage year. He was born on November 25.

Chapter 1

A village boyhood

Great things are done when men and mountains meet
(William Blake, *Gnomic Verses, 1*).

Angelo Giuseppe Roncalli was born at 10.15 a.m. on Friday November 25, 1881, in the matrimonial bed at Via Brusicco 42, in the village of Sotto il Monte, ten miles from Bergamo, just off the road from Bergamo to Lecco. The 1,200 inhabitants worked on the land, and lived in scattered, roomy but spartan houses, which all had individual names. The Roncalli house was known as the Palazzo. But there was nothing very grand about it. They shared the ground floor with their six cows.

Giovanni Battista (John Baptist) Roncalli and Marianna (née Mazzola) were contemporaries, both born in 1854. They had grown up together in Sotto il Monte and were married on January 23, 1877 when they were twenty-three. It may seem an odd time of year to get wed, but in this intensely Catholic milieu it was natural to marry on the feast of the Espousals of Joseph and Mary. It was also a time when there was nothing much to do on the farm. Their model was the Holy Family of Nazareth whose actual house was believed to have been angelically transported to Loreto on the Adriatic coast, sometime in the twelfth century. Their honeymoon treat was to walk to Bergamo and back.

Ten months after the wedding Marianna had her first child Caterina (1877–83), quickly followed by Teresa (1879–1954) and Ancilla (1880–1953). Above the matrimonial bed hung a large picture of Our Lady of Sorrows. In the earliest surviving photographs Marianna looks prematurely aged, and she went on to have eight more children after Angelo; but she out-lived her husband by nearly four years. He died July 28, 1935, and she followed him on February 20, 1939.

Angelo was born in the first-floor bedroom. The single window does not let in much light. The walls are four feet thick and outside runs the three-arched gallery which gives on to an inner courtyard. Next door, at right-angles, was 'the girls' room'. It was somewhat larger and boasted a cut-down version of a steeply inclined 'Renaissance' fireplace. A large kitchen and storerooms completed the other sides of the quadrangle. The house was better adapted to the summer months, when life could be lived out of doors.

On Angelo's birthday a bitter wind blew down from the Alps, and rain and hail made the roads muddy and impassable. Giovanni, his father, was delighted that, after three girls, he now had a son and heir, someone to help him in the back-breaking work in the fields.

Equally delighted was 'Uncle' Zaverio, the brother of Angelo's grandfather. In this patriarchal society, he was the senior male, the *reggitore*, the man in charge. Unmarried, literate and pious, his first concern was to have Angelino – the diminutive was used throughout his childhood – baptised as soon as possible. Naturally, Zaverio would be his godfather. He went off to find the parish priest, but he was away in Bergamo. Zaverio decided to wait for him in the cold and empty church. He had recited all fifteen decades of the rosary and the litany of Our Lady before Fr Francesco Rebuzzini got back. So as darkness fell Angelo was wrapped in shawls, carried down the wooden steps and taken the eighty yards to the church of Santa Maria di Brusicco. It belonged to the parish, but was not strictly the parish church (Cugini, p. 23). So not yet a day old Angelino was baptised in the name of the Father, the Son and the Holy Spirit. There was no fuss, no special ceremony or celebration. Uncle Zaverio joined the men for a glass of wine. 'Tonight we are thirty-two', he announced. He meant that there were already thirty-one members of this distinctly 'extended family'.

This hasty baptism was not due to anxiety about his state of health. Angelo Roncalli was baptised on the day of his birth not because he was a weakling but because it was the custom in the diocese of Bergamo. It was 'the way things were done'. Of the Roncalli children, ten were baptised on the day they were born; the remaining three, having been born during the night, were baptised the next day (*Secolo*, p. 23). It was the first instance of what was to become a pattern in the life of Angelo Roncalli. 'Nature' and 'grace' were not in opposition or conflict: instead they formed one inseparable interweave. He was born into a human family, and that very same day was 'born into grace', welcomed into the family of the Church. His civil existence began four days later when his birth was officially registered. The mayor's secretary distractedly got the order of names wrong and called him Giuseppe Angelo. This strengthened his bond with St Joseph.

Throughout Angelo Roncalli's life this nondescript church of Santa Maria di Brusicco remained his own church in a special sense. There his parents had been married. There he was baptised, and would make his first communion. And there he sang his first solemn Mass on August 15, feast of the Assumption, after his ordination in Rome. Built about 1450, it is, as Roncalli later said, 'not much to look at, but inside what richness' (*Letture*, p. 47). The walls bear traces of early frescoes that have not quite vanished. Now a plaque commemorates Sotto il Monte's most famous son.

The Roncallis had lived in the same village, though not the same house, since the fifteenth century. Angelo's historical researches later showed that the family had arrived in Sotto il Monte from the Valle Imagna to the north-west in the year

1429. A certain Martino Roncalli had built a solid-looking house which still exists. It was known as Camaitino, the dialect form of *Casa Martino*, Martin's house. Angelo's sense of history led him to rent this house and use it as a summer retreat – except when prevented by war – between 1925 and 1958.

The name Roncalli is said to derive from the Italian word *ronchi*, a terrace for vines cut into a hillside. It was an appropriate name because from the back of Camaitino Angelo could see the rising ground, vineyards below, woods above, which gave Sotto il Monte its name: beneath the mountain. At the top of the hill was the tower and church of San Giovanni, the earliest parish church. From what became his study at Camaitino Roncalli could see the new parish church and then the plain beyond, known as the 'island' (*l'Isola*) because it lay between the two rivers Adda and Brembo. The River Adda had once been the border between the Duchy of Milan, ruled by the Spaniards, and the Republic of Venice, to which Bergamo belonged until the French Revolution. It remained, in opera scenarios and sometimes in fact, the frontier between tyranny and liberty.

Like most of the inhabitants of Sotto il Monte, the Roncallis were share-croppers. Their landlords were Count Ottavio, Guido, Maria and Don Giovanni Morlani of Bergamo. Don Giovanni Morlani was prior of Santa Maria Maggiore in Bergamo. Later he became Angelo's patron and financed his seminary education. He ended his days as a canon of St Peter's in Rome.

The share-cropping system meant that the Roncallis led a precarious life. Half their produce went to the landlords, and they had to live off the rest. They extracted what profit they could from their five hectares. Their cows produced milk and veal. Their vines yielded a rough, non-exportable wine. They grew kale as animal feed. But the silkworms were their most important and fluctuating asset; mulberry bushes provided the leaves to feed them. Male and female tasks were clearly distinguished. The women looked after the silkworms, the kitchen-garden, the piggery and the chicken run (*Secolo*, p. 28), as well as the cooking. The men looked after the farm. It may sound like a formula for self-sufficiency, worked out over so many centuries.

But there were so many mouths to feed. The number sitting down to *polenta* – a dish of maize flour – was rarely less than thirty. Besides Giovanni Battista and his brood, there was his cousin Luigi who had ten children. Then there were the survivors of an earlier generation like Zaverio. Their whole economy was vulnerable to the hazards of the weather, price fluctuations, and to international trade factors that were entirely beyond their control. They were poor because they were dependent.

The main consequence of their poverty was that there were too many of them in too small a space. They lived on top of each other, and there were sometimes demarcation disputes. Without some sense of Providence, they could hardly have borne it. Another child meant another mouth to feed. But Angelo liked to recall the old Lombardy proverb, 'God blesses big pots more than little ones'. And he exhorted them in one of his earliest letters home to see the hand of God in their poverty. 'We must never feel saddened by the very straitened circumstances in which we live; we must be patient, look above and think of paradise . . . Think of what the good Jesus did and suffered for us. He endured great poverty, he worked from morning to night' (*Journal*, pp. 253–4). The Roncallis worked 'from morning to night', being woken in the morning by the Angelus bell from the village church or the Franciscan convent at Baccanello on the hill. 'Uncle' Zaverio was the chief waker-up: 'Time to get up, Angelo, "The Angel of the Lord declared unto Mary" ' (*Secolo*, p. 27). He gave the ritual answer: 'And she conceived by the Holy Spirit. Hail Mary, full of grace . . . '

As pope, Roncalli looked back on his childhood with affection but without romanticism:

> We were poor, but happy with our lot and confident in the help of
> Providence. There was never any bread on our table, only *polenta*; no wine
> for the children and young people; only at Christmas and Easter did we
> have a slice of home-made cake. Clothes, and shoes for going to church, had
> to last for years and years . . . And yet when a beggar appeared at the door of
> our kitchen, when the children – twenty of them – were waiting
> impatiently for their bowl of *minestra* [vegetable soup], there was always
> room for him, and my mother would hasten to seat this stranger alongside
> us (*Familiari*, I, p. 8).

The Roncallis knew their bible: 'Do not neglect to show hospitality to strangers, for thereby some have entertained angels unawares' (Hebrews 13.2). They treated the stranger as a Christian brother.

It was a traditional, patriarchal society that would change more in Angelo's lifetime than it had in the previous 400 years. Life was monotonous and laborious. But it had the rhythm of the changing seasons and took colour from the liturgical year. They celebrated the great feasts of the Christian calendar and went annually on pilgrimage by donkey-cart to the Madonna del Bosco (Our Lady of the Woods) across the River Adda (*Secolo* p. 27). But besides the feasts of Christmas, Easter and Pentecost, almost every month had its special 'devotion'. January was for the child Jesus; March, St Joseph; June, the Sacred Heart; July, the Precious Blood; October, the Rosary, November, the 'faithful departed'.

They were a close-knit family, the Roncallis, the largest in the village, but they were undemonstrative. 'Our old people were a little gruff [*burberi*]', Angelo later wrote to his brother Giuseppe, 'but they were serious-minded and good' (*Familiari*, I, p. 565). The same day he wrote to his sisters: 'In our family we are not much given to external shows of tenderness. And it's better that way' (*Familiari*, I, p. 566). They were like the North Italian peasants described in

Alessandro Manzoni's novel, *I Promessi Sposi* which is set in this region. They loved each other, but they had no concept of romantic love. When Renzo eventually brings his bride, Lucia, back to his village, after hair-raising adventures, the neighbours comment: 'After so much time and so many speeches, we expected something better than this . . . She's just a peasant girl like so many others' (*I Promessi Sposi*, p. 538). The men of Sotto il Monte had a practical, matter-of-fact attitude to marriage and children. They expected their women to be industrious and reliable. Emotion was diffused in daily fidelity.

The first important date in Angelino's life came when he was eighteen months. His brother Zaverio was born on May 12, 1883. Each Roncalli baby slept and was suckled in the matrimonial bed, moving out only when the next child came along. So, as Roncalli put it, 'when the child [himself] no longer needed his mother, it was grand-uncle Zaverio who looked after him and shared with him, by word and example, the attractive power of his religious spirit' (*Secolo*, p. 25).

Henceforward, Zaverio took charge of him. Zaverio was already fifty-nine (he lived to 88), had never had a family of his own, and, says Angelo, 'devoted himself to his godson, without intending to make a priest of him' (*Secolo*, p. 25). Zaverio, more usually known as Barba, was a reading man, familiar with the meditations of Fr Luis da Ponte S.J. and a subscriber to *l'Eco di Bergamo*, a Catholic paper founded in 1880 to counter 'secularist' propaganda. Through Barba, the whole family was kept in touch with a wider religious world. He was involved in the beginnings of Catholic Action in Bergamo. He read the *Bolletino Salesiano* published by Don (later Saint) John Bosco in Milan and was a 'co-operator' of the Salesians, a member of their 'extended family' (*Secolo*, p. 25). That meant that he was interested in new methods in the apostolate and the missions (or 'foreign missions' as they were then known). Zaverio cut out of the *Bolletino Salesiano* a picture of 'Our Lady Auxiliatrix' and placed it above Angelo's bed (*Secolo*, p. 34).

But Angelo's mother, Marianna, still played an essential role in his life. His earliest distinct memory is of her. It can be dated very precisely: November 21, 1885, feast of Mary's Presentation in the Temple. She set off for the shrine of the Madonna delle Càneve (or delle cantine). It was only about a kilometre away, but the track towards it wound uphill, and she had to coax along Teresa, 6, Ancilla, 5, Angelo, 4, while carrying Zaverio, 2, in one arm and Maria Elisa, 1, in the other. She was also pregnant again. By the time they reached the shrine Mass had already started and the tiny chapel was packed out. Unable to enter, she lifted up her children one by one and let them look through the grille of the window so that they could see the Madonna (*Secolo*, p. 47). Seventy-six years later, the whole episode was still fresh in the mind of Pope John. He recounted it to a group of pilgrims:

The shrine of the Madonna in my native village is at the end of a rough track, among the trees, at a point where one can go no further. It is still a place of pilgrimage today, especially for young people going off for military service or emigrants setting off to look for work. And old people go there too, so they can remember the kindness of Mary and renew their hope... My mother lifted me up and said: 'Look, Angelino, look how beautiful the Madonna is. I have consecrated you wholly to her'. This is the first clear memory that I have of my childhood (*Rosario*, pp. 15–16).

Marianna was then 28. He loved her with simplicity until her death and beyond: 'What a mother! what a simple and lucid conscience, that she kept into extreme old age, loved and venerated by her ten children and the whole parish' (*Secolo*, p. 25).

At the age of five (or six) Angelino learned his first poem by heart:

Quanto è soave al cuore	How sweet to the heart
il nome tuo, Maria.	is your name, Mary.
Ogni dolcezza mia	Every joy I have
Da quel tuo nome vien.	comes from your name.
Che bella idea di amore	What a fine idea of love
da quel tuo nome appresi	I learned from your name.
che bei desiri accesi	What fine desires are kindled
mi vien destando in sen.	and awakened in my breast.

He still knew it by heart in the last year of his life. A month before the Council began, he wrote it down in his Journal and explained:

These lines are the beginning of the first poem I knew as a child, and I learned it from the Second Reader then in use in the village school. I did my first year's schooling in the old village schoolhouse at the right-hand corner of the so-called Piazza, as you come from Guardina. Opposite was the shop [*Bütiga* – a local word] of Rosa Bonanomi and her sister, Marianna, who was an invalid. That must have been in 1886 or 1887. The next year, with the completion of the school buildings, the new school was opened at Bercio, and I was among the first to attend it (*Journal*, p. 347).

The 'new' school was the result of the Casati law on public education. Primary education, but for three years only, became in principle universal and compulsory; and state schools replaced the hit-or-miss system of parish schools.

Thus in 1888, when nearing seven, Angelino unwittingly found himself caught in ideological cross-fire. The new state schools were designed to forge a new national consciousness. While raising educational standards, they would also overcome the 'regionalism' that flourished in Italy and transform it into a truly modern state. The physical unity of the peninsula had been achieved with the final collapse of the Papal States in 1870; it remained to bring about its psychological unity. Thanks partly to the intransigence of Pius IX who declared himself 'the prisoner of the Vatican' and forbade Catholics, in a famous phrase, to be 'either electors or elected', the new Italian 'Establishment' was liberal and anti-clerical. Garibaldi, a notorious Freemason, had called his horse Mastai – Pius IX's family name. School-teachers were in the front-line of the battle for a new Italy, freed from ignorance and superstition.

The man entrusted with this missionary task in Sotto il Monte was a certain Signor Orbè, complete with monocle and side-burns. It was uphill work. Orbè had to teach the first three years together. He found the peasant children stubborn and slow on the uptake. His brightest pupil, Angelo Roncalli, was already under the spell of the parish priest, and preferred church to school. One incident is recorded. An essential feature of the Casati law on education was that schools should be regularly inspected. The inspector arrived at Sotto il Monte and asked the class: 'Which is heavier, a quintal of straw or a quintal of iron?' 'A quintal of iron', chorused the class, except for Angelo who said they weighed the same: a quintal is a quintal (Cugini, p. 37). It was not evidence of any great precocity. But he was different.

Signor Orbè was fighting a losing battle. Angelo was already serving early morning Mass daily. He was on hand to hold the salt and the candle whenever there was a baptism. In 1888 'Uncle' Zaverio was the only member of the parish to go to Rome for the fiftieth anniversary of Pope Leo XIII's priestly ordination. Angelo begged to be allowed to accompany him, but was considered too young (Cugini, p. 31). Zaverio had acclaimed Leo as *il Papa-ré* (the Pope–King). This was one of the first mass pilgrimages, made possible by the spread of the railways, which persuaded Leo that the workers wanted him to say something on 'the social question'; three years later, he published the encyclical *Rerum Novarum*, the 'workers' charter'. Zaverio's pilgrimage to Rome confirmed the judgement of the Roncallis that the Pope was being dealt with most scurvily and unjustly by the new Italian state. His portrait was a constant reminder of that injustice.

1889 was a most important year for Angelo. On February 13 he was confirmed by Mgr Camillo Guindani, bishop of Bergamo, at Carvico, the next-door parish. Two weeks later, March 3, *Laetare* Sunday, he made his first Communion. This was an exceptional privilege, since it was only later, in the pontificate of Pius X, that children were encouraged to make their first Communion so young. He remembered the day well:

> I was allowed to make my first communion at the age of eight, without any special ceremony, on a cold Lenten morning, in the Church of Santa Maria di Brusicco. Only the children, the parish priest, Rebuzzini, and his curate,

don Bortolo Locatelli, were present. I like to recall one detail which remained in my heart.

After the ceremony the neo-communicants went to the presbytery to be inscribed one by one in the Apostleship of Prayer; and Fr Rebuzzini gave me the honour of writing out the list of names of my companions. This was the first writing exercise I can remember doing, the first page of so many that would proliferate in half a century of living with pen in hand (*Secolo*, p. 26).

The Apostleship of Prayer had been promoted by the French Jesuit, Henri Ramière in 1861. Its members pledged themselves to say the 'Morning Offering' every day 'in union with the Sacred Heart'. They offered all the 'prayers, works and sufferings' of the coming day for some intention (e.g. the 'foreign missions') approved by the Pope. It was another bond with the 'lonely prisoner of the Vatican'. It was also a way of sanctifying everyday happenings.

One of Angelo's playmates was a girl cousin, possibly Camilla, daughter of Luigi. One day, as an adventure, they crept up a creaking staircase to see a dead old woman. They found her lying there in a darkened room, lit only by an oil lamp, her mouth agape, the last remaining tooth visible. Curiosity turned to terror. They fled (*Cugini*, pp. 32–3).

Angelo's father, Giovanni, played little part in his life. He was eclipsed by other 'father-figures', first Zaverio and then, increasingly, by Fr Rebuzzini. Giovanni, with his crew-cut hair and moustache, was austere and the least demonstrative member of the family. Angelo remembered him as an exemplar of industry and goodness: 'My father is a peasant who spends his days digging and hoeing, among other things, and I, far from being better than my father, am worth much less, for my father is at least simple and good, while I am full of malice' (*Journal*, p. 92). This remark, made in the fervour of a retreat at the Roman seminary in 1902, tells us more about himself than about his father. But there is one sun-lit memory of his father which remained with him till his death. On August 6, 1889, they walked together the six kilometres to Ponte San Pietro for the eleventh feast of the Bergamo Catholic Action. The church was large, resplendent with gold, lit by innumerable candles. For a child it was a magical spectacle. 'In the imagination of the country people', wrote Davide Cugini, 'Ponte San Pietro was like the Paris of the plains' (Cugini, p. 32). But Angelo was too small to see the parade, so his father hoisted him onto his shoulders. Pope John recalled the incident when, for the first time, on November 4, 1958, he appeared on the *sedia gestatoria* (or portable papal chair): 'Once again I am being carried, carried aloft by my sons. More than seventy years ago I was carried on the shoulders of my father at Ponte San Pietro . . . The secret of everything is to let oneself be carried by God, and so to carry Him [to others]' (*Letture*, pp. 53–4). Roncalli moved spontaneously from homely events to their spiritual meaning.

The Catholic Action rally at Ponte San Pietro on that sweltering August day is a reminder that the diocese of Bergamo pioneered this form of Christian 'presence to the world'. Catholics, on papal orders, had withdrawn from the official political life of Italy. But they remained concerned about 'social problems' and invented a network of movements and organisations to work for justice. Italian unification had not brought prosperity to the peasants and the working-class. High taxation and growing unemployment in the 1880s led to emigration to, in order of preference, Latin America, France, Tunisia, the United States. The statistics of emigration in Angelo's boyhood told the grim story: 1880, 20,000; 1887, 127,000; 1888, 196,000. When Catholics pointed out that the lot of peasants and workers was worse than before unification, they were accused of 'clerical demagogy' (Fonzi, p. 80). An alliance began to develop between the 'intransigents' – those Catholics who felt that the Pope had been ill-treated – and the peasants and workers. *Il Popolo* of Milan claimed that the new Italy had 'abandoned the peasant to the arbitrariness of capital which callously proceeded to exploit his isolation, his weakness and his poverty' (Fonzi, p. 82).

Thus, although Italian Catholicism of the 1880s was still associated with the reactionary conservatism that had marked the pontificate of Pius IX, it was beginning to have a potential for changing society. Angelo wrote the following note for Zaverio's funeral card: 'He was truly the 'upright man' of Holy Scripture . . . Throughout the vicissitudes of a turbulent age, to the end he held fervently and affectionately to the enthusiams of his youth: devotion to the Sacred Heart, the cause of Christ, the Church and the Pope, and he was a humble but convinced apostle of Catholic Action in this rural milieu' (*Familiari* I, p. 34). A typical institution of rural Catholic Action was the credit bank. It took the Roncallis twenty more years to save enough to get a mortgage on their own house and farm. They were sustained by the thought that to be property-owners, even on a small scale, was more in accord with human dignity than to be share-croppers. Some critics thought that Pope John's encyclical, *Mater et Magistra*, gave a disproportionate amount of space to agricultural problems. Now we know why.

Angelo later confessed that 'he could never remember the time when he didn't want to be a priest'. The first person he told about it was his cousin Camilla. He was both alarmed and delighted at the idea. He had observed Fr Francesco Rebuzzini very carefully, noting the way in hot weather the rigid white collar pressed round the neck and sweat gathered. But Rebuzzini had also been observing Angelo. One day he said to him: 'Don't be a priest, Angelino. You see how high and sharp this collar is. It digs into the neck and sometimes really hurts' (Cugini, p. 33). So he'd already guessed.

Rebuzzini had been at Sotto il Monte since 1872 and was to die there. He knew his peasant congregation intimately, and shared in their joys and anxieties. He was a cultivated man and illustrated the *mystique* of the Bergamo diocesan clergy: it little matters if one is in obscurity and one's talents are not given scope – provided one can be sure that this is God's will. As the fictional parish priest, not otherwise very admirable, says in *I Promessi Sposi*: 'It's the parish priests who pull the cart along' (p. 564). Angelo never forgot the text, alleged to be from St Bernard, which hung on the wall of Rebuzzini's study:

> Peace within the cell; fierce warfare without.
> Hear all; believe a few; honour all.
> Do not believe everything you hear;
> Do not judge everything you see;
> Do not do everything you can;
> Do not give everything you have;
> Do not say everything you know.
> Pray, read, withdraw, be silent, be at peace (*Journal*, p. 440).

Christian faith is here turned into a 'practical wisdom'. Rebuzzini was not to know it, but it was the perfect formula for a Vatican diplomat.

Meanwhile in 1890, Rebuzzini looked on as the Roncallis made rather a mess of Angelo's education. He had outgrown Signor Orbè's class, and his companions had already left school. Zaverio arranged for him to have Latin lessons with Don Pietro Bolis, parish priest of Carvico. An impressive and rather frightening man, with huge hands, he spared neither rod nor child. Angelo remembered this year with dread: 'After a few Latin lessons the merciless don Bolis invited me to translate Book I of Caesar's *Gallic War*. I had to translate and find the nominatives and the accusatives, and if I made a mistake, he gave me a slap. Sometimes he made me kneel down outside as a punishment for an error' (Cugini, p. 39). After a year of blows and Caesar, Angelo was considered ready to go as a day boy to the episcopal college at Celana, founded by St Charles Borromeo as a pre-junior seminary. This meant leaving home for the first time and staying with relatives at Ca'di Rizzi di Pontida. Even though he came back home for the weekends, he felt keenly the pain of parting and described it fifty years later to console a cousin who had left home to become a Sacred Heart sister: 'My father came with me as far as the Faida woods, just before the Villa d'Adda, where he left me to make my own way to Celana. I was alone in the woods and it was cold and, thinking of the warmth of the family I had just left, I felt for the first time the pain of separation' (*Familiari* I, p. 561). He pulled himself together. But he added that each time he returned home to Sotto il Monte

> My heart was endangered, and I had to leave as quickly as possible so as not to reveal my inner emotion. And it is right that this should happen. We are made to love each other eternally. It goes without saying that this feeling

should find expression and be a cause of sorrow. Thus we merit the sweetness of final reconciliation (*Familiari*, I, p. 561).

The Roncallis may have been undemonstrative. But they were vulnerable and not stoic. Angelo was nearly nine when he went to Celana. It was an unhappy year. He was younger than the rest of his class. He still had to walk six kilometres daily there and back. His Latin master, he recalled, 'managed to make me forget what little I knew: it was a disaster' (Cugini, p. 47). To make matters worse, the atmosphere at Ca'di Rizzi was unpleasant. As Capovilla puts it tantalisingly, 'it was unsuitable for one of his sensitivity and strict education' (*Cronologia*, p. 516). An argument about an inheritance had poisoned the atmosphere. So to spare him the humiliation of failure in the end-of-term exams and remove him from the obnoxious relatives at Ca'di Rizzi, he went home.

At this point Don Rebuzzini took over. Throughout the summer of 1892 he acted as Angelo's tutor and prepared him properly for entry into the junior seminary at Bergamo. It now became apparent that he had a taste and an aptitude for study that his previous teachers had failed to awaken. This period also brought them closer together. Rebuzzini had before him a ten-year-old who was setting off to the seminary just as he had done in the 1840s; and Angelo had found his father-figure.

Even so he remained deeply attached to his family and never lost touch with them on all his wanderings. He was a 'rooted' man, 'true to the kindred points of heaven and home'. In 1930 he wrote to his parents: 'Ever since I left home, towards the age of ten, I have read many books and learned many things that you could not have taught me. But what I learned from you remains the most precious and important, and it sustains and gives life to the many other things I learned later in so many years of study and teaching' (*Secolo*, p. 28).

Chapter 2

A Counter-Reformation seminary

In the art of your native city, you had already found all the lessons needed by
a diplomat. Your painters, above all the great portrait painter Lorenzo
Lotto, had taught you psychology; the statue of Torquato Tasso,
reminding you of the beauty of your hills, evoked the poetry of far-away
lands; and the tomb of Colleoni contained the remains of a man of heroic
wisdom. Your love of history led you to interest yourself in the glorious
series of Bishops of Bergamo

(President Vincent Auriol, January 15, 1953, *Mission to France*, pp. 181–2).

Hardly anything remains of the Bergamo seminary, junior and senior, where
Angelo Roncalli arrived as a boarder in November 1893, shortly before his
twelfth birthday. It was rebuilt on a lavish scale in 1964. As pope he was to have
consecrated the new chapel, but he died before it was completed. But the old
chapel remains, its dome the highest point of the hill-top city. Inside it has been
much re-arranged, the position of the altar has been changed, and so Our Lady in
Glory now looks down from the painted vault sideways on.

Yet the old chapel, with its heady evocative smells of incense and flowers,
remains the best link with Angelo Roncalli and the seminary founded by St
Charles Borromeo, archbishop of Milan, who had been canonised in 1610 as 'the
model of a bishop according to the Council of Trent'. Roncalli later wrote the
history of the Bergamo seminary: work on it plunged him into his favourite
historical period, the Counter-Reformation in Lombardy. After all, the city of
Trent was only a hundred kilometres away. But what he later wrote about, he
first experienced.

Trent brought about a revolution in studies for the priesthood. It invented the
seminary or 'seed-plot' as a place of formation, spiritual and theological, for future
priests. It caught them young. It segregated them from 'the world'. It tried to
protect them from whatever was troublesome or tempting. The very first entry in
Angelo's journal is a transcription of Trent's *Decretum de reformatione*, canon 1, on
the 'model priest':

> It is in every way fitting that clergy who have been called to the service of
> the Lord should so order their lives and habits that in their dress, gestures,
> gait and conversation and all other matters they show nothing that is not
> grave, controlled and full of religious feeling; and let them also avoid minor
> faults, which in them would be very great, so that their actions may win
> the respect of all (*Journal*, p. 4).

16

Naturally, this is not all that Trent says about the priesthood. It is the most external view of the priest, and emphasises respectability – not a quality greatly prized by the more relaxed mediaevals educated, if at all, in the turbulent world of the university. Even in 1575 a certain Canon Corregio was observed 'going through the streets of Bergamo playing a lute', and he was suspected of keeping a mistress (*Atti*, III, p. 223). That was precisely the sort of behaviour Trent tried, on the whole successfully, to put a stop to. Control and self-discipline were the key words. The spontaneous and the impulsive must be curbed. The natural man, the 'old Adam', must die the death.

The second entry in Angelo's journal is a quotation from Ecclesiasticus 3.27: 'It is good for a man to bear the yoke in his youth' (*Journal*, p. 4). He began his journal in 1895, at the age of fourteen, and kept up the practice for the rest of his life. Eighty printed pages are devoted to the minor seminary at Bergamo. It is the most fully documented period of his life. He began his journal on the advice of Canon Luigi Isacchi (1839–98), who held the office of spiritual director. Its purpose was three-fold: to remind himself of his resolutions, to record his moments of grace or spiritual insight, and to maintain a critical weather-eye on his faults and back-slidings. The latter function tended to prevail. In the 1970s diary-keeping as a means of spiritual progress was 'discovered' in the United States (the Progoff method). But in Bergamo in the 1890s not all spiritual directors agreed with it. In November 1898 Isacchi died and his successor, Canon Quirito Spampatti, was distinctly cool. Angelo noted: 'As for my habit of making these jottings, as I had done from last year until this last month, the new director does not seem to think so highly of this as the other did. In short, one thinks in one way, one in another. That is why there is such a gap between my last entry and today's' (*Journal*, p. 62). But despite this, sixteen-year-old Angelo carried on. He needed this communication about the things of God.

He was not writing for posterity. We can only eavesdrop on his inner conversation. The portrait that emerges is of a serious-minded, intense, painfully scrupulous adolescent, tempted only by gossip or *gourmandise*. His aim in life is to become a holy priest. The only 'events' were the tonsure, June 18, 1895, by which he became officially a 'cleric'; the minor orders of door-keeper and reader, July 3, 1898; the minor orders of exorcist and acolyte, June 25, 1899. We learn very little about his literary studies during the first five years or the content of the theology that he began on November 3, 1898. He led a sheltered life on which public events hardly impinged: no newspapers were allowed. The seminary was a fortress, a self-contained world of its own.

But his self-portrait is incomplete. Simply to live in Bergamo was a liberal education. History lay about him as he walked round the city, never without a companion. The seminary was at the highest point of the upper city with its narrow streets, tiny squares, massive sixteenth century walls, plashing fountains, and everywhere the lion rampant of St Mark as a reminder that Bergamo had known Venetian rule for 350 years. Legend said that St Alexander, the city patron, had been killed in 288 on the very spot where the church of San Alessandro in Colonna now rose. At the Congress of Vienna Bergamo was assigned to Austria. Italian patriots had been executed in the *fara* (an old Longobard word for an open space) until the arrival of Garibaldi in 1859. Looking down from the seminary garden, Angelo saw the new city, with its broad, tree-lined avenues, the railway station linking Bergamo to Milan and Brescia, and the textile factories beyond.

Roncalli came to love Bergamo and would talk endlessly about its beauties. Though it had never had a university or a court, it was justifiably proud of its musicians and artists. Gaetano Donizetti, the composer of over sixty operas, had lived and died in via Arena, a stone's throw from the seminary. Painters like Lorenzo Lotto, Paolo Cavagna and Gian Battista Tiepolo had filled the countless churches with martyrdoms and madonnas. The greatest Bergamesque painter was Giovanni Battista Moroni, best known for his portraits, astute psychological studies of priests, nobles and sometimes ordinary tradesmen in the last quarter of the sixteenth century. Moroni's sitters were the contemporaries of Charles Borromeo, who had visited and reported on every parish and religious house in Bergamo in 1575. Angelo did not yet know that editing the *Acta* of St Charles Borromeo would be the main scholarly work of his life.

Yet in his walks around the city, in cassock and soup-plate hat, he was laying the foundations for that intimate knowledge of its churches and piazzas that would console him in exile and sustain his research. It is true, that, as a seminarian, he had to keep 'custody of the eyes', another form of self-discipline. He resolved to behave 'with the greatest decorum when I am passing through towns or other places full of people, never looking at posters or illustrations or shops which might contain indecent objects, bearing in mind the words of Ecclesiasticus, "Do not look around in the streets of the city; nor wander about its deserted sections" ' (*Journal*, p. 17). His rigorism extended at that date even to religious art which might, 'however slightly, offend against piety': one might be drawn to brood morosely over the repentant Magdalen's previous career rather than give thanks for her conversion. Yet it is difficult to believe that Angelo walked round Bergamo looking merely at his boots.

His seminarian's eye was disapproving of much of what he saw. His 'image' of Bergamo in 1895 is often the projection of fears instilled in him by his spiritual guides. So he exhorts himself to avert his gaze especially from 'those who hang around inns, or are intemperate, particularly in drinking; those who wish to be admired as revengeful, quarrelsome men, swift to draw a weapon . . .; those who go to gaming houses or gamble in public' (*Journal*, p. 7). These deplorable characters of 1895 could have stepped right out of the pages of the *Acta* of Charles

Borromeo – except that then they included priests. In 1575 the parish priest of San Alessandro in Colonna complained that 'clergy were to be seen in the square, talking to riff-raff, that the servants of the canons played cards while their masters sang office, that these same servants bore arms even while they vested the canons, and that too much noise came from the sacristy of San Vincente and Santa Maria Maggiore' (*Atti*, III, pp. 220–1). The Counter-Reformation was omnipresent. Angelo met it again in what became his favourite novel, *I Promessi Sposi* by Alessandro Manzoni. He was already reading it – selectively – in the seminary. It is set around 1630 when Frederigo Borromeo, cousin of Charles, had succeeded him as archbishop of Milan. 'It is not only the first modern Italian novel; for Italy it is all Scott, Dickens and Thackeray rolled into one' (Archibald Colquhoun, *The Betrothed*, Dent, London, 1951, p. 575). That is kindly meant. *I Promessi Sposi* also made an important contribution to the formation of a common Italian language and style, making Tuscan the norm. This is why it became a schoolbook. For Angelo, as we have already seen, it held an additional interest because it was set in familiar territory. But he valued above all Manzoni's religious spirit: sincere, serious, crowned by compassion and charity. In the 1930s he recommends the reading of its final chapter to a troubled priest. In Manzoni he found a style, a spirituality, a psychology and a humour that met his needs and saved him from narrowness.

The bishop of Bergamo, Camillo Guindani, lived at this date in the seminary fortress. Looking out from its ramparts, he saw rather more than Angelo. He knew that the problems of contemporary Bergamo were not knife-drawing or gaming in the streets so much as strikes and lock-outs. Guindani was a leader in social action. In 1893 he published a full commentary on Leo XIII's *Rerum Novarum* which stressed the novelty of this somewhat ambivalent encyclical and applied it to the local circumstances. In 1895 he held a follow-up meeting at the seminary to see what had been achieved.

It really was astonishing. Bergamo's claim to lead Catholic Action in Italy was vindicated. Fr Niccolò Rezzara, the priest in charge of social action, reported that the diocese had over 200 associations with over 40,000 members. They included 50 study circles, 104 mutual assistance projects, 43 co-operatives and credit banks (Dreyfus, p. 32). In this way the Church in Bergamo, though still excluded from politics, demonstrated that it was concerned for justice as well as charity. It sought to serve the poorest members of society, victims of the unrestrained *laissez-faire* capitalism deplored by *Rerum Novarum*. If, in the process, it dished the socialists, that was a bonus, not the aim. Angelo was already inscribed in the diocese of Bergamo as a 'cleric'; if he wanted to be a priest in the diocese his theology would have to have a social dimension. 'Uncle' Zaverio had disposed him to understand that. There was already talk of 'Christian democracy'.

But not all the Bergamesque clergy were united behind Bishop Guindani (see *My Bishop*, p. 129). He was the former pupil and special friend of the bishop of

Cremona, Geremia Bonomelli, the stormy petrel of the Italian episcopacy. One of his pamphlets, *Italy and the Reality of Things*, had been placed on the Index of Forbidden Books in 1889. It was a plea for reconciliation between the papacy and the new Italian state. The 'conciliarists' held that the pope should cease sighing for the *ancien régime*, accept the loss of the Papal States as a liberation for the Church, and permit Catholics to take their place in Italian political life. Seen in this light, Catholic Action and the lay movement known as *Opera dei Congressi* were a dress-rehearsal for the return to full political involvement. But that was not the mood in the Vatican where 'intransigence' still prevailed. Bonomelli, in this as in other matters, had said the right thing at the wrong time. Some felt that Guindani, too, was excessively 'modern' and conciliatory. From the time he began to think about it, Angelo was spontaneously 'conciliarist'.

He caught a glimpse of the Italian Church as a whole in September 1895 when he spent five days in Milan for the third National Eucharistic Congress. It was a display of Catholic muscle as well as an act of piety. There he saw for the first time Cardinal Andrea Ferrari, archbishop of Milan, his metropolitan and later spiritual guide. Also present among a galaxy of cardinals was Giuseppe Sarto, patriarch of Venice and the future St Pius X. Angelo recorded one of his edifying remarks: 'I was much more fortunate and lived much more happily when I was a simple country curate than now when I am seated on the Patriarchal throne of Venice' (*Journal*, p. 436). That foreshadowed the melancholy that Sarto brought to his tense pontificate.

Milan was already the financial and publishing capital of Italy. The Banco Ambrosiano was founded in this same year, 1895, by the far-sighted Mgr Giuseppe Tovini, for the support of charitable and pious works; prospective share-holders had to produce their baptismal certificates. *Il Popolo*, the Catholic daily, was the rival of the 'liberal' *Corriere della Sera*. The most dynamic – and most menacing – political movements began there. Angelo was more struck by Milan's historical associations. Here St Ambrose had baptised St Augustine on Easter Sunday 387. At an altar on the left-hand side of the cathedral was the crucifix carried in procession by both Charles and Frederigo Borromeo as a talisman against the plague. If his heart always remained in Bergamo, Milan, with its prestigious Ambrosian Library, contributed to his intellectual formation. He always thought of himself as a 'Lombard': '*Anch'io sono Lombardo*' (*Quindicesimo anniversario*, p. 50).

Back in the seminary after this five-day excursion, Angelo copied down the 'Little Rules' of the Sodality of the Annunciation of Mary Immaculate. As a cleric, he was automatically enrolled in it. The Sodality, originally a kind of Jesuit 'third order', was an association for developing the spiritual life among laypeople. It had a long tradition in the Bergamo seminary. Its records date back to the seventeenth century. By the time Angelo arrived it was still a flourishing institution with its statutes, periodic meetings, election of officers and special feast-days. But in Bergamo it had another more surprising feature. It had two levels of membership: ordinary members and a special group from whom more was expected. Only the élite received the hand-written 'Little Rules' designed for 'a seminarian who wishes to advance in the way of perfection'. So already Angelo was regarded as a spiritual high-flyer. He belonged to an élite of an élite.

It might be thought that the Sodality, conceived in this way, would lead straight to favouritism, jealousy among outsiders, and arrogant smugness on the part of the elect. But it makes more sense when we recall that not all the students at the Bergamo Seminary had the same degree of commitment. Some did not intend to become priests and were merely at the seminary for their high-school education; others were clerical students but lived at home and came to the seminary only for classes and worship; Angelo was a full-time boarder with no life outside the seminary. It was the 'secular' students who were most likely to be heard 'singing love-songs', a hazard that recurs with some frequency in Angelo's notes. So he was in a sense 'more committed' than most of the others. His journal makes it clear that for him the moral life was not a matter of choosing between good and evil; that question had already been decided. It was a matter of opting for the better and the best, according to the Ignatian formula, *Ad majorem Dei gloriam*, 'to the *greater* glory of God'.

It was in this spirit that Angelo, not content with the 'Little Rules' provided for him, devised his own 'Rules of Life' which were more detailed and covered every aspect of his waking time. It was a rigorous and exhaustive programme. He maps out what he has to do daily, weekly, monthly, annually, concluding with a final section devoted to 'at all times'. Angelo's 'Rules of Life' were rules for life. Capovilla says: 'He copied them out by hand, in minute writing, kept them always by him and constantly observed them, even when he was Pope' (*Journal*, p. 4). So however fastidious the exercise, some account of his 'Rules of Life' must be given here. They mattered so much to Angelo.

Daily he devoted 'at least a quarter of an hour to mental prayer' on rising. He heard or preferably served Mass, read 'thoughtfully' a whole chapter of *The Imitation of Christ*, examined his conscience and prepared the next day's meditation before going to bed. In addition there were visits to the Blessed Sacrament, five Hail Marys and Our Fathers 'between six and nine o'clock in the evening in honour of the five wounds' (of Jesus on the cross), not to mention 'brief, fervent invocations' (known at the time as 'ejaculatory prayers'). He says nothing about his studies in the 'Rules of Life' but in 1896 seemed to regard them as an opportunity for ascetical self-denial: 'As regards studies I will apply myself to them with love and enthusiasm to the best of my abilities, taking care to give due attention to all subjects without distinction, never offering the excuse that I do not like any of them' (*Journal*, p. 14).

His *weekly* tasks included confession and communion. The fact that he went to Mass daily but to Communion only weekly was a relic of Jansenist influence in Bergamo: Pius X opened the way to daily communion a decade later. He fasted on Fridays and Saturdays, when he would also perform some penance.

Monthly he saw his spiritual director, set aside a day 'for more profound recollection' and reflection on how well he was keeping his rules. He invited one of the most 'exemplary and zealous youths' to tell him 'with frankness and charity about any faults he had noticed'. He also chose a special patron saint for each month.

Annually, he would make a retreat in the seminary, choosing Carnival time in order to be praying harder while the world revelled. He would make an annual general confession. A touch of humanity comes in with the resolution at the end of term 'to give some souvenir to his companions and accept one from them, to help us all pass the time profitably in the Lord' (*Journal*, p. 7). Roncalli was, in fact, always good at remembering anniversaries and feast-days, and performing small thoughtful kindnesses. Life, as the spiritual writers said, is made up of little things.

Angelo stated his project in his 'Rules of Life'. But it was threatened on all sides. 'Occasions of sin' lay in wait to entrap him. Life became a kind of obstacle-race in which coming through unscathed was the goal. His seminary companions posed the first threat, because dangerous 'particular friendships' might arise. So he counter-attacks: 'On no account or pretext must you use the intimate *tu* in talking together or lay your hands on each other, or run after, push or strike each other, even in jest, nor should you indulge in other careless actions, words or gestures which might provoke scorn or be the cause of even greater danger' (*Journal*, p. 7). He exhorts himself to avoid 'those whose speech contains impure suggestions, filthy or cynical words, or dialect expressions' (*Journal*, p. 7). Later he relented a little about dialect and the intimate *tu*, but he remained punctilious in such matters.

Women generally represented a major source of trouble. So they too were simply to be avoided, *vitandae*. Nor was he talking merely about seductresses, *femmes fatales* or women of the streets. The ban also applied to relatives and 'holy women': 'I will be particularly cautious, avoiding their familiarity, company or conversation, especially if they are young women. Nor will I ever fix my eye on their faces, mindful of what the Holy Spirit teaches us: "Do not look intently at a virgin, lest you stumble and incur penalties for her" ' (*Journal*, p. 18). This was yet another quotation from Ecclesiasticus (9.5). It did not occur to Angelo to wonder why this rather world-weary Jewish sage should be expected to throw light on preparation for the Christian ministry. He took it all aboard.

He also believed that he was called to 'holy purity' as a condition of 'the angelic ministry of the priesthood' (*Journal*, p. 16). Angelo Roncalli strove to be angelic.

Yet 'angelism', the denial of the embodied human condition, is a heresy. But he was merely echoing one of the assumptions of his age. His models were the 'three angelic youths', three Jesuit students who died young: Aloysius Gonzaga (1568–91, beatified 1605, canonised 1726); Stanislaus Kostka, a Pole (1550–68, beatified 1660, canonised 1726); and John Berchmans, from the Low Countries (1599–1621, beatified 1865, canonised 1888). Though subsequent biographers, notably C. C. Martindale S. J., scraped off the hagiographical barnacles and showed that each of them was an individual personality of considerable strength and charm, in the 1890s they were presented as anaemic plaster saints. Alleged to be the patrons of youth generally, they were of little use except to young religious or seminarians.

But precisely, Angelo was a seminarian, always a seminarian, never off-duty, always being watched: 'I am never alone, even when I am by myself: God, Mary and my Guardian Angel see me; and I am always a seminarist' (*Journal*, p. 19). Even his sleep was supervised. He dealt with the problem of what moralists called 'involuntary nocturnal emissions' in the recommended manner:

> I will likewise observe the greatest modesty with regard to my own body at all times . . . To remove any occasion for these movements, however innocent, at night before falling asleep, I will place the rosary of the Blessed Virgin round my neck, fold my arms crosswise on my breast, and see that I find myself still lying in that position in the morning (*Journal*, p. 18).

In this way, he believed, he would remain 'pure as an angel'. And since self-indulgence in one realm of physical appetites so easily leads to laxity in another, he will be austere in eating and drinking as well: 'As regards the drinking of wine, I will be more than moderate, because in wine lies the same danger as in women: "Wine and women lead intelligent men astray" ' (*Journal*, p. 18). Inevitably the tag came from Ecclesiasticus (19.2).

Clearly Angelo had a long way to go to reach spiritual and human maturity. The Bergamo seminary was for him a 'total institution' as defined by Michael Hill: 'Total commitment is demanded of its members, and considerably more obedience than is required in the Church at large' (*The Religious Order*, p. 6). Angelo was consciously trying to programme his life according to the pre-established, tradition-stamped model. One critic, Paul Johnson, can hardly contain his incredulity at the craziness of it all: 'The wonder is that Roncalli survived this debilitating atmosphere of static, mindless religiosity, with his intellectual common sense, and his spontaneous spirituality, more or less intact' (Johnson, p. 16).

Such astonishment is misplaced. Angelo's mature spirituality was a development, not a rejection, of his seminary formation. He led a rigorously structured and regimented life. But, as John Henry Newman remarked, in religious matters we may have to begin with externals; the fault would lie not in starting there, but in remaining there and assuming that externals were the whole of religious life. He was obeying rules, but he was also assimilating values. At the age of fourteen he already knew that fidelity to the discovered will of God was at the heart of the Gospel. So he could write: 'Let your will be mine, and let my will ever respond to yours, in perfect harmony. Let me desire what you desire and hate what you hate, and let me desire and hate nothing but what you desire and hate. Let me die to all that is of this world and for your sake rejoice to be despised and ignored in this generation' (*Journal*, p. 11). It was an echo of the Beatitudes: 'Blessed are those who mourn, for they shall be comforted . . . Blessed are the pure in heart, for they shall see God. Blessed are the peacemakers, for they shall be called sons of God' (Matthew 5.4, 8–9). In maturity he loved to quote St Gregory Nazianzen (whom Dante echoed): *Voluntas Dei, pax nostra* (God's will is our peace). In adolescence he characteristically preferred to quote Thomas à Kempis: 'You are the true peace of the heart, you are its only resting place . . . In this peace, in this very peace which is yourself, the one, supreme, eternal God, I will sleep and rest' (*Journal*, p. 11; *Imitation*, Book 3, ch. 15). On this point he never wavered; it provided the contemplative ground-bass of his life.

There is no evidence to suggest that Angelo was miserable at the seminary. Life was austere, but he was where he wanted to be. On the other hand the long summer holidays spent with his family at La Colombera – they had moved to this nearby but larger eighteeen-roomed house on November 21, 1893 – proved increasingly irksome. He had a growing sense of misunderstanding and alienation. The root of the trouble was that some members of his family thought he 'wanted to be a priest to escape having to work on the land' (*Familiari* I, pp. 482–3).

The first sign of trouble came in June 1898. A busybody Franciscan from Baccanello, who was always dropping in at La Colombera, picked up the domestic gossip. It was said that Marianna was giving her eldest son preferential treatment and choicer food. Angelo was not enjoying his holiday anyway. He resented the constant bickering, and was frustrated at not being able to write for two days running, first because he had no candle and then because he had no ink (*Journal*, p. 38). He had neither sought nor expected any preferential treatment. The matter would have ended there, had not the Franciscan taken it into his head to delate Angelo to the rector of the seminary, the austere Don Giacinto Dentella. By the time the tale-bearers had done their work, the original charge had been transformed. Angelo noted: 'My superiors have received an account, I think exaggerated, of my having behaved arrogantly during the vacation, and I have been duly rebuked. So I have had to humble myself against my will' (*Journal*, p. 25). On July 19, 1898, back home again, he walked over to Baccanello to meet the friar who had delated him; but he was coldly received (*Journal*, p. 30). It was a minor injustice, but keenly felt. The atmosphere of La Colombera was subtly poisoned. Home was no longer the same.

He could always turn to Don Rebuzzini, his old teacher, the parish priest. On Saturday evening, September 24, 1898, he met Rebuzzini and exchanged routine greetings with him: *Arrivederci*. But next morning, while preparing for Mass, Don Rebuzzini tried to kneel down, fell back on his head, and died. Angelo saw him lying there on the ground, 'his mouth open and red with blood, his eyes closed' (*Journal*, p. 49). He seemed 'like a statue of the dead Jesus, after he had been taken down from the cross'. This was not just pious hyperbole: the theme of the priest as *alter Christus*, another Christ, was commonplace in Counter-Reformation piety.

Angelo was 'heart-broken', but instead of weeping he felt turned to stone (*Journal*, p. 49). He drew what lessons he could. It was consoling to think that 'although death took him unawares, he had been preparing for it for the last seventy-three years' (i.e. all his life). 'If only my death could be like that', wrote the sixteen-year-old Angelo, meaning 'while preparing for Mass'. He felt orphaned by the death of Fr Rebuzzini. The expression occurs three times within a few pages of his journal. 'I am left an orphan to my immense loss' (*Journal*, p. 51), he wrote on Tuesday morning, September 27; and two days later he sketches out a prayer with an allusion to John 14.18: 'O God, do not leave us orphans'; and finally, 'if my Father has gone, Jesus is still here and opens his arms to me, inviting me to go to him for consolation' (*Journal*, p. 51).

Now since his own father, Giovanni Battista, was still very much alive, this language can only mean that the Church had replaced his family as his 'true home', and the spiritual paternity of Don Rebuzzini had eclipsed the physical paternity of his actual father. Nor was this a feeling Angelo had merely when he was sixteen and impressionable. In 1962, rereading his account of the death of Rebuzzini, he added a heading in which he called him 'the saintly guardian of my childhood and vocation' (*Journal*, p. 52). Don Rebuzzini was his first 'model' of the priesthood – and he found that he could not improve on it. Rebuzzini had spent the last twenty-six years of his life at Sotto il Monte. The life of an obscure diocesan priest, living contentedly in this insignificant pre-Alpine village, could be a path to holiness that put into perspective ecclesiastical ambition and careerism.

Don Rebuzzini bequeathed to him his copy of the *Imitation of Christ*. Or to be more truthful, Angelo managed to purloin the book while the effects were being cleared up ('I have succeeded in obtaining' – *Journal*, p. 51). It was a Latin edition, published in Venice in 1745, with notes by Enrico Sommali S. J. Angelo already knew the *Imitation of Christ*, the most widely diffused and translated book of spirituality ever published. But he treasured this well-thumbed copy because Francesco Rebuzzini had used it since he was a seminarian, in Bergamo, so many years before. Angelo's sense of tradition was not an abstraction: it was embodied in precise, nameable people. He returned to the seminary and began his theology on November 3, 1898.

On May 21, 1899, he preached his first sermon. It was largely a stylistic exercise, intended only for his peers. It was the eve of Pentecost. His appointed theme was 'Mary in the Cenacle'. He began:

> This place, which gathers us for prayer and study, our seminary, *is* the upper room, the cenacle. We who live here in the exercise of ecclesiastical virtues, our gaze fixed on the altar, *are* the new apostles who, renewing the miracles of the first Pentecost will lead back the scattered sheep to the sweet embrace of Jesus, the Good Shepherd (*Rosario*, p. 89).

No great claims need be made for this as a piece of prose: but his writing already has the smooth cadences he learned from Manzoni. And he anticipates his prayer for the Council so many years later: 'Renew thy wonders in this day, as by a new Pentecost' (Abbott, p. 793).

Thereafter his sermon wanders off into a prose poem that frustrates all efforts to provide a passable translation. The gist of it is that the dawn breaking over the Vatican Hill illumines the white hairs of a valiant old man – Leo XIII – and then, sweeping over the Mediterranean, lights up a grotto in a hillside. This is Mary, *quasi aurora consurgens*, arising like the dawn. We have arrived in Lourdes. Angelo was quoting the Canticle of Canticles 6.10: 'Who is this that looks forth like the dawn, fair as the moon, bright as the sun?' His words were not meant to be exegesis. Yet they bring to the figure of Mary a poetry and a feeling that enrich her in the imagination, and yet leave her humble, everyday reality intact. Everyone should be writing poetry at seventeen; the seminarian writes on Mary, about whom he is allowed to *feel*.

September 17, 1899, was a turning-point in his life, though no one knew it at the time. He had escaped from the oppressive atmosphere of La Colombera and walked the five kilometres to Ghaïe di Bonate Sopra for a celebration in honour of the *Madonna Addolorata*, Our Lady of Sorrows. The parish priest, Alessandro Locatelli, had befriended him after the death of Don Rebuzzini. While he was there, Mgr Giacomo Radini Tedeschi, a canon of St Peter's Rome at the age of forty-two, turned up. He and Locatelli had studied together in Bergamo. They compared notes. *O quam sit dispar exitus* – how different their fates were. Locatelli was a modest parish priest, while Radini Tedeschi already had an important national role: he was animator of the *Opera dei Congressi*, the umbrella movement for Catholic social action, and he was organising the mass pilgrimages for the coming Holy Year of 1900. He radiated energy and excitement. In Rome he was talked about as a future Secretary of State. If Angelo were to go to Rome he could join Radini's study and action group, the *Circolo dell'Immaculata* (Our Lady's Club) (*My Bishop*, p. 32). But at this stage going to Rome was a distant mirage. It wasn't something he could choose to do. Still, he had made his first contact with an influential member of the Roman Curia. Since there was no orderly 'career structure' in the Church, much depended on the old-boy network and chance meetings.

In the seminary he was beginning to pick up minor posts of responsibility. Early in 1900 he was put in charge of Gregorian chant or plain-song. Its revival, largely the work of the Benedictines at Solesmes in France, was a first step towards liturgical reform. The austerity and directness of plainchant was coming to be preferred to baroque embroidery. He was also 'prefect' which meant that he had to keep an eye on his companions. One of his charges, referred to only by his initials, A.G., later abandoned the ministry, and Roncalli traced the beginnings of trouble to the Bergamo seminary. A.G. in 1900 was spending 'entire days with eyes cast down so much so that he would not look his companions in the eyes at recreation' (*Pasqua*, 1976, p. 51). Angelo intervened:

> I warned him that custody of the eyes could never be excessive while out walking or in his contacts with the outside world, but that the rigorism he practised was out of place within the seminary; that it would not last; that it would be a tyranny to live for ever in this way; and that he should avoid excess (*ne quid nimis*) in everything other than the love of God (*Pasqua*, 1976, p. 52).

This was written in 1932. Hindsight may be at work in the editing of his memories. But it suggests that his assimilation of seminary values was neither wooden nor mechanical. He knew about the perils of inhuman 'straining'.

But while Angelo was advancing on all fronts at the seminary, at home a crisis was brewing in the summer of 1900. While everyone else was out in the vine-yards, he was at his books but was overcome by boredom, *accidie*: 'Although I racked my brains to try to study with some profit, I could not get anything done. I felt out of sorts with everything, bored stiff with sermons and reading, with everything in fact' (*Journal*, p. 80). Five days later, on August 29, 1900, a most painful incident occurred. The precise details elude us, but the journal conveys the feeling:

> My mother was rather hurt by something I said (which, I confess, might have been put more gently) rebuking her curiosity about a certain matter. She was deeply offended, and said things to me that I would never have expected to hear from my mother for whom, after God, Mary and the saints, I bear the greatest love of which my heart is capable.
> To hear her tell me that I am always uncivil with her, without gentleness or good manners, when I feel that I can say with all sincerity that this is not true, has hurt me too deeply; she was distressed because of me, but I was

very much more distressed to see her grieving and, to put it bluntly, giving way like that. After so much tender love, to be told by my mother that I dislike her, and other things that I have not the heart to remember any longer, oh, this was too much for the heart of a son, and of a son who feels the most profound natural affection (*Journal*, p. 82).

This was the nearest Angelo came in his seminary days to a crisis, defined in the strict sense as 'a crucial period of increased vulnerability and heightened potential' (Erikson, *Identity: Youth and Crisis*, p. 96). He showed that he was not an emotional zombie by feeling deeply hurt; but from now on he would be less dependent on his mother. It is interesting that he did not think of appealing to his father to smooth out the misunderstanding. He was growing up, and growing away.

Perhaps to cheer him up, the curate at Sotto il Monte, Don Ignazio Valsecchi, invited him to go to Rome for the Holy Year pilgrimage from September 12 to 19, 1900. For the first time he saw Rome and the ninety-year-old Pope Leo XIII. It was a particularly tense moment. As September 22, thirtieth anniversary of the breach of Porta Pia which signalled the end of the Papal States, came round, the anti-clericals intensified their campaign against the Pope. Rival demonstrations were organised round the statue of Giordano Bruno in the Campo dei Fiori where he had been burned as a heretic. It was enough to make anyone intransigent. But Angelo reflected on the papacy in the light of St Gregory the Great: 'Before this majestic figure, I feel renewed enthusiasm and affection for the Pope, the great Leo XIII, against whom the most grievous, wicked and diabolical insults are being hurled these days' (*Journal*, p. 83). Despite the polemical atmosphere, he already saw the essence of the papacy as service: 'Is it not the greatest honour for a holy man if people say of him that he is the servant of God? Surely your pontiff, your vicar on earth is proud to be called by this name: the servant of the servants of God' (*Journal*, p. 68, with reference to St Gregory the Great, *Epistolarum* XIII, 1, P.L. LXXVII, 1254). On his way back from Rome he stopped at Assisi with its vivid memories of St Francis, patron of Italy, and at Loreto. On the eve of the Council, in October 1962, he redid these pilgrimages and recalled his first visit to Loreto in 1900. On September 20 he received Communion at two o'clock in the afternoon and 'poured out my soul in prolonged and deeply moved prayer'. But the 'painful circumstances of the time . . . turned the pilgrimage to bitterness'. He had to shut his ears to the mocking gibes coming from the square outside the basilica (*Rosario*, p. 138).

Good news awaited him when he returned from Loreto. He was invited by Bishop Guindani to sit for a Rome scholarship exam. This had been founded in 1640 by Canon Flaminio Cerasola to provide for ten to fifteen Bergamesque theology students at the Roman College (*Secolo*, p. 120). Angelo passed and was accepted. His fellow-students, as a thank-you gift for the way he had fulfilled the office of prefect, presented him with the four Latin volumes of the *Treatise on the Church of Christ* by Fr Louis Billot S.J. Though one of the most celebrated Roman professors of the time, Billot was not the most attuned to modern thought. Yet there was a widespread feeling in the Church that there could be a new synthesis of scholarship and theology. The mood of optimism was expressed by Bishop Geremia Bonomelli in a book called *Il Secolo che nasce – The Century that is Being Born*. Undeterred by his earlier brush with the Index, he declared:

> Remove the mind from the light and air of a proper liberty, deprive it of the stimulus of research – which will never be without its fatigues and risks – and it will become timid, uncertain, lazy, unproductive, looking only to the past, running along pre-established tracks, and incapable of moving forwards towards new horizons (Quoted in *Chiesa e Stato nell'ottocento*, II, p. 418).

After the safe haven of Bergamo, Angelo hoped to find 'the stimulus of research' in Rome. We do not know what his exact feelings were. His seminary journal, unaccountably, dries up at this point. Its last words had been written on September 7, 1900: 'Recollection, prayer and, for the rest, holy joy, *santa gioa*' (*Journal*, p. 84).

Chapter 3

A Roman education

There is no other social organism which so attracts and absorbs a man as the Church of Rome. Rome remains always greater than any Roman, whether he be Roman by birth or Roman by service

(Don Giuseppe De Luca, *Il Cardinale Bonaventura Cerretti*, p. 89.)

Angelo arrived in Rome by the overnight train from Bergamo at 6.30 a.m. on January 4, 1901. With him were two other Bergamo scholarship winners, Achille Ballini and Guglielmo Carozzi. At this time there were two Romes which stared at each other uneasily. There was the Rome that had become the capital of Italy in 1871. It was symbolised by the new public buildings on the Via Nazionale and the frock-coated statesmen who strutted in stone along the Corso Vittorio Emmanuele. On the Capitoline Hill the monument to King Victor Emmanuel, known officially as 'the altar of the republic' but popularly as 'the wedding-cake', was already rising allegedly to challenge the dome of St Peter's. This 'Rome of the Freemasons' contrasted with ecclesiastical Rome, city of the catacombs, drenched in the blood of martyrs, endowed with innumerable baroque churches (one for every day of the year, said legend) and religious houses, home of the popes and their civil service, the Roman Curia. The two Romes were not on speaking terms with each other. Each pretended the other did not exist. Each survived by resenting the other. That, in essence, was 'the Roman Question' which was not resolved for another thirty years.

Angelo and his two companions clip-clopped along in a horse-drawn carriage from the station to the Roman seminary in Piazza San Apollinare, just to the east of Piazza Navona and a good stone's throw from the Tiber. He settled in quickly. He had a room to himself. The bed was rather hard, but he thought that no bad thing. He had all he needed: a table, a wardrobe, bookshelves *and* a radiator. With a radiator in his room and electric lighting on the streets, introduced only the previous year, it seemed to him that Rome was in the van of progress and modernity. That, at least, is the impression he gives in his first letter home (*Familiari*, I, pp. 3–5). Because of his youth – he was only nineteen – he was enrolled in the first year of theology. The lectures caused him no bother. He already felt like 'an old hand' ('*una persona vecchia del Seminario*').

It was not all study. They were allowed out for walks around the city in their purple cassocks, looking like the bishops that most of them, except by mis-adventure, eventually became. They learned the archaeology and geography of

Rome. They sometimes had meetings with students from other ecclesiastical colleges. On January 10, less than a week after his arrival Angelo tells his astonished family about going to Propaganda Fide, the missionary college in the Piazza di Spagna, where 'forty clerics recited their own compositions in forty different languages' and 'some were white, some yellow, some red, and some had hands and faces as black as coal' (*Familiari*, I, p. 4). If that sounds like Babel, harmony was restored on January 31 when he attended a performance of Lorenzo Perosi's *Il Natale* (Christmas), the Italian answer to Georg Friedrich Handel's *Messiah*.

They even had – carefully selected – visits to the theatre for plays which expressed Christian values. On February 17, 1901, Angelo saw a dramatised version of the novel by the Polish writer, Henryk Sienkiewicz, *Quo Vadis?* (*Cronologia*, p. 518). St Peter, fleeing Rome during Nero's persecution, meets Christ along the way. Peter asks, '*Quo vadis*, where are you going, Lord?' Jesus replies: 'I am going to Rome to be crucified a second time'. Crestfallen, Peter returns to Rome to stand in for Jesus. A Polish pope was to quote this same novel at his inauguration Mass in 1978. But in 1901 Sienkiewicz's message seemed to be supremely topical. Although in fact Pope Leo XIII would die tranquilly in his bed, it suited Catholics to regard the 'insults' to which he was daily subjected in the liberal press as a form of persecution, unparalleled since the time of Nero.

Angelo rather enjoyed the pomp and pageantry of the Vatican. It was the only free entertainment he had. He liked his ceremonies to be long and grand. He was present in April 1901 when Pope Leo created ten new cardinals, including the Bergamesque, Felici Cavagnis (*Cronologia*, p. 518). Though Leo was unbelievably ninety-one, Angelo learned from him how a proper pope should behave. He tells his parents how, on his first Sunday in Rome, he received a personal blessing from the Pope in St Peter's. But he was careful not to hug his joy unto himself. He wrote home: 'In that solemn and moving moment, I thought of all of you, and all our relatives, benefactors and friends; and he, the good old man, included all of you in his blessing' (*Familiari*, I, p. 4).

Although Leo XIII, the 'good old man', repeatedly foiled those who predicted his proximate demise, it was evident that he could not live for much longer. 'Informed circles' (that is, clerical gossip) said that his successor would undoubtedly be Cardinal Mariano Rampolla, then Secretary of State and general factotum. Mgr Radini Tedeschi was a protegé of Rampolla, who made him ecclesiastical assistant (in effect chaplain) to the Mary Immaculate Club. Angelo naturally gravitated towards this '*circulo*', of which Radini Tedeschi was the life and soul: 'There were those long evenings spent in his company . . . by that valiant band of Romans – still vigorous and highly respected men today – in pleasant and cheerful conversation or, more often, in the hard work which he encouraged us by word and example to undertake for the success of the various projects he so capably directed' (*My Bishop*, p. 32). Radini Tedeschi's initiatives included soup kitchens and hostels for the poor as well as recreation centres for soldiers. Angelo found life in Rome exhilarating. He didn't have time to feel lonely, still less home-sick. He found the staff of the Roman seminary welcoming. He became a life-long friend of the rector, Mgr Vincenzo Bugarini, and the tutor and from 1902 vice-rector, Mgr Domenico Spolverini. When he returned to Rome in 1921 he took Bugarini, by then old and retired, into his apartment; and he says of Spolverini: 'He always showed an affectionate interest in me... and when I returned to Rome in 1921 he received me as tenderly as a mother her child' (*Journal*, p. 170, fn. 16). It was a tradition at the Roman seminary that superiors kept in touch with their old boys, and watched them advance in their careers with much pride and pleasure.

There were 'characters' too, who provided the stuff of anecdotes for later reunions. Don Ignazio Garroni, the bursar, was a 'grumpy but kindly man' ('*un burbero benefico*'), who prowled round the refectory vainly urging the students to 'Eat less, eat less' (*Lettere*, p. 86). Angelo was humiliated by having to borrow from him from time to time even though they were only 'small debts' (*Journal*, p. 136). His poverty was real and meant that he had to make do with second-hand reach-me-downs: 'Since I became a seminarian I have never worn a garment that was not given to me out of charity by some kind person' (*Ibid.*, p. 94).

The outstanding eccentric, however, was Canon Oreste Borgia. He slept in a hammock and was reputed to levitate. He always arrived late for meals and appeared to eat nothing; this was a ploy to allow him to slip unnoticed (he fondly believed) into the kitchen where he made up food parcels for a group of pious but impoverished old ladies. The irreverent seminarians called them 'the twelve stars of the Madonna' (*Lettere*, p. 86).

Roncalli recalled these memories on November 27, 1958, when he visited the Lateran College, successor of the Roman seminary. He could still reel off the names of his eleven professors. The most famous was Riccardo Tabarelli (1859–1909) who contributed to the revival of Thomism stimulated by the encyclical *Aeterni Patris* (August 4, 1879). Tabarelli liked to stress personal responsibility for sin and virtue. 'Devils? What devils?' he would enquire in his treatise on grace, 'We are the devils. We are the responsible ones' (*Journal*, p. 262). His most notorious professor was Umberto Benigni, later to mastermind the spying campaign against the 'Modernists'. But at this date he appeared to be – and probably was – a serious historian who tried to apply the method of Hippolyte Taine ('the man, the moment and the milieu') to the social ideas of the Church, but without succumbing to Taine's determinism. Benigni believed, quite rightly, that history was the crucial discipline and yet that it was 'the Cinderella of the seminaries' (see Poulat, p. 214). We will meet him again. He contributed to Angelo's choice of history as his special field.

The first semester sped by. 'Here in Rome, I can say I have all that I need', he noted (*Journal*, p. 86). He was happy and spiritually fulfilled: 'This is the first retreat I have made since I came to Rome. How am I? I cannot complain about the graces Jesus has sent me, the indescribable joys, the moments of sheer delight which shed their radiance over all the rest' (*Journal*, p. 86). Twinges of social inferiority sometimes afflicted him; but he used them to keep his feet on the ground ('certain rebuffs to my pride').

He had no sense of intellectual inferiority. On June 25, 1901, he sailed through his exams and was awarded a prize for an optional paper in Hebrew (*Cronologia*, p. 518). But then the comfortable world he was fashioning crashed about him.

He was ordered to report to the Umberto I Barracks in Bergamo for compulsory military service. On November 30, 1901, he became plain Private Roncalli, Angelo, Number 11331-42, sir, in the 73rd Infantry Regiment, the Lombardy Brigade. The fact that clerics had to do military service at all seemed to him 'an unjust and barbarous imposition' (*Journal*, p. 94). It was one of the irritants that kept 'the Roman Question' alive. By paying 1,200 *lire* the diocesan Curia in Bergamo at least got his service reduced to twelve months. But that was quite long enough seriously to interrupt his studies. And he hated it from the start.

He called it 'the year of Babylonian Captivity' and 'the year of conflicts' (*Journal*, p. 88 and p. 108). After less than a month he wrote despondently to his Rector, Mgr Bugarini:

> My life is one of great suffering, a real purgatory; and yet I feel the
> Lord is very close to me, with his holy and provident care, beyond all
> expectations. Sometimes I am amazed at myself, amazed at the happy
> solution of this difficult and appalling problem, and I can only explain it by
> the thought of so many good and dear people who are praying for me, and
> of my beloved Madonna della Fiducia [Our Lady of Confidence] whose
> lovely image is always on my breast (*Journal*, p. 357: December 23, 1901).

The image of Our Lady of Confidence, a copy of the picture painted by the Venerable Clara Isabelle Fornari, born in 1697, was an object of special devotion at the Roman seminary. It became the only thread of continuity throughout the college's subsequent wanderings. Angelo kept a copy of this picture on his writing desk all his life (*Journal*, p. 120, fn. 57).

Yet his military purgatory had some redeeming features. He was stationed in Bergamo, and so could go home on week-end leaves and at Christmas. The army appreciated him. He was promoted corporal on May 31, 1902, and sergeant on November 30. He scored high marks on the rifle range (*Cronologia*, p. 518). One has to admit that during the summer manoeuvres at Presolana he was arrested and confined to barracks. But that was not his fault: his men proved 'insubordinate' which in military jargon covers a multitude of crimes. This lapse aside, the officers and especially Colonel Enrico Campo, his C.O., treated him with respect and 'allow me the fullest liberty to pursue my religious practices' (*Journal*, p. 358). Whatever the theory of Church–state relations, the actual practice was humanised in typical Italian style. Angelo reports also that his fellow conscripts, mostly from Bergamo or Brescia, gave him 'marks of respect and affection', and 'compete in doing those little services that at least save me a lot of bother' (*Journal*, p. 358). Did they clean his boots? So what was the problem?

Bluntly, the 'brutal and licentious soldiery' confronted him with the raw facts of sexuality for which he was not prepared. He simply did not know how to handle barrack-room boasting about brothel exploits. This explains his wildly extravagant language when he was rid of it all:

> O the world is so ugly, filthy and loathesome! In my year of military service
> I have learned all about it. The army is a running fountain of pollution,
> enough to submerge whole cities. Who can hope to escape from this flood
> of slime, unless God comes to his aid . . . I did not think that a reasonable
> man could fall so low. Yet it is a fact. Today, after my brief experience, I
> think it is true that more than half of all mankind, at some time in their
> lives, become animals, without any shame (*Journal*, pp. 92–3).

He wrote that in December 1902 shortly after he was demobbed.

His chastity had been tested. He realised that priests and future priests were not immune to temptation: 'And the priests? I tremble when I think that not a few, even among these, betray their sacred calling' (*Journal*, p. 93). He draws 'realistic' conclusions: 'Now nothing surprises me any more: certain stories make no impression on me. Everything is explained'. He resolves to be 'more scrupulous than ever about this matter, even if I become the laughing-stock of the whole world' (*Ibid.*). He learned the truth of John Milton's maxim: 'I cannot praise a fugitive and cloistered virtue, unexercised and unbreathed, that never sallies out and sees her adversary, but slinks out of the race . . . ' (*Areopagitica*). He said good-bye to 1902 with a sigh of relief and a sense of providential protection:

> I shall always remember 1902: the year of my military service, the year of
> conflicts. I might, like so many other poor wretches, have lost my vocation
> – and I did not lose it. I might have lost holy purity and the grace of God,
> but God did not allow me to do this. I passed through the mire and by his
> grace I was kept unpolluted. I am still alive, healthy, robust as before, better
> than before . . . Jesus I thank you, I love you (*Journal*, p. 108).

It wasn't quite his last word on the army. The experience of the First World War made him more sympathetic to these peasant conscripts caught up in a conflict they did not comprehend; and as pope he boasted cheerfully of having reached the rank of sergeant. But he was not joking in 1902.

To mark his return to the Roman seminary, Angelo began a ten-day retreat directed by Fr Francesco Pitocchi, a Redemptorist, who had just arrived as 'spiritual father'. It was unusual to give this post to a religious. But Pitocchi was unusual in a number of ways. Born on September 21, 1852, at seventeen he wanted to join the Jesuits, was told to wait, got himself ordained a diocesan priest in 1875 at the age of twenty-two, and joined the Redemptorists ten years later. He edited the correspondence of St Alphonsus Liguori, founder of the order, and published a slim volume of the saint's maxims under the revealing title *Certain Paradise* (*Il Paradiso assicurato*, Cuggiani, Rome, 1890). Then in 1896 his health broke down. A combination of digestive troubles and nervous spasms in the neck muscles made him a permanent invalid. He snatched what little sleep he could in a hammock. He was unable to say Mass or have any public ministry. Despite or because of his sufferings, he was regarded as a spiritual guide of the highest quality. It was all he could do, and it was the best he could do (see Battaglia, Giuseppe, Unpublished paper on Pitocchi given at Istituto per le scienze religiose, Bologna, November 14, 1981). Angelo remained attached to Pitocchi until his death on June 13, 1922.

The December 1902 retreat followed closely the *Spiritual Exercises* of St Ignatius as they were then conceived both by Jesuits and Redemptorists. Angelo noted down what he had heard Pitocchi say. The 'first principle and foundation' established that the purpose of creation was the praise, reverence and service of the Lord. Meditations on sin showed how far one had departed from God's plan. There followed a series of exercises designed to help the retreatant to assimilate the values of Christ expressed in the Beatitudes so as to be ready to follow him in poverty and humiliation. This led to the 'election' or decisive choice for Christ, made only when the will had been purified and the 'spirits discerned'. Does the prompting come from Satan or the Holy Spirit? The Passion and the Resurrection (skimpily dealt with) confirmed this resolution and released the retreatant on the world a changed and converted person. That was the theory. It was often highly effective, despite a somewhat mechanical use of the *Exercises* that was, as subsequent work has shown, entirely foreign to Ignatius and his first companions.

Yet Angelo, despite being preached at five times a day and told how to feel, responded to the *Exercises* in a personal way. Ignatius had been a soldier and cast his meditation on the Kingdom of Christ in military imagery. Fresh from his army service and just twenty-one, Angelo welcomes this aspect of the *Exercises* with enthusiasm: 'I am the King's page, and go with him everywhere; I am admitted to his secrets' (*Journal*, p. 89). He pictures himself as a knight, called to fight in the battles of Christ the King:

I boldly enlist in the ranks of your volunteers. I dedicate myself to your service, for life or death. You offer me your cross as a standard and weapon.

I place my right hand on this invincible weapon and give you my word,
swearing with all the fervour of my youthful heart absolute fidelity unto
death. So I, whom you created your servant, have become your soldier. I
put on your uniform, I gird on your sword, I am proud to call myself a
knight of Christ. Give me a soldier's heart, a knight's valour (*Journal*, p.
93).

And so on. The motto of the 73rd infantry regiment had been *Acerrimus hostibus*
('Most fierce to the foe'). He transposed this easily enough into the spiritual
realm. But since the signal for battle had not yet been sounded, he was waiting in
his tent, where the chief enemy was the relentless *ego* (see *Journal*, pp. 93–4).

But there was in this retreat something more fundamental, which Angelo
derived not from Fr Pitocchi but from his own experience: he thought of God not
as Father so much as Mother. The theme was traditional but rare; it belonged to
that current of tradition that had gone underground. Yet here it colours Angelo's
whole perception of God:

It really looks as though God has lavished upon me his most tender and
motherly care . . . (*Journal*, p. 91).
He (God) took me, a country lad, from my home, and with the affection of
a loving mother he has given me all I needed . . . and he still cares for me
without respite, day and night, more than a mother cares for her child
(*Ibid.*, pp. 95–6).

No doubt this reflected relationships within his own family, where the busily
caring mother was contrasted with the taciturn father; but it is more important as
an instance of the way Angelo exploited his own experience to understand God
better. In fact, at this stage, his actual mother, Marianna, was more alarmed at the
idea that he was out on the streets of Rome at night when there were thieves
about. He gently tells her not to worry (*Familiari*, I, p. 12). Marianna had been
transcended; the essential lay elsewhere.

He came closer still to it on the evening of December 16, 1902, when he had his
first conversation with Pitocchi:

He gave me a kind of motto as the conclusion of our first meeting. He
repeated it often, calmly but with insistence: 'God is everything: I am
nothing' [*Dio è tutto: io sono nulla*]. This became like a touchstone which
disclosed to me a new and unexplored horizon, full of mystery and spiritual
fascination (*Giornale*, 5th edition, p. 471).

That was written nearly twenty years later. 'God is everything: I am nothing'
marked a decisive movement not because the formula taught him something he

did not already know but because, coming from a man who lived it, it struck home with great force. In Newman's language, it ceased to be a 'notional' truth and was 'realised'. In terms of the *Spiritual Exercises*, it represented a fundamental option, a choice of God as the over-riding truth of Angelo's existence.

He returned to his studies in January 1903 with renewed enthusiasm: 'Tomorrow the lectures begin again: I feel a need and a passionate desire to study' (*Journal*, p. 110). His mind had lain fallow throughout his military service. Now it was hyper-active, and on January 8, 1903 he expresses an almost Faustian thirst for learning: 'I feel a restless longing to know everything, to study all the great authors, to familiarize myself with the scientific moment in all its manifestations' (*Journal*, p. 111). No one at this date was talking of 'modernism' or 'modernists': for that we have to wait until the encyclical *Pascendi* condemned them (September 8, 1907). Alfred Loisy's *L'Evangile et l'Eglise* had appeared in November 1902. But Angelo was thinking in more general terms of what he called 'the forward, upward movement of Catholic culture' (*Journal*, p. 110). This, together with his reference to 'the scientific movement in all its manifestations', evokes the heady intellectual atmosphere of the period, when Catholic scholars were striking out in new directions and looking for some kind of synthesis between Catholicism and 'modern thought'. The description is vague, but it is no vaguer than it was in some of its advocates.

That Angelo was on the side of those who wanted to reconcile faith and contemporary thought becomes clear in his reflections after the funeral of Cardinal Lucido Parocchi (1833–1903) who had been archbishop of Bologna and then, since 1884, cardinal vicar of the diocese of Rome. In other words he looked after the diocese of Rome on behalf of the Pope who, because of the 'Roman Question', could not set foot in it. Parocchi was a learned man, had founded the review *La Scuola Cattolica*, and had worked for reconciliation with Italy through the *Opera dei Congressi*. He was one of Angelo's heroes:

> Cardinal Parocchi was the sort of figure we very rarely come across in the records of the Church. The bare mention of his name was enough to silence those who accused the Church of ignorance; before him even unbelievers reverently bowed their heads, and men of science faltered when they had to speak in his presence. His erudition extended into every field of knowledge ... Opinions may differ about Cardinal Parocchi's political views: I know that some malicious insinuations have been made – but no one will ever question his courage and his enthusiastic loyalty to Church and Pope ... Oh, if only I had his learning and his fortitude, I would be well content (*Journal*, p. 114).

'Conciliarists' like Parocchi were accustomed to being accused of 'disloyalty to the Holy Father'. Angelo was not mistaken in his estimate of Parocchi. Giuseppe

Toniolo, the leading Catholic sociologist of the time, called him 'a man of exceptionally liberal views' (*Journal*, p. 113, fn. 48).

But now a new generation of Catholic scholars was emerging. At the Roman seminary, the most brilliant student was Ernesto Buonaiuti. Chance had thrown them together during Angelo's first semester, January to July 1901. The custom was to draw lots for places in chapel and the refectory and companions for walks. Buonaiuti drew Roncalli, so they had many walks together around Rome. Buonaiuti was already a scholar and conscious of his worth. He was impatient with the petty restrictions of the Roman seminary. One piece of idiocy caused him great amusement. He had asked permission of the vice-rector, Spolverini, to read Augusto Conti's *History of Philosophy*, a safe and reputable work, graced even with an *imprimatur*. Spolverini thought about it and eventually gave his permission, but only after tearing out the pages concerning Peter Abelard: his love for Héloise and subsequent castration were not fit reading for a seminarian. Buonaiuti was later excommunicated as a 'Modernist' and later still hailed as a 'prophet'. That may account for the ambivalence of Roncalli's attitude towards him. As Pope he sometimes admitted that he had learned a lot from 'Don Ernesto' (Andreotti, p. 66). But to Capovilla he edited his memories of 1901–4 and claimed that he 'never discussed theological, biblical or historical questions with him, and never read any of the underground works of his that were circulating' (*Dodicesimo anniversario*, p. 118).

One wonders what, then, they did talk about, since Buonaiuti could hardly keep silent on the questions that were churning him up. But Angelo would recoil from jokes about Abelard and Héloise, and would have been disconcerted to hear what Buonaiuti thought about the type of priest the Roman seminary was producing. 'For my professors', Buonaiuti wrote in his memoirs, 'the ideal priest should and could be nothing other than the authorized administrator, in due bureaucratic form, of a number of magical gestures which would bring consolation to human anguish' (Dreyfus, p. 37). He dreamt of a priest who would embody 'the missionary tradition of the Church in the modern world' and of a Church that would be 'perpetually revivified by the free circulation of charismatic gifts' (*Ibid.*). Yet in his own more conventional way, Angelo shared this same vision.

In the attempted reconciliation between science and faith, the key discipline was history. The lesson of the nineteenth century – of John Henry Newman as much as of Charles Darwin – was that an end-result could only be understood by tracing its development in time. 'Look at the process as well as the result', advised Lord Acton. This had consequences for every branch of theology. And already there was beginning to be controversy between those who 'took history seriously' and the neo-scholastics who believed that they worked *sub specie aeternitatis* and so eluded historical questions.

Now Umberto Benigni (1862–1934) was professor of Church History at the Roman seminary. He receives one mention in the Journal. On January 7, 1903 he advised his students to 'read little, but read well' (*Journal*, p. 111). Yet he had more influence on Angelo than that suggests. Though fat, rather repulsive-looking and afflicted with a stammer, his competence as an historian and a teacher was unquestioned. One witness says of him that he was 'strong in his first-hand knowledge of sources and bibliographical information, vivid in his exposition which he conducted in Italian not in Latin, and sensitive to critical problems' (Michele Maccarrone, quoted in Poulat, p. 174, fn. 6). Buonaiuti offers a less flattering portrait in which hindsight knowledge of Benigni's later career as grand inquisitor no doubt plays a part:

> In his lectures and conversation he showed a lively and broad intelligence which, however, was cold and sterile as steel. I came to know him well. I told him, more than once, about my enthusiasm for a priesthood dedicated to the laborious transformation of minds in an age that was pregnant with novelties and dramatic changes. Each confidence of mine was greeted with a sceptical and ironical smile, as though it were no more than the product of an over-excitable mind and juvenile illusions. Mgr Benigni understood the Church as a military hierarchy characterised by bureaucratic uniformity (Poulat p. 185).

Buonaiuti was a prejudiced witness. Yet there is no reason to doubt him when he reports Benigni saying: 'My friend, do you really believe that men are capable of any good in this world? History is one long and desperate spewing up, and the only thing for this humanity is the Inquisition' (*Ibid.*).

The only question is *when* Benigni made what Buonaiuti calls this 'terrible remark'. The change that came over him can best be expressed as a move from optimism to pessimism. In his early period, Benigni was fascinated by the social impact of Christianity and strongly favoured 'Christian democracy' which he said should be called 'Christocracy'. Thus Léon Harmel, the French industrialist who introduced profit-sharing into his factory in the 1890s, says of Benigni:

> His first volume, which covers the first four centuries to Constantine, is finished . . . This book is a real revelation. He has managed to prove from contemporary sources that the spread of Christianity depended on the social movement. It was through the development and application of democratic ideas that the Christians recruited so many followers among the slaves and humble people. So much so that the priests who today are concerned with trades unions and co-operatives are doing no more than follow in the footsteps of their early predecessors (Poulat, p. 178).

Volume I of Benigni's *Storia sociale della Chiesa* (*Social History of the Church*) did not appear until 1907. But he had tried out the material in lectures long before then. Angelo was enthusiastic about this aspect of Benigni's work. He retained Benigni's optimism, and never followed him into pessimism. But he saw Christian democracy as another way of expressing the priest's mission of service: 'Jesus stooped to wash the feet of the twelve poor fishermen. This is _true democracy_, of which we ecclesiastics should be the most eloquent examples' (_Journal_, p. 97).

Angelo's spirituality was maturing under the double impact of his military service and his progress in theology. He decides that his idea of holiness as the literal imitation of the lives of the saints, was mistaken:

> I used to call to mind the image of some saint whom I set myself to imitate down to the smallest detail, as a painter makes an exact copy of a Raphael picture. I used to say to myself: in this case St Aloysius would have done so and so; he would not have done this or that. It turned out, however, that I was never able to achieve what I had thought I could do, and this worried me. The method was wrong. From the saints, one must _take the substance, not the accidents, of their virtues_ . . . I must not be the dry, bloodless reproduction of a model, however perfect (_Journal_, p. 113).

Angelo was approaching ordination to the sub-diaconate which took place on April 11, 1903 in St John Lateran. He was now irrevocably committed to celibacy. The 'angelism' he had professed in the Bergamo seminary was abandoned. Instead of suppressing emotions, he seeks to harness them to the love of God:

> I must not let my head be turned in good fortune nor let myself be soured by the bitter moments of life. This does not mean denying that the senses or impulses of nature exist. The enjoyment of God's love, the sweet and total abandonment to his will, must absorb all else in me or, rather, _transform and sublimate_ all the desires of my lower nature (_Journal_, p. 136).

The background to this concept of 'sublimation' was Thomist rather than Freudian: grace builds on, and does not destroy, nature. Yet Angelo's use of the term shows up the inadequacy of the Freudian definition of sublimation as 'the gratification of instinctual impulses, usually aggressive or sexual in nature, through the substitution of socially acceptable behaviour for prohibited drives' (_Fontana Dictionary of Modern Thought_, 1977, p. 610). The deepest impulses are redirected into safe channels. But this overlooks the fact that they can be turned to creative account, as in the artist, or to service, as in the committed celibate. Without some such positive idea of sublimation, Angelo's celibacy would have been nonsense. He had already grasped this at the age of twenty-one. His remaining sixty years must be seen in this light.

Meanwhile, in the spring of 1903 international events began for the first time to engage his attention. On February 20 Leo XIII celebrated the twenty-fifth anniversary of his pontificate. Legend had it that after St Peter no pope would last for so long. But the tabu had been broken first by Pius IX and now, even more remarkably in view of his advanced age and fragile health, by Leo XIII. 'A great day today', noted Angelo, 'he has survived all his persecutors, amazingly youthful for his ninety-three years, to explain the works of God to an astonished world' (*Journal*, pp. 119–20). Although constricted in Italy, Leo XIII had pursued a policy of reconciliation wherever he could. He had patched up the quarrel with Germany after the disastrous *Kulturkampf*, sought the friendship of England, made peace with Switzerland, done his best to rally nostalgic French monarchists to the Third Republic, kept an eye on Russia (introducing the 'prayers for the conversion of Russia' recited, until Vatican II, at the end of every Mass), and even written to the emperor of China inviting him to protect missionaries.

Now all this patient diplomatic work, ably seconded by Cardinal Rampolla, began to bear fruit. On April 29, 1903 and then on May 2, the streets of Rome were alive with 'flags, festoons, decorations, glittering uniforms, plumes, soldiers, military reviews' (*Journal*, p. 128): first King Edward VII, of Great Britain and Ireland, and then Kaiser William II of Germany, were on their way to see the Pope. This was dramatic and unprecedented. Angelo wasn't quite sure what to make of Edward VII who was 'King of one of the greatest nations', and he moralises about the vanity of fame and the applause of crowds: *Sic transit gloria mundi* ('Thus does wordly glory vanish' – words once used at papal coronations) (*Journal*, p. 129). Kings and emperors pass. They are like 'specks of dust' (*Ibid.*). God's judgement will humble them.

Yet Angelo reads both visits as Providential events, bearing a message from the Holy Spirit:

> It is highly significant . . . that an heretical King of Protestant England, which has persecuted the Catholic Church for more than three centuries, should go in person to pay his respects to the poor old pope, held like a prisoner in his own house. It is *a sign of the times* that, after a night of storms, we see the new dawn rising from the Vatican, a slow but real and sincere return of the nations to the arms of their common father who has long awaited them, weeping over their foolishness . . . (*Journal*, p. 130).

After Edward VII, Kaiser Wilhelm or William II:

> This event is indeed extraordinary and of great significance. It is truly an act of Divine Providence, a real triumph for the papacy. A Protestant Emperor, after centuries of hostility, ascends the Vatican staircase with unusual, almost unique ceremony and splendour, and humbles himself before the greatness of

the papal throne . . . the Emperor, applauded and admired, who, if he were not a heretic, would be the Charlemagne of modern times . . . (*Journal*, p. 132).

Was Angelo, obsessed with the papacy as the centre of the world, exaggerating? Yes and no. The real reason for the visit of king and emperor to Rome was to woo Italy. Edward VII's political masters wanted to draw Italy into their *Entente* with France. Kaiser William's chancellor, von Bülow, wanted to strengthen Italy's membership of the Triple Alliance with Austria-Hungary which, with ups and downs, dated back to 1882. In 1903 neither the *Entente* nor the Triple Alliance were strictly incompatible; but within twelve years Italy would have to make up its mind where its true interests lay. One thing was clear at this date: 'The Roman question had ceased to count in international diplomacy' (Seton-Watson, p. 331). No one, not even Leo XIII himself, imagined that Italy was about to be broken up and the Papal States restored. So Edward VII and William II could pay their courtesy visits to the Vatican without annoying overmuch their brother King Victor Emmanuel III. To that extent Angelo was mistaken.

But he was not altogether wrong if one thinks, as he did, that 'God holds the keys of men's hearts and, through all the intrigues of human politics, finds a means of making known the glory of his name and the glory of the Catholic Church' (*Journal*, p. 130). This conviction was not susceptible of proof. It presupposes a distinction between the foreground of history in which great men orate and have their reasons, and a background on which one sees cast the shadow of God's hand. Roncalli's own pontificate makes sense only in the light of this distinction between the apparent and the real stage of history.

Then, within three months of the crowning triumph of his pontificate, Leo XIII died. Instead of going to the villa house of the Roman seminary at Roccantica, Angelo stayed on in Rome to follow, from afar, the conclave. The central issue was: continuity or change? Rampolla was the candidate of continuity. Leo XIII's heritage was impressive. First there was the reconciliation with the nations of Europe demonstrated by the visits we have just examined. Secondly, he had contributed to the revival of Catholic scholarship, opened the Vatican Library, made John Henry Newman a cardinal, encouraged an enlightened Neo-Thomism, and declared that 'the Church has nothing to fear from truth'. Thirdly in his encyclical *Rerum Novarum* he had displayed a qualified interest in democracy and defended the rights of workers to band together in trades unions. Rampolla was the standard-bearer of these causes. He was prepared to take up and develop this inheritance. Angelo – not that, as a seminarian, he mattered – supported the same line.

At first (though none of this was known at the time) Rampolla carried all before him. There were 63 cardinal electors. He needed therefore 42 votes. In successive ballots Rampolla got 24, 29, 29 and then 30 votes. There comes a time in a conclave when a candidate gets stuck: being unable to rise any further, he is condemned to sink. That is what happened to Rampolla. His defeat is usually attributed to the veto of the Austro–Hungarian Emperor Franz-Joseph conveyed through the cardinal archbishop of Kraków, Kniaz de Kolzielsko Puzyna. But there was also a curial faction implacably opposed to Rampolla which sought a change from what they saw as the weak and accomodating policies of Leo XIII. This opened the way for Giuseppe Sarto, patriarch of Venice, who made a great point of stressing his humility. After the fourth ballot he declared: 'I shall renounce the cardinalate and become a Capuchin friar' (Falconi, p. 13). However, he did not carry out this threat and strolled home with 50 votes in the sixth ballot (*Quale Papa?* pp. 132–4). Asked the ritual question 'By what name do you wish to be called?' he replied without hesitation: 'Pius, trusting to the help of the holy popes who have honoured this name by their virtues and defended the Church with strength and gentleness' (Falconi, p. 14). This was ominous. The last Pius, Pio Nono, had turned his back on the modern world and in his *Syllabus of Errors* (1864) denounced those who fondly hoped to reconcile the Church with 'progress and modern civilisation'.

Angelo had been present at the 'white smoke' in St Peter's Square on August 14, 1903. Special editions of the papers were rushed out within half an hour. On his way back he passed by the church of San Giovanni dei Fiorentini, just across the Tiber. There he found an old woman intently studying photographs. 'I don't know anything about this Pius X', she said, 'but at least he's handsome' (*Corriere della Sera*, January 3, 1959: Pope John told this story at an audience). But Pius X was not just a pretty face. There were other aspects of his character that were less agreeable. Angelo was present at the coronation in St Peter's on August 9, 1903. He never forgot the impression the new pope made on him: 'The Pope came in to a hurricane of applause and *vivas*. For a moment he lowered his head a little, and when he looked up again his eyes were filled with tears. And the crowd fell silent' (*Letture*, pp. 51–2).

Angelo did not comment in his journal on what he called 'these grave and extraordinary events' (*Journal*, p. 145). He was more immediately concerned about his ordination to the diaconate at St John Lateran on December 18, 1903 and his ordination to the priesthood, due in 1904. His Bergamesque companions, Ballini and Carozzi, had led the way, being ordained on July 25, 1903 (*Cronologia*, p. 519). Pitocchi had the good sense to forbid him to make any additional 'retreat resolutions' (*Journal*, p. 145), and assigned him the desultory task of producing a summary of the autobiography of Maria Celeste Crostorasa, a seventeenth-century nun who founded an institute that eventually became the female arm of the Redemptorists (Battaglia, p. 4). This may have been his attempt to make spirituality prevail over theological enquiry.

Certainly Angelo was becoming aware of a tension between the 'scientific movement', into which he had plunged with so much ardour, and his ambition to be a 'good priest'. He stated the dilemma clearly on March 7, feast of St Thomas Aquinas: 'In our enthusiasm for study, if often happens that piety has to take second place; we behave as though we thought the time given to devotional exercises was wasted. And yet St Thomas, before becoming the greatest scholar of his age, was a saint; and it was because he was a saint that he reached such a lofty height of wisdom' (*Journal*, pp. 122–3). The dilemma was sharpened with the new pontificate. There were already signs that Pius X would conduct an offensive against what he considered 'excessive' criticism. In December 1903 Angelo was looking for a *via media*, a middle way between intellectual integrity and compliance:

> I do not despise criticism, and I shall be most careful not to think badly of critics or treat them with disrespect. On the contrary, I shall love it. I shall study new systems of thought, their continual evolution and their trends; criticism for me is light, is truth, and there is only one truth.
>
> But I shall always try to introduce into these discussions, in which too often ill-considered enthusiasms and deceptive appearances have a part to play, a great moderation, harmony, balance and serenity of judgement, allied to a prudent and cautious broad-mindedness.
>
> On very doubtful points I shall prefer to keep silent, like one who does not know, rather than hazard propositions which might differ in the slightest degree from the Church's orthodoxy. I will not be surprised at anything even if certain conclusions, while preserving intact the sacred deposit of the faith, turn out to be rather unexpected. Surprise is the daughter of ignorance (*Journal*, p. 153).

He swings dialectically to and fro, torn between 'the atmosphere and light of the modern age' (*Journal*, p. 153) and the example of the 'good old Bergamesque priests of old . . . who neither saw or desired to see further than could be seen by the Pope, the Bishops, the common sense and mind of the Church' (*Ibid.*). It was a cruel and, some would think, an unnecessary dilemma. But Angelo felt it deeply.

If 1902 had been the testing year of military service and 1903 the exhilarating year of intellectual expansion and international events, 1904 was the year of immediate preparation for ordination. There were three minor events along the road. In January 1904 he attended a lecture by Marc Sagnier, leader of *Le Sillon*, the French Christian Democratic movement. He was destined to be condemned by Pius X, to the great joy of the atheist Charles Maurras, who joined in hounding him with his book, *Le Dilemme de Marc Sagnier* (see Richard Sutton, *Nationalism, Positivism and Catholicism. The Politics of Charles Maurras and French*

Catholics 1890–1914, Cambridge, 1982, p. 91). On June 9 he was present when his compatriot, Carozzi, defended theological theses against all comers in the Vatican's Sala Clementina; Angelo had been the first choice for this academic exercise (known as 'the public act') but had declined the honour for reasons unknown (*Cronologia*, p. 519). On July 13 he was awarded his doctorate in theology – easily come by in Rome – and his written exam was supervised by Eugenio Pacelli, the future Pius XII.

He made his pre-ordination retreat at the house of the Passionist Fathers on the Coelian Hill. From his window he could see the Colosseum, St John Lateran and, stretching lazily out beyond, the Appian Way with its catacombs. There he reread the words he had written two years before and would underline in red when he became pope. He felt that he had been brought to Rome so that 'I may live under the protection of his Vicar, alongside the very fountain of Catholic truth and the tomb of his apostles, where the very soil is stained with the blood of his martyrs, and the air is filled with the holiness of his confessors' (*Journal*, p. 95). Every afternoon he practised saying Mass in the room where St Paul of the Cross, founder of the Passionists, had died. On the eve of his ordination he prayed in St John Lateran, mounted the 'Holy Stairs' on his knees, and then went on to St Paul's without the Walls (*Journal*, p. 169).

Early in the morning of August 10, 1904, feast of St Lawrence, the vice-rector, Spolverini, collected him and they went by cab to the church of Santa Maria in Monte Santo, on the Piazza del Popolo. But Spolverini couldn't stay, and so during the ordination ceremony Angelo's assistant was Ernesto Buonaiuti (*Dodicesimo anniversario*, p. 118). The ordaining bishop was Giuseppe Ceppetelli, titular patriarch of Constantinople. Throughout his life, Angelo, now Don Roncalli, always celebrated the anniversary of his ordination. In 1912 he recalled it in this way:

> When all was over and I raised my eyes, having sworn the oath of eternal
> fidelity to my superior, the Bishop, I saw the blessed image of Our Lady to
> which I confess I had not paid any attention before. She seemed to smile at
> me from the altar and her look gave me a feeling of sweet peace in my soul
> and a generous and confident spirit (*Journal*, p. 170).

He had no anxiety about the irrevocable step he had taken. He was in his right place. Most of the students from the Roman seminary were away at the holiday Villa at Roccantica. The college was deserted.

He wrote letters to his parents and 'Uncle' Zaverio to thank them and share his joy. They had been unable to scrape together the money for the train fare. He would be in Sotto il Monte by August 15 to say Mass in the church of his baptism on the feast of the Assumption. He wrote to Camillo Guindani, bishop of Bergamo, pledging obedience. Then he went on a round of churches – he lists seven but says there were 'many others' – beseeching his favourite saints 'to help me to keep ever alight in my heart the flame of this memorable day' (*Journal*, p. 171).

The next day, August 11, Spolverini accompanied him to the crypt of St Peter's where he celebrated his first Mass. He was free to choose the texts, and opted for the 'votive Mass' of Sts Peter and Paul. Texts and setting conspired to make him commit himself totally to 'the service of Jesus and of the Church'. He used the words of St Peter himself: 'Lord, you know everything; you know that I love you' (John 21.17). He wasn't to know that he would himself be buried where he said his first Mass. His account goes on: 'I came out of the church as if in a dream. On that day the marble and bronze popes aligned along the walls of the Basilica seemed to look at me from their tombs with a new expression, as if to give me courage and confidence' (*Journal*, p. 171). Spolverini had arranged an audience with the living Pope, Pius X, which took place towards midday. Kneeling, Angelo stammered out a few words about his village and the vow he had taken in the crypt. Pius placed a hand on his head, and almost whispering in his ear said: 'Well done, well done, my boy . . . this is what I like to hear. I will ask the good Lord to grant a special blessing on these good intentions of yours, so that you may remain a priest after his own heart' (*Journal*, p. 172). Pius blessed him paternally and began talking to a Pole. But then he turned back and asked Angelo how soon he would be home. 'For the Assumption' was the answer. The Pope said: 'Ah, what a feast that will be up there in your little village, and how those fine Bergamesque bells will peal out on that day' (*Ibid.*). And so it turned out.

But Sotto il Monte saw him for less than two weeks, and he spent the months of September and October with his Roman seminary friends at Roccantica, savouring his priesthood and the daily intimacy with Christ in the Eucharist. He began further studies in canon law on November 4, 1904. The Roman term starts late, but on a symbolic feast, that of St Charles Borromeo. He was named 'prefect' of the freshmen, which was an honour but rather tiresome. He was busier than ever, helping Mgr Radini Tedeschi to prepare the Congress, November 30 to December 4, to commemorate the fiftieth anniversary of the definition of the Immaculate Conception. But his first months as a new priest were not a period of unalloyed happiness.

His mother was complaining that he didn't love her any more. He hadn't written to her and, what's more, she alleged that her husband was withholding Angelo's letters. He hadn't sent her any money. And he had sent a photograph to the parish priest but not to the family. Don Angelo patiently tried to clear up these misunderstandings in a long letter. He refused to believe that his father had withheld any letters. He didn't have any money: it had all been swallowed up in the expenses of his first Mass at Sotto il Monte, he had to buy new shoes and a soutane for his ordination, and canon law books were particularly expensive. He advises patience and promises to send a photograph, though he adds that 'being neither pope, cardinal nor bishop but a simple priest', he does not see why his portrait should be all over the place (*Familiari*, I, p. 19). He protests his undying love: 'Even if I were pope, you would always remain for me the greatest lady in this world. So, I beg you, please don't doubt my love and the tender memories that I will always have of you. Believe me, distance, far from weakening filial love, makes it more vivid, gentle and affectionate' (*Ibid.*, p. 18). The purpose of this letter dated January 1, 1905, was to reduce the growing gap between himself and his mother; yet it provides evidence of how deep the estrangement was becoming.

Nor were his first attempts at public speaking back in Rome a great success. On December 8 Fr Pitocchi had prevailed upon him to give a talk on the Immaculate Conception to the Children of Mary in a rich Roman suburb. He wrote it out in advance, but on rereading it, found it 'too fancy, too flowery and full of high-sounding words' (Pepper, p. 41). So he tried to make it simpler, but got confused and lost his way:

> My talk was a disaster. I mixed up quotations from the Old and the New Testaments. I confused St Alphonsus with St Bernard. I mistook writings of the Fathers for writings of the prophets. A fiasco. I was so ashamed that afterwards I fell into the arms of Fr Francesco and confessed my mortification (*Ibid.*, p. 41).

He still remembered the fiasco as Pope, and told the story to the sculptor, Giacomo Manzù.

Then something happened that made him forget his mother's grumbles and his oratorical failures. Without any initiative on his part, his life suddenly took a new and wholly unexpected direction: that pattern would recur. He was merely at the end of a long chain of events.

Pius X had stunned the Roman Curia by appointing a thirty-seven-year-old Spaniard educated in an English seminary, Rafael Merry del Val, as his Secretary of State. He made it clear that he was repudiating both the policies and the men of the previous pontificate. The first victim was the defeated candidate in the conclave, Cardinal Rampolla. He resignedly prepared for death (it did not come) and lived 'like a king in exile' (De Luca, p. 90). He was too close to the spirit of Leo XIII for comfort. In his *Memoirs*, Merry del Val cruelly explains that Rampolla would not have been elected pope, even if the Austrian veto had not operated (Newman Press, Westminster, Maryland, 1951, p. 1). Pius dealt with the institutions as harshly as with the men of Leo XIII.

In July 1904 he dissolved the *Opera dei Congressi*. This was a bitter blow to Count Giovanni Grosoli, its last president, and 'the hardest moment in the life of its chaplain, Radini Tedeschi' (see Gabriele De Rosa in *Linee*, p. 51). Angelo said later that 'it came like a thunderbolt in a clear sky'. Pius X was not interested in social doctrine and despised democracy, whether Christian or not (see his encyclical *Vehementer*). He saw the *Opera dei Congressi* as 'modernism' in its social form. Since the main goal of his pontificate was the suppression of 'modernism', the *Opera dei Congressi* had to go. And with it had to go Radini Tedeschi, another 'Leo XIII man'. Bishop Guindani of Bergamo had died in October 1904. Radini Tedeschi was appointed to succeed him.

This was exciting news for Angelo, since he already had links with Radini Tedeschi. It first leaked out on January 8, 1905, after the beatification of Jean-Marie Vianney, universally known as the Curé d'Ars. There was a certain irony in this timing. The Curé d'Ars was a humble village priest, innocent of theology, who tramped the muddy lanes in his hob-nailed boots (still reverently preserved) and struggled in single-handed combat with the Devil. His beatification was a conscious judgement on presumptuously critical theologians, sophisticated religious priests who looked down their elegant noses on the diocesan clergy, and on all those tempted by intellectual pride. Roncalli had noted down some of his maxims when at the Bergamo seminary. One of them seemed particularly apt now: 'Those who humiliate us are our real friends, not those who praise us' (*Journal*, p. 436). Pius X, however, contrived to pass off Radini Tedeschi's banishment to Bergamo as a promotion. It was nothing of the kind for someone used to being at the decision-making centre. But Radini Tedeschi accepted the appointment with good grace and his obedience, so creative in its results, had a profound effect on Roncalli.

The bishop-elect needed a secretary. He asked the rector of the Roman seminary, Bugarini, to bring along to his flat, Corso Vittorio Emmanuele 21, his Bergamesque students. They imagined they were merely going to present their homage to the new bishop. He took two of them, Roncalli and Carozzi, and tried them out for a week, setting them to deal with the abundant correspondence that followed upon the news of his appointment. He selected Roncalli. Thus at twenty-four Angelo, the village boy, became secretary to an aristocratic bishop exactly twice his age. On January 29, 1905, Pius X ordained Radini Tedeschi bishop. Angelo acted as chaplain, holding the Book of the Gospels on the bishop's shoulders to signify the burden he would have to bear. For Angelo it meant the end of canon law; and it meant going home.

Chapter 4

Into the whirlwind of Modernism

Controversy, at least in this age, does not lie between the hosts of heaven, Michael and his angels on the one side, and the powers of evil on the other; but it is a sort of night battle, where each fights for himself, and friend and foe stand together

(John Henry Newman, 'Faith and Reason contrasted as Habits of Mind', in *Sermons, chiefly on the Theory of Religious Belief, preached before the University of Oxford,* 1843)

Angelo left Bergamo for Rome as a hopeful young seminarian in 1901. He returned at the start of April, 1905 as secretary to the newly appointed bishop. It was a post requiring the utmost tact. Though he had so far 'done nothing' as a priest to justify his early promotion, his regular contact with the bishop led the Bergamesque clergy – including his old seminary professors – to suppose that from now on he would have some 'influence'. On closer analysis, they were a cliquish lot. Opinion in the diocese, already divided under the two previous bishops, was far from unanimous about the appointment of Radini Tedeschi, who could be malevolently regarded as a Roman careerist whose career had unexpectedly gone wrong. Roncalli was to write the biography of Radini Tedeschi whom he always called, with pride and affection, 'My Bishop'. He hints at these quarrels with characteristic understatement: 'When Mgr Radini Tedeschi came to Bergamo he found, still smouldering, the ashes of the disputes which had saddened his two immediate and illustrious prodecessors, Mgr Speranza and Mgr Guindani, and naturally those who represented the two parties would have liked to have the new bishop on their side' (*My Bishop,* p. 129). Roncalli relates an old clerical chestnut about earlier bishops. One didn't know how to say 'no' to anyone; another couldn't bring himself to say 'yes'; and a third hovered uncertainly between 'yes' and 'no' (*Ibid.,* p. 105).

Radini Tedeschi had none of these problems. He knew exactly what he wanted to do. He was authoritarian, and something of a martinet; 'In the government of his diocese this military spirit was very apparent in his insistence on discipline which was to be maintained in everything, down to the smallest detail' (*Ibid.,* p. 106). He was not in the habit of turning a blind eye. He was convinced that 'a strong and vigorous government does less harm than a weak one' and 'abhorred popularity won by compliance and surrender' (*Ibid.,* p. 106). Angelo, whose own temperament was very different, was able to observe at close quarters the way Radini Tedeschi exercised his episcopal authority. It was part of his ecclesiastical

49

education to discover that holy men could differ among themselves, and that obedience and loyalty, though essential, did not magically solve all problems. But he was 'the Bishop's shadow', as he was nicknamed, and learned discretion the hard way.

The bells of Bergamo echoed from the upper town on April 9, 1905, when Radini Tedeschi entered Bergamo in triumph and took possession of his cathedral. Angelo wrote an account of it for the local paper, *l'Eco di Bergamo*. It was his first piece of journalism, and for the next decade he wrote regularly for this staunchly Catholic paper.

But having taken possession of his diocese, Radini Tedeschi, accompanied by his secretary, immediately departed on a national pilgrimage to Lourdes. They set sail from Genoa on April 29, 1905, stayed in Marseilles, Lyons, Paray-le-Monial and Montpellier as well as Lourdes. They returned via Rome where Radini Tedeschi addressed the 13th National Eucharistic Congress on June 5. They had an audience with Pius X on June 29 and in July Don Roncalli spent a few days at the Radini Tedeschi family home in Piacenza. It might be thought that Radini Tedeschi was reluctant to take charge of his diocese. But as the Bergamesque clergy waited apprehensively for his first move, he was laying his plans.

The visit to France was a pilgrimage, of course. But it also gave the pilgrims an opportunity to measure the impact of Pius X's policy towards France. Leo XIII's attempt to rally Franch Catholics to the Republic had been rejected as 'appeasement'. The new policy was one of confrontation. It was expressed with admirable clarity by Merry del Val:

> If only one could persuade the French that their salvation lies in battle. They should oblige us to restrain them, to moderate their ardour. But instead we have to push them. Yet they are on the battlefield and the front line. Men in that position are generally only too anxious to fight. But *they* just want to surrender. I am thinking particularly of the leaders, the intellectuals who are actively involved (Larkin, p. 124).

So France became the testing ground of the new pontificate. Pius X saw France as a country where bishops were feeble, Catholic political leaders like Marc Sagnier compromising, and theologians like Loisy were undermining the foundations of faith. He challenged all three groups. The French government resonded with increasing petulance, culminating in the 'Law of separation of Church and State' on December 9, 1905 (Text in Larkin, pp. 227 *et seq.*). The religious orders were expelled. Pius lost the battle with the French state. He then fell back on the battle within the Church.

These were alarm bells for a not very distant future, but they did not affect Radini Tedeschi as, in the autumn of 1905, he at last began to put his plans for the diocese into effect. Angelo sincerely admired his methodical energy. He discreetly noted: 'His fiery apostolic eloquence, his determination, his innumerable projects and extraordinary personal activity may have given many people at first the impression that he intended to make the most radical changes and was inspired only by the desire to introduce innovations' (*My Bishop*, p. 48). Was this first impression, then, mistaken? No and yes. He explains: 'He did not concentrate on carrying out reforms so much as on maintaining the glorious traditions of his diocese, and interpreting them *in harmony with the new conditions and needs of the time*' (*Ibid.*, p. 48). This was precisely Roncalli's own ambition when he became Pope more than fifty years later, and he expressed it in the same language: the revivifying of tradition through *aggiornamento* (a word only inadequately rendered by 'adaptation' or 'up-dating').

Radini Tedeschi's first priority was the pastoral visitation of the diocese. It had 352 parishes and a population of half a million. The Bishop began his visitation with the cathedral in Bergamo on December 8, 1905 and concluded it in 1909. In that time it was calculated that he had distributed Communion to a good third of his flock. Angelo was always at his side. Those priests who 'had dreaded his arrival' were won over (*Ibid.*, p. 49).

Radini Tedeschi was a great builder. He restored and redecorated the cathedral – rather too ornately for Roncalli's taste. He had a purpose-built retreat-house set up at Martinengo. Finding his episcopal palace 'an ugly, inconvenient and insanitary building', he had a new one designed and moved into it on November 21, 1906. There Roncalli lived for the next eight years. He thought it was 'a noble and graceful building' which did not clash with 'the jewels of Renaissance art, the Colleoni Chapel and the Baptistery' among which it was set. But inside it was very simple, 'the home of one who must set an example to others' (*My Bishop*, pp. 51–2). Radini Tedeschi also modernised the seminary, installing running water and central heating. Physical education, unheard of in Angelo's time as a student, became compulsory. Chemistry and other science labs were added. Around the diocese tumble-down parish churches were rebuilt. Roncalli learned to care for ecclesiastical plant.

Radini Tedeschi, finally, was an organiser of great ability. He laid particular emphasis on Catholic Action in the social sphere. In other words, he carried on exactly where the now suppressed *Opera dei Congressi* left off. Roncalli says this explicitly: 'He grieved for the disappearance of the Opera, but always remained faithful to its ideals ... He shared with his friends the desire ... to direct its rejuvenated energies into new social organisations required by the new conditions of the times' (*My Bishop*, p. 77). Radini Tedeschi's very first pastoral letter was devoted to Catholic Action. It stated principles to which his secretary remained devoted for the rest of his life:

Catholic Action must be founded on a wider awareness of the needs and

conditions of times, men and events. It must be directed towards the formation of wise and well-informed consciences, full of prudence in doing good work which must be brought to a conclusion without unjustifiable delay or imprudent haste. It must show due regard for Christian social reforms, and for the need to respect the rights of everyone and the obligations which no one can honourably reject. It must be particularly active wherever justice and charity are most obviously neglected . . . It must harmonise authority and freedom, find its unity in the co-operation of all men for the common good and in the mutual trust between all men and social classes; its purpose is to restore all things in Jesus Christ (*My Bishop*, p. 78).

That could be considered a sketch for Pope John's social encyclicals, *Mater et Magistra* and *Pacem in Terris*.

But Don Angelo, though the 'Bishop's shadow', had his own independent existence. His contributions to *l'Eco di Bergamo* sharpened his style and gave him an eye for contemporary events. They also brought him into contact with Count Giovanni Grosoli who ran a chain of 'Christian Democratic' newspapers. From October, 1905 he subscribed to one of them, *Il Momento* of Turin. In June, 1905 Pius X, with his encyclical *Fermo Proposito*, dispensed Catholics from the *non expedit*, that is, allowed them to vote in the November elections wherever Church interests demanded it. As Italian Catholics re-entered Italian political life, the role of the Catholic press became more important than ever. Pius X was an avid newspaper reader, scrutinised articles for their orthodoxy, and was not above 'planting' pieces written by himself or his private secretary, Giambattista Bressan. Having suppressed the *Opera dei Congressi*, Pius did not much like Grosoli, its last president, and poured scorn on Christian Democracy. Radini Tedeschi was tarred with the same brush.

Pius X favoured papers like *Riscossa*, edited in Milan since 1890 by three priest brothers, Andrea, Gottardo and Jacopo Scotton. It was the organ of the 'intransigents'. Their proud motto was *Frangar, non flectar*. They would rather break than bend before the winds of change. Don Roncalli repudiated this attitude, and modified the motto to *Flectar, non frangar* (I will bend, but not break) (*Letture*, p. 397). But in 1906 the 'intransigents' were in command, confident that they had the support of the Pope. They specialised in attacks on 'modernism' in Lombardy. There was some evidence that their charges were not entirely unfounded. In 1906 the French Protestant, Paul Sabatier, made a journey through upper Italy and found that Alfred Loisy was influential in Turin, Novara and Bergamo. He wrote to Loisy: 'In Milan you know that our friends are going to found a review, a sort of Italian *Demain*, called *Rinnovimento*. Poor Pius X. I met Fogazzaro too, in good physical and spiritual health, full of vigour and determined to win through' (Loisy, *Mémoires pour servir à l'histoire religieuse de notre temps*, II, p. 476). Fogazzaro was the author of a novel, *Il Santo*, in which he had imagined a pope of Franciscan simplicity who would go out among the people. Though hardly an incitement to rebellion in the Church, its reforming implications were deemed subversive, and in 1905 it was placed on the Index of Forbidden Books. But the Scotton brothers didn't mind who they attacked. Their principal local target was Cardinal Andrea Carlo Ferrari, archbishop of Milan.

Don Roncalli first met Ferrari on September 4, 1905, and despite the difference of age – Ferrari was fifty-five, Roncalli twenty-four – and rank, they became friends. Ferrari had been Archbishop since 1894. They met almost once a month until Ferrari's death in February, 1921. He was not technically a spiritual director, but Angelo consulted him on important decisions. Ferrari was no 'modernist' in the manner of Loisy, but he was a 'conciliarist' in Italian politics, much influenced by Antonio Rosmini (whose *Five Wounds of the Church*, once placed on the Index, was the breviary of Italian 'liberal' Catholicism). He believed that only adaptation would permit the Church to reach the dechristianised working class, and encouraged theologians, clerical and lay, to work for the reconciliation of faith and learning (see Carlo Snider, *L'Episcopato del Cardinale Andrea Carlo Ferrari*, vol. I, Vicenza, Neri Pozza, 1981). Roncalli shared in all these ambitions, and remained faithful to Ferrari. The proof is that on February 10, 1963, in the presence of a large number of pilgrims from Lombardy, he signed the decree introducing the beatification cause of the cardinal.

But in 1906 it was dangerous to be associated with Ferrari. Pius X did not like him, set his watch-dogs on him, and made leaden-footed jokes about the tediousness of his sermons: 'Preach away, preach away, and it won't even be noticed if you bore the pants off everyone' (Snider, p. 361). Pius X, with his 'peasant simplicity', could be crude as well as unjust. Jesuit historian Domenico Mondrone claims that further study of the relationship between Pius X and Ferrari would show 'how far a well-orchestrated campaign of calumny can take over the mind and affect the judgement of a saint' (*Civiltà Cattolica,* July, 1981, p. 159). That is much too charitable. We know that Roncalli was preoccupied with this problem. In 1959 he read carefully through the historical *Disquisitio* prepared for the beatification of Pius X (Typis Polyglottis Vaticanis, 1950).

The contact with Ferrari led him to make an important historical discovery on February 23, 1906. While the bishops were preparing the 8th Provincial Council in the Episcopal Palace, Piazza Fontana, 2, their secretaries had time on their hands. Don Roncalli was browsing in the archiepiscopal library, full of memories of St Charles Borromeo. He describes what happened:

Suddenly I was struck by thirty-nine parchment bound volumes which bore the title: *Archivio Spirituale – Bergamo.* I explored them: I read them through on successive visits. What a pleasant surprise for my spirit! To come across such rich and fascinating documents concerning the Church of Bergamo at the most characteristic period of its religious renewal (*rinnovimento*), just after the Council of Trent, in the most ardent period of the Counter-reformation (*Atti*, III, p. xxx).

Two questions come to mind about this discovery of what was treasure trove for a budding historian. Why were the thirty-nine volumes not in the Ambrosian Library round the corner, where they would certainly have been catalogued by its indefatigable prefect, Mgr Achille Ratti, the future Pius XI? And why had no one noticed them before?

Here is a hypothesis. They were in the archiepiscopal library rather than the Ambrosiano because they belonged to the personal archives of the archbishops of Milan. They suddenly 'became available' to Don Roncalli because Ferrari believed that they would throw light on how St Charles Borromeo set about the reform of a diocese after the Council of Trent. Pius X was starting to 'reform' dioceses by imposing on them apostolic visitors of his choice. The Borromeo archives showed, on the contrary, that the constitutional way to reform a diocese was by meticulous episcopal visitation of all its parishes and religious houses followed by a diocesan Synod. In the mind of the Council of Trent, the bishop, not some curial interloper from Rome, was the proper agent of reform. 'History', Roncalli liked to say, 'is the teacher of life' (*Magistra vitae*). He quoted this in his opening speech to the Council on October 11, 1962.

Roncalli, at any rate, had discovered his scholarly vocation: editing the thirty-nine volumes of St Charles Borromeo. He began teaching church history at the Bergamo seminary the following November. By 1909 Radini Tedeschi set up a commission of seminary professors to edit the texts. But, as Roncalli wryly notes, 'as usually happens with committees, the work fell almost entirely upon one person' (*Atti*, III, p. xxxi): himself. Don Pietro Forno helped until his death in 1938. But it took a lifetime. The five volumes appeared in 1936, 1937, 1938, 1946 and 1957. The patient, steady work suited his temperament. The fact that it was local history did not make it unimportant. Most Italian history, anyway, is local history, and the 'Romans' play less part in it than foreigners imagine. As Arnoldo Momigliano, the great cultural historian, remarked, 'Each Italian city has a history in which the Romans played only one part – German feudal lords and Christian Bishops were no less important' (*Terza contributo*, p. 151). That was certainly true of Milan and Bergamo. This work also meant that Roncalli saw the Council of Trent not as an anti-Protestant polemic, but as a reforming Council in a world he knew well. As he plodded round after Radini Tedeschi on his pastoral visits to parishes, notebook in hand, he was reliving the pastoral visitation of St Charles Borromeo.

In September and October, 1906 there was a diocesan pilgrimage to the Holy Land. It was no jet-age four-star hotel joyride. Much of it was done on horseback. In Tiberias, a welcoming volley of rifle shots from some well-meaning Arabs startled the horse of a fellow pilgrim. It reared and threw its rider to the ground. The road between Nazareth and Cana was no more than a dusty track. Roncalli wrote rather tartly in one of his regular despatches for *l'Eco di Bergamo*: 'But we are under the Turks here, don't forget, and though the Turkish government knows all about extortion and incredible injustice, it knows nothing about roads' (Elliott, p. 52). He would get to know a lot more about Turkish roads thirty years later.

But Roncalli's report on the pilgrimage is not confined to travelogues. The *Spiritual Exercises* had taught him to visualise in imagination the places where Jesus had lived. It was the first step towards contemplation. Now he is seeing them for real. He is moved, and it affects his prose. They were up at 4.30 one morning to take a boat across the Lake of Tiberias:

> I shall never forget the enchantment, the heart's ease, the spiritual relish I discovered this morning floating upon these waters. Little by little, as our small boat stood out into the lake, the first light of dawn lent colour to the water, the houses and then the surrounding hills. We did not speak, but our hearts were stirred. It was as though we could see Jesus crossing this lake in Peter's boat. Jesus was before us and we could see him; unworthy though we were, we sailed towards him and our prayer, silent though it was, was eloquent and spontaneous . . . As we touched the shore the sun appeared (Elliott, p. 53. Translation modified).

Christological controversies were raging in Europe. The Holy Office was already extracting propositions from the works of Loisy in preparation for the decree *Lamentabili*. One condemned error stated: 'It may be granted that the Christ shown by history is much inferior to the Christ who is the object of faith' (DS, 3429). Roncalli's pilgrimage to the Holy Land helped to preserve him from the ruinous disjunction (later developed by Rudolf Bultmann) between the 'Jesus of history' and 'the Christ of faith'.

In Jerusalem he struck an ecumenical note. The 'confused disorder of people, objects, languages, rites and beliefs that surround the church of the Holy Sepulchre' caused him 'pained astonishment'. He prayed for the day when 'the separated brothers' would be reunited (Dreyfus, p. 47). But this interlude was soon over. The new academic year was beginning, and he had to lecture in the seminary on Church history.

Don Roncalli could hardly have begun to teach the subject at a less propitious time than in November 1906. Far from being a quiet grove of Academe in which dusty scholars exchanged even dustier papers on topics that concerned only themselves, history was at the fiery heart of the contemporary philosophical debate. The first question was: does God act in human history (sometimes put in the form: Is there a supernatural element in history?)? Anyone who answered 'no' to either question was denying the possibility of divine revelation, which happens in time ('suffered under Pontius Pilate'), and declaring himself agnostic. The more difficult set of questions came next: How does one *know* that God is acting in history? Or: Is this divine action accessible to the critical tools of the historian?

Alfred Loisy was reputed to have said that 'God is not an actor in human history', a remark which was, to say the least, ambivalent. The French historian, Louis Marie Olivier Duchesne, director of the Ecole Française in Rome since 1895, was writing a *History of the Early Church*. He was later accused of 'ignoring the supernatural dimension of history' and placed on the Index. Part of Duchesne's 'doubt' was methodological: he did not want to press history to say more than it could say. The knife-edge between survival as a Catholic scholar and condemnation is illustrated by the fact that in 1906, Benigni praised Duchesne's first volume unreservedly: 'We do not need to wait for the Italian translation to commend the work to all college and seminary libraries and to the cultivated clergy who will find in Duchesne's most recent work a synthesis which combines science and orthodoxy, two qualities not easily found together these days' (Poulat, *Catholicisme*, p. 219). Don Roncalli's aim was precisely to combine science and orthodoxy. The difficulty of the enterprise at that date was that historical science was held to be 'critical', while orthodoxy was often 'uncritical': it was enlightenment versus obscurantism.

To overcome that false dilemma, Don Roncalli looked for a 'model' of historical writing in which science and orthodoxy were seen to be reconciled. He studied the *Annali* of Cesare Baronius, Oratorian, friend of St Philip Neri, and founding father of modern church history. He was not exaggerating the importance of Baronius, as the following judgement of Momigliano shows:

> From the sixteenth to the eighteenth century ecclesiastical history (especially of the early Church) was treated with a much greater display of erudition, with much more care for minute analysis of the evidence than any other type of history. There is no work in profane history comparable with the Magdeburg Centuriators and the *Annali* of Baronius (*Terzo contributo*, p. 101).

Modern secular history (including Edward Gibbon) derives from church history.

Roncalli learned from Baronius that, alongside the patient grind of the archivist, necessarily concerned with fastidious details, the historian also needs a vision of the whole. Writing as a historiographer, he shows that Baronius took account of 'the supernatural dimension' of history without loss of intellectual integrity:

Considering facts in the light of ideas, Baronius was able to weave into a unity all the scattered threads even of secular history, and to bring out its wonderful ordering towards the triumph of the sovereign idea which dominates the history of the world, that is the action of Divine Providence through which human actions converge towards the victory of the City of God, the Church. For that reason the *Annali* occupy a midway place between the *De Civitate Dei* (413 and 417) of St Augustine and Bossuet's *Discours sur l'histoire universelle* (1681); they are far superior to the contemporary histories of Guicciardini and Machiavelli, and from this point of view are surpassed perhaps only by Giovanni Battista Vico's *Principii di una Scienza Nuova* (1725 and 1730) whose work, however, is not free from obscurities. One can see that fresh studies could profitably be made on Baronius comparing him with other contemporary historians (*Linee*, p. 64).

Roncalli never got any further with the project implicitly announced in that final sentence. But he remained faithful to his central insight: the 'Christian idea', acting somewhat in the manner of Hegel's *Geist* or Spirit, works itself out in human history, not without ups and downs, not without human collaboration (for there is nothing deterministic about Roncalli's view of history). The 'prophets of gloom', denounced at the start of Vatican II, 'behave as though they had learned nothing from history . . . They behave as though at the time of the former Councils the *Christian idea* was fully vindicated' (Abbott, p. 712). Roncalli's attempt to 'pierce through the shimmer of relativity on the surface of history' (Arnold Toynbee) made a crucial impact on his view of the modern world; for if God is still at work in human history and all history is *Heilsgeschichte*, salvation-history, then this presence ought to be detectable through the 'signs of the times'.

However, this was not a view of history that was fashionable, or even understood, at the court of Pius X. It believed that the modern world was riddled with errors. Pius went over to the attack on April 17, 1907, with an allocution directed against 'religious neo-reformism'. Rebels are abroad in the Church, Pius proclaimed, 'who profess and disseminate in subtle form monstrous errors' on the evolution of dogma, on the need to return to the pure Gospel stripped of theological explanations and conciliar definitions, on emancipation from the Church, though not so openly as to risk excommunication, and, finally, on the need for adaptation to the times. Taken together these errors constitute 'not a heresy, but the compendium and poison of all the heresies' (for this, see Daly, p. 191). The attack gathered pace. On July 3, 1907 the decree *Lamentabili* listed sixty-five unattributed errors (though fifty-three of them were derived from Loisy). It was difficult, indeed impossible, to deduce a positive content from *anathemata* cast in a negative form. Error 65, for example, stated: 'Modern

Catholicism can be reconciled with true science only if it is transformed into a non-dogmatic Christianity, that is to say, into a broad and liberal Protestantism.' Did that leave room for other attempts to reconcile 'modern Catholicism with true science' that did not fall into this manifest error? The answer was by no means clear. But an atmosphere of anxiety and suspicion was generated in which the presumption was that 'errors' were omnipresent, and menacing.

But *Lamentabili* was mere skirmishing compared with the encyclical *Pascendi* which appeared on September 8, 1907 (AAS, 40, 1907, pp. 593–650). It acted as the Syllabus of Errors for the early twentieth century. It may be said to have invented 'Modernism' as a system in order better to condemn it. *Pascendi* recognised this in its introduction: 'It is one of the cleverest devices of the Modernists (as they are commonly and rightly called) to present their doctrines without order and systematic arrangement, in a scattered and disjointed manner, so as to make it appear as if their minds were in doubt and hesitation, whereas in reality they are quite fixed and steadfast' (Daly, p. 195). The author of *Pascendi* (in fact Fr Joseph Lemius O.M.I. working to the orders of Pius X conveyed by Merry del Val) claims a remarkable insight into the hidden motivations of those he seeks to destroy. He credits them with a synthesis they had not previously achieved, and obligingly spells it out for them. The two errors at the heart of the system are agnosticism, defined as 'the restriction of knowledge to phenomena', and its correlative, 'immanentism'. Since the source of religion cannot be found outside man or in the objective order, it must necessarily be sought within man, in therefore his wholly subjective needs, impulses, aspirations, or so-called 'religious sense'. *Pascendi* did not deign to argue to try to refute this position. Its author appeared to believe that mere statement would be sufficient repudiation.

That is not, however, what happened. 'Modernists' (some now began to accept the label) declared that they could not find themselves in the incriminated system. *Pascendi* was talking about someone else, possibly some imaginary theologian. They had not been hit; they had not even been grazed ('*Nous ne sommes pas même effleurés*', wrote Maurice Blondel, Daly, p. 205). Where the encyclical was precise, it did not concern them; where it was vague, it was so indiscriminate that no one at all need feel wounded by it. 'The Modernist', *Pascendi* confidently explained, 'includes in himself a manifold personality; he is a philosopher, a believer, a theologian, an historian, a critic, an apologist, a reformer'. Few could escape belonging to one or other of these categories; no one could embrace them all. Everyone had a bolt-hole.

The discussion about who was or was not condemned by *Pascendi* could have gone on for a very long time, with all the suspects protesting their aggrieved innocence. But Pius X had thought of that, and included in the encyclical a *disciplinary* section of the utmost severity. It said:

Anyone who is in any way found to be tainted with Modernism is to be excluded without compunction from those offices, whether of government or of teaching, and those who already occupy them are to be removed. The same policy is to be adopted towards those who openly or secretly lend countenance to Modernism, either by extolling the Modernists or excusing their culpable conduct, or by carping at scholasticism or the *Magisterium* of the Church, or by refusing obedience to ecclesiastical authority or any of its depositories; and towards those who show a love of novelty in history, archaeology or biblical exegesis; and finally towards those who neglect the sacred sciences or appear to prefer the secular sciences to them.

Pascendi was a catch-all net in which anyone in any scholarly field could be trapped. So that these harsh provisions would not remain a dead letter, other measures were taken: 'councils of vigilance' were set up in every diocese; Umberto Benigni was encouraged by Merry del Val to create a secret network of informers; 'apostolic visitations' (what Ferrari called 'apostolic vexations') began in suspect dioceses. That meant, in the first place, Italy, which was always more immediately affected by Vatican decisions.

In November 1907 it was announced that those who opposed *Pascendi* would be excommunicated. The ordinary process of 'reception' of an encyclical was short-circuited. Even those who agreed that there was a need to condemn some of the wilder theories that were circulating might have thought that *Pascendi* was badly drafted, ill-conceived, and wrongly timed. Was that 'disagreement'? The witch-hunt drew perilously close to Bergamo. The Milanese review, *Il Rinnovimento*, was condemned and the reforming group led by Tommaso Gallerati Scotti was dissolved (*Utopia*, p. 393). It is not unfair to speak of a reign of terror. Even 'thought-crime' (graphically described by George Orwell in *1984*) was now being hunted down.

In this context the lecture given by Don Roncalli at the Bergamo seminary on December 4, 1907, to commemorate the third centenary of the death of Baronius, was dramatic (text published as Angelo Roncalli, *Il cardinale Cesare Baronio*, Edizioni di Storia e Letteratura, 1961). He was just twenty-six. He had been professor of church history for only a year. Trip-wires abounded. He knew exactly what was at stake: a loose or incautious phrase might have wrecked his career for good. Yet he shows a surprising coolness. He speaks as someone who has read widely in his field, has assessed the evidence dispassionately, and is capable of making up his own mind on controversial issues. His appointed theme was 'Faith and Scientific Research'. So although Baronius was the pretext, his real subject was the place of historical scholarship in the Church in the year 1907, just four months after *Pascendi*.

This was Roncalli's finest hour to date. He defended 'historical criticism' and spoke of the 'wonderful progress that has been made in scientific history in the last few years' (Alberigo, p. 401). He claimed that Baronius 'has quite rightly been hailed as the founder of historical criticism'. This was a shrewd and legitimate move. It meant that he could assert that the Church had been the first in the field of historical criticism. This had been overlooked because, as he explained, 'some scholars, especially in Germany, believe that they have a monopoly of truth – to the great damage of the faith and Catholic truth, as though the Church feared the light that might come from the results of such criticism'. But, he went boldly on, it was the Church that had opened the way to this kind of research. The tradition started by Baronius had been continued and developed by Bellarmine, Petavius, Tomassino and the French Maurists (*Ibid.,* p. 401). Their work would have brought credit, he adds, 'to the Academies of Berlin and Vienna'.

Not content with this defence of 'historical criticism', he went out of his way to use the now suspect language of 'renewal' (*rinnovimento*). He drew an analogy between the late sixteenth and early twentieth century and made it plain that he considered the 'general renewal of Catholic scholarship' (*il rinnovimento della scienza cattolica*), promoted by Baronius, to be still on the agenda. It was precisely this capacity for 'renewal' that made Baronius 'a man of his time – we would say today a "modern man" – in that he had intuited profoundly the needs of the Church and the society of his time' (*Linee,* p. 64). This was quite enough to arouse the interest of the delators who, he knew, were somewhere in his audience.

So, dialectically, he offered them a 'pound of flesh'. He talked clearly about 'Modernism', though without actually naming it. He did not need to. In the Bergamo seminary in December 1907 everyone knew perfectly well what he meant:

> It seems to me that the abandonment of these deep convictions of faith (i.e. that history has a supernatural factor) is one of the main causes of the strange movement of ideas which until recently troubled Catholic consciences and caused grave concern. Certain poor deluded souls – I think it right to call them so – judged the Church and Christianity by criteria that were all too human. Thus the illogical and unjust application that German theological rationalism made of its critical conclusions to the traditional doctrine of the Church, was an attack on its perennial consistency – no doubt with the praiseworthy intention of saving it. The result, however, is that out of fear they have recourse to other systems of thought which, by a strange irony, lead to a destruction of the scientific method and a dreadful regression into subjectivism of the worst sort. Woe to the day on which such doctrines prevailed (*Linee,* p. 66).

That could be considered as an endorsement of *Pascendi* in the broadest sense. But unlike *Pascendi*, Roncalli recognises the good intentions of these thinkers ('with the praiseworthy intention of saving it') and speaks as though the problem were now happily resolved ('until *recently* troubled Catholic consciences'). *Pascendi*, on the contrary, attributed motives of vainglory and pride to the Modernists, and said that they were an ever-present and insidious menace.

Don Roncalli, moreover, distanced himself from *Pascendi* in another way. The encyclical had presented Modernism as an organised conspiracy of well-nigh diabolical cunning; Roncalli, writing more in sorrow than in anger, presents it rather as one strand in the development of Western European thought:

> The remarkable historical period which, prepared by the pagan renaissance,
> started with the German Reformation is still unfinished at the dawn of the
> twentieth century. The problems which worried the Church then and the
> tremendous difficulties which beset it, are the problems and difficulties of
> the Church today – except perhaps that they have become even more
> disturbing. The empiricism of Bacon and his school, which dominated
> European science in the seventeenth century, led scholars to the strangest
> conclusions about Christianity and the Church. In the name of positivistic
> studies Catholics were attacked from all sides. The least of the charges was
> that of obscurantism: the Church was said to be locked into narrow-
> minded and ancient formulations that had lost all meaning (*Linee*, p. 65).

The questions posed by history, he seems to imply, will not go away because they have been declared 'errors'.

Don Roncalli could not have spoken in this way and risked Roman censure unless he had allies. His first ally was his bishop, Radini Tedeschi. But Radini Tedeschi had a wide circle of friends. Among them was Cardinal Désiré Mercier of Malines-Brussels. He had visited Bergamo on May 4, 1906, and Don Roncalli had shown him round the city (*Cronologia*, p. 522). After teaching a revived form of Thomism in Louvain for nearly a quarter of a century, he had been made primate of Belgium out of the blue in 1906. He was open to the best in modern thought, corresponded with many scholars throughout Europe, and acted as a kind of under-ground clearing house for all those who believed that condemnations alone were not the best way to deal with Modernism. Dubious scholarship had to be met by better scholarship. In a footnote to the published version of his Baronius lecture, Don Roncalli quotes a speech given by Mercier along these lines in Louvain on December 8, 1907. So they were exchanging off-prints. Privately, Mercier did not have a high opinion of Pius X. In 1908 Wilfrid Ward, one of his many correspondents and editor of *The Dublin Review*, wrote to the Duke of Norfolk: '(Cardinal Mercier) thinks the Roman theology quite impossible: yet though he is hand in glove with the Pope he clearly does not give him the least inkling of this view' (*Bishops and Writers*, p. 58).

Don Roncalli's ally in Milan, Cardinal Ferrari, went public. In a pastoral letter in 1908, he denounced the 'anti-Modernists' who, he said, were just as bad and just as 'modern' (the word now having lost all meaning) as those they attacked: 'In certain reviews and newspapers warding off Modernism involves excesses. These anti-modernist zealots (*zelanti*) discover Modernism all over the place, and even manage to throw suspicion on those who are very far removed from it' (Tramontin, I, p. 72). That did not endear him to Pius X. Roncalli spent three days with Bishop Bonomelli in Cremona June 1 to 3, 1908. The old volcano was not yet extinguished. He had tried to persuade Cardinal Rampolla that the intellectual crisis 'should not be met with repressive and negative measures', that the mood of fear was bad for scholarship and the Church, and that 'an honest and fruitful liberty' was needed if Catholic scholars were to progress (Tramontin, I, pp. 85–6). Rampolla agreed, but was powerless to influence events. Even more remarkably, Bonomelli, already in 1908, looked forward to an ecumenical council: 'Perhaps a great ecumenical council, which would discuss rapidly, freely and publicly the great problems of religious life, would draw the attention of the world to the Church, stimulate faith, and open up new ways for the future' (*Ibid.*, p. 86). Almost exactly fifty years later, Roncalli took up Bonomelli's idea in almost identical terms.

One of the first casualties of *Pascendi* was Giacomo Della Chiesa, the future Benedict XV. He was working in the Secretariat of State. His principal crime was that he remined on friendly terms with Cardinal Rampolla. Merry del Val told him curtly that this was 'bad diplomacy' on his part, and Della Chiesa was exiled to Bologna as archbishop. Shy and unprepossessing in appearance, he found the anti-clerical atmosphere of Bologna a strain, and the Pope refused to give him the cardinal's hat that normally went with the appointment. Pius relented only in the spring of 1914 (see Trevor, pp. 71–2). In June 1908 there was an 'apostolic visitation' of the Bergamo seminary and another for the whole diocese in July and August. Don Giuseppe Moioli, the New Testament professor, was sacked. The others including Don Roncalli survived; but they became uncomfortably aware that there were spies in their midst. One of them (though they may not have known this at the time) was Mgr Giovanni Mazzoleni, a cathedral canon, who regularly wrote to his old seminary friend, Cardinal Gaetano De Lai, now head of the all-powerful Consistorial Congregation (it dealt with the appointment of bishops and supervised the administration of dioceses). Mazzoleni's haul of Modernists was meagre. He concentrated on manifestations of 'social modernism', by which he meant excessive affection for the now discredited 'Christian democracy'. The best he can do is to report on the senior common room at the seminary. The priests are reading newspapers of a 'modernising tendency'. He has heard disloyal remarks such as: 'The "Roman Question" is definitely *dépassé*', 'The Vatican is merely stumbling forwards and doesn't know what to do', and 'Another pope would not behave in this way' (*Disquisitio*, p. 172). None of these remarks was particularly outrageous and, with hindsight, we can say that they were all true. But they were dangerous at this time, and Mazzoleni judged them worth delating.

He also reported that some were trying to excuse Pius X by suggesting that his advisors were acting without his authority. 'It's all the fault of Merry del Val', was the commonest remark, but De Lai, Cardinal Vives y Tuto or 'the Jesuits' were sometimes invoked as scapegoats (*Ibid.*). As though wearying of such arguments, Don Roncalli busied himself with the Borromeo archives and in October, 1908 visited Venice for the first time, in search of documents. But on November 18, 1908, he had a chance to meet Pius X and see for himself how obsessed the Pope was with his anti-Modernist campaign. It ought to have been a joyful occasion. Radini Tedeschi was leading a delegation from Bergamo to congratulate Pius on the 50th anniversary of his priestly ordination. Don Roncalli carried the tray containing their offering of 25,100 *lire* in gold coins. He never forgot the impression the Pope made on him: 'After the address of homage, Pius X spoke with such anxiety about the perilous times we were living through and of the insidious traps that the evil one lays for the good faith of Catholics, that he completely forgot to thank us for our gift' (*Letture*, pp. 272–3). By the time Roncalli reported this he was already Pope himself and Pius X had been canonised. So his comment on the ungrateful pontiff has special weight: 'Certainly holy, but not fully perfect in that he let himself be overwhelmed by anxiety and showed himself so anguished' (*Ibid.*).

Radini Tedeschi's optimism, by contrast, was unquenched. He had not given up hope of forming a more theologically literate clergy. In January, 1909 he launched *La vita diocesana*, consciously modelled on Mercier's *La vie diocésaine*. Though his Roman seminary friend Guglielmo Carozzi was nominally the editor, it was Roncalli who did much of the work. In 1953 he claimed that 'most of the unsigned articles can be attributed to the humble author of these lines' (*Lettere*, p. 498).

In autumn 1909 800 workers at a textile factory at Ranica, just outside Bergamo, went on strike. They had founded a union known as 'the Workers' League'. Management responded by sacking the chief union official and putting the factory on short time. The strike was designed to secure his reinstatement and a guaranteed 'contract of employment' for the future. It began on September 21, 1909. There was very little in the union coffers. After a month *l'Eco de Bergamo* started a fund to support the strikers. Radini Tedeschi made the first contribution of 500 *lire*. The right-wing press was furious. 'The Bishop's alms', thundered *Perseveranza*, 'is a consecration of the strike, a blessing given to a frankly socialist cause' (Dreyfus, p. 50). Pressure was put on Pius X to disavow this somewhat improbable candidate for the role of 'red bishop'.

Radini Tedeschi had no option but to support the strike. His whole concept of Catholic Action was at stake. In 1906 he had founded the Labour Office (*Ufficio del Lavoro*) which acted as the trades union council for the Bergamo region (*My Bishop*, p. 85). It was inaugurated in the Rubini Theatre with some pomp. It was based in the People's House (*Casa del Popolo*) where Don Roncalli gave popular lectures on church history. The right of workers to band together in trades unions was clearly stated in Leo XIII's *Rerum Novarum*. So Radini Tedeschi's support for the Ranica strikers was consistent with everything he had been trying to do.

Don Roncalli sprang to his defence with an article in *La vita diocesana* in November 1909 (text in *Pasqua*, 1976, p. 17 *et seq.*). It is a mini-treatise on the right and duty of the Church to 'intervene in politics'. 'The priest who lives in the light of the teachings of the Gospel', he writes, 'could not pass by on the other side of the road'. The Bishop led the way because he had 'a duty of charity towards the weak who were suffering for the triumph of justice'. The parish priests had joined in and 'sustained the workers' cause to the end'. Roncalli denounces as old-hat the 'liberal' notion that 'a bishop should not embrace the cause of the oppressed'. This was to overlook that in the Gospels 'Christ's *preference* goes to the disinherited, the weak and the oppressed' (*Ibid.*, p. 19). Here he adumbrated one of the main themes of 'liberation theology' in the 1970s. And he forestalls the objection that a priest should be the minister of peace and reconciliation by saying: yes – but not at any price, and certainly not at the price of injustice.

One may be quite sure that the indefatigable Mazzoleni sent a copy of this article to Cardinal De Lai. It entered the files marked 'Roncalli'. Next to it, both spiritually and alphabetically, was the file of 'Radini Tedeschi'. Even the discreet circumlocutions of *My Bishop* cannot conceal that something was gravely wrong: 'Gradually, as a result of various incidents, he (Radini Tedeschi) came to suspect that with the Pope he no longer enjoyed the esteem of former years, and so he feared that more credit was given to informers' reports than his own concerning the true state of the diocese' (*My Bishop*, pp. 133–4).

Despite this knowledge, Radini Tedeschi pressed on with his plans. From April 26 to 28, 1910 a diocesan Synod was held in the cathedral, the first since 1724. Don Roncalli was its deputy secretary. He thought the Synod was the high point of Radini Tedeschi's episcopate, 'the outcome of the first five years of his labour, and the inspiration of the five years that followed it' (*My Bishop*, p. 95). It was not a democratic affair, and there was no debate: that, in any case, would have been impossible in the pontificate of Pius X when gatherings of clergy were forbidden. It suited Radini Tedeschi's temperament – he had been professor of canon law at Piacenza – to compose the decrees of the Synod single-handedly in advance. The function of the Synod was to applaud the five sections which dealt with Faith, the Sacraments, Divine Worship, Clerical Discipline, and Morality. Radini Tedeschi preached four sermons in the course of the Synod to drive home its lessons. Don Roncalli thought it was a great success:

> Every decree, which had perhaps at first met with criticism or opposition, now found its right place in the diocesan Code of Canon Law and was seen to be eminently natural and opportune. So it always is in this world. New measures annoy those who must make some sacrifices to obey them, but, once they have been accepted, there is always general surprise that they had not been thought of before (*My Bishop*, p. 93).

It should perhaps be added that there was at this date no systematic Code of Canon Law; so Radini Tedeschi was meeting a need. Roncalli called Synods as patriarch of Venice and bishop of Rome. The 'Council' was merely an extension of the synodal principle to the universal Church (and indeed was always called *Synodus* in Latin).

One decree of the Synod had a special interest for Don Roncalli. On November 3, 1909, Radini Tedeschi had formally set up a diocesan congregation known as Priests of the Sacred Heart. Since the new congregation was closely modelled on the Oblates of St Charles Borromeo, and Roncalli was becoming an authority on him, he was involved in the preparatory work. The Synod decree defined its goals:

> The general purpose of this institute will be to form and have available priests who will have a special concern for their own perfection and will be of special help to the bishop in the fulfilment of his pastoral ministry, placing themselves in strict dependence on him as the Oblates of St Charles do in the diocese of Milan. The particular purpose will be to help the bishop in missions to the people, in the *Spiritual Exercises* for clergy and laity, with special emphasis on the Christian education of youth in colleges, schools, oratories and suchlike ... (*Pastore*, p. 38).

The decree concludes comprehensively that the Priests of the Sacred Heart 'will fulfil all other offices that the bishop sees fit to entrust to them'.

Don Roncalli thought of joining the new institute forthwith. It would involve no new obligations, but would be 'a new and constant encouragement to persevere in all my former intentions to sanctify myself' (*Journal*, p. 187). But throughout the year 1910, when he had a lot of work to do in connection with the third centenary of the canonisation of St Charles Borromeo, he hesitated on the brink. He offered some hint of an explanation later:

> I confess that certain difficulties arose which weakened my good intentions about this. But they were due to human respect and were caused, for the most part, by my pride ... I care nothing for the judgements of the world, even of the ecclesiastical world. My intention, before God, is upright and pure (*Journal*, p. 192).

Some clergy may have felt that the new Congregation would result in a two-tier clergy of first- and second-class priests; others may have thought that, as bishop's secretary, he didn't need any closer bonds with him – he was already the favourite son. But we don't know.

What we do know is that during his 1910 retreat made at Martinengo with the bishop, he passed the severest and most conventional judgement on 'Modernism' that ever came from his pen. When set alongside his Baronius lecture it is puzzling. Our Lord had shown him in prayer 'the wisdom, timeliness and nobility of the measures taken by the Pope to safeguard the clergy in particular from the infection of modern errors (the so-called Modernist errors), which in a crafty and tempting way are trying to undermine the foundations of Catholic doctrine' (*Journal*, p. 188).

Word for loaded word, especially adjective for adjective ('infection', 'crafty', 'tempting'), he was echoing what Pius X wanted good seminary professors to believe. Modernism was not an intellectual problem, to be debated and resolved through argument: it was rather a moral and spiritual problem, to be resolved by authority and obedience to it. Moreover, despite the punitive measures of the last three years, it had not yet been overcome:

> The painful experiences of this year, suffered here and there, the grave anxieties of the Holy Father and the pronouncements of the religious authorities have convinced me, *without the need of further proof,* that this wind of Modernism blows more strongly and more widely than it seemed at first sight, and that it may very likely strike and bewilder even those who were at first moved only by *the desire to adapt the ancient truth of Christianity to modern needs.* Many, some of them good men, have fallen into error, perhaps unconsciously . . . (*Journal*, p. 189, italics added).

Roncalli was here placing on the altar and slaying the ideal of adaptation and *aggiornamento* that was his own as well as that of Radini Tedeschi, Ferrari, Bonomelli and Mercier. How could he be so supine?

The answer can be seen by looking at the dates. The retreat was made from October 2 to 10, 1910. On September 1 the 'Anti-modernist Oath' had been published (DS nos. 3537–50: trans. in Daly, pp. 235–6). It was a fiercely uncompromising text. It left no loopholes for interpretation. It had to be taken by clerics on the reception of minor orders, office-holders when they took up office, and professors at the start of the academic year. So Don Roncalli was due to take it the following November. It laid particular emphasis on the fixity of doctrine ('transmitted to us in the same sense and meaning from the Apostles' and 'the absolute and immutable truth first preached by the Apostles') which the historian no less than the philosopher or the reader of Newman's *Essay on Development* found difficult to accept. One clause attempted to put an end, once and for all, to any

kind of debate in the Church: 'With like respect I submit and adhere whole-
heartedly to the condemnations and all the prescriptions which are contained in
the encyclical letter *Pascendi* and in the decree *Lamentabili* especially those which
bear on the history of Dogma.' This was a considerable novelty. As Archbishop
Mignot of Albi wrote:

> They are organising a white terror . . . We used to believe that in order to be
> a good Catholic it was sufficient to believe all the truths which God revealed
> or the Church taught . . . It seems now that more is needed, namely that the
> Church should tell us not only what must be believed, but *how we should
> think* . . . The Pope is demanding an absolute assent to formularies which are
> *not of faith,* at least in all their parts, so that authority *binds us* while *not
> binding itself* (De la Bedoyère, pp. 210–11).

But Mignot, a considerable theologian, was writing in private to Baron von
Hügel. Such thoughts could not be expressed publicly, certainly not in Italy,
without the sanction of excommunication falling on the utterer. The 'Anti-
modernist Oath' was designed as an either–or ultimatum addressed to all in the
Church.

In such a crunch-situation, Don Roncalli inevitably had to side with the Pope.
As a priest–professor, there was no way he could elude the Oath. He quotes the
maxim of St Alphonsus Liguori, 'The Pope's will: God's will' (*Journal*, p. 190).
But this remark was less Ultramontane than it superficially appeared. St
Alphonsus made it in the context of the suppression of the Jesuits on July 22,
1773. He liked the Jesuits, used the *Spiritual Exercises* of St Ignatius, and was
bafflled by Pope Clement XIV's action. So 'The Pope's will: God's will' could be
considered in 1910–11 as an expression of acceptance combined with incompre-
hension ('in days of uncertainty and sadness' – *Journal*, p. 190). Roncalli refers to
Modernism as 'this devastating whirlwind' (*Ibid.*, p. 189). In a whirlwind one
cannot see very clearly. It causes what Newman called 'a night battle, where each
fights for himself, and friend and foe stand together'.

In the teeth of the whirlwind, Don Roncalli clung to the papacy and to the
faith of the church, but tried to disentangle this faith from the quarrel between
'Mediaevals' and 'Moderns' by stressing that 'the Church contains within herself
the eternal youth of the truth and of Christ, and is of all ages' (*Journal*, p. 189). This
theme would remain very dear to him. The church demonstrates its perennial
youthfulness by its capacity for renewal. Perhaps there wasn't much evidence of
this in 1910–11. But almost contemporaneously the French Catholic poet,
Charles Péguy, was hymning in *Eve, 'Dieu lui-même jeune ensemble qu'éternel'*
(Péguy, p. 711).

In the summer of 1911 the Lombardy Seminaries had another Apostolic
Visitor, Tommaso Boggiani O.P. He spent June 3 to 5 in Bergamo. We do not

know what his secret report contained. But his report on Milan and Cardinal Ferrari was published in 1974. A sample:

> As far as modernistic ideas go, or ideas approximating to modernist theses, it is certain that they are widespread among the clergy, especially the younger priests. The cardinal cannot be unaware of this, but he remains too tolerant. One result is that he has accepted the role of honorary president of a high school congress to take place next September at Saronno 'in this year so dear to Italians as the fiftieth anniversary of our national epic', as the letter of invitation puts it (Bedeschi, *Modernismo*, pp. 101–2).

Boggiani moved with breath-taking ease from an unfounded generalisation to a trivial and insignificant piece of evidence: it would be difficult to deduce from *Pascendi* and *Lamentabili* that an Italian bishop should not celebrate fifty years of Italian unity. The only reason he mentioned it was that it comes under the heading of dangerous talk already seen in the Bergamo common room. It implied that 'the "Roman Question" is *dépassé*'.

That autumn, 1911, Don Roncalli had first-hand experience in Bergamo of what the anti-modernist campaign really meant. It was less agreeable on one's own door-step than when contemplated in the quiet of a retreat. The cause of the trouble was a famous Jesuit, Fr Guido Matiussi, professor of theology at the Milan Faculty and thorn in the flesh of Cardinal Ferrari. He had anticipated *Pascendi* with an article in 1902–3, *Il veleno Kantiano* (see Daly, p. 166), in which he presented Thomism as the only true antidote to the poison of Immanuel Kant. His two lectures at the Bergamo seminary set the whole city and diocese by the ears. The pros and cons were debated in the press. Radini Tedeschi asked Don Roncalli for a private report (found in *Decimo anniversario*, pp. 57–62). Study of it will permit further *nuances* to our understanding of Roncalli's attitude to Modernism.

He begins by saying that 'the good father' (no irony intended) had made a bad impression from the start. He insulted his audience by not preparing his lectures. They were so disorganised that he couldn't remember what he had said on the previous occasion, and was incapable even of summing up at the end. Evidently Matiussi had trusted his talent for improvisation. He had gathered together a few thoughts on the short train journey from Milan to Bergamo.

Worse still, Matiussi's persistently harsh and polemical tone was offensive. He saw nothing positive in anyone. Denouncing the lurking presence of Modernism had become his vocation. The result was a jaundiced and distorted view of life. 'The truth and the whole truth has to be stated', wrote Roncalli, 'but I could not understand why it had to be accompanied by thunderbolts and stormclaps from Mount Sinai rather than by the calm and serenity of Jesus on lakeside or mountain' (*Decimo anniversario*, p. 58). He admits that this could be simply due to a difference of temperament. However hard he tried, he could not 'enter into the system' of Matiussi, 'such was the utter contrast (*repugnanza*) between his character and mine'. Matiussi was 'too absolute and one-sided' in his judgements: the result was that the students failed to grasp how the principles he expounded 'could be combined with other principles that were equally true and of the greatest importance for Catholicism' (*Ibid.*, p. 59). The 'Catholic Thing', Roncalli knew, is to hold onto 'both ends of the chain' and to allow complementary truths to stand in creative tension with each other.

As an example of Matiussi's one-sidedness he cites his treatment of the act of faith. Following Billot in his *De Ecclesia* (the same work that Roncalli had received as a gift from his fellow students in Bergamo), Matiussi argued that only the 'external proofs' of Jesus' mission – miracles and the fulfilment of Old Testament prophecies – really counted in the act of faith; 'internal proofs' – appeals to religious experience or prayer – were dismissed as 'subjective' and leading to the dreaded 'immanentism' said to be advocated by Maurice Blondel, Matiussi's current *bête noire*. This account of the act of faith has been described as 'the apologetics of the robot': 'Man, given the appropriate external circumstances, is programmed to believe' (Daly, p. 17). The believer becomes a passive, inert *tabula rasa*. Against this, Roncalli hinted that if everything labelled 'experience' is to be ruled out of court in the act of faith, then theology becomes a kind of geometry, faith the conclusion to an argument, and the theologian a desiccated logician. Here his 'spirituality' saved him from the one-sided excesses of the anti-Modernists, for it taught him to verify his insights in prayer. It took courage for a twenty-nine-year-old professor in a provincial seminary to say this, even in a private note, against powerful 'Establishment' theologians such as Billot and Matiussi. It also showed that Roncalli had a clear grasp of the theological issues involved in the anti-Modernist campaign. He was far from being the theological simpleton some have imagined.

But it was in his treatment of individuals that Matiussi really became offensive and unjust in the eyes of Roncalli. He denounced Duchesne, concentrating on the 'Loisy-type errors which his work contains, and which have been admitted' (*Decimo anniversario*, p. 60). Matiussi was better informed than Roncalli on Duchesne. His condemnation was in the pipe-line. His *History of the Early Church* was placed on the Index on January 12, 1912, just four months later. Matiussi's allusion to 'an element of Kantianism in a certain prelate' was, correctly, taken to be a reference to Cardinal Mercier. But most offensive of all were his disparaging remarks about the late Leo XIII and 'the young men of Christian democracy'. This did not go down well in a diocese which had been the most socially committed in Italy. Roncalli concluded his report with the hope that in future Matiussi would moderate his tone, not misapply his undoubted gifts, and so contribute 'to the dear and noble cause, the preservation of Catholic doctrine from all error' in accordance with the mind of Pius X (*Ibid.*, p. 61).

The uncomfortable truth, however, was that Matiussi, far from being some maverick lone ranger, was much closer to 'the mind of Pius X' than Don Roncalli. The Bergamo spies began to denounce not Matiussi but the hostile reception he had received. An anonymous cleric known as L.F. wrote to the rector of the Bergamo seminary to say that Matiussi's lectures had 'opened his eyes'. They had struck a decisive blow against Duchesne, against the 600 members of the Bergamo priests' association (the *Unione*) and against 'modernist fellow travellers' (*simpatizzanti modernisti*) generally. 'Now I have understood', wrote L.F., 'how right and necessary is intransigence in matters of principle and orthodoxy'. He concluded: 'Have not our *dilettanti* prepared a new drama?' (*Decimo anniversario*, pp. 55–6). By that he meant fresh condemnations. But L.F. was a minor character.

Much more serious was Mazzoleni's letter to De Lai at the Consistorial Congregation. He reported that the president of the *Unione* had made a 'vehement protest' against Matiussi's lectures. Moreover, *l'Eco di Bergamo* had said that Matiussi used 'intemperate language' in speaking of Leo XIII and Christian Democracy (*Decimo anniversario*, p. 56. Letter dated September 28, 1911). The paper went so far as to say that Matiussi made 'a sinister impression' on the seminarians. And, the Bishop *had done nothing about all this*. Moreover, our man in Bergamo reports that the Rector and professors Roncalli and Biolghini were using Duchesne's *History of the Early Church*. The rot was spreading. Researches in a Bergamo bookshop revealed that twenty-six priests had ordered copies of Duchesne's forthcoming volume in Italian translation. Mazzoleni's final thrust was that though Duchesne was clearly influential, 'it will be very difficult to arrive at the truth', presumably on the grounds that those attacked would try to do a cover-up (*Ibid.*, p. 57).

Roncalli's report was dated the next day, September 29, 1911. Soon the Matiussi affair was arousing controversy well beyond the diocese of Bergamo. *L'Unità Cattolica* of Florence attacked *l'Eco di Bergamo*, and its editor received a letter of thanks from Bressan, the Pope's secretary. Bressan also wrote to Matiussi himself on October 7, 1911:

No. 1096
The Holy Father has noted what you said in your kind letter of the 3rd inst. But even apart from it his Holiness was fully informed and completely approves of what you said at the Bergamo Seminary, and is very happy that you should have put your finger on the wound. No one will dare to ask you for a retractation, not even on the question of whether what you said was 'opportune' or not. This is because the truth has the right to be preached always and everywhere. This applies *l'Eco*'s comments on your remarks on democracy. So you can be of good heart and rest assured that everyone,

when they have had time to think about it, will be ashamed of this uproar and – it is hoped – will learn from it. His holiness blesses you etc. (*Utopia*, pp. 409–10).

Pius X backed this up on December 10, 1911, with a personal letter to the archbishop of Florence, Mistrangelo. He was writing to him because *l'Unità Cattolica*, the Pope's favourite newspaper, was in his diocese. Pius X dismissed *l'Eco di Bergamo* as a minor paper that was nothing to boast about, and explained that 'for all the esteem I have for the clergy of Bergamo, it contains a lot of dead wood (*zamorra*), and in no other diocese has Duchesne's *History* been so widely diffused and praised' (*Disquisitio*, pp. 112–13). He attacked the Bishop of Bergamo for his 'moderation'.

It was at this point that Don Roncalli finally joined the diocesan Congregation of the Priests of the Sacred Heart. On November 4, 1911, feast of St Charles Borromeo, he asked to be admitted. Two days later he made his vow of obedience to the bishop and promised to live in poverty of spirit. These were temporary vows. He renewed them annually until 1917 when they became 'perpetual'. When he became a bishop himself, he remained an 'honorary' member and continued to correspond with the Superior throughout his life. So from November 1911 Don Roncalli was a diocesan religious (see *Pastore*, p. 43), a fact which has escaped most of his biographers. He bound himself to Radini Tedeschi, then, at a time when his bishop was in dire difficulties. Radini Tedeschi concealed his distress: 'This suspicion (that the Pope did not esteem him) was truly a crown of thorns which afflicted him profoundly, although few people were aware of it and he knew how to hide his grief in public' (*My Bishop*, p. 134). Among those who were aware of his grief was his secretary.

Yet they survived 1912 without too many alarums. 'Uncle' Zaverio died in May, at the age of eighty-eight. Cardinal Ferrari contrived to get Fr Matiussi S.J. removed from Milan; in the Vatican this was regarded as further evidence of Ferrari's lack of orthodoxy; Matiussi was rewarded with Billot's chair at the Gregorian University. Radini Tedeschi's health became a source of concern; he needed longer periods of rest. But in the summer he was fit enough to set off on a journey to Munich and Vienna for a eucharistic congress. They stayed at nunciatures; Don Roncalli made his first contacts with Vatican diplomats, without any feelings of envy; in Munich he met Mgr Giuseppe Pizzardo. From Vienna he pushed on to Kraków and to Budapest, both at that date within the Austro-Hungarian Empire.

While he was away, one of Radini Tedeschi's friends, Cardinal Maffi of Pisa, who had kept silent for two years, tried to protest to Pius X about the anti-Modernist campaign. He wrote confidentially to Cardinal De Lai on July 31, 1912:

They (the right-wing press) deplore the fact that the Pope is not loved and obeyed, that fervour is in decline and pilgrimages are less popular etc. But the guilty ones are those who try to impose love with beatings (*imporre l'amore a bastonate*), who treat sincere enthusiasm with mistrust and the suspicion of imposture, who claim a monopoly of orthodoxy and so on. But enough (*Disquisitio*, p. 96).

This perspicacious letter never reached Pius X. De Lai replied that he would not show it to the Pope, in order to spare his feelings. De Lai was of course right. 'Kindness is for fools', Pius once said to someone who begged him to show compassion towards a supposed Modernist. 'They want to be treated with oil, soap and caresses', he said on another occasion, 'but they should be beaten with fists. In a duel, you don't count or measure the blows, you strike as you can. You do not wage war with charity' (Falconi, p. 54). Don Roncalli had complained about 'the thunderbolts and storm-claps' of Fr Matiussi. It was more difficult to object when they descended from the Pope.

Yet no one can say that the Lombardy bishops did not try to conform. As the year 1913 approached, they conceived the idea of writing a pastoral letter to commemorate the 1600th anniversary of the Edict of Milan. This was the measure by which the Emperor Constantine had agreed to tolerate Christianity within the Roman empire; it marked the end of persecution and the catacombs. Ferrari asked Radini Tedeschi to draft a text. He said he was too tired and proposed his secretary, Don Roncalli. Ferrari thought this was a good idea. So Roncalli set to work, basing himself on the writings of Bishop Bonomelli, and in particular his delightfully entitled, *Seguiamo la ragione, Questioni morali e sociali del giorno (Let's Follow Reason, Contemporary Moral and Social Questions) (Lettere*, p. 548). Roncalli's eye was more on 1913 than 313. His draft was toughened up by the Lombardy Bishops to make it an outright attack on the educational policies of Premier Giovanni Giolitti's Radical Party government. The government was opposed to private (i.e. Catholic) schools and to the introduction of religious education into state schools. The final version of the pastoral, called 'The sixteenth centenary of the Edict of Milan and the liberty of religion in the school', received the *nihil obstat* of the Secretariat of State without which it could not have been published. It compared Giolitti with Diocletian, the most notorious persecutor of Christians in all history (so far).

This was too much for Bonomelli, the advocate of 'conciliation', who refused to sign it. At the age of eighty-one, this was the bishop of Cremona's last stand. On October 25, 1912, he wrote to a friend:

The good cardinal (i.e. Ferrari) has begged me again and again to sign *pro bono pacis* [for the sake of peace]. I refused, because I could not publicly approve of what I in conscience reject. The cardinal explained the situation to the Pope. The Pope said: 'Then let it be published without the signature

of Cremona and people will judge for themselves'. So let them judge for
themselves! Only the other day Pietro Giacosa wrote a savage article in
Corriere della Sera against the pastoral. Is all the wrong on his side? Far from
it (*Lettere*, p. 549).

Pope John's only comment fifty years later was: 'And to think that I based the
pastoral letter on his own writings' (*Ibid.*). But one senses a sneaking admiration
for Bonomelli's refusal to be intimidated.

The row over the pastoral letter was not unconnected with the preparations for
the General Election of October 26, 1913, the first to be held on universal
suffrage. Giolitti needed Catholic support. It was revealed only after the election
that the *non expedit* ban on Catholic voting had been relaxed in 330 constituencies
(two thirds of the total), and that consequently 228 deputies including those of
Bergamo had been elected with the aid of Catholic votes. This was known as the
'Gentiloni Pact'. The Vatican pointed out that it was not a formal agreement on
the national level, but did not deny that it existed. Anti-clericals and socialists
were furious at this revival of political clericalism. But the General Election of
1913 proved that, whatever the theoretical position, the heat had gone out of 'the
Roman Question'. Even Merry del Val admitted privately that 'it would be a
cause of extreme embarrassment to the Vatican to have to govern even the
Leonine City' (Seton-Watson, pp. 388–9). So the broader claim to the Papal
States had been abandoned. This was something novel in Vatican–Italy relations.

But nothing had changed in the anti-Modernist campaign. On June 1, 1914
Don Roncalli was in Rome with the seminary rector to discuss finance with
Cardinal De Lai. As they were leaving, De Lai called him back and said:
'*Professore*, please be careful in the teaching of Scripture'. Roncalli was too
flabbergasted to explain that he had never taught scripture and that his work had
been in church history, apologetics and patristics. Perhaps it was a case of
mistaken identity. Roncalli was deeply distressed and rushed straight to the Gesù,
the Jesuit church, where he renewed all the vows of his youth. He wrote a reply
to De Lai at the Albergo del Senato the next day, June 2, and had it delivered by
hand. He corrected the mistake about the teaching of Scripture and protested his
fidelity 'to the directives of the Church and the Pope always and in everything'
(*Decimo anniversario*, pp. 63–4).

On June 12, 1914, De Lai answered apparently in friendly fashion: 'I am sorry
you were so disturbed by my advice to you. It was not a reproach but a salutary
warning'. But then he revealed the real cause of his displeasure:

> According to information that has come my way, I knew that you had been
> a reader of Duchesne and other unbridled authors, and that on certain
> occasions you had shown yourself inclined to that school of thought which
> tends to empty out the value of tradition and the authority of the past, a

dangerous current which leads to fatal consequences etc. (*Decimo anniversario,* p. 65).

De Lai had written that letter a hundred times. The mechnical phrases fell from his pen, illuminating nothing, creating a mood of apprehension in the receiver. He signed off: 'I bless you in the Lord, Yours most affectionately in Jesus Christ, ✠ G. card. De Lai, Bishop of Sabina'.

Don Roncalli did not find it easy to reply. His letter went through several drafts and had many corrections – all of which he preserved. By June 27 he was ready to post it. 'I do not believe that the information comes from anyone who knows me' he began. He was prepared to deny all the charges *on oath*. In particular:

> I have never read more then 15 to 20 pages – and even then just as a sampler – of volume I of the *Histoire Ancienne de l'Eglise* (second edition, Paris, 1906). I have never seen the other two volumes. I have therefore *not read a single line* of Duchesne's history translated by (Nicola) Turchi, and never had them in my hands or among my books. I knew the French prelate a little, but I never had any sympathy with him even when he made corrections intended to put to rest doubts about his orthodoxy. I was fairly familiar with the ideas of Turchi who for some months was a fellow student at the Roman seminary, but he never confided in me. I remember more than once expressing my feelings of mistrust and antipathy towards him to my fellow seminarians (*Decimo anniversario*, p. 67).

There is only one word to describe Roncalli's letter to De Lai: grovelling. In his anxiety to please his inquisitor he has forgotten the 'Note on Duchesne' that appeared in *La Vita Diocesana* in September, 1911. It was unsigned but he admitted authorship. In it he said that he did not want to take sides in the controversy about Duchesne, and 'confined himself to reading and studying' (*Decimo anniversario*, p. 62). Duchesne's book, he pointed out in 1911, had an *imprimatur* not from any diocese but from the diocese of Rome itself. So in 1911 he emulated the attitude of *Civiltà Cattolica,* and prudently abstained from judgement (*Ibid.,* p. 62). It is also relevant that as a professor of church history, he *ought* to have read Duchesne who, as we have seen, was praised by Benigni (p. 56 above) for his 'synthesis of science and orthodoxy'. But now that his back is to the wall, Roncalli obliterates these memories.

He goes on and on. Mgr Spolverini, by now rector of the Roman seminary, will bear witness that he 'never ever read a single modernist book, pamphlet, or review, except for Fogazzaro's *Il Santo* that I flicked through before it was condemned to help me in my confessional ministry' (*Ibid.,* p. 68). He ended by reporting that Radini Tedeschi's health was completely restored – an optimistic diagnosis – and kissing his eminence's sacred purple. In a postscript he mentioned that he was enclosing an offprint of his lecture on Baronius. This might have been considered imprudent.

Pope John reread this letter to De Lai on December 14, 1961, and noted that it concurred with the copy he had always kept by him. But in 1914 Don Roncalli was like a soldier who, having come unscathed through a long and arduous war, narrowly escapes being wounded on the eve of the armistice. For the whirlwind of Modernism had blown itself out. It ended with the death of Pius X. From the whole tragic episode Roncalli drew the conclusion that there were other and better ways of dealing with 'error' in the Church. But another whirlwind was brewing up, the whirlwind of war.

Chapter 5

The Great War

What candles may be held to speed them all?
Not in the hands of boys, but in their eyes
Shall shine the holy glimmers of good-byes

('Anthem for Doomed Youth', Wilfrid Owen).

The First World War, known to contemporaries as the Great War because it surpassed all previous conflicts, broke out on August 1, 1914. Italy was not involved until May of the following year, but already the dark shadow fell across the whole of Europe. On August 20, 1914, the day Brussels fell to the advancing Germans, Pius X died broken-hearted, it was said, by a war he had foreseen but had been unable to prevent. Two days later, Don Roncalli was kneeling at the bedside of the dying Radini Tedeschi:

> As the curfew sounded from the tower, Monsignor lay on his death-bed with as much dignity as if he were seated on his episcopal throne during a solemn ceremony. As I knelt beside him . . . I remembered the first service I ever performed for him when, on the day of his solemn consecration in the Sistine Chapel, I held the Book of the Gospels, representing the yoke of Christ, against his shoulders, while the august hands of Pius X were laid upon his head to confer upon him the fulness of the priesthood and the strength of the Holy Spirit. Ten years had been spent in his company since that day, and it seemed to me a great privilege and blessing, that I shall never forget, to be able to assist him to the end and to witness a death so precious in the eyes of the Lord.
> The last prayer we heard him murmur was:
> 'O my crucified Jesus, I offer you willingly – yes, willingly, O Lord – the sacrifices of my life in union with your sacrifice on the cross . . . in expiation for my own sins and those of my people, for holy Church, for the new Pope you will give to her, for my priests, my city and my diocese, all religious everywhere, all who suffer, all who loved me as well as those who felt no love for me, for all those dearest to my heart, for my relations and friends near and far – for my country . . . '
> At this point he opened his eyes and seemed to be gazing far away as he added, with a strong and clear voice, 'and for peace, and for peace' (*My Bishop*, p. 142).

Shortly before his own death, Pope John noted in his diary: 'I reread in my volume on Mgr Radini, written in the thick of the World War in 1916, the account of the last days of my Bishop and his final prayer, peace, peace . . . I would like that to be my last prayer as Pope' (*Letture*, p. 497).

The deaths of Radini Tedeschi and Pius X added to the feeling that the lights were going out all over Europe. Shrewd old Fr Francesco Pitocchi, his spiritual director at the Roman seminary with whom he still corresponded, said that Don Roncalli would suffer more from the death of Radini Tedeschi than from that of Pius.

The truth was that many were glad to see the back of a pontificate which had been a disaster for the intellectual life of the Church. To a senator who wondered at the impressively devout crowds who flocked to pay their last tribute to Pius X as he lay in state in St Peter's, Cardinal Ferrari remarked: 'Yes, but he will have to give an account before God of the way he let his bishops down when they were attacked' (*Disquisitio*, p. 129). Cardinal Mercier, now an international figure who embodied the heroic resistance of 'gallant little Belgium', wrote a pastoral letter in which he spoke of the 'wounded souls' and 'human wretchedness' to which the pontificate had led; and he denounced the 'free-lance knights of orthodoxy who imagine that, in order to obey the Pope more humbly, one has to attack the authority of the Bishops' (*Per Crucem ad Lucem*, pp. 66, and following). So Ferrari and Mercier were among those cardinals who hoped that the September 1914 conclave would produce a pope who could put an end to the atmosphere of repression. In the midst of a fratricidal European war, the Church had to have a different set of priorities.

The Curia, however, did not agree, and with Cardinal De Lai acting as king-maker, supported Cardinal Alberto Serafini, a Benedictine and assessor at the Holy Office, who could be relied upon to continue making orthodoxy, narrowly conceived, the most important task of the papacy. So the Curia bitterly opposed first Cardinal Maffi of Pisa, believed to be close to the House of Savoy, and then Cardinal Della Chiesa of Bologna, who began to gather in the 'Austrian' vote. The Curia said that Della Chiesa was a mediocre man and a mere bureaucrat (he had been under-secretary of state in Rampolla's time). They argued that his election would be an insult to the memory of Pius X. Even when Della Chiesa managed to reach the thirty-eight votes needed to win the election, the curial faction accused him of voting for himself. The accusation was shown to be groundless. So Giacomo Della Chiesa became Pope Benedict XV: the last arch-bishop of Bologna to become pope, Prosper Lambertini, had taken the name Benedict in 1740; but Della Chiesa may have also been influenced by the fact that the hero of Fogazzaro's novel was called Benedict. The reality of war had already come home to the conclave: cardinals from opposing sides were present and civil with each other, and Cardinal Louis Billot had already lost two nephews at the front. Two days after an economy-style coronation in the Sistine Chapel – pomp would have seemed blasphemous at such a time, Benedict announced his intention of making peace his main concern: 'We are firmly resolved . . . to leave nothing undone which may lead to the speedy ending of this calamity' (Holmes, pp. 2–3). In his first encyclical, *Ad Beatissimi*, he called for a halt to the anti-modernist campaign: 'There is no need to add epithets to the profession of Catholicism. It is enough for each to say, *'Christianus mihi nomen, Catholicus cognomen'* ('Christian is my name, and Catholic is my family name'). What matters is to live up to these names in one's life' (*Popes of the Twentieth Century*, p. 132). This was aimed at Umberto Benigni's espionage network, the *Sodalitium Pianum*, which always insisted on *'integral* Catholicism' and was quick to note its absence in theologians or bishops. The extraordinary situation was reached in which Benedict believed it had been abolished, whereas it had been reconstituted with the blessing of Cardinal De Lai in the summer of 1915 (*Ibid.*). But the worst was over.

The election of Benedict XV helped to console Roncalli for the death of Radini Tedeschi. Della Chiesa had great esteem for Radini Tedeschi and thought him 'worthy to become pope' (*Letture*, p. 497). But still the loss of his father-figure was hard to bear, and Roncalli had a sense of being orphaned once again. His whole priestly life had been lived out as the bishop's secretary. Now his life seemed empty. He began to gather materials for the biography of Radini Tedeschi whom he always called, with *pietas*, simplicity and capital letters, My Bishop (*il Mio Vescovo*). It was an occupation, but it was not a job. It was highly unlikely that the new bishop, whoever he was, would want him to continue as secretary. Secretaries were expendable. In his September 1914 retreat he drew the obvious conclusion: 'I have entered this new period of my life' (*Journal*, p. 200).

He resolved to get up at half-past five every morning and to give his 'whole attention to the seminary without neglecting pastoral work' (*Journal*, p. 200). One note has a special poignancy:

> I shall make a point of giving my new bishop, whoever he may be, that reverence, obedience, and sincere, generous and cheerful affection which, by the grace of God, I was always able to feel for his unforgettable pre-decessor . . . Naturally my different position will mean a different relation-ship, but whatever it is, it will be inspired by those feelings of respect, prudence and exquisite delicacy which are the fine flower of love. May my behaviour give the new bishop some satisfaction and comfort, so that I may not be an obstacle but a tool with which to build (*Journal*, p. 201).

That stated the problem perceptively if a little preciously. By a nice irony, the preacher of this autumn 1914 retreat was Luigi Maria Marella, then bishop of Bobbio, who in 1915 became bishop of . . . Bergamo.

But Roncalli was perturbed about the 'new situation'. The proof is that he interrupted his retreat for 'a flying visit to Milan to ask Cardinal Ferrari for some advice about how to handle certain matters with the new Bishop' (*Journal,* pp. 201–2). We do not know what these 'certain matters' were; but he emerged from the meeting consoled and cheered up. He went to pray at the tomb of St Charles Borromeo in the Duomo (cathedral), reminded himself that as a priest of the Association of the Sacred Heart he was bound in a special way to his bishop, renounced 'fantastic dreams, ... thoughts of honours, positions *etc.*', and prepared himself for sacrifices to come (*Ibid.*).

Freed from his chores as Bishop's secretary, Don Roncalli was able to spend more time on study and prayer. He gave courses in church history at the seminary and also at the *Casa del Popolo,* an adult education centre. The titles of his lectures reveal the range of his intellectual interests: The Church, Science and the School; Christianity and Graeco-Roman Science; Schools in the Barbarian Period to Charlemagne; Astrology, Alchemy and the Intellectual Aberrations of the Middle Ages; the University and Scholasticism; the Church and the Renaissance; the Church and Modern Scientific Thought; Modern Struggles for Freedom in Education; Origins of Modern Universal Education; Great Christian Educators. It was history with one eye on the present state of Italy. It had an underlying apologetic purpose: to justify the claim of Italian Catholics to have Church schools supported by the state (which did not happen). It was also a typical reflection for a time of crisis, when values were in the melting-pot and the foundations of society seemed to be shaken: to improve the quality of education often seems to be the answer.

In a letter of February 5, 1915, he recommends the reading of St Francis de Sales' letters in a time of crisis: 'He will do your spirits good, bringing to you that calm, that sweet, gentle and generous resignation that transforms pain into an element of priestly fervour, and zeal for the divine and noble cause for which we are ordained' (*Pastore,* p. 84). Gentleness with oneself was what he always valued in François de Sales. This was a letter of condolence addressed to the new superior of the Priests of the Sacred Heart, whose mother had died. But it contained a message that would be more widely relevant as Italy hesitated on the brink of war.

There was intense debate between the 'neutralists' and the 'interventionists'. For Italy to join the war on the side of the *Entente* (Britain, France and Russia) would mean abandoning the Triple Alliance with the Central Powers (Germany and Austro–Hungary) to which it was pledged. The Treaty of London was secretly negotiated as an inducement to Italy to come into the war on the side of the Entente: post-war territorial gains were promised. This strengthened the hand of the 'interventionists' in the government, but since the arrangement was confidential, it was of no help in winning over public opinion. Pope Benedict XV was a 'neutralist'. So was Don Roncalli. He remained deeply sceptical about 'the gains' of war. 'Official' Italy, the frock-coated men who ruled from Rome, had little claim to represent the Italy of Catholic peasants for whom they had done so little. Besides, if Italy joined the Entente, its bedfellows would be Protestant England, free-thinking France and autocratic Russia; and its potential enemy would then be Austria, the only combatant with which it had a common frontier. But Bergamo and Venice, especially, had strong cultural links with Austria, and had been part of the Austro-Hungarian Empire between the fall of Napoleon and the unification of Italy. For Roncalli's grandparents, war with Austria would have been a civil war.

So Italy stumbled into a war that could hardly be called popular. Mobilisation was ordered in May 1915. On May 19 Don Roncalli was called up, and became a hospital orderly stationed in Bergamo. On May 24 Italy declared war on Austria–Hungary, though not on Germany, and there were sharp engagements on the north-eastern front. Bergamo was tranquil and unchanged. Don Roncalli began to grow a moustache which soon bristled formidably on his upper lip. Though there was no question of 'hiding his priesthood', he did not want to appear odd or singular among his peer-group. Despite his portliness, he cut a fairly dashing figure in his uniform.

But he was not very warlike. His first wartime letter is to his brother, Zaverio, who was two years younger. It gave fraternal advice on how to get invalided out. As a hospital orderly and a scholar, Don Roncalli had time to master the regulations. Unfortunately they had just been changed. Until a few months previously, it was enough to be lacking sixteen teeth to be declared unfit for military service. Now, apparently, one could fight with any number of teeth, or indeed none at all; after all, one did not have to bite the enemy. So defective teeth will provide no let-out *unless* they are a symptom of 'gastric disturbances' and being generally 'run-down'. Even then, they could only exempt one from active service in the front-line (*Familiari*, I, p. 39). But by September 17, 1915, he learned that all his efforts had been in vain: Zaverio was passed 'fit for war-service' (*Ibid.*, p. 42). Now being a hospital orderly was no sinecure: the casualties began to come in in growing numbers. His cousin, Battista Mazzola, had just died in Verona: he had been hit by an Austrian hand grenade.

The war placed Don Roncalli in a new relationship to his family. As Bishop's secretary he had been very busy and rather 'grand'; not exactly aloof, but too immersed in his work to visit them and too near to need to write. The war made him the family link-man, writing consoling letters, arranging meetings, seeking to decipher the hand of God in these terrible events. But though he is the only educated person in the family, he is just as baffled by war as they are. He had a special concern for Zaverio who by December 12, 1915, was in Brindisi, possibly about to embark for Albania or Macedonia. Don Roncalli, as usual, recommends calm: 'If the Lord is with us, who can be against us? We won't fear either hunger or cold or malaria or Albania or the Germans, will we?' (*Familiari*, I, p. 43). But Zaverio never set sail from Brindisi, so Roncalli thought of taking a train to see him there. Practical as ever he lays his plans. Zaverio must be sure to get leave for the day. Angelo's train will arrive at 5.33 p.m. and depart next morning at 7.37 a.m. Italian wartime trains seem to have been remarkably punctual. 'Let me know the name of your captain', he writes, not unwilling to pull rank in a good cause. But he never went to Brindisi. That's war: order, counter-order, disorder.

He couldn't even get home to Sotto il Monte. He had planned to take his friend Don Giacomo Testa to see his parents in January, 1917; but the road from Bergamo was impassable and the carriage got stuck in the mud. If it was like this in the foothills of the Alps, it wasn't difficult to imagine what it was like up in the mountains at the front. The weather relented a little and on February 5, 1917, he was able to go home. Everyone was there. Only Maria, Zaverio's wife, was missing. 'Mother and the sisters provided a lunch that surpassed all my expectations', he wrote to Zaverio (*Familiari*, I, p. 45); he knew how much they had to pinch and scrape in wartime. He had prudently invited Count Morlani's steward to dine and found him 'a really good man'. So he was already thinking about buying outright the house and farm for his father and his brothers; but like most other decisions at the time, it had to be postponed until that distant horizon, 'when the war is over'.

The next day he underwent another medical inspection and was passed fit 'for the rigours of war'. 'Will I have to go to the front?' he mused: 'If they send me, I will be happy, because I hope to do a bit of good there' (*Familiari*, I, p. 46). Those were not bellicose feelings. A week later, he wrote to Zaverio's wife, Maria, and returned to the theme of 'good out of evil': 'My heart tells me that Zaverio will return safe and sound from the present tempest. But, my good Maria, we have to know how to merit this grace from the Lord through perfect tranquillity of soul in this time of tribulation, fully convinced that the Lord uses even painful events for our good' (*Ibid.*, p. 47). Zaverio, meanwhile, had been transferred from Brindisi and was now in Piacenza, much nearer to the front-line and also to Bergamo. But Don Roncalli can't get away because he is 'up to my eyes in work among the troops'. To Zaverio himself he writes: 'Keep up your spirits and your confidence in God; with God it is always good, whether at the front or not' (*Ibid.*, p. 48).

On May 6, 1917, Don Roncalli wrote to Zaverio to say that he had looked up his whereabouts on a local map – the name was a military secret – and thought it a good, defensible position 'that will greatly strengthen our artillery'. The war was coming closer all the time. And for the first time Don Roncalli speaks more precisely about how he sees 'duty towards our country':

We don't go in for a lot of arguments and all the useless chatterings that

some shirkers indulge in, do we? We know that love of our country is love
of our neighbour, and that this implies the love of God. That's really all
there is to say: and we accept willingly the sacrifices the war imposes,
keeping our eyes fixed on high, and in this way we will merit blessings for
ourselves, our family and our country [*patria*] (*Familiari*, I, pp. 48–9).

It is not a very sophisticated argument; but he is trying to give his brother at the
front a motive for hanging on. Moreover, Zaverio was a peasant like most of the
men whose wounds he was tending, and he was learning from them. Angelo
knew how resentful they sometimes felt at being merely cannon-fodder while
urban munitions workers ('the shirkers') enjoyed the luxury of discussing 'war
aims'.

Don Roncalli no longer sees the conscript army as a sink of iniquity, as he
priggishly did during his military service in 1901. He came to know these simple
men and appreciate their unnoticed qualities. Caring for the troops is his entire
life, he tells Zaverio, and 'I have learned that with a little patience and the grace of
God, they can all be won over' (*Familiari*, I, p. 49). The wounds of anti-
clericalism were superficial and could be healed. Most of Roncalli's diaries for the
wartime period were lost. But this page survives and allows us to see him at
work:

> March 8, 1917. How dear to me is Orazi Domenico as he struggles with a
> violent crisis of bronchial pneumonia in a room not far from mine. He's
> nineteen and comes from Ascoli Piceno. A humble peasant with a soul as
> limpid as an angel's. It shines out from his intelligent eyes and his good and
> ingenuous smile. This morning and evening, as I listened to him
> murmuring in my ear, I was deeply moved: 'For me, Father, to die now
> would be a blessing: I would willingly die because I feel that by the grace of
> God my soul still remains innocent. If I died when I were older, who
> knows how lumpish I'd become. And then, when you die older, the
> separation is more painful: it costs a lot to give up wife, children and home.
> But what does it cost me to die now?' A moment later, he said to me 'I'd
> like to die now, Father, with you beside me, so that I can remain
> completely the Lord's until my last breath'. But I, on the other hand, dear
> Menicuccio, pray the Lord that he may grant you many years of life. The
> world needs such chosen, simple souls who are a fragrance of faith, of
> purity, of fresh and holy poetry. And we priests need them too to feel
> encouraged to virtue and zeal (*Decimo anniversario*, p. 27).

But a month later, Domenico Orazio Menicuccio, the nineteen-year-old peasant
from Ascoli Piceno, died suddenly while undergoing an operation.

Don Roncalli tried to console himself with the scripture text that the liturgy applied to the Jesuit 'boy saints': 'He was snatched away lest wickedness should change his understanding or guile deceive his soul' (Wisdom 4.11). 'So long as Italy has such sons who go straight to heaven', he reflected, 'it will not lack God's blessings' (*Decimo anniversario,* p. 27). But this had very little – indeed nothing – to do with heroism on the battlefield or whether the cause being defended was just. Roncalli as a young priest moralised war: but the fact that it could evoke virtues did not make waging it legitimate. Forty years on, he would sometimes speak of his time in the army: 'After days of intensive work, when all one's limbs were aching, I would return to my room, fall down on my knees, and tears of consolation would run down my cheeks. What tremendous reserves of moral energy are present and at work among our people' (*Ibid.,* p. 28: Capovilla reporting). This was what the war meant for Sergeant Roncalli, hospital orderly turned chaplain.

While still close to the events, he spoke about them in an address given on September 9, 1920. It is worth giving rather fully since it is the only description we have of his work as a chaplain:

It seemed as though the war would destroy the last remnants of faith and ancestral piety. Bless the Lord that this did not happen. War is and remains the greatest evil, and he who has understood the meaning of Christ and his Gospel of human and Christian brotherhood can never detest it enough. It would be naïve to expect very much from war as a contribution towards the moral progress of our people. Yet it was a great test of the worth of peoples, and besides the brutality and wretchedness some of us endured, it is fair to dwell upon the consoling episodes that gave the lie to our pessimism. Oh! the long vigils among the bunks of our dear and brave soldiers spent in hearing their confessions and preparing them to receive the bread of the strong in the morning! The hymns to Mary that rose up around simple, improvised altars; the sublime solemnity of the Mass celebrated in the fields; the hospital feast-days, especially Christmas, Easter and the month of May, where the poetry of one's own village church flourished again, and the tender memories of distant wives and mothers mingled with the anxious hope for an end to the harsh sacrifice!
Humble priests, generously fulfilling their duty towards their motherland [*patria*], but still more aware of a higher duty towards the Church and souls, how many times did we lean over our dying younger brothers and listen to the anguished breathing of the nation expressed in their passion and agony. It is impossible to say what the priestly heart felt in such moments. It often happened – permit me this personal memory – that I had to fall on my knees and cry like a child, alone in my room, unable to contain the emotion that I felt at the simple and holy deaths of so many poor sons of

our people – modest peasants from the Marche, Garfagna, the Abruzzo or Calabria – who died with the sacrament of Christ in their hearts and the name of Mary on their lips, not cursing their harsh fate but joyfully offering the flower of their youth for God and their brethren.

It was indeed from such spiritual contacts that I, along with many others better than myself, had the consoling impression and the firm conviction – whispered from one to another during our brief encounters: No, it is not true that Christian Italy is dead. *Non est mortua puella, sed dormit* [The child is not dead but sleeps: Matthew 9. 24] (*Rosario*, pp. 126–7).

Of course this post-war view represents experience mediated and no doubt adjusted by hindsight. It omits the raw experience of war: not Roncalli weeping in his room but men dying with their guts splayed out, stoic peasants doing their duty for incomprehensible reasons.

But pulpit-rhetoric apart, the text is faithful enough to experience to show that Roncalli, unlike many military chaplains in the First World War, never glorified war or justified it because of its bracing and stimulating effects. 'War is and remains the greatest evil' he says without any ambiguity. Yet somehow God was present in it. It permitted him personally to discover the youth of Italy in a way that would have been impossible had he remained merely a seminary professor. It permitted Italy to discover 'nationhood' although it was still a young country – not yet fifty years old – and still a collection of cities and provinces with very different histories. And it permitted Roncalli to discover himself in Italy by providing evidence of a religious revival that helped to overcome the antagonism between Church and State that had bedevilled its origins. So the war pointed the way towards the resolution of 'the Roman Question' and 'reconciliation'.

But all this was wisdom after the event. In the summer of 1917 Don Roncalli was proved wrong in his prediction that 'the war will be over much sooner than is believed' (*Familiari*, I, p. 51). He gladly associated himself with Benedict XV's appeal for 'a just and speedy peace'. These optimistic hopes proved unfounded, and were soon to be cruelly mocked by events.

Pope Benedict's appeals for peace were brushed aside as irrelevant. He had never wanted Italy to get involved in the war, foreseeing (correctly) awesome consequences if its principal enemy, Austria–Hungary, were to be destroyed and dismembered (Seton-Watson, p. 472). On the Western front in 1917 a stalemate had been reached. The allies and the Germans were pounding each other for a few yards of muddy trenches. Benedict tried to profit from the sense of having reached an *impasse* by offering an honourable way out. On August 1, 1917, he addressed a note to all the belligerents urging them to accept 'a just and lasting settlement', to abandon the empty hope of 'victory' as a war aim, and to put an end to 'the useless struggle' (*Ibid.*). His hope was that frustration and weariness would bring the nations of Europe to their senses. One of Benedict's agents in this diplomatic initiative was forty-one year old Mgr Eugenio Pacelli, the future Pius XII. He liked to recall – much later – that he had been ordained archbishop on May 13, 1917, the very day on which Our Lady appeared for the first time to three peasant children near Fatima in Portugal.

But no one else seemed to have received the message, and Benedict's well-meant initiative not only failed; it rallied everyone against him. In Italy, his remarks about 'the useless struggle' undermined national morale and suggested that Catholics were unpatriotic and disloyal. Benedict was dubbed Maldetto XV (Accursed instead of Blessed) and charged with 'defeatism'. Nor was he any more acceptable to the Western Allies. Britain and France did not believe that he was truly impartial, blamed him for his 'silence' about the martyrdom of Catholic Belgium, and called him the *Boche* (or German) Pope. The fiery prophet Léon Bloy declared in *Au seuil de l'apocalypse* that 'he deceived . . . infallibly', and the Baron Friedrich von Hügel, after the war, suggested that he ought to abdicate *(Popes of the Twentieth Century,* p. 123). The Germans, on the other hand, were convinced that Benedict XV was pro-French, the *Franzozenpapst.*

As for Austria–Hungary, which Benedict was trying to protect, it was disinclined to sue for peace precisely at the moment when Russia, its principal enemy, ceased to be a serious fighting force in the events which prepared the October Revolution. Whatever the wider meaning of the October Revolution in 1917, its immediate effect was that the Austrians could now concentrate all their energies and vast armies on the Italian front. Benedict's intervention had little chance of success. Yet Roncalli never forgot it, and mentioned it in a footnote to *Pacem in Terris* (footnote 59 to No. 112). More profoundly, it led him to think about the timing and efficacy of papal pronouncements.

These events had immediate consequences in October, 1917. The Austrians now stiffened by seven hand-picked German divisions, broke through with overwhelming force, took 300,000 prisoners in two weeks, inflicted heavy casualties, and drove the Italians back to within fifteen miles of Venice. This was Caporetto, the greatest battle on the Italian front during the entire war. It was a rout, later compared by General Cadorna's wife to the collapse of France in 1940 (Seton-Watson, p. 480). This was an exaggeration, but one sees the point. The seventy-mile retreat had left a million and a half Italians under Austrian occupation. Four hundred thousand refugees clogged the roads and had somehow to be housed and fed. The Italian commander, General Cadorna, blamed the defeat on the lack of fighting spirit among the troops ('they cravenly withdrew without fighting or ignominiously surrendered' said his communiqué). The retreating troops were 'decimated' (that is, one in ten was taken out and shot) *pour encourager les autres.* Despite this, one witness reported that the retreating men 'gave the impression of people returning home at last after a long job of work, laughing and chattering'. The soldiers 'naïvely imagined that this was the way to end the war, and there were shouts for peace and for the Pope' (Seton-Watson, p. 479; also Ragionieri, pp. 2038–41).

Don Roncalli was no great military strategist – censorship did not help – and it took him some time to realise what was happening. As late as October 5, 1917 – three days after the enemy attack was launched – his optimism was still undented and he hoped for an early end to the war, 'despite the babbling of the newspapers and especially the pestiferous *Corriere della Sera* which we can dispense ourselves from reading' (*Familiari*, I, p. 57). But the Milanese newspaper had a better grasp than Roncalli of the political weaknesses that loomed behind the military defeat. By October 27, 1917, the truth could no longer be concealed. Everyone knew that something mighty and terrible was in train. Don Roncalli wrote his most sombre letter ever to his brother Zaverio: 'I think that we have arrived at the gravest moment of our war, and I hope that our cause will go well, that is that there should be victory and a just and lasting peace' (*Ibid.*, p. 58).

The shock of Caporetto brought about a revival of patriotism. *L'Osservatore Romano,* the Vatican newspaper, now editorialised about the Catholic's duty to resist the enemy. Prayers were offered not merely for 'a just peace' but for 'victory' (Seton-Watson, p. 482). Don Roncalli shared in this changed mood. Now that so much Italian territory was under foreign rule, the whole game was changed and one had to speak of an invasion. So he wrote to Zaverio on November 22: 'Now the enemy is in the house, he has to be chased out at whatever cost, otherwise things will be bad for us. Everyone should stay in his own house. We are all guilty, but today it is our duty to make evey sacrifice to see that the Germans [*Tedeschi*] clear out of Italy' (*Familiari*, I, p. 60). Caporetto simplified the issue of patriotism; it was now more evidently true that it was a form of solidarity with a people and a matter of neighbourly and brotherly love. But that merely intensified and made even more inscrutable the providential design that lay hidden in the war. And even at the highest pitch of patriotism, Don Angelo does not lose his even-handedness: 'We are all guilty'.

As the Bergamo hospitals filled up with the wounded of Caporetto, he had a more personal cause for worry. His youngest surviving brother, Giuseppe, was missing. (Luigi, born in 1896, had died at the age of two.) He was twenty-three, thirteen years younger than Angelo, who felt very protective towards him. He wrote to Giuseppe, always known in the family as Pino or Giuseppino, on November 5, 1917:

Dearest Giuseppino,
When your card arrived yesterday our father was here in Bergamo on business. You can imagine how much we are all with you in thought and heart especially now that you are in danger. It consoles me to know that you are resigned to what is happening. You know that our resignation is

neither cowardice nor weakness, but is rather courage and strength.
It is founded on God who sees and hears everything, who sustains and
makes us joyful and content and preserves us from all evil even under
cannon fire. Yet when they hear talk of patriotism many soldiers just shrug,
smile or even curse. Not so we. We do our duty and keep our gaze on high.
The men who have governed and are governing us are not worthy of our
sacrifices, but the imperilled nation merited them; men pass, the nation
[*patria*] remains. A sacrifice for one's country is a sacrifice for God and for
our brothers; and when you come back – soon, I hope – you will see that
nothing, nothing at all has been lost by your sufferings. . . . Where are you?
In a trench on the Tridentine front? Let me know, if you can, without
failing in your duty (*Familiari*, I, p. 61).

Roncalli's contempt for politicians reflected the current 'Catholic' judgement
that they did not truly represent the country; and his remark that the privations of
the troops would not prove vain reflects his hope that in the post-war period it
would be recognised that Catholics had earned the right to take part in public life.

But this letter to Giuseppe was never delivered. A month later, on January 6,
1918, there was still no definite news about him. He told Zaverio that 'tears well
up in my eyes when I think of Giuseppino, and I cannot resist the impulse of
tenderness that comes over me' (*Familiari*, I, p. 63). His enquiries about Giuseppe
have led nowhere: he could be 'already in paradise, but is more likely in a prisoner-
of-war camp'. Sergeant Roncalli fights back the tears with the brisk command:
'Yes I must, I want to be strong'. For now the whole family is dependent on him
for news and comfort. He tries to keep up their morale: 'Let others prattle away,
we go in for sacrifice. That's the way to love one's country, unlike so many others
who have the word *patria* on their lips but not in their heart' (*Ibid.*, p. 64). He
gives Zaverio all the latest gossip. He has been to Sotto il Monte where there is a
new parish priest. But he was beginning to wonder whether any of his letters to
his brothers were getting through.

There is a three month gap in his correspondence at this point. It starts again
with a letter to Zaverio on April 17, 1918, with the good news that Giuseppino is
a prisoner-of-war somewhere in Austria. Pino's routine postcard (cross out what
does not apply) was dated February 19, 1918. His only complaint was that he was
hungry and lacked bread. 'It seems that in Austria', Roncalli writes to his brother
Zaverio, 'the food situation is worse than it is here' (*Familiari*, I, p. 65). That
meant it was very bad indeed. In Italy, bread was rationed, and in large cities
meat, sugar, fats and olive oil were also rationed; two days a week were declared
'meatless' (Seton-Watson, p. 487). In Sotto il Monte his mother had actually been
sending bread-parcels to Giuseppino; Angelo joined in this exercise so as not to disappoint her, knowing full well that it was a waste of time. But it was a gesture.

Apart from the fate of Giuseppe, the war now faded out of Roncalli's correspondence until it was over. This was partly because he had less to do in the hospital. In April 1918 he reported: 'I am almost without patients here'. The Italian front was relatively quiet. He shared the conventional view that the war would be decided elsewhere: 'The battle at present being fought in France seems really to be decisive and likely to bring about an end to the war. Let's hope it all ends well for us, and tht it is not too bad for the others. We are all guilty, and we have all suffered' (*Familiari*, I, p. 65). Against this background, he began to pick up the threads of his future. He saw Cardinal Ferrari in Milan on January 31, 1918, and stayed on to give a lecture to the Union of Catholic Women on St Catherine of Siena. But he was not neglecting his military duties. He addressed the troops five days later on Torquato Tasso's poem *La Gerusalemme Liberata* (*Jerusalem Saved*) (*Cronologia*, p. 536).

Normality, it seemed, was flooding back. The war was being settled elsewhere. Don Roncalli was given his post-war job. On February 27, 1918, Bishop Marella decided he would become warden of a Student Hostel (*Casa dello Studente*) to be housed in a *palazzo* not far from the Seminary. This was a new venture. He had to start from scratch. Roncalli threw himself with enthusiasm into the novel task of setting up his own place at the age of thirty-seven. He started to buy furniture, paying a 5% rate of interest on the loan he took out to pay for it. He hoped that his sisters Ancilla and Maria would come and keep house for him (*Familiari*, I, p. 65). All the members of the family would be welcome at any time.

But distinctions had to be made. On May 27, 1918, he thanked Zaverio and his wife, Maria, for their gift of 250 *lire*, but sent it back: they can't afford it. His father had been typically generous, he says, and there was no question of sending *his* money back. More was still needed for kitchen equipment, so he borrowed again from the Piccolo Credito Bergamo, the local Catholic bank, and expected to repay his debts within two to three years. He was jauntily confident: he didn't mind the expenses because they were all 'one-off' (*Familiari*, I, p. 67).

Thus, while Don Roncalli was thinking about pots and pans and domesticity, Pope Benedict XV risked another rebuff by exploring the chances of a separate peace between Italy and Austria–Hungary (Seton-Watson, p. 492). Neutral Switzerland acted as intermediary. These efforts, however, were doomed to failure because Italy was now thoroughly locked in to the alliance with England and France, and because the Central Powers thought that the Italian front offered the best terrain for one last, desperate offensive. It began in June, 1918, and after initial successes, was thrown back by an army that had been completely re-organised and re-equipped after the humiliation of Caporetto.

Two further facts are worth mentioning, because they foreshadowed future events. The left in Italy, always mistrustful of 'patriotism', now advocated a 'revolution through defeat' on the model of the recent Russian Revolution. At the other end of the spectrum, the Italian army was stiffened by a new breed of shock troops, who did not have tedious trench duties but were kept fit for more spectacular and heroic operations. Known as the *arditi* because they were on fire for Italy, they wore black shirts, despised the peasants because they fought with fatalistic resignation, and 'lived in an atmosphere of bombs and flames' (Seton-Watson, p. 498). They were the forerunners of the Fascists. They were worlds apart from Roncalli's stoic peasants.

His prediction that the war would be won in France was not fulfilled in quite the way he expected. Italian honour was involved. The Italian government could not afford to end the war with so much of its territory still occupied by the enemy. It was in a bad bargaining posture. To have any influence at all in the post-war peace settlement and to implement the vague Treaty of London, it needed a victory.

So on October 24, 1918, the first anniversary of Caporetto, the Italians attacked in numbers across the River Piave. At first they met with fierce resistance. The weather was against them, and flood waters swept away the pontoons. But after five days the town of Vittorio Veneto was taken (it gave its name to the battle) and the Austrians began to retreat. The retreat became a rout – Caporetto in reverse – as the Austrian army, made up of so many different nationalities now determined to go home and achieve independence, disintegrated. The Czechs, the Yugoslavs and the Hungarians revolted. The Italian government had its victory at the last gasp.

Italy could take its place at the conference table with some dignity. Benedict XV, however, was excluded from the peace conference according to article 15 of the London Treaty – the Soviets had made its terms public in order to embarrass the capitalist powers (Seton-Watson, p. 493). On the Italian front, the armistice was signed on November 3, and the cease-fire came into force the next day at 3 p.m. (*Ibid.,* p. 503). On the Western front the guns fell silent at 11 a.m. on November 11, the eleventh month. 1918. The Great War was over.

We have Don Roncalli's diary for these last, dramatic days:

November 4, 1918. The victory of our arms has been truly grandiose. We shouldn't boast about it because we are all sinners . . .

November 10, 1918. Great religioso-patriotic demonstrations. An incredible crowd, devout and orderly. I'm glad to see Catholics taking part in such demonstrations. We have to recover from such a long period of sloth: the fear of the accidental has made us neglect the substance, to the disadvantage of the Church and our own cause. Where there is no question of compromise and everything to gain, the intelligent thing is to *be present* so that no one can claim to act without us, and so the abuse of patriotism at the expense of Catholics would cease . . .

November 11, 1918. The latest news is that Kaiser William II has
abdicated. There's someone who liked to say *Domine, domine* (Lord, Lord),
and yet treated the Lord as though he were an equal. I remember seeing him
in Rome in 1903 when he was frantically acclaimed by delirious crowds.
What a difference between then and now (*Letture,* p. 407).

He visited his brother, Giuseppe, now repatriated but gravely ill at
Montegrotto near Padua. Roncalli was in fact demobilised on December 10,
1918, though the official papers releasing him from the army were dated February
28 and March 15, 1919 (*Cronologia,* p. 537). He had had enough of the army and,
in the new mood of national reconciliation, a priest could slip unobtrusively away,
with a wink to his superior officer. He destroyed his army uniform, glad to be rid
of it.

Chapter 6

Towards Propaganda and Fascism

And the flags. And the trumpets. And so many eagles.
How many? Count them. And such a press of people.
We hardly knew ourselves that day, or knew the City.
This is the way to the temple . . .

(T. S. Eliot, *Coriolan* (1920), from *Collected Poems 1909–1962*, p. 139).

For Don Roncalli, as for Italy as a whole, 1919 was a time of relief and hope, enthusiasm and new plans. There was a widespread yearning for change and a utopian desire for better things. The returning soldiers expected at least to find work if not 'homes fit for heroes'. Italy had ended on the winning side in the war; it hoped therefore for a share in the spoils and an important role at the conference table. Catholics, their contribution to the war now recognised, re-entered political life. The Vatican gave permission for Don Luigi Sturzo, a Sicilian priest, to found the Partito Popolare Italiano (henceforward PPI or Popolari). It presented its manifesto on January 18, 1919. Though Cardinal Pietro Gasparri, Secretary of State, had vetoed the use of 'Catholic' or 'Christian' in its title, and although it was not a 'confessional' party, it embodied the aspirations of the Catholic peasants and workers. Don Roncalli supported it enthusiastically from the outset.

There was a sense – wholly deceptive, as it turned out – of a new age dawning. 'We are awakening as if to the light of a new day', Roncalli wrote (*Journal*, p. 208). On January 30, 1919, Fr Agostino Gemelli, one of the leaders of the PPI, called on him. Still in the uniform of the army doctor he had been, Major Gemelli talked about setting up a movement to be called the Association of Mothers of the Fallen. An innocent enough project, it seemed, and Roncalli could not be expected to guess that this 'cult of the dead' would lead Gemelli later to become an ardent Fascist (Gemelli gave his name to the hospital in which Pope John Paul II was treated in 1981). In 1919 Roncalli found him 'very Franciscan' and tried to interest him, without much success, in what was becoming, on his own admission, his *idée fixe*: 'The need to popularise study of the liturgy and encourage living participation in it' (*Memorie*, p. 431). In this respect he was ahead of his time.

Three weeks later, in February 1919, he met Don Giovanni Rossi, secretary to Cardinal Ferrari, who was bubbling over with the plan to found a Catholic university along the lines of Louvain. Naturally this would be in Milan, which was much more intellectually exciting than Bergamo, even than Rome. 'In Milan there's something going on in every field' (*Memorie*, p. 435). Ferrari himself, despite throat-cancer and old age, was full of optimism about the prospects for Catholicism in post-war Italy. The 'Law of Guarantees' had defined the position of the Church and the Vatican in the state. But, Ferrari maintained, the Church had two far more solid guarantees than that: the promise of Christ that the gates of hell would not prevail, and massive popular support. He concluded:

> President Wilson, like Kaiser William II before him, has gone to Rome and knelt before the Pope, despite opposition, because he knows the Pope has the support of millions of organised Catholics who really matter. If we can let that voice make itself heard in Italy in proper constitutional form, then we will have assured the triumph of the Church, of Christ and of the Pope (*Memorie*, p. 435).

'Golden words', commented Roncalli in his diary. Triumphalist words too.

On the personal level, he had plenty of reasons for optimism. He had survived the war with his confidence in God's goodness unshaken: 'In four years of war, passed in the midst of a world in agony, how good the Lord has been to me' (*Journal*, p. 206). On May 9, 1919, his father was at last able to get a loan to buy La Colombera, the family home since 1892. It cost 57,000 *lire*. It was an exceptionally good year for silk-worms, and they were able to sell the whole lot and make a down payment of 11,000 *lire*. The Roncallis were still poor, but they were no longer dependent on Count Morlani. Since land reform was on the programme of the PPI, the Roncallis were among its 'natural' supporters.

Professionally, too, Don Angelo was happy. His work as warden of the new *Casa dello Studente* in the Palazzo Marenzi, via San Salvatore, in the upper city, was engrossing and satisfying. He had just over forty students. Education was the best way to prepare the future and fulfil his vows, now permanent, as a member of the Association of Priests of the Sacred Heart. Socialists and Fascists were already competing for the new generation, so in forming his students 'as generous apostles of truth and goodness, I shall at the same time be cherishing the best hopes of our families and our country' (*Journal*, pp. 208–9). He was spiritually content, seeing his work in the light of the Emmaus story: 'So often, in the evening, when I turn over in my mind the events of the day spent in looking after my dear students, I feel in me something of the awe which fell upon those two disciples on the way to Emmaus, as if in contact with the divine' (*Journal*, p. 208). He thought there could be no higher vocation than that of 'forming a new generation in the spirit of Jesus' (*Ibid.*). Maybe he was working in obscurity, but God and his students made up 'not a bad public' (as Thomas More says in *A Man for all Seasons*).

There were, of course, problems. Roncalli's notes for January 28, 1919, record a minor tragedy, a Bergamesque *Romeo and Juliet* in which he was unable to play Friar Laurence. One of his students, M.S., fell in love with a girl glimpsed at a window opposite the Hostel. It was nobody's fault, Roncalli thought. It was just that M.S. was 'dazzled by his first, unexpected, spontaneous feelings' and 'enjoying his first love-idyll' (*Memorie*, p. 430). M.S. was expelled, as a warning to the others: falling in love was not part of the programme of the Student Hostel. It was already under attack from conservatives who were ready to pounce on the first sign of laxity or softness. Roncalli tried to mitigate the blow by fixing a place for M.S. at the Collegio San Alessandro, where he would be removed from the window and temptation. The boy shed copious tears.

Roncalli, puzzled by his 'taciturnity', pondered 'the mystery of adolescence and youth' (*Ibid.*). At 38, he was rather out of his depth: his own adolescence and youth had not included the experience of human love, unless we count filial love. But he could feel the pain of it: 'How often the mystery of the youthful soul comes home to me with such suffering that I feel an ineffable tenderness' (*Memorie*, p. 431). Circumstances cast him in the role of defender of the institution and heavy-handed father. But he thought of himself rather as a mother, just as he had previously thought of God as Mother (cf. p. 36): 'I shall love my students as a mother her sons, but always in the Lord' (*Journal*, p. 208).

He was in demand as a preacher. In April he held three 'pulpit-dialogues' with Don Carozzi, his Roman seminary companion. One of them feigned ignorance and evoked crushing replies from the 'Catholic'. It was a diverting and popular form of apologetic entertainment. He saw, twice, the film *Christus*, was at first disappointed but on balance decided it was 'a contribution of modern art and industry to Christ's glorification' (*Memorie*, p. 442).

Giuseppe Toniolo, sociologist and theoretician of Christian democracy, died in May 1919, and Count Giuseppe Dalla Torre (who would spend almost his entire life working for *l'Osservatore Romano*) eulogised him in words that Roncalli carefully noted down:

> Amid the material and moral ruins of the modern age brought on by
> liberalism and socialism, the heirs of the French Revolution, Professor
> Toniolo discovered the latent energies impelling the people towards Christ,
> the source of true restoration, and towards the Church, the mother of true
> civilisation. So he devised a programme for Italy to enable it to link up with
> its glorious past and fulfil once again its tasks and mission in the world
> (*Memorie*, p. 448).

That would remain part of Roncalli's mature historical analysis. It involved an optimistic reading of the nineteenth century and a rejection of the world-denying gloom of the Syllabus of Errors (1864). It pointed towards the 'reconciliation' of Church and state in Italy. When as pope Roncalli took possession of his cathedral, St John Lateran, he quoted Toniolo's prediction about Italy ' . . . that one day Christ will return in triumph on the shoulders of his people' (*Vent'Anni*, p. 69).

But it was not happening just yet. Roncalli records his sadness on June 19, 1919, as the Corpus Christi procession wound its way through the upper city and past the Student Hostel. There was one magnificent, joyous white banner, the standard of Catholic Youth – but no one was behind it. He resolved that next year his forty students would march behind that banner. And so they did (*Memorie*, p. 451). Exactly forty years later, he reread this passage in the Vatican Gardens and was deeply moved (*Letture*, p. 65).

Besides much preaching and his work at the hostel, Don Roncalli was also chaplain to the Union of Catholic Women. The title of its newsletter, *Gigli e Rose*, did not suggest a very radical movement. He already knew a real Catholic feminist, Adelaide Coari, who had worked with Bishop Radini. She despised the lilies and roses world of sewing circles that so often passed for female Catholic Action, and held that women should learn their rights and engage in direct social action. She was now working in Milan. We will meet her again when she starts to correspond with Roncalli.

The Union of Catholic Women was going well in Bergamo, especially in the upper city: by June 1919 the youth group had over fifty dedicated members, and Don Roncalli was stirring up 'the more sluggish parishes' (*Memorie*, p. 450). He was no longer scared of women, but he still kept firmly to the rule he had given himself in 1910 when he was first appointed chaplain to the Union: 'The work I am doing requires great delicacy and prudence, as it frequently means dealing with women. I intend, therefore, that my behaviour shall always be kind, modest and dignified so as to divert attention away from myself and give a richer spiritual quality to my work' (*Journal*, p. 193). He had a similar problem with the students in 1919. They became attached to him personally. He resolved it in the same way. He saw himself as 'a small instrument', never out of the hands of the Lord. That did not mean having 'the hardness and deadness of a stone' but rather being 'transparent with grace and doctrine, and so bringing life and encouragement' (*Memorie*, p. 473).

Though Roncalli shared in the triumphalist optimism of the post-war period, he was critical of its cruder manifestations. He attended a prize-giving at the local Jesuit school where the aggressive and smart-alec style of the student contributions shocked him. It reminded him too much of Fr Matiussi's 'one-sidedness':

> The essays read out by the students were combative and full of battle-cries. They always seem to have the whip in their hands. They have the spirit of Elijah and very little of the Sacred Heart. If any of our adversaries had been present, I doubt that they would have been convinced or attracted to us. This seems to me to be lacking in perfection. Or am I wrong? I could be (*Memorie*, p. 451).

Despite the polemical atmosphere typical of the period, Roncalli believed that opponents should always be treated with respect. Bludgeoning was not the Christian way.

He entertained private doubts about his bishop, Luigi Marella. He was kind and meant well but 'he doesn't understand certain situations and hasn't the courage to do the things that would bring him great honour; so he withdraws, bewildered, into his shell' (*Memorie*, p. 432). That was in February 1919. Two months later, Marella is said to be 'shy and terrified of everything that is new'. He responds to problems day by day, as they come up, instead of 'following a plan and carrying it out with energy' (*Ibid.*, p. 444). Marella, in short, was not Radini Tedeschi. Don Roncalli, as the biographer and former secretary of Radini Tedeschi, was in a difficult position. Any criticism coming from him could be interpreted as nostalgia for 'the good old days' when he had influence. So he avoided gossip. On June 8, 1919, he met Bishop Marella by chance on the funicular railway that links the upper and lower cities. 'Has the seminary rector said anything?' asked the bishop, cryptically. He hadn't, but next day Roncalli learned that he had been appointed spiritual director at the seminary from the start of the next academic year.

It was a position of trust, but not of any great prestige. It meant that the absurd worries about his alleged 'modernism' had been put to rest. In his retreat for 1919 he disdained all ambition: 'Honours and distinctions, even in the ecclesiastical world, are "vanity of vanities" ' (*Journal*, p. 207). He lectures himself on their essential frivolity: 'Anyone who has lived in the midst of such stupidities, as I did in Rome and in the first ten years of my priesthood, may well say that they deserve no better name' (*Ibid.*). Was he protesting too much? Taking out an insurance against disappointment? Certainly, when a conference of the newly founded National Union of Catholic Women (*Unione Femminile Italiana*), was announced for October 1919, he leaped at the chance to go to Rome and began to feel a certain nostalgia: 'To tell the truth I gladly welcome this opportunity to have a bath of *romanità*, and to offer my ministry among the students and seminarians to the tombs of the Roman saints' (*Memorie*, p. 464).

He set off for Rome on October 26, 1919 with rather more precise aims: to attend the conference, and to present the Student Hostel scheme to the Curia and, if possible, the Pope. The journey began badly. At Milan railway station his wallet, containing 800 *lire*, was stolen. He tried to make light of the incident by thinking up an apt scripture comment ('You joyfully accepted the plundering of your property', Hebrews 10.34). But he was mortified, not so much at losing the money as at his incompetence. He should not have been so absent-minded. He was tired out on arrival in Rome, and found the conference a bore. He went for long walks, admiring the modern art in the Galleria Borghese and discovering that Rome had changed much: new and expensive villas now covered the hill of Parioli. He sought out old friends, like his former rector, Mgr Bugarini. On

November 1 he had a long conversation with Mgr Franceschini, parish priest of San Rocco, on 'the perennially awkward problem of pastoral work in Rome' (*Memorie*, p. 467). Very few priests came from the diocese of Rome (only two were to be ordained in 1925); the popes, though technically bishops of Rome, could not act as true pastors, at first because they were also its temporal rulers and after 1870 because they were confined to the Vatican; and now the spread of the suburbs meant that the churches were where the people were not. Don Roncalli stored up these impressions for the future. As pope, he would try to be bishop of Rome.

But his 1919 visit cured him of any lingering nostalgia: 'I must confess that the older I get, the less I like the Roman atmosphere. I'm like a pilgrim here; and even though there is a lot of good to be done, I wouldn't want to live here' (*Memorie*, p. 498). Yet he couldn't leave, because he was still waiting for an audience with Pope Benedict XV. He saw Mgr Tedeschini, Under-Secretary of State on October 29, and was relieved that he didn't ask too many questions about Bergamo (*Ibid*. p. 466). That ought to have been enough. He had explained how the Student Hostels – two others were planned – were financed: a limited company was founded under the title of Opera San Alessandro with a board of twelve and the bishop as president. He went over the same ground in a letter to the Pope dated November 5, 1919 (*Pastore*, pp. 85–7) describing the work as a response to 'the new demands of a new age' (*tenendo conto dei nuovi tempi e delle nuove esigenze*), a phrase that would have raised hackles ten years earlier. But still the audience did not come. He spent a whole morning kicking his heels in the ante-chamber and began to feel impatient: 'This blessed audience is becoming a positive torture for me' (*Memorie*, p. 468).

Finally, at noon on November 6, 1919, he saw the Pope, being ushered in by Canon Pietro Morlani, brother of his parents' former landlord. It went well:

> The Pope was so good. He asked me some questions about the workers' movement in Bergamo, and let slip a certain anxiety about it. He listened when I talked about my work with the students, and blessed it along with the work I am starting at the seminary. He made a most agreeable and affectionate impression. The blessing of the Pope is precious and will strengthen me (*Memorie*, p. 469).

Roncalli had audiences with all the popes of the twentieth century. He found Benedict XV the most sympathetic. But this audience took place in the midst of a fierce electoral battle. Nowhere was the conflict sharper than in Bergamo.

The Pope's anxieties about Bergamo were brought on by its supposed drift left-wards. When Roncalli got home there was only one more week of campaigning to go. His committment to the PPI was total. He saw it as 'the expression of the claims of the Christian spirit in public life' (*Memorie*, p. 470). The symbol of the

PPI was a white cross on a blue shield; they were crusading for justice (after 1945 their spiritual heirs, the Christian Democrats, used a red cross on a white shield). Don Roncalli was overjoyed at the local result. In Bergamo the *Popolari* had won five out of six seats. That was better than the national performance. The *Popolari* won 100 seats in the Chamber compared with 156 Socialists and 252 Liberals and their allies. They held the balance of power. For a party less than one year old, this was a resounding success. It was made all the sweeter in that the Fascists of Mussolini, an ex-socialist nationalist, were badly mauled. Informed opinion claimed that the *Popolari* had eaten into the Socialist vote, and so prevented a revolution.

But the election of November 16, 1919, settled nothing. The extreme left sought to create a 'revolutionary situation' through strikes and factory occupations. The Fascists fed on discontented nationalism, the disillusion of ex-servicemen, and set their bully-boys roaming the streets while claiming to be the party of 'order'. The crunch of marching boots was the background music to the twenties in Italy far more than the Charleston or the jazz of New Orleans.

Don Roncalli was more immediately concerned with the affairs of the Priests of the Sacred Heart. The superior, Mgr Luigi Drago was a man of fiery temperament, described by contemporaries as a 'Prussian' who 'attacked in order to defend' (*Pastore*, p. 47). Roncalli was the tactful, diplomatic second-in-command, entrusted with the task of writing to Pope Benedict XV on the tenth anniversary of their foundation (text in *Pastore*, pp. 89–90). The letter was dated January 29, 1920. They were, he said, only a small band. In a post-script he listed them all by name: nine were living in community ('interns') while eighteen others (including himself) were dispersed around the diocese ('externs'). He craved a blessing and, if possible, a few personal words from the Pope. Benedict exceeded all expectations with a Latin letter dated April 13, 1920, which pointed out that quality rather than quantity was what mattered (*Pastore*, pp. 91–2).

This somewhat banal and desultory exchange shows how committed Don Roncalli was to the Priests of the Sacred Heart. When under attack, they could quote the papal letter as a talisman. The correspondence also served to bring the name of Roncalli to Benedict's mind, though this was far from being its purpose. But not many diocesan priests, even in Italy, would have written to the Pope twice within two months. In September 1920 he suddenly became much more widely known. He was chosen to address the sixth National Eucharistic Congress. Held in Bergamo, its theme was 'The Eucharist and Our Lady'. Superficially, this looked like an introverted and 'churchy' topic, a matter of getting the balance right between the centrality of Christ and a Marian piety which threatened to run wild. But this first post-war Eucharistic Congress was also an opportunity for the Italian Church to define its position in society. From May 1920 onwards industrial troubles had multiplied. Yet the mood of the

Congress was one of optimism. A contemporary account catches something of
the atmosphere in which Don Roncalli delivered the most important speech of his
life so far on the afternoon of September 9, 1920:

> The Rubini Theatre was more crowded even than the day before. Not a
> single corner was free. The stage itself was packed with bishops and
> notables. The scene cannot be described: hearts are full of joy; enthusiasm,
> restrained by reverence, shines out on all faces. The eucharistic hymn is
> sung, the president recites the prayers and sums up the work done during
> the morning. Then Professor Don Roncalli begins to speak . . . His speech is
> many times interrupted by applause, and at the end the audience, deeply
> moved and enthusiastic, gave him a standing ovation (*Rosario*, p. 131,
> quoting the official *Acts* of the Congress).

The speech was an outstanding success. It can be considered as an instance of
Roncalli's mariology and as a commentary on the 'signs of the times' as they
appeared in 1920.

His mariology is unremarkable and sound. He expounds the motto of Lourdes,
Ad Jesum per Mariam ('To Jesus through Mary'), to show that Mary's role in salvation-history cannot be understood without reference to her Son. Thus she cannot be considered as a rival to Jesus or a threat to his role as 'the one mediator'. His
exposition is solid rather than brilliant, buttressed by patristic quotations and
vivified by poetry borrowed from the Song of Songs. The sermons of St Bernard
guided him through these ambivalent regions. When the Song of Songs (sometimes known as the Canticle of Canticles) declares that 'as a lily among brambles,
so is my love among maidens' (2,2), Don Roncalli enquired rhetorically, 'Who
can fail to discern in the delicate image of the lily Mary Immaculate, beautiful and
resplendent?' (*Rosario*, p. 120). It would be churlish not to. Besides, the image
had a long history. But when the lily is flanked by the apple-tree whose 'highly
nutritious fruit' is said to be 'evidently' the Eucharist, it is tempting to think than
allegorical exegesis, unchecked, obscures as much as it adorns.

But Don Roncalli had one well-founded argument to establish a link between
Mary and the Eucharist. It comes at the end of Matthew's genealogy of Jesus:
'Mary, of whom Jesus was born, who is called Christ' (Matthew 1.16). *Caro
Christi, caro Mariae*: the flesh of Christ comes from the flesh of Mary. To establish
the link between Mary and the Eucharist, Roncalli explained, there is no need to
follow those brash modern painters who depict Mary receiving communion at the
hands of St John. An unnecessary invention. It is enough to go back to the ancient
antiphon, *Ave, verum corpus, natum ex Maria Virgine* ('Hail true body, born of the
Virgin Mary'). If Jesus is born of Mary, and if the Eucharist is his body and blood,
then there is an intimate connection between Our Lady and the Eucharist.

But it was not the mariology that won Roncalli a standing ovation. He earned it by his patriotic fervour and his cry, based on his wartime experience as chaplain (see p. 84 above), 'No, Christian Italy is not dead' (*Rosario*, p. 127). Anti-clericals were saying that support for the *Popolari* had been drummed up by the clergy who were acting as its recruiting sergeants. But in Bergamo, he replied, Catholic Action is a *populist* cause and this 'vast and powerful organisation is merely the spontaneous emanation of the religious feeling of the people' (*Ibid.*, p. 128). Its purpose was to bring to bear the principles of Catholic social doctrine, 'derived from the Gospels', on all the contemporary questions: unemployment, poverty, class-war, labour unrest, inflation. He admitted that 'the economic problem is the great unknown quantity of this agitated time' (*Ibid.*, p. 129). He had no technical solutions to offer. But he knew that any solutions would have to be fair and equitable if they were not to fail.

Don Roncalli was not speaking in a vacuum. Only the previous month the Red Army had been driven back from the gates of Warsaw in a battle known as 'the miracle of the Vistula'. The victory was commonly attributed to Our Lady of Czestochowa. But now, Italy itself was being threatened:

> While we are gathered here for this Congress, our Italy is going through one of its blackest and most terrible hours. New barbarians are standing at the gates of our city. You have seen the red banners, symbols of violence, fluttering in sinister fashion above the factories where the people – sometimes gullible but always good at heart – are waiting for work. What is going to happen? Are we perhaps on the eve of a social revolution (*Rosario*, p. 131)?

They were not. But it was a reasonable enough question. For six months the government of 78-year-old Giolitti had been struggling with wage-demands. The traditional remedy of 'standing firm' did not seem to work any more. Lock-outs were countered by factory occupations by the workers. Red guards were posted at the gates. The aim was to show that the workers could run the factories as well as their managers. The young Marxist theoretician, Antonio Gramsci, explained at fervent factory meetings that Italy was in that terminal state known as 'pre-revolutionary'. One big push, and the façade of bourgeois society would collapse. The Russian Revolution of 1917 provided the model and the inspiration. The bourgeoisie was alarmed, and looked to the right for protection.

Roncalli stayed calm. The peroration, which won him his standing ovation, was an invitation to hope. He told the story of the Polish Dominican St Hyacinth who had carried the Eucharist many miles to escape the Tartar hordes; but the statue of Our Lady proved too heavy for him, so he entrusted it to his parishioners and together they reached the safety of Kraków. The relevance was clear:

> Our spirits are not apprehensive. Our hearts are firm, even if the revolution should come. In the midst of universal ruin, salvation lies in our hands.

Behold, we priests will raise aloft Christ in his sacrament, and will bless the swirling river of humanity. You laypeople will strap upon your backs the image of the Madonna, and will face with sure steps the abyss, the tempest, death itself. God will renew his miracles. We will bring to safety the sacred pledges of civilisation, the Holy Eucharist and the Madonna, the dearest objects of our faith and love, and after the agonising struggle, will lay them on the altar of the *patria* (*Rosario*, p. 131).

It was not very clear. But crystal clarity cannot be demanded of a peroration. Don Roncalli was keeping his options open: without either advocating or damning the revolution, he was trying to say that the Church should be present, somehow, in the very necessary work of the reconstruction of society.

But already, in this month of September 1920, the prospects of revolution were fading. The workers were prepared for a defensive occupation of the factories, but not for armed insurrection. Gramsci and the far-left did not have the popular support they needed. One of the aptest comments came from Gaetano Bensi, a Milanese trades union leader: 'Revolutions are not made by first summoning an assembly to discuss whether one should or should not make a revolution' (Seton-Watson, p. 565, fn. 2). Roncalli's speech at the Eucharistic Congress established him as a forceful orator and a potential leader. It won him a modest national reputation. He was now a distinctly 'promising' priest. Though 39, he was young for his profession. A great career could be confidently predicted for him – but it would almost certainly mean leaving Bergamo.

The first hint of a move came in a letter from Cardinal William van Rossum, the Dutch Prefect of Propaganda Fide, to Bishop Luigi Marella. (After Dr Josef Goebbels had blackened the term 'propaganda', the department was rebaptised Congregation for the Evangelisation of Peoples, an unwieldy mouthful that has not caught on). Van Rossum said that he had his eye on Don Roncalli for the post of national director of the Propagation of the Faith. Though many dioceses, including Bergamo, had a flourishing organisation to support the work of the missions, elsewhere in Italy the work was badly organised or totally unknown. Van Rossum wanted an organiser, an animator and a fund-raiser. He knew that Don Roncalli was doing important work as founder and warden of the Student Hostel, but Bergamo's loss would be Rome's gain (*Natale, 1970*, pp. 10–11). Van Rossum's letter was dated December 6, 1920.

Bishop Marella handed it on to Don Roncalli, who was cast into 'perplexity and pain' (*Ibid.*, p. 14). He was happy in Bergamo; and he was not sure that he would be happy in Rome. At the same time, he did not want to resist 'the will of God', if it were shown to be truly God's will. He wrote to Bishop Marella and Cardinal Ferrari stating his misgivings and asking their advice. It was not any lack of zeal for the missions that made him hesitate. On the contrary: 'Over and above spreading the Kingdom of Christ in the world, which is the principal task of the Church, I am convinced that one of the best and surest means of re-invigorating faith among the tepid believers of the West is to interest them in the Catholic missions in the East' (*Natale, 1970*, p. 12). Middle East or Far East? Why only the East? What has happened to Africa? This curious limitation (which might be a slip of the pen) anticipated his own work in the Balkans and the Middle East.

But despite his love for the missions, he felt that a mistake had been made somewhere. He did not have the organising ability he was being credited with. Van Rossum must be confusing him with Radini Tedeschi, the master organiser. Finally – humility's last throw – he declared that he did not have the right temperament for the post. He is 'someone who doesn't get much done; by nature lazy, I write very slowly and am easily distracted in my work' (*Natale, 1970*, p. 13). His self-description concludes: 'The active life of exterior movement to which I have so far been condemned was never my ideal; I would have preferred a life of recollection and study in a monastic cell, with a taste for the direct ministry of souls but peacefully and without fuss' (*Ibid.*). Giuseppe Roncalli O.S.B. was a fantasy he indulged in from time to time.

No one paid any very great attention to these protestations of unworthiness. Bishop Marella replied to Van Rossum that replacing Roncalli would not be easy and pleaded for delay (*Natale, 1970*, p. 17). The letter that mattered came from Cardinal Ferrari. On December 15, 1920, he wrote to Don Angelo:

> You know how much I love you: it is another debt towards Mgr Radini Tedeschi. Precisely for that reason, here is my clear and unhesitating judgement: the will of God is as plain as can be, since the 'red' pope (the Prefect of Propaganda) is the echo of the 'white' pope; and both are of God. So go ahead. Whenever God calls, one goes, without hesitation, abandoning oneself in everything to his divine and living Providence.
>
> Most affectionately in Jesus Christ
> ✠ Andrea C. card. archb. (*Natale, 1970*, p. 15).

By now Ferrari was a dying man. This lent added force to his words.

But the whole Milanese Curia at Piazza Fontana, 2, was on Roncalli's side and thought his qualities had at last been recognised. Don Giovanni Rossi congratulated and embraced him in the Lord (thirty-eight years later, he was one of the first to be told about the project for an Ecumenical Council). Don Alessandro Macchi, second secretary, described how Cardinal Ferrari, on reading his letter on his sickbed, 'stammered a few words and with a magnificent gesture let us understand how splendid he thought the decision was' (*Ibid.*, p. 16). Macchi added 'From his bed of pain, he rules the diocese with the serenity of a Saint' (*Ibid.*). It was Macchi who used a capital letter. If no man is a hero to his valet, few bishops are saints to their secretaries.

Before this barrage of good advice, Roncalli's resistance crumbled. His frankest letter was to Don Paolo Giobbe, who had been his prefect at the Roman seminary and was now rector of the Propaganda Fide College. (He was made a cardinal by Pope John on December 15, 1958.) Roncalli admitted that 'this sudden change in the direction of my life has left me astonished and terrified'. He felt a pronounced aversion for the new post. He didn't want it at all. Yet on one side is 'Thy will be done' and on the other 'self-love and the reasons of the heart' (*Natale, 1970*, p. 18). But once Roncalli had set up the problem in this way, it was already resolved. 'Self-love' which would have kept him in Bergamo had been undermined. He accepted the job.

The appointment was confirmed in a letter from Van Rossum to Bishop Marella of January 10, 1921 (*Natale, 1970*, p. 21). Don Roncalli's first meeting with Van Rossum was a success. He decided to begin work at Propaganda on January 18, 1921, feast of the Chair of St Peter. This was a deliberate choice based on his historical knowledge. Peter's chair symbolised the authority which is carried on in the pope. Our talk of 'cathedral' (from *cathedra*) and see (meaning 'seat') derives from Peter's chair, from the 'holy see'.

Roncalli was now a curialist, in the direct service of the Apostolic See. Propaganda Fide, his particular branch of the Curia, was being expanded and re-organised as a direct result of initiatives taken by Pope Benedict XV. His encyclical *Maximum Illud* (November 30, 1919) was devoted to missionary activity in the much-changed post-war world. Germany had lost all its African colonies: Benedict's representatives had saved their missions from total extinction at the Versailles Peace Conference, a fact that irritated Giolitti, since it involved treating the Pope as a serious partner in international dialogue.

Benedict's encyclical stated three fundamental principles of missionary work. The first was that a local or 'native' clergy should be ordained as soon as possible; and from this indigenous clergy it was expected that bishops would soon emerge. The second was that European missionaries – there were at the time few others – should cast off every form of nationalism. This was aimed particularly at the French. Even the anti-clerical leaders of France had declared that 'anti-clericalism is not for export' and used missionaries to turn Africans into polished Racine-loving 'overseas Frenchmen'. More widely, the religious differences of Europe had been exported to the 'colonies' where they made very little sense. 'Remember', concluded Benedict, 'that you have to make citizens not of any country upon this earth, but of the heavenly *patria*' (Holmes, p. 23 and following). He was ahead of most secular pundits of the time, who were still thinking of a God-given destiny propped up by neo-Darwinian arguments which convinced them that with their maxim-guns they were the 'fittest'; and he was already looking forward to the end of the colonial era which Roncalli was to hail as one of the 'signs of the times' in his encyclical *Pacem in Terris*.

The third principle stated by Benedict in *Maximum Illud* brought Roncalli to Rome. Not everyone could travel to the missions, but everyone was to be involved in missionary work. Missionary 'consciousness' was to be raised by prayer, sacrifice and financial involvement. Roncalli directed this operation in Italy. He discovered an Italy that he hardly knew, and as he moved round the country had to learn tact in dealing with apathy in the South and existing missionary organisations in the North like the Missionary Union which felt threatened by the new centralism. The work also enabled him to travel round Europe to consult other missionary bodies, so that he gained a more 'universalist' view of the Church than would ever have been possible in Bergamo.

But this did not happen all at once. Don Roncalli had arrived in Rome, but was in no hurry to set up house there. He returned to Bergamo to pack and on his way saw Cardinal Ferrari for the last time on January 21, 1921. Throat cancer made Ferrari speechless, but, as Roncalli put it, he 'accepted this cross and continued to speak with eyes and pen'. One of his last acts was to authorise the setting up of the Catholic university of the Sacred Heart in Milan. On February 2, 1921, feast of the Purification of Our Lady, Ferrari died as the last notes of the evening Angelus rang out from the cathedral. It is Roncalli who records these details in an obituary he wrote at the time (*Dodicesimo anniversario*, p. 111 and following).

Ferrari was, he said, a master of spirituality and the defender of the poor. Those who attended his funeral on February 7, 1921, realised just how deep his influence had been on all sections of the Milanese population, believers and unbelievers. Nothing like it had been seen since the funeral of St Charles Borromeo. Ferrari had been appointed archbishop of Milan in 1894, and had been content to remain there, considering his diocese the 'finest and most beautiful garden he could wish for'. In eulogising Ferrari, Roncalli was drawing his own self-portrait:

> He always preferred to affirm rather than to deny, to act rather than to criticise. Pettiness was foreign to him. He overcame every obstacle with unvanquished constancy, drawing his inspiration not from worldly criteria but from the Christian faith and piety that filled the depths of his spirit . . . He sought the Kingdom of God and its justice, and nothing else. He knew that he had to become holy in order to make others holy (*Dodicesimo anniversario*, pp. 113–14).

These lessons were Ferrari's dying legacy to him. All Roncalli's spiritual guides were now departed. Radini Tedeschi had died in 1914 and now Ferrari in 1921. He was orphaned once more. Subsequently he would have many 'spiritual directors' but no more true father-figures or models of the episcopal ministry. From now on his memories of Radini Tedeschi and Ferrari would fuse with the accounts of great bishops in history to shape his concept of episcopacy.

As he set about his work at Propaganda, other, more minor, sub-episcopal dignities came his way. In March 1921 the cathedral chapter of Bergamo voted unanimously to make him an honorary canon (*Pastore*, p. 97). It was a way of saying 'thank-you' and an indication that they didn't expect to see him back: his Roman career was now properly launched. Roncalli, however, saw it rather as another tribute to the memory of Radini Tedeschi. But he was Canon Roncalli for less than two months since on May 7, 1921, he was made a 'domestic prelate of his Holiness'. This allowed him to wear red piping on his soutane and to be addressed as *Monsignore*. He took it rather pompously in a letter home: 'What difference does the colour of a soutane make? . . . this dignity is a great responsibility' (*Familiari*, I, p. 75). But given his post at propaganda, not becoming a domestic prelate would have been a slight. It went with the job.

Rome had its compensations. On March 28, 1921, he met a future *beatus*, Don Luigi Orione, founder of a missionary order (beatified by John Paul II on October 26, 1980). He attended sessions of the Italian parliament, felt the growing tensions and realised the risk of seeking authoritarian solutions. But most of the time he was on the road, the itinerant pedlar of the importance of the missions. He managed to time his movements well. So he chanced to be in Milan on September 8, 1921, when Achille Ratti took possession of his see. Roncalli was keenly interested in the succession of Ferrari, and was surprised by the Ratti appointment. Here was someone who had spent his entire life among books, first as prefect of the prestigious Ambrosian Library in Milan and then as prefect of the Vatican Library. Roncalli had known him in Milan. Ratti had helped him by photocopying documents on St Charles Borromeo (at the time an expensive and elaborate process). But they had not been close. In 1918 Ratti had been thrown to the wolves as Vatican diplomatic representative (he was not yet Nuncio) in newly independent Poland. Roncalli wasn't quite sure what he thought of Ratti as Ferrari's successor. The man was aloof, reserved, enigmatic.

Finally Roncalli's flat-hunting in Rome proved successful. He had turned down a seven-roomed apartment because it would have cost 15,600 *lire* a year (*Familiari*, I, p. 76, letter of August 3, 1921). He accepted a flat in Via Volturno 58, for 6,000 *lire* a year. Though not very close to Propaganda, it was handy for the railway station. He was able to offer hospitality to his old seminary rector, Mgr Vincenzo Bugarini, who had nowhere to go in retirement and felt unwanted. His knowledge of Oriental languages was considerable, but unfortunately he had never committed it to paper. To remedy that would be the work of his retirement. Mgr Roncalli brought down his sisters Ancilla and Maria by one of the few trains that were still running – there was another strike (*Familiari*, I, p. 78, letter of November 13, 1921). They became his housekeepers. They found Rome very expensive compared with Sotto il Monte, but their cooking delighted Bugarini and *Monsignore* their brother showed them the sights of Rome beginning, naturally, with the churches he knew so well (*Familiari*, I, p. 79).

But then he was off over Christmastide, from December 17 to January 8, to see how missionary activity was funded and organised in France, Belgium, Germany and Holland. In Germany he saw the effects of runaway inflation and reported to his family: 'Think of the Germans and the Austrians whose money is worthless. They are far worse off than we are. But for the most part they are good people. And they will haul themselves up again before we do, because they work hard while we spend our time in strikes and revolutions' (*Familiari*, I, 81). This mythic contrast between the hard-working German and the indolent Italian had a long literary history.

No sooner was he back from his travels than on January 22, 1922, Pope Benedict XV died. For the first time since 1870 flags were flown at half-mast on government buildings. Yet his achievements, though considerable, were not widely appreciated. His pleas for peace had gone unheard. He had emptied the Vatican coffers, partly to provide 'humanitarian' aid to Soviet Russia. Though obviously unable to remove all inquisitors from key posts, he had put an end to the anti-Modernist campaign. He had witnessed the foundation of the PPI and seen the return of Italian Catholics to the mainstream of political life. And he had given new impetus to missionary activity. In the long-term, he proved to be one of the most enlightened and 'prophetic' popes of the century. The conclave had as usual to decide whether to continue or cancel out his policies. It needed fourteen ballots to reach a compromise conclusion, and was the most protracted and bloodiest conclave of the century.

Thanks to the diary of the cardinal of Vienna, Gustavo Piffl, it is possible to reconstruct what happened (*Quale Papa?* p. 138 and following). Roncalli's superior, Van Rossum, made the first move. He thought the time had come to elect a non-Italian. Unfortunately the foreigner he proposed, Merry del Val, was more Roman than the Romans, and his election would have meant a return to the rigours of Pius X, whose Secretary of State he had been. La Fontaine, patriarch of Venice, was another former inquisitor who could plausibly claim to inherit the mantle of Pius X, but was that what the fifty-three cardinals really wanted?

The alternative was Pietro Gasparri, author of the 1917 Code of Canon Law and Secretary of State under Benedict whose policies he would continue but without Benedict's imprudences. A vote for Gasparri would be a vote for sagacity. But since neither side would give way, the conclave was deadlocked. Thirty-six votes were needed to win. Merry del Val reached 17, La Fontaine peaked at 23 and Gasparri at 24. As they faded, Ratti, Archbishop of Milan for only five months, came through the middle. But it was a bruising contest. One witness, on oath during the beatification process for Merry del Val, reported that Gasparri had said that 'during the conclave Merry del Val's ambitions knew no bounds so much so that he incurred excommunication' (*Quale Papa?*, p. 142). Cardinal De Lai, whom we last met in 1914 deploring Duchesne, had acted as election agent for

Merry del Val. When his candidate failed, he tried to impose on Ratti the condition that he would have Gasparri as his Secretary of State. But it is against conclave rules to make deals in advance. In theory, De Lai was excommunicated too. Ratti, unoriginally, took the name of Pius XI.

At least one person was overjoyed at Ratti's election. Duchesne, the venerable church historian, was now 79 and in the last year of his life. He had known Ratti as librarian in Milan and Rome. He felt his whole life's work was vindicated. With his Breton faith undimmed he had survived being put on the Index of Forbidden Books and he now looked forward to an era of flourishing scholarship in the Church. Enclosed in his vast black cape (the *pèlerine*) he followed the *sedia gestatoria* as it bore the new pope into St Peter's to the sound of silver trumpets. Giuseppe De Luca takes up the story: 'Hearing the very words which rang out for Gregory the Great and Gregory VII and seeing his friend bent beneath so great a burden, he felt his old heart beat faster' (*Lettere*, p. 34). Roncalli was more guarded in his judgement. The truth was that no one knew where Ratti stood on important questions. He had successfully avoided showing his hand in all the disputes that had raged with such passionate intensity over the last thirty years (see Tramontin, I, p. 146). In the 'night battle' he had prudently made himself invisible. It was known that in Poland he had conceived a detestation for Bolshevism, as Communism was then known. And in Milan he had just time to issue one pastoral letter on the need for 'reconciliation' with the Italian state; but by now that was a conventional view, requiring neither courage nor originality.

At first the new pontificate made no difference to the work of Roncalli at Propaganda Fide. Pius XI was as concerned as his predecessor that the missions should prosper. He gave Van Rossum and his team an early vote of confidence. They had been preparing a *motu proprio* which worked out the details of the reorganisation of missionary work. Pius XI published it at the first possible moment, on March 3, 1922, under the title *Romanorum Pontificum*. It was an unashamedly centralising document which transferred the headquarters of missionary work from France to Rome. Roncalli worked on it and even claimed to be its author (*Gran Sacerdote*, p. 134). Even if that were not literally true, he made a contribution towards it and it was his first 'papal document'. He had already learned the lesson that the role of the pope was to prompt and sign documents rather than compose them.

Mgr Roncalli's first comment on Pius XI came in a letter to Don Antonio Guerinoni, a Bergamesque working in the nunciature in Madrid:

The new Holy Father is well. I saw him again in a long audience a few days ago. He had the goodness to treat me with the trust that befits an affectionate friend of Mgr Radini Tedeschi and the prefect of the Ambrosian

Library. Yet I get between his feet as little as possible, and feel shivers run down my spine every time I have to go through those Vatican halls. Despite my constant and heart-felt attempt to serve the new pope as best I can, I don't envy – indeed I feel compassion – towards those who have to work in the Vatican. The Pope is truly good and wise; he shows that he has the Spirit with him (*Gran Sacerdote*, pp. 135–6. Letter dated July 21, 1922).

That proves only that he had not lost his distaste for waiting about in Vatican ante-chambers. He kept out of the way because he was happy with his work and wanted to continue with it.

They moved house again July 1922. Their new flat was a charming roof-top eyrie cut into the facade of the church of Santa Maria in Via Lata. 'My crow's nest', he called it in a letter to Guerinoni (*Gran Sacerdote*, p. 134). Finding it, he told his mother, was 'an answer to prayer' (*Familiari*, I, p. 82). It was much more convenient for his office in Piazza di Spagna. Mgr Bugarini, now an established member of the household, moved along with them and pulled his weight. His knowledge of the Italian church proved invaluable. So many bishops had passed through his hands at the Roman seminary. Roncalli was able to assure Michele Zezza, archbishop of Naples, that 'Mgr Bugarini often thinks of you' and remark on the coincidence that the two great maritime sees, Naples and Genoa, were both ruled by ex-alumni of the Roman seminary. But Bugarini had only another eighteen months to live.

By any criteria, Mgr Roncalli was a success at Propaganda Fide. He saw his work not in bureaucratic terms but as helping the pope, as the 'father of the family', to provide for the needs of all the missions (*Gran Sacerdote*, p. 139, letter to the vicar general of Parma, March 20, 1924). He more than doubled the collections for Propaganda, from 400,000 *lire* in 1920 to over a million in 1922 (Trevor, p. 123). He made friends for life with his colleagues Dieci and Rusticoni. He skilfully avoided ruffling the feathers of Fr Paolo Manna, for example, superior of the institute of foreign missions in Milan (*Gran Sacerdote*, p. 139, letter of December 2, 1924). Anything he had achieved at Propaganda, he said, had been built on Manna's work; and his wartime book, *Salviamo le missioni* (*Let's Save the Missions*), had sounded the tocsin which led to 'the post-war resurrection of missionary energies' (*Ibid.*). But as he looked back later over his time at Propaganda, he saw it in a different light. Writing to his successor, Zanetti, he said: 'I am convinced that if there were any good fruits of my work, that was because I took up this ministry out of pure obedience. Then the Lord gave me the grace to love it, and I left with sorrow . . . ' (*Gran Sacerdote* p. 152, letter of May 29, 1929). The pattern was becoming familiar: distaste, obedience, attachment and then the wrench.

It wasn't all hard work. In May 1923 he travelled throughout Sicily, a whole new enchanted world for a northerner like himself. The newspapers reported hail-storms near Bergamo, he wrote home, but Sicily

> is like a garden. Now that I've been all round the island, I can truly say that
> it's a semi-paradise. The streets are not very clean, but then they lack water;
> for the rest they live very well here. The Sicilians I've met have been good,
> friendly, hospitable. The women go about with a modesty and reserve that
> we in upper Italy have no conception of (*Familiari*, I, p. 78).

Travel, he concluded, gave him 'an extraordinary appetite'. He had not yet joined the weight-watchers.

In his letters home Mgr Roncalli usually steered well clear of politics. But as he travelled round the country, he was able to gauge the shifting national mood. The last letter quoted was written from Catania in Sicily. He would have been told how the Fascists had broken up the Corpus Christi procession there the previous year with cries of *Abbasso il Papa* (Down with the Pope) (Trevor, p. 124). But now Mussolini was in power and had apparently shed his anti-clericalism. The 'march on Rome', which was later hailed in Fascist mythology as an act of dashing heroism, was really the resolution of a fairly routine political muddle. Those Fascists who were not halted by driving rain arrived by train. Mussolini himself appeared in Rome on October 30, 1922, not in the uniform of the saviour of the nation but in the frock-coat and top-hat of the traditional politician. Only the irresolution of the army and King Victor Emmanuel III's sudden and unexpected change of mind let the Fascists into the city. An elderly prelate who had watched the Italian army march in fifty-two years previously remarked sadly, 'In 1870 we defended the city better' (Seton-Watson, p. 629).

Mussolini played down his atheist and anti-clerical past. He knew that to hold and extend his power in Italy, he would have to woo the Church. His package of pro-clerical proposals included the introduction of religious education into primary schools, the appointment of official military chaplains, improved salaries for the clergy, and the return of the crucifix to public buildings. These were all measures no Liberal government had even contemplated. The Vatican was favour-ably impressed. Pietro Gasparri, Secretary of State, was able to have his first secret meeting with Mussolini on January 20, 1923 (Pollard, p. 48). Mussolini promised, among other things, to 'deal with the problem of Freemasonry', still dedicated, it was believed, to the final liquidation of the temporal power of the papacy. Gasparri promised in return to prepare a list of 'unreliable and mistaken men' in the Vatican service who were trying to build up the *Popolari* as an alternative to the Fascists. But nothing was known of this secret deal, which marked the beginning of the complicated minuet that would lead, eventually, to the Lateran Pacts of 1929.

Nothing was known about the deal, but its effects were soon felt. In July 1923 Don Luigi Sturzo was ordered to resign as secretary of the PPI, and he went into exile in London. He was succeeded by a young layman from Trentino, Alcide De Gasperi, whose first political experience had been gained in the Austrian parliament. But the writing was on the wall for the *Popolari*, and the only force that could conceivably have checked the Fascists was emasculated. Pius XI and Gasparri had decided that an apolitical Catholic Action was the best form of Christian 'presence' to the world. The doomed *Popolari* made their last stand under De Gasperi at the elections of April 6, 1924.

For the first (and last) time Mgr Roncalli had some advice for his family on an election. Using the typewriter bequeathed him by Mgr Bugarini, who had just died on February 14, 1924, he said:

> I recommend everyone not to get too excited about the elections. Vote
> when the time comes. Now it is better to let things be. Keep quiet and stay
> at home; think it out for yourselves, and let everyone do what they think is
> right. I, for example, remain faithful to the *Partito Popolare*; but because of
> the post I have with the Holy See I can't and musn't make any public state-
> ments at all. For that reason I won't be coming to Bergamo to vote
> (*Familiari*, I, p. 96, letter of February 24, 1924).

So Roncalli had made up his mind early on what he would do. And he was going against *l'Osservatore Romano*, now edited by Giuseppe Dalla Torre, which had welcomed the march on Rome and Mussolini's pro-clerical package, and devoted more space to Catholic Action than to the *Popolari*. But Roncalli retained his independence of judgement. Two days before the election he wrote again to his family:

> I might have come to see you for the elections, but to tell the truth I
> preferred to stay here for reasons you will well understand. *In my conscience
> as a priest and a Christian, I don't feel I can vote for the Fascists*. Everyone has
> the right to think as they believe. In the end we'll see who was right; do
> what seems good to you. My advice is this: if there is freedom to vote, vote
> for the PPI list. If there is danger of trouble, stay at home and let the world
> go its own way. Of one thing I am certain: *the salvation of Italy cannot come
> from Mussolini even though he may be a man of talent*. His goals may perhaps
> be good and correct, but the means he takes to realise them are wicked
> (*iniqui*) and contrary to the law of the Gospel. Therefore and as a conse-
> quence – as Uncle Barba would have said, He who survives will see
> (*Familiari*, I, p. 98, April 4, 1924. Italics added).

The warning to stay at home in case of violence was needed. The Fascists hung about the polling booths and intimidated the electors. The campaign headquarters of the PPI were attacked. Even so, the *Popolari* still won 40 out of 375 seats, compared with 42 for the Socialists and 17 for the Communists. But the Fascist landslide meant that the power of the *Popolari* was now broken. Its leaders would go into exile, prison or hiding.

The Vatican dropped the *Popolari*. This brought together in despondency those curialists who had pinned their hopes on the PPI. Roncalli now met for the first time Giovanni Battista Montini, the future Paul VI. Montini's father, Giorgio, was editor of *Il Cittadino di Brescia*, and a PPI member of parliament. But after the kidnap and murder of the Socialist deputy, Giacomo Matteotti, in June 1924, he never set foot in the chamber again, believing rightly that the Fascists would stop at nothing to secure their hold on power. His newspaper was suppressed. Giovanni Battista, just back from a spell in Poland, was now at the Secretariat of State. He had to report to Giuseppe Pizzardo, head of the Italian section, on 'the spiritual and moral condition of the young' and to gather material he became student chaplain at the university. This whole milieu, more cultivated and sophisticated than anything Roncalli had previously known, was solidly anti-Fascist. Montini sensed a kindred spirit, sought him out, and invited him to address his students. This was their first documented contact (*Quinquagesimo anniversario*, pp. 57–8). Over the next three decades they became good friends.

Roncalli's sermon in Bergamo Cathedral on September 1, 1924, was a lament for the *Popolari*. According to the point of view adopted, it could be described as the most injudicious or the most courageous, the finest or the most foolhardy sermon he ever preached. The tenth anniversary of the death of Bishop Radini Tedeschi was the pretext. As his biographer and former secretary, Roncalli was the obvious choice as preacher. But the presence of the civic, political and military establishment turned it into a political event of some significance. The memory of 'My Bishop' moved Roncalli to an eloquence he had not displayed since the eucharistic Congress of 1920. But the changed context made it even more dramatic. His listeners were concerned only with his answer to one question: what did he think of Fascism?

Roncalli's chosen theme was patriotism or 'true love of one's country'. Some of those present might be asking of Radini Tedeschi, whom they had not known: 'What did he do for his country? Was he so immersed in churchy affairs that he did nothing?' (*Pasqua 1976*, p. 30). We are always being invited, he remarked rather loftily, to bless this or that cause and to lend our support to 'various movements of minds'. As churchmen, he went on, we have to be patriotic, because 'patriotism is a form of brotherly love'. But patriotism cannot be used as a protective cloak to cover everything a government does. The Church uses a different yardstick in determining 'the true good of a country'. Its greatness is not measured by 'military enterprises, diplomatic agreements or economic successes' about which the Fascists constantly orated, even if so far there was nothing much to show. A country should boast only of 'justice embodied in law' (*Ibid.*, p. 31). *Iustitia regnorum fundamentum*: justice is the foundation of kingdoms. He did not need to add that the Matteotti affair had illustrated rather 'injustice embodied in law'.

Patriotism, then, as he understood it, did not exclude a certain distance from the state, a standing back from immediate issues and the use of longer-term criteria. This 'distance' was a condition of the Church's freedom. Roncalli cried:

> O leave us the holy freedom of our peaceful and lofty ministry . . . Leave to us the guardianship of the fundamental laws of civilisation, which are the Ten Commandments and the Gospels; from this source derives the doctrine which enlightens and inspires every noble action, leading to sacrifice and heroism. Leave this to us. And *do not ask us for anything more* (*Pasqua, 1976*, p. 31: italics added).

It was a warning that there were limits to what could be asked of the Church. Roncalli plunged on, almost recklessly. Bergamo in the past had the reputation of being 'intransigent'. So it was. But this did not rule out good relations with the civil authorities. Radini Tedeschi had always behaved 'as a perfect gentleman' towards them. His contribution to the debate on education had been described by Giuseppe Toniolo as 'the most complete treatment of the question written in Italy or elsewhere' (*Ibid.*, p. 32). Mention of Toniolo was dynamite for he had been the advocate of 'Christian democracy' and Catholic populism that were now regarded as enemies of the regime.

Finally, Roncalli commented directly on the government's 'concessions' to the Church: 'We are happy at the return of the crucifix and the catechism to primary schools, while hoping soon for the fuller joy of seeing the return of Catholic teaching to middle and senior schools' (*Pasqua, 1976*, p. 33). Mussolini had no intention of surrendering control over education beyond the primary stage. Roncalli cut the 'concessions' down to size by insisting that they were not enough and attributing them not to Fascist generosity but 'to the champions of the just cause of educational freedom in Italy such as Radini Tedeschi'. Just to compound his error, he again quoted Toniolo who had remarked: 'A cause can be considered already victorious when men of such quality as Radini Tedeschi enter the lists on its behalf' (*Ibid.*, p. 33). After such effrontery, it was only a matter of time before the Fascist police caught up with Roncalli and – in the discreetest possible manner – invited the Vatican to remove him.

He had misjudged the mood in the Vatican. Just over a week after his Bergamo sermon, Pius XI denounced with some asperity any 'opening to the left' on the part of the *Popolari* (see Giovanni Martina in De Gasperi, *Lettere sul Concordato*, p. 123). In Germany and Belgium Catholic parties were already co-operating with non-Communist Socialists. Pius XI did not want that to happen in Italy. Thus any hope of an anti-Fascist alliance faded away. Mussolini was given a clear run. Roncalli opposed this policy for as long as he could not because he was of a rebellious nature – no one was less rebellious; he made his stand out of fidelity to the memory of Radini Tedeschi and the Christian democracy Toniolo had expounded. It made him look old-fashioned, naïve perhaps, and unaware of the eddies of history. But at least he was more principled than the 'realists' in the Vatican who could come to terms with almost anyone.

But his Bergamo sermon had no immediate consequences. Bishop Luigi Marella stayed with him in Rome on October 1, 1924, and they no doubt speculated on what might happen. His career seemed secure. He was a member of the commission to prepare the coming Holy Year, 1925. In addition to his work at Propaganda, he began to lecture in patristics at the Pontifical Lateran Athenaeum (his old *alma mater* in new dress) from November 1924. It was quite usual for curialists to double up with academic posts. It kept their minds stretched and filled in the afternoons. Roncalli had taught patristics in Bergamo, and was not by Roman standards badly prepared for the task. His lectures 'were popular and even applauded' (Trevor, p. 131). But it was all over for him in Rome.

The high hopes he had entertained in the spring of 1919 when he destroyed his army uniform, said 'goodbye to all that' and supported the *Popolari*, had all vanished. The new uniform was a black shirt, and the sound of marching boots led away from the temple.

Chapter 7

Ten hard years in Bulgaria

'You will tell the truth – you will speak well of us. We Bulgarians like to be praised'. It is very easy to praise them: for their kindness, for their hospitality and friendliness

(David Martin in *The Religious and the Secular*, p. 131).

On the evening of February 17, 1925, Cardinal Pietro Gasparri, Secretary of State, summoned Mgr Roncalli and told him that he had been appointed apostolic visitor to Bulgaria. After this spell in 'purgatory' – he was assured that it would not last long – he would formally enter the Vatican diplomatic service and take up a congenial posting in Argentina where more than a tenth of the population was Italian. It sounded both enchanting and fishy.

Roncalli objected, with perfect truthfulness, that he had had no diplomatic training and knew nothing at all about Bulgaria. Surely there must be someone better prepared for this mission. Gasparri dismissed this by saying that his name had been put forward by Cardinal Giovanni Tacci, of the Congregation for the Oriental Churches, who presumably knew the field and had settled on him. Roncalli tried another objection: his sisters, Ancilla and Maria, would be very upset at him leaving Rome just when they were all properly installed. Shrugs from Gasparri. Roncalli had one final question, in his mind the most decisive: 'Was the mission to Bulgaria a matter of obedience?' It was indeed, and when Pope Pius XI heard his name mentioned he had said: 'Splendid, this is the man sent by Providence'. But even papal approval did not put his mind completely at rest, and he left saying he would think it over. All this Roncalli noted down the same evening (*Quindicesimo anniversario*, p. 27).

Later he used to recall that Gasparri did not seem to be very well-informed about Bulgaria and that his briefing was perfunctory. Gasparri had said to him:

Listen, *monsignore*, I'm told the situation in Bulgaria is very confused. I can't tell you in detail what's going on. But everyone seems to be fighting with everyone else, the Moslems with the Orthodox, the Greek Catholics with the Latins, and the Latins with each other. Could you go there and find out what is really happening? (*Corriere della Sera*, March 29, 1959, Pope John in conversation with Indro Montanelli).

It did not take Mgr Roncalli very long to discover that to say 'the situation in Bulgaria is confused' was a considerable under-statement.

Just as he had predicted, the news filled his sisters Ancilla and Maria with alarm and despondency. 'Groans, tears, endless lamentations' he noted in his diary. But they calmed down a little after saying the rosary (*Quindicesimo anniversario*, p. 27). Roncalli felt responsible for them. They had built their world around him, and now it had come crashing down. In Rome as house-keepers to their priest-brother, they had a role and were appreciated. Back in Sotto il Monte as two maiden aunts with nothing to do, they would be a burden on the by now aging parents. Roncalli assured them that whatever happened he would continue to look after them financially.

But it wasn't only the Roncalli sisters who wept at the prospect of Bulgaria. Roncalli himself confessed in a letter to Cardinal William van Rossum, his superior at Propaganda, that after meeting Gasparri 'I shed many tears during the night, and even now – nearly a week later – when I think of it alone, especially in prayer, tears begin to well up in my eyes again' (*Quindicesimo anniversario*, p. 33). He had an audience with Pius XI on February 21, 1925. Pius was paternal but hardly more illuminating than his Secretary of State. Roncalli's diary records the Pope's words:

> Your name was suggested to me for this visitation. I was very happy about it. I was told that your title of monsignor would be enough, but I replied 'it is not a good thing when an apostolic prelate goes to a country and has to deal with bishops without being one himself'. I don't want a repeat performance of what happened to me in Poland. I was embarrassed at episcopal meetings when I had to take my place as the representative of the Holy Father, having precedence over the Polish Bishops and archbishops. So I decided you should be consecrated archbishop (*Quindicesimo anniversario*, p. 11).

So Roncalli became an archbishop because of humiliations undergone by Mgr Achille Ratti in post-war Poland. The truth, however, was the Polish bishops did not reject Ratti because of his junior rank: they could not see what he was doing in Poland at all. On one occasion, they excluded him from a meeting, and the man who shut the door on him was Archbishop Adam Sapieha, mentor and predecessor of Karol Wojtyla, the future Pope John Paul II (see George Huntston Williams, p. 83). Pius XI never forgot this slight and ostentatiously did not make Sapieha a cardinal.

In any case his remarks had little bearing on the situation in Bulgaria. Poland had a Catholic tradition with a strong and determined hierarchy anxious to impose itself now that the country was at last independent and united. Bulgaria, on the other hand, was an Orthodox country, rumoured to have some 60,000 Catholics of varying rites. Its two bishops would have welcomed any visitor, whatever his rank, as a sign that they had not been abandoned. But if he knew nothing very helpful about Bulgaria, Pius XI could at least provide a parting gift, the *Scintillae Ignatianae*, a collection of maxims of St Ignatius arranged for day-by-day reading. Ignatius was not given to sparkling epigrams, so the gift may have been a recognition that in Sofia Roncalli would need all the spiritual consolation he could muster.

On March 3, 1925 *l'Osservatore Romano* announced that Angelo Roncalli would be ordained archbishop with the title of Areopolis, the ancient Roman city whose ruins still stand between the Dead Sea and the Red Sea. He made a retreat at the Villa Carpegna. He was consecrated on March 19, feast of St Joseph, in San Carlo allo Corso, the Milanese church dedicated to St Charles Borromeo. His family were present, looking stiff and awkward, and the next morning he took them down to the crypt of St Peter's for his first episcopal Mass, and then presented them to Pius XI. Thus he repeated, in detail, the pattern of his priestly ordination twenty-one years previously.

But there was a difference. In 1904 he imagined he saw Our Lady smiling down at him. In 1925 there were no smiles, only intimations of crosses to be borne. This is how he remembered it five years later:

> The profound and lasting impression that I received during the whole ceremony of my consecration as bishop in Rome in San Carlo allo Corso on March 19, 1925, and since then the difficulties and trials of my ministry in Bulgaria during these five years as Apostolic Visitor, without any consolation save that of a good conscience and a rather sombre prospect for the future, convince me that the Lord wants me all for himself along the royal road to the cross . . . (*Journal*, p. 231).

The apprehensions he felt on the day of his episcopal ordination were well-founded.

Yet he was, in some fairly obvious sense, being promoted. His career was well and truly launched – even if towards unknown and possibly hazardous seas. During his retreat he pondered what the liturgy of episcopal ordination has to say about the bishop. Its most interesting feature theologically is the way it presents the Pope not as the 'Vicar of Christ' (a modern, that is to say thirteenth-century concept) but as in a sense the 'vicar of Peter'. Roncalli resolved 'in all things to show fidelity, submission and obedience to the Blessed Apostle Peter and the Roman Pontiff' (*Journal*, p. 219). He racked his brains dutifully over a distinction made by St Thomas Aquinas. The bishop, unlike the religious, is said to be 'in a state of perfection already acquired (*acquisita*), not still to be acquired (*acquirenda*)' (*Journal*, p. 218). That did not get him very far. The most important fruit of this pre-ordination retreat was the reassurance that 'I have not sought or desired this new ministry; the Lord has chosen me, making it so clear that it is his will that it would be a grave sin for me to refuse. So it will be for him to cover up my failings and inadequacies. This comforts me and brings tranquillity and confidence' (*Journal*, p. 218).

He was able to say exactly the same thing at every other change of direction in his life – including being elected Pope. His episcopal motto, borrowed from Cesare Baronius, summed up his attitude: *Obedientia et Pax*. The path to peace lay through obedience.

Yet this 'edifying' interpretation of his appointment cannot have banished entirely the suspicion that he was the victim of a plot or of some secret wheeler-dealing. Dom Lambert Beauduin O.S.B., a good friend and then professor of fundamental theology at San Anselmo in Rome, used to maintain that Roncalli 'was relieved of his teaching post at the Lateran on suspicion of Modernism' (see Trevor, p. 132). This theory has had wide currency. But a month's teaching would not have given the inquisitors very much to work on. And at this date more attention was being paid to political than to theological unorthodoxy. As we have seen, Roncalli's sermon on Radini Tedeschi on September 1, 1924, marked him out as an unrepentant supporter of the PPI (the *Popolari*). That was enough to despatch him to Bulgaria where he could do no harm.

Beauduin had a great and permanent influence on Roncalli. He had vision. He was the founder of the 'liturgical movement' (Villain, p. 216), and was also a pioneer of social action and ecumenism. His knowledge and love of the Orthodox Churches had led him to take an interest in Bulgaria. In this same year, 1925, he realised his heart's desire of founding a Benedictine Priory wholly dedicated to Church unity: it began at Amay-sur-Meuse and transferred to Chevetogne in 1939. Beauduin's ecumenical concern was not limited to the Orthodox. Cardinal Mercier asked him to prepare a paper for the Malines Conversations with the Anglicans. He drew a parallel between the situation of the ancient patriarchates of the East and the pre-Reformation Church in England. Its title, *'L'Eglise Anglicane unie, non absorbée'* (The Anglican Church, united, not absorbed), became famous and anticipated the ecumenical dialogues that would follow Pope John's Council. In 1925 Beauduin was helpful in a more precise way. On March 22, 1925, he introduced Roncalli to a fellow Benedictine, Dom Constantin Bosschaerts, who would go with him to Sofia as temporary secretary.

Other friends rallied round, notably Don Giovanni Battista Montini who dropped in for a long conversation the day before Roncalli left Rome for Bergamo (Fappani-Molinari, Letter of Montini, April 9, 1925). Between them, they managed to make some sense of his appointment. Its ecumenical importance was evident. St Cyril – known for most of his life as Constantine the Philosopher – devised the Slav alphabet which is still called Cyrillic after him. He went to Rome to ask Pope Hadrian II to approve his newly created Slav liturgy and died there in 869. His disciples St Clement (Kliment) and St Naoum used this liturgy to evangelise Bulgaria. A thousand years later Bulgaria was an Orthodox country in a unique situation. Its hierarchy had been in schism from the ecumenical patriarch in Constantinople since 1872, and though it had traditionally looked to Moscow for leadership, the Moscow patriarchate was now powerless and persecuted. So Bulgarian Orthodoxy was adrift, and could go anywhere. It was beginning to take an interest in the burgeoning 'ecumenical movement' of Protestant inspiration.

Again, Roncalli and his friends were able to piece together the reasons why someone was needed in Bulgaria. Bulgaria had made the mistake of choosing the defeated side in the First World War. It had been punished by losing territory and its traditional friends. It was therefore isolated and biddable. As early as 1923, Kristov Kalkov, the future minister of cults, had an audience with Pius XI and meetings in the Secretariat of State. The possibility of a concordat was aired. Then in 1924 the Vatican librarian, the energetic French ex-cavalry officer Mgr Eugène Tisserant, had gone to Sofia in search of manuscripts and rare books. After the upheavals of war and the closing of many Russian monasteries, there were rich pickings. It was Tisserant who had suggested that an envoy should be sent to discover the needs of the small minority of Catholics of Slav rite.

So it was possible to see Roncalli's mission to Bulgaria in a very positive way. It had three dimensions – ecumenical, diplomatic and pastoral. Though rather off the beaten track, it was no disgrace to be sent there. And it wasn't for very long.

One matter of great personal importance was resolved just before he left Bergamo. Baron Gianmaria Scotti agreed to rent Archbishop Roncalli part of Camaitino, the house of an earlier Roncalli. This meant that Ancilla and Maria could live there, look after the house and not be a burden on the parents. And Roncalli would have a place to stay during his summer holidays. Except when war made it impossible, he managed to spend about a month there every summer until 1958 when he was elected Pope. Camaitino became his great bond with Sotto Il Monte. He could hardly have descended any longer upon his already overcrowded parents. He loved Camaitino. His letters to Ancilla and Maria over the years are filled with details about tiled floors and new curtains and furnishings. The books he couldn't transport were there too. On a clear day, he could see the spire of Milan Cathedral from his balcony. That helped him to concentrate on his work on St Charles Borromeo, which was now years behind schedule. But all that was for the future. On April 23, 1925, he said good-bye to all his family and his new acquisition and set off for Sofia.

It was the age of the train. He boarded the Simplon Orient Express, the world's most famous train, in Milan. It combined opulence, mystery, exoticism and scandal in about equal proportions, which is why novelists have loved it. The Orient Express was to play an important part in Roncalli's life. For the next thirty-three years he went back and forth along its route – Sofia, Constantinople, Paris, Venice, with Milan as the constant point of departure. He enjoyed his journeys. 'In the train', he tells his sisters, who had never been on such a luxurious journey, 'you can relax, read, pray, observe the beauties of nature and the variety of people' (*Familiari*, I, p. 205). John Dos Passos has described the Orient Express as it was at this time rather more vividly:

> Between meals I sit in the privacy of my little green compartment full of nickel nobs and fixings, occasionally interrupted by passport men, customs agents, detectives, secret police or by the porter, an elderly Belgian who breathes heavily like a locomotive, a man irrevocably exhausted by too many miles of railroad, by too many telegraph poles counted, by too many cinders brushed off green plush seats. At stations I walk up and down with a brittle little Frenchman smoking the local cigarettes; he talks knowingly about Bucharest, love, assassination, triangular marriage and diplomacy. He knows everything and his collars and cuffs are always spotless (*Orient Express*, Jonathan Cape, London, 1928, p. 15).

After two days on the Orient Express, Roncalli arrived at Sofia station. He was already rather portly, and was easily recognisable in his long black top-coat, soutane and soup-plate hat. He was greeted by Mgr Peev, a Bulgarian Capuchin friar who was Latin bishop for the south of Bulgaria. Sofia was still dazed, recovering from the shock of a terrorist bomb that had left more than a hundred dead and a thousand injured amid the ruins of the ancient church of Svata Nedela.

The foreign minister, forewarned of his arrival, did not want him to pass by the devastated church because it would give a bad impression of his country. So Roncalli went directly to the modest residence at Liuline Street 7, next door to the diminutive church of the Ascension. Over supper Bishop Peev and young Fr Stefan Kurtev began his initiation into Bulgarian complexities. First they dealt with the events of the last two weeks that had culminated in the Svata Nedela outrage. On April 13, 1925, King Boris III had narrowly escaped assassination while out hunting in the mountains. Nine suspects were arrested and summarily hanged. The next day the 'revolutionaries' killed General Constantin Gheorghiev, confident that the king would attend his funeral in the Svata Nedela church. A pillar at the base of the central cupola was stuffed with explosives. The king survived the blast, but the casualty lists made this the greatest man-made catastrophe since the war. All that had happened in the two weeks before Roncalli arrived.

To explain King Boris' precarious position, they had to delve a little deeper into Bulgarian history. After nearly five centuries of Turkish rule, independence had been regained in 1878 though it was not ratified until 1908. In the First Balkans War (1912), Bulgaria led the alliance against the Turks, the hereditary enemy, and won some impressive victories; but the defeat of the Central Powers in 1918 meant that Bulgaria lost much territory, including the precious right of access to the Aegean. That was when Boris succeeded his father who abdicated in disappointment. It was a time of great tensions. The Communist Party, stimulated by the success of the October Revolution next door in Russia, was founded by Georgi Dimitrov (later to be the hero of the Reichstag fire trial in Dresden). In 1923 the Agrarian Prime Minister, Alexander Stambolisky, was murdered in a right-wing coup, and from then on the Communists refused to have anything more to do with 'bourgeois' politics and waited for the 'contradictions of capitalism' to topple the regime. King Boris tried his best to balance the opposing forces, but their differences were about personalities rather than policies. Bulgarian politics were determined by coups rather than by consent.

There was not much that Archbishop Roncalli, the first papal representative in the country for over five centuries, could do about Bulgarian history. But he could help to cope with disasters. His first and highly characteristic act was to ask King Boris to allow him to visit those wounded in the Svata Nedela attack. Permission was granted. But immediately the Holy Synod, governing body of the Bulgarian Orthodox Church, criticised the apostolic visitor in its newspaper, *Tzarkoven Vestnik* (Dreyfus, p. 75). Roncalli's arrival meant, it suggested, that Latin 'imperialism' and 'proselytism' would be stepped up. Bulgarian Orthodoxy was the object of a devious Roman plot.

Yet the 62,000 Catholics of Bulgaria hardly posed a very serious threat. Moreover, they were divided among themselves. There were said to be about 48,000 Latins who were mostly urban and 14,000 Uniates of the Slav rite who lived in rural areas. Many of the Uniates were refugees from Macedonia and Thrace (as Roncalli noted in a lecture in 1954: *Natale, 1975*, p. 19). Their last bishop (or exarch) had died in 1924. The Latin Catholics were divided into two dioceses: the Dutch Bishop Jan Theelen C.P. ruled from Rustchuk in the north where all the clergy except three were Passionists like himself; Mgr Peev administered the southern diocese of Sofia–Plovdiv where all the priests except three were Bulgarian (*Irénikon*, 1928, p. 420). Tact was needed to get these disparate groups to work together. In addition, French sensibilities had to be attended to in Sofia where there were many French religious orders, chiefly Assumptionists, Vincentians, Christian Brothers, and Capuchin Franciscans. Roncalli's mission was to put some flesh on the bare bones of these statistics and give a first-hand report on the needs of the Bulgarian Catholics.

So he set about visiting the scattered mountain parishes of his 'Slav rite' Catholics. He knew hardly any Bulgarian, and used Fr Stefan Kurtev as interpreter. They travelled by mule, on horseback or in jolting carts. Cars were hardly ever seen in these poor areas, and roads were bad. Rivers were crossed on primitive-looking rafts. Everywhere he went he kept his soup-plate hat firmly fixed on his head. As he said in his 1954 lecture, 'I went to seek them out in the most distant villages, I entered their modest homes and became their neighbour'

(*Natale, 1975*, p. 19). The echo of the 'good shepherd' who seeks out the lost sheep was perhaps unconscious here; but it says as much about Roncalli's theology of the episcopacy as his most elaborate retreat reflections. He 'became their neighbour'.

He later thought that he was received 'with affection and joy' because he was the Pope's representative. Yet sometimes he was made sharply aware of the contrast between the pomp of Rome and the poverty of these Bulgarian villages. He wrote in a 1929 letter:

> My heart breaks when I think that you in Rome can devise no further ways of making the triumph of Jesus in the Eucharist, carried in the arms of his Vicar, more spectacular, while here we don't even have oil to light the lamps in the chicken-coops we use as chapels. But these poor lamps are a beginning (*Gran Sacerdote*, p. 153. Letter to his successor at Propaganda, from Jambol, May 29, 1929).

It does not occur to Roncalli that something of his success was due to his own personality. Yet soon he was known among the Catholic Bulgarians as *Diado*, the good father. Small boys out spying would rush home with the news that *Diado* was on his way. He brought concern to a forgotten people. And he never forgot them. In 1949 he was able to write: 'I still keep a fine collection of photographs of these beautiful country places, and when I am tired I look through them again. Believe me, when I remember those dear people, my heart is moved and my eyes are full of tears' (*Mission*, p. 93. Letter to Bishop Stefan Kurtev dated January 14, 1949).

Apart from fading photographs, music is the most potent stimulus to memory. The Bulgarians had, along with the Russians, the finest church music of the Orthodox Church, and the Uniates had continued their tradition. In his 1954 lecture Roncalli explained:

> At the start I found it difficult to join in their prayers and worship, but suddenly I understood that this compenetration of hearts and voices was a great door by which one could reach these Slav brothers who were so open-minded, upright and sincere in their feelings. As I joined with them in singing their grieving lamentations, which were the echo of centuries of political and religious slavery, I began to feel myself more catholic, more truly universal (*Natale, 1975*, p. 19).

Like the Negro spirituals of the United States, Slav music was moving because it was the expression of centuries of suffering and humiliation. The Uniates had another reason for suffering because, as Roncalli wrote, 'they had so often had to suffer trials and persecutions for their faith from the Orthodox' (*Gran Sacerdote*, p. 153).

His round of visits over, Roncalli had – in theory – completed his work in Bulgaria. In October 1925 he led a party of Bulgarian pilgrims to Rome. They had an audience with Pius XI on October 14, 1925, which at least proved that they existed. Pius replied to the usual compliments with the exhortation: 'Honour and love our representative: may he be for you the Pope's eye, heart and hand' (*Mission*, pp. 105–6). This was found puzzling: was the Pope's representative a spy in their midst, or was he, if not a friend at court, a friend of friends at court? This question haunted Roncalli's diplomatic career.

But in 1925 his presence in Rome enabled him to present his report to the Congregation of the Oriental Churches in person. His main recommendation was that the Uniates of Slav rite needed a bishop. He proposed Fr Stefan Kurtev for this office, despite his youth: he was only thirty-four. Although the Congregation should have trusted Roncalli as the man on the spot, it took a year to rally to his judgement. Roncalli and Kurtev made a retreat together at St Paul's without the Walls in November 1926, under the direction of the Abbot, Dom Ildefonso Schuster O.S.B. Roncalli noted in his *Journal* the 'strange fact' that his many trials were 'not caused by the Bulgarians for whom I work but by the central organs of ecclesiastical administration' (*Journal*, p. 222). They were caused, in short, by the Roman Curia.

Despite these hazards, Stefan Kurtev was ordained bishop for the Bulgarians of the Byzantine Slav rite in San Clemente on December 5, 1926, in the presence of Archbishop Roncalli. San Clemente – entrusted to the Irish Dominicans – was chosen because it had the tomb of St Cyril, brother of St Methodius.

Kurtev naturally took the name of Stefan Cyril. The only problem about Bishop Stefan Cyril was that he had been born into an Orthodox family, gone to school with the Assumptionists at Mustrackli, and then become a Catholic. To the Orthodox he was therefore a living illustration of Roman 'proselytism'. Roncalli could not take too much trouble over his protégé. He fussed over his episcopal coat-of-arms. He didn't want any imitations of bastardised French models but something properly 'Oriental' (*Gran Sacerdote*, p. 145). Since the name Kurtev in Turkish means 'wolf', he thought that a counter-punning motto about the 'Good Shepherd' was indicated. So Bishop Stefan Cyril acquired the motto *Polaga Dusciata si* ('He lays down his life'), a fair summing up of his remaining thirty years.

With the appointment of Kurtev Roncalli had fulfilled the first part of his mission and worked himself out of a job: he no longer needed to make pastoral visits to the scattered Bulgarian Catholics. The next item on his agenda was to provide them with a seminary of their own. So long as all priests had to go abroad for their clerical studies, the Church would appear as irremediably 'foreign'. In December 1929 he acquired a site for a seminary, and paid a quarter of a million *lire* for 30,000 square metres (*Familiari*, I, p. 209). At that date, the exchange rate was

18 or 19 *lire* to the US dollar. He hoped that work would be started on the building in the following spring, but in February 1930 he reports rather wearily that 'Rome has changed its mind once again' (*Familiari*, I, p. 218). The seminary was never built. No one in the Vatican seemed to share his sense of the importance of the project. He pulled himself together with a cheerful, 'well, that's one less problem for me', but he was disappointed. Part of his difficulty with the Curia was that he had to deal with three departments – the Secretariat of State, Propaganda Fide and the Oriental Congregation – whose views did not always co-incide. Everyone seemed to have forgotten that he had been sent to Bulgaria on a temporary mission. No one mentioned Argentina any more. The provisional was beginning to look dangerously permanent.

Having done what he could for his flock, Roncalli had more time to devote to the second and more testing goal of his mission in Bulgaria: 'To make known and loved the Pope and the Catholic Church among the great mass of the Orthodox', as he put it in his 1954 lecture (*Natale, 1975*, p. 18). He had already met the president of the Holy Synod, Archbishop Stefan Gheorghiev. The ecumenical patriarch of Constantinople refused him the title of 'patriarch': and this had led to schism. The Bulgarian Orthodox Church was a state Church. It had stiffened national morale and kept identity alive throughout the five centuries of Turkish rule. The bonds between language, culture, religion and nationalism were therefore very strong. By the same token, a suspicion of 'disloyalty' hung about the Catholics, simply because they were an anomaly. Bulgarian Orthodoxy was a populist form of religion, lacking much of an intellectual tradition. The same was true of the Catholics of the Slav rite, and though the 'Latins' were more urban and sophisticated, they struck Bulgarians as 'foreign'. The Orthodox saw the monarch as the patron and protector of the Church. So although King Boris, a Saxe-Coburg, had been brought up a Catholic, he had to become Orthodox in order to succeed to the throne. *Raison d'état* demanded his conversion.

It was to this Church that Roncalli had to try to commend 'the Pope and the Catholic Church'. History made it uphill work. But Roncalli's attempts to dissipate prejudice and improve relations were an ecumenical apprenticeship that proved invaluable later on. Although 'ecumenism' was frowned upon in the Vatican at this date, Roncalli learned its ground rules from experience. The most basic rule of all was that one could not expect to begin a dialogue with condemnations. Friendliness in Christ was the starting-point, along with a capacity to listen and learn. What Roncalli found in his own experience was theologically confirmed by Dom Lambert Beauduin in his review *Irénikon*.

Roncalli's first ever letter on ecumenism quotes *Irénikon*. It is equally significant that it should have been addressed to a laywoman, Adelaide Coari, and not to a fellow cleric. We have already met Signorina Coari. Roncalli was sufficiently involved to write a letter commending her to Fr Enrico Rosa, editor of *Civiltà*

Cattolica (*Gran Sacerdote*, p. 142). He explained that she was now engaged in teacher-training in Milan, was the sort of person who did not fit easily into Catholic organisations, and would greatly profit by 'direction from a shrewd and intelligent priest'. He added that Pope Pius XI had known her in Milan and 'appreciates and encourages her up to a point – *juxta modum*' (*Ibid.*). Pius' reservations were no doubt explained by the fact that Coari was interested in everything new – the feminist, the biblical and the ecumenical movement – and even more by her concern for the fate of Ernesto Buonaiuti, Roncalli's old seminary acquaintance, now triply ex-communicated.

Roncalli wrote to Signorina Coari on May 9, 1927:

> I am very pleased that you are interested in the union of the Churches and delighted that you like the spirit of charity found in the Belgian review *Irénikon* [he spells it *Irenicon*]. So we agree about that. As for knowing how to deal with the Orthodox, we Catholics have a lot to learn, and should accept without hesitation Pius XI's recommendation in this sense. What a great thing it is to understand and show compassion.
>
> A month ago I had an interesting meeting with the Ecumenical Patriarch Basil III, the successor of Photius and Michael Cerularius. How times have changed! But Catholics are impelled by charity to hasten the day of the return of the brethren to the unity of the one fold [*il ritorno dei fratelli alla unità dell'ovile*]. You follow me? By *charity* – this rather than by theological discussions. By the charity praised by St Paul in I Corinthians 13.4 (*Dodicesimo anniversario*, p. 49).

It took a long time for Roncalli to shed the concept of 'return' (*ritorno*) which was found offensive by the separated brothers. It is more important to understand what he means here by the primacy of charity – which has sometimes been taken to imply an anti-intellectual attitude which belittles theology.

Beauduin had developed the idea of the primacy of charity in *Irénikon* (June–July 1928, pp. 226 and following). His article was a tribute to Cardinal Mercier, one of Roncalli's heroes. Beauduin argued that Mercier had discovered his ecumenical vocation simply by thinking about what it meant to be a Catholic bishop: he was first of all responsible for his own diocese, but as a member of the episcopal college he also shared in 'the solicitude of all the Churches'. He could not therefore remain indifferent to the scandal of Christian divisions. His special interest was in the Orthodox Church. He soon realised that Orthodox Christians were not to be persuaded by apologetic arguments of a scholastic nature. Syllogisms left them cold. The only way forward was through 'the primacy of charity'. What was needed, wrote Beauduin, was 'a living apologetics that requires no other miracle than love' (*Ibid.*, p. 229).

Nor could it be said – Beauduin went on – that Mercier was anti-intellectual.

On the contrary, in every field he touched he stressed the need for professional competence. He was alive to the best in modern thought, and had a horror of parochialism. The influence of Mercier and Beauduin can be seen in Roncalli's pontificate. In the 1920s they inspired in him an approach to ecumenism that was simply not available in the Vatican at that date. For fifty years Catholic ecumenism was an underground stream. Roncalli was sympathetic to it because it matched his own experience in the East.

His meeting with the ecumenical patriarch, Basil III, took place on March 25, 1927. Basil's main preoccupation, at that time, was to organise a Pan-Orthodox meeting in the hope of reconciling the Russian Orthodox at home and abroad and of ending the Bulgarian schism. But he knew his limitations. He was not an Oriental pope but a symbolic point of reference endowed with convenor's rights. He also had a wider ecumenical vision. He recognised the Old Catholic and Anglican hierarchies (on the basis of eighth-century precedents and later events in Russia). He longed for 'reconciliation and communion' even with the Church of Rome, and made the following remarkable statement to Mgr Denis, head of the Orthodox Church in Poland, who visited him early in 1928: 'If I live long enough, I will myself go to the Pope of Rome to beg him to have pity on the persecuted Church everywhere . . . and together we will fight the anti-Christ' (*Irénikon*, March–April, 1928, p. 192). It is a reasonable guess that he said something similar to Roncalli in March 1927.

Roncalli's ecumenical apprenticeship consisted in getting to know Orthodox Church leaders who were merely a generalised abstraction to the Roman Curia – interchangeable bearded orientals with an incomprehensible history and an unknown language. One of his friends was Stepanosse Hovagnimian, archbishop of Nicomedia, Armenian patriarch in Bulgaria. When Roncalli met him in 1927 he was already eighty years old. He embodied living history. With about 50,000 of his Armenians he had escaped the Turkish massacres of 1896 and the even more terrible massacres of 1915. Constantinople refused to recognise him, so he sought out Roncalli and told him how, back in 1893, he had received the delegate of the Holy See in his cathedral with the honours due to a patriarch (*Irénikon*, p. 422). When Pope John addressed the Observers on October 13, 1962, just as the Council began, he recalled that he had given 'this venerable old prelate' a medal of Pius XI's pontificate: 'When a short time later he was dying, he asked that the medal should be placed upon his heart. I saw it there myself, and the memory moves me still' (DMC, vol IV, 1962, p. 607).

Roncalli's pastoral work and ecumenical meetings made him painfully aware of the problems of the Uniates, the term used to describe those Christians of Oriental rite who were in communion with Rome. Though relatively small in numbers (apart from the four million Ukrainians) they had great symbolic importance because they illustrated the truly Catholic nature of the Church. It was also hoped, rather more optimistically, that they would build a bridge between East and West. In the 1920s the Congregation for the Oriental Churches – it had been split off from Propaganda only in 1917 – did everything it could to encourage the Uniates who were its charge. Roncalli was in correspondence with Fr Cyril Korolevkij, professor at the Greek College in Rome, who had written a passionate plea for the Uniates called *Uniatismo* (it appeared, naturally, in *Irénikon* in 1927). Korolevkij was a colourful and controversial figure. Of mixed Slav, Latin and French origins, he had been ordained in 1902 in Damascus, Syria, by the 'Patriarch of Antioch and all the East'. An immensely learned man, he did not have the highest regard for Italian scholarship in the field of Slav studies. He constantly clashed with the Congregation for Oriental Churches. He argued strongly against the excessive 'Latinisation' of the Uniate Churches – a complaint that has been heard as long as they have existed. Roncalli wrote that he found the articles 'a little too iconoclastic' and was more optimistic than Korolevkij about the chances of adapting some Latin devotions for the Uniate Churches. Otherwise he endorsed with enthusiasm Korolevkij's articles on the Uniates and thought they would 'help the cause of unity by preparing Catholics to understand what it means' (*Gran Sacerdote*, p. 146. Letter from Sofia, July 13, 1927). Unity would not mean absorption.

One thing saddened him, however. The Uniate Churches were poor and understandably preoccupied with mere survival. They felt psychologically squeezed between the Orthodox who saw them as a 'Latin' bridgehead and Latin Catholics who, often enough, felt socially superior to them. So Roncalli makes a plea for some indulgence towards them. One should not be for ever dwelling on their defects – Korolevkij tended to rant about the ignorance of the married clergy – but should encourage them 'by paying attention to the real good they have done and their generous and energetic commitment' (*Gran Sacerdote*, p. 146). He had been appalled to read a sweeping attack on the Uniates in the Belgian *Revue des idées et faits*: 'Heavens above! We want to bring about union with the Orthodox, and yet at the very earliest stage we set a bad example of disunity and quarrelling between Catholics toiling in the same field. So what is built up by one hand is torn down by the other' (*Gran Sacerdote*, p. 146).

While Roncalli was writing to Korolevkij in July 1927, he received a copy of *l'Osservatore Romano*. It contained the Holy Office decree forbidding Catholics to take part in the Lausanne Conference on Faith and Order (*Gran Sacerdote*, p. 147; for the Conference see Bell, pp. 29 and following). Roncalli accepted this decision without demur:

> The ban (on attending the Faith and Order Conference) seems a little harsh to the Orthodox; but it is perfectly logical for us. These conferences, over and above the good faith of some who take part in them, are the beginning

of a new form of Protestantism. The decree of the Holy Office will
undoubtedly help to clarify the situation (*Ibid.*, p. 147).

It was relatively easy to accept exclusion from a particular meeting, even if the
grounds – the fear of 'a new form of Protestantism' – seem with hindsight somewhat far-fetched. The Orthodox in Bulgaria were at this date so far removed from
any such temptation that the Holy Synod strongly disapproved of the YMCA as
'working on an inter-denominational basis harmful to Orthodoxy' (*Irénikon*,
1928, p. 548).

Roncalli found it more difficult to defend the encylical *Mortalium Animos* of
January 6, 1928, where Pius XI spoke ironically of 'congresses where all, without
distinction, believers and unbelievers, even those who have unhappily rejected
Christ and denied his divine nature and mission, are invited to join in the discussion'. *Mortalium Animos* had enormous influence. It remained substantially in
force until Roncalli himself became pope. It seemed to slam the door on the whole
ecumenical movement. It was widely taken as a rebuff to other Christians, who
traced its source to the arrogant belief that Rome was 'the one (i.e. sole) true
Church'. Dr George K. Bell, Anglican bishop of Chichester, has a chapter on the
Vatican in his history of the World Council of Churches: it is called 'The Refusal
of Rome' (Bell, p. 67).

Yet *Mortalium Animos* made no difference to Roncalli's personal dealings with
Orthodox leaders in Bulgaria and Constantinople. The need for 'the miracle of
love' and 'the primacy of charity' remained. *Irénikon*, obviously embarrassed by
the encyclical, sought out a German Jesuit, Fr Friedrich Muckermann, who
explained that its 'apparently harsh tone was a sign of love' and its real target was
'exaggerated intellectualism and interminable discussion which lead to scepticism'
(*Irénikon*, July–September, 1928). He concluded ingeniously that *Mortalium
Animos* was not a condemnation of ecumenism as such, but only of one particular
ecumenical method – that which 'minimised faith' by seeking to base unity on a
'least common denominator'. Laborious though such casuistry may seem,
another South German Jesuit, Augustin Bea, had recourse to very similar arguments in the 1960s to justify Pope John's new approach to ecumenism.

In Bulgaria these theoretical debates were rendered otiose by a severe earthquake on April 14, 1928. The tremor was felt in Sofia, but its main epicentre was
in the mountainous region of Plovdiv where most of the Uniate Catholics lived.
Roncalli was on the spot the day after to assess the situation, returned to Sofia to
cable the Vatican for aid, and three days later was organising food and blankets for
the most needy. The shock had been terrible, and he was afraid for his life. It was
ironic that the blow had fallen so heavily on the Uniates, as he wrote to Fr Pietro
Carrara, the bishop of Bergamo's secretary, on April 26, 1928:

Fifteen days ago there were at least a few oases on which one could rest

one's eyes in this otherwise completely Orthodox milieu. But now there is
desert and utter desolation. We will have to start again to rebuild on a
bigger scale. What has become of our poor dreams, dear Don Pietro, in the
face of the terrible wrath of God expressed through the fury of nature?
(*Dodicesimo anniversario*, p. 54).

To his sisters, Ancilla and Maria, he brought what reassurance he could:

Don't be afraid for me when you hear the news about the earthquake in
Bulgaria. It was a long way from here. In the last few days I have been to
see its effects. What a pitiful sight! Last night I was at Plovdiv when
another very violent tremor caused immense destruction throughout the
whole city. I spent the night out of doors like everyone else. Now I have
come back to Sofia to get on with the relief work . . . 'From the scourge of
earthquakes, deliver us Lord' (*Familiari*, I, pp. 162–3).

The Pope had sent half a million *leva* 'which created a very good impression in
Bulgaria'. But the needs were endless. The earthquakes had been followed by
heavy rain; the people refused to go back to their cracked and threatened houses;
the wooden huts that had been promised them had not yet arrived; the mud was
already deep and further floods were anticipated (*Familiari*, I, p. 164). It was the
familiar train of disasters that follow upon an earthquake.

The Italian people was sympathetic: they had plenty of experience of earthquakes themselves. *L'Eco di Bergamo* had not forgotten its former correspondent,
Roncalli, and got up a subscription for the victims. Thanks to this disaster,
Bulgaria briefly made the headlines. Roncalli did not regard the earthquake as an
intellectual puzzle about the goodness of God; nor did he adopt Dr Pangloss'
attitude that 'everything was for the best'. He saw it as imposing on him a
practical task, a chance to exercise 'the corporal works of mercy'. Only a month
before on March 6, 1928, he had urged Ancilla and Maria to 'spend yourselves in
visiting the sick. That is a good thing that you can do. It is one of the most beautiful works of mercy . . . The Lord responds with mercy to those who are charitable' (*Familiari*, I, p. 155). Now he had to apply this lesson himself. He concludes
his letter about the earthquake to his sisters: 'As I've told you, not only am I well
but I am happy to be here amid so much suffering provided I can bring help and
comfort in the name of the Lord who made us all brothers' (*Familiari*, I, p. 164).
Perhaps he wouldn't have put it that way in a report to the Vatican, but in
addressing his sisters, the truth was pared down to its essentials.

After these – literally – earth-shaking events, Archbishop Roncalli spent
Christmas 1928 quietly in Constantinople. He was getting to know the city well.
It had far richer historical memories and greater ecumenical importance than
Sofia. He felt drawn to the place for a variety of reasons. The one he revealed to his
family in his Christmas letter was frankly 'triumphalistic':

Everything in Constantinople is on a bigger scale and more beautiful than in
Sofia. There are more than 30,000 Catholics. There are religious men and
sisters and Catholic schools of every kind. This does not prevent it being the
capital of Islam and of the Schism. But the number of Catholics can sometimes give the feeling of being in a Catholic country. All the more since the
churches are beautiful and the Catholics certainly frequent them in large
numbers. At midnight Mass, for example, the cathedral of the Holy Spirit
was packed out, and there were many communions including men and
young people. By its situation, Constantinople is certainly the finest city in
the world (*Familiari*, I, p. 178).

Writing at the same time to Pietro Grasso, bishop of Tortona, on his priestly
jubilee, Roncalli can take all that as read and concentrate on the new trends that
are emerging, what he called later 'the signs of the times':

I would be delighted to have you with me in this marvellous city of
Constantinople that I am getting to know quite well. I wish you were here
to discuss the great problems concerning the future of the Church – problems which are seen in a completely different and very interesting perspective from here, in this central but now almost spent heart of
Orthodoxy, amid the imposing but desolate ruins of the Byzantine period,
and on the threshold of the mysterious world of Islam in which there are
new stirrings whose direction is in the hands of God (*Gran Sacerdote*, p.
151).

In 1928 the 'new stirrings' in Islam referred not to the oil-confident religious
revival of fifty years later but on the contrary to the secularising policies of
Atatürk who was determined to drag Turkey into the twentieth century. The
judgement on the decline of the Phanar, home of the ecumenical patriarch, was
harsh but accurate. Yet the patriarch's symbolic importance remained. Living in
the Balkans gave Roncalli insights into such problems that would not have been
possible had he been limited to Bergamo or Rome.

But the price he paid was exile, and he began to feel its burden. As he
approached the twenty-fifth anniversary of his ordination in 1929, he went
through a crisis that had many elements: a sense of being forgotten and
abandoned; a feeling of frustration at getting nowhere with his plans for the
Bulgarian Church; and the distressing thought that his career was in the dol-
drums. Or, as he put it himself during his 1930 retreat at Rustchuk in the
Passionist house that over-looked the Danube and the burning waste-gas of the
Rumanian oil-fields beyond:

The trials, with which in recent months the Lord has tested my patience,
have been many: anxieties concerning the arrangements for founding the

Bulgarian Seminary; the uncertainty which has now lasted five years about the exact purpose of my mission in this country; my frustrations and disappointments at not being able to do more, and the enforced restrictions of my life as a complete hermit, in contrast to my longing to work directly ministering to souls; my interior discontent with what is left of my natural human inclinations, even if so far until now I have succeeded in keeping them under control (*Journal*, p. 229).

This was Roncalli in his most sombre mood, though the retreat ends with him quoting the maxim of St Francis de Sales, 'I am like a bird singing in a thicket of thorns' (*Ibid*., p. 232). Obedience was becoming a cross to be borne. His motto was *Obedientia et Pax* and he had gone to Bulgaria believing that obedience would lead to peace. Now he finds at least as much truth in the motto of Mgr Giuseppe Facchinetti, the first superior of the Priests of the Sacred Heart, *Semper in Cruce, obedientia duce* ('Under the guidance of obedience, always on the cross') (*Journal*, p. 233).

How he resolved this crisis can be seen in his correspondence with Don Pietro Forno (1887–1938), the Bergamesque priest who was helping him with his edition of the *Atti* of St Charles Borromeo. But what brought them even closer together at this period was that they were both going through a time of trial. The nature of Forno's 'trial' is not made clear, but since Capovilla says that it was caused by 'the defects of his remarkable intellectual qualities and his frank and impetuous character' (*Dodicesimo anniversario*, p. 50) and since he wanted to migrate to another diocese, one may infer that he was having difficulties with his bishop. Like Roncalli he felt passed over, unappreciated.

In a letter from Sofia dated April 8, 1928, Roncalli makes use of a revealing historical parallel to their situation:

Before going to sleep I've been reading Pastor's lives of the Popes. How many encouraging examples for you and me there are in these volumes. In the chapter on Paul IV, for example, we read how card. Morone – one of the greatest servants of the Church in the sixteenth century, a great diplomat, a man of exquisite courtesy, upright, pious, etc. – was held prisoner in Castel San Angelo under this pope, no doubt a holy but an impetuous man, and there he (Morone) had to remain and put up with the most humiliating trials until the death of Paul who was, I repeat, a holy man who did a lot of good (*Dodicesimo anniversario*, p. 51).

This bed-time reading encouraged the fantasy that he himself, confined to Sofia for no good reason, resembled Cardinal Morone, locked up in the Castel San Angelo on a whim of Pope Paul IV. Yet he still finds it difficult to criticise a tyrannical pope, even a long dead one. An ironical post-script to this tale is that on

November 11, 1962, the opening day of the Council, Pope John read out, as canon law prescribed, the profession of faith of Paul IV. Those observers who found its tone offensive and knew that Paul IV had been described as 'the most sinister pope in history' (Hans Kühner), would have been consoled to discover that Roncalli disapproved of his treatment of Cardinal Morone.

After this dodgy historical parallel, Roncalli tries to console his fellow-sufferer Forno with the thought that from time to time we all need a 'stroke of grace' (*un colpo di grazia*):

> You remember what I told you last year about the troubles I had with my ministry in Bulgaria? Well, when I was in Rome I had a stroke of grace which restored perfect peace to me. It is not that the reasons why I suffered last year have gone away. No, they are still there, or have perhaps diminished just a little. But I was granted a *raison d'être*, a reason for being and suffering; and so I love and suffer willingly . . . Since I was ordained bishop I have recited every day one of the prayers of St Ignatius. I enclose a copy. It happened that one morning, when I was suffering the most, it seemed to me that this prayer had been very precisely answered. This reflection, too, brought me peace and contentment (*Dodicesimo anniversario*, pp. 51–2).

What was the 'Ignatian prayer' said daily by Archbishop Roncalli? He tells us in his retreat notes for 1930. It was the prayer, 'O eternal Lord of all things' which concludes the meditation on the Kingdom of Christ. 'To tell the truth', Roncalli confesses, 'I found it hard to say this prayer' (*Journal*, p. 230). It is indeed difficult for anyone with ambition to say that they want to 'imitate Christ in bearing all wrongs and all abuse and all poverty, both actual and spiritual' (*Exercises*, No. 98).

But there was a further step, and Roncalli took it in 1930. He decided to add the prayer which concludes the meditation on 'three degrees of humility'. It differs from the Kingdom prayer in that poverty with Christ is now positively *preferred*, and not merely borne:

> Whenever the praise and glory of the divine majesty would be equally served, in order to imitate and be in reality more like Christ our Lord, I desire and choose poverty with Christ poor, rather than riches; insults with Christ loaded with them rather than honours; I desire to be accounted worthless and a fool for Christ, rather than to be esteemed wise and prudent in this world. So was Christ treated before me (*Exercises*, No. 167).

Of course one does not reach this height of identification with Christ simply by uttering the words; but they are a start and point in the right direction.

Roncalli's 'stroke of grace', then, was not some new intellectual insight. It involved a shift of perspective in which the familiar took on a new aspect. A letter written to his former secretary at Propaganda, Mgr Giovanni Dieci, on May 5,

1928, clearly refers to the same experience: 'There is nothing heroic in what has happened to me and in what I have thought it my duty to do. Once you have renounced everything, really everything, then any bold enterprise [*audacia*] becomes the simplest and most natural thing in the world' (Alberigo, p. 430). Nothing could make clearer the meaning of 'renunciation' as seen by Roncalli. It is an act of letting go in God in order to be with Jesus more intimately. It does not involve running away or world-denying timidity. It leaves the one who embraces it poised and stripped for action. It is renunciation for freedom. It was this attitude that permitted him to launch the 'bold enterprise' of the Council at the age of 77, when common sense would have said that it was folly.

The practical conclusion in the late 1920s was that he would not intrigue to get another posting. Whenever people in Rome said to him, 'But haven't you been in Bulgaria rather a long time?', he changed the subject (*Familiari*, I, p. 209). Unfortunately Forno received no comparable 'stroke of grace'. In February 1929 Roncalli writes to him less as a colleague than as a spiritual director who has to try a dozen different ways of saying the same thing:

> You say that you would like me to be given a big diocese in which there
> would be a job for you as well. Nothing doing. Bulgaria is my cross, and
> I'm sincerely ready to stay here until I die, if obedience wanted it. I let
> others waste their time dreaming about what might happen to me. You
> should do the same. The idea that one would be better off somewhere else is
> an illusion. Read the last pages of Manzoni's *I Promessi Sposi*. Simple words:
> but popular wisdom of the highest level (*Dodicesimo anniversario*, pp. 56-7).

Manzoni and the *Spiritual Exercises* of St Ignatius combined to teach him that a right decision was followed by the gifts of the Spirit. As he wrote to Dieci: 'By the Lord's grace I continue to love obedience though it ties me here to a work that brings so few consolations, and involves me in activities so exactly contrary to what I really would want to do if I follow my natural tendencies. But peace of heart is not lacking; and so I live content' (Alberigo, p. 430). In August 1929 he celebrated the twenty-fifth anniversary of his priestly ordination. He guessed (wrongly) that the second part of his life as a priest would be shorter (*Pastore*, p. 159). He wisely went on a diet.

Roncalli in Sofia was not completely cut off from Italian life. Letters and papers took about five days to arrive. Most summers he was able to spend about two months in Italy. In the summer of 1929 he went to Prague, Czestochowa, Gniezno and Berlin where Mgr Eugenio Pacelli was nuncio. So he was not unaware of what was happening in Europe. The Fascist regime in Italy was now an outright dictatorship and made increasingly totalitarian claims. Roncalli began to feel that there was something to be said for being in Bulgaria after all. He wrote to Pietro Forno:

It seems to me a great Providence that I am out of Italian affairs. I follow all
the papers, and find the whole thing painful. I think one should pray a great
deal for the Holy Father and say as little as possible. It is truly a great comfort for us Catholics to see the rights of Holy Church defended with such
dignity and fearlessness by the Pope. Yes, in this Pope too one must
admire the '*digitus Dei*' [the finger of God] (*Dodicesimo anniversario*, p. 52).

That was the conventional view in 1928. Pius XI was bravely standing up to the
dictator Mussolini. The issues on which they monotonously clashed – Catholic
Action, youth movements, education – revealed a deep and irreconcilable
antagonism between a freedom-loving Church and an increasingly totalitarian
state. Pius XI challenged the Fascist claim to have a monopoly of Italian
partiotism. It was not difficult for Roncalli to take the side of the heroic Pope.

But then on February 11, 1929, came the startling news that the Pope and
Mussolini had done a dea'. Known as the Lateran Pacts, there were in fact three
related agreements: a Treaty between the Holy See and Italy which acknowledged
the sovereignty of the Vatican over its pocket-handkerchief territory in Rome; a
financial convention which provided compensation for the loss of the Papal States
in 1870; and a Concordat which would govern the future relations between the
Holy See and Italy. Many Catholics were disappointed by these measures. The
image of an heroic Pope courageously resisting the dictator gave way to that of a
pragmatic Pope ready to come to terms with anyone. The ex-*Popolari* were
particularly bitter. In exile in London, Don Luigi Sturzo found the Lateran Pacts
like the curate's egg, 'a mixture of good and bad': good because they settled the
tedious 'Roman Question' once and for all, but bad because the reconciliation had
been achieved with a Fascist regime whose ideology was fundamentally anti-
Christian. Sturzo and Alcide De Gasperi (soon to be immured for his own safety in
the Vatican) distinguished between the Treaty which they accepted and the
Concordat which they found ambivalent. The Concordat seemed to grant certain
rights to the Church but only in exchange for political docility.

One of the sharpest critics of the Lateran Pacts was Mgr Giovanni Battista
Montini. He thought the agreement was merely a pseudo-reconciliation, a non-
event from which Mussolini had gained a great deal of favourable publicity.
'Almost all thinking people', Montini wrote, 'are unhappy and full of
reservations' (Fappani-Molinari, pp. 259 and following). He decided to spend still
more time on FUCI, the Catholic Student Movement which, in time, would
provide the link between the *Popolari* of the 1920s and the Christian Democrats
after 1945. But all this criticism of the Lateran Pacts was confined to private letters
and conversations. The standard public response was one of great rejoicing.
L'Osservatore Romano, in a notorious and never-to-be-forgotten phrase declared
that 'Italy has been given back to God, and God to Italy' (February 12, 1929).

Away in Sofia Roncalli had no difficulty in following the official line. As a quasi-Vatican diplomat he had the task of explaining the Lateran Pacts to King Boris who – though Roncalli didn't know this – had a special interest in Italian events: he was thinking of marrying Princess Giovanna of the House of Savoy. Roncalli's enthusiasm for the Lateran Pacts was unfeigned. He accepted them at face-value. He did not have Montini's feeling for the long-term consequences. Unlike the ex-*Popolari*, it was the *fact* of 'reconciliation' that impressed him, while *with whom* it was achieved was secondary. He saw in the event the realisation of the dreams of his mentors – Giuseppe Toniolo, Bishop Geremia Bonomelli and Cardinal Ferrari.

Roncalli's first comment on the Lateran Pacts came in a letter to Don Pietro Forno who, though still in crisis, had shown enough humour to suggest that he was coming through. Roncalli wrote on February 18, 1929:

> You can imagine with what rejoicing for the cause of the Holy See and of Italy I followed the events of Rome. They seem more like a dream than a miracle of justice and God's goodness. Don't you find here a lesson and an encouragement for you as well? One protests in due form, waits and suffers; and then the Lord intervenes, bringing joy, liberation and salvation (*Dodicesimo anniversario*, p. 57).

So the signing of the Lateran treaties illustrated a universally applicable 'law' of the spiritual life: the papacy has lived patiently through its time of trial, and has now been rewarded.

Six days later he wrote to Ancilla and Maria with equal enthusiasm. He presents 'reconciliation' between the Pope and Italy as a Roncalli family tradition:

> You can imagine how I followed the rejoicing in all Italy over the *peace* arrived at between the Vatican and the Quirinal. Think what a joy that would have been for the deceased members of our family! Let us bless the Lord! Everything that free-masonry, that is, the devil, had done against the Church and the Pope in the last sixty years – all that has been over-turned. We live among men with a thousand faults. The awkward consequences will be seen later on. There will be other troubles. But meanwhile we should have the courage and the loyalty to recognise the miraculous aspect of these events and the incalculable good that they can bring for Italy and for everyone. It means that someone who stayed away from church and was not a practising Catholic because of patriotism, no longer has that excuse. Every difficulty has been removed. Once again, let us bless the Lord (*Familiari*, I, p. 185. Letter dated February 24, 1929).

The emphasis on the defeat of Freemasonry is explained by the anti-clerical, masonic element in the *Risorgimento*: Garibaldi called his horse Mastai, the family name of Pius IX. Roncalli's most far-sighted remark is the most incidental: the 'awkward consequences' he predicted began to be felt almost as soon as the ink was dry on the Pacts. The reconciliation between Catholics and Italy that so delighted him had been achieved largely on paper.

Still, the Vatican and Italy now had diplomatic relations and a forum in which to air difficulties. The first nuncio of the Holy See to Italy was Mgr Francesco Borgongini Duca, Roncalli's contemporary at the Roman seminary. His opposite number, De Vecchi, Italian ambassador to the Holy See, was firmly convinced that Borgongini Duca was 'the leader of the pro-*Popolari* faction in the Vatican' (Pollard, p. 119). If true, this would help to explain why he thought of Roncalli for the prestigious post of archbishop of Milan – and also why Roncalli proved politically unacceptable.

Only the rumour is documented. Cardinal Eugenio Tosi, Ferrari's successor, had died on January 7, 1929, just a month before the Lateran Pacts. The new appointment would be made under the Concordat rules, which gave the state a role. No sooner was Tosi in his tomb than gossip began to appoint Roncalli to Milan. On February 10, 1929, only three days after Tosi's death, he wrote to Ancilla and Maria: 'Rumours are going the rounds linking my name with Milan. Don't believe them. Pray the Lord that I may be preserved from dignities and responsibilities greater than those I already have. One should not waste time imagining things. On the reverse side of greater honours lie also great and incredible sufferings' (*Familiari*, I, p. 182). If they hear anyone talking about him going to Milan, they are to change the subject. This was the appropriate response from someone who had embraced 'the royal road of the cross'. Yet it could not be denied that the appointment would have made sense. He came from Lombardy. At 48, he was the right age for a long and fruitful episcopal ministry. As the historian of St Charles Borromeo he had a thorough knowledge of the best traditions of the Milanese Church. He was in some sense the heir of Cardinal Ferrari, to whom he had been devoted. Add to these advantages the fact that he had been conveniently absent from Italy throughout the previous four years, and so had a clean political sheet. On February 19, 1929, he reports that rumours of his appointment were coming thick and fast from Milan, Bergamo and Rome (*Familiari*, I, p. 183). He claimed to find the whole thing amusing (the stories 'put me in a good humour').

In the event Cardinal Ildefonso Schuster O.S.B. was appointed cardinal archbishop of Milan in August 1929. The long delay between February and August suggests a battle royal behind the scenes. One of Mussolini's main concerns was to prevent any revival of the *Popolari* or any promotion for those associated with them. 'We will not permit', he said in June 1929, 'the resurrection of parties or organisations that we have destroyed once for all' (Pollard, p. 111). Schuster was politically reliable; Roncalli was not. On the first anniversary of the Lateran Pacts,

Schuster was heard to declare that 'right from the start Catholic Italy and the Pope have blessed Fascism' – a statement so outrageous and false that *l'Osservatore Romano* issued a *démenti* in the form of a *Rettifica*, a term reserved for the gravest of blunders (Pollard, pp. 263–4).

Roncalli wrote to Schuster to congratulate him on his elevation 'to the prestigious see of St Ambrose'. Schuster would have heard the rumours too, and been grateful for this letter from a good loser. Roncalli, however, apologises for not being able to attend Schuster's solemn entry into Milan on September 8, 1929, even though he was in near-by Bergamo. He makes some excuse about a previous engagement. It may be presumed that Signorina Adelaide Coari, herself from Milan, regretted that Schuster had been preferred to Roncalli. Certainly in his next letter he tries to reconcile her to Schuster by stressing that he is a Benedictine and that 'monastic life takes away all preoccupation with one's own *ego* . . . and so the monk is liberated for the tasks that Providence gives him' (*Dodicesimo anniversario*, pp. 58–9). This may seem a rather incomplete account of Schuster's merits, but Roncalli had a firm principle that he would not quarrel with appointments once they were made. Still less would he denigrate a supposed rival.

His letter to Adelaide brought her Christmas greetings. It must have given her great pleasure because her friend the archbishop placed her spontaneously on the same level as himself:

> Neither you nor I, dear Signorina Coari, have had the advantage of a monastic education. Yet as we become older we have to try to adapt our lives to the monastic spirit which can bring us, over and above order, peace and interior joy, new energies to have a good apostolate. You see? You have already done so much. Opening the door to Clemente Rivera was a highly apostolic act. These good things and the others that you report in the bulletin of your action group, are they not an excellent form of apostolate? (*Dodicesimo anniversario*, p. 59).

Rivera was a Milanese poet whom Coari had converted. (He later became a Rosminian priest.) She was sufficiently influential in Milanese society to introduce him to the new cardinal just before Christmas. Roncalli always encouraged her unofficial ministry, one that a later generation might have called 'charismatic'.

That same Christmas, 1929, Roncalli also sent greetings to Mgr Borgongini Duca who had been ordained archbishop so that he could take up his post as nuncio to Italy. He welcomes him into the 'episcopal fraternity' and feels it justifies him using the familiar '*tu*' (*Quindicesimo anniversario*, p. 51). He contrasts his own humble work with his friend's awesome task of 'setting up a whole new order of relationships on which the future good of Catholic life in Italy depends' (*Ibid.*, p. 52). He prays that the nuncio might receive 'the grace of great calm in the sometimes vexations and irksome matters that you are involved in'. So far, so banal. But then comes an intriguing remark: 'For me it is a great joy . . . and also a pleasant diversion to follow you in your various activities. Obviously I can only judge by what appears outwardly. But from time to time I manage to see *quod intrinsecus latet* [what lies behind]' (*Ibid.*, p. 51). As a diplomat, Roncalli had to learn to distinguish between appearance and reality. But had he, in distant Sofia, correctly guessed at the power-game that was going on behind the smiling faces? 'Reconciliation' soon proved to be a facade behind which tough battles went on for every inch of the ground.

This was something Roncalli could allude to in a letter to the nuncio to Italy. But he kept such worries hidden from his family. He didn't want to burden them. He was more frank with his sisters, Ancilla and Maria. From time to time he wondered about them coming out to join him in Sofia, but always decided against it as they would have to contend with an unknown language and strange food and, anyway, they were needed at home to look after the parents, now in their seventies. Ancilla and Maria had no interest in politics. On feast days, he wrote to the whole family. His long letter for Easter, 1930, is a mini-homily on the peasant's lot, full of nostalgia for Sotto il Monte that he would never see again in the spring:

> My dearest parents, brothers and sisters, and all the family,
> Though I keep in touch with all of you through Ancilla and Maria at
> Camaitino, it's a pleasure for me to send you a special greeting for Easter.
> It is the same year by year – a foretaste of the blessings and the peace of the
> Lord; but one might almost say that spring gets more beautiful as one gets
> older. The years go by, and the old people keep their good health and the
> love of the children and grandchildren. Isn't that a great grace? I know that
> there has been illness here and there. But you don't want to put the doctors
> and the specialists out of work, do you? But on the whole the health of the
> members of the family has been good, and one should be glad about that.
> Then the grandchildren grow in number and age, and that is the first
> blessing on any household. Even if Mussolini doesn't give you one of his
> agricultural prizes, the Lord will certainly grant you one, since as the holy
> bishop card. Barbarigo used to say, he blesses big pots but not little ones.
> Within a few weeks the countryside will be full of spring blossoms. Let's
> hope the harvest will be abundant again this year . . .
> As for me I continue to be well and to live peacefully and happily, without
> any thought other than to do the will of the Lord. In part I owe this tran-
> quil disposition and ability to let myself go in the arms of Providence and
> obedience to being born in the country, into a family that is poor in material
> goods but rich in faith and the fear of the Lord, and that is used to the

simple realities of nature coming round day by day and year by year. So a sound organism, without any desire for extraordinary things, since what the Lord has given us every day according to nature is already so beautiful and wonderful.

Now it has to be added that science can develop nature and make it docile in the service of the Lord and also for our convenience. You will have heard of the recent discovery of Marconi – who by the way is a good Christian and a friend of the Holy Father. Soon we will be in intimate communication so that we'll not only hear each other at a distance but be able to see each other in pictures. Just think that every evening with the little radio that I have in my study I can hear very clearly speeches, music, news, coming effortlessly over vast distances.

All these things existed from the creation of the world, but up till now the Lord has kept to himself the secrets of the earth and the air, to console us but also to humble those who in the past thought they were very knowing and who in their ignorance insulted sacred things. That was a good remark of Marconi to the Archbishop of Genoa: he said that he had done no more than seek out the laws of God in the book of nature . . . La Colombera is getting to be a true Noah's Ark.

I bless each and everyone.

Aff:ly your son, brother, cousin and uncle.

✠ A. G. archb. (*Familiari*, I, pp. 220–2).

Roncalli was not just flattering his family when he said that he owed his equable temperament to them. They were his link with ordinary human experience, and the long patience of centuries. One can see why he devoted so much space to agriculture in his social encyclical, *Mater et Magistra*. At the same time he was open to the new: Signor Marconi's invention was an early form of television. Next year, 1931, Marconi inaugurated Vatican Radio.

Meanwhile Bulgaria leapt into the headlines. Italy had long had ambitions in the Balkans, and a royal marriage seemed an excellent way of cementing relations with Bulgaria and extending Italian influence generally. King Boris III was an eligible batchelor of 35, while King Victor Emmanuel III's daughter, Princess Giovanna, was unattached and docile. Though Victor Emmanuel was anti-clerical and had opposed the Lateran Pacts, he was now drawn – officially at least – into the new mood of 'reconciliation'. Not only Church and state, but Church, state and royal family would work hand in hand. Since Boris was an Orthodox Christian, a dispensation was needed. It was arranged by Borgongini Duca. The wedding took place amid great rejoicing according to the Catholic rite at Assisi on October 25, 1930. The royal couple had given written undertakings that their children would be brought up as Catholics. Naturally Roncalli, as apostolic visitor to Bulgaria, was present as a guest – though he had not negotiated the dispensation. Later that day he had an audience with Pius XI who presented him with a gold medal for King Boris. Italo–Bulgarian friendship and reconciliation all round had been sealed, as it were, with a kiss for the bride.

But the romantic idyll did not last long. Roncalli made his way back in leisurely fashion, spending the night with the Jesuits in Trieste and arriving in Sofia on October 30. The next day King Boris and his bride, now Queen Giovanna, had a splendid Orthodox marriage ceremony in the cathedral of Alexander Nevski in Sofia. This 'second marriage' made Pius XI furious. On Christmas Eve he denounced the royal couple who had given the most solemn undertakings and then gone back on their word. A choleric man, he felt betrayed. And quite unfairly the apostolic visitor in Sofia, Roncalli, had to shoulder part of the blame for what had happened.

The fuss over the Bulgarian marriage showed that Pius XI and Roncalli had completely contrasting temperaments. While the Pope waxed indignant and dramatised the situation, his apostolic visitor stayed cool, looked for a diplomatic solution, and played down the forceful papal statements. He wrote to Bishop Jan Theelen on December 27, 1930:

> More painful for me is the sense of the uselessness of my attempts to persuade the King to make a simple declaration that would have explained the significance of the October 31 marriage, a declaration that would have averted the solemn words of the Pope that cannot have been very pleasant for his Majesty. But for everyone else, and perhaps for the King himself, the incident could be providential in that it makes it clear that the Pope does not trifle with the Lord and sacred things. In any case, as you will notice, the Holy Father's language could not have been more balanced and kind (*Familiari*, I, p. 243).

But Pius XI thundered on. On the last day of 1930 he published his encyclical *Casti Connubii* which defended the sanctity of Catholic marriage against all those who dared to break its rules. Of course he had other targets besides the Bulgarian royal family. He also denounced (though not by name) the Lambeth Conference, the Anglican assembly, which had rather tentatively approved of birth-control.

Pius XI renewed his tirade against royal promise-breakers in March 1933. Boris and Giovanna had their first child, Princess Maria Luisa, in January and she was baptised by Metropolitan Stefan Georghiev. The apostolic delegate – the office had been raised to this diplomatic dignity on September 26, 1931 – wrote an official letter of protest to King Boris: 'I think of the pain of the Holy Father and of all good Catholics around the world; and then I myself grieve that no real advantage can accrue either to your royal family or to the Bulgarian people from these continued outrages [*soprusi*] to the human conscience . . . (*Familiari*, I, pp. 285–6.

letter dated January 15, 1933). Capovilla calls this letter 'an energetic protest'. It seems rather to be written under orders from Rome and to have a touch of more-in-sorrow-than-in-anger. The consequence, however, was that Roncalli was banned from court for a year.

He did what he could to soften the blow for the wholly innocent Queen Giovanna. That the natural rejoicing over her first-born should have been marred by an ecclesiastico–political dispute was hard to bear. Roncalli invited her to go to Mass privately at the Apostolic Delegation (rather than in a public church). On March 19, 1933, feast of St Joseph, the very day on which Pius XI was denouncing yet again those who violated the sanctity of Catholic marriage, he gave her a handsome missal as a sign that she was not included in the Pope's displeasure (Trevor, p. 157). A more experienced Italian exile than she, he treated Giovanna with kindness and thoughtful chivalry.

It was difficult to extend the same indulgence to King Boris. But Boris was capable of defending himself. A few days after Roncalli's protest, he explained his position:

> You know perfectly well, your excellency, that by family and baptism I was a Catholic. If I have acted as I have twice over, it was solely out of concern for the interests of my country. The Holy Synod was beginning to doubt my loyalty towards the Orthodox Church. The Communists seize upon anything that can turn the people against me. I have to do all I can for this torn and divided country (Dreyfus, p. 83).

Once the initial *raison d'état* argument for King Boris's conversion to Orthodoxy had been accepted, the rest followed. It was difficult to refute his case. He could continue to rule in Bulgaria only as a loyal and faithful Orthodox Christian. In any case, Roncalli, as a keen student of *Irénikon*, would have been perfectly aware of the validity of the Orthodox sacraments from the point of view of Catholic theology. It was his duty to carry out papal policies. But he could have been forgiven if he sometimes felt that Pius XI was making a mountain out of a molehill. There were – in 1933 – graver European matters that should have attracted his attention.

But Pius XI was not the easiest of popes to work for. He was impatient and easily carried away by his immediate emotions. Ludwig von Pastor, Austrian ambassador to the Holy See and the historian whom Roncalli used as bedside reading, said in an official memo that 'he almost always went against the advice that was given him' (Stehle, p. 81). One source has a story which confirms this picture: 'After the Orthodox baptism of Prince Simeon, heir to the Bulgarian throne, Pius XI kept Roncalli kneeling before him for forty-five minutes as a penance . . . But some years later, Pius XI put this right. He explained that although as Pope Pius XI he could not apologise, as plain Achille Ratti he could'

(Bergerre, p. 75). The story would have been more edifying if Pius XI rather than Achille Ratti had actually been able to apologise.

What is not 'legendary' is that in the vague forum of 'public opinion', it was widely believed that Roncalli had behaved naïvely over the Bulgarian marriage. He was too good, too trusting for the real world. He ought to have realised that King Boris never intended to keep his promises. This charge pursued him right up to the spring of 1942, when it was put to him by an Italian officer in Greece. Roncalli replied rather indignantly: 'No, I won't have that. I told the Secretariat of State quite clearly that they should not trust any guarantees given by King Boris. No doubt he was sincere, but the Bulgarian Orthodox Church would never have consented to the baptism of the heir-apparent according to the Catholic rite' (Trusso, Fr Francesco OMI, Diary quoted in Caprile, *Ancora Su Giovanni XXIII*'). So in the end the truth of the matter was that Roncalli had not been taken for a ride. His only 'failure' was his inability to make King Boris' position understood in Rome. In any case, the diplomatic sulks did not last very long. On September 11, 1934, he met King Boris and Metropolitan Stefan at a reception for the Fourth Congress of Byzantine Studies held in Sofia. Between them, and somewhat painfully, they had put Bulgaria on the map of Europe.

It was time for Roncalli to think of leaving. The same thought had finally penetrated the Vatican. In 1933 there was gossip about him moving down the line of the Orient Express to Constantinople, where the apostolic delegate, Mgr Carlo Margotti, had been something of a disaster. This 39-year-old Milanese contrived to antagonise simultaneously both his clergy and the Atatürk government. His removal was a matter of time.

But by 1934 Constantinople was no longer the attractive proposition it had seemed six years earlier. Atatürk imposed tight police restrictions on all Christian activities. Roncalli wrote to Andrea Cesarano who had been his first guide to Constantinople and, since 1931, archbishop of Manfredonia:

> The news I have about the way the Turkish government is dealing with Catholics is alarming for the Church's future on the Bosphorus. Recently I was asked by Rome if I were prepared to go to Constantinople as the eventual successor of Mgr Margotti. I replied that I was always ready to go where obedience demanded, even if that meant doing a provisional stint in hell; but as to whether I liked the idea or not, I had no illusions about the place. I believe that Constantinople is a good post for someone content to hold together what remains of the beleaguered Catholic flock, while waiting patiently for the doors to be opened for an apostolate among the Turks (*Quindicesimo anniversario*, p. 72).

The last remark suggests that Roncalli had been hoping for something rather more adventurous than a patient holding operation. Yet the transfer from Sofia to

Constantinople was a promotion and made sense: he was becoming an expert on the Balkans. It was the only move in his life that he knew about well in advance. He was prepared for Turkey in a way he had never been for Bulgaria. So it was with some confidence that he looked to the future: 'It's a whole new world that will open up for me, and I need to prepare myself for it. The past has gone for good. So for me it's new circumstances, and new arrangements' (*Dunque circonstanze nuove: provvidenze nuove*) (*Ibid.*). But he was jumping the gun. It was not until November 17, 1934, that he was officially informed of his transfer to Constantinople by the undersecretary of state, Mgr Giuseppe Pizzardo. The same day he had a meeting with the new Secretary of State, Cardinal Eugenio Pacelli, who didn't mention it (*Cronologia*, p. 560).

So his Christmas homily in Sofia in 1934 became his farewell to Bulgaria. It has something of the sadness of Newman's 'parting of friends' sermon. Some of the friends – the 'separated brethren' – were not even present, and he hesitated before addressing them indirectly. But then he explained to the Orthodox why he had to keep a certain distance: 'Divergencies in faith between us on one of the most fundamental points of Christ's doctrine, reported in the Gospels, I mean the unity in the Church of Christ of all believers with the successor of the Prince of the Apostles, imposed on me a certain reserve in my contacts and personal dealings with them' (*Natale 1975*, p. 9). For papal representative this was a very scaled-down and modest version of papal claims: they are merely 'one of the most fundamental points', and the unity sought is 'with' Peter not 'under' him. Subtleties, perhaps: but ecumenical advance depends on sensitivity to such nuances.

Roncalli gives the impression in his farewell sermon that he is trying to justify his behaviour not only to the Orthodox but equally to his own brethren, some of whom kept alive the ancient feuds, and to his superiors in Rome:

> I think that I have been well understood by them (i.e. the Orthodox). The respect I've always tried to have for everyone, both in public and in private; my unbroken and non-judgemental silence; the fact that I never stooped to pick up the stones that were cast at me from this or that side of the street – all this leaves me with the clear certainty that I have shown everyone that I love them in the Lord with that fraternal, heart-felt and sincere charity that is taught in the Gospels . . . *Via caritatis, via veritatis* (The way of love is the way of truth) (*Natale*, 1975, p. 9).

Declarations of love from the pulpit can so easily seem mawkish or embarrassing. They only work if the hearers sense that the language and the feelings are authentic. Roncalli passed this test.

He was leaving Sofia for Constantinople. His historical imagination took wing and he recalled that the fourth-century Emperor Constantine had at first thought of establishing his imperial capital, the 'second Rome', in Sofia ('*Roma mea est*

Sardica'), until in the end strategic considerations led him to Constantinople. So in some sense Roncalli was following in the footsteps of Constantine who had great plans for Bulgaria. He paid the Bulgarians another compliment by announcing that the Holy See had agreed to change his rather meaningless episcopal title of Areopolis for that of Mesembria, 'a marvellous place, a veritable jewel of Bulgaria', as he put it. Until he became patriarch of Venice, he would carry the memory of Bulgaria with him in the hauntingly beautiful name of Mesembria.

He concluded his sermon with the 'Irish custom' of leaving a lighted candle in the window at Christmas to show Jesus and Mary that the family was waiting for them:

> Dear brothers, nobody knows the paths of the future. Wherever I may go,
> if a Bulgarian passes by my door, whether it's night-time or whether he's
> poor, he will find that candle lighted at my window. Knock, knock. You
> won't be asked whether you're a Catholic or not; the title of Bulgarian
> brother is enough. Come in. Two fraternal arms will welcome you, and the
> warm heart of a friend will make it a feast-day. Such is the charity of the
> Lord whose graces have made life sweet during my ten year stay in
> Bulgaria. *Pax hominibus bonae voluntatis* [Peace on earth to men of good will]
> (*Natale, 1975*, p. 11).

The archbishop of Mesembria was given a great send-off from Sofia on January 4, 1935. Representatives of the king and the archbishop were present. It made a striking contrast with the way he had slipped in anonymously ten years earlier. Judged by that criterion, his mission to Bulgaria was successful. In his private *Journal* he used more rigorous standards. He wrote in August 1934: 'What has Mgr Roncalli been doing during these monotonous years at the Apostolic Delegation? Trying to make himself holy and with simplicity, kindness and joy opening a source of blessings and graces for all Bulgaria, whether he lives to see it or not . . . The rest does not matter' (*Journal*, p. 239).

Chapter 8

The innocent suspect

Let me remind you of the old maxim: people under suspicion are better moving than at rest, since at rest they may be sitting in the balance without knowing it, being weighed together with their sins

(Franz Kafka, *The Castle*, chapter 5).

Archbishop Roncalli arrived in Istanbul – revived name for the city, imposed by Atatürk – on January 5, 1935. He was met at the station by Mgr Angelo Dell'Acqua, his new secretary, a Milanese. His first duty was to report to the police. From now on he had the Kafka-like experience of being a suspect wherever he went. But he brought a human touch to his arrival by paying an unscheduled courtesy call on Vali Muhidden Ustundag, the city governor. Ustundag, who had known Roncalli's predecessor, the austere and unbending Margotti, was at first icy cool; but he succumbed to the new man's charm and they ended up drinking *raki* together on the terrace overlooking the Bosphorus. It was a good start to what was a daunting assignment: how to be Vatican representative in an Islamic country that was busily rejecting Islam and all religion as retrograde.

The next day, the feast of the Epiphany, he formally 'took possession' of his cathedral of the Holy Spirit. It is a modest, barrel-vaulted church in basilica style, built in 1846. In its courtyard stands a rare statue of Benedict XV, revered in Istanbul as the 'protector of the East' during the First World War. Roncalli's next significant act was to bring to a close the Octave of Prayer for Christian Unity on January 25, 1935, feast of the Conversion of St Paul. He preached a sermon in French that he had evidently prepared with great care. In it he announced his policy for Constantinople – he still preferred the old name.

He now had direct pastoral responsibility for the 35,000 Catholics who lived in and around Istanbul. They included 'Latins' of various nationalities – in order of importance French, Italian, German and Austrian – as well as a rich variety of 'Uniates': Armenians, Chaldeans, Syrians, Maronites, Melkites, Bulgarians and Greeks. The 'Uniates', if not exactly at home, were at least near enough to their places of origin to feel nostalgic. The list of Churches sounds rather like the peoples present in Jerusalem on the day of Pentecost; and Roncalli knew that it would need a comparable miracle to unite them. But that was his ambition.

He addressed himself above all to the 'young people' who he knew were present. He offered them a doctrine of the Church that was much broader and more 'patristic' than Vatican I. He said:

143

Our Lord has built his Church on the foundation of the Apostles, to whom
he gave the command to preach the Gospel to everyone. The Church is not
bound to this or that nation; but all the nations, without distinction, are
called to rally to its standard. In Jesus' Church there are not first- and
second-class citizens. All peoples are invited equally to sit down at the same
banquet of heavenly doctrine and to share in the grace that saves, sanctifies
and rejoices the heart (Alberigo, p. 437).

True, there was a *caveat*:

In founding his Church, Jesus gave it the mark of unity, the seal of divinity,
which distinguishes it from various human enterprises and institutions. He
did not found the various Christian Churches but his Church, *ecclesiam
meam*. And having created it, he sent it forth to win over the world (*Ibid.*).

Seen in this light, 'disunity' was a 'laceration of the divine plan', an anomaly, a
scandal. So Roncalli prayed along with millions of others, along with 'the Holy
Father in Rome whose arms are ever open', for the 'return of unity' (*le retour de
l'unité*). This was subtly different from the 'return to unity' which the Orthodox
feared as a Roman imposition. His prayer was for a goal beyond human powers
alone. He admitted that the movement towards it was constantly threatened by
human egoism. But he insisted that it was there, as an horizon of hope.

Quite evidently Roncalli had gone to Istanbul with a very clear idea of what his
task was: first to unify his own mixed bag of a flock, and then to seek good
relations with the 100,000 or so Orthodox Christians who still clustered around
the ecumenical patriarch, Photius II, in the Phanar. From the start he established
his authority by the reasonableness of what he said. He succeeded because of the
simple contrast between his approach and the prickly high-handedness of his
predecessor.

It was less easy to establish good relations with the Turkish authorities. This
was not because he was ill-disposed towards them, but because they were in the
process of creating a thoroughly secular state. The heirs of the 'Young Turks' had
broken the power of the caliph and the mullahs; they saw no reason why the
power of the Christian priests should survive. Within a month of Roncalli's
arrival, *La Vita diocesana*, the diocesan weekly, was suppressed, along with every
other kind of publication that could conceivably be construed as 'religious propaganda'. He wrote, not without humour, to auxiliary Bishop Andrea Bernareggi
of Bergamo on February 3, 1935:

I don't know what I'm going to say in my Lenten pastoral letter or
whether it will be published. All that's left for me to talk about is prayer
and liturgy. Even the theological virtues are banned. I hope that at least it
will still be possible to talk about charity. But to have any dealings at all

with the Turks, as the recent earthquake in the island of Marmara showed, can be dangerous (Alberigo, p. 440).

This was to become a familiar pattern in the post-war Communist countries: the Church would be allowed to exist provided it was confined to the sacristy.

Mustafa Kemal, who gave himself the name of Atatürk, 'father of the Turks', should not be thought of as a benevolent Fabian reformer. He dealt most savagely with all opposition. His biographers, who are not unsympathetic to him, open one chapter with this chilling sentence: 'Having hanged every prominent man in the country known to be opposed to his policies, and imprisoned lesser rivals, Mustafa Kemal could now take stock' (Orga, p. 272). Taking stock in 1935, Atatürk decided to launch an attack on Christian religious dress. This was entirely logical. Atatürk's policy was 'Westernising' at least in outward forms. Since Moslems had to sacrifice the fez in the name of modernity, it followed that Christians should abandon their soutanes and habits. The fez, after all, being brimless, was very suitable for Moslem prayer; and the very phrase 'to put on a hat' meant to apostasise from Islam. So Atatürk made his Westernising intentions plain by appearing one day in a panama hat (Orga, pp. 260–3).

Christians had to follow this secularising example. Religious habits were abolished by a law which came into force on June 13, 1935. Roncalli did not take this measure too tragically. He wrote to the retired bishop of Bergamo, Marella, on April 13, 1935:

Even the difficulties which afflict us also help us to love religious life. As you know from June all the priests and monks and friars here will have to go about in secular dress. It's a great trial for everyone. We'll be happy enough if it stops there. Let's hope there's no imitation of what is happening in Mexico (*Quindicesimo anniversario*, p. 78).

In Mexico priests were being hunted down and shot: Atatürk's anti-clericalism did not go so far. In the end, the loss of religious dress was the least of Roncalli's worries. 'What does it matter', he remarked to Dell'Acqua, 'whether we wear the soutane or trousers as long as we proclaim the word of God' (Dreyfus, p. 93). The main result was to provide posterity with memorable photographs of Archbishop Roncalli in bowler hat and sober suit, looking for all the world like a Lombardy businessman who found it difficult to cut down on the *pasta*.

A much more serious problem was the government pressure on Christian schools. The Christian Brothers closed down four of their eight schools in his first year. The Sisters of Our Lady of Sion were forced to close two schools, but managed to expand the one nearest the cathedral. The Vatican urged Roncalli to resist these pressures. But there was not much he could do. He had no official diplomatic status, and nowhere to deliver his protests. It was painful to witness the destruction of this educational work. He wrote to Marella: 'The present generation of Levantines had a first-class religious education in the numerous foreign schools that have flourished up till now. Who knows what will happen tomorrow?' (*Quindicesimo anniversario*, p. 78).

These difficulties, however, drove Roncalli back upon the pastoral work that he preferred. Compared with Bulgaria, he was now in his element 'blessing, conse-crating, preaching' as he told Marella (*Quindicesimo anniversario*, p. 77). The Apostolic Delegation at 87 Olçek Sokak Street also needed attention. He began work on the chapel, redecorated his study, reordered the archives and the library. He tried to give the Delegation the atmosphere of a religious family. His faithful servant, Luigi Bresciani, who had followed him from Sofia, looked after his material needs. There were readings at meals from Fr Faber's *Spiritual Conferences*. He saw himself as the father of his little family. 'The exercise of pastoral and fatherly kindness', he noted, 'such as befits a shepherd and a father, must express the whole purpose of my life as Bishop' (*Journal*, pp. 246–7). Roncalli was always a well-organised and methodical worker. But the only time he had for personal work was between the hours of ten o'clock and midnight (*Journal*, p. 246). On one side of his desk was the Philips radio; on the other the Siemens telephone. Photographs of his family, numerous in his bedroom, were excluded from his study on the grounds that a Vatican representative should be 'like Melchizedek, without father or mother' (Righi, p. 21).

Yet it was there in July 1935 that he received the news that his father was dying. He tried to console his mother with the thought that 'when someone is gravely ill in the house, it is as though Jesus himself becomes visibly our guest, and that he sits there bringing comfort, blessings and holiness' (*Familiari*, I, p. 353. Letter dated July 25, 1935). But before this letter arrived in Sotto il Monte, Giovanni Battista Roncalli had died at the age of 81 – exactly the age his son would reach. Angelo – he became a little boy once again – went alone to the chapel 'to weep like a child' ('*a piangere come un bambino*'). That was on the day the telegram came. 'Now', he wrote, 'I am a little better, but tears keep welling up in my eyes' (*Ibid*., p. 353).

But there was no question of returning for the funeral. There wasn't time, and in any case he was needed in Turkey at this particularly tense moment in the life of the Church. He insists so much on the pressure of work that one suspects his mother had reproached him for his absence. Yet his only thought was to console her. But did he choose the right approach? In his letter home he says:

> As soon as the news of the death was made known people began to 'phone the Delegation. Tomorrow four Istanbul papers and *l'Osservatore Romano* will carry the news. Hundreds of Masses will be offered for the repose of his soul, and thousands of communions. A solemn requiem Mass is being

prepared for Thursday in the cathedral. I think it will be a most imposing ceremony. In all this you can find some compensation for my inability to be present at Sotto il Monte in person (*Familiari*, I, p. 357).

The Requiem Mass he celebrated for his father on August 1, 1935, was indeed 'most imposing'. A choir of 75 performed a Mass by Lorenzo Perosi, who remained his favourite 'modern' Church composer. He drew consolation from the fact that if his parents had not made the sacrifice of their son to the Church, no one would ever have heard of 'our poor, dear father, and who would have prayed for him?' (*Ibid.*).

He was on firmer ground when he assured his mother that although Giovanni Battista had died at 81, 'yet I still think he died too young'; and he predicted (falsely) that she would reach the age of 90 (*Familiari*, I, p. 354). Better still, when he returned home in September, he took her by car on pilgrimage to her favourite Marian shrines, notably the Madonna of Tears at Treviglio (*Cronologia*, p. 563). He treated his mother with great gentleness thereafter, installed her with Ancilla and Maria at Camaitino, and wrote to her directly more often than before.

He devoted the rest of his holiday in autumn 1935 to keeping his Roman friendships in good repair. He had long conversations with Borgongini Duca who was still nuncio to Italy (*Quindicesimo anniversario*, p. 76). He got another view of the Italian situation from Mgr Giovanni Battista Montini when they had dinner together at the home of Emilio Bonomelli, a Brescian like Montini, who re-designed and wrote the history of the papal gardens at Castelgandolfo. He took his newly appointed secretary, Mgr Gustavo Testa, along with him to meet Mgr Cesare Orsenigo, nuncio in Berlin. On October 17, 1935, there was a Roman seminary reunion at the retirement home in San Martino in Cimino, near Viterbo, of Mgr Domenico Spolverini, their former rector. Among the dozen guests were four who later became cardinals and heard Roncalli announce the Council (Ottaviani, Tardini, Fumasoni-Biondi and Roberti). The lunch was somewhat overshadowed by the fact that Spolverini knew that he was dying of cancer of the liver. 'And he is only 63', noted Roncalli, who was himself fifty-four (*Familiari*, I, p. 363). Most of Roncalli's friends had higher posts in the Curia or the Vatican diplomatic service than he had. He knew that some of them considered him 'unlucky' to have got out of Bulgaria only to land in Turkey (Alberigo, p. 439: letter to Bishop Bernareggi of February 3, 1935). Roncalli replied, as he always did, with the principle that obedience was the surest way to know God's will. But in this autumn of 1935 the conversation cannot have been confined to such personal matters.

For on October 2, 1935, Italy invaded Abyssinia. It was a coldly calculated and long-prepared move against the last sovereign state of Africa. According to Mussolini, its purpose was to win Italy 'a place in the sun', to provide an outlet for emigration from the *Mezzogiorno*, to display the martial virtues that were part of the ideology of Fascism, and to demonstrate that Italy was now a 'world power'. It was a popular war, even rallying to the government some previously dissident intellectuals like Benedetto Croce. The Vatican was embarrassed. *L'Osservatore Romano* pretended that nothing was happening.

However, on the very day the League of Nations discussed sanctions against Italy, Pius XI declared that 'the hopes, the demands, the needs of a great and good people should be recognised and satisfied' (Ragionieri 2, p. 2250). This piece of Vaticanese was taken to mean that Italy had a right to a colonial empire. It was a shocking remark because it totally ignored the hopes and the needs of the people of Abyssinia who, incidentally, had a long Christian tradition. The people of Abyssinia were now to be massacred, bombed and (it was later learned) gassed into submission. Though the Vatican abstained as far as possible from the conflict, the Italian clergy did not always show such restraint. There was a new form of *union sacrée*. Bishops blessed the departing troops. On November 18, 1935, all the mothers of Italy, from Queen Elena herself to the humblest peasant, were invited to donate their wedding rings for the war effort. This melodramatic and largely symbolic gesture would have been unimaginable, wrote one historian, 'without the help of the Church's network of contacts and powers of persuasion' (Ragioneri, 2, p. 2250).

It seems unlikely that Marianna Roncalli would have been prepared to surrender her wedding ring so soon after the death of her husband. Archbishop Roncalli's only comment on the war came in a letter to Ancilla and Maria who – it was sometimes a sore point – did not have wedding rings:

> In these last months the whole world has been in turmoil. We have to pray for this agitated world, and especially for our Italy. These are big questions: reason about them too much, and there's a danger of getting them wrong. But it's clear that the old fairy-tales are making a come-back. The big fish wants to eat the little fish. The little fish says the sea is big enough for everyone. Enough: let's hope and pray the war will soon be over because it is, after all, a war (*Familiari*, I, p. 366).

So much for Mussolini's bombastic orations: he was nothing more than a big fish trying to devour a little fish. For this cartoonist's-eye-view of the situation, Roncalli needed to be far away and able to stand back from events. In Italy they were being bombarded with propaganda about how the benefits of civilization were being brought to a benighted African people. In the process the ancient Ethiopian Church was systematically destroyed. In this manifestly unjust war, it was the Italians who were the barbarians.

Ancilla and Maria had more mundane and maiden aunt worries. What should they do about the continued arrival of *l'Osservatore Romano*? He advised them to read it and pass it round to other members of the family. He would pay the subscription (*Familiari*, I, pp. 370–1). The Vatican newspaper may not have been heroically out-spoken, but it remained the last independent paper in Italy. The sisters' next problem concerned women, or more precisely a woman, described simply as Signora G., wife of the builder who had constructed the church at Sotto il Monte in 1902. So in 1936 she cannot have been in the first bloom of youth. On her way to Tripoli, Libya, she proposed to stop in Rome and call on him, and she had told other women in Sotto il Monte that 'Mgr Roncalli has great sympathy with her'. No doubt Signora G's boasting was wholly innocent. But it was enough to make Roncalli clamber upon his high horse: 'Don't worry about the certain lady you mention. I don't think she will see me. I have never seen her and have never spoken to her *alone* (*sola*). So there is no need to worry. I know the score, and the Lord has always protected my honour' (*Familiari*, I, pp. 385–6: letter of December 12, 1936). This seems a little excessive, especially coming from someone who claimed to follow Radini Tedeschi's principle of acting 'as if there were no women in the world' (*Journal*, p. 294); but perhaps he laid on the indignation to reassure his sisters that they had no need to fear a rival claim on his affections.

His problems in Turkey were of a different order. He decided at the start of 1936 to introduce a few words of Turkish into worship. From January 12, 1936, the 'Divine Praises' ('Blessed be God, blessed be his holy name' etc.) were to be recited in Turkish. It was a small change, indicative of his desire that the Church should make its home among the Turkish people; but as his pontificate showed, any change of principle can have an importance far beyond its immediate effect (e.g. when he added the name of St Joseph to the Canon of the Mass, he showed that the text was neither immutable nor inviolable). In 1936 the 'changes' were not appreciated by everyone. In his diary he records:

> When the *Tanre Mubarek olsun* [Blessed be God] was recited, many people left the church displeased . . . [But] I am happy. On Sunday the Gospel in Turkish before the French Ambassador; today the Litany in Turkish before the Italian Ambassador . . . the Catholic Church respects everyone. The Apostolic Delegate is a bishop for all and intends to honour the Gospel which does not admit national monopolies, is not fossilised, and looks to the future (Trevor, p. 169).

Roncalli saw his linguistic innovations as a way of making the Church more genuinely 'Catholic'. He was denounced to Rome. In his October 1936 retreat he remarks that 'the difference between my way of seeing situations on the spot and certain ways of judging the same things in Rome hurts me considerably; it is my only real cross' (*Journal*, p. 244).

On other fronts he was moving cautiously forwards. He was represented at the funeral of the ecumenical patriarch, Photius II, and congratulated his successor, Benjamin I on his election. But he did not actually meet Benjamin until three years later, As for the Turkish government, he told Borgongini Duca that he continued to 'live dangerously. I keep a proper distance, and it has been confirmed that this is the best way to be respected or at least tolerated' (*Quindicesimo anniversario*, p. 76). Though not regarded by the government as an accredited diplomat, he made regular journeys to Ankara when he could – he needed police permission – and made himself known to sympathetic ambassadors. In 1935–6 these included the British, American, French, Dutch, Belgian, Polish and Italian ambassadors. He had to be careful about devoting too much time to the Italian ambassador, Carlo Galli, since he represented a technically 'foreign' state. On the other hand, he was on particularly good terms with successive French ambassadors and the Polish ambassador, Michael Sokolnicki, who may have been involved in an intrigue to have him sent to Poland as nuncio. Certainly the retiring nuncio, Cardinal Marmaggi, whom he met in Rome on November 13, 1936, wanted him as his successor. It was another of his endless might-have-beens. Roncalli did his best as an unofficial diplomat, but his diplomatic style was original, owing more to the Gospels than to Machiavelli. In his 1936 retreat at Ranica, Bergamo (where the strike had been in 1911) he stated his method: 'Above all I wish to render good for evil, and in all things try to prefer the Gospel truth to the cunning of human politics' (*Journal*, p. 244). Without realising it, he was, however, laying solid foundations for his diplomatic activity during the war when Turkey's neutrality made it a meeting-ground for all the contending parties, and Istanbul ceased to be a backwater.

Maxims about returning good for evil were handy in his dealings with the Greek government. Greece was his responsibility just as much as Turkey, and it was his headache. He was even more 'suspect' in Orthodox Greece than in post-Islamic Turkey. Part of the trouble was that Margotti, his predecessor, had behaved tactlessly in Greece. He had slipped clandestinely into the country and then driven around in a car ostentatiously flying the papal flag. This did not win him many Greek friends. Roncalli took exactly the opposite line. He made sure his papers were in order and when granted a visa kept his visits as discreet as possible. He knew that the Greek mistrust of the 'Latins' whom they still called 'Franks' was founded in the terrible experience of the crusades. In scholarly correspondence about the likely whereabouts of the remains of St Demetrius of Salonika, he concedes that almost anything was possible in the thirteenth century 'when the Venetians and the crusaders were stealing everything they could lay hands on' (*Quindicesimo anniversario*, p. 82). In the folk-memory the 'Franks' had robbed, raped and pillaged. Mussolini's aggressive Mediterranean policy re-opened the old wounds. In 1923 Italy had briefly occupied the island of Corfu after a bombardment that killed many Greek refugees. Roncalli told Davide

Cugini: 'In Athens we don't ride about in a carriage. The bombardment of Corfu is still echoing in Greek ears. No doubt my predecessor was a very acute man, but he was also too optimistic' (Cugini, p. 54). For all these reasons, the Greeks found it difficult to distinguish between the Vatican and the Italian government.

To add to the complications there were the Latin-rite religious, mostly French, who after Greek Independence in 1832 had flocked in to run schools and hospitals. The last straw was a handful – some 2,000 – of Greek 'Uniates' who had been repatriated from Turkey by the Treaty of Lausanne in 1923. Since they challenged the national consensus by their very existence, they were regarded as – so to speak – a Trojan horse. The identification of 'being Greek' and 'being Orthodox' was almost complete.

Apart from encouraging the local Catholics to hold firm, the main purpose of Roncalli's mission to Greece was to discover what form of Vatican representation the Greeks would be prepared to accept. The short answer was none. The monarchy had been restored with the aid of the military in 1935, and Roncalli hoped that general elections of January 1936 would enable him to clarify his position with the new government.

But the elections resolved nothing either for Roncalli or Greece. General Metaxas became prime minister even though he had only six followers in parliament. Greece was under economic pressure from Germany and political pressure from Italy. Mussolini, irritated by Greek opposition to the Abyssinian war in the League of Nations, revived his claim to Albania. On the pretext of forestalling a *coup d'état*, from April 1936 Metaxas abolished parliament, began to govern by decree, declared a state of emergency, and used the army to put down a general strike (Woodhouse, pp. 230–1). It was not the most propitious moment for the arrival of a Vatican envoy who happened to be an Italian and was based on Istanbul. It would have been difficult to devise a more daunting set of obstacles.

So Roncalli was understating things when he wrote to his mother on May 24, 1936: 'There are so many things to fix (*combinare*) in this country; but since the people are all Orthodox and are frightened of the Holy See and the Pope, one has to act slowly, cautiously, and with extreme sensitivity' (*Familiari*, I, p. 378). He met King George II the day after writing this letter. The meeting was friendly but inconclusive. The king was a constitutional monarch with little power to influence events. Approaches to the government got him nowhere either. Metaxas, a strong-arm nationalist who saw no reason to pander to the 'Franks' thought the Pope was the ally of Mussolini. The 'Uniates' were refused permission to build a church, and all marriages except Orthodox marriages were made illegal. Roncalli took all this calmly, and tried to make light of his difficulties: 'Now I think I have made some sort of progress; but I have to wait for orders from Rome. This is natural enough: as representative of the Pope, I must know and follow his mind in everything. In Rome, no one is in any hurry, and

that too is a form of Providence. It means that all I have to do is to wait' (*Ibid.*).
But a year later, nothing had changed. On June 19, 1937, he wrote to his family:
'You know how I stand with the Turks. But the difficulties with the Greeks are
greater. These splendid people give me fine words; but as you know the
Orthodox are afraid of the Pope. So I need a lot of patience. You know I think it
better to exceed in this direction. One slip could compromise everything'
(*Familiari*, I, p. 408). He always seemed to stay in Greece longer than he had
planned.

He used the delays to indulge in spiritual tourism. He got to know about Greek
monasticism by going round the monasteries. Here is how he describes to his
mother a visit to Mount Athos:

> Up there are more than twenty huge monasteries and as many small ones: it
> is unique in the world. Women are not allowed, and since the mountain
> rises abruptly from the sea, it would be difficult for them to land anyway.
> Once there were about 10,000 monks; now there are only about 2,000.
> When you get up there you find a most extraordinarily luxuriant
> vegetation, but there are no roads. One has to take the most difficult paths
> on horseback, and this made me entrust myself to St Joseph and my
> ancestors – as I always do – so as not to fall off. I didn't fall off once. I was
> there for three days and it takes at least five hours by horse or mule to get to
> the top; so one's bones get shaken up, and then there was the bad food and
> sleeping on hard beds etc. . . . But this diversion did me good. I returned to
> Athens fitter than ever (*Familiari*, I, p. 379. The visit to Mount Athos was
> May 17–20, 1936).

But he had overestimated his fitness. In December 1936 he fell ill in Athens with
nephritis. Back in Istanbul he was soon cured thanks to what Capovilla calls 'the
energetic interventions' of Dr Lorando who also gave him a complete medical
check-up.

He reported all the gory details to his family (*Familiari*, I, pp. 386–7). His
general state of health was pronounced good. But the illness had been a scare or
what he called 'a grave warning'. He saw 'signs of old age in my thinning hair'.
He reflected that in December 1937 he was the age that Radini Tedeschi had been
when he died, 57, and that every extra year beyond that was an uncovenanted
grace (*Journal*, pp. 244–5). The thought of mortality did not depress him, but
prompted him to 'wisdom, joy and calm' in the short time that lay ahead. Yet he
reported a curious conversation with Don Pietro Forno, co-editor of the *Acta* of
St Charles Borromeo, when they met for what turned out to be the last time on
October 7, 1937:

To think that Don Pietro said to me then: 'My health is so good and I am bursting with energy'. So we moved on from topic to topic: the uncertainty of the future, the warning signs of old age, the always terrible and mysterious judgement of God. 'I'm not afraid of the Lord' – he interrupted me as he did when he was on good form – 'I'm not frightened. Who have I served through my life? Mahomet perhaps? No, I served Jesus crucified and dying for me' (*Dodicesimo anniversario*, p. 50: the text comes from the introduction to volume II, Part I, of the *Atti della Visita Apostolica de S. Carlo Borromeo*).

In fact Forno died in November 1938 while saying Mass. Roncalli thought this a great grace. Forno was outlasted by his 88-year old mother, something that Roncalli points out to his own mother. He had been, despite or perhaps because of his 'crisis', one of Roncalli's best friends. 'Don Forno was full of rude health and energy – and sometimes a little too gruff' (*Familiari*, I, p. 447). Among his gear was discovered a mitre belonging to Roncalli. Had Forno, the plain, bluff man, dreamt of being a bishop? We do not know. We do know that from now on Roncalli was always interested in the last words of the dying and of the exact time of the arrival of 'sister death'. He used St Francis' term with great naturalness.

Sister death was busy just about then. Kemal Atatürk died on November 10, 1938 – Roncalli regretted that he was unavoidably absent in Greece – and few thought that Pope Pius XI could last much longer. First he was seen to be 'limping badly' (*Familiari*, I, p. 408) and then in November 1937 Roncalli gave a pessimistic diagnosis to his family: 'I saw the Pope the day before yesterday at the opening of new premises for the Roman College at St John Lateran. Those who saw him when he was ill say that he now seems to have resurrected. But for me who saw him a year ago, he seems to be much, much worse' (*Familiari*, I, p. 415). Pius was 80. He had begun to doze off during audiences, and often missed what was said to him. But he was not finished yet. Irish historian D. A. Binchy noted at this time that there was 'some mighty force in him, some spiritual dynamo charging the feeble battery' (Binchy, p. 71). Twice in March 1937 Pius XI roused himself with two forceful encyclicals, *Mit Brennender Sorge* (March 14, 1937) and *Divini Redemptoris* (March 19, 1937). The sub-titles explained their purpose: 'On the situation of the Catholic Church in Germany' and 'Against Atheistic Communism'.

With these encyclicals Pius XI dealt a blow to the two collectivist systems, Nazism and Communism. Though usually placed at opposite ends of the 'left' and 'right' spectrum, they both resulted in repressive dictatorships in which the rule of law was suspended and the individual human person was subordinated to the omnipotent state. Moreover, both their leaders, Adolf Hitler and Joseph Stalin, presented themselves as heroic saviours of the nation and encouraged a preposterous 'personality cult'. But despite these similarities, Pius XI did not quite put both dictatorships in the same bag. The emphasis in *Divini Redemptoris* fell on the 'intrinsically evil' nature of atheistic Communism, with which no Catholic could collaborate; in *Mit Brennender Sorge* Pius eloquently complained that the Church's rights were being violated, but that could be remedied if the Concordat were properly applied. Communism, in short, was a hopeless case; the Nazis, though behaving very badly, were not quite irredeemable.

Roncalli may have been alluding to these questions in his Epiphany sermon in Istanbul in 1938. God works out his purposes whatever the 'great men' who appear to dominate history imagine they are doing: 'History ebbs and flows. The designs of the Lord not human plans shape the philosophy of history: all peoples, all ages, even those which seem most hostile, work for the triumph of Christ' (Alberigo, p. 447). This Epiphany sermon was a meditation on the transiency of things. It was prompted by the simple fact that in this city created by the Emperor Constantine, nothing was left of him – not even the name he gave it. The two basilicas of Saint Irene and of the Holy Apostles had vanished. The column, surmounted by the emperor dressed as Apollo, with the nails of the true cross forming his halo, was no more. There was now no trace of the villa near Nicomedia where Constantine was baptised by Eusebius in 337.

Roncalli drew the conclusion that the Kingdom of Jesus is not tied to particular buildings or monuments or places. The Church has great freedom with regard to all external forms. So there is no need to sigh for the past, for 'in the divine plan, what is material and therefore changeable of its very nature, is not important' (Alberigo, pp. 446–7). In view of the fact that later 'progressives' have blamed Constantine for subordinating the Church to the political power, it is ironic that Roncalli's reflections on Constantine led him to the conclusion that the Church should travel lightly. It was a lesson he learned amid the ruins of Turkey. Having a sense of tradition did not mean carrying the past as a heavy burden. Roncalli's letters at this time are full of references to the need for the Church to be adaptable and able to respond to new needs. He wrote to Mgr Luigi Drago on February 21, 1938, that he was happy to be in Istanbul because 'I can work in my own style, that is in the style of a Church that is both teacher of all and always modern according to the demands of the times and the places' ('*chiesa maestra a tutti e sempre moderna secondo le esigenze dei tempi e delle località*') (Alberigo, p. 448). That simple phrase provides a bridge between the Roncalli who in 1908 sympathised with the aspirations of 'Modernism' and the reforming Pope John of 1958. And the bridge was constructed not out of speculative theories but out of pastoral concern.

These reflections went on against an increasingly gloomy international background. It looked as though history would repeat itself and that a Pope would die on the outbreak of a European conflict. Italy's growing *rapprochement* with Germany made war more than ever likely. Despite their common emphasis on 'charismatic' leadership – the *Führer* and the *Duce* – there were differences between the two right-wing ideologies, and it was not inevitable that they should have become allies. The most significant sign of their new friendship was Hitler's visit to Rome in May 1938. The swastika, a twisted and perverted version of the cross, was seen for the first time in the streets of Rome, a sinister portent. Pius XI roused himself for another bout of indignation: 'It is not found out of place or out of season to raise up in Rome, on this feast of the Exaltation of the Holy Cross, the symbol of another cross which is not that of Christ' (Holmes, pp. 73–4). Preferring not even to be in the same city as Hitler, he then departed to Castelgandolfo. *L'Osservatore Romano* studiously ignored the visit, and the Vatican museums were shut for its duration. But despite papal displeasure, Hitler's visit to Rome was a great success, and henceforward Italian domestic and foreign policies were more closely aligned with those of the Germans. In particular Mussolini began to persecute, not very efficiently, Italy's 40–70,000 Jews. Though he pretended this was essential to preserve the purity of the Italian race, privately he thought the idea of Italian racial purity was nonsensical. But it was politically expedient (see Mack Smith, pp. 257–8). Cardinal Schuster of Milan who had welcomed the Fascists had his eyes opened. If the hope had been to 'Christianise' Fascism, now it was on the contrary being 'nazified'.

For this reason the strengthening of the alliance between Germany and Italy led to increasing tensions between the Church and the Fascists. The anti-clerical strand in Fascism was revived. Roncalli had personal experience of this when he went home to Bergamo in mid-August 1938. The episcopal palace of Bishop Andrea Bernareggi, who had taken over from Bishop Marella in 1936, was daubed at night with insulting slogans. The offices of Catholic Action, the last national organisation not incorporated into the Fascist state, were attacked. The bishop was not able to communicate freely with his clergy. Roncalli was the chief guest preacher at the regional Eucharistic Congress held at Ardesio from August 29 to September 4, 1938. But it was not a moment for escapist piety. It was one of the few occasions when the priests of Bergamo had been able to gather freely round Bernareggi. They entrusted Roncalli, as an outsider and an archbishop, with the task of expressing their solidarity with the bishop. It took the form of a letter addressed to him. Since he was in the midst, that might have seemed rather redundant; but it was designed to reassure him that he was not alone.

The letter is an important piece of evidence about the Church–state clash at the time, but it was not a ringing clarion-call to action of any sort (text in *Dodicesimo anniversario*, pp. 72–4). More in sorrow than in anger, Roncalli deplores the outrages heaped upon this good man, and claims that successive bishops of Bergamo have always known how to 'render nobly to Caesar what is Caesar's and to God what is God's'. Local pride prompted him to find the attack on Catholic Action particularly unfortunate, since 'Catholic Action already existed in Bergamo while the rest of Italy slept' (*Ibid.*, p. 73). He boldly asserts that bishops of Bergamo have always concentrated on their religious mission and thus 'made the most precious contribution to our well-being and to the glory of our dear country' – which might have been considered an attempt to steal the Fascists' clothes. But the criticism stops there. There was no suggestion that the Church should become a focus of opposition to a regime to which the clergy of Bergamo, at the time, could not imagine an alternative. Roncalli was no doubt additionally cautious in that as a Vatican diplomat 'he ought not to have involved himself in such grave events of a local nature' (to borrow Capovilla's phrase).

Perhaps not. But it was good that he should have made himself the spokesman for those who believed that something terrible was about to happen (in clericalese 'felt with terror that the world was entering a new phase of serious and tremendous responsibility for all' – *Ibid.*, p. 74). The Munich crisis came within a month. But as war approached, all language tended to limp lamely behind events. From Istanbul Roncalli wrote to his brother Giuseppe and proposed this simple guide to truth: 'What you hear in church is certain truth. Everything else you hear may contain some truth, but is usually made up of untruth and falsehood. One has to know the difference (*saper discernere*). Meanwhile it seems that political matters are going better. Let's put our trust in God' (*Familiari*, I, p. 430: letter of April 28, 1938). But such nostrums were being offered also on the highest level. Roncalli's final meeting with Pius XI was devoted to the impending conflict. In his panegyric of Pius, he reports the Pope as saying: 'I am not afraid for the future of the Church. She only wants to be free. I know well what fate may well await her – sorrow and persecutions; but she will always have the last word, because she embodies the divine promises. But, on the other hand, I tremble for the nations . . .' (Dreyfus, p. 94). And he went on to list the doom-stricken nations, contrasting the unprincipled nature of the dictatorships with the irresolute weakness of the democracies.

Pius XI died on February 10, 1939. There was much speculation in the Vatican about a speech he had been preparing for the next day, the tenth anniversary of the signing of the Lateran Pacts. Roncalli was as intrigued as anyone by the *novissima verba*, the last words, of Pius XI. When he became pope, he had the archives searched and found the draft of this never-delivered speech, written in a hand that was already trembling. Exactly twenty years later, in February 1959, he published parts of it in a Letter to the Bishops of Italy.

He explained that the final weeks of Pius XI's life had been 'full of disappointments, and this makes it understandable that the aged pope should express himself in a language of justified resentment' (*Lettere*, p. 103). That hardly prepares one for the blistering tone of what follows:

You know how badly the Pope's words are treated. People read our allocutions or addresses – not only in Italy – in order to falsify their meaning, sometimes inventing altogether and attributing to us the most utter nonsense and absurdities. Recent and past history are so perverted in a certain press that it is said that there is no persecution in Germany, and this denial is accompanied by false and calumnious allegations of mixing in politics, just as Nero's persecution used the charge of setting fire to Rome . . .

Take care, dearest brothers in Christ, and never forget that there are observers and tale-bearers (call them 'spies' and you will be nearer the truth) . . . who will listen to you in order to denounce you, having understood nothing of the matter in hand or got it all wrong. They have in their favour – one must remember how Our Lord thought of his executioners – only the great, sovereign excuse of ignorance (*Lettere*, p. 105).

Clearly, Pius XI was determined to go out on a high note. Roncalli quoted him twenty years later to put the historical record straight and to show Pius' attitude to the Lateran Pacts. With his dying breath he was not proposing to scrap the Concordat with Italy, despite great provocation. This brought out the permanent validity of the Lateran Pacts. If they provided the legal basis for the defence of the Church against a sometimes hostile dictatorship in 1939, they were an even better basis for collaboration with a friendly Italian government in 1959.

It is difficult to know what Roncalli really felt on the death of Pius XI. It seems that he admired him more than he loved him. He remarked that had Radini Tedeschi lived, he would have been the same age as the Pope – which perhaps suggested that in his judgement Radini Tedeschi would have made a better pope. But his response to the death of Pius was complicated by the fact that his mother was also dying at the same time. Despite the urgent pleas of his family, he could not return for the end. He was 'like a soldier, under orders' (*Familiari*, I, p. 459). He had to stay in Istanbul because the death of a pope and the election of a new one meant a round of formal condolences and official visits. All this had to be done in person. It would be bad form to ask Mgr Gustavo Testa to stand in for him. Already his absence on the death of Atatürk the previous November had been remarked upon. But then he had the excuse of obedience. It must have seemed in-comprehensibly self-important in Sotto il Monte, where the diplomatic minuet was another world.

All they knew was that Angelo, having missed the death of his father, was now going to miss the death of his mother. Ancilla and Maria – for once we have their side of the correspondence – give a touching picture of Marianna Roncalli in her last months, as she lay bedridden;

Frequently she would recall her children, and especially you who are so far away; and you should have seen how, poor thing, she came to life again when she got a letter from you. She wouldn't entrust it to anyone else; she wanted to take it in her hands and read it for herself. But then thinking she might make mistakes, she would have it read by Enrica, and murmur: It's understandable that he can't come, but let's hope that he might. But if the Lord abandons me here, and I know how to do his will, we'll meet together in Paradise (*Familiari*, I, pp. 459–60).

So Marianna Roncalli died, of 'flu, at the age of 85, on February 20, 1939, during the *novemdiales* or nine days of mourning for the deceased pope. Angelo paid for her to have a splendid funeral, explaining that after all 'she is the mother of a Bishop' (*Familiari*, I, p. 460). Telegrams of condolence poured in from prelates, including Cardinal Pacelli, and Roncalli adds, 'my reply was perhaps the last message he received before he became Pope' (*Ibid.*, p. 467). He chose the photograph for her funeral card, and wrote a prose-poem to go on the back of it (text in *Familiari*, I, pp. 475–6: English trans. in Trevor pp. 180–1).

Roncalli had few comments on the conclave – the shortest of the century so far. Eugenio Pacelli, the Secretary of State, was elected, predictably enough. 'Being pope today', Roncalli remarks, 'is enough to turn your hair as white as your soutane' (*Familiari*, I, p. 465). He declares himself 'most happy' with the outcome and is convinced that 'the Lord had a hand in this election' (*Ibid.*, p. 467). He had no thought that he would be present at the next conclave, still less that he would be elected. In March 1939 he followed Pius' Coronation Mass on Vatican radio, and continued to marvel at this modern device.

The election of Pius XII indirectly enabled him to secure an historic 'first'. A representative of the Ecumenical Patriarch, Benjamin I, was present at the *Te Deum* for the new pope. On May 27, 1938, Roncalli went along to the Phanar to thank Benjamin who embraced him warmly and declared, in faultless Latin: '*Haec est dies quam fecit Dominus*' – 'This is the day which the Lord has made', the Latin Easter greeting (Righi, p. 151). Roncalli had met an earlier patriarch in 1927, but that visit had been private and unofficial. In the Orthodox tradition the 'kiss of peace', the embrace, has great symbolic value. After an enmity lasting so long the 'kiss of peace' between Benjamin and the Pope's representative, Roncalli, prefigured the embrace between the brother patriarchs, Athenagoras and Paul VI, in Jerusalem in January 1965. The Christian East and the Christian West, Constantinople and Rome, were finally able to meet in the land of their common origin.

That happy outcome was a good illustration of Roncalli's ecumenical method, as he outlined it to the Reverend Austin Oakley, personal representative of the archbishop of Canterbury to the ecumenical patriarch and the first Anglican he came to know. He thought in the long-term. One could not expect to batter down the walls of Christian divisions, but, said Roncalli, 'I try to pull out a brick here and there'. He also applied in the same context the maxim '*Gutta cavat lapidem*' – the drop of water eventually hollows out the rock (Trevor, p. 177).

Roncalli's meeting with the ecumenical patriarch was one of the few pieces of good news in 1939. On Good Friday – April 8 – Italy invaded Albania. It took about a week to overcome the army of King Zog, during which time a son and heir was born to him and named Skanderbeg after Albania's national hero. King, Queen and infant Prince fled to Greece which thought it was next on the list. Yet Roncalli's next letter home – from Istanbul on April 22, 1939 – ignores these events and shows him in his most 'patriotic' vein:

> I'm feeling happier now because the skies are clearing. I don't believe that we will have a war. For our part we try to be at peace with everyone, not speaking ill of anyone and not getting mixed up in political matters.
> It's true that there are some who like to speak ill of Italy, but they are wrong. There are arrogant people among us, and there is no lack of exaggeration; but as a country Italy is organised and respectful of religion and still the best place to be (*ancora dove si sta meglio*). There is no need to bother about what third and fourth parties are doing. As you know, I stay out of politics, but I cannot deny what I think and feel (*Familiari*, I, pp. 470–1).

Roncalli was not exactly beating the Fascist drum, but he was giving them, as *Italians*, the benefit of whatever doubt was going. He was never as pro-Fascist as, say, Fr Agostino Gemelli O.F.M., Rector of the Sacred Heart University in Milan; but neither was he by this date markedly anti-Fascist. His old PPI (*Popolari*) instincts no longer held him back and, anyway, their cause seemed now forlorn. He accepted Fascism because it was there. His denial of an interest in politics is symptomatic: it almost always means an acceptance of the *status quo*. It would be anachronistic to blame Roncalli for holding such views; it would be dishonest not to mention that he held them.

'I don't believe we will have a war', Roncalli wrote optimistically in April 1939. On May 22, 1939, Hitler and Mussolini signed the 'Pact of Steel', a remarkably nonchalant document in which the *Duce* accepted the German terms 'without fixing their purpose or their limits' (Ragionieri, 2, p. 2272). War was now inevitable; the only question concerned its timing and occasion. Pius XII had become pope just in time to utter vain exhortations to peace. His last-minute appeal, broadcast on August 24, 1939, was brushed aside as irrelevant, setting a pattern that would recur frequently in the next five years. The key sentences of the message are worth recalling; since they defined what would be Vatican policy throughout the war: 'It is by force of reason and not by force of arms that justice makes progress. Empires which are not founded on justice are not blessed by God. Statesmanship emancipated from morality betrays those very ones who would have it so. The danger is imminent, but there is yet time. Nothing is lost by peace;

everything may be lost by war' (Holmes, p. 122). The last epigrammatic sentence was attributed in curial circles to Giovanni Battista Montini. The problem about all such exhortations to morality was and remained in the passage from the general to the particular. Who was founding an empire not based on justice? Who was the unjust aggressor? So long as these questions remained unanswered, the Vatican was striking a pacific attitude but not really saying very much. Yet to answer them would mean taking sides, and so abandoning the even-handed neutrality that the Pope sought to maintain. This problem was never really resolved, and perhaps was insoluble. But the result was that both sides thought the Vatican was less sympathetic towards them than it should have been.

As the war machines clicked into gear, Roncalli had a meeting on August 2 with the new German ambassador to Turkey, Franz von Papen. They got on well. If the concept is not too absurd, von Papen represented the smiling, Catholic face of Hitler's Germany. We will meet him again. Then Roncalli flew to Rome via Athens and Brindisi to report to Cardinal Maglione, the new Secretary of State, and the substitute under-Secretary, his old friend, Giovanni Battista Montini. Roncalli had thoughtfully written to congratulate him on his appointment. So he was in Italy on 'the day war broke out', and saw Pius XII on September 5. But Italy was not yet in the war. Roncalli was now in the habit of flying everywhere, and arranged to be met at Milan airport by the parish priest of Sotto il Monte, who was instructed to come alone in his car because 'I have a lot of luggage and don't want to be packed in like a sack' (*Familiari*, I, p. 478). He was now an important ecclesiastical personage. The changing of the guard at the Curia gave him fresh hope: 'I received an extremely benevolent and encouraging welcome in Rome' (*Journal*, p. 252). This had led to gossip that 'greater things are in store' (*Ibid.*, p. 249). But he saw such flattery as a form of temptation, and changed the subject: 'I smile, and pass on to something else'. In Sotto il Monte he visited his mother's tomb, and saw to it that everything was in order.

On his way back to Turkey he made a more unexpected pilgrimage. On September 17–18 he was the guest of Carlo Margotti, the predecessor in Turkey and Greece who had bequeathed him so many acute problems and irate Franciscans, now archbishop of Gorizia. Margotti's achievement in Gorizia, scene of some of the fiercest battles of the First World War, had been to complete the 'Italianisation' of a Church that had been to a great extent Slovene. So with the 'patriotic' Margotti, he visited the shrine of the Madonna di Monte Santo, 'from which can be seen vast areas of the theatre of operations during the first world war' (*Familiari*, I, p. 479). The next day, they went to the military cemetery of Redipuglia 'where lie hundreds of thousands of dead soldiers'. It was a desolating experience, all the more since it now seemed that the slaughter of that first conflict would be repeated and 'the finest flower of the youth of Europe destroyed' (*Ibid.*). Though Italy was not yet at war, Margotti tended the sacred flame of Italian heroism just to be prepared. In a crisis, people tend to reach into their stock of clichés from the past.

But it was the internationally-minded Roncalli who arrived in Istanbul in time to organise a committee to aid Polish refugees on the day Warsaw fell – September 28, 1939. What tradition called 'the corporal works of mercy' would be from now on at the top of his agenda. Yet the war seemed very far away when he made his retreat November 12–18, 1939. The beauty of the scene enchanted him, and for once in a while he records some visual impressions:

> Every evening from the window of my room here in the Jesuit residence, I see a cluster of boats on the Bosphorus; they come round from the Golden Horn in tens and hundreds; they gather at a given spot and then they light up, some more brilliantly than others, offering a most impressive spectacle of light and colour. I thought it was a sea festival for Bairam (one of the two great annual Moslem feasts) which occurs about now. But it was simply the fleet organised to fish for *bonito*, the large fish which is said to come from far away in the Black Sea. These lights glow throughout the night, and one can hear the cheerful voices of the fishermen.
> I find the sight very moving. The other night, towards one o'clock, it was pouring with rain, but the fishermen were still there, undeterred from their heavy toil (*Journal*, pp. 251–2).

Then, as though to off-set any aesthetic self-indulgence that would be inappropriate in wartime, he moralises the scene and reminds himself that as a 'fisher of men' he should show no less zeal and courage than these Turkish fishermen (*Ibid.*).

But the thought of the war, however remote, kept on breaking in. In the East, Germany and the Soviet Union, accomplices at last, had cynically carved up Poland, and began to destroy its élite of priests and intellectuals. In the West it seemed that nothing much was happening. It was the period known as the '*drôle de guerre*' or the phoney war, the *Sitzkrieg* (stationary war) that preceded the *Blitzkrieg* (war of rapid movement). The main consolation for Roncalli, as he sat down to write his letter home on Christmas Day, 1939, was that Italy had not yet been drawn into the conflict. He attributed this non-belligerency to Mussolini's political shrewdness – it was a common propaganda theme at the time:

> I wish you a happy new year. Who knows what mysteries are in store for us. Think of all the unfortunate people who are at war, the Poles and those poor Finns and the Germans themselves and the Russians. What do the troops know about all this? They suffer and die, causing grief to countless families. It is the leaders who are responsible. It is they who are obstinate, and they're all the same.

We're blessed in Italy. This time we really must admit that *Il Duce* is guided
to act for the good of Italy. I think the Lord wants in this way to reward
both rulers and subjects for the reconciliations with the Church.
And now there is this celebration of peace in the meeting of the Pope and
the King. Who could ever have imagined that it would go so well? The
chief merit for this belongs to the courageous soul of the late Pius XI. He
knew when to resist and when to give way without being afraid of anyone.
Good for him. And we have to be grateful to Mussolini . . . The popes were
always ready for reconciliation, but there was never anyone on the side of
the state who would accept this (*Familiari*, I, pp. 489–90).

This letter is disconcerting only if read out of context. Roncalli was stating half-
truths, without the qualifications they needed. Mussolini had indeed contributed
to the reconciliation of Church and State – even if for his own reasons and as a
means of control over the Church. A few days later, on December 28, 1939, there
was a meeting at the Quirinale between Pius XII and King Victor Emmanuel III
which seemed to set the seal on that good relationship – even though the
monarchy had tended to be anti-clerical and 'Voltairean'. And on September 1,
1939, Mussolini had declared that 'Italy will not take the initiative in any military
operations' – even though his peace-loving attitude was strictly provisional and
motivated largely by a lack of military preparedness. With hindsight it is easy to
see how each of these 'signs' was ambivalent. But he was writing home, to
reassure his worried family. He was the only one who had any experience of the
wider world. He was as optimistic as he could be. This had the disadvantage that
he was constantly being refuted by events.

In 1940 the Vatican ordered him to devote more time to Greece. He paid three
visits there between January and May. Greece continued to be his cross. Though
he claimed to love the Turks and admire their 'natural qualities' (*Journal*, p. 252),
he has no comparable passage about the Greeks. There were times, indeed, when
he wished someone else would take over from him: 'I confess I would not mind if
it were entrusted to someone else, but while it is mine, I want to honour the
obligation at all costs. "Those who sow in tears shall reap in joy"'. It little matters
to me that others will reap' (*Ibid.*). So, despite the vexations, he soldiered on. But
the deteriorating political situation made his mission more difficult than ever.
Metaxas was still in power. As a Greek patriot, he was deeply distrustful of
German and Italian intentions in the Mediterranean. The Italian occupation of
Albania was virtually complete, which meant that Greece had Italian troops along
its northern border. It was not a time when Roncalli's protestations of neutrality
and universal love were likely to carry much weight. He was more than ever the
'suspect'.

The British government also began to take an interest in him. Later, after

Italy's entry into the war, Vatican diplomats of Italian nationality – that is, the majority of them – were treated as 'enemy aliens' (*Actes et documents*, 4, Introduction). In neutral Turkey, Roncalli was spared this indignity. But in a city where everyone was carefully watching everyone else, it would not have escaped notice that he met von Papen again on January 26, 1940. Roncalli saw in him the Catholic aristocrat with a pious wife who did the flower arrangements in the Delegation chapel and sometimes swept the floor.

The Vatican knew rather more about von Papen's past and was not so easily taken in. He had been one of the 'government of barons' who accepted the end of the Weimar Republic in the foolish belief that they could 'control Hitler'. Not remarkable for his courage, von Papen had shown a certain bravery in 1934 when he made a speech critical of the Nazis. But the murder of the aide who helped him draft the speech brought him back to his senses. He was sent to Austria to prepare the *Anschluss* or union of Austria and Germany. This was not a particularly 'Nazi' cause, and many German and Austrian Catholics welcomed the idea of a 'Greater Germany'. It was of a different order from later territorial claims. Having dealt satisfactorily with Austria, von Papen was despatched as ambassador to Turkey early in 1939. It was not a top post, but neither was it an irrelevant side-show: Turkey guarded the Dardanelles with an efficient army of two million men, and would form the German right flank in any eventual conflict with the Soviet Union. In April 1940 von Papen was proposed as German ambassador to the Holy See. Pius XII consulted Konrad von Preysing, bishop of Berlin, who said no. Von Papen was thought to be too shifty. Pius refused his *agrément*. Von Papen remained in Turkey.

Roncalli had to follow the instructions of the Secretariat of State. They were simple. The Vatican was neutral, even if that meant being equidistant between the two contending parties and making no moral discrimination between them. There was certainly no belief that the 'English' were morally superior or more idealistic. Here, for example, is how Roncalli's superior, Mgr Domenico Tardini, minuted a request from Lord Halifax in 1940 that the Vatican should publicly dissociate itself from the Axis powers:

A curious fellow, Lord Halifax, half a preacher [*predicozzo*]. The mysticism of the Foreign Office comes down to the interests of Britain (Utilitarianism). He professes to be defending religious interests, but in fact seeks political goals. He tries to get the Holy See to say that Nazism is as bad as Communism, forgetting that only yesterday the British government was courting the Communists. His purpose is evident: to provoke the Holy See into a statement useful to England and damaging to the Axis (*Actes et documents*, 4, No. 166).

This mistrustful attitude towards British intentions would have been picked up

by the British Embassy in Ankara, despite Austin Oakley's assurances that Roncalli
was a man of peace and genuinely neutral.

As the phoney war dragged on, there were changes at the Delegation. Mgr
Gustavo Testa, whom Roncalli regarded as his spiritual son, departed and was
replaced by Mgr Vittorio Ugo Righi, who owed his Christian names to his
parents' regard for the French poet, Victor Hugo. Roncalli lapses into Bergamesque dialect to describe him: *L'è pui do no got*, 'he's hardly there at all', a reference
to the fact that Righi was tiny (*Familiari*, I, p. 491). His letters home are filled
with domestic details. He has bought some new carpets in Rome and gives
instructions to Ancilla and Maria about where to put them (*Ibid*., p. 497). He
worries about his twelve-year-old nephew, Battista, son of Giovanni, who wants
to enter the seminary but is not very bright (*Ibid*., p. 482). It was as though the
war would somehow go away, if one didn't talk about it. What was there to be
said, anyway? On March 26, 1940, he wrote to Giovanni 'as for the war, we hope
there won't be an attack, but many think it won't be long in coming' (*Ibid*., p.
502). But soon he bowed to the inevitable and wrote to Giuseppe, 'we are
entering into the "vale of tears" of the *Salve Regina*' and he quoted one of his
favourite texts from Manzoni's *I Promessi Sposi*: 'The Lord never disturbs the joy
of his sons, except to prepare them for another, greater and more certain joy'
(*Ibid*., p. 506: the Manzoni quotation comes from Chapter 8). Roncalli was on
his way by ship from Athens to Istanbul when the 'attack' finally came.

The word evokes the First World War, when the generals would order 'the big
push' after due artillery 'softening up'. It was not like that in 1940. On May 10
the Germans invaded neutral Holland, Luxembourg and Belgium, thus circumventing the Maginot Line. They swept all before them. Roncalli did not think he
was breaking with neutrality in presenting his condolences at the Netherlands
Legation on May 15. The French Army was routed, much of the British
Expeditionary Force escaped via the beaches of Dunkirk, and Paris fell on June 14.

For Roncalli personally, the decisive date in this critical month of June 1940
was not the 22nd, when the Franco–German armistice was signed in the famous
railway carriage at Compiègne, but the 10th, the day Italy entered the war. Only
six months before he had thanked God for Mussolini and believed that his protestations of non-belligerency were sincere; now that card-house of hope collapsed.
It was a blow partly because he had always loved France – even though largely
from a distance and through the eyes of Radini Tedeschi – but even more because
Mussolini had not kept his word.

Next day, June 11, 1940, he received Mgr Joseph Guillois, a Frenchman and his
episcopal chancellor, solemnly gave him the kiss of peace, and because he did not
trust himself to improvise, read out the following text written the night before:

A day of sadness. Italy has declared war on France and England . . . War is a terrible *periculum*, danger. For the Christian who believes in Jesus and his Gospel it is an iniquity and a contradiction. 'Deliver us, O Lord, from famine and war'. I think that today my duties of wisdom, moderation and charity have become more grave than ever. I must be the bishop of all, that is the *consul Dei*, God's consul, father, light, encouragement for all. Nature makes me want the success of my dear country; grace fills me more than ever with the desire to seek and work for peace (*Letture*, p. 286).

This was when Roncalli's war really began. How he tried to be a man of peace in time of war will be the subject of the next chapter.

Chapter 9

God's consul

Mussolini speaks from the balcony of the Palazzo Venezia. The news of the war does not surprise anyone and does not arouse very much enthusiasm. I am sad, very sad. The adventure begins. May God help Italy!

(Count Galeazzo Ciano, Mussolini's foreign minister and son-in-law, *Diaries*, p. 264, June 10, 1940).

Italy's entry into the war was a bitter blow for Archbishop Roncalli. It made his tightrope walk of neutrality considerably more difficult, especially in Greece. The war was unpopular with the Italian people who had not been consulted about it. Nor was it altogether welcome to the Germans, since it opened up vast new fronts in Africa and the Balkans that, from a strategic point of view, would have been better left quiescent. Many Italians consoled themselves with the idea that the war was practically over: it seemed reasonable to expect that an isolated Britain would soon seek a negotiated peace. Roncalli half-shared this wide-spread view. On June 21, 1940, he wrote home:

> Let's hope that the war with England will soon be over. Otherwise it will be a very bad look-out for our cousin in the navy [Peppino Roncalli]. All of you should remember what Bishop Bernareggi wrote on the outbreak of war. His were golden words. At a time like this one should speak little, pray a lot, and impose some sacrifices on oneself.
> General Pétain put it very well yesterday. One of the causes of the French defeat was their unbridled enjoyment of material pleasures after the Great War. The Germans on the other hand began to impose limitations and sacrifices on themselves, and so were prepared and strong. It's another form of the parable of the wise and foolish virgins (*Familiari*, I, pp. 508–9).

The bishop of Bergamo's 'golden words' came in a pastoral letter and were straightforward enough: 'The duty of Catholics in wartime is this – to obey'. They should also tighten their belts. Roncalli must have been one of the few people in Europe capable of presenting the German rearmament policy ('Guns before butter') as an illustration of how to be an evangelical wise virgin.

The Vatican's assessment was more sophisticated. Two days after Roncalli's letter home, Mgr Domenico Tardini, head of the foreign section of the Secretariat of State, discussed the situation with Pope Pius XII and Cardinal Maglione. Tardini's appreciation was couched in his usual brisk style:

1. Above all the special duty of HH (his Holiness) is to help avoid further bloodshed and ruinous destruction, since it is perfectly clear that the struggle with England will be murderous in the extreme.
2. There is a chance that Hitler, having won a great victory in France and worried about Russian moves in the East, will now be ready to try to settle with England; all the more since Hitler must realise that an attack on England will be a risky and a bloody enterprise.
3. There is a chance that England, now alone and in imminent danger of attack, would prefer to negotiate to avoid catastrophe and a long, ferocious struggle (*Actes et documents*, I, pp. 499–500).

Tardini was vastly more experienced than Roncalli in the diplomatic task of assessing future intentions. But he was wrong about what 'England', under Winston Churchill, was likely to do. Yet at the time and to outsiders, a negotiated peace seemed the most sensible and probable outcome.

Such was the background to Roncalli's long conversation with von Papen on August 12, 1940. He reported on it the next day (*Actes et documents*, 4, pp. 105–11). It was his most important diplomatic despatch to date, and he knew it. Von Papen had just returned from Berlin where he found Hitler 'more calm and reflective after the victory that he had ever seemed before'. Since the fate of the world depended on what Hitler was thinking or feeling, a knowledge of his latest position was a vital piece of intelligence. According to von Papen, Hitler's more pensive position was this:

> He repeated that it had never been his intention to annihilate England, but rather to make it behave more reasonably towards Germany . . . He would deeply regret having to pass over to an all-out attack; but the attack would surely come, and he would be happy if, after the first blows, England decided to negotiate an agreement.
> The way the English and the French are completely deceived about German war resources – von Papen went on – is painful to behold. They have a spirit of hatred and detestation of Germany that we Germans have never had towards them. We have tried and will continue to try to treat them with respect, and not with the contempt they habitually display towards us.

It would be exaggerating the importance of these remarks to say that through von Papen Hitler was 'flying a kite' and hinting that Germany, at least, would welcome papal mediation to put a stop to the war. It is more likely that von Papen was simply engaging in diplomatic propaganda, stressing for the benefit of the Holy See the contrast between the 'reasonable' Germans and the obsessed, hate-inspired English.

That the object of the exercise was to encourage the Vatican to think well of

Germany becomes clear when von Papen moved on to outline his vision of the present and post-war position of the Catholic Church in Germany:

> It seems to von Papen that the clergy and the faithful should pay great attention to the *transformatio ab imis* (the change from below) that is taking place, and the way the robust and enthusiastic forces of Catholicism are called to collaborate with it, making a contribution that can only be of advantage to the Church of tomorrow – especially in comparison with the Protestants who are an inert mass without internal cohesion or organisation.

Roncalli noted that von Papen made the next remarks 'in a more lively tone'. Not surprisingly. He had reached the heart of the matter:

> Despite the various estimates that may be made of Hitler's character . . . there are still so many open possiblities, and the future could be rich in surprises. One of them could be that after the war Catholicism would become the 'formative principle' of the new German social order, rather in the way Mussolini had wisely endowed Italy with the concordat and social legislation inspired on some points by the great teaching of Leo XIII.

Von Papen was overplaying his hand here. The notion that Mussolini was inspired by the social teaching of the Church was a pleasant fantasy; and the picture of a Hitler domesticated into Catholicism was even more fantastic.

But it was all part of von Papen's diplomatic propaganda. To pursue his military aims. Hitler needed docile Catholics, and in 1940 he had begun to relax his anti-Church policy with that in view (see Helmreich, p. 348). The whole shimmering prospect that von Papen dangled before Roncalli depended on German Catholics being involved ever more closely in 'the cares, the sufferings and the joys of this great and noble nation'. Von Papen expected the war to be over by November 1940 (they were in August). Then there would be something for Italy too. In the redrawn German map of Europe, Italy would replace France as 'the major responsible power' in the Middle East, be conceded the island of Corsica and some territory around Nice, and the 'Tunisian' problem would be solved in favour of Italy. Even though technically incorrect, it was shrewd of von Papen to address Roncalli as an Italian. If Italy really did replace France in the Middle East, then many of the problems he had experienced as apostolic delegate in Bulgaria, Turkey and the Lebanon would disappear.

Though Roncalli gives it as his opinion that von Papen was 'a sincere and a good Catholic', he was not listening altogether uncritically. He pressed von Papen on two points. First, was he distinguishing clearly between Hitler's views and his own? What von Papen was saying made some sense as the wish-fulfilment of a German Catholic who still hoped that Hitler could be 'controlled'. But could he really speak for Hitler? The other crucial question was about Hitler's sincerity. Von Papen tried to reassure him on both points. Finally, Roncalli put the most decisive question of all. German Catholics had good reason to dislike and mistrust Hitler 'in view of the raging Nazi spirit which has subverted not only every treaty but the religious tradition of Germany as well'. Von Papen's theory of a privileged place for Catholicism in the thousand-year *Reich* (Empire) would crumble if there were radical incompatibility between the pagan ideology of Nazism and Christianity. Von Papen does not seem to have had much of a reply to this objection. He extricated himself as best he could by talking about the 'collective psychology' of the Germans compared with the individualist French. It seems that von Papen was clutching at straws.

Roncalli added one last detail, of great importance for the future. While he was closeted with von Papen, his secretary, Righi, was out walking in the embassy garden with Baron Kurt von Lersner. His exact role was not easy to pin down, and it changed. He was supposed to be von Papen's cultural attaché, but this was a cover to allow him to negotiate a commercial treaty with the Turks. Later he became the Istanbul agent of Admiral Wilhelm Canaris. As a Lutheran, he was an admirable foil to the Catholic von Papen. Roncalli came to like him and trust him. When the two Vatican diplomats got back home to the Delegation, they compared notes and reported:

> Together we were allowed to glimpse an outline of the reconstructed
> Europe of tomorrow: for example, Alsace-Lorraine and Luxembourg would
> be absorbed into Germany; Belgium and Holland with their independence
> restored but demilitarised. The same to be said of the new Poland and the
> protectorate of Bohemia and Moravia. Finally the cost of the war for the
> two Axis powers would be borne by the colonial possessions of Belgium
> and Holland in the form of raw materials . . . France would restore the
> former German colonies and pay war indemnities. Both von Papen and
> Baron Lersner foresee the end of the war by this autumn.

It was Roncalli's duty to transmit accurately what he had heard, not to comment on it. But at the same time, there is something sinister in this calm recital of the consequences of Hitler's *Neue Ordnung* or New Order. He fully expected to have to live with it. When Roncalli's report arrived in the Secretariat of State, Tardini minuted it: 'This fellow has understood nothing' (*'Questo a capito niente'*). The good-natured Roncalli had been too gullible, and had been taken for a diplomatic ride.

Matters of high politics were strictly excluded from his letters home. He told his sisters, instead, how he was rebuilding, at his own expense, the Apostolic Delegation. 'The nasty little entrance you used to know', he wrote, 'has been replaced by a large atrium with four columns' (*Familiari*, I, p. 514–15). It looked out over the garden which was ablaze with roses and magnolias. He had icons in the chapel and the text *Ad Jesum per Mariam* was inscribed above its door. He always maintained that mariology was the key to unity with the Orthodox. The *Theotókos* (the Mother of God) remained part of the common heritage despite subsequent theological quarrels (see Righi, p. 272). So the Delegation became a kind of haven in a world at war. Turkish neutrality meant that Roncalli became, as he put it, the Vatican's postman for the whole of the Middle East and beyond (*Familiari* I, p. 557). What he does not tell his sisters, however, is that on the very day he was writing to them, September 5, 1940, he had met a party of Polish Jews who brought grim news from Nazi-occupied Poland. He helped them on their way to the Holy Land. Von Papen's assurances about the 'independence' of Poland were already exposed as nonsense.

A month later – according to von Papen, the war ought to have been over – he began the most sombre retreat of his life at the villa house of the Sisters of Our Lady of Sion. It was at Terapia and overlooked the Bosphorus. But this time there were no twinkling lights of fishing boats out at sea. Following a suggestion of Pius XII, he took Psalm 51, the *Miserere*, as the basis of his meditations. So he was praying this Jewish prayer, in the midst of a community dedicated to ministering to Jews, at a time when the first inkling of the terrible fate that awaited them had begun to emerge. Some things became clearer to him.

The first was simply that no nation can claim to have God on its side. This 'murderous war that is being waged on land and sea and in the air' was certainly no crusade: 'It has been asserted, and is still being asserted, that God is bound to preserve this or that country or grant it invulnerability and final victory, because of the righteous people who live there and the good they do. We forget that although God has made the nations, he has left the constitution of states to the free decisions of men' (*Journal*, p. 257). War, then, results from human choices: it is not like some inexplicable, inevitable natural catastrophe. Men go to war because they want to: 'War is desired by men, deliberately, in defiance of the most sacred laws. That is what makes it so evil. He who instigates war and foments it is always the "Prince of this world" who has nothing to do with Christ, the "Prince of peace" ' (*Ibid.*). But the devil cannot be used as an alibi. Roncalli remembers the teaching of Tabarelli at the Roman seminary: 'Devils? What devils? We are the devils. We are the ones responsible' (*Ibid.*, p. 262).

But then the mystery of evil deepens. Why should men desire what is so evidently opposed to the common good? Roncalli's answer is that war-lust is stimulated and sustained by nationalism, especially the nationalisms that are based on theories of 'racial purity'. Nationalism is the perversion of patriotism: 'Patriotism, which is right and may be holy, may also degenerate into nationalism ... The world is poisoned by morbid nationalism, built up on the basis of race and blood, in contradiction with the Gospel. In this matter, which is of burning topical interest, "deliver me from men of blood, O Lord" ' (*Journal*, pp. 270–1).

There is a third strand in Roncalli's mediation on war in November, 1940: through it he rediscovers the specific mission of the Church. For the promises of God that have *not* been given to any of the nations *have* been given to his Church, to the 'race of believers', the new race which embraces all the nations (*Journal*, p. 257). Yet God's promises to the Church, 'though they preserve her from final defeat, do not guarantee her immunity from trials and persecutions' (*Ibid.*). The proper response to a promise is hope. The Church is in the world as the community of hope. It is a sign of hope in that it proclaims to the world that in God's design the nations should live in harmony, and in its own life anticipates this harmony. He quotes St Robert Bellarmine: 'Among those things that have been revealed to us, we have hardly anything greater, or from which we may better discover the greatness of God, than the founding of the Church' (*Ibid.*, p. 272). The reason is that the nature of the Church tells us something about the nature of God. Roncalli then sketches what he calls his 'vision' of the Church: 'It is not seen as a historic monument of the past, but as a living institution. Holy Church is not like a palace that is built in a year. It is a vast city that must one day cover the whole universe' (*Ibid.*). Roncalli's wartime mediation foreshadows the ecclesiology of Vatican II: he sees the Church not merely as an institution but as the living people of God, in movement, on the march, a sign and a light to the nations, *Lumen Gentium*.

The practical conclusion in 1940 was that, as bishop in Istanbul, he should be 'above all nationalistic disputes' (*Journal*, p. 270). He reminded himself that 'words move, but examples draw' (*Ibid.*, p. 269), thus tracing a difficult line in which he would be genial with all and yet keep his conversation insubstantial. This retreat disposes of the illusion that Roncalli's cheerfulness and *bonhomie* came naturally to him. True, he recognises that he has a 'happy disposition' that saves him from the excesses of those zealots who 'fling themselves like living flames into their eager labour for souls' (*Ibid.*, p. 274). But he still has to work at cheerfulness. He makes his own the motto which summed up the spirit of the Sisters of Our Lady of Sion: *l'abnégation souriante*, renunciation with a smile.

Yet there was something rather forced in the cheerfulness of his next letter to Ancilla and Maria. He rattles on about what it feels like to reach sixty and reports his latest attempts to keep his weight down. In the evening he has only soup and fruit, with no bread or wine. For breakfast nothing but coffee and fruit. At lunch, however, he 'eats like a good Christian'. He claims that this regime is working well. He is in the best of health, has slimmed a little, and retains 'the freshness and agility of youth' (*Familiari*, I, p. 525). The war breaks in as he wishes them a happy Christmas. For the first time since he arrived in Turkey he will not be singing Midnight Mass. Though Turkey is not at war, a black-out has been imposed on Istanbul as a precaution against air-raids. So at Christmas 1940 with *bellum in terris* (war on earth) he did not sing *pax in terris* (peace on earth). That seemed right.

As part of his keep fit at sixty campaign Roncalli started to go for afternoon walks around the strangely deserted city. Most of the men of military age were away in the army. The removal of the capital to Ankara – Atatürk had been pursuing some atavistic memory of a Hittite capital 4000 years before – had deprived Istanbul's European quarter, Pera Beyoglu, of its vitality. The city seemed moribund. It was like a museum. This had its compensations for those who stayed behind. Roncalli's afternoon walks became archaeological excursions. He particularly loved the Studion, near the Golden Gate, once a centre of monastic arts and sciences; its precious library was vandalised by the crusaders in 1204. He used to say the rosary among its ruins. He found plenty of traces of Byzantium in Istanbul, and became something of an expert on Greek inscriptions.

He became known to ambassadors and visiting scholars as a man of erudition. Turkey was just the place for someone with historical imagination. The first great Councils – Ephesus, Chalcedon, Constantinople – had all been held there. Roncalli kept beside him on his desk a list of the 856 (*sic*) episcopal sees which had once flourished in 'Asia Minor' (Righi, p. 94). He thought it would be a good joke to send to his old friend Borgongini Duca, Nuncio to Italy, a post-card from Eraclea of Europe of which he was titular bishop. 'We are here under your juris-diction', Roncalli wrote from the straggling village, Eregli, that was all that remained. Then there was Antioch, once the cultural rival of Rome, and equally the city of St Peter, where the followers of Christ were first given the nickname 'Christian'. Roncalli also became familiar with the Greek fathers, especially St John Chrysostom, priest of Antioch, who was press-ganged into becoming bishop of Constantinople and died in exile. He was the patron of the Catholics of Istanbul. Roncalli preached on him at the conclusion of the Octave of Prayer for Church Unity in 1941 (text in Alberigo, pp. 458–63). Living in Turkey gave him a sense of Christian origins and a knowledge of the Oriental tradition. He was delivered from the narrowness of Roman theology.

But his plunge into the past, though it could be used to divert – in both senses – ambassadors of scholarly leanings, could not provide an escape from the present. Early in 1941 von Papen was back with news that the understanding between the Axis powers (Germany and Italy) and the Soviet Union was complete. Since he had just seen Hitler, Molotov, the Russian Foreign Minister, and King Boris of Bulgaria, this seemed like authoritative inside information, and Roncalli hastened to transmit it:

> The Triple Pact grows ever stronger, and the basis of a *new order* in Europe is already laid down. Some nations have already joined the Pact; others are on

their way. The door is open for all those who want to join, also for
Turkey . . .
I got the impression [Roncalli is now speaking in his own name] that once
England is liquidated, the Axis and Russia will not give excessive
importance to Turkey and that its independence could be guaranteed in the
future redrawing of the map of Europe (*Actes et documents*, 4, pp. 273–4).

Once again the new order and its consequences are accepted with what looks like
equanimity. The use of the typically totalitarian word 'liquidated' is chilling. And
there was a lack of political perceptiveness in swallowing uncritically von Papen's
assurances about the solid friendship that bound Germany and the Soviet Union
together. Within six months Operation Barbarossa, the Nazi attack on Russia,
was launched to prove the hollowness of that claim.

But Roncalli was now in deep water, caught up in plots and counter-plots. The
Baron von Lersner was up to something, and Roncalli begins to do favours for
him and report his conversations. Von Lersner was an anti-Nazi who secretly
wanted the removal of Hitler so that a deal could be done in the West (see *Actes et
documents*, 4, pp. 367–8). But the removal of Hitler could only be achieved on the
hypothesis that there existed 'good' Germans who were prepared to take the risks
involved. This was precisely what the allied doctrine of 'unconditional surrender' –
already applied in practice – excluded. Though the United States was not yet in
the war, President Franklin D. Roosevelt's moral and economic support for
Britain strengthened British resolve to fight on to the bitter end. On January 6,
1941, Roosevelt declared that he would not deal with the Nazi regime and that
'no one can tame a tiger or turn it into a charming kitten' (Dreyfus, p. 97).

This robbed the anti-Nazi Germans of hope. It made von Lersner very angry
indeed. Roncalli reports him saying: 'No one loves peace any more. Roosevelt has
now torn off the mask. His first statements suggested sincerity. But he was play-
acting to secure re-election. Once he won, he behaved like everyone else' (*Actes et
documents*, 4, p. 382). Now that Roosevelt had joined the baying pack, Lersner
was forced to look elsewhere for moral leadership and peace initiatives. He
attributed the following remark to 'an important Turk', but it was clear that these
were his own views: 'Today, the greatest man in the world, much greater than
Hitler or Churchill or Mussolini, would be the one who had enough moral
influence to bring governments to consider concrete peace proposals' (*Ibid.*, p.
380). But there was only one candidate for this historic role: Pope Pius XII.

Roncalli's report remains as detached as usual. But it would be surprising if he
did not feel a certain *frisson* of excitement. For here was a German Lutheran
proposing papal mediation to end the war. What Benedict XV had been rebuffed
for attempting in August 1917 was now being offered to his successor. Moreover,
to demonstrate his sincerity, von Lersner casually revealed details of German plans

for the Balkans. The next month, March, German troops 'peacefully' entered
Bulgaria and in April twenty-one divisions fell upon Yugoslavia and Greece, to
help out the Italians who were being held. This was impressive, but it was not
impressive enough. It was known in the Secretariat of State that the allies would
not depart from their policy of 'unconditional surrender', and that the language of
'peace' was regarded as treasonable in Nazi Germany. So nothing could be done.

There was a division of opinion within the Secretariat of State. Tardini
continued to denounce 'unconditional surrender' as barbarous and iniquitous.
Montini, on the other hand, had a better understanding of why it was insisted
upon. That Roncalli was aware of this difference in broad terms is shown by the
fact that he wrote a *private* letter to Montini recommending von Lersner to him.
Von Lersner was due in Rome with his Protestant wife. Roncalli wrote: 'Is he
obeying someone else's orders? Is he the victim of an illusion? I don't
know . . . He loves his country; but he deplores the modern anti-Christian
theories; he doesn't belong to the party; he has links with army officers' (*Saggio*, p.
32. Letter dated April 23, 1942). Presumably Roncalli wrote – unusually – to
Montini because he had already had enough abuse from Tardini about his naïveté.
He was prepared to be naïve for peace.

But what he did not know was that Montini had already concluded that the
insistance on 'unconditional surrender' meant that Italy could only achieve a
separate peace by switching sides. Italy's only alternative to continuing the war on
the German side was to dump Mussolini, abandon the Axis, and wager on an
Allied victory (see *La Repubblica*, September 7, 1983: interview with ex-Queen
Maria José of Savoy). This was also the view of Alcide De Gasperi, who was
immured in the Vatican. But since such a scheme was perilous, treacherous even,
it is unlikely that anyone would risk talking about it to a Vatican diplomat in such
a nest of spies as Istanbul. In any event, Roncalli was completely taken by surprise
when it actually happened.

He was also taken by surprise by the German attack on Russia on June 22,
1941. Only three days earlier he reported that Germany had signed a non-
aggression pact with Turkey. Roncalli saw it merely as a feather in von Papen's
cap and not as a necessary securing of the right flank before the attack on Russia:
'In my previous reports I hinted at the possibility of such a surprise. It crowns the
tenacious and fortunate endeavours of von Papen . . . It is a step towards peace,
and it demanded an act of courage on the part of Turkey in view of its commit-
ments to Great Britain' (*Actes et documents*, 4, p. 560). Roncalli shared in von
Papen's success with some enthusiasm. The same day – June 19, 1940 – he wrote
to his sisters: 'Here we are still out of the war: this very day a treaty was signed
between Germany and Turkey who will not grab each other by the throat. What
more can one ask? I believe that Italy will now do the same. Now try to say that
your brother was not a prophet!' (*Familiari*, I, p. 543). But his prophetic gifts

were strictly limited. Not only had he failed to foresee the long-planned Operation Barbarossa, but on the word of von Papen had frequently informed the Vatican that the relationship between Germany and Russia was in good shape.

Von Papen and von Lersner flattered Roncalli by taking him into their confidence. But they did not tell him everything. The weakness of his one-sided reliance on German sources became apparent. The British, for example, did not take the Non-aggression Pact between Germany and Turkey too tragically. They realised that the Turks had to place their own national interest first, and that meant playing for time. It was not that Roncalli got on badly with the British ambassador, Sir Hughe Knatchbull-Hugessen (later to be notorious as the victim of the Albanian spy known as 'Cicero'). It was simply that when they met, they met for tea. They never discussed strategic or political matters; their talk was confined to technical questions about – for example – the transmission of Vatican correspondence, aid for starving Greece or Italian refugees in the Middle East. Unlike von Papen, Sir Hughe did not think it was any part of his mission to win over the apostolic delegate to his country's cause (Righi, pp. 202–3).

It would have required superhuman powers of detachment – or consummate acting skill – to hide all signs of partisanship in such a complicated situation. In a report to the Vatican Roncalli claimed to be on good terms with all the belligerents by being *nec procul, nec prope* (neither too distant nor too close). He said nothing about his relations with von Papen, but admitted being close to the Italian Embassy. The reasons for this were 'well understood, and do not deprive me of my freedom to express my mind and that of the Holy See with frankness on topical problems in the light of the Gospel' (*Actes et documents*, 5, pp. 463–4). Privately he thought that he could steer even-handedly through his divided community by displaying what he calls 'the gravity and loveable dignity of the elderly prelate who diffuses an air of nobility, wisdom and grace' (*Journal*, p. 255). Faced with internecine quarrels between French Gaullists and Pétainists, he again adopts the grand patriarchal matter: 'I read in the Old Testament that Jacob also had sons who disagreed among themselves. But he, the father, *rem tacitus considerabat* – pondered the matter in silence' (Trevor, p. 186). It was a text he would make use of as Pope, by which time he was old enough to play the patriarchal role more successfully.

Just when he thought he had found a method for dealing with the problems of Istanbul, he was ordered to Greece. This time he was told to stay as long as was necessary finally to resolve the question of Vatican diplomatic representation. In seven years he had got nowhere. It was ironical and galling that German and Italian military occupation, combined with Greek desperation, were needed to make a solution look possible. His dependence on the Germans was such that he needed a visa from von Papen to travel to Greece, and used German air transport for most of the journey. Greece was in chaos. He was told he would have to go via

Sofia. This raised questions of protocol, since he could not pass through Sofia unnoticed. The Secretariat of State ordered him to 'make contacts' in agreement
with Mgr Giuseppe Mazzoli who had succeeded him as apostolic delegate in
Bulgaria. So what had been a mere stop-over became an important diplomatic
mission. He met King Boris, Queen Giovanna, leading politicians, and the
Orthodox metropolitan, Stefan. These were all old acquaintances. His patient
work during ten years in Bulgaria now paid off.

King Boris revealed that the Russians had been putting pressure on him to
attack Turkey, the traditional Bulgarian enemy. He resisted their blandishments
and threats. This inevitably brought him closer to the Germans. But Boris would
say very little about the Germans. He preferred to steer the conversation towards
Italy, 'in which he has complete confidence', and to reminisce about King Victor
Emmanuel III, his father-in-law. Boris claimed that the Lateran Pacts had made
the royal family better disposed towards the Church. Though Victor Emmanuel
was prone to 'Voltairean gibes' at the Church's expense, he was slowly changing
in old age. When Boris told him that last time he was in Rome he had gone
incognito into St Peter's, said his prayers at various altars and kissed the foot of St
Peter's statue, Victor Emmanuel said: '*Bravo*, you did well' (*Actes et documents*, 5,
pp. 91 and following).

King Boris then talked about 'the Serbian disaster', meaning the collapse of the
Yugoslav government. He attributed it to 'the bankruptcy of the alliance between
Balkan Orthodoxy and Freemasonry'. He recounted the story of the Serbian
Orthodox patriarch, Gavrilo Dozić, who had allegedly fled to some rocky
mountain refuge 'with a stock of ham to keep him from hunger and a vast
collection of records, especially those of Josephine Baker, the famous black dancer,
to keep him from melancholy'. But this tale of the pusillanimous patriarch was a
calumny, a product of the German propaganda machine. The truth was that
Patriarch Gavrilo was arrested in a monastery, brutally beaten up, and eventually
sent to Dachau for refusing to collaborate with the Nazis (Alexander, pp. 10–11).
That Roncalli should have repeated the calumny without raising any critical
questions about it is scandalous. Contained in an official report, it would have re-
inforced the Vatican prejudice against the Serbian Orthodox.

King Boris, however, drew from the episode the conclusion that the Bulgarian
Orthodox Church would have to revise its alliances after the war. As a result,
Catholic–Orthodox relations would be better. Roncalli saw an opening here, and
ventured a personal touch:

> With a smile I suggested that we live in an era of undreamt of surprises and
> historic changes, and that one shouldn't be surprised if, one day, a pope of
> Rome restored to the King of Bulgaria one of the ancient crowns given to
> his predecessors (*Ibid.*).

Boris modestly replied that he was unworthy of so great an honour. By the time Roncalli became pope, it was too late for such gestures: Boris and the monarchy had been swept aside.

The most astonishing feature of this interview was the way King Boris asked the papal diplomat to help him deal with the anglophile leanings of the Orthodox metropolitan, Stefan. Boris was very indiscreet. 'I wanted to save him', said the King, 'and now he has started making pro-monarchist speeches that I find rather amusing. All things considered, *monsignore*, do try and see him'. Roncalli sought out the metropolitan and reported to Rome on his meeting:

> He showed himself still somewhat under the spell of the Anglo-American organisations which on the pretext of charity [*sotto il velo di beneficenza*] pursue the illusion of world peace through the union of Christians. He recalled a conversation with Pacelli in Berlin and still appreciated his charm. He accepted with good grace my suggestion that the Orthodox should try not to have polemics on every page of their newspapers (*Ibid.*).

This embarrassing text was not published until 1969. It shows that, at sixty, Roncalli still had a lot to learn about ecumenism.

He was on surer ground when he urged the Vatican to support Bulgaria's border claim against Yugoslavia. The Bulgarians wanted Ochrida, site of the monasteries of Sts Clement and Naoum, disciples of St Cyril and Methodius. 'Poor as they are', King Boris explained, 'they represent the Jerusalem of the Bulgarian nation'. Roncalli comments: 'It is the highest wisdom not to upset or offend against the psychological characteristics of different peoples'. The truth was that Bulgaria, so far, had done rather well out of the war: Romania had ceded to it Southern Dobrouja, and after the German occupation of Yugoslavia and Greece just three months earlier – in April, 1941 – Bulgaria gained Western Thrace and Southern Macedonia from Greece and seized Northern Macedonia from Yugoslavia. All Bulgaria's gains depended on its alliance with Germany and the acceptance of Hitler's 'New Order'. The *Blitzkrieg* or 'lightning war' against Russia was going well. Minsk fell on June 28, 1941. By July 9 the northern armies were hurtling towards Leningrad. But the prospect of victory and permanence did not make the 'New Order' any more morally acceptable.

Sofia, however, was a tranquil interlude. Roncalli's work was now in devastated Greece. Travel by road was difficult: so many bridges had been blown up in a desperate attempt to slow down the German advance. So whenever possible, Roncalli travelled by air, keeping the statistics of his flights with all the gratitude of the survivor. In 1941 he was on eight flights, bringing his total up to fifteen. In Greece he found hunger as well as destruction. The spring crops had not been planted, and the British had imposed a food blockade. Roncalli summarised his impressions in an early report to the Vatican:

Athens, which I am visiting for the seventeenth time, looks completely
different. The signs of foreign domination are everywhere: from the
Acropolis and from the best-known monuments flutter reminders of defeat
and national humiliation. On the broad sunlit streets is the usual vigorous
and colourful Athenian crowd. But if you look closely at them, they seem
like people returning from the cemetery after a funeral, and they know they
are going back to a house of desolation where new sorrows await
them . . . At Salonika they are still not too badly off compared with Athens;
and it also seems that life is tolerable in the country and on the islands. But
here we are in a situation where *parvuli petunt panem*, children beg for bread,
and there is not enough bread. Strict rationing has been imposed on the city,
quite inadequate for the ordinary nutrition of a young person, a robust man
or a mother with children (*Actes et documents*, 5, pp. 99–100).

Roncalli's sympathy with the defeated Greeks comes through very clearly in this
passage; and he soon translated it into practical help. But his very presence was
ambivalent and his status uncertain. He was the unrecognised papal representative, and yet he was in Greece only by favour of the Germans and the Italians.
One of his first acts was to call on the Italian General Geloso and on the German
commander, Wilhelm von List. To the Greeks he must at first have appeared in-
distinguishable from the occupation establishment.

He reverted to being an Italian, especially when he discovered that there were
Bergamesque troops in Athens. On July 28, 1941, he wrote home: 'There are
many good soldiers here from Bergamo. Their chaplains speak highly of them.
They are part of the occupying forces, and naturally prefer that to being at the
front. But they are good soldiers who have already been at the front and won
honour for themselves' (*Familiari*, I, p. 546). One senses a certain embarrassment
here. It is not clear on what front the Bergamesque troops had won honour: the
Italians had been pushed back by the Greeks who only succumbed when the better
equipped and more determined Germans arrived; and a preference for belonging
to an occupying force does not indicate a high level of heroism or military
ambition. In another letter Roncalli claimed that the many Italian troops and
officials he met in Athens 'are very good and kind, and make our dear country
loved where before there was so much anger against us' (*Familiari*, I, pp. 549–50).
The judgement may seem over-optimistic, complacent even: but an independent
witness speaks of 'the most compassionate military occupation that history
records' (Levi, p. 217).

To adjust the balance, Roncalli also visited the German wounded and the
British prisoners of war. But the hungry, defeated Greeks were his main concern.
He explained how he saw his role in a despatch to the Vatican dated August 4,
1941. He wanted to emulate 'one of those ancient bishops who earned the title of

consules Dei, 'God's Consuls'. This was the expression he had used on the day Italy entered the war. Now he defined a 'God's Consul' as 'a bishop who has the holy freedom to present himself to the conqueror in the name of a spiritual authority, and in the name of the interests of the conquered people' (*Actes et documents*, 5, p. 125).

As autumn 1941 began to close in, Greece's most urgent need was for food. There was no lack of foreign assets and 360,000 tons of grain, already paid for, were awaiting shipment from Haifa in Palestine. But they needed an Allied safe-conduct which was not forthcoming. Someone was needed to persuade the British that their blockade was doing more harm to their allies, the Greek people, than to their enemies, the German and Italian occupying forces. On September 9, 1941, a group of Greek laymen approached Roncalli and asked him to get the Holy See to intervene. He was willing, but he did not want to offend the new metropolitan of Athens, Damaskinos George, who was acting as regent for the government-in-exile in London. Greek suspicions of the 'Italian' Vatican remained, and he could not simply go along and present himself to the metro-politan. Roncalli played his discouraging hand with great skill and tact.

His first move was to send along Mgr George Calavassy, the Greek Uniate bishop, to sound out Damaskinos. Despite their theological differences, they were both pastors who could be counted to put the interests of the Greek people first in its hour of desperate need. Calavassy was made welcome. He reported that Damaskinos was ready 'to turn over the page and believed that everyone, clergy and laity, should work together along the path of fraternal charity' (*Actes et documents*, 5, p. 129).

Thus encouraged, Roncalli met Metropolitan Damaskinos in conditions of some secrecy at the home of a Lipsia university professor, Georgakis, who also acted as interpreter, Damaskinos speaking no language other than Greek. Calavassy was also present. From an ecumenical point of view it was an historic encounter. Roncalli soon discovered that Damaskinos was a man of great passion who had vowed at his enthronement to make relieving the wretchedness of the Greek people his first concern. The German and Italian authorities had agreed to let the grain through. Damaskinos believed that there was 'no one better than the Holy Father to persuade the English and American governments to honour their obligations, for this work transcended the war and belonged to the most elementary manifestations of brotherhood between peoples' (*Actes et documents*, 5, pp. 212–13). They talked together for exactly two hours and towards the end evoked 'a new order of relationships and contacts between the Catholic and Orthodox clergy'. Roncalli ended his report: 'In short, we began with a handshake, but said farewell with a heart-felt embrace and with sincere joy in our hearts' (*Ibid.*).

Roncalli made a quick dash by air to Rome where he saw Maglione, Secretary

of State, on October 8 and Pius XII two days later. He was then able to spend a
few days at Camaitino – his only wartime visit – and had a second audience with
Pius on November 11, 1941. It would be comforting to report that the papal
intervention succeeded, and indeed one biographer assures us that it did: 'The plan
was put into action, the ships passed through, and the Greeks were saved from the
worst effects of the famine' (Trevor, p. 190). But Righi, who was closer to
events, says bluntly that the scheme failed (Righi, p. 210). What is true is that
Roncalli's Roman lobbying alerted the Vatican to the needs of Greece and that aid
was sent on a scale sufficient to make *some* difference. Condensed milk and
medicines, bought in Switzerland, were shipped directly to Piraeus; and sixteen
'Providence Centres' dispensed soup to all comers in Athens (Righi, p. 227). 'I
live in the exercise of charity', wrote Roncalli on February 19, 1942, 'charity for
all' (*Familiari*, I, p. 570).

But the needs outstripped the resources, and Roncalli was under no illusion
that the trickle of Vatican aid could 'solve' the problem of famine in Greece. Back
in Istanbul for the Feast of St John Chrysostom, he wrote home on January 15,
1942:

> Ah! Greece is a place of desolation. I told you something about it when I
> was home. Since then the situation has become and is becoming more
> serious than ever. Pray to the Lord and get the children to pray that you
> may be spared such post-war horrors. War is nasty and the plague is nasty;
> but famine is something even more horrible to live through. I repeat what I
> already said to our young people: you have to get used to mortifications and
> to pray for the many old people, children and the sick who simply die of
> exhaustion. I foresee an even sadder spring for this poor people that has
> suffered for so long, and is now so humiliated and distressed. I organised
> some relief work with Mgr Giacomo Testa. The Holy Father sent me half a
> million *lire* to begin with. But what's needed here is the gift of miracles
> (*Familiari*, I, p. 568).

He did not possess the gift of miracles. But at least he had Mgr Giacomo Testa, his
fellow Bergamesque, whom he could trust to look after the relief work.

Roncalli, meanwhile, had to return to Ankara for his spring round of diplomatic visits. His other important engagement was on May 17, 1942, Whitsunday.
He always liked to celebrate Pentecost in his cathedral, dedicated to the Holy
Spirit; there was pomp and clouds of incense and afterwards forty guests were
entertained to lunch at the Delegation. On this Whitsunday the theme if his
homily was the way the Holy Spirit gives life to the Church. His long stay in the
East made his thinking more Spirit-centred than was customary in Roman
manual-theology.

The Spirit first of all animates the *whole* Church: 'The Spirit is poured out on the whole Church – and even the simplest faithful and the humblest souls share in the Spirit, sometimes super-abundantly and to the point of heroism and holiness' (Righi, p. 255). Against this background Roncalli sets the figure of the bishop, whom he describes in language borrowed from St Paul at Ephesus: 'You who have been established as pastors to feed the flock of Christ' (Acts, 20.28). Paul, he pointed out, had summoned the bishops of Asia Minor to Ephesus; and these very local references bring to life what was later known as 'collegiality'; Ephesus was after all not so very far from Constantinople. He has a very 'high' but at the same time scripturally-based view of the episcopal office, and conjures up the long line of bishops throughout the centuries:

> Men of God and men of the people, always teaching, ruling, blessing, sanctifying, consecrating; witnesses and creators of that *perennial youthfulness* of the One, Holy, Catholic and Apostolic Church which does not fear perils and contradictions, which *does not forget its own past, because it knows how to find in the past the certainty of mastering the future* – in the Holy Spirit, who is 'Lord and Giver of life' (Righi, p. 255; italics added).

This is what Roncalli meant by his 'philosophy of history'. It involved the paradox of saying that the Church must go back in order to go forwards, that it is new because it is ancient, youthful because it is old. Tradition is not the dead hand of the past weighing down on the present; it is the guarantee of continuity in a living organism, made young by the abiding and dynamic presence of the Holy Spirit. All these ideas would find their fulfilment in his pontificate.

But on Pentecost Sunday, 1942, he had the duty of celebrating the twenty-fifth anniversary of the episcopal ordination of Eugenio Pacelli, Pope Pius XII, then uneasily reigning. It was an anniversary that no papal diplomat could possibly miss. Roncalli reminded his congregation that Pacelli had been ordained bishop in 1917, at the very time when the three peasant children at Fatima had their first vision of Our Lady. But that was not really what he wanted to say. If the episcopacy must be seen aginst the background of the whole people of God, showered with the gifts of the Spirit, then the papacy itself must be seen against the background of the whole episcopal college. Only in this way would the papacy become intelligible to those Orthodox or Protestant Christians who rejected its claims as extravagant, unfounded or even blasphemous.

Roncalli went on: 'All the Apostles received an *equal mandate* from Jesus, but Jesus entrusted to Peter a pre-eminent place as pastor and father' (Righi, p. 255). Carefully avoiding any 'Vicar of Christ' terminology (a thirteenth-century innovation), he calls the pope repeatedly 'the Bishop of Rome' and speaks of his 'seat' (*sedes*) and 'chair' (*cathedra*) (See Tillard, p. 92 and following, for the importance of this usage). This was a return to an earlier tradition, *before* the division of East and West. It was another instance of going back in order to go forwards. Long before he became pope himself, he had already thought much about the office, and clarified his vision of an essentially *pastoral* papacy. He concluded his Pentecost sermon:

> Whatever concerns the Bishop of Rome makes the hearts of believers in Christ beat faster, wherever they may be, scattered throughout the world, without distinction of language or race or nationality: for he is the *sign of union* amid so many passions and conflicts of interest, and represents an *invitation* to order, gentleness and reconciliation (Righi, p. 255).

He was speaking, of course, of Pius XII, but it is legitimate to see the passage as prophetic. The papal ministry is for service, not power.

The same is true of the episcopal ministry. In July 1942, Roncalli was back in Greece to confirm those Italian soldiers who had somehow slipped through the parish net. There were moving incidents. Some of the troops disobeyed orders and shared their bread ration with Greek children who begged for it. Their only explanation – and it was enough – was 'We have little children of our own' (Righi, p. 229). Another time he visited the headquarters of the Italian Eighth Army and reviewed the troops in company with the General and his staff. A corporal broke ranks, approached Roncalli, knelt and kissed his ring. 'What is it, my son?' asked Roncalli. The corporal replied: '*Monsignore*, may I embrace you in the name of all of us?' He did so, to applause from the men (Righi, *Ibid*.). This very 'Italian' event on a remote hillside in a devastated country says as much about Roncalli as the most elaborate treatise on his idea of episcopacy. He managed to create an atmosphere in which such things could happen and seem natural.

But he also reflected on the episcopal office during his next retreat made at the Delegation October 25–31. This was partly because he turned the retreat into a collegial exercise – like St Paul at Ephesus – by inviting Kiredjian the archbishop of the Armenians, along with the ordinaries of the Greek, Melkite, Syrian and Bulgarian rites (*Journal*, p. 278). The French director of the retreat, Fr René Follet S.J., also prompted him to think about episcopacy by giving him St Isidore of Seville's portrait of St Fulgentius. This Latin text described a model bishop from the patristic era. Roncalli kept it beside him and read it often. In Paris in 1947 he calls it 'a wonderful passage' and applies it detail by detail to his work at the Nunciature (*Journal*, p. 290). It confirmed his move from a juridical towards a pastoral concept of the bishop.

According to Isidore, the bishop is above all a *teacher*, not an administrator, 'set in authority for the education and instruction of the people for their good'. His language should be 'pure, simple, open'. His primary duty is 'to read the sacred scriptures'. Then comes one of those carefully balanced antitheses which recall the Rule of St Benedict's treatment of the abbot's authority (Chapter 64): 'Every bishop should be distinguished as much by his humility as his authority, so that he

may neither cause the vices of his subordinates to flourish through his own
excessive humility, nor exercise his authority with excessive severity' (*Journal*, p.
281). This was not a merely theoretical question for Roncalli: how to combine a
sense of humility or truth before God with a non-authoritarian manner was
something he continued to ponder. He would be neither a doormat nor a tyrant.
But authority itself is set in the context of charity. Isidore says that 'charity excels
all other gifts, and without it all virtue is nothing'. It will be seen in the bishop's
'caring for the poor and clothing the naked', in short, in the 'corporal works of
mercy' that Roncalli had been engaged upon in Greece. He still had this ideal of a
bishop before his eyes when he became bishop of Rome.

The next problem he tried to face during his October 1942 retreat was even
more pressing and urgent. 'We are all more or less tainted with *nationalism*', he
concedes, adding: 'It is one thing to love Italy, as I most fervently do, and quite
another to display this affection in public' (*Journal*, p. 280). How was he to resolve
this problem, given that even God's consul could not pretend to be an abstract
man from nowhere? He gives it as his opinion that 'the Italian clergy, especially
the secular clergy, are less contaminated by nationalism than others', but he
provides no evidence for this judgement. (This does not mean that it was ill-
founded: one could argue, for example that the 'regional' or 'provincial' tradition
of Italy, combined with its late accession to nationhood, preserved it from the
arrogant and aggressive nationalism found elsewhere.) Roncalli's answer to
nationalism was to bind himself as closely as possible to the supranational Holy
See, whose representative he was. This gave him a practical guide to conduct:

> Holy Church, which I represent, is the mother of nations, of all nations.
> Everyone with whom I come into contact must admire in the Pope's repre-
> sentative that respect for the nationality of others, expressed with gracious-
> ness and mild judgements, which inspires universal trust. Great caution
> then, respectful silence, and courtesy all the time (*Journal*, p. 280).

Roncalli's behaviour reflected this counsel of perfection. In a fiercely partisan
world, some were irritated by the way he seemed to float above controversies and
abstain from moral judgements. Yet his readiness to talk with everyone was
impressive. It was so different from what was on offer elsewhere. It permitted
another way of looking at the terrible events that were being lived through.

Roncalli called this alternative way of looking at the world his 'philosophy of
history'. It was another task he assigned to the bishop. It was a development of his
Baronius lecture of 1907, but now the problem was much more harrowing and
the stakes were higher. 'Is it possible for God to act in human history?' could be
considered an academic – which is not to say unimportant – question in 1907. But
by 1942 the presence or absence of God had become a more demanding question
going to the very root of Christian faith. Was God silent in this terrifying

conflict? Was he indifferent to pain and injustice on this prodigious scale? Could they have any 'meaning'? Roncalli resolved to reread St Augustine's *City of God*, a work written at a time when civilisation seemed to be collapsing, 'and to draw from his doctrine the necessary material to form my own judgement' (*Journal*, p. 281). His provisional guess was that war, willed by men (as we have seen), is an evil that carries with it its own condemnation:

> We are living through great events, and chaos lies ahead. This makes it all the more necessary to return to those principles which are the foundation of the Christian social order, and to judge what is happening today in the light of what the Gospel teaches us, recognising in the terror and horror which engulf us the terrible sanctions that safeguard the divine law, even here on earth (*Journal*, *Ibid.*).

It was the line of reflection that lay behind *Pacem in Terris*. Its starting point was a sentence from the *City of God*: 'Peace is tranquillity in the order of all things, ordered obedience in fidelity to the eternal law'. War was 'unnatural' in the strict Thomist sense of 'not according to reason'. It was *alienum a ratione*, a madness.

In late 1942, the madness reigned unchecked and Roncalli, in his role as God's consul, had the experience of failure. In December he made repeated appeals to Field Marshal Wilhelm von List, the German commander in Greece, to spare the lives of a group of Greek partisans. But the orders could not be changed. The executions went ahead as planned.

Though no one knew it, the turning-point of the war had been reached. Early in 1943 the Germans, surrounded at Stalingrad, suffered their first serious defeat — cynically sacrificing the Italian expeditionary force. By the end of February German and Italian resistance in North Africa was practically over. The number of prisoners held by either side was now about the same. Tracing prisoners of war became Roncalli's main work during this period. Along with the Red Cross, the Vatican acted as a clearing house for information about prisoners of war on all sides. The Russians, however, did not join in this scheme, for the chilling reason given by Ernst von Weizsäcker, German Ambassador to the Holy See: 'The Soviet regime is not interested in the fate of its own prisoners of war because it considers them traitors' (*Actes et documents*, 9, p. 238). So one could not bargain information about them in exchange for news of the German and Italian prisoners in Russia. But Roncalli was ordered by Tardini to do what he could on March 18, 1943. He thought that if anyone could pull it off, it would be Roncalli. Tardini minuted: 'He's a peaceable man, and has good relationships with the diplomats including the Russians' (*Actes et documents*, 9, p. 190). So Tardini's judgement about his naïveté did not exclude the recognition of other qualities.

It was Roncalli's first formal contact with the Russians. He set about his work with a proper regard for diplomatic *nuances*. Rather than risk a rebuff by going to

the top and speaking with the ambassador in Ankara, he preferred to start with
the consul general in Istanbul, Nicholas Ivanov. They had a fascinating discussion
on the Soviet Union's attitude to religion. Ivanov claimed to be interested in
religion as a cultural reality. Roncalli reported to the Secretariat of State:

> He explained the position of the Russian government at the present time.
> Unlike the Catholic Church, the Russian Orthodox Church never existed as
> a society independent of the civil authority. When under the Czars it
> showed a desire for independence, it was crushed by the state. At the time
> of the Bolshevik Revolution the Church represented conservatism and
> reaction to the new ideas. Hence the violent persecution. Now a number of
> years have passed by; the new political system has taken root; the Orthodox
> Church no longer arouses fear; so a way is being sought to adapt it while
> respecting liberty of conscience (*Actes et documents*, 9, p. 236).

Of course Roncalli knew that the more lenient treatment of the Russian
Orthodox Church was born of a desire to unite the nation and stiffen morale in
what the Russians called 'the Great Patriotic War'. In this same year the Moscow
Patriarchate was restored and transferred from a log-cabin in an unpaved street to
the former German Embassy. But sometimes people are actually convinced by
their own propaganda. Roncalli was alert to this possibility, and did not forget his
conversation with Ivanov. He had met a Russian diplomat who did not sport
horns and a tail.

But on the substantive issue of the prisoners of war held in the Soviet Union,
Roncalli got nowhere, either with Ivanov or the ambassador. He surmised,
correctly, that they were acting under orders from Moscow. A note of disappointment, almost of despair, creeps into his report to the Vatican: 'I will continue to
keep you informed, though I feel a wrench in my heart at the gloomy prospect of
persistent refusal by the Russians, unless the Lord, having listened to so many
prayers, grants a miracle' (*Actes et documents*, 9, p. 238). He was now working
closely with Raymond Courvoisier, director of the Red Cross in Ankara, who
was able to confirm Moscow's unremitting hostility. So there was nothing he
could do. He had spent three months banging his head against a diplomatic brick
wall. For the first time he complained to the Secretariat of State:

> Requests come flooding in to the Delegation from parents who imagine
> that we are somehow in communication with Russia. We are already over-
> loaded with work, and to answer every request is an additional burden.
> Perhaps it would be better to publish the true state of affairs in the press. In
> this way fruitless anxieties would be avoided (*Actes et documents*, 9, p. 309).

He asked permission to forward such requests to the Red Cross in Geneva.
    There was no happy outcome to this story, but there was an ironical postcript.

In August 1943 thousands of cards arrived in Turkey allegedly from prisoners in Russia. Roncalli suspected a propaganda trick:

> Are these cards genuine? Why do they come from some camps and not from others? Can one hope for a regular exchange of information? What is one to think of the special conditions of the Italian and Romanian prisoners who are supposed to be amazed at their good treatment? I don't know what the answers are (*Actes et documents*, 9, p. 391).

Nor do we, even with benefit of hindsight. He was right to suspect that the witness of Italian and Romanian treatment to their favourable treatment had something to do with the attempt to get their countries to switch sides. Roncalli was learning. In this matter he was neither duped nor naïve.

But it was another failure on the part of God's consul to modify the harshness of war. Still, he learned to talk to Russians, and found some of them personally sympathetic even if officially unhelpful. And he had learned to collaborate with another international organisation, the Red Cross, which some in the Vatican regarded as 'too humanitarian' and a rival. Roncalli never saw it that way.

He needed Raymond Courvoisier and the Red Cross (known as the Red Crescent in Turkey so as not to upset Islamic susceptibilities) in the other task which now engrossed him: aiding Jews. Von Papen, speaking on oath to the postulator of Pope John's beatification cause, claimed that he 'helped 24,000 Jews with clothes, money and documents' (see Zizola, in *Oggi*, April 13, 1963). It is difficult to translate charity into statistics. It would be better in this context to follow the Talmudic verse which says, 'He who saves a single life, saves the world entire' (Keneally, p. 371). Roncalli had been made aware of the problem at a relatively early stage of the war, through refugees from Poland. The fate of the *Struma* continued to haunt him. The *Struma* left the Rumanian port of Constanza in December 1941 carrying a human cargo of 769 Jewish refugees. It was mysteriously blown up by a mine, and there was only one survivor, Zelia Stolaric. In 1943 Mother Marie Casilda, a Sister of Our Lady of Sion, wrote to Roncalli from Bucharest about the fate of the *Struma*. She refused to believe that the Turks had simply blown the ship up. She imagined it must have been a legal cover-story to mask the rescue of the Jews who were now safe in some secret camp. Roncalli let her down gently. Her version of the story was wishful thinking. But, 'We are dealing with one of the great mysteries in the history of humanity. Poor children of Israel. Daily I hear their groans around me. They are relatives and fellow-countrymen of Jesus. May the Divine Saviour come to their aid and enlighten them' (*Actes et documents*, 9, p. 310: Letter dated April 14, 1943). To describe the holocaust as a 'mystery' is the right place to begin thinking about this ultimate in horror: it belongs to the mystery of iniquity.

Istanbul played a key-role. Turkey was still neutral, and the last escape-route out of Nazi-occupied Europe led through the Balkans and via Istanbul. It also led to Palestine, then under British mandate. But the British argument against accepting more than a limited number of refugees in Palestine was that 'there might be spies among them', and that Jewish expansion ought to depend upon Arab consent that was unlikely to be forthcoming (see Wasserstein, Bernard, *Britain and the Jews of Europe, 1939–1945*). Istanbul was at the cross-roads of information if not of immigration. Roncalli was better informed than his superiors in the Vatican. The Jewish organisation had offices in Istanbul and was desperate for help. Chaim Barlas of the Jerusalem Jewish Agency met him on January 22, 1943. It was the first of many meetings that culminated a year later in a visit from the Grand Rabbi of Jerusalem, Isaac Herzog.

Roncalli, however, did not have much freedom of action. Most of the time he was merely the link-man who forwarded requests to the Vatican. In January 1943 Chaim Barlas asked him to transmit three very modest but basic requests. Would the Vatican sound out neutrals like Portugal and Sweden to see if they would grant temporary asylum to Jews who managed to escape? This would involve no financial liability. American Jewry would look after them. Second, would the Vatican inform the German government that the Palestine Jewish Agency had 5000 immigration certificates available? Finally Barlas wanted Vatican Radio to declare loud and clear that 'rendering help to persecuted Jews is considered by the Church to be a good deed' (*Actes et documents*, 9, pp. 87–8). That such a statement was thought necessary was a measure of how deep the roots of Christian anti-Semitism were. Though Roncalli's task here was simply to transmit, not to explain or justify, there is no reason to believe that he regarded these requests as anything other than reasonable and fulfillable.

The Vatican thought otherwise. Its reply came in the form of a letter from the Secretary of State, Cardinal Maglione, to Fr Arthur Hughes, now *chargé d'affaires* in Cairo, Egypt. Hughes, a British priest, had replaced an Italian suspected of spying. Hughes worked closely with Roncalli. They conferred in Istanbul on January 12, 1943. Maglione's answer was disappointing, pompous and disconcerting. The Holy See had helped Jewish emigration in the past by taking soundings and providing subsidies, but 'unfortunately this help has increasingly encountered no slight difficulties which, for the time being, are insurmountable'. Since no 'subsidies' had been requested, it was impossible to understand why 'taking soundings' should run into such insurmountable difficulties. Maglione said nothing about what Vatican Radio might do, and was distinctly cool about 'the transfer of Jews to Palestine, because one cannot prescind from the strict connection between this problem and that of the Holy Places, for whose liberty the Holy See is deeply concerned' (*Actes et documents*, 9, p. 137).

Hughes was told to keep this last remark confidential. Wisely. There would have been a scandal if it had got out that the Vatican was opposing the return of

Jews to Palestine out of a concern for the 'Holy Places'. Maglione's words were worse than any of Pius XII's 'silences'. Yet they represented the firm and considered position of the Vatican. On May 4, 1943, Maglione wrote to Mgr William Godfrey, apostolic delegate in London, to say that 'the religious feelings of Catholics throughout the world would be offended and they would fear for their rights if ever Palestine came to belong exclusively to the Jews' (*Actes et documents*, 9, p. 272). What made Maglione's remarks even more inept was that the very next day the Secretariat of State received a report from Poland which said that while the pre-war Jewish population of Poland had been four million and a half, there now remained only about 100,000 Jews, 'including those brought from elsewhere'. There was a hint about how this remarkable population decline had been achieved: 'It is said that hundreds of people are sometimes locked up in lorries where they die under the effects of gas' (*Ibid.*, 9, p. 274). This was out of date. The technology of death was being improved all the time. Meanwhile the 'Holy Places' were being kept safe for Christian pilgrims.

Roncalli was not a party to such callous indifference. He did what he could. He managed to give some practical help to the Jews of Slovakia. Capovilla sums it up: 'Through his intervention, and with the help of King Boris of Bulgaria, thousands of Jews from Slovakia who had first been sent to Hungary and then to Bulgaria and who were in danger of being sent to concentration camps, obtained transit visas for Palestine, signed by him' (*Cronologia*, p. 578). That he did succeed, and rapidly, in this affair is proved by the fact that on May 22, 1943, Chaim Barlas thanked Roncalli for his intervention (*Actes et documents*, 9, p. 307). No doubt this is where most of the 24,000 came from. And he must have had at least the connivance of von Papen.

Two months later, Roncalli tried to use the same channels again. He wrote to King Boris on June 30, 1943, in an ambiguous style designed to flatter his prejudices and yet lure him into compassionate action:

> I know that it is only too true – according to what I read coming out of Bulgaria – that some of the sons of Judah are not without reproach. But alongside the guilty, there are also many that are innocent; and there are many cases where some sign of clemency, over and above the great honour it would bring to a Christian sovereign, would be a pledge of blessings in time of trial (*Actes et documents*, 9, p. 371).

Boris replied that he would do his best, but pointed out that his own position was threatened. Roncalli annotated his reply: 'The King says that to deal with individual cases arouses the jealousy of others. But he has done so in the past, he really has' (*Ibid.*). This letter to Roncalli was almost King Boris' last free act. On August 28, 1943, he died mysteriously during a return flight from Germany after seeing Hitler. It was assumed that he was killed as an unreliable ally. His six-year old son, Simeon, succeeded him. With Boris's death went Roncalli's last slim chance of influencing events in the Balkans.

In the midst of these dramatic events, on July 26, 1943, Roncalli acquired a new Secretary. The pint-sized Mgr Righi departed to be replaced by the giant (or so he seemed) Irishman, 30 year old Mgr Thomas Ryan. 'He comes from good farming stock like ourselves', Roncalli told his family, 'and he speaks Italian just like us' (*Familiari*, I, pp. 629–30). The Secretariat of State may have believed that Ryan, as an Irishman, ought to get on better with the Allies. However that may have been, he spoke English and began to teach Roncalli the rudiments of the language. It was now evident that the United States was the dominant partner in the anti-Nazi alliance. A sign of this was the two-way visit to Istanbul, May 14–16, 1943, of Francis Spellman, archbishop of New York and chaplain general to the U.S. army. Spellman who had worked in the Secretariat of State in the 1930s, was an old friend. He had kept Roncalli supplied with Mass stipends throughout the depression years (see *Familiari*, I, p. 246, where one reads of cheques deposited in the National Bank, Whitman, Mass.). His visit intrigued the press and had reporters crowding to the Delegation. No one believed that Spellman was in Turkey merely to see the spring flowers. On May 18, 1943, President Ismet Inönü received him, which suggested that he had some diplomatic or political role. But the signs remained ambivalent. The presidential visit – the first time since the collapse of the Ottoman Empire that a Turkish President had welcomed a Catholic prelate – had been set up by the U.S. Ambassador, Steinhart, which meant that Spellman was being honoured as an American rather than as an archbishop. But on the other hand he pleased Roncalli by staying at the Delegation, and so 'heightened the prestige of the Holy See'. That is from Roncalli's report to the Vatican. It throws no light on any covert motive for the visit, and attributes the 'fantastic press speculations' to 'the impatient aspiration for peace'. In Turkey, he explained, there were only two topics of conversation: the Russian threat, and the prospects for peace (*Actes et documents*, 7, p. 353). Spellman gave what he called a 'press conference' in which he was tantalisingly silent on both questions. He preached, first in Italian, then in English, in the cathedral of the Holy Spirit and then departed to Baghdad accompanied by more press speculation.

Throughout this time there were dramatic events in Italy, as the scenario envisaged by De Gasperi and Montini came to pass. Roncalli followed the news with anxiety and attention. The war in North Africa was over by May 13, 1943. 'Everyone knew' that the invasion of Italy was next on the Allied agenda. It duly came. On the night of July 9–10 the Allies landed in Sicily and met with little resistance, some Italian regiments joyfully surrendering while others simply melted away. It was the end of the road for Mussolini. He was arrested, having forgotten to shave. It was July 25, 1943. 'By midnight, the news had spread through Rome and the whole complex fabric of fascism, which people had taken to be so strong and durable, disintegrated in minutes' (Mack Smith, p. 347). There began the curious inter-regnum of the aged Marshal Badoglio who was under the spell of King Victor Emmanuel. Although Badoglio introduced himself to the nation on this same July 25 with the inauspicious slogan, 'The war goes on' (*La Guerra continua*) he soon began to negotiate with the Americans through neutral Lisbon while swearing to the Germans that he was doing nothing of the kind. It could not last.

On September 8, feast of the Birthday of Our Lady, Italy signed the armistice which took it out of the war. Confusion reigned. As King Victor Emmanuel fled to Switzerland with as much loot as he could carry, a Committee of National Liberation was founded. It was an alliance of Communists, Christian Democrats (including many of Montini's former students), Liberals and Socialists. Its aim was to oppose the Nazis who overnight had become the occupiers instead of the allies of Italy. There was an hiatus of power. The Germans swiftly poured in eight divisions to hold the line in the south. The Badoglio government played for time, and then submitted to the inevitable. Italy declared war on Germany on October 13, 1943.

This was a startling reversal. What did they think of it in Sotto il Monte? Where did true patriotism lie? Where was duty now? Roncalli shed no tears over Mussolini and had no problems in accepting the Badoglio government. He happened to know the new foreign minister, Raffaele Guariglia, who had been ambassador in Turkey. Indeed, Roncalli had a last conversation with him in August 1944 shortly before he left for Rome. 'His presence in the government', Roncalli told his brother Giovanni, 'inspires great confidence in me', and he went on:

> I follow Italian events from here. You know my attitude, and you can imagine what I am thinking. In all human persons and institutions, there is a mixture of the good and the bad, the high and the low. If there was error in the past, now is the time of expiation. One has to try to take everything with gentleness of judgement and language. Anyone can make a mistake in the choice of means towards an end in itself the best and most elevated. Sometimes the outcome of a war depends upon the smallest thing: a lemon skin can make a giant slip. The fact that Italy could pass without disturbance in a couple of days from one political constitution to another, means that common sense and dignity count for more than the mere victory of brutal or overwhelming power. So there's no need to speak about anyone with bitterness (*Familiari*, I, pp. 627–8: letter dated August 4, 1943).

So 'common sense and dignity' were the true victors. It is understandable that Roncalli should want to avoid the bitterness and desire for revenge that are inseparable from switching sides. He sensed, correctly, that there was going to be an undeclared civil war in Italy. In his next letter to his 'apolitical' sisters on August 23, 1943, he is even more 'abstentionist' or 'agnostic':

> The important thing is that we should all behave well, according to the maxims that I have so often repeated: don't talk too much, pray a great deal; look on the bright side (*cercare il lato meno triste*); in everything follow the decisions of the government and concentrate on one's own affairs, while having a sense of sharing and solidarity for the good of Italy and the peace of the whole world. I feel confident that worse is not to come, especially for you who live in the country and are far away from the major lines of communication (*Familiari*, I, p. 630).

But both these letters were written before the armistice and Italy's declaration of war on Germany. By October 16, 1943, when the reversal of alliances was completed, he has little to say to his family except that they should keep their heads down:

> I have no need to repeat the advice I gave you already about the events that have convulsed the life of our dear country. There is no need to comment on them: now the war, a great punishment of the Lord, has been brought down on the heads of Italians. This is not the moment to be apportioning blame. We have to suffer, be silent, and do our own duty in the painful circumstances of the present. But above all and always we should remain at the disposition of the duly constituted government, and behave like ants who continue to work away even when the temporal order is about to burst into flames. Each one of us should be intent on the duties of his own household or milieu, letting the soldier be a soldier, and leaving politics to those who want to be politicians; your business is to pray, suffer, obey, and be silent, silent, silent. This sacrifice will bring down on you a blessing in time (*Familiari*, I, pp. 633–4).

These were early days, but one cannot say that Roncalli's imagination was fired by the prospect of the Italian resistance movement. He did not see it as a second *Risorgimento*, in which Italians could purge their guilt and contribute towards their own liberation. 'Letting the soldier be a soldier and the politician a politician' was a prudent, unheroic recipe for a quiet life.

But Roncalli's refusal of partisanship can be read more positively as a commitment to peace. He genuinely believed that there would have to be reconciliation in the end. So on October 16, three days after Italy's declaration of war on Germany, he goes out of his way to remark that 'my relations with the Germans, in Greece and in Turkey, were always good and remain good now' (*Familiari*, I, p. 633). His sense of 'the mixture of the good and the bad' in all human persons and institutions preserved him from the kind of 'manichaeism' which sees in opponents the personification of the devil. Von Papen remarked that even when Roncalli 'could see no alternative to a German defeat' he nevertheless 'forwarded to the Vatican my pleas that the Allies should recognise the difference between the Hitler régime and the German people' (*Memoirs*, London, 1952). The other side of the coin was that on November 25, 1943, he sent a nephew a photograph of himself with Archbishop Spellman, adding the note: 'You see how the Holy Catholic Church brings together as brothers the sons of the most distant regions, and so prefigures the great peace that we await' (*Familiari*, I, p. 637).

But there was still a bitter struggle before that goal was realised. The immediate consequence of Italy switching sides was that the country including Rome became in effect German-occupied. It was urgent therefore to get the remaining Italian Jews out of the country as soon as possible. Many were put on ships heading for Palestine. Roncalli *protested* to Cardinal Maglione, not at the fact that they were helped to escape, but at their destination. Since this was the only instance of Roncalli questioning the wisdom of a Vatican decision, his feelings must have been very strong. On September 4, 1943, he wrote to the Cardinal Secretary of State:

> I confess that this convoy of Jews to Palestine, aided specifically by the Holy See, looks like the reconstruction of the Hebrew Kingdom, and so arouses certain doubts in my mind . . . That their fellow Jews and political friends should want them to go there makes perfect sense. But it does not seem to me that the simple and elevated charity of the Holy See should lend itself to the suspicion that by this co-operation, at least an initial and indirect contribution is being made to the realisation of the messianic dream.
> Perhaps this is no more than a personal scruple that only has to be admitted to be dissolved, so clear it is that the reconstruction of the Kingdom of Judaea and Israel is no more than a utopia (*Actes et documents*, 9, p. 469).

After this outburst, Roncalli never referred to the matter again. But his scruple was rather disconcerting. Before the state of Israel existed, it was easier to make a distinction between 'helping Jews' and 'helping Zionists' and to prefer the former activity. Roncalli did so for what at the time were considered valid theological reasons: since the true Messiah had already come, it was impossible to envisage the return of the people of Israel as a whole to their ancient homeland. Yet it was an insensitive argument because in 1943 the problem was to find any country at all that would take those who had escaped the extermination camps.

Roncalli's practice was better than his theology. He continued to help Jews on their way to Palestine. In February 1944 he had two meetings with Isaac Herzog, grand rabbi of Jerusalem, about the fate of the 55,000 Jews of Transnistria, a Rumanian-administered province made up of territories seized from the Soviet

Union in 1941. A bleak and inhospitable region, it became a kind of penal colony for deported Jews. As the German eastern front began to crumble, the Jews were shunted westwards towards the extermination camps. The last hope was that the Vatican would be able to intercede with the Rumanian government. This time Roncalli pulled out all the stops, and earned the following testimonial from Rabbi Herzog:

> Before leaving, God willing, this evening, I want to express my deepest gratitude for the energetic steps that you have taken and will undertake to save our unfortunate people, innocent victims of unheard of horrors from a cruel power which totally ignores the principles of religion that are the basis of humanity. You follow in the tradition, so profoundly humanitarian, of the Holy See, and you follow the noble feelings of your own heart. The people of Israel will never forget the help brought to its unfortuante brothers and sisters by the Holy See and its highest representatives at this the saddest moment of our history (*Actes et documents*, 10, p. 161: letter dated February 28, 1944).

Herzog, who had been chief rabbi in Dublin from 1925 to 1936, also sent 'the blessings of Jerusalem and Sion' to Roncalli and Ryan. Roncalli was deeply touched. On March 23, 1944, he was able to report to Chaim Barlas that all the matters raised had been taken up by the Holy See, and he concluded his letter: 'May God be with you, bringing you grace and prosperity. Always at your service, and at the service of all the brothers of Israel' (*Actes et documents*, 10, p. 188).

He was to echo these words on October 17, 1960, when he met 130 U.S. Jews led by Rabbi Herbert Friedman. He told them his favourite story about Joseph recognising his brothers:

> I am your brother. Certainly there is a difference between those who admit only the Old Testament as their guide and those who add the New Testament as the supreme law and guide. But that distinction does not abolish the brotherhood that comes from a common origin. We are all sons of the same Father. We come from the Father, and must return to the Father (Righi, p. 197).

His wartime experiences in Istanbul proved that these were not empty formulas.

In the spring of 1944 Roncalli had to liaise with Ira Hirshman, Istanbul agent of the 'War Refugee Board', set up in Washington on January 22, 1944. Though its purpose was to aid all victims of Nazi persecution, its main work was with Jews (*Actes et documents*, 10, p. 191). There were occasional demarcation disputes, not caused by Roncalli but by the Secretariat of State, still punctilious about its neutrality. Tardini had to remind Harold H. Tittmann Jr, American *chargé d'affaires* to the Holy See, that although the Vatican might act in parallel with the U.S. government, it would also have to be seen to be independent of it 'for obvious reasons'. He added that the Vatican attitude towards the setting up of a Jewish state in Palestine was unchanged (*Actes et documents*, 10, p. 293). This meeting took place on May 26, 1944. The situation on the ground was getting more and more desperate, as the last escape routes were systematically sealed off. Under Admiral Horthy the Jews of Hungary had been relatively unscathed. But on March 23, 1944, the Germans entered the country on the pretext of securing their lines of communication, and began deporting Jews to Auschwitz. Only the city of Budapest remained under Horthy's control. In October Horthy was arrested, Hungary was ruled by the Fascist Cross Arrows, and Adolf Eichmann arrived to oversee personally the last phase of the 'final solution'.

The limits on Roncalli's ability to help Jews were now cruelly apparent. There was very little room left for manoeuvre. He was almost powerless. Supposing a group of Jews by some miracle were to be sprung from the Nazi trap, who would provide the transport? On March 31, 1944, Jenke, one of von Papen's aides in Ankara, cabled the *Auswärtiges Amt* or Foreign Office to say that 'for some time' he had been dealing with the Red Cross about 'some 1500' Jews who were trying to get from Rumania to Palestine. Under pressure from the Americans, the Turks had put the steamer *Tari* at their disposition (ADAP, p. 596). A week later von Thadden replied from Berlin. The numbers have now swollen to 7000, 'mostly children'. The Rumanians want to let them go, but cannot provide a ship. The Swedes have a ship ready, but cannot get it into position. There remained the Turks as the last hope. On April 25, 1944, Mgr Dell'Acqua, Roncalli's former Secretary now in the Secretariat of State, wrote a despairing memo which probably referred to this attempt to find a ship:

> I do not think that Mgr Roncalli can do anything in this matter. His position vis-à-vis the Turkish government is very delicate. The government considers the Apostolic Delegate to be a 'distinguished guest', and no more. Further, I think that if the refugees boarded a Turkish ship, that would mean the Turkish government had given its permission. One could think about an approach towards the German Ambassador in Ankara, von Papen, in view of the good relations which exist between him and Mons. Roncalli; but it does not seem to me to be opportune (*Actes et documents*, 10, p. 243, fn. 4).

But the friendship with von Papen was now of no avail. Von Papen got his orders from Berlin on April 6, 1944. They were clear, and illustrate Hannah Arendt's views on the 'banality' and 'bureaucratisation' of evil. Von Thadden made three points. First, there are so many Rumanian Jews. The release of 7000 is being asked for now. This could be the thin end of the wedge. In any case, von Thadden went on, the German view is that Palestine is an Arab country, and so Jewish emigration there is not to be encouraged. Finally, such a concession would 'upset our counter-espionage and our sea strategy' (ADAP, doc. 320). This was almost the exact mirror-image of the British reasoning (see p. 187 above). Yet one or two ships still managed to get through. In July 1944 Roncalli reports the arrival of a ship from Transnistria 'with 730 passengers, including 250 orphans' (*Actes et documents*, 10, p. 355). But that was a far cry from the 55,000 the grand rabbi of Jerusalem had been hoping for six months earlier.

The most useful thing Roncalli could do was to forward to the Vatican diplomats in Hungary and Rumania the 'Immigration Certificates' issued by the Palestine Jewish Agency. They conferred no real rights, but they sometimes worked and were better than nothing. It was these 'Immigration Certificates' that gave rise to the myth that Roncalli issued 'baptismal certificates' to Jews. This story was popularised by Ira Hirshman in his book *Caution to the Winds* (New York, 1962). Yet Roncalli's letter to Mgr Rotta, Nuncio in Budapest, dated August 16, 1944, shows its inaccuracy: 'Since the "Immigration Certificates" we sent you in May contributed to the saving of the lives of the Jews they were intended for, I have accepted from the Jewish Agency in Palestine three more bundles, begging your excellency to pass them on to the person they are intended for, Mr Milkos Krausz' (*Actes et documents*, 10, p. 391). The last name should be Moshe Kraus, Budapest Secretary of the Jewish Agency. The mistake proves that the letter was written by Roncalli himself. He was always a little uncertain about the spelling of foreign names.

On the other hand, it is extremely unlikely that he personally drafted the frigid letter to Ira Hirshman dated only two days later. It is the first and only wartime document from the Delegation in Istanbul to be written in English, a language Roncalli had certainly not mastered despite Ryan's coaching. It reflected the position of the Secretariat of State and hinted in its last sentence that Roncalli had been acting with too much independence in financial matters:

It is not the intention of the Apostolic Delegation to make any further representations on behalf of the Jewish people in Hungary; the only means of doing so is through the papal Secretariat of State, and it seems certain that the Vatican is doing its utmost, both directly and through the Apostolic Nuncio in Budapest, to ameliorate the conditions of the oppressed peoples . . . There is no evidence that the Vatican has been instrumental in procuring special treatment for persons who are Jewish by definition but Christians by faith. The dispositions, however, promulgated by the Hungarian government on July 8 (see enclosed copy) do distinguish between Jews in religion and converted Jews . . . Owing to the political nature of the accusations brought against the persons mentioned in the lists, the Apostolic

Delegation feels that it is not in a position to take any action in the matter . . . Owing to various inconveniences that have arisen in the past out of the forwarding of sums of money on behalf of oppressed peoples, the Apostolic Delegation regrets that it cannot be of any assistance in the transmission of funds to Hungary or to any other country (*Actes et documents*, 10, p. 389 and following: letter dated August 18, 1944).

Roncalli signed this chilling letter. The only defence of its bureaucratic, Pilate-like handwashing was that on August 2, 1944, Turkey broke off diplomatic relations with Germany, and on August 5 von Papen and his family headed for home. So Roncalli no longer had any means of direct contact with the potential enemy, and reverted to his role as a 'tolerated guest' in Turkey. From the Vatican point of view, had he shown *trop de zèle* in helping Jews and poured too much money into the bottomless pit of bribery?

Von Papen – it was his redeeming feature – had certainly helped Roncalli in his work for Jews. As nuncio to France Roncalli wrote an unsolicited letter to the President of the International Tribunal on Nazi war crimes at Nuremberg. It probably saved von Papen's life. Roncalli wrote: 'I do not wish to interfere with any political judgement on Franz von Papen; I can only say one thing: he gave me the chance to save the lives of 24,000 Jews' (Zizola, *Oggi*, April 13, 1983). Von Papen reported this on oath to the Pope John beatification tribunal. He also described their last meeting in Turkey:

> When I had to leave – recalled by Berlin – he came to greet me at the first stop after the main station. For ten minutes we paced up and down on the platform like old friends. In the end, I knelt down and asked for his blessing. I did this because I thought it would be the last time I would see him, since the Allies would certainly hang me. Then the Apostolic Delegate put a letter in my hands. Now it is in the American Archives. I read it in the train. A brother could not have written with greater cordiality (*Ibid.*).

Von Lersner, meanwhile, lingered on in Turkey and plotted with George B. Earle, former governor of Pennsylvania and ambassador to Bulgaria: they both wanted a separate peace with Germany as a bulwark against Soviet expansion. Roncalli transmitted messages from von Lersner, who now called himself by the codename 'Marmara', to Berlin via the nuncio in Berne – until Tardini told him to stop it. His second telegram contained military information (see Graham, Robert A., *Civiltà Cattolica*, May 1, 1982, p. 228).

One event stands out like a beacon in this otherwise grim year of 1944. Roncalli's Pentecost sermon gleams with the conviction that the war is drawing to a close, that it is time to think of post-war 'reconstruction', and that the Holy Spirit is still at work in the world, mysteriously but powerfully. The Spirit is fire or dove: the first image suggesting energy, the second gentleness. Only the Spirit can break down the barriers set up by races and nations. Left to itself, humanity regresses and begins to resemble 'one of those iron-age villages, in which every house was an impenetrable fortress, and people lived among their fortifications' (Righi, p. 259). Europe had become an iron-age village, with modern technology adding its refinements to the industry of death.

Surveying his mixed congregation, Roncalli went on to say that we can all find plausible reasons for stressing differences in race, religion, culture or education. Catholics in particular liked to mark themselves off from the 'others' – 'our Orthodox brothers, Protestants, Jews, Moslems, believers or non-believers in other religions'. The list was comprehensive enough for Istanbul. However:

> My dear brothers and children, I have to tell you that in the light of the Gospel and the Catholic principle, this logic of division does not hold. Jesus came to break down all these barriers; he died to proclaim universal brother-hood; the central point of his teaching is charity, that is the love which binds all men to him as the elder brother, and binds us all with him to the Father (Righi, p. 259).

'Catholic' should be a unifying, inclusive term – not a mark of exclusive distinction. So he prayed for 'an explosion of charity' to realise this vision. He pictured 'the double order of nature and grace' as a mighty musical instrument on which the Spirit played. The act of preaching itself is a gift of the Spirit, for 'he (the Spirit) pours out the gift of persuasion and so, vibrating with the grace of the Spirit, every language should be at his service'. Only in this way could true civil-isation, *civiltà*, born at the foot of the cross, be built up; it could not be founded on 'material usefulness or the spirit of domination'.

It was the most 'visionary' or 'utopian' homily delivered by Roncalli in Istanbul. Yet it came from a darkened and grieving world. It also had the cadences – but this was unconscious – of someone who was saying farewell. It was as though the wheel had come full circle. This was the message he had been sent to Istanbul to deliver. He had said it in his first sermon there on January 25, 1935 (see p. 144). The difference was that by 1944 he had pitted his hope against catastrophe and dereliction.

On December 6, 1944, out of the blue, Roncalli received a telegram from Tardini announcing that he had been appointed nuncio to France. Mgr Joseph Guillois, who had been with him the day Italy declared war on France, congrat-ulated him on this happier occasion. But Roncalli's feelings were more mixed, as his diary recalls:

> Late at night Tardini's coded telegram arrived, like a thunderbolt. I was astonished and dismayed. I went to the chapel to ask Jesus whether I should

elude the burden and the cross, or just accept it; but as calm returned I decided to accept according to the principle *non recuso laborem* [I do not refuse work]. That was how I spent the night between the feasts of St Nicholas and St Ambrose, two men who were called to the episcopacy and became great saints and sanctifiers (*Lettere*, p. 287).

His amazement and apprehensions were justified. Forgotten in the East for nearly twenty years, he was moving from what, but for the war, would have been a minor diplomatic post to the most prestigious Nunciature in the Pope's gift. Just as well he had always got on with the French ambassadors to Turkey – there had been no less than five during his time there. He liked to tease them by asking the meaning of a splendid Gobelins tapestry which hung in the main reception room of their Embassy.

It depicted Cardinal Flavio Chigi, nephew of Pope Alexander VI, apologising to King Louis XIV for some trivial offence caused by his uncle. The ambassadors found this embarrassing, but Roncalli turned it into a *bon mot*: 'It was not easy to be nuncio to France at the time of the absolute monarchs. It's a lot better now that much of the nineteenth century anti-clericalism has gone and Church and State, each in its own order, can work together for the good of the French people' (Righi, pp. 267–8: quoting Fr Gauhier Dubois O.F.M. Cap.). But it was by no means certain that he would find General Charles de Gaulle easier to deal with than Chigi found Louis XIV.

Chapter 10

Difficult mission to France

They order, said I, this matter better in France
(Laurence Sterne, *A Sentimental Journey*, 1768).

Frenchmen are just like Italians, minus their good humour
(André Frossard, 1983).

The train of events which led Archbishop Roncalli unexpectedly to Paris began at 9 a.m. on June 30, 1944, when General Charles de Gaulle had an audience with Pope Pius XII. Familiar with *grandeur*, de Gaulle was impressed: 'Pius XII judges everything from a point of view that transcends human beings, their enterprises, and their quarrels'. From this lofty level he surveyed the destiny of the world, and especially Europe. Pius XII feared that liberated France would relapse once more into its age-old feuding, and grieved over the sufferings about to befall the German people, but, de Gaulle adds, 'it was the action of the Soviets in Poland today and in the whole of Eastern Europe tomorrow that filled the Holy Father with most anxiety' (*Mémoires de Guerre*, 2, pp. 233–4).

But France and the Holy See did not see eye to eye on everything. For the next five months a symbolic battle raged around the nuncio to France, the bearded, ascetic and uncommunicative Mgr Valerio Valeri. De Gaulle demanded his removal on the grounds that he had been close to the Vichy regime of Marshal Philippe Pétain (see *Actes et documents*, 11, p. 38 and following). Pius refused. He defended the strict juridical position: his nuncios were appointed to *states,* not to particular governments or heads of state. Valeri, he pointed out, was already nuncio to France at the time of the Popular Front in 1936. He had outlasted two very different regimes. He could cope with another.

Though technically correct, this approach ignored the passionate feelings that were running high as France was gradually liberated. For de Gaulle a new and better France was coming to birth in which anything that smacked of 'collaboration' with the Nazis had to be ruthlessly purged. On the local level there was much trigger-happy settling of old scores. No one suggested that Valeri had done anything noteworthy wicked. But he had remained loyal to Pétain and that was enough. He had to go. Pius would not budge. An *impasse* was reached.

The decisive month, militarily and politically, was August, 1944. On August 20 German troops broke into Pétain's bedroom at the Hôtel du Parc in Vichy and shipped him off to Germany. Valeri and the Swiss ambassador were on hand to record the old man's last indignant protest (Cartier, p. 129). Though this was a courtesy it would have been indecent to refuse, it made de Gaulle more determined than ever to remove the nuncio. This seemed all the more logical in that Vichy's ambassador to the Holy See had already resigned and been smoothly replaced by de Gaulle's personal envoy, Hubert Guérin. After the liberation of Rome there had been a general about-post of diplomats: those who had taken refuge in the Vatican now emerged, and their places were taken by the ambassadors or ministers of Germany, Japan and Finland.

Paris was liberated in August, after a messy insurrection and very little destruction. The French were granted the honour of being the first into the city. Away in Istanbul, Roncalli celebrated the feast of St Louis, king of France, not realising that it was the decisive day in the liberation of Paris and that, for the first time in four years, the tricolor fluttered from the Eiffel Tower. The next day, August 26, 1944, de Gaulle led his forces down the Champs-Elysées and into the cathedral of Notre Dame for a *Magnificat* in thanksgiving for the liberation of Paris. God had indeed toppled the mighty from their thrones. But it was a far from untroubled celebration.

Shots rattled round the nave, One looked in vain for Cardinal Emmanuel Célestin Suhard, archbishop of Paris. He was held prisoner in his own palace, suspected of 'collaboration'. Like most French bishops he had welcomed Pétain in the confusion and despair of defeat, and supported his 'national revolution' until its subjection to Germany and anti-semitic element became clear. The resistance movement had divided French Catholics. Those who continued the Christian Democratic tradition of Marc Sagnier – Georges Bidault and Maurice Schuman, for example – became ardent Gaullists and contributed to the rethinking of French institutions that had gone on in exile. If Suhard was locked up in his palace, one could see in Notre Dame the Dominican Fr Raymond Bruckberger in his white habit and, in dress uniform, Rear-Admiral Thierry d'Argenlieu, a Carmelite priest. It was an indication of the divisions within the French Church with which Roncalli would have to deal.

Pius XII, meanwhile, stood by Valeri and refused to name a new nuncio. This was politically unwise. September, October and November passed by, and the Vatican had still not officially recognised the new regime in France. To Pius' mortification, the Russians stole a march on him. They were the first to recognise de Gaulle, and so were able to have their ambassador to Vichy confirmed in office. This forced Pius' hand. The end of the year was approaching and tradition had it that the papal nuncio, as dean of the diplomatic corps, should present the New Year greetings to the head of state. In the absence of a nuncio, the task would fall to the most senior man present, who chanced to be the Russian ambassador. This would never do. To avert such a *contretemps*, Pius decided to give way and appoint a nuncio quickly.

His first choice was Archbishop Joseph Fietta, since 1936 nuncio to Argentina, who was telegraphed on December 2, 1944. He replied the next day, declining Paris on health grounds. Tardini despatched the fateful telegram to Roncalli on December 5 (*Actes et documents,* 11, p. 633, p. 637 and p. 639). It had all been done at great speed, and Roncalli was the second choice for France. He was the stop-gap. Not much was known about him in Rome. One reporter asked a curial prelate what he knew about Roncalli and was told: 'He's an old fogey' ('*Une vieille baderne*' – Bergerre, p. 45).

The 'old fogey' so suddenly catapulted to the Vatican's most prestigious diplomatic post was now sixty-three, and perfectly well aware that he did not come out of the top drawer of Vatican diplomats. He had not been at the Ecclesiastical Academy where they were trained. To his friend Giacomo Testa, he quoted the maxim of Teofilo Folengo (1496–1544): 'Where horses are lacking, the donkeys trot along' ('*Ubi deficiunt equi, trottant aselli*' – Alberigo, p. 470). He kept this tag in mind when people congratulated him on his new post. And he wondered how it had come about.

On his way through Rome he asked Tardini, confidentially, 'who had picked out my name from the vast sea of the Vatican diplomatic service'. Tardini gruffly replied that it was all the Pope's doing, and hinted that he did not approve (Alberigo, p. 472). Tardini's biographer confirms this suspicion: 'When Roncalli arrived in Rome in haste and anxious to be on the banks of the Seine, Tardini, his immediate superior, did not waste time on compliments, nor would he accept any thanks. He said that he had no part in the appointment which was the result of the direct intervention of the Pope' (Nicolini, p. 183). Later the story was put about that Roncalli, a second-rater, had been chosen to snub de Gaulle. But Pius XII, though obstinate, was not irresponsible. It was comforting for Roncalli to know that the Pope had singled him out. Pius said: 'I want to make it clear that I was the one who acted in this nomination, thought of it and arranged it all. For that reason you may be sure that the will of God could not be more manifest or encouraging' (Alberigo, p. 472, letter to Giacomo Testa, February 7, 1945). But while encouraging him, it also bound him to Pius by an extra tie of loyalty.

If little was known about Roncalli in Rome, he was almost totally unknown in Paris. Cardinal Suhard awaited the arrival of the new nuncio with some apprehension. His own position was far from secure. He knew that his name was on a government list of bishops to be removed. The Pope had given way on the matter of the nuncio: would he hold out on the bishops? There was much ugly baying for blood. Suhard also knew that Rome was watching attentively the experiment, begun the previous year, of sending priests to work in the factories and dockyards of France. Pius XII supported the idea in general, but on condition that Suhard personally supervised the experiment and was answerable for it. Where would the nuncio stand on the priest-workers?

Suhard was relieved to get a letter commending Roncalli from Mgr Giovanni

Battista Montini, the substitute or second in command at the Secretariat of State. Montini was widely and correctly believed to be Francophile. He wrote on December 23, 1944:

> In announcing officially this nomination to your eminence, I am quite sure
> that you will be delighted to learn of it for you know, at least by
> reputation, the excellent qualities of the new Representative of the Holy See
> in France. He has distinguished himself not only in his earlier missions in
> Turkey and Greece, but also in the pastoral ministry, as assistant to a great
> Bishop, Mgr Radini Tedeschi, whose well-deserved fame has spread beyond
> the boundaries of the diocese of Bergamo (*Mission,* p. 3).

It is far from evident that the mention of Radini Tedeschi would mean very much to Suhard. The fact that he had been in Paris in 1893 as a legate was not fresh in everyone's memory. However, Montini's blessing on the new man was important because it suggested that Roncalli was closer to him than to Mgr Alfredo Ottaviani who reigned at the Holy Office (see Guitton, p. 26). And that further meant that he would not be systematically hostile to the kind of pastoral experiments that Suhard wanted to encourage.

Once the decision had been taken, events moved swiftly. Roncalli left Ankara on December 27, 1944, was bundled in and out of aeroplanes and transported 'like Habakkuk' as he put it (*Dodicesimo anniversario,* p. 81) on a series of short-haul flights that took him to Beirut, Lydda, Cairo, Benghazi, Naples and finally Rome on the afternoon of December 28. Without pausing to rest he had meetings that same day with Tardini and Montini who now formed a dyarchy in the Vatican, Pius XII having dispensed with a Secretary of State. Next day he had an audience with Pius and a meeting with the ousted Valerio Valeri who, though now officially out of favour in France, had drafted Roncalli's New Year speech for him. Roncalli always felt that his predecessor Valeri had been unjustly treated and voted for him in the 1958 conclave as a mark of respect. Then he had lunch at the Palazzo Taverno with Guérin, de Gaulle's man in Rome.

He left Rome at 10 a.m. the next day in a plane specially provided by the French government, could see nothing of Paris except the Eiffel Tower shrouded by the mist, and landed at the Villa Coublet military airport at two in the afternoon. He installed himself in the Nunciature at 10 avenue Wilson, and that same evening presented his respects to Georges Bidault, foreign minister, at the Quai d'Orsay. December 31 was a Sunday. He rested most of the day, but had his first meeting with Suhard in the evening. Next morning he presented his credentials to de Gaulle, provisional president of the Republic, at the Elysée Palace and thus was in position, by eleven o'clock, to the right of the Russian ambassador, Bogomilov, who, in a sense, was the cause of all this frenzied agitation throughout the last four days.

He had a pleasant surprise. There was a familiar face in the crush. Menemencioglu, the Turkish ambassador, had been telling everyone what a splendid fellow Roncalli was and basked in the glory of having helped to prepare him for his present mission. Since the Turks had paid no attention to him while he was in Turkey, here was a paradox that needed some explanation. Menemencioglu later elegantly declared: 'I would like you to inform the Holy Father that the Turkish government would like to pay the Nuncio in Paris the honours it was unable to confer on the Apostolic Delegate in Istanbul' (Alberigo, p. 471 – letter to Giacomo Testa). Roncalli murmured an apology to Bogomilov, and arranged that his first exchange of diplomatic courtesies would be with the Russian embassy. He then launched into his Valeri-prepared greetings. Conventional and second-hand though the speech was, it constituted the first formal act of recognition of the new French government by the Holy See. *Monsieur le Président*, Roncalli began,

> ... Thanks to your political sagacity, this beloved country has recovered her liberty and at the same time her faith in her own destiny. We do not doubt that the New Year will see further progress and fresh triumphs. So once again, France resumes her place among the nations. With her clear-sightedness, her zest for work, her love of freedom and her spiritual ardour, of which I was an admiring witness during my long years in the Middle East, she will be able to indicate the way which, in union of hearts and justice, will at last lead our human society towards a time of tranquillity and lasting peace (*Mission*, p. 6).

Uttered on January 1, 1945, these words were not banal. They meant that in the eyes of the Vatican the Vichy regime had been an aberration in which France had lost her liberty and her place among the nations. The quarrel about legitimacy was over: full and ungrudging recognition was given to the provisional government. At the same time there was a hint ('union of hearts and justice') that the work of *épuration* or purging should be carried out with restraint and without splitting the nation irrevocably.

Roncalli's first appearance in France was a minor triumph. He had mollified de Gaulle and shown consideration for the Russian ambassador. But it was a *diplomatic* triumph, largely unnoticed outside a narrow circle of professionals. This was to be Roncalli's fate throughout his difficult mission to France. As nuncio he was responsible for relations with the French state which remained separate from the Church. Though all his instincts were pastoral and apostolic, he had to learn to keep them in check. He could not act as 'principal bishop' as he had in Istanbul. It was not his role, and the French Church would have resented it. If he travelled in France, it was by episcopal invitation.

But he naturally tried to introduce himself to the French Church on his arrival in Paris. On the feast of the Epiphany, January 6, 1945, he wrote what he called, 'a humble and simple letter' to all the bishops of France. He gently praised Valeri, treated the bishops with respect, and let them understand that he was not going to act as a ferocious new broom. It worked. 'About a hundred bishops' replied to his letter. While appreciating that he had to tread cautiously with the government, those whose heads were likely to roll felt that the new nuncio was on their side.

He introduced himself to a wider public on January 21, 1945, with an address at St Joseph des Carmes, the church of the Institut Catholique. It was the Octave of Prayer for Christian Unity once more, and Fr Louis Bouyer, of the Congregation of the Oratory, had already preached at pontifical vespers. So Roncalli was merely adding a few improving thoughts. He succumbed to a little burst of rhetoric as he tried to link his last words in Constantinople with his first in Paris: 'These shining points, Constantinople and Paris, which stand for two worlds and two civilisations, are spanned, as it were, by a brilliant rainbow upon which glow the last words of Jesus' farewell prayer, "That they may all be one" ' (John 17.21: *Mission*, p. 8). Roncalli's French was always a little haphazard, and his poetic efforts sometimes caused merriment. He was philosophical about this, and wrote to the parish priest of Sotto il Monte, Fr Giovanni Biroloni, on February 20, 1945:

> I am beginning to preach here and there, as I did in Istanbul. This pleases the French, even if I cannot imitate to perfection either Bossuet or Mabillon. They consider that speaking their language is a sure sign of respect and affection, and so they willingly forgive me errors or uncertainties of style. Nothing else matters so long as the Lord's Gospel is proclaimed (*Mission*, pp. 16–17).

A more candid account of Roncalli's early efforts to preach in French is given by Denise Aimé-Azam. He liked to frequent his 'parish church', St Pierre de Chaillot. He preached there during some solemn ceremony, but the microphone was defective and nothing but loud shrieks and wails emerged from it. Roncalli descended from the pulpit and spoke from the centre aisle: 'Dear children, you have heard nothing of what I was saying. That doesn't matter. It wasn't very interesting. I don't speak French very well. My saintly old mother, who was a peasant, didn't make me learn it early enough' (Aimé-Azam, p. 27). There was general hilarity. The parish priest of St Pierre de Chaillot, the improbably named Canon C. Glamorgan, shared with the nuncio a great devotion to St Philip Neri who was famed for his sense of humour. The truth was, and Roncalli admitted it, that whatever knowledge of France he had was due to Bishop Radini Tedeschi who 'spoke French elegantly, knew her history perfectly and well understood her genius' (*Mission*, p. 179).

His letters home were reassuring and vague. On February 20, 1945, he wrote from Paris for the first time:

> I sleep better in Paris than in Istanbul. Not that I need much sleep here, and am content with little. There are important questions to be dealt with on which depends the good of the Catholic Church in France. I do my best, knowing that I am here at the explicit and personal desire of the Holy Father. And so I feel alert and serene in everything I do (*Familiari*, II, pp. 9–10).

He offers few clues about his work. He lives in 'a princely palace with everything one might need, two secretaries, three nuns, three staff, five servants and a splendid car' (*Ibid.*, p. 14). The car was a black Cadillac. In this privileged world, he kept himself humble by remembering La Colombera and Sotto il Monte.

He was well aware of the delicacy of his mission. The 'important questions' he had to deal with formed a set of inter-related problems. He felt he was 'walking on live coals' (to Cardinal Alfredo Ildefonso Schuster of Milan, *Mission*, p. 25). For his family he varied the metaphor and spoke of 'thorns amid the roses' (*Familiari*, II, p. 14). His most difficult immediate problem was how to deal with the government's request for the removal of allegedly 'collaborationist' bishops. How he resolved it can be studied in the work of André Latreille, who was 'director of cults at the Interior Ministry' during the relevant period from July, 1944 to August 1945 (*De Gaulle, la Libération et l'Eglise Catholique*, Cerf, Paris, 1978). The story has often been mythologised. It can now be told plainly.

As early as July 26, 1944, the Interior Ministry had drawn up a list of prelates 'who had caused the greatest scandal during the occupation'. The list had twenty-five names, included three cardinals – Suhard (Paris), Gerlier (Lyons) and Liénart (Lille) – and among the bishops were Beaussart, auxiliary of Paris and Courbe, head of Catholic Action. So as to appear constructive, the Interior Ministry thoughtfully produced another list of six bishops worthy to become archbishops, and twenty-two priests who were good bishop material. It was a well-meaning but clumsy gesture: it looked as though the new regime was attacking the freedom of the Church to make its own appointments.

By the time Roncalli arrived in Paris the harshness and sweeping nature of these charges was realised. So the word 'collaborationist' was dropped, and the accusation was that the bishops had preached submission to Vichy – which was undeniable – and that 'a fair number of prelates had publicly taken positions favourable to German propaganda'. But the charges remained vague, were often based on unfounded local denunciations, and they ignored subsequent behaviour. One of the incriminated bishops, Gabriel Pinguet of Clermont was actually in Dachau. Cardinal Gerlier of Lyons was never allowed to forget that he had once said: 'Today France is Pétain, and Pétain is France'. But later he had written a vigorous pastoral letter against the treatment of the Jews and protested to the *Wehrmacht* against the massacre of hostages. Gerlier in short had redeemed himself. Others had done the same.

Thus by January, 1945 the original list of twenty-five had been whittled down to a dozen or so. 'Find me ten or twelve', Georges Bidault urged Latreille on January 28, and he was particularly insistent that the heads of Feltin and Beaussart should roll. De Gaulle was less vengeful. Latreille had an interview with him on January 30 and noted in his diary: 'On the matter of the Bishops, he heard me out and agreed that it would have to be a limited operation, maybe four or five; but he did not seem to understand the difficulty of getting the documents together and presenting them to Rome. That seemed so simple . . .' (Latreille, p. 51). The problem facing the nuncio was not simple and it had two aspects. The Vichy regime had been 'legitimate' and so obeying it was no crime, even retrospectively. It would be against justice to treat the bishops as scapegoats. Then there was the Church–state problem: was the new French government trying to appoint bishops on political grounds?

What Roncalli thought about these questions can be gathered from Latreille's account of their first meeting on February 17, 1945:

> He welcomed me with amusement and cordiality. A very lively talker, stout, friendly, words tumble forth from him so that it is hard to get a word in edgeways. Yet he says he really does want to be well-informed. He tells me the likely way the Vatican is interpreting the events: the bishops have committed no fault, and though they might have made some mistakes, are they not the victims of a handful of wild men?
> I explained to him not so much the attitude of the government as that of the Catholics in the Resistance movement. The Bishops bore a heavy responsibility. The silence of the majority and the declarations of some had given the impression that they had failed to apply the principles of papal doctrine to the time we live in. So there was a crisis of conscience for the French, especially for those who had been in the Resistance.
> And today there is a natural reaction. It is not hostile to the Church, but it cannot be ignored without exposing the Church to 1) serious internal divisions, 2) a revivial of anti-clericalism, and 3) the scornful indifference of part of the people.
> I managed to make myself understood. The Nuncio admitted that public peace had to be secured and that *odium plebis* (being hated by the people) could be an argument against an offending prelate. But we have to say exactly what we want, and we have to produce evidence. And we mustn't expect the new nuncio to become the Torquemada of the French Bishops (Latreille, p. 60).

They met again a week later on February 26, 1945. Now that he had discovered that Latreille had ten children, Roncalli was more forthcoming and showed him photographs of his own family. There was still no documentary evidence on the bishops. The nuncio was more concerned about another matter. De Gaulle wanted to appoint the philosopher Jacques Maritain as his ambassador to the Holy See. It was a shrewd move, for neither his Catholic nor his Gaullist credentials could be questioned.

It is a sign of the tenseness of Franco–Vatican relations that Mgr Tardini managed to make an issue out of Maritain's appointment. Roncalli had asked for his *agrément* and explained; 'The famous writer, Jacques Maritain, the foreign minister – Bidault – told me, has been chosen as an exponent of Catholic thought and to show the government's desire, both now and in the future, to bring out a Catholic conception of France' (*Actes et documents*, 11, p. 626: dated January 13, 1945). It seemed an innocent enough proposal. But in 1944 Maritain had travelled through Latin America on a lecture tour in which he spoke of human rights and Allied war aims. His lectures were gathered in a volume called *Derechos Humanos (Human Rights)*. To speak of 'human rights' in certain Latin American countries was to tread on egg-shells: the nuncios of Chile and Argentina reported that Maritain had left a wash of controversy in his wake. So even when Tardini eventually granted Maritain's accreditation, he could not resist adding in his blunt Roman Borgo way that 'the Holy See would have preferred someone not involved in public party political controversies' (*Ibid.*, p. 679).

This was to inflate the Maritain affair out of all proportion. On January 23, 1945 Roncalli had a 'long conversation' with de Gaulle and, on orders from Tardini, presented the acceptance of Maritain as ambassador to the Holy See as yet another 'concession' to France – the first 'concession' being the removal of Valeri. De Gaulle somewhat wearily repeated that the removal of Valeri implied no hostility towards him as an individual, and that he had indeed been honoured on his departure with the *Légion d'Honneur* (*Actes et documents*, 11, p. 686). As for Maritain, de Gaulle confided, 'vigorous and incisive as he is with pen in hand, in practical matters he is humble, shy and clumsy'. Accordingly, he added confidentially, but Roncalli passed it on, Maritain's stay in Rome would be brief and he would soon be replaced by 'someone better qualified and formed in the best' traditions of the French diplomatic service' (*Ibid.*, p. 687). Despite de Gaulle's disparagement, Maritain, back in Paris by April 11, 1945, remained at his post in Rome for three years. There his friendship with Mgr Montini ripened.

Germany was over-run and finally capitulated unconditionally on May 8, 1945, V–E day. On June 24 Roncalli was due to preach in Lyons on the 700th anniversary of the First Council of Lyons. His historian's imagination was stirred by the great Basilica of St Jean, which nestles at the foot of the hill of Fourvière, where the Jesuits had their most important theological college. But the timing of the event and the presence of Cardinal Gerlier and fifteen bishops turned it into something of a victory celebration. It was important that Roncalli should get the mood right.

He presented Lyons I in 1245 as a stage in the Church's struggle for emancipation from temporal rulers, from 'the protector who had become a tyrant', from, in short, the Emperor Frederick (*Mission*, p. 31). This was relevant because, Roncalli insisted, the Church's freedom was not the first move in a power-game but a condition for the exercise of its ministry: 'It is not a manifestation of power or human domination, but a service rendered to the apostolate of the Gospel, the apostolate of love'. Secondly, he pointed out that Lyons I was a *reforming* Council, which had compared the evils threatening the Church to 'the five wounds of Christ' on the Cross. He glanced in passing at Lyons II in 1274 whose aim was to bring about reconciliation between the Greek and Latin Churches, 'all the more interesting to me because of the twenty years I passed in the East' (*Ibid.*). So in Roncalli's mind a Council – this one or some future one – had three features: service, reform, and unity.

Then he quoted the account of the dramatic end of Lyons I given by Matthew Paris. From his throne Pope Innocent IV pronounced this terrible condemnation: 'The Lord Frederick, ex-emperor, unworthy of the empire and the royal sovereignty, is dispossessed by God of all power to rule and reign'. Whereupon he 'threw down the smoking taper he held in his hand and stamped it out. All those present then threw their tapers to the ground in imitation of the papal gesture. Upon which the defender of Frederick, Thaddeus de Suesse, cried out in terror, "Oh fatal day, day of wrath! of calamity and misery!" ' (*Mission*, p. 33). Uttered in June, 1945 these words had a special force and significance which Roncalli brought out in his peroration: 'My brothers of Lyons, the days of wrath, calamity and universal misery have passed over our own heads. But God has abased the proud who sought to conquer the world. He has struck down those who were responsible, and the formidable armies. The head of Christendom has not needed to repeat the words of Pope Innocent' (*Ibid.*, p. 34). His hearers could supply for themselves the missing names of 'the proud who sought to conquer the world': Adolf Hitler poisoned and incinerated outside his Bunker in Berlin; Benito Mussolini exhibited upside down in the Piazzale Loreto in Milan; and their minions. Roncalli calls the Pope 'the head of Christendom' (*de la Chrétienté*) which has an archaic, mediaeval flavour but avoids 'the head of the Church', already proscribed by Yves-Marie Congar O.P. as near-blasphemous, for Christ alone is 'the head of the Church' according to St Paul.

Then Roncalli glimpsed a vision. Though he had presented the Church's role as one of service rather than domination, the plain meaning of Innocent IV's crushed taper was that he had power even in the secular realm. So Roncalli reverses the image of the crushed tapers, and in so doing transforms it:

> Let us gather up all the blessed tapers which this terrible hurricane had extinguished. Let us light them again with a new flame and, gathered joyfully round our father, the august pontiff Pius XII, like the soldier pilgrims of old, reform the procession of the church and march forwards to the music of our hymns (*Mission*, p. 34).

There is some pulpit-rhetoric here, though the crusading spirit was aptly associated with Lyons and Charles Péguy had revived interest in it. But the Lyons sermon had a deeper long-term significance.

It showed that Roncalli had thought deeply about conciliar history. He held that Councils should be positive rather than negative, and that condemnations were no longer needed. The remark that Pius XII 'had not needed to repeat the words of Pope Innocent' adumbrates what he said in his inaugural speech to the Council: the Church did not need to condemn errors since 'men were condemning them of themselves' (Abbott, p. 716). Finally, although the gathering round the Pope sounds more like a rally than a council, the idea that a council should be called in which the world would be stunned to admiration by the spectacle of former enemies now embracing each other was envisaged in 1948 (see pp. 310 ff. below). But all that was, as the Germans say, *Zukunftsmusik*, music of the future, in 1945.

Roncalli was brought back to earth by a meeting with the left-wing mayor of Lyons, Edouard Herriot, who liked to recall Gerlier's *faux-pas* by saying, 'Today Lyons is Cardinal Gerlier, and Cardinal Gerlier is Lyons'. He became president of the National Assembly and a good friend of Roncalli. A further jolt was the news – it turned out to be false – that Mgr Domenico Menna, bishop of Mantua from 1928, 'had been shot by his own people who accused him of having supported Fascism' (*Mission*, p. 35). This he reported in a letter to a mutual friend, Mgr Cesare Orsenigo who had slogged through his war as nuncio in Berlin. He also told Orsenigo about an open-air evening Mass on the vast esplanade which stretches from the Trocadéro (now the Palais de Chaillot) to the Eiffel Tower. They were celebrating, if that was the right word, the return to France of concentration camp survivors and prisoners of war. Roncalli described the scene: 'Many thousands were present, including all those who have returned from the German camps of suffering and death: a great crowd of women in mourning; and a hundred priests, still dressed as prisoners, distributed Holy Communion. So we live among tragic spectacles of suffering and death, and the hope of new life' (*Mission*, p. 36). It might – should – have occurred to him that these prisoners in prison garb were unlikely to accept confinement in their fortress-like presbyteries from now on.

That discovery was soon to come. Meanwhile he did what he could to ensure that all prisoners returned home as soon as possible. He visited the Germans still held at Douai. He worked with three French priests, Mgr Rhodain and abbé Le Meur of *Secours Catholique* and the remarkable abbé Desgranges who founded, or rather refounded, the *Fraternité de la Merci* for the redemption of all captives, including political prisoners (Aimé-Azam, p. 77). This was controversial. But the three of them had already grasped that the basis of the new Europe they could see emerging would be Franco–German reconciliation. Roncalli agreed.

Meanwhile the question of the 'collaborationist' bishops had been largely taken out of his hands. Ironically, this was partly the result of his success in getting Maritain accepted as French ambassador to the Holy See. De Gaulle and Bidault negotiated through Maritain directly with the Holy See – in practice Tardini – to such good effect that by June 1945 the Vatican had accepted that 'some' bishops would have to go. Roncalli was by-passed. The mood in France was changing. The immediate passions of the liberation began to simmer down. The offending bishops, whoever they were, no longer posed a threat to public order. There had been no incidents since Roncalli arrived in France.

Moreover the Christian Democrats in the *Mouvement Républicain Populaire* (MRP, construed by the satirical magazine, *Le Canard Enchaîné*, as the *Mouvement des Révérends Pères*, that is, the Jesuits) had done well in the municipal elections, and seemed the only political party capable of rallying the Catholics and defeating the Communists. A long conversation with the justice minister, Pierre-Henri Teitgen, convinced Roncalli that the sacrifice of a few bishops would improve relations with the government. Further talks with M. de Saint-Hardouin, of the Quai d'Orsay, whom he had known in Istanbul, suggested that since the questions of subsidies for Catholic schools would soon have to be faced, it was prudent not to fight hopeless battles.

So on July 27, 1945, seven prelates 'of France and the Empire' were discreetly removed. They went out with neither a whimper nor a bang. They were spared humiliation, given pension rights in their former dioceses, and the reasons for their departure were not made public. The seven were Archbishop de la Villerabel of Aix-en-Provence, Bishops Dutoit (Arras) and Auvity (Mende), the auxiliary bishop of Paris, Beaussart (so Bidault got his man), and the apostolic vicars of Rabat, Saint Pierre and Miquelon, and Dakar. In the end it was a meagre haul. Legend usually attributes this success to Roncalli's cunning delaying tactics. But as we have seen in January, 1945, when he arrived in Paris, de Gaulle said he would be happy with 'four or five'; and in any case Roncalli was not the chief agent in the matter. But Latreille goes to the other extreme of inaccuracy when he remarks: 'At the time we did not know how far Pius XII's ambassador was condemned to prudence by the lack of esteem in which his superior (*patron*) held him' (Latreille, p. 71). The point was not, however, that Pius did not personally esteem his nuncio to France: it was rather that he treated all subordinates as mere extensions of his will. As he frequently remarked, 'I want executants, not collaborators' ('*Io non voglio collaboratori, ma esecutori*' – Nicolini, p. 146). Pius' men were used to finding that the Pope had gone over their heads.

There was another embarrassing instance in the summer of 1945. No cardinals had been created since the start of Pius XII's pontificate in 1939; war-time difficulties, it was said, made a consistory impossible. Now that the war was over, de Gaulle and Bidault wanted the Pope to reward with a cardinal's hat the three archbishops who had most clearly dissociated themselves from Vichy, Jules Saliège of Toulouse, Petit de Juleville of Rouen, and Clément Roques of Rennes. Their promotion would clearly be seen as a political event. Roncalli was opposed to it. He explained why to Jacques Dumaine, then head of protocol at the Quai d'Orsay:

> Their names were put forward by the government, and they are fine men . . . But there are difficulties. For instance Mgr Salièges, the Archbishop of Toulouse, has been paralysed for six years and cannot utter a word, while Mgr Petit de Juleville, the Archbishop of Rouen, suffers from agoraphobia. Only Mgr Roques is active and able to speak, so the situation is not very promising. Your ministers tell me that a priest should be judged by his intelligence, his priestly virtues and his courage. I tell them that physical presence is also important, even within the church – and especially at a Consistory (*Quai d'Orsay 1945–1951*, quoted Johnson, p. 64).

Roncalli was not mistaken about the impression of decrepitude conveyed especially by Saliège. The trio would not cut a good figure at the Consistory. He was always a stickler for presentation, for what the army calls 'good turn out'; and yet it was a curiously 'worldly' judgement coming from him, and suggests that he had not yet grasped the qualities of heart and intelligence that were masked by Saliège's paralysis.

Even odder is the fact that by mid-October, 1945, when the nomination of all three men had been confirmed and publicly announced, Roncalli exclaimed with every appearance of satisfaction, '*our* three candidates, *our* three candidates are through' (Latreille, p. 72). One can only suppose that he had put the case against, been over-ruled by Tardini or the Pope, and loyally if belatedly accepted the wisdom of their choice. This pattern was to recur during his time in France. It was the reason why some had difficulty in knowing where he stood personally on controversial questions. But as a diplomat he accepted that his first duty was towards Pius XII. In the late 1940s this idea was unfashionable in France.

On December 31, 1946, Roncalli was back again at the Elysée Palace to present the good wishes of the diplomatic corps to the President. These speeches punctuated his stay in France. This time he devised another burst of poetry which confirmed his reputation as a 'character': 'In a few days time the door of your home will be adorned with a fine bouquet of orange blossom', by which the Nuncio simply meant that de Gaulle's daughter, Elizabeth, was getting married (*Mission*, p. 48). He was not to know that, within a month, de Gaulle would huffily resign. On January 26, 1946, he withdrew to Colombey-les-deux-Eglises to await his recall. He felt himself as the leader of the nation, not of a party. A series of coalition governments succeeded in excluding both the Gaullists and the Communists who, with five million votes, were the largest single party. Pius XII was not unhappy about this.

For many observers, Roncalli was little more than the local agent of a highly political pope. This was especially true of those whose profession was spying. Roncalli was now important enough to be the object of their attentions and, in some cases, of their inventions. The OSS – Office of Strategic Studies, ancestor of the US Central Intelligence Agency (CIA) – has a number of reports about Roncalli. They are implausible. So on January 5, 1945, 'Vessels' (a collective name) cabled to Magruder that 'Mgr Roncalli has informed the Vatican that de Gaulle government will do all it can to support those Spanish elements seeking to end the regime of Franco'. It is unlikely that Roncalli, as he began to familiarise himself with the French situation, should have plunged into a wholly new set of problems, and equally unlikely that within five days of arriving in Paris would have been able to pronounce so confidently on French intentions. These were confidential intelligence reports, destined for the files (they were declassified on October 18, 1978).

The Communists presented to the public the picture of a highly political Roncalli in *Documenti Segreti della Diplomazia Vaticana* (Secret Documents of Vatican Diplomacy) published in Lugano in 1948. The sub-title, *The Vatican Against World Peace*, gave the game away. The 'secret documents' consist of reports from Vatican diplomats, including Roncalli. They were published without commentary. How they were acquired is not explained. According to the fourteen despatches allegedly sent from Roncalli in September and October, 1946, the 'Church' switched from Bidault's MRP to de Gaulle's new *Rassemblement du Peuple Français* (RPF). On October 1, the MRP sent a mission to Rome to stop this move, but to no effect. In the referendum of October 13, the new Constitution was accepted and the Fourth Republic inaugurated. It turned out to be more like the third Republic than anyone had imagined.

Most of this was intelligent guesswork rather than inside information. The *Secret Documents* were later demonstrated to be forgeries. They were the work of Virgilio Scattolini, sometime playwright and author of saucy novels, who later became part-time film critic for *l'Osservatore Romano* (Hoffmann, p. 257). The fact is that Roncalli was not in Paris between September 7 and October 22, 1946, when he is alleged to have written his fourteen reports. He spent most of this period at Sotto il Monte or Bergamo. In any case, politics did not dominate his thinking to the extent that the spies imagined.

An authentic letter to Montini shows what his real state of mind was at this time:

> Your excellency,
> I have been here at Sotto il Monte for three days. After receiving your telegrammed permission to leave, I set off after initiating the new auditor, Mgr Silvio Oddi, whom I knew quite well and for whom I am grateful. From my reports to H.E. (his excellency) Tardini and to you which should have arrived in the Vatican, you can deduce that I didn't think it harmful to the interests of the Holy See for me to be away for a few weeks leaving the counsellor in charge. Mgr Vagnozzi will perform very ably according to the instructions I left him.
> Since the weather is so lovely here on my hillside, and I can have a proper rest among my books and papers, and since there is no urgent business and it would be inconvenient for me to come to Rome twice, I thought I would stay on here for another week. I can leave for Rome on September 22 and stay for two weeks.
> All this, of course, provided there are not difficulties for the Holy Father, whose desires I wish to serve above all else... (*Saggio,* pp. 40–1).

That is not the tone of a man obsessed by the twists and turns of French politics. He was glad to be away from it all, and content to leave Egidio Vagnozzi (later to be apostolic delegate to the United States) in charge.

Another indication of Roncalli's detachment from immediate political concerns is that on September 27, 1946, after his audience with Pius XII, he nonchalantly went off to the Vatican Library to see what material there was on Gerolamo Ragazzoni, bishop of Bergamo from 1577 to 1592, who had also served as nuncio to the French court (*Letture,* p. 594). That Roncalli should be interested in such a figure, linking Bergamo and Paris and living in the historical period he had made his own, was natural enough. But it showed a capacity to distance himself from the problems of de Gaulle and the MRP.

Of course Roncalli did have contacts with MRP leaders and other political figures during his early years in France: that was his job. He also chanced to be in Rome on October 1, 1946, when the MRP delegation put its case. He does not seem to have been present. Aimé-Azam recalls that apart from Robert Schuman, the MRP leaders regarded Roncalli as a *polichinelle* or puppet, someone manipulated by the Roman Curia or, in Balzac's vocabulary, a man 'lacking in principle and character'. In his September 27 audience with the Pope, Pius had recalled the old saw about the nuncio being 'the hand, the eye and the heart' of the Pope in France. The maxim could be given a charitable interpretation, as Roncalli did in 1949 (*Mission*, p. 106). But to some it sounded ominous and sinister, as though the nuncio were merely a papal spy in France.

Those who bothered to meet him found a different Roncalli to the political intriguer who stalks the pages of the *Secret Documents*. He was friendly, unassuming, loquacious and inclined to go on and on about Bergamo. Anyone who mentioned a 'red hat' got slapped down. 'Hats', he said to someone who wondered when he would become a cardinal, 'hats – I prefer to look at ladies' hats' (Aimé-Azam, p. 42). He felt most at home in his corner room with its bay window from which, as in tourist pictures of Paris, the Eiffel Tower could be seen. The chimney was Victorian gothic. His huge desk was in the darkest corner of the room. He sat his visitors in the light. From time to time, he would emerge from his lair and pace up and down, hands in his belly-band, talking volubly. Denise Aimé-Azam, to whom we owe this description, relates how one day Roncalli wanted to find a book by John Henry Newman which he knew was on the bottom shelf. Down went the portly nuncio on hands and knees, all dignity gone. He didn't find the Newman, but fished out instead an English translation of Dom Guéranger's *Année Liturgique* and explained, somewhat bizarrely, 'I use this to brush up my English' (Aimé-Azam, p. 61). He became a well-known figure in his *quartier*. He picked up the daily gossip in conversation with Yvette Morin who ran the newspaper kiosk on the corner of avenue Moreau and avenue Pierre I de Serbie. He knew her story. She was Jewish and her mother had been at Ravensbrück. Later Pius XII told him that it was undignified for a nuncio to walk the streets of Paris.

As in Istanbul, Roncalli did what he could to improve the plant that he had inherited. He describes 10 avenue Wilson in a letter to Montini:

> The Nunciature of Paris, bought from the Prince of Monaco in 1921 in the time of Mgr Cerretti, is certainly decorous; it is no better than the principal residences of diplomats in Paris, in fact far more modest, but that is as it should be. On the whole it is a worthy and noble residence.
> What surprised me, however, as soon as I saw it, was the unsatisfactory nature of the dining room used for great occasions. Mgr Valeri tried to improve it, giving it a cement roof with a terrace on top which allows one to take a few steps in the open air in the summer, to say one's office or to meditate in solitude. But the dull white walls remained, not much relieved by a large picture of St Peter's Square, certainly painted with good intentions . . . but more suitable as the drop-curtain of a small country theatre than a room to be used by diplomats (*Mission*, p. 115: letter dated March 10, 1950).

He remedied the bareness of the dining room by acquiring, thanks to a legacy, two tapestries woven in the Vatican workshops in the seventeenth century. One depicted 'Pope Urban VIII in the middle of the thirty years war praying with members of his court' and the other 'Pope Urban examining a plan of fortification for the Leonine City or some other town' (*Ibid.*). Roncalli assured Montini that the tapestries were a good investment. Cheaply bought, they were now worth millions. Cardinal Nicola Canali, top financial man at the Vatican, had approved. Later, Roncalli had an unnamed painter execute Roman scenes on the panelling, and Mgr Bruno Heim (subsequently the first pro-nuncio to the United Kingdom) designed the coats of arms of the last three popes.

But in post-war France this preoccupation with interior decoration appeared irrelevant, risible and even blasphemous in a man of God. Priests working in the industrial suburbs despised those who lived in the *beaux quartiers* and wondered how they could possibly understand the workers' problems. As nuncio Roncalli was limited by what he saw from his bay window. Whatever tourists might think, Paris was not summed up in the Eiffel Tower. True, Roncalli knew that there were 'unbelievers' somewhere way out there. In an early letter to his family he explains that 'Paris is a city of five million inhabitants, and many of them lead a life that is completely cut off from the Church'. Then he added, to soften the blow, 'Quite a number still go to Church, and they are very fervent' (*Familiari*, II, p. 14).

Those Parisians 'completely cut off from the Church' were largely the workers. Despite the efforts of the Young Christian Workers (known as *Jocistes* in France), it was estimated that only one per cent of working-class males went to Mass. France had become a *pays de mission*, a mission land. Cardinal Suhard had discovered the 'dechristianisation' of France when he became bishop of Bayeux and Lisieux in 1928. As early as 1929 he told a seminarian: 'There is a whole region around Caen, containing all our great factories where Christ is unknown; this is our true mission territory. Day and night this thought haunts me: I long for missionaries' (*Chronicle*, p. 17). As archbishop of Paris, he could do something about this longing. In 1941 he founded the *mission de France*, a new style seminary whose aim was to prepare hand-picked young priests to work effectively in a working-class milieu. He chose Lisieux for its base because St Theresa was the patron of the missions. In 1943 he started another seminary along the same lines for the capital, the *mission de Paris*.

But something unforeseen and unwelcome changed everything. In the course of 1942 800,000 young Frenchmen were marched off to forced labour in Germany (*Service de Travail Obligatoire* – STO). The Germans refused to allow chaplains to accompany them. Suhard took advice from, among others, the young Jesuit Jean-Marie Leblond who assured him that 'there is nothing in the Church's tradition to prevent priests working with their hands and earning their living'. So Suhard secretly assigned twenty-five priests to join the *déportés*. Most of them were soon discovered and two perished in concentration camps (*Chronicle*, p. 18). They were the first priest-workers.

Other priests had comparable experiences in prison camps or the resistance movement. They discovered that an immense cultural gap yawned between the Church and the workers. The Latin language and the ancient rites did not speak to the workers. The priests returning from the prison camps had learned fraternity and solidarity and were unwilling to be mere props of an unjust social order. They wanted to be identified with, not separated from, the workers. Roncalli had lamented that he could not preach in the style of Bossuet or Mabillon. The 'new priests' ridiculed such ambitions. They wanted to use every-day language to relate the aspirations of the workers to Gospel values. There was a good deal of romantic *ouvrièrisme* in these attitudes.

But on a deeper level, it was their understanding of Christianity itself that had changed. In work and prison camps priests and Catholic Action militants discovered a faith that was 'heroic' – leading to prison or death; 'total' – for faith had to cope with all the problems of daily living; and 'anomic' – because they had to improvise liturgies in strange places. This description comes from Emile Poulat who adds that 'when the prisoners returned from Germany, whether they were priests or laymen, believers or unbelievers, they brought with them an incommunicable experience'. So on their return, there was a problem of re-insertion. They were unable to settle down into the old pre-war routine. Inevitably, they shocked the bourgeoisie.

As nuncio Roncalli had to listen to the complaints of middle-class Catholics who believed that the priest-workers were Communists in all but name. They supplied him with stories of a shock/horror nature. Fr X has said Mass in a boiler-suit. Instead of saying *Dominus vobiscum*, Fr Y greets the congregation with '*Salut, les copains*' ('Hi, pals'). Fr Z translated *Ite Missa est* as 'Go, the Mass of the world is beginning'. The desire to save the Church freed Roncalli's informants from scruples about slander or detraction. The habit of denunciation to Rome was a French tradition. Mgr Montini once quoted the remark: 'Out of any two French Catholics one is sure to be packing his bag to go to Rome to denounce the other' (Guitton, p. 26). In the nature of the case, it was the alarmed bourgeoisie who called on the nuncio. Those complained about wrote him off and declared that he was 'in the pocket of the conservatives'. Roncalli was thus trapped. He knew that the real target of the delators was not the priest-workers themselves so much as Cardinal Suhard who 'weakly allowed their excesses to continue unrebuked and unchecked'. But Suhard remained loyal to the project he had started and in which he saw the salvation of the working class.

As was his duty, Roncalli forwarded to Rome the reports he thought were serious. But the Vatican did not reply with one voice. Mgr Alfredo Ottaviani at the Holy Office was hostile to the priest-workers and eagerly accepted the denunciations. In 1947 he addressed the following set of questions to Cardinal Suhard:

Do the priest-workers fulfil the obligations of the priesthood (saying the divine office, keeping the promise of chastity)? Was evening Mass really necessary? Why this new form of apostolate? Did it not harm the traditional ministry of the priest? Were there not other ways of reaching the masses? (*Chronicle,* p. 51: Suhard replied on February 15, 1947).

The French felt that such questions came from a bureaucrat who had never seen the inside of a factory. Moreover, they had a nastily inquisitorial flavour of 'guilty until proved innocent'. The other voice in the Vatican was that of Mgr Montini. He had been heard to say: 'When so much is at stake, risks must be taken, lest one should be guilty of failing to do all that is possible for the salvation of the world' (*Chronicle,* p. 51).

Where did Roncalli really stand on this question which dogged him throughout his eight years in France? The French would dearly have liked to have known. A letter written as pope permits one to reconstruct his position. His natural inclination was to agree with Ottaviani that the two states of life, priest and worker, were in the end incompatible. On the other hand, like Montini he understood the generosity, self-sacrifice and zeal which led priests to want to do factory work. So his letter to Cardinal Maurice Feltin, dated October 8, 1959, is mildness itself. It contained '*suggestions* made in the Lord' and hoped that 'the desire to preserve in all circumstances the fervour, piety and sacred character of the priesthood' should not exclude 'coming close to the workers and bringing them the breath of light and grace' (*Lettere,* p. 171). In 1964 Montini, by then Pope Paul VI, approved a modified form of 'priests at work'.

In the late 1940s, however, the priest-worker debate was only a particular form of a much wider question. How much pastoral initiative could be left to the local Church? Had the French Church, thanks to its intellectual endeavours, earned the right to offer leadership to the rest of the Church? Had the twentieth century, as Gertrude Stein claimed, happened in Paris? And how well informed was Roncalli, as nuncio, about what was going on?

It was a time of great intellectual effervescence in the French Church. The Jesuits at Fourvière and the Dominicans at Le Saulchoir were renewing theological studies through a return to scripture and the fathers. Henri de Lubac's *Catholicism* dazzlingly showed the social dimension of salvation as a counter-blast to the distorted collectivisms of Nazism and Communism. Yves-Marie Congar defined the nature of 'reform' (*Vraie et fausse réforme dans l'Eglise*), and laid the foundations for the ecumenical theology the Council would find indispensable (the collection *Una Sancta*). Etienne Gilson on St Thomas Aquinas and Henri Marrou on St Augustine proved that at last Christian themes could be at home in secular universities. At the review *Esprit* Emmanuel Mounier and his friends were already denouncing French colonialism.

Moreover, there was talk of a 'Catholic renaissance' in literature, of which the poet Paul Claudel and the novelists Georges Bernanos, François Mauriac and the half-American Julien Green were the best-known representatives. Catholicism was intellectually respectable. It was all the more influential in that the Parisian vogue at the time was for the despairing nihilism dubbed 'extentialism' typified by Albert Camus' Sisyphus, absurdly pushing his boulder up the hill, and Jean-Paul Sartre's Roquentin experiencing nausea (*la nausée*) as he contemplated the roots of a tree trunk. But Sartre had been in prison-camp with Jean-Marie Leblond S.J. and in 1948 Camus addressed the Paris Dominicans and urged them to seek Christ 'in the blood-stained face of history in our own age'. It was an exciting time to be in Paris.

There is no evidence that Roncalli shared in any of this excitement. He admired the collection of patristic texts edited by de Lubac and Jean Daniélou, *Sources Chrétiennes,* and used its edition of the sermons of St Leo the Great. Like Blaise Pascal's *honnête homme,* he gleaned most of his knowledge of theology from conversation. Secular writers fared even worse than theologians. His one exercise in literary appreciation – an extended commentary on the last of La Fontaine's *Fables* – was on his own admission a failure (*'Parve felice la presentazione': Pasqua, 1978,* p. 30). Apart from the historian Henri Daniel-Rops, Paul Claudel was the only author he saw with any regularity. But by now the former ambassador to China was thoroughly *bien-pensant* and had repented of the youthful follies evoked in *Partage de Midi.* Roncalli flicked through and marked a few passages in Claudel's *Accompagnements* (1949), but they were merely banalities about the papal office (*Letture,* p. 63). The poet endowed the pope with a 'luminous tongue'. Roncalli's copy of Charles Péguy, on the other hand, was well-thumbed, especially the *Mystères des Saints Innocents.* He underlined the passage where God says, 'I don't ask much of men. Just the heart', and another in which He says: 'The submission of all the slaves in the world/is not worth the proud look of a free man' (*Letture,* p. 353). But Péguy, though he had been rediscovered, was hardly a contemporary writer. He had been killed at the head of his men in 1914 during the first 'Battle of the Marne'.

When Bernanos, who had claimed part of the prophetic inheritance of Péguy, heard that the nuncio had attended a lecture on his novels, he assumed that they were about to be put on the Index of Forbidden Books (*Combat pour la Liberté,* II, p. 646). He was exaggerating their importance in Roman eyes. But when André Gide *was* placed on the Index shortly after his death in 1951, Mauriac protested vociferously. It looked as though the Holy Office – Ottaviani again – unable for fear of ridicule to take on the living, preferred to condemn dead authors. Mauriac may also have felt that he might soon follow Gide on to the Index. It seemed that the only interest of the Vatican and its representative in literature was as material for burning.

As for Pierre Teilhard de Chardin S.J. who was by now living in New York but whose visits to Paris were always the signal for intellectual coteries to gather, Roncalli felt out of his depth. The evidence is that he could only make feeble jokes about his name. He called him Teilhard de Chapardas (*chaparder* being slang for to 'purloin' or 'nick'). The story comes form the oral tradition of *Etudes*, the Jesuit review at 15 rue Monsieur. One day Roncalli remarked to Robert Rouquette S.J., who also worked on *Etudes*: 'This Teilhard fellow . . . why can't he be content with the catechism and the social doctrine of the Church, instead of bringing up all these problems?' When Rouquette replied that the Church could do without another Galileo affair, the Nuncio grew angry (Rouquette, I, p. 315).

Roncalli's lack of real involvement in French intellectual life was partly due to ignorance. Aimé-Azam guesses that his picture of France and the French was derived from St Francis de Sales which, by 1949, was rather misleading (Aimé-Azam, p. 54). The fact is that he simply did not have the background of French culture that was needed to keep pace with the rapidly spinning turn-table of wit, allusion and knowingness that makes up 'conversation' in Paris. It had no place for memories of Bergamo. Besides, he was in his late sixties, and was overwhelmed by the mass of paper-work he had to do. In December 1947 he made a retreat with the Jesuits at Clamart, a Paris suburb. He complains ruefully about not being able to read all the books he has acquired:

> I have filled my room with books that I would love to read; all of them serious books dealing with Catholic life. But these books are a source of distraction which often creates a disproportion between the time I must give to current affairs, to writing reports for the Holy See and similar matters, and the time that I can actually spend in reading. A great effort is needed here, and I shall set about it with all my might. What is the use of all this anxiety to read, if it is harmful to my immediate responsibilities as Apostolic Nuncio? (*Journal*, pp. 289–90).

There speaks the man of duty. The need to write his 'reports' dominated his waking hours, but without really engaging his deepest self. A candid friend or confessor might have pointed out that the first task of a nuncio (as of any other diplomat) was to understand the country to which he had been sent, and that sharing in its intellectual and cultural life was the best, indeed only, way to that end.

But it was not really lack of time that stopped Roncalli from reading as much as he ought. The proof is that he always managed to keep up his reading of history. The Bollandists in Brussels, for example, continued to think of him as a serious scholar and eagerly awaited the completion of his much-delayed work on St Charles Borromeo (*Mission*, pp. 142–3: letter to Fr Baudouin de Gaiffier S.J., July 5, 1951). If he was neglecting Borromeo, he devoured anything to do with the

Paris Nunciature. Two works in particular interested him. On May 29, 1949, he thanked Mgr Jacques Martin for his work on *La Nonciature de Paris et les affaires ecclésiastiques de France sous le règne de Louis Philippe.* Roncalli was particularly fascinated by the chapter on 'Episcopal Nominations'. 'Ah!' he exclaims, non-committally, 'our own times, in spite of difficulties here and there, are more fortunate' (*Mission*, p. 103). Martin went on to become prefect of the Pontifical Household (a post he still held in 1984).

In one case Roncalli asked to be sent a book (*Mission*, pp. 102–3). Mgr Bonaventura Cerretti had been the first of the new series of nuncios to France after diplomatic relations were restored in 1921. An anonymous biography had appeared in 1939. But at least in the Roman Curia, 'everyone knew' that its author was Don Giuseppe De Luca, a wit, man of letters, and admirer of Lytton Strachey's *Eminent Victorians.* He had planned to write a book on Cardinal Pietro Gasparri which would have taken the lid off the Vatican between 1890 and 1930. His Cerretti book was merely 'the orchestra tuning up for the symphony'. But the symphony was never finished. Roncalli befriended this awkward curialist, and made the fortune of his publishing house by assigning to it all the rights of his *juvenilia* after he became Pope. The reason why the obscure *Edizioni di Storia e Letteratura* occurs so much in the bibliography of this book is simply that Roncalli took a fancy to the enigmatic De Luca.

He came to know the history of the Paris Nunciature intimately. This knowledge gave him perspective, and so made him philosophic, about his own difficulties. They were neither so tragic nor so rare as he might be tempted to believe. He plunged further back into French history, reading the letters of St Francis de Sales who was, he says in 1947, 'my great teacher' (*Journal*, p. 290). He wrote to Montini on May 9, 1950, and aptly quoted St Francis: 'Whatever is written about us, let us never forget that just as our enemies are wont to exaggerate our defects, so our friends are wont to magnify us in their praise; and in the end we are no other than what we are in the sight of God' (*Mission*, p. 124). He suggested that Pius XII might like to see this text (*Saggio*, p. 51). Double-edged though it was, Montini, the substitute, managed to 'lay it before the Pope' on June 1, 1950 (*Ibid.*, p. 51). Pius made no comment.

Roncalli's historical curiosity never flagged, and France offered him a rich store of memories. It was natural that he should be drawn to Avignon where the Palace of the Popes still stands as a gaunt and impressive ruin. In Avignon he astonished the archivists with his knowledge of the papacy in exile and even more by his interest in John XXII, the last 'legitimate' Pope John. Without having 'if-I-were-pope-fantasies', he was already persuaded that it would be a good idea to rescue the name John – both Baptist and Evangelist – for the papacy. After his election he told Cardinal Feltin that he had chosen the name 'in memory of France and in memory of John XXII who continued the history of the papacy in France'

(Bergerre, p. 70). In short, Roncalli preferred his historical studies to contemporary works. One reason may simply have been that, as nuncio, he was uncomfortable with so much modern writing on the Church.

So, for example, Cardinal Suhard's great pastoral letter, *Essor ou déclin de l'Eglise* (Progress or Decline of the Church), published on February 11, 1947, seemed to sum up the swaggeringly confident mood of French-Catholicism. It was known that Suhard had consulted Dominican and Jesuit theologians in its drafting. It appeared as the manifesto of the 'new Church' that was emerging. (In Oxford, a decade later, a club of Catholic intellectuals gave itself the name 'the Suhard Society'.) But behind the scenes there was a furious row. Pius XII was very angry.

He was annoyed because the sweep and scope of Suhard's pastoral were so wide-ranging that, in Vatican eyes, he seemed to be setting up a rival *magisterium*. It was up to the Pope, not the Archbishop of Paris, to decide whether the Church was advancing or declining. That could lead to a slippery discussion on the difference between an *ex officio magisterium* and one of competence. Secondly, the pastoral letter, once again seen from Rome, looked like another bid for independence, and proof of the inexorably 'Gallican' or separatist tendencies that lurked just beneath the surface in France. In every pontificate there is a Church that Rome likes to suspect. Under Paul VI in the late 1960s this was the Church in the Netherlands. In the 1940s the French Church was the fall-guy. But thirdly, and decisively, Suhard's pastoral led to demands for the adaptation (Italian *aggiornamento*) of Church life to contemporary needs. It led to a call for new forms of ministry and apostolate. But since Pius XII did not believe that the Church was in need of radical reform, such language was *anathema* to him.

Where did Roncalli stand? Or, more appropriately, on which fence did he uncomfortably sit? He was loyal to Pius XII, and rationalised his loyalty by denouncing – in private – French arrogance. Aimé-Azam remembers him saying:

> You know about the chosen people and what its fault was throughout the
> Bible: to believe that to be chosen was enough, and that to be chosen
> dispensed one from all effort. This is wrong. One must *respond* to God,
> always and everywhere. Now because France is 'the eldest daughter of the
> Church', it imagines that it can do anything without *faith* entering into
> what it does. This is a mistake, and I am fearful for France (Aimé-Azam, p.
> 55).

There is a parallel passage in his December, 1947 retreat:

> I am delighted to praise these dear, good Catholics of France, but I feel it
> part of my mission not to conceal, through a desire not to be
> uncomplimentary and unpleasant, a certain disquiet concerning the real state
> of this 'eldest daughter of the Church' and some of her obvious failings. I

am concerned about the practice of religion, the unresolved question of the schools, the lack of clergy, and the spread of secularism and communism. My plain duty in these matters may come down to a matter of how much and how far. But the Nuncio is unworthy to be considered the ear and the eye of Holy Church if he simply praises all he sees, including what is troublesome and wrong (*Journal*, p. 291: December 1947).

This is Roncalli at his most severe and censorious. He is the 'eye and ear' of the Holy See. Something has happened to his 'heart and hand'. No *bonhomie*, no diplomatic bluff, no amount of engaging chatter about Bergamo could disguise the fact that he did not like much of what was happening in France. This gave rise to what Rouquette called 'the Roncalli mystery': how was it that a man who appeared so conventional and conservative in France could turn out to be a pope that astonished the world? This question can be focused by asking about Roncalli's relationship with Cardinal Suhard.

There are two contradictory versions of how they got on. For Capovilla 'the relations between Cardinal Suhard and the papal representative were always most cordial and affectionate' (*Mission*, p. 104). That sounds too good to be true, and anyway Capovilla was not in Paris. A slightly better-placed witness was Robert Rouquette S.J. who said that Cardinal Suhard 'was afraid of the Nuncio and always emerged from meetings with him looking gloomy and unhappy' ('*sombre et inquiet*': Rouquette, I, p. 315). But even Rouquette was not at the key-hole all the time. Certainly, what Roncalli often had to convey was 'bad news' as denunciations about the latest escapade of the 'new priests' reached Rome.

An example was that of the enthusiastic abbé Boulier, a man who chafed under the restriction of being a parish priest in Monaco. He had gone to a Communist-inspired 'peace meeting' in Poland in November, 1948. He made the inevitable meal-ticket speech. In his peroration he declared: 'If we, who are engaged upon the struggle for peace, are asked "Who are the Communists among us?", we will reply, "All of us" ' (*Chronicle*, p. 52). This remark brought the roof down in Warsaw. It nearly brought the roof down over Suhard in Paris as well. The 'new priests' were routinely anti-American and opposed to 'Western militarism', but Boulier had gone further than that. Rome expected Suhard to do something.

On February 5, 1949, Cardinal Suhard issued a solemn statement in which he denounced 'habitual and close collaboration with Communism' (*Chronicle*, p. 53). On March 5, 1949, *l'Osservatore Romano* pointed out that 'it is not just "habitual and close collaboration" that is to be avoided. The greatest vigilance is needed even in small actions where there is any risk of error' (*Ibid.*). This was regarded in France as an offensive remark. It was believed to be (though it was not) a rebuke without precedent to a cardinal. It suggested that *l'Osservatore Romano* was blessing those French Catholics who, all along, had been saying that Suhard was irresolute and 'soft on communism'.

On March 17, 1949, Roncalli invited all the French cardinals and archbishops to the Nunciature to discuss the *affaire* Boulier. He warned them that Ottaviani at the Holy Office was very fierce on Communism and could quote on his side *Divini Redemptoris* (1937). It had declared that 'Communism is intrinsically evil, and no collaboration can be allowed with it'. The French prelates knew that, and were upset at the presumption that they were in some way 'pro-Communist'. Roncalli worked through Montini to such good effect that *l'Osservatore Romano* of March 31, 1949, carried an article which praised the *mission de Paris* and in particular Cardinal Suhard 'who has full responsibility for it'. Even though this changed the subject, it could be considered a kind of apology. 'Placing' articles in *l'Osservatore Romano* was the way inner-curial battles were waged. At this point Montini was successful in trying to explain 'from the inside' what the priest-workers were trying to to, and showing that their primary motivation was not to engage in politics but to be with Christ in poverty: 'But only one thing is necessary for these men, who are seeking God in poverty, for themselves and for others: and that is to know that they are following in the footsteps of Christ, the Lord of the humble and the poor' (*Chronicle,* p. 53). In this instance Roncalli had 'made known' the views of the French episcopacy without revealing his own. He had been of positive service to them. Yet the mystery of his own intentions remained. After a good lunch at *Etudes,* cigar in hand, he cheerfully described to the Jesuits the Vatican attitude towards France as 'a half-turn to the left followed by a half-turn to the right' (Rouquette, I, p. 315). They laughed dutifully, wondering where his real convictions lay.

If there was any disagreement between Roncalli and Suhard, both men took pains to cover it up. They met often, and there was always the telephone. In the single month of December, 1948 – made critical by the abbé Boulier's foolish outburst – they were seen in public together on five occasions. The most moving was the ceremony in Notre Dame on December 5, the fiftieth anniversary of Suhard's priestly ordination. He spoke eloquently of his love for the *mission de Paris*:

> The first task is to save the souls of the people of Paris: it is for these masses that I will have to answer on the day of judgement. This is the thought that weighs me down, day and night. When I see these crowds of people my heart is wrung. I constantly meditate on how to break down the barrier which separates the Church from the masses – for unless it is broken down, Christ cannot be given back to the people who have lost him. That is why we have entrusted the *mission de Paris* to specially chosen priests, who are in the vanguard of the Church's progress (*Chronicle,* p. 52).

This was a valedictory. Suhard was seventy-five and felt that he had not long to live. Nuncio and Cardinal came together again on December 29, 1948 to protest against the imprisonment of Cardinal József Mindszenty in Budapest – proof, if any were still needed, of their resolute anti-Communism. It also proved that whatever the *mauvaises langues* might be saying – and Paris had its quota of malicious tongues – no wedge could be driven between Roncalli and Suhard.

They continued to work in tandem up to Suhard's death on May 30, 1949. The most bizarre joint function they attended was a lunch on April 3 with 'three thousand people over seventy years of age, gathered from the city parishes' to celebrate the fiftieth anniversary of Pius XII's priestly ordination. Roncalli hastened to write to the Pope about it:

> Once the Pope was hailed as *salus Italiae,* the salvation of Italy, and there were some who refused to acknowledge this title. This is no longer the case. It is now magnified, and arouses echoes in the whole world. It is no longer the Pope, the 'salvation of Italy' but the Pope 'the salvation of the whole world' . . . The Catholic poet of France, Paul Claudel, coins a happy phrase in a recent book: 'The parish priest of the world'. This very day I met the aged poet at the poor people's dinner in honour of your Holiness. I reminded him of his words. He was delighted (*Mission,* p. 101).

One can take this as a piece of court-flattery or as a prophetic statement about how he, Roncalli, would transform the papacy. It is a fact that Italy took second place in his pontificate. Suhard did not think in such terms. His final pastoral letter appeared in mid-April. Its title was 'The Priest in the City' (*Le Prêtre dans la Cité*) and it showed that Suhard was to be optimistic, tenacious and defiant to the last: 'The Christianisation of this new world, the modern urban world, calls for a complete intellectual renewal; it will perhaps be a long time before we are able to outgrow the methods of mediaeval Christianity' (*Chronicle,* p. 55). This was Suhard's last will and testament.

Was Cardinal Ottaviani, perhaps, still purveying 'the methods of mediaeval Christianity'? It was too late to ask that question now. On May 29, 1949, Roncalli visited Suhard on his death-bed and saw that he was fading fast. He attended the funeral in Notre Dame on June 8, 1949, and no doubt remembered the day, nearly five years earlier, when Suhard had been kept out of his own cathedral. To Bishop Pierre Brot, Suhard's auxiliary and literary executor, Roncalli wrote: 'Almost five years of spiritual contacts had set the seal on a brotherly love that not even the slightest shadow has disturbed: we understood each other so well' (*Mission,* p. 104). No one is on oath in a letter of condolence, and much of this one is written in mortuary slab prose – 'this illustrious pastor', 'the incomparable prelate' and so on. But there is no need to doubt Roncalli's sincerity: he thought he got on well with Suhard. Yet there is irony in the remark: 'We understood each other so well'. Suhard understood that the role of the nuncio was to keep the Vatican informed about what was going on; Roncalli understood that the head of a local Church had to respond to its pastoral needs. Suhard bequeathed Roncalli a *rochet* or surplice, for which he was grateful.

He had inherited a surplice from Suhard: what else had he inherited? Suhard summed up the mood of French Catholicism at the time. He was open to the modern world and ready to learn from it. He believed that there should be a dialogue with Communists and other men of good will and that it could not begin with fulminations. He wanted a renewal of the Church on all levels, a reanimated, active laity and a priesthood adapted to modern industrial life. These were all factors which influenced Roncalli in the long run, even if his first reaction and duty as nuncio was to be suspicious of their novelty. But there is a lot of Suhard in Pope John's pontificate. The 'French' or 'Suhardian' ideas lay fallow in his mind, waiting the time when they would be seen as pastorally necessary, evangelically based, and justified as a response to history.

Roncalli wore Suhard's *rochet* for the first time on June 29, 1949, when he ordained forty-nine priests in Notre Dame. Once again, he was acting as stopgap. These were all 'Suhard priests' who had mostly been through prison or labour camps. Had he lived, he would have ordained them himself. For Roncalli, this ordination Mass in Notre Dame was the high point of his mission to France. He confided in his diary:

> In the story of my life this feast of St Peter will remain a solemn
> memory . . . Several times I was nearly overcome by emotion, but I managed
> to control myself. Everything was enchanting. At the end I gave the solemn
> papal benediction; and in the sacristy I said a few words to the newly
> ordained, whose attitude edified me so much. I commented upon my
> archiepiscopal motto, *Obedientia et Pax* [Obedience and Peace] and on Yves
> de Chartres' remark to Pope Urban II: '*Cum Petro pugnare et cum Petro
> regnare*' ['To fight with Peter and to reign with Peter'] . . . For the first time
> I wore Cardinal Suhard's surplice (*Cronologia*, p. 614).

However, there was more to this episode than meets the eye. Roncalli was edified by the new priests, because it was feared that some would disapprove of him replacing their beloved Suhard. There could have been a demonstration. His private appeal in the sacristy for them to 'fight with Peter' was made in the knowledge that the Holy Office was about to publish a decree which would cause consternation in France and seem like the repudiation of Suhard's entire mission. Pius XII signed the decree the next day, June 30, 1949, and it came out, with unconscious humour, on July 14, anniversary of the storming of the Bastille. It excommunicated all those who 'knowingly and with full consent defend the materialistic doctrines of Communism'. No surprise there. But the decree also included in the ban those who collaborated 'in any way' in actions that would lead to a Communist regime (see *Documentation Catholique*, No. 1048, July 31, 1949). Though apologists argued, probably correctly, that the decree was 'really' aimed at Eastern Europe or Italy, the French saw it as an attack on themselves and a rejection of Suhard's attempt to come to terms with the modern world. The Vatican had cynically waited for his death to reveal itself as a politically conservative and essentially anti-Communist institution. As nuncio, Roncalli was guilty by association.

He chose this moment to go on a long tour of the provinces, leaving the interpretation of the decree to others. He went to Lille, Saint-Wandrille, Vannes, Ars (where the *curé* came from) and La Louvesc. Pius XII later complained about his absence from Paris at critical moments. He told Mgr Marella on his appointment as nuncio to France: 'Above all, don't be like your predecessor Roncalli – he was never there' (Bergerre, p. 70). During Roncalli's diplomatic absence, the four French cardinals patiently explained what the Holy Office decree did *not* mean:

> By condemning the action of communist parties, the church is not taking the side of capitalism; on the contrary, in the very idea of capitalism there is a kind of materialism that is rejected by Christian teaching . . . We are also well aware of the sadness that workers will feel at this condemnation of Communism. We know that they see in the Communist Party above all a resolute champion against the social injustice from which they suffer . . . We are moved by their sorrow, and wish to remove the painful impression that the church is unsympathetic to their aspirations (*Chronicle*, pp. 55–6).

But if that were what the Holy Office decree really meant, it would have been simpler for it to have said so. Taken naïvely, it sounded extremely negative, and one would hardly have guessed that 'in capitalism there is a kind of materialism'. Pius XII offered no guidance on the matter. Pope John's own 'social' encyclicals, *Mater et Magistra* (1961) and *Pacem in Terris* (1963) would be an attempt to redefine the Church's position on socialism and communism. As Nuncio he had no comment.

But he was not neglecting his work while on his peregrinations. He did not leave France until he had found a successor for Cardinal Suhard. The translation of Maurice Feltin, archbishop of Bordeaux, to Paris was announced on August 15, 1949. Two years younger than Roncalli, Feltin came from the northern slopes of the Alps, from the village of Delle. Roncalli called on his relatives there on August 20 on his way home to Italy. They had something in common: they were both mountain village boys from opposite sides of the Alps, and shared a certain rugged spiritual commonsense and a weight problem. They were made cardinals together in 1953, continued to correspond, and Feltin, as president of Pax Christi,

the Catholic peace movement, initiated him into the critical thinking about
nuclear weaponry that is found in *Pacem in Terris*.

Roncalli had an audience with Pius XII at Castelgandolfo on September 6,
1949. One might have expected some discussion of the impact of the Holy Office
decree, but that does not figure in Roncalli's diary:

> In the name of France I thanked his Holiness for the welcome he had given
> to Frenchmen of both high and humble condition who were so edified
> when they visited him. With what spiritual joy I heard him say: 'But that is
> my great concern and consolation – to welcome these men of the world,
> even if they think differently. Isn't this the way the pastor should live? Am
> I not here for sinners, for those who have gone astray? They are all equally
> sons' (*Letture*, p. 437).

This paternalistic version of the pastoral office – let the sinners come to me – was
in complete contrast with the 'identification with the oppressed' that was the
basis of pastoral work in France. It was also in complete contrast with Pope John's
habit of declaring to visitors to the Vatican, 'I am your brother Joseph'. But ten
years earlier he treated the Pope as an oracle.

The appointment of Feltin began the second phase of Roncalli's difficult
mission to France. They got on well, though Feltin did not claim a close
friendship with the Nuncio. Feltin's portrait of Roncalli is more *nuancé* and
perceptive than any we have so far seen:

> He was always friendly, understanding and sought to smooth out difficult
> problems; but when action was needed, he did not lack decisiveness and
> firmness of character. His goodness was not soggy but strong [*ferme... non
> molle*]. Furthermore, he could be subtle, perspicacious and far-sighted; and I
> could give plenty of examples of the way he slipped through the grasp of
> those who sought to exploit him (Bergerre, p. 69).

In 1950, Feltin's first year of office, 'those who sought to exploit' the nuncio
were the conservatives or *intégristes* as they were locally known. It was a Holy
Year, and crowds of pilgrims flocked to Rome. Pius XII with his upturned gaze,
his rimless spectacles, his arms extended to embrace the world, seemed to embody
the very essence of the papacy as it was then conceived. The *intégristes* were
delighted. But others in France were disenchanted. Almost every decision taken
by Pius XII in 1950 appeared to be aimed at the French Church.

The first blow was the apostolic exhortation, *Menti Nostrae*, on the
sanctification of priestly life. Pius XII expressed his sadness at 'the alarming spread
of revolutionary ideas' among some priests who, he averred, 'were not highly
distinguished for learning or austerity of life' (Holmes, p. 185). This was
evidently an allusion to the priest-workers, but its mandarin aloofness caused

much irreverent merriment by the time it reached them. Anyone who thought that life in a modern factory was insufficiently 'austere' was not really in touch. As for 'lack of learning', the priest-workers accepted the charge, adding however that book learning cut them off from the workers and that there were other equally valuable forms of knowledge. But *Menti Nostrae,* though it exhibited deep disapproval of the priest-workers, did not put an end to them: they remained the responsibility of the French bishops. The axe did not finally fall until 1953 by which time Roncalli was gone.

But *Menti Nostrae* was mere skirmishing compared with the mighty encyclical letter *Humani Generis* which appeared on August 12, 1950 at a time when most of the theologians it incriminated were away on lecture tours or on holiday. Its impact may fairly be described with the over-worked phrase, 'theological bombshell'. The fall-out was considerable. It had much the same effect as *Pascendi* forty-three years before. And as in 1907 the fact that the encyclical mentioned no names meant that suspicion knew no bounds. Who will be next? was the question theologians asked themselves as they returned from their summer holidays.

In order to determine 'against whom' *Humani Generis* was written, the only course was to consider which theologians lost their jobs. Using this criterion, the attack seemed to be directed principally against the Jesuits at Fourvière, Lyons, where the three Henris – de Lubac, Rondet and Bouillard – were all forbidden to teach. And there were many others who were 'guilty by association'. Henri de Lubac (made a Cardinal in February, 1983) suffered the cruellest fate: not only was he banned from teaching, but he was forbidden to live in a house where there were students, lest they be corrupted by his pernicious influence. In practice it meant that he was deprived of the life-blood of a proper library. De Lubac was held to be the leader of *la théologie nouvelle* ('the new theology'). Its principal novelty was a meticulous return to the patristic sources. However, he addressed this patristic literature having in mind the questions posed by Maurice Blondel: grace was to be found in nature though it was not of nature (*in natura sed non ex natura*). This theme had been dealt with in his 1946 book *Surnaturel* which argued forcefully against any two-decker view of nature and grace, as though grace were stuck onto nature from the outside. *Humani Generis* attacked a caricature of this position when it said: 'Others destroy the truly gratuitous character of the supernatural order by suggesting that God cannot create rational beings without ordaining them to the beatific vision and calling them to it' (D–S, 3981).

Another group banned from teaching was made up of those, again mostly Jesuits, who were believed to have fallen under the spell of Teilhard de Chardin. Though he had been forbidden to publish, since 1924, except on strictly scientific matters, his lecture notes and speculations were circulating in *samizdat* form and copies hastily duplicated in evil-smelling purple ink were eagerly passed from hand to hand. Like the theologians mentioned in the previous paragraph, Teilhard was deemed to have fallen into 'immanentism'; but he was also guilty of what *Humani Generis* called 'the conjecture of polygenism', that is the idea that the original human beings were a group rather than a single couple (D–S, 3897).

The Dominicans at Le Saulchoir were just as severely hit as the Jesuits of Fourvière. Marie-Dominique Chenu had a book put on the Index in 1942: he had maintained that the study of St Thomas Aquinas could only gain if attention were paid to his historical background. This inoffensive truism was anathema to those scholastic theologians who claimed to 'prescind' from the dimension of time and utter only 'eternal verities'. Chenu was also rumoured to be theological advisor to priest-workers in the Paris region. He was the first to develop systematically the idea of 'signs of the times' (see his article in *La Nouvelle Revue Théologique*, *'Les Signes du temps'*, January, 1965, pp. 29–39) that Pope John was to make his own. But Chenu had been talking about the need to detect the Holy Spirit at work in secular history from the 1940s. A passage in *Humani Generis* seemed to be aimed directly at Chenu. The encyclical is ironic about those who imagine that 'theology should constantly exchange old concepts for new ones, in accordance with various philosophies that it uses as instruments in the course of time' (D–S, 3822). Chenu had said nothing of the kind, but the cap fitted approximately. Yves-Marie Congar, another Dominican who believed in historical theology, was also sacked but he was told by his Master-General that it was for 'false irenicism'. He was in Greece when *Humani Generis* appeared. He was sent into miserable exile in Cambridge, and not allowed to talk with Anglicans or even his brother Dominicans at Blackfriars, Oxford. The director of the Editions du Cerf, the Dominican publishing house, was fired. The Dominican review, *Jeunesse d'Eglise*, was suppressed. Fr Jérôme Hamer O.P. was brought down from Belgium to become regent of studies at Le Saulchoir. (In 1984 he became prefect of the Congregation of Religious.)

It is difficult to know what Roncalli thought about this wave of repression. On the scholasticism versus history issue his sympathies were with Congar and Chenu, as his opening address to the Council makes clear: 'The substance of the ancient deposit of faith is one thing, the way in which it is presented is another' (Abbott, p. 715). But that future event was of no consolation to either theologian in 1950. Roncalli was not directly involved in the purge. On August 21, ten days after *Humani Generis*, he left for Italy and did not return until mid-October. Back in Paris, he was unaccountably silent: his memoirs have a six-months gap between July and December, 1950. In any case, Roncalli was let off the hook in another way. Since most of the ousted theologians were religious, the task of disciplining them could be safely left to their major superiors. Besides, *Humani Generis* had a delayed action effect: some of its victims were not dealt with until late in 1953, by which time the Dominican Master-General, Emmanuel Suarez, a notoriously bad driver, had died in a car accident, and Roncalli was packing his bags to leave France. So there was little he could do about the censured theologians except counsel patience, raise his hands aloft, and shrug.

Pius XII chose this moment to define the bodily Assumption into heaven of the Virgin Mary in a solemn ceremony in St Peter's Square. It was November 1, 1950 the feast of All Saints. The definition was controversial for a number of reasons. It raised the question of the relationship between the *magisterium* and history, and of tradition and scripture. It was the first (and possibly last) exercise of infallibility as defined by Vatican I, and even then did not meet that Council's implicit conditions: whereas Vatican I thought that a definition could be used to put an end to controversy and crisis in the church, in this instance bishops from all over the world were said to be 'almost unanimous' (D–S, 3902), which made the definition redundant. It set up an additional barrier to ecumenism. It was an act of defiance of the world. This last aspect was well brought out by Cardinal Giuseppe Siri, who was close enough to Pius XII to be considered his dauphin. Siri explained that the definition of the Assumption 'was an act of courage because Pius XII challenged directly with an infallible definition a world that did not like teachers' (Siri, on 25th anniversary of Pius XII's death, October 8, 1983, p.4). This made it sound like an act of ecclesiastical *machismo*. French theologians, still reeling from *Humani Generis,* saw it as a loyalty test.

Roncalli had no problem in accepting the definition of the Assumption. He had celebrated the feast since childhood. Ten years after the definition he wrote: 'As Nuncio to France, I was one of those fortunate enough to be present at the ceremony in St Peter's Square. I felt no anxiety about this doctrine, having always believed it; during my years in Eastern Europe my eyes were constantly drawn to images of the "falling asleep of the Blessed Virgin Mary" in churches of both Greek and Slav rite' (*Journal,* p. 337). Roncalli's constant meditation on the Assumption brings out Mary's closeness to us. She is with us not above us. She is the first of disciples and the leader in faith. He concludes his meditation: 'The mystery of the Assumption brings home the thought of death, of *our* death, and it diffuses within us a mood of peaceful abandonment; it familiarises us with and reconciles us to the idea that the Lord will be present at our death agony, to gather up into his hands our immortal soul' (*Rosario,* p. 56). This is a far cry from using the Assumption to teach the world a lesson.

In the last phase of his mission to France, 1951–2, finding French Catholics quarrelsome and argumentative, Roncalli devoted more time to those 'outside' the Church. Not having to pay attention to *ukases* from Rome, they were better placed to appreciate his qualities of heart and understanding. Certainly President Vincent Auriol, who had been finance minister in the 1936 Popular Front, found him congenial. While most French Catholics saw the nuncio's role in terms of the inner life of the Church, the traditionally anti-clerical socialists and radicals understood just how much he had contributed to the good relations between France and the Holy See in this post-war period. The protracted debates on Catholic schools (*écoles libres*) were never allowed to degenerate into bitterness. The 1951 legislation solved the problem amicably (though not finally): Catholic schools received some public funds on the grounds that, with the birth-rate booming, the state system could not otherwise cope (see Jackson, J. Hampden in *A Short History of France*, Cambridge, 1959, p. 208). For Roncalli 'the maintenance of peaceful relations between Church and State' was 'the *primary object* of the Apostolic Nunciature' (*Mission*, p. 180). Judged by this criterion, his mission to France was a success. The virulent Church–state quarrel was over. Moreover, he had learned that he could get on with other than Christian Democratic politicians, a lesson he took home to Italy where it was a novelty.

Roncalli reached out even further in 1951 when he was appointed official Vatican observer to UNESCO. He addressed its General Conference on July 11, 1951. Though a young organisation ('hardly disengaged from the swaddling bands of its infancy' as he put it), it was acquiring a definite shape. It was not just an international museum-keeper, nor should it attempt to impose educational programmes on the whole world. Its role was, he said, 'to kindle active energies and widespread co-operation in the interests of justice, liberty and peace, for all the peoples of the earth, without distinction of race, language or religion' (*Mission*, p. 144). If this involved some overlap with the mission of the Church, so much the better. Roncalli did not consider international organisations as rivals to the Church. But neither did he preach to UNESCO.

He kept his sermon for a special Mass in Saint Pierre de Chaillot. He gave the Catholics working in UNESCO the ground rules for dialogue with unbelievers and other believers. The starting-point was the altar inscription in the Athens market-place: 'To the unknown God' (*Ignoto Deo*). There is an anonymous search for God, and wherever there is justice and truth, grace is also present. As usual, Roncalli had a maxim to express the attitudes which followed: 'To look at each other without mistrust; to come close to each other without fear; to help each other without surrender' (*'Se regarder sans se méfier; se rapprocher sans peur; s'entr'aider sans se compromettre'*: *Mission*, p. 146, where the words are attributed to Cardinal Lecot at the Elysée Palace in 1893). It was not a bad motto for any international organisation. It helped to shape his pontificate. It was in France and at UNESCO that he learned that it was possible to set aside ideological barriers and address 'all men of good will'.

One particular race had a special claim on his attention: the Jews. His wartime memories were still vivid. In Algiers cathedral in March, 1950 he spoke of the Jews as 'the children of promise' (Romans 9.8), 'whom I so often met in Eastern Europe, sometimes in moments of grief, but always in the mutual exchange of human and fraternal charity' (*Mission,* p. 120). The basis for serious theological dialogue was 'to contemplate the people of Israel in the light of Abraham, the great patriarch of all believers'. He had many Jewish friends in Paris, and rejoiced when one of them, Antonio Coën, returned to the faith of his ancestors after a bout of Freemasonry (Aimé-Azam, p. 107). He became very interested in Simone Weil, and in 1952 wrote to her father, Dr Bernard Weil, with the idea of visiting the austere room – it had a sleeping bag but no bed – where she used to work (*Ibid.,* p. 114). He read *La Connaissance Surnaturelle* and greatly admired it. He was moved by her final note which begins, 'I believe in God, the Trinity, the Incarnation, Redemption, the Eucharist and the Gospel . . . ', but then explains why she must remain 'on the threshold' (*au seuil*) of the Church. Roncalli treasured this text, and gave a copy of it to Cardinal Augustin Bea before it was published in 1962 (in *Pensées sans ordre concernant l'amour de Dieu*).

Roncalli's departure from Paris was as unexpected as his appointment there. On November 14, 1952, he received a letter from Montini marked 'private and confidential'. It was rather puzzling. In the name of Pius XII Montini asked whether he would be prepared to succeed the patriarch of Venice, Carlo Agostini, in the event of his death which was imminent. No one at all was to be told or consulted. So Roncalli had to confide in his diary: 'I prayed, thought about it, and answered *Obedientia et Pax* [Obedience and Peace]. A totally unexpected new direction to my life. I remember St Joseph and follow his example. So I push my donkey off in a new direction and bless the Lord' (*Pasqua, 1978,* p. 28). He wrote to Montini the same day, expressing his readiness to obey 'in true freedom of spirit' (*Saggio,* p. 57). Yet he was put in an awkward position. He could not actually wish for the death of Agostini, yet if the old man hung on or recovered, Roncalli might find himself falling between two stools. He neatly covered both eventualities in his reply to Montini: 'I pray that the Lord may cure the Patriarch of Venice, and grant him many years to come. But if I should succeed him, may I be granted the grace to merit the ancient saying about St Mark as the *discipulus et interpres Petri*' ('disciple and interpreter of Peter', *Saggio,* p. 57). For the pastorally-minded Roncalli Venice would be a marvellous fulfilment of a dream of youth. The four hundred years of shared history between Venice and Bergamo meant that it would be like going home. But it was not yet in the bag.

On November 29, 1952, he received a telegram from Montini to say that the Holy Father had decided to 'elevate him to the sacred purple' at the Consistory on the coming January 12, 1953. Feltin of Paris and Grente of Le Mans were also to be created cardinals (*Saggio,* pp. 57–8). He reacted calmly to this not unexpected news. It meant that it was now certain he would be leaving Paris, if not for Venice, then for the Roman Curia – a prospect that did not fill him with unmitigated joy. Moreover, he was worried by the news received the same day that Ancilla, 'who has always been the most precious treasure of my household'

(*Ibid.*, p. 59) was dying of cancer. He asked permission to make a quick journey to Sotto il Monte to see her. This was granted. On the night express to Milan the thought of Ancilla and the cardinal's hat jostled in his mind, and he wrote in his diary:

A restful night in the train. O Jesus, how human am I! How thankful I am for the faith that gives me clarity of vision and immortal hopes, and how thankful I am that a time which could lead to temptations of vanity and self-satisfaction should become instead a period of union with the cross. O *crux, ave, ave* ['Hail, hail, o cross'] (*Pasqua, 1978*, p. 29).

By December 12 he was at Ancilla's bedside. Though the doctors had given her only a few weeks to live, she lingered on for another year until November 11, 1953.

Back in Paris the news that he was to become a cardinal – but not that he might be going to Venice – had become public knowledge. The round of official congratulations began with the prime minister, Antoine Pinay, and President Auriol, who said it would make a sad leave-taking. When Feltin, shortly to be his brother cardinal, called to congratulate him, he found Roncalli uncharacteristically 'sad, gloomy and troubled'. Feltin asked, 'All the same, aren't you really glad about it?' Roncalli replied: 'No, I'm not at all happy because I wanted to stay in France. I love France and I love Paris, and I hoped to stay a little longer. I can't really see myself in Rome, going along day after day to meeting after meeting and concerned with administration. That's not what I'm good at. I'm really a pastor' (Bergerre, p. 69). What he couldn't tell even Feltin was that he would escape this curial fate only if Agostini died. By Christmas the patriarch of Venice was sinking fast. Roncalli prayed for him, but added in his diary: 'If I should succeed him, I unite my prayer with his sacrifice which is already a good preparation for my sacrifice' (*Pasqua, 1978*, p. 29). That was on Christmas Day, 1952. Four days later he opened his copy of *Le Figaro* at breakfast and learned that Agostini had died. 'With this death', he noted, 'the new direction of my life indicated on November 14, the feast of St Josephat, begins. I await my instructions from the Holy See' (*Ibid.*, pp. 29–30). He had narrowly escaped the Roman Curia.

Becoming a cardinal and patriarch of Venice did not go to his head. He reminded himself that 'there have been rogues and saints among the cardinals' (*Pasqua, 1978*, p. 29) and that being a cardinal was an honour, not another sacrament, 'not even a sacramental' as he explained to Cardinal Saliège (*Mission*, p. 176). He resolved to prepare himself spiritually for the office. His inner life was simplifying itself. He found it helpful to return to Book III, chapter 23, of *The Imitation of Christ*. Its subject is 'the four things that bring great inward peace' and its maxims, so evangelical in spirit, are essential for understanding Roncalli:

Choose always to have less rather than more.
Seek always the lowest place and to be beneath everyone.
Seek always and pray that the will of God may be wholly fulfilled in you.
Behold, such a man enters within the borders of peace and rest
(*Pasqua, 1978*, p. 45: letter to Mgr Gustavo Testa, then nuncio in Berne,
dated December 2, 1952).

To those who met him then and later, Roncalli seemed to enjoy the 'great inward peace' of which *The Imitation of Christ* speaks. They could only guess at the price he paid for it.

He had arrived in France in December, 1944 in haste and without fuss. He left nine years later with all the leisurely and elaborate rituals of official leave-taking. On January 15, 1953, President Vincent Auriol, making use of a special privilege that used to belong to 'Catholic' heads of state, handed over his red biretta. He then decorated Roncalli with the *Légion d'Honneur* and made a speech. Auriol's key sentence was this: 'Your experience enabled you to appreciate the role of France in the world and made you understand, long ago, the traditions of justice and tolerance which have always been the honour of our nation and which were to unite, in answer to Pope Leo XIII's solemn appeal, all the spiritual families of France around the Republic' (*Mission*, p. 182). The tribute was deserved and nicely judged. In 1893 Leo XIII had urged French Catholics to 'rally to the Republic'. The France–Vatican clash in the pontificate of Pius X made that difficult if not impossible. Now, by 1952, those wounds were healed and French Catholics, if one discounted a few impenitent monarchists and survivors of *Action Française*, had rallied to the Fourth Republic.

While Auriol was conferring the red biretta on him in Paris, in Rome his appointment as patriarch of Venice was finally announced. Some French people were offended that 'their' cardinal, instead of going to an influential post in the Curia where he could defend the French Church, was heading for Venice. The 'image' of Venice was of a toy-town city with canals and lagoons, of unearthly beauty but fairy-tale irrelevance to the modern world.

On February 5, 1953, Roncalli organised a farewell dinner at the Nunciature to which he invited Edouard Herriot, president of the National Assembly, and the eight men who had been prime minister during his time in France: Georges Bidault, Félix Gouin, René Pleven, Edgar Faure, André Marie, Robert Schuman and Antoine Pinay (Dreyfus, pp. 118–19). They all came. Capovilla quotes a remark that went the rounds: 'Only under the nuncio's roof could French politicians of such diverse views meet each other in a friendly way' (*Mission*, p. 185). One could equally reflect on how quickly political figures pass into oblivion.

General Georges Vannier, Canadian ambassador, paid tribute to Roncalli in the name of the diplomatic corps on February 19, 1953. The chill of the cold war meant that no East Europeans turned up, but – Roncalli counted them – 'fifty-nine colleagues were present' (*Pasqua, 1978*, p. 31). Vannier's baroque conceits rivalled Roncalli's own rhetoric. The nuncio, he suggested, summed up in his person the three characteristic products of Bergamo: wine, silk and steel. The wine evoked 'the warmth of your heart and the vivacity of your spirit'. Silk hinted at 'a sense of nuances' and made clear that he would never be 'one of those severe, Goya-type cardinals'. Vannier warmed to his theme: 'No, you have the strength tempered with grace that we find in the paintings of Raphael'. Finally the steel stood for 'the firmness of character which makes no compromise where truth is concerned' (*Mission*, p. 186). It was not such a bad portrait. But one is left wondering why the French Church did not see Roncalli the way the diplomats did.

Four days later, on February 23, 1953, he left France. His diary records:

> Left France for good [*partenza definitiva*]. Got up at 4.30 a.m. after a good night's sleep. Sorrow at departure, but sweetness in union with God and a sense of 'goodness turned into love'. Holy Mass at 6 a.m. A silent, emotional farewell at 7.30, with a few tears here and there . . . I bless the Lord and thank him *pro universis beneficiis suis,* for all his kindness to me (*Pasqua, 1978,* p. 31).

That evening he was in Milan. The next day he saw his dying sister Ancilla and on February 25, 1953, went by train to Rome where he was greeted at the station by Mgr Angelo Dell'Acqua, his former secretary in Istanbul. He saw Tardini briefly and had a 'very long conversation' with Montini who forwarded a note to Pius XII, who was too ill to receive him. The triangle of Venice–Milan–Rome had dominated his life so far. At last he was going home to be the pastor he had always wanted to be. He was seventy-one. It seemed likely to be his last posting.

Chapter 11

The seasons of Venice

Venice is a seasonal city, dependent more than most on weather and temperature. She lives for the summer when her great tourist industry leaps into action, and in winter she is a curiously simple, homely place, instinct with melancholy, her piazzas deserted, her canals choppy and dismal

(James Morris, *Venice*, p. 203).

The consistory of January 12, 1953, was the second and, as it turned out, the last of the pontificate of Pope Pius XII. Though no one realized it at the time, it completed the college which would elect his successor, and therefore the next pope was somewhere among their number. Roncalli was pleased to see Valerio Valeri made a cardinal. Of the new intake of twenty-four, ten were Italian. At the time this was widely hailed as a move towards 'internationalization': *only* ten were Italian. Eight of them were destined to spend the rest of their lives in the Roman Curia. The exceptions were Roncalli and Giuseppe Siri, archbishop of Genoa since 1946. Still only forty-seven, a man of some brilliance, he was considered not only to have the ear of Pius XII but to be his dauphin or secretly designated successor. He would be one of Roncalli's rivals in the conclave of 1958. Political significance was read into the nomination of 'Iron Curtain' cardinals, Alojzije Stepinac of Zagreb, Yugoslavia, and Stefan Wyszyński of Gniezno-Warsaw, Poland. Both were under house arrest and unable to come.

Even before he left Paris, Roncalli was beginning to build up his team for Venice. The vicar general, Mgr Erminio Macacek, came to see him on February 3, 1953, bringing with him Don Loris Capovilla. Born in 1915 in a small mainland town near Padua, Capovilla lost his father and knew poverty before entering the Patriarchal seminary in Venice. Small, vivacious and energetic, he had 'done a bit of everything' since his ordination. He had been army chaplain, broadcaster, journalist, editor of the diocesan paper, *La Voce di San Marco*. He was not Roman-trained. Roncalli took to him at once and made him his secretary. They were not parted until his death. In Capovilla Roncalli got much more than a secretary: he got a spiritual son, a literary executor, a *confidant* and a Boswell.

Roncalli wrote to the mayor of Bergamo on January 17, 1953. After his not very happy attempt to expound La Fontaine, he was obviously delighted to be back in a world where the name of Alessandro Manzoni meant so much. Manzoni, in fact, had never been far from his thoughts in Paris, since it was there that the novelist had been converted; and Roncalli contrasted the fate of the layman Manzoni with that of Lorenzo Mascherone, a Bergamesque priest, poet and mathematician who lost his faith there (*Dodicesimo anniversario*, p. 89). Now once more he could quote Manzoni and be sure of being understood. In his letter to the Mayor of Bergamo he recalled the scene in which the hero, Renzo, reaches the River Adda at daybreak and sees walls and towers in the distance:

Is that Bergamo?
The city of Bergamo, replied the fisherman.
And the bank over there belongs to Bergamo?
To the land of St Mark.
Then long live St Mark, cried Renzo, already beginning to feel like a Bergamesque (*Pasqua, 1978*, pp. 62–3).

Long live St Mark, disciple and interpreter of St Peter, Roncalli equivalently cried, already beginning to feel like a Venetian. The four centuries of common history, he told the mayor of Bergamo, 'formed the character of our people on the pattern of Venice, and set up a current of sympathy between the East and the West of the Serenissima'. Roncalli remained fundamentally a regionalist: 'Today all the regions of the peninsula make up one Italy. But within this attempt to establish brotherhood between all Italians, respect for the particular character of each region enriches us all with a spiritual beauty that makes one exult and rejoice' (*Ibid.*, p. 63). He was clearly going to enjoy being a pastoral man in Venice. He had waited a long time for this chance.

He took possession of his diocese in the grand style on March 15, 1953. He did not disdain pageantry or find it tiresome. Young Albino Luciani, whom he ordained bishop of Vittorio Veneto on December 27, 1958, eventually became patriarch of Venice on February 8, 1970. He abolished the procession of gondolas which had been the traditional accompaniment to the entry of the patriarch. Roncalli was not so puritan. Venetians enjoyed processions. Many gondoliers had freshly repainted their boats. Roncalli introduced himself that same afternoon to the people of Venice with characteristic directness:

I want to talk to you with the greatest frankness. You have waited
impatiently for me. Things have been said and written about me that
greatly exaggerate my merits. I humbly introduce myself.
Like every other man on earth, I come from a particular family and place. I
have been blessed with good physical health and enough common sense to
grasp things quickly and clearly; I also have an inclination to love people,
which keeps me faithful to the law of the Gospel and respectful of my own
rights and those of others. It stops me doing harm to anyone; it encourages
me to do good to all.
I come from a modest family and was brought up in contented and blessed

poverty – a poverty that has few needs, builds up the highest virtues and prepares one for the great adventure of life.

Providence took me away from my native village and led me along the roads of East and West. It allowed me to come close to people of different religions and ideologies, and to study grave and menacing social problems. Yet Providence also allowed me to maintain a balanced and calm judgement. I have always been more concerned with what unites than with what separates and causes differences . . .

I dare not apply to myself what Petrarch, a lover of Venice, used to say of himself. Nor have I tales to tell like Marco Polo when he returned here among his own. But strong bonds bind me to Venice. I come from Bergamo, land of St Mark, the land where Bartolomeo Colleoni was born. Behind the hills of my youth lies Somasca and the cave of St Jerome Emilian.

No doubt the great position entrusted to me exceeds all my capacities. But above all I commend to your kindness someone who simply wants to be your brother, kind approachable and understanding . . .

Such is the man, such is the new citizen whom Venice has been good enough to welcome today with such festive demonstrations (Alberigo, pp. 207–10).

It was irresistible. Roncalli at seventy-one had a charism that was not merely explained as the sum of his goodness, sincerity and charm. It was difficult to dislike him. Meeting the painter, Giuseppe Cherubini, a majestic and imposing figure with a long flowing beard, Roncalli shook hands instead of having his ring kissed and explained: 'We're both patriarchs – you by your magnificent beard, I *ad literam*, literally' (Cugini, p. 58). It was a quip, but it had the ring of truth.

Venice took to the patriarch, and the patriarch took to Venice. He loved its traditions and the links with Byzantium. On his first Easter Sunday evening he had reached the end of benediction in St Mark's Basilica, all dark, gleaming and mysterious. He thought there was nothing more to come when suddenly the seminary choir burst into a haunting oriental-inspired litany which, Capovilla thought, 'seemed to reawaken the angels and the saints looking down from the mosaics of the gilded cupolas'. Roncalli turned to the canon on his right and asked, 'What next?' The ancient replied in Venetian: '*Eminensa, andèmo a l'altàr de la Nicopeja a ralagrarse co la siora Mare, perchè son Fio xe ressucità*' ('Let's go, your eminence, to the Nicopeia altar to congratulate Our Lady on her son's resurrection') (*IME*, pp. 94–5). The Madonna of Nicopeia is a mysterious icon, reputed to have been painted by St Luke; it was removed from Constantinople in 1204. The Nicopeia Madonna was not the only memory of the time when Venice 'held the gorgeous East in fee'. The East was present in the design and décor of the

Basilica and in the Convent of the Mechitarist Fathers, an Armenian order who had lived on the San Lazzaro island since 1715.

Familiar with the history of the city, Roncalli knew that it had fallen from its former glory. Now it had crumbling palaces and pockets of poverty. It came to life during its festivals – of cinema, painting and music – when it provided a picturesque décor for international jet-setters. In the summer it was crowded out with tourists, artists, *nouveaux riches* or homosexuals (lured by the memory of Baron Corvo and Thomas Mann) who irritated or were preyed upon by the 400,000 who made up Roncalli's flock. But the population of the historic city was declining as the young looked for work in Marghera and Mestre, by now large industrial towns. Roncalli made his first visit to Porto Marghera within a few days of arriving. He said Mass for the victims of industrial accidents. He recorded in his diary: 'Made a deep impression on me, and was well received' (*Pasqua, 1978*, p. 34 – March 27, 1953). As patriarch he saw another Venice that the tourist posters preferred to ignore.

The contrast between magnificence and poverty continued to strike him. He made his first retreat as patriarch at Fietta, the villa house of the Venice seminary. He was joined collegially by the fifteen bishops and auxiliaries from the eight dioceses of which he was now metropolitan. His notes make it clear that Venice was no sinecure: 'Despite the ecclesiastical splendour that surrounds me and the veneration shown to me as cardinal and patriarch, I already have two painful problems: lack of funds, and the throng of poor people who want work and financial help' (*Journal*, p. 305).

He made a similar remark to his sister Ancilla on May 15, 1953: 'The Venetians are indeed very good, courteous and affectionate towards their Patriarch. But there is also great poverty here' (*Familiari*, II, p. 333). Later, as Christmas approached, and the piazzas were full of returning 'migrant workers', he wrote to Maria: 'In Paris I had plenty of work, but it was as nothing compared with here . . . I'm like the mother of a poor family who is entrusted with so many children' (*Ibid.*, p. 344).

As usual in a new place, he liked to get his domestic arrangements sorted out as soon as possible. His palace, a nondescript building on the left of St Mark's Basilica, gave onto the piazzetta dei Leonicini, so called because of the two rusty lions who guarded it. It was, he told Mgr Bruno Heim who was now in Vienna, 'a modest but welcoming place' and guests could always be squeezed in somehow (*Pasqua, 1978*, p. 79). But the guest rooms were cold and draughty in winter (*Familiari*, II, p. 344). Heim, an heraldic expert, advised him on his coat of arms: a lion of St Mark on a white ground. He preferred not to live in the rooms on the first floor, once occupied by his predecessor, Blessed Pius X, and installed himself on the second floor. He knocked down a wall and had a new partition built so that his bedroom opened onto his study. He looked onto the inner courtyard. It was very tranquil, especially at night when he liked to work on the history of Venice and his long-delayed final volume of the *Atti* of St Charles Borromeo's visitations. 'With this work', he told David Cugini, 'which has gone on for forty years, I hope to leave to our grand nephews and nieces a little sign of affection for Bergamo and win respect for my humble name' (Cugini, p. 56). He meant that he would be remembered for these four volumes. He could not have been more wrong. The four volumes of the *Atti* helped him measure the rate of inflation. The printing of volume I cost 2,000 *lire*; volume IV was going to cost 2 million *lire*. 'I'll have to find the money in Bergamo', he explained, 'because, you know, I'm not a capitalist' (*Ibid.*).

Over the door to his study he placed the words '*Pastor et Pater*' (Shepherd and Father) as a reminder of how his authority should be exercised (Alberigo, p. 249). He persuaded Cardinal Adeodato Piazza, prefect of the Consistorial Congregation, to give him an auxiliary bishop, and was pleased with Mgr Augusto Gianfrancheschini who had been a parish priest in the inner city (*Pasqua, 1978*, p. 8: letter to Piazza, June 19, 1953). In Guido Gussi, a twenty-two-year-old from the nearby fishing village of Caorle, he found the perfect batman who eventually accompanied him to Rome. Guido was frustrated because he was not often called upon to drive the Fiat 1400 that the Catholic Bank of Venice had presented to the patriarch. It wasn't much help in the city of canals. And Roncalli preferred to take the *vaporetto*, the water bus. House-keeping, finally, was looked after by discreet nuns from the Istituto delle Poverelle in Bergamo.

He would dearly have liked to have had his two sisters, Ancilla and Maria, as his housekeepers now that he was at last back in Italy. But his first two years in Venice were overshadowed by a secret distress: both Ancilla and Maria were dying of stomach cancer. As Ancilla's x-rays brought further bad news, he wrote to her that he had thought of complaining to God, like Job, but then 'I hadn't the heart, convinced as I am that you and I are essentially united in the will of the Lord, and so we will merit many graces in this life. Just imagine the graces of the life to come' (*Familiari*, II, p. 338). This letter was written from Rome on October 22, 1953. He was aware of the irony. Here he was at the pinnacle of his profession, having received 'the highest mark of honour for an ecclesiastic on earth' (*Ibid.*), while his beloved sister was dying. The remark shows that at this stage he had no thought of becoming pope. On October 19, 1953, he was appointed to three Roman Congregations – Oriental Churches, Propaganda Fide, and Religious. He was assiduous in meeting cardinals and called on twelve in a few days (*Cronologia*, p. 654). He neither envied nor wanted to change places with them. To Heim he had quoted the remark of Sarto, the future Pius X: 'I prefer to be a cardinal in the forest rather than a cardinal in a cage' (*Pasqua, 1978*, p. 79).

He also met three French Cardinals, Feltin, Gerlier and Liénart, who were in Rome to save what they could of the priest-worker experiment. Roncalli's successor, Mgr Paolo Marella, had arrived in Paris on June 1, 1953, with orders to suppress the priest-workers altogether (*Chronicle*, pp. 63 and 77). Now that Roncalli was himself on the receiving end of curial instructions, he felt more sympathetic towards the French. He continued to keep his friendships in good repair. But his thoughts kept coming back to Ancilla.

His last letter to her is dated November 8, 1953, just three days after the French Cardinals and their fateful audience with Pius XII and three days before her death. He wrote very simply:

> Dear Ancilla,
> Today I took possession of my titular church of Santa Prisca, so I'm now a fully-fledged cardinal. But my heart carries around a wound – the thought of my dear sister. I say to the Lord, *Fiat voluntas tua* [Thy will be done], but saying it costs me a lot; how much more costing it must be for you who are so tried and suffering . . . Dear Ancilla, you have done so much good in your life, and all those who know you bless you. Remain in patience, in abandonment to God, in the certainty that all will be turned into great joy and blessings. I'll come and see you on Friday or Saturday next, the 13th or the 14th, but I can't say exactly when. Affectionately (*Familiari*, II, pp. 340–1).

But he was not able to keep his promise. On November 11, 1953, while he was inaugurating the new junior seminary at Fietta, Ancilla died. He did see her on November 13 as she lay in an unadorned coffin in his house at Camaitino. The patriarch knelt among the peasant women gabbling their *Ave Marias* and prayed for his sister whose life had been one long round of domestic drudgery, relieved only by the recurrent feasts of the Church. Before the coffin was finally sealed, he kissed her on the brow, and said to Capovilla 'That's the second time I've done that – the first was when I knew she was dying' (*IME*, p. 52).

Then they trooped off to the village graveyard and laid Ancilla – the servant – to rest alongside their parents, Giovanni and Marianna. A vicious wind lashed the cypress trees and scattered the autumn leaves. Roncalli would not be buried here. He had already revised his will and arranged to be buried, along with earlier patriarchs, in the crypt of St Mark's. The other members of his family would all come to rest here in the Sotto Il Monte cemetery, Teresa in 1954, Maria in 1955. But there was no time to linger. They had to hurry back by train to Venice. It was already dark, and Roncalli was in a pensive mood. Capovilla heard him murmur, '*Guai a noi se fosse tutta un illusione*'. With the rhythm of the train and the rain beating down on the windows, the mysterious remark, 'Woe to us if it's all an illusion', was imprinted on Capovilla's memory because 'it revealed a disconcerting aspect of genuine humanity in my patriarch, who was normally always so strong and self-controlled' (*IME*, p. 53). Whether Roncalli was thinking of the pomp of Venice, Ancilla's wasted years or eternal life itself, his doubt brought him closer to common humanity. It was a backcloth against which faith could shine out.

But he did not repine, and was soon writing two letters in three days to Mgr Giovanni Battista Montini about a plan he had at heart. The Giorgio Cini Foundation had recently completed the restoration of the Benedictine Abbey on the island of San Giorgio, just across from the Doge's palace and the basilica. Roncalli was glad to be chairman of the Cini Foundation Committee. It was just the sort of project to appeal to him. It involved the rescue of a neglected island and the conservation of a church of great beauty designed by Andrea Palladio. San Giorgio was steeped in history. Its first church was built in 830. It was there in 1800 that the conclave met to elect Pope Pius VII, who was later bullied and humiliated by Napoleon. But San Giorgio was far from being merely a museum. It was now a cultural centre with concerts and symposia and an open-air theatre. It had a technical school run by the Salesians and the Marina orphanage. Roncalli assured Montini that this was the kind of work – cultural and conservationist but at the same time charitable and socially useful – that was once the pride of Italy. And these different facets were brought together in the prayer of the Benedictines, who had returned to San Giorgio after a long absence. The whole operation was 'a miracle of resurrection – an island rising up to a new and glorious life – like a poem' (*Saggio*, p. 64: the two letters are dated 10 and 12 December, 1953). The story of San Giorgio was a metaphor for Roncalli's thinking about the Church: with deeply traditional roots, but of contemporary relevance.

This work led him into friendship with Count Vittorio Cini. It was largely to encourage Cini that Roncalli asked Montini to solicit for the patriarch the title of 'commendatory abbot', that is caretaker-abbot until such time as a proper one is appointed. It was granted. Cini was also paying for the restoration work in the patriarchate (*Saggio*, p. 65). So Roncalli was already well in with the Venetian 'establishment'. Like all Italian bishops, alongside his ecclesial role, he had an indirect 'civic' function. He met prefects and mayors, city and provincial councils, chiefs of the police and the fire-brigade. He organised a Mass for journalists on the feast of St Francis de Sales. He welcomed the rugby team 'Faema' at the Patriarchate and blessed the oil-tanker 'Marilen' at Porto Marghera. He was becoming a well-known personage, a civic asset, a Venetian landmark.

He was also involved, willy-nilly, with politicians and especially the dominant Christian Democrats. In the pontificate of Pius XII bishops were expected to support the Christian Democrats as a way of keeping the Communists permanently out of power. Elections were fought on a simple 'Rome or Moscow' ticket. Roncalli did not find this altogether congenial. He had been in Rome shortly before the April 18, 1948 election and attended a youth rally in St Peter's Square. He was disconcerted to hear Carlo Caretto, a young Catholic Action leader, denounce the politicians present – including the Christian Democratic party secretary, Alcide De Gasperi – as too timid and feeble in their opposition to Communism. It was a frank display of Catholic muscle, and the 'green berets' of Catholic Action recalled earlier and more sinister attempts to forge 'strength through unity' (*Utopia*, Ital., p. 383). Roncalli saw this as an abuse of Catholic Action:

> That's not what the Lord wants. The Christian steers clear of clash and rhetoric . . . One has to move cautiously. There's a whole web of relationships with the entire political class that demands delicate respect and a sense of duty. As witnesses to Christ, our first task is not struggle [*lotta*] but sowing the good grain, not victory but suffering (*Letture*, p. 351).

Catholic Action and pastoral work were twisted out of true when they were subordinated to politics. One simply could not measure the advance of the Kingdom by the number of votes won for the Christian Democrats.

But by the time Roncalli arrived in Venice the 'system' was firmly in place and well-oiled. Dr Luigi Gedda, head of Catholic Action and the Pope's man, had set up 'civic committees' which in effect turned every parish into a recruiting and propaganda office for the Christian Democrats. Hovering in the background was the threat of excommunication for all those who co-operated with Communists in any way. Mgr Alfredo Ottaviani, of the Holy Office, used to boast that 'you can say what you like about the divinity of Christ but if, in the remotest village of Sicily, you vote Communist, your excommunication will arrive the next day' (*Magister*, p. 52). In private, Montini and his friends were critical of this systematic anti-Communism. It dispensed (or appeared to dispense) the Christian Democrats from any concern for the social justice they had been founded to defend; and it pushed them to the right, where the only possible allies were the the Neo-Fascists. But if Montini thought in terms of political strategy, Roncalli saw the problem in more spiritual and human fashion: his mission was one of reconciliation.

In his very first address in Venice he had said he would 'stress what unites rather than what divides'. Political parties, on the other hand, were there to stress what divides: they are by definition partial and partisan. So if Roncalli were to be the patriarch of all Venetians and not just of the Christian Democratic voters among them, he would have to try to disengage himself from party political squabbles and be even-handed in his approach. He made this quite clear the first time he went to the city hall to meet the Council:

> I find myself in a house that belongs to the people as a whole, and I am glad to be here, for the place is in good order. I am happy to be among busy people, for only the man who works to a good purpose is truly a Christian.

Indeed, the only way to be a Christian is by being good. That is why I am
happy to be here, even though there may be some present who do not call
themselves Christians, but who can be acknowledged as such because of
their good deeds. To all I give my paternal blessing (Trevor, p. 242).

So Roncalli knew all about the 'anonymous Christians' later identified by Karl
Rahner: all good acts are borne by the grace of Christ, even if this is not explicitly
recognised. In practical terms it meant having respect for all who engaged in
politics.

The first test of these high-minded attitudes came in the run up to the elections
of June, 1953. But Roncalli was not altogether a free agent. He had to harmonise
what he said with the bishops of his province not to mention the known desires of
Pius XII. The imminence of the election was indeed one reason why Pius had
urged him to get to Venice sooner than he would have preferred (see *Pasqua, 1978*,
p. 67: 'The Holy Father has let me know his desire that I should arrive as soon as
possible . . . but I can't just run away from Paris'). His eve-of-poll declaration,
when it eventually came out on May 30, 1953, was full of studied under-
statements. 'We don't need a lot of words to understand each other', he told the
Venetians. A wink was as good as a nod. He avoided the crusading tone and contented himself with clarifying where duty lay: 'Above all, we must vote, we must
all vote, and we must not throw our votes away. As Christians and Catholics you
cannot and should not campaign on behalf of those who profess anti-Christian
doctrines which the Catholic Church has condemned and condemns' (Alberigo,
p. 211). Taken rigorously, that would exclude only the Communist Party in so far
as it was 'Stalinist'. Roncalli recalled that the experience of fifty years of 'trying to
create social justice without Christ's Gospel' had not been very successful. Only
die-hard Communists would dispute that truism. It was interesting that a bishop
should recognise that the Soviet Union had been 'trying to create social justice' at
all. And Roncalli has a cryptic phrase to suggest vaguely that the situation could
change: 'The tactical requirements of a debate so full of imponderables might
indicate a different attitude in circumstances so far not very clearly foreseeable'
(*Ibid.*). In sheer elusiveness that almost equalled some of the later statements of
Aldo Moro, master of the elliptic style. But the main point was that Roncalli's
pre-electoral statement was milder than that of most Italian bishops. He uttered
no dire threats of excommunication and tried to write as a pastor offering
elucidation rather than as a prince–bishop imposing his will.

No doubt it was vain to imagine that elections could ever lead to reconciliation.
But on February 11, 1954, there was an anniversary that spoke explicitly of
'reconciliation': it was twenty-five years since the signature of the Lateran Pacts.
Roncalli preached on this theme at 6.30 p.m. in St Mark's, and became overnight
a national figure. His life-long meditation on the meaning of history led him to

tackle two questions: what should Italian Catholics, in 1953, think of Mussolini? how does the Church come to change its policy on important issues?

The problem posed by the Lateran Pacts, especially the manner in which they were secretly negotiated and suddenly announced, was that the Church had quite simply changed its mind. It gave up its age-old claim to the restoration of the Papal States. But one can defend the right cause at the wrong moment, and what makes change possible is the admission that God is still mysteriously at work in the world. Roncalli patiently explains 'It was natural that the Popes should feel it their duty to defend themselves, whatever the cost, until the day when there was a new sign from heaven, which would find a response in the papal conscience and so put an end to its otherwise justified claims and assertions' (Bertoli, p. 19). So the reconciliation of the Italian Church with the Italian nation became the prototype of the reconciliation between Church and 'world' more generally. The art was to 'discern the signs of the times'.

But then there was a difficulty. It looked as though Mussolini himself was being presented as the 'new sign from heaven'. That was hard to swallow. Two days before the Duce's death, Cardinal Schuster of Milan 'counselled him to repent of his sins and was upset to find him far removed from feelings of penitence' (Mack Smith, pp. 370–1). How could such a man be a 'sign from heaven' still less 'the man of Providence' as Pius XI was alleged to have called him?

On the second, controverted point, Roncalli put the record straight by quoting the exact words used by Pius XI in 1929: 'We should say that we have been nobly assisted by the other party. And perhaps there had to be someone like the man whom Providence put in our path, someone free from the obsessions of old and out-moded ways of thinking.' Pius XI meant that Mussolini, from whatever motive, had rid himself of the anti-clerical prejudice that had kept the 'Roman Question' simmering. And there is an important *nuance* between calling someone 'a man of Providence' and saying that 'Providence put him in my path'. Roncalli's commentary on Pius' remark was listened to in intense silence. He knew how to keep an audience in suspense:

A sad thought wells up from the depths of my spirit. May I say to you with confidence and as a father to his children, a few words that may help us towards understanding and forgiveness?
Consider: the man whom Providence put in the path of Pius XI, the one who, because of his freedom from out-moded ideas, was able to grasp more clearly and with greater intuitive penetration the problem of Reconciliation, this same man later became a cause of great sorrow to the Italian people. It would be inhuman and unChristian to deprive him of this title of honour despite the immense calamity [*immensa sciagura*] he brought upon us. He was firm and decisive in drawing up and ratifying the Lateran Pacts. So we

have to entrust this humbled soul to the mystery of divine mercy which
sometimes chooses vessels of clay for the realisation of its plans, and then
breaks them, as though they had been made for this purpose alone.
My brothers and sisters, I know that you can read my heart. Let us respect
the broken fragments of this vase, and draw profit from the lessons it
teaches us (Bertoli, pp. 18–20).

The Lateran Pacts, in other words, were Mussolini's 'redeeming feature', and
remained so despite the subsequent tragedy. It needed courage to state such simple
truths in 1954 when Mussolini was a tabu topic and his memory was execrated.
Yet so long as Italians and the Italian Church in particular had not come to terms
with this part of its recent history, there would be falsity, uneasiness and the threat
of returning demons. Roncalli exorcised the past with compassion.

It was axiomatic that only the Neo-Fascists had a good word to say for
Mussolini. So predictably the left-wing press read Roncalli's sermon as an attempt
to rehabilitate the hated dictator. But it was something much more profound –
more like a healing of the Italian national psyche. This was recognised by
Montini, whose anti-Fascist credentials were never in doubt, who wrote to congratulate and thank Roncalli for his address (*Saggio*, p. 66: letter of March 5,
1954).

Montini was increasingly his Roman *confidant*. They wrote to each other
frequently. Included in their correspondence is a letter written by Roncalli on
Easter Sunday 1954, that was never sent, though the draft was carefully
preserved. Capovilla speculates that it was withheld because it was 'too self-
revealing' (*Saggio*, p. 70). Another reason for withholding it could be that
Roncalli's attempt to lower the ideological temperature in Venice was having
some success: 'The relationship of the Patriarch with all the civil, military and cultural authorities is excellent, and such that one may hope to have a good spiritual
influence upon them. People of opposed ideologies argue among themselves but
keep their respect for each other' (*Saggio*, p. 69). It may have occurred to Roncalli
that such sentiments were bound to appear naïve to the Roman Curia. Set in a
position where he was supposed to give decisive leadership, he was once again
being too good-hearted. That he had defused traditional hostilities in Venice was a
good thing in itself, but it could be attacked as compromise by the time it reached
Rome. And it was important not to upset Pius XII now that he was said to be so
gravely ill.

Not so ill, however, that on this same Easter Sunday, April 18, 1954, Pius was
able to announce the date for the canonisation of Blessed Pius X, May 29, and
make an important statement on atomic weapons. He called them:

new, destructive weapons of unheard-of violence, arms likely to bring down
a dangerous catastrophe upon the whole planet, to encompass the total

extermination of all animal and vegetable life and all the works of man over even vaster areas, arms that are capable, with their long-lasting radio-active isotopes of polluting for a long time the atmosphere, the earth, the very oceans, even though they may be very far from the zones directly affected and contaminated by nuclear explosions (*Saggio*, p. 69).

Pius' rhetoric – based on the principle that everything must be said thrice – and his display of pseudo-scientific knowledge (those 'radio-active isotopes') could not hide the gravity of the situation. The French were known to be testing atomic bombs in the Pacific. Roncalli took the Pope's statement seriously enough. He refers to 'these memorable and awesome words directed against the abuse of nuclear energy, which is the terror (*spavento*) of all who live in this tragic and mysterious age'. It was Roncalli's first documented mention of the nuclear threat (*Saggio*, p. 69). It suggests that one can recognise the originality of *Pacem in Terris*, while conceding that it owes more to Pius XII than is commonly supposed.

Despite this burst of activity at Eastertime, Pius XII's illness continued to cause anxiety. It was believed – and he certainly believed – that he was mortally ill. He had already vouchsafed his 'dying words' to Cardinal Giuseppe Siri: '*Depositum custodi, depositum custodi*' ('I have kept the deposit of faith') (Siri, address to Synod, October 9, 1983). A conclave was therefore imminent. Roncalli would have to think about it. It occurred to others, if not also to himself, that he was a candidate and *papabile*.

Roncalli's first mention of the Pope's precarious state of health came in a letter to his whole family dated March 3, 1954. After noting that 'despite the burden of work', his own health was excellent, he went on:

The great worry just now is for the health of the Holy Father. It seems that he suffers from the same illness that our own Ancilla suffered from, a stomach tumour as it is called. This explains why he can be fed only by injections. Like our dear, departed Ancilla, he will have perhaps only a few months, but in the end he must give in like all mortal beings.
I owe the Holy Father infinite gratitude for having named me Patriarch of Venice and still more cardinal. Join with me in praying that the Lord may long preserve this great Pope.
To tell you the truth, his death would cause me great bother: I would have to interrupt for at least a month the splendid work that I have begun with my pastoral visitation. I don't want to change my programme for this year (*Familiari*, II, p. 353).

A conclave would be a nuisance because it would interfere with his pastoral plan: visitation of all the parishes to be followed by a Synod of the whole diocese. He regards the death of Pius XII as an inconvenience rather than a great loss. There is a notable lack of emotion about this passage, as though Roncalli felt that Pius XII had done his work and should not cling immoderately onto life.

Yet the illness of Pius XII hung sombrely over 1954, overshadowing the more predictable events: it had been declared a 'Marian year' – it was the 100th anniversary of the definition of the Immaculate Conception of the Virgin Mary; and Blessed Pius X was due to be canonised on May 29. Roncalli's judgement had mellowed or grown more prudent over the years. In 1951, year of the beatification, he had written an article in *France Illustration* extolling Pius X as 'a bright and sure light amid the uncertainties of modern thought', adding with uncharacteristic brutality that 'those who opposed him sank by the wayside or reaped only the whirlwind' (*Mission*, p. 138). In another passage in the same article there is just a hint of the 'anguished' Pius X whom he found so lacking in serenity (see above, p. 63): 'Pius X conquered all hearts because he gave himself with constant willing devotion that reminds us of St Vincent de Paul, with a smile that was frank and joyful, but more often *tinged with a veiled and gentle sadness* such as was seen in the eyes of St Francis of Assisi' (*Ibid.*, p. 139: my italics). It was evident that Roncalli, who had not been critical of the beatification was unlikely to get worked up about the canonisation in 1954, even though he knew full well that most of the biographies of Pius X involved 'rose-tinted spectacles and lashings of whitewash' (Marrou, p. 343.)

He threw himself into the preparations for the canonisation with a will. The chapel and study of Sarto on the first floor were restored to their 1903 state as a memorial. There were still surviving relatives about, and on May 16, 1954, Roncalli gave first communion to some of Pius X's grand-nephews and nieces. He told Montini that he preached almost every day, and rarely failed to mention Pius X, even if briefly (*Saggio*, p. 70). He presided over the inter-diocesan committee which pleaded that the mortal remains of the new saint should 'go on pilgrimage' to the cities where he had once been known. Roncalli's energy pulled this off, despite difficulties about security (*Saggio*, p. 75). Cardinal Francis Spellman from New York came for the feast of the Ascension – always celebrated with great panache in Venice as the marriage of the city and the sea – and they were together in Rome for the post-canonisation triduum. The canonisation was a matter of great local pride in Venice. As Patriarch, Roncalli asked for and was given a role in the Roman ceremonies: on May 31, 1954, he celebrated Mass before the tomb of Pius X in Santa Maria Maggiore. Then he hastened home to dedicate a church to the new saint in Maghera. Since St Pius X was anti-intellectual, it was assumed that he would be popular with the workers. All in all the canonisation brought, in the time-honoured phrase, 'great honour to the Church of Venice'. And throughout this period Roncalli was increasingly dependent on Montini as his friend in high places.

They were in correspondence again over the Marian year. Roncalli had no prob-

Giovanni Battista Roncalli, Angelo's father (1854–1935).

Marianna Roncalli, née Mazzola, his mother (1854–1939).

Angelo Roncalli on his arrival at the Roman seminary, January 1901.

Angelo's 'year' at the Roman seminary, 1901; he is at the right hand end of the back row.

Medical Corps: sergeant and chaplain in the First World War.

Consecrated bishop at San Carlo allo Corso, Rome, March 19, 1925.

In the saddle in Bulgaria.

On the balcony at the Apostolic Delegation, Sofia.

Confirming Italian servicemen, Greece, July 16, 1942.

Presenting the diplomatic corps' New Year greetings to President Charles de Gaulle, January 1, 1945.

The Patriarch on the Grand Canal. Arriving in Venice in traditional style, March 15, 1953.

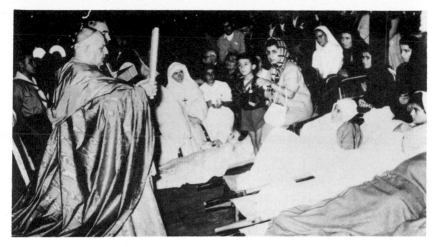

Blessing the sick. Marian year celebrations, 1954.

The last audience with Pius XII, March 27, 1958. On the right, Roncalli's secretary, Don Loris Capovilla.

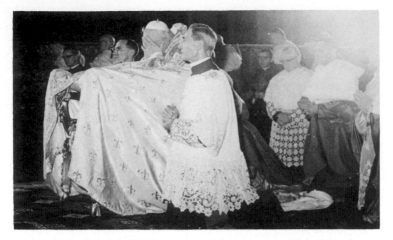

Pope John in prayer on the day he announced the Council at St Paul's-without-the-walls, Rome, January 25, 1959.

Christmas Day, 1959, wearing the fur bonnet he revived.

Honouring his secretary, Capovilla, in the papal library.

President de Valera of Ireland, St Patrick's Day, 1962.

HM Queen Elizabeth II and HRH Prince Philip, May 5, 1961.

President Dwight D. Eisenhower, December 6, 1959.

Chancellor Adenauer, January 22, 1960.

With leaders of the Italian Church; from left to right Giovanni Battista Montini, Milan; Giovanni Urbani, Venice; Alfonso Castaldo, Naples; Pope John; Giuseppe Siri, Genoa; Giacomo Lercaro, Bologna; Maurilio Fossati, Turin.

With the Benedictines at San Anselmo, November 25, 1959.

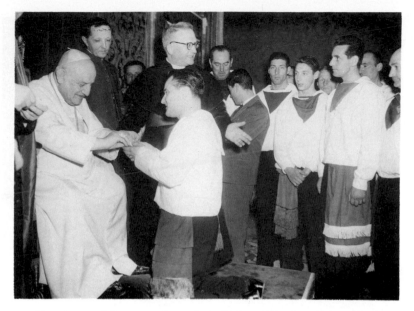

Venetian gondoliers are welcome in the Vatican. When in Venice, Patriarch
Roncalli used to present the prizes at the end of their annual regatta.

In the printshop of the Vatican Polyglot Press.

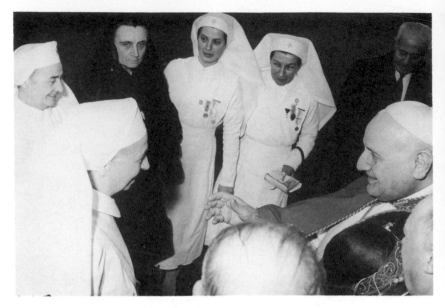

A joke with nurses.

A walk in the formal garden at Castelgandolfo.

Urbi et Orbi, Easter 1961.

Leaving St Peter's on the opening day of the Council, October 11, 1962, having made the 'speech of his life' (photo by Tony Spina).

Giacomo Manzù, sculptor, at work in Pope John's study (photo by Tony Spina).

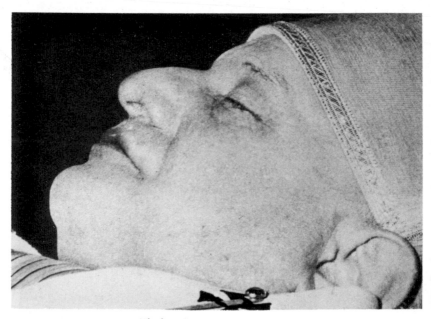

The last photograph, June 3, 1963.

lem about celebrating the 100th anniversary of the definition of the Immaculate
Conception; in 1904 he had helped Radini Tedeschi celebrate the half century of
the definition. However, he did not hold the view, common among mariologists
in the pontificate of Pius XII, that one could not have too much of a good thing
and 'could not honour Mary too much'. There was a search for new and more
extravagant titles. Invited to sign a petition in favour of a new feast, *Regalitas
Mariae*, the Queenship of Mary, Roncalli politely declined:

> I beg you to forgive my silence so far which is evidence of my uncertainty
> and the fear that such a feast could prejudice the great action already under-
> taken towards the refashioning of the unity of the Catholic Church in the
> world. When Jesus was dying, he said to John, 'Behold your mother'. That
> is enough for faith and the liturgy.
> All the rest may be – and no doubt is for the most part – edifying and
> moving for devout and pious souls; but for many, far, far more, however
> well disposed towards the Catholic Church, it would be merely irritating
> and – as the modern phrase is – counterproductive. . . . Meanwhile, I am
> happy to say *Salve Regina, Mater misericordiae* [Hail holy Queen, Mother of
> mercy] (Alberigo, p. 489: letter dated April 22, 1954).

He prudently added, however, that should 'the supreme authority of the Church'
decide to set up such a feast, he would be among the first to celebrate it. This was
just as well since six months later the encyclical *Ad Coeli Reginam* established the
feast of the Queenship of Mary and directed that it be kept on May 31. Yet
Roncalli's objection of principle remained on the record. It was most unusual for
an Italian prelate to oppose a new Marian feast on *ecumenical* grounds. There were
limits to his mariology, and the ground was being prepared for the sound and
sober mariology of the Council.

Despite this misjudgement, he was invited by a letter of Montini to go to
Beirut, in the Lebanon, as papal legate at the National Marian Congress (*Saggio*,
p. 73: letter dated June 15, 1954). The Lebanon was an old haunt. He had known
it, he claimed somewhat loosely, 'from my youth' (*Ibid.*, p. 74). But it was a great
honour and a mark of trust. It meant that Pius XII, or just possibly Montini, had
not forgotten Roncalli's diplomatic past and still cast him in a modest international role. But before he could set off for Beirut, he was preoccupied with a
more personal celebration.

The 50th anniversary of his ordination fell on August 10, 1954. These fifty
years had flashed by. He regarded the anniversary as a private event to be marked
by extra prayer and recollection at Sotto il Monte. He thought he was entitled to
some peace and had been fêted enough in Venice and Bergamo when he became a
cardinal. He did not want another fuss. In a letter to the Venetians he gave explicit
orders that 'there should be no celebration, either liturgical or cultural, of this

anniversary' (*Pastore*, p. 339: letter dated August 10, 1953). Naturally enough, his orders were ignored.

This caused him to write one of the most incensed letters of his life. It was addressed to his nephew, Don Battista, son of his brother Giovanni, who was still on the long road to ordination. Battista had already tried his uncle's patience by shilly-shallying about his vocation and fussing about the difficulties of study (see Alberigo, p. 482: letter to G. Battaglia dated September 28, 1951). But now there was a sudden change of gear. Don Battista, who had certainly meant well, received this thunder-bolt from his uncle patriarch on August 2, 1954. It is revealing as an instance of what could make Roncalli really angry:

> Dear Don Battista,
> When I got back to Venice I heard from Mgr Loris (Capovilla) that cele-
> brations are being planned for my priestly jubilee. *I have told you many times
> that there are to be no festivities for me*. I intend to take part in the ordinary
> celebration of the Assumption at Sotto il Monte: I will celebrate a low Mass
> at 7 or 8, and will be present at the High Mass and take part in the
> procession later in the afternoon. But I do not want, I do not desire that
> *anything more should be done than in previous years*. So: no guests from
> Bergamo or anywhere else, whether clergy or laity, friends or relations: I
> want to be *alone, alone*, with my family and the dear parishioners of Sotto il
> Monte. Have you got that? Tell also dear Dom Mario (Minola) that he has
> no need to put himself out for me. Why do you have to offend me and
> make me suffer? Are you trying to stop me from coming at all?
> Don Loris will come from Venice and that's all. I've had enough public
> celebrations in my life already: they are far in excess of anything I have
> deserved in the last half century. Enough is enough [*basta, basta*]. I can't
> avoid some kind of manifestation here in Venice on September 30 and
> December 8. But then these are my spiritual children.
> Two meetings, one with the clergy and another with the laity, and that's
> all. I don't want anything from Bergamo. They did far too much for me
> when I became a cardinal last year. Let's turn our thoughts to living well
> and dying well. Beneath the flowers in the cemetery the earth has not yet
> settled on the graves of our dear sisters Ancilla and Teresa. And should we
> be thinking of a feast? You understand me, dear Don Battista? Let it be
> understood by others. I'll be at Camaitino with Don Loris and Guido the
> day after tomorrow. Arrange everything with simplicity, and you will be
> blessed.
>   affectionately,
>   Ang. Gius. cardinal
> (*Familiari*, II, pp. 357–8; italics in the original).

After this avuncular wigging, Don Battista did what he was told. He was soon to find that the advantages of having his Uncle Angelo in high places were not unmixed. Roncalli hated nepotism.

So Roncalli celebrated the fiftieth anniversary of his ordination, in the place where he was born and grew up, in comparative peace. Here is how he described the day:

> A wonderfully bright sky after merciful night showers. The sound of the *Angelus* from San Giovanni roused me at once with a *Laus tibi, Domine* [Praise to you, O Lord]. There followed an hour of prayer in the chapel with the breviary lessons about St Laurence in my hand, on my lips, in my heart: pages that are a poem. What is my poor life of fifty years of priest-hood? A faint reflection of this poem: 'My merit – God's mercy' (*Journal*, p. 307).

Another note, written the same day, shows how he used his Breviary as a prayer of intercession for all those he had known: 'Every day as I say my Breviary, I think of all the places I have been in: at Prime I pray for France; at Terce, Turkey; at Sext, Greece; at Nones for my beloved Bulgaria. And I pray for all, the living and the dead' (Righi, p. 103). It is characteristic of Roncalli that his heart could expand to meet new demands. On this clear day after night rain in August 1954 he celebrated fifty years of mercy, fifty years of graces bestowed. In Venice he had come home to port.

One reason he wanted to lie low for his golden jubilee celebration was that gossip and speculation continued to present him as eminently *papabile*. His tran-quillity at Sotto il Monte was disturbed by a French would-be prophet, Gaston Bardet, who not only predicted that he would become pope but guessed the name he would choose when elected. Bardet sent him the proofs of a book he had written, with a request for a preface. Roncalli replied from Sotto il Monte on August 26, 1954, in pained tones:

> My Dear Friend,
> I received your letter with the page proofs for which you invite me to write a preface. For some weeks I have been very worried about this, so much so that I haven't been able to think about anything else. But because your soul, as I can see, is in great ferment, I gathered my thoughts in fervent prayer and now have the courage to tell you openly about the painful doubt that has been afflicting my heart for some time (Capovilla, Archives).

After that courteous introduction, Roncalli told Bardet bluntly that he was 'the victim of a serious and dangerous hallucination', and that the words of Jesus applied: 'Get thou behind me, Satan'. Having 'tested the spirits', he concludes that Bordet's 'mish-mash [*groviglio*] of predictions bears all the marks of the "spirit of confusion" '. So he thinks it better that they should not meet. He quotes the example of Donna Prassede in *I Promessi Sposi* 'who meant well, and thought she read in the heavens what in fact was contained within her head' (*Ibid*).

But Bordet was not so easily brushed aside. He went to Venice, had a meeting with Roncalli, repeated his predictions and said, in Capovilla's hearing, that his pontificate would be marked by 'doctrinal interventions and disciplinary reforms'. Roncalli was still worried by Bordet as late as January 1955. He referred to him in a letter to his sister, Maria:

> Some mad Frenchman, who has revelations and second sight, has even given the name I will take when they make me pope. Mad, mad, the whole lot of them. I'm thinking rather of death. I have a full programme of work for this year and also for next year, the centenary of St Laurence Justinian who was the first Patriarch of Venice (*Familiari*, II, p. 368).

So Bordet was unceremoniously dismissed as mad; but a disturbing flicker of doubt remained.

It was all perfectly ridiculous. He had the Lebanon to think about. He flew out on October 19, 1954 and returned in leisurely fashion by ship a week later. As papal legate, he made two important speeches. He listened *on his knees* to the radio message of Pius XII (*Cronologia*, p. 672). He enjoyed the trip, as did Guido Gussi, now firmly established as his driver and factotum. He met the Melkite patriarch, Maximos IV Saigh, who would play an important part in the Council, and the 92-year-old Maronite patriarch, Anthony Arida, who made him feel distinctly youthful (*Familiari*, II, p. 360). With a conclave looming, such innocent remarks about his own physical fitness at seventy-three could seem loaded. The speculation would not go away.

On November 10, 1954, he wrote to Maria and asked, pointedly, 'Who wants to be more than a cardinal?' So he expected to die a cardinal. He went on: 'I have become insensible to everything, and if the Lord called me swiftly, I would not want to complain. His will is enough for me. Obedience and peace' (*Familiari*, II, p. 361). His contemporaries had been dying one after another. He had preached five funeral orations in as many months. His old friend, Cardinal Francesco Borgongini Duca, nuncio to Italy for so many years, had just died. Roncalli was present at a memorial service for him on November 4, at which the young Christian Democrat M.P., Giulio Andreotti, gave the panegyric (*Cronologia*, p. 673). But the one person who seemed loath to die was Pius XII. Even cardinals had no inside information about the Pope's state of health. Roncalli was only repeating press gossip when he told Maria that 'the Pope seemed to be about to die, and then he got better, only for a relapse to follow'. There were rumours of some expensive new treatment. Roncalli was not sure whether it was worth it:

I have little confidence that the Holy Father will be cured; despite so many doctors and medicines and so much expense. His life is a miracle, but miracles, as you know, only last a very short time. And perhaps we are all wrong, my dear Maria, to complain. At our age, to be alive at all is a bonus (*Familiari*, II, p. 366: letter dated January 8, 1955).

So he still expects a conclave shortly. And he is fit: 'Among the old people here the Patriarch is the most vigorous and is regarded with wonder by the good people of Venice' (*Ibid.*, p. 368). That was for his sister Maria only. Yet this constant emphasis on his own physical fitness makes little sense except as a hint to the college of cardinals. He was not presumptuously seeking election, far from it, but the word was passed round that he was in good shape and available.

But there was to be no conclave for another four years. The expensive new treatment from the Swiss specialist appeared to work. Pius XII recovered or, more accurately, survived. How far he was in charge was much debated. Then, in November 1954, something happened that left Roncalli utterly disconcerted: his friend Giovanni Battista Montini was abruptly removed from his post at the Secretariat of State and sent off into exile as archbishop of Milan. This was, of course 'a great honour'. But in plainer language it meant that Montini had been sacked from the Roman Curia after nearly thirty years. Nor could he be said to be 'acquiring the pastoral experience needed to equip him for the papacy', since there was never any intention of making him a cardinal, though this was the tradition of the ancient and prestigious see of Milan. It was a daunting task for someone whose health was frail, and who had never managed a diocese, still less one so huge and complicated. Why had Pius XII done this? What did it all mean?

Roncalli first heard the news at noon on November 3, 1954, while at Pompeii for a meeting of Italian cardinals and archbishops. It was publicly released the next day which, appropriately enough, was the feast of St Charles Borromeo. Capovilla describes Roncalli's reaction: 'He was dumbfounded (*interdetto*). On the one hand he rejoiced that Montini would succeed not only Schuster but St Ambrose, St Charles Borromeo and Cardinal Ferrari; but on the other hand he was sad to see him removed from Rome and the immediate service of the Pope' (*Saggio*, p. 15). On his way back to Venice Roncalli stopped in Rome and called on Montini. He was struck, Capovilla noted, 'by the air of departure, tinged with sadness, that already hung about the apartment' (*Ibid.*). It was all very well to say that the Curia's loss was Milan's gain, but what puzzled Roncalli was that Pius XII in extreme old age should deprive himself of his most efficient aide. As he remarked to Capovilla: 'Where else will we find someone capable of writing a letter or drafting a document in the way he can?' (*Ibid.*). Was there some shady intrigue in the background?

Roncalli's congratulatory letter contains a hint of his bafflement. Since he arrived in Venice Capovilla had noted that the relationship between these 'two courteous men' 'went beyond the bounds of protocol', and that they had 'lived out their friendship with prudence and discretion' (*Saggio*, p. 14). Now they shared a cross:

> Today and forever your episcopal ordination seals your excellency's conse-cration to the pastoral ministry . . . We will understand together the *sacramentum voluntatis Christi* [the sacrament of Christ's will] of St Paul. This imposes on us the veneration of the cross, but it also brings along with it a fountain of ineffable consolation here below, so long as life and the pastoral mandate last (*Saggio*, pp. 80–1: dated December 12, 1954).

He then invited Montini to come to Venice and preach on the feast of the Ascension. Last year he had Cardinal Spellman. This year the archbishop of Milan.

But despite Roncalli's persuasiveness, Montini was able to plead a multitude of tasks in his new diocese and he could not come just yet. Two anecdotes from 1955 suggest that Roncalli had Montini in mind as successor to Pius XII. Answering a question put to him at a meeting of academics on the Isola San Giorgio he said: 'If Montini were a cardinal, I would have no hesitation in voting for him at the con-clave' (*Lettere*, p. 40). Later two cousins, Giovanni and Candida Roncalli from Milan, came to stay with him at the Patriarchate. He said: 'Look what happened to little Angelo, the son of Battista Roncalli, a farm-worker: he became Patriarch of Venice and a cardinal of the Holy Roman Church. The only thing left now is for him to become pope, but that won't happen, because the next pope will be your Archbishop' [i.e. Montini] (*Ibid.*). This was a common opinion among pundits. The only thing wrong with it was that Montini was not yet a cardinal, and therefore would be excluded from the next conclave.

Montini's banishment was a mystery at the time. Many fanciful explanations have been offered for it. The true story is worth setting down because of its bearing on the conclaves of 1958 and 1963. The illness of Pius XII in 1954 put the question of his succession on the agenda. It also meant that effective control of the Roman Curia passed into the hands of the five influential cardinals – Pizzardo, Piazza, Ottaviani, Canali and Micara – who were known as 'the Pentagon' (Falconi, p. 243). They did not like Montini who was, they believed, 'too liberal'. He was opposed to Luigi Gedda and the 'civic committees'. He was favourable to the 'opening to the left'. He had tried to get the scandalous Catholic novelist Graham Greene to write in *l'Osservatore Romano*. He had defended the cata-strophic priest-worker movement. He had been intimate with Alcide De Gasperi, the Christian Democratic leader, who died on August 19, 1954, out of favour with Pius XII. (Roncalli was unable to go to De Gasperi's funeral at Trent, but he sent along his auxiliary Gianfrancheschini and Capovilla.) Thus in the small world of the Roman Curia Montini's enemies gathered their evidence and awaited their opportunity.

Yet so far he had avoided preparing any rope by which he might be hanged. But then he made a false move, prompted, characteristically, by his desire to stay in touch with the young. He attended a secret meeting of the Catholic Youth Movement (GIAC) at the Villa Carpegna in Rome. Its purpose was to scupper Gedda's alliance with the Neo-Fascists which was having – they believed – the most harmful effect on the Church. But Gedda was the favourite of Pius XII. The Pope used to repeat his predecessor's maxim that 'Catholic Action is the apple of my eye'. There being no other way to protest, Marco Rossi, president of GIAC, resigned. This was unheard of. Leaders of Catholic Action were nominated by the Pope and not supposed to resign (*Quale Papa?*, p. 153).

Rossi's letter of resignation was delivered to Montini, as was right and proper: he dealt with Italian affairs while Tardini covered the rest of the world. Rossi explained why he thought the reactionary and Fascist tendencies of Luigi Gedda were a grave danger for the Church. Montini kept the letter on his desk, wondering what to do about it. But when the news of Rossi's resignation was leaked, Montini was accused of 'concealing information from the Holy Father'. His motive had been to protect Rossi from his own impetuousness. But in Curial eyes he had behaved unforgiveably. His removal in November 1954 followed inevitably. It had political significance in Italy. It was a swing to the right (masked as 'restoring the unity of views' in the Curia); and it was also part of the pre-conclave manoeuvrings (any future pope who thought of having Montini as his Secretary of State would be well advised to think again) (*Quale Papa?*, pp. 152–4). Everything, of course, continued to be done 'in the name of the Pope' and 'by his supreme authority'. But Pius XII was increasingly remote and ailing. Real power had drifted away from him. With the departure of Montini, Roncalli had lost his best friend at court. Angelo Dell'Acqua, once his secretary in Istanbul, was still there as '*sostituto*' in the Secretariat of State. He was friendly enough, but he did not have the calibre of Montini.

But Roncalli never dwelt on disappointment for long. His pastoral letter for Lent 1955 revealed no trace of any anxiety. Always the historian, he points out that the habit of writing Lenten pastorals began in the eighteenth century – precisely the period when papal encyclicals began. Roncalli's pastorals, like those of Ferrari and Suhard, were lengthy and substantial works, prepared in consultation with theologians. One could say they were dress rehearsals for encyclicals. In 1955 Roncalli warned once more – this was by now a routine – against 'the impossible marriage of the Christian and Marxist concept of society' (Alberigo, p. 216). But his main concern was with *renewal* which he saw as a process of perpetual rejuvenation. He wanted to say – it was a reflection of his own experience – that while the curve of bodily existence declines and moves

towards its inevitable end, the spirit can grow younger. He quoted a favourite
maxim from St Gregory the Great: '*Studet per desiderium semper incohare*' ('The
spirit wants always to start afresh'), and quoted the example of St Anthony the
hermit, all of whose teeth were intact at the age of 105. This was, in every sense of
the term, a sore point: the Roncallis' teeth were bad. But that was a joke. Roncalli's
1955 pastoral showed a concern for the renewal of the individual, the Church and
society that was deeply rooted in St Paul ('be transformed by the renewal of your
mind' Romans 12.2) and set the programme of his eventual Council.

But in Lent 1955 he was more concerned with the 'Mission to Venice'. This
enterprise was made possible by 'the peaceful resolution of the Roman question'
(Alberigo, p. 219). Fifty years before it would simply not have been possible to
have thirty-five young laypeople addressing the Venetians on the streets, bridges
and squares of the city (*Familiari*, II, p. 375). The laity were backed up by
twenty-five priests who preached more conventionally in churches. This symbolic
division of labour expressed the then current theory of Catholic Action: the clergy
acted on the faithful while the laity dealt with the world. It was an inadequate
theory. But at least it was an attempt to avoid having a mission which simply
'preached to the converted'. And it also allowed Roncalli to bring to Venice his
old friend Don Giovanni Rossi, Ferrari's secretary in Milan more than thirty years
before, who became founder and director of *Pro Civitate Christiana* at Assisi, a
movement which formed lay people in theology and sent them out into the
'world'. Roncalli judged that the Lent 1955 Mission had been a success. His
criterion was that there were clear signs of 'spiritual renewal', that fresh energies
had been released, and that there was a rediscovery of 'the perennial youthfulness
of Christian and religious life' (Alberigo, pp. 234–5).

Many others were at work in the same field of renewal and reform. Roncalli
met 'prophets' like the anti-Fascist Don Primo Mazzolari who looked forward to
a more fraternal papacy, shorn of pomp and authoritarianism. He came to know
and admire Cardinal Giacomo Lercaro, archbishop of Bologna, a liturgical
reformer who led a life of Franciscan simplicity and later turned his episcopal
palace into an orphanage. Roncalli had him over to preach for Holy Innocents
1955 (*Saggio*, p. 86). 'He knows', Roncalli noted, 'how to create at once an
atmosphere of happiness' (Trevor, p. 248). But it would be wrong to think that
all Roncalli's guests were of one tendency, or that he was trying to build up a
'faction' of like-minded people in the church. He also had along Cardinal
Giuseppe Siri of Genoa to address Catholic Action. At the same time, he knew
who his friends were, and was not averse to giving them some publicity. So he
invited the Venetian, Giovanni Urbani, then head of Catholic Action, to address
his Synod; and in 1956 the literary priest, Don Giuseppe De Luca, gave a lecture
on St Laurence Justinian at San Giorgio (*Saggio*, 87). Montini was present at it,
suggesting that hidden affinities were at work.

Less sympathetic to Roncalli and his friends was Fr Riccardo Lombardi S.J. He was the best-known preacher of the day. Known as 'God's microphone', a sobriquet that gave him pleasure, he filled the squares of post-war Italy with his ringing denunciations of Communism. He was a keen supporter of Luigi Gedda's 'civic committees' and had founded a crusading movement of his own known as 'For a Better World'. The phrase was taken from a speech of Pius XII to the Catholics of Rome (February 10, 1952). Lombardi was also a reformer in some sense. One of his more endearing habits was to call on curial cardinals and enquire what Jesus Christ would do if he were sitting in their chair. Some threw him out for impertinence. But he could not be easily shaken off. He believed that reform had to start at the top, and that then it would trickle downwards. He talked much about the need for an ecumenical council, and indeed liked to quote Pius XII's forthright prediction: 'The next Pope will call a Council' (see Rotundi, Virgilio, 'Padre Lombardi' in *Civiltà Cattolica*, February 2, 1980). Lombardi was powerful because he was believed to have the ear of Pius.

So the bishops of Roncalli's region, Triveneto, thought it prudent in 1955 to invite Lombardi to give them their annual retreat. But as they gathered at the Villa Torreglia, Padua, on May 20, 1955, they were rather wary and their disquiet grew as the week went on. Lombardi seemed to make his 'Better World' movement the norm of renewal in the Church. Everything else, including the *Spiritual Exercises* of St Ignatius, was subordinated to it (*Journal*, p. 310). Roncalli, self-censoring even in his *Journal*, tried hard to be fair to Lombardi, and called him 'an élite religious, edifying and fervent to the point of exaltation'. But then came the reservations. He was worried by Lombardi's 'historical judgements and his one-sided view of the state of the modern world . . . and his aggressive, pessimistic, trouble-shooting tone' (*Giornale*, p. 342; *Lettere*, pp. 142–3: these remarks were unaccountably omitted from the English translation of the *Journal*, p. 310). Roncalli applied his favourite text, I Thessalonians 5.21: 'Test everything, hold fast to what is good'. He was not sure that the Better World movement, despite pontifical approval, passed that test.

But he did not confine his complaints to the privacy of his *Journal*. On November 6, 1955, six months after the retreat, he wrote on behalf of the bishops of Triveneto to Mgr Angelo Dell'Acqua, substitute at the Secretariat of State. It is a letter of some obscurity, though as Capovilla remarks, perhaps with unconscious humour, 'the attentive reader will be enlightened by it' (*Lettere*, p. 143). The bishops had discussed their retreat experience and the 'Better World' movement generally. Their main objection to the 'Better World' was that it seemed to ignore the 'ordinary norms of pastoral government' laid down by the Council of Trent. Lombardi was constantly summoning meetings of bishops, ostensibly to 'inform' them about his movement. Thirty-eight bishops had attended his course at Mondragone in August 1955. But what are these assemblies of bishops? They

have no status in canon law. Meetings of bishops are the ordinary mode of government in the Church; but meetings of bishops to promote a particular movement
are unheard of and could be divisive. To make adherence to the Better World
movement the criterion of fervour in a bishop is abusive. No doubt, Roncalli concludes, the Better World movement has its uses as a stimulus to the laity, but he
wonders whether it is not 'trying to inspire new formulas of authentic reform
which go beyond the competence of individual bishops or groups of bishops'
(*Lettere*, p. 145). So he asks for 'an authoritative word'. But there is no evidence
that Pius – who was being aimed at through Dell'Acqua – replied. Lombardi continued his work. Few could object to a 'Better World' in general. It was the way
it was done that caused problems: Lombardi sometimes had priests and nuns play
party games on the floor in order to rediscover 'the spirit of childhood'.

During the Lombardi retreat, he wondered whether he was not too easy-
going: 'I am always tempted to indulge my peaceable instincts which lead me to
prefer a quiet life rather than take risks' (*Journal*, p. 309). Six months later his
peaceable instincts were tested. He received a letter from Cardinal Pizzardo,
secretary of the Supreme Congregation of the Holy Office, dated January 5, 1956.
It concerned Dr Vladimiro Dorigo (whose name it misspelt), editor of *Il Popolo del
Veneto* (which it incorrectly described as 'the Catholic daily paper of the region').
The Holy Office scribe even contrived to get Roncalli's name wrong, addressing
him as Cardinal Giuseppe Roncalli instead of Angelo Giuseppe. But if the letter
was riddled with inaccuracies and vague, it was also menacing, since it demanded
action on 'the complaints that have come to the Holy See concerning the social
and political direction of *Il Popolo del Veneto*' (*Utopia*, Eng., p. 212). Dorigo was
the immediate target, but Roncalli was also on trial. Would he comply, defend or
distinguish?

He began by trying to get the facts straight. In consultation with the other
bishops of the province, he pieced together a picture of Dorigo that was at odds
with that dreamed up by the Holy Office. He had been one of the associates of
Marco Rossi (see p. 255 above) and had resigned with him from GIAC in 1954.
He then became editor of *Il Popolo del Veneto* and faithfully reflected the line of the
Venetian Secretariat of the Christian Democrats. They belonged, Roncalli
explains to the Holy Office, 'to that wing of the party which impatiently calls for
the realisation of social reforms'. They saw the reigning 'centrist coalition' as an
obstacle. Dorigo and his friends advocated a modest form of the 'opening to the
left': an exclusively Christian Democrat government (*monocolore*) that could rely
on the Socialists to support it when it put forward reforming legislation. But this
was not yet an acceptable line within the Christian Democrats on the national
level, and there was talk of replacing Dorigo as editor of the paper. But, Roncalli
assured the Holy Office, Dorigo's limited 'opening to the left' in no way implied
'the least adherence to Communist doctrine which, on the contrary, has been

repudiated more than once' (*Utopia*, Eng., pp. 213–14).

He concluded that the Dorigo affair was internal to the Christian Democrats and should be left in their hands. Hence, 'any direct intervention by ecclesiastical authority would give rise to unfavourable impressions and comments' (*Utopia*, Eng., p. 214). Roncalli was trying to keep his distance, to behave with that 'reserve' (*riserbo*) in political matters that marked his papacy. In his conversations with Dorigo he stuck to general principles: 'I have met him only three times and our conversation was confined to the broader aspects of sociology and Christian life, without touching on particular controversies or everyday problems'. His portrait was favourable: 'Dr Dorigo is an intelligent young man of unblemished life and fervent religious observance, a stranger to any selfish calculations but very firm, possibly obstinate, in his ideas, which he defends with unusual dialectical skill' (*Ibid.*, p. 215). It was a defence of Dorigo, and it seemed to work. The Holy Office belatedly recognised that since *Il Popolo del Veneto* was a Christian Democrat and not a 'Catholic' paper, action against it was more difficult.

But if the immediate threat to Dorigo was averted, the pressure on Roncalli to show toughness remained. It came not only from the 'Pentagon' but from some of his fellow-bishops who wanted an outright condemnation of *Il Popolo del Veneto* because its supporters, the left-wing Catholics, were active and wreaking havoc in their dioceses. Roncalli disliked condemnations and continued to believe that what a Christian Democratic newspaper did was none of his business. But he was being urged to do something. In the end he wrote a pastoral letter, dated August 12, 1956, in which he deplored the 'opening to the left at any price'. This was, he declared, 'a most serious doctrinal error and a flagrant violation of Catholic discipline'. The error was 'to join those who support the Marxist ideology which is the negation of Christianity and which cannot be harmonised with the values of the Christian Gospel'. Moreover, it was illusory to champion the 'opening to the left' on the grounds that it would lead to economic and social reforms and greater social justice. This was Roncalli's harshest intervention in political affairs while in Venice. It was not his style. How can it be explained?

Most simply by pressure from the bishops of his province. He knew they were going to take action anyway. His August 12, 1956 statement was his 'pound of flesh', the limit to which he was prepared to go. This can be deduced from the fact that his colleagues adroitly issued a communiqué expressing their agreement with his letter, but hardening it and taking it a stage further:

> We declare our full solidarity with the thought and action of the Patriarch and we invite all our faithful, especially the young, to be on the watch against propaganda which is carried on in the subtlest way by some either in person or through the political weekly *Il Popolo del Veneto*. Therefore, we warn against the reading and diffusion of the said weekly (*Utopia*, Eng., p. 219).

Roncalli did not *sign* this document. Obviously not, it might be said, since it was addressed to him. But that was a subterfuge, designed to conceal the fact that the patriarch refused to condemn Dorigo and *Il Popolo del Veneto*. Despite buffetings from events, his resolution of the previous year still held firm: 'Watchful kindness, patience and forbearance get one along much further and more quickly than severity and the rod. I have no illusions or doubts about this' (*Journal*, p. 309). But in laying aside 'the rod', Roncalli risked the charge of 'foolishness'. He had long been familiar with 'the third degree of humility' described in the *Spiritual Exercises* (see p. 130 above) and had opted to be 'a fool with Christ rather than be esteemed wise and prudent in this world' (*Exercises*, No. 167). His 1956 retreat proves that he had thought about this and made his decisive choice (or 'election'): 'I would not mind being thought a fool if this could help people to understand what I firmly believe and shall assert as long as I live, that the Gospel teaching is unalterable and that in the Gospel Jesus teaches us to be *gentle and humble*; naturally this is not the same thing as being weak and easy-going' (*Journal*, p. 312). Whatever people thought of him, whatever the rebuffs, Roncalli was going to gamble on goodness.

He carried this conviction into everyday life. He reached out towards those who were considered opponents if not enemies. The thirty-second Congress of the Italian Socialist party was due to meet in Venice on February 1, 1957, under its secretary Pietro Nenni. In a Candlemasday exhortation called 'The Light of Christ in the History and Life of Peoples' Roncalli, speaking as Venetian and patriarch, welcomed the Congress. The city had a tradition of hospitality, and St Paul recommended a bishop to be *hospitalis et benignus* – hospitable and kind (*Letture*, p. 45). He hoped the Venetians would appreciate as he did 'the exceptional importance of this event, which is of great moment for the immediate future direction of our country'. In the definitive edition of his Venetian writings, *Scritti e discorsi*, this banal sentiment was dropped. It did not do for an influential Italian prelate to suggest that a Socialist Party Congress might matter for the country's future. But Roncalli had gone much further than that. He deplored the 'gap' that had opened up between Christian and secular culture, and prayed that the Congress might help to bridge it: 'It is certainly inspired – I am willing to believe – by the desire to bring about the mutual understanding that is needed to improve living conditions and social prosperity' (*Ibid.*). These innocent welcoming remarks caused a furious row. Roncalli had perpetrated another *gaffe*. He was publicly praised by *L'Unità*, the Communist paper, for providing the basis for co-operation between Catholics and the left, and privately though courteously rebuked by Dell'Acqua (*Utopia*, Eng., p. 221). There was once more talk of his naïveté. He was too easily exploited. He was too good to be trusted in a cruel and wicked world.

But he refused to be budged from his policy of charity first. He explained why in a letter to Don Fausto Vaillanc, a priest from Val d'Aosta, who had sprung to his defence in diocesan papers:

> I am so grateful to you for your help in so many ways. I see that you understand me very well. In time, and given patience, everything comes full circle. Even my first statement – judged *as a whole* and not by phrases torn out of context by the malignant scissors of my enemies – would have contributed to greater sincerity and courtesy. Isn't courtesy the first aim of charity?
>
> The truth is that the balanced attitude [*contengo misurato*] of the humble Patriarch – I have honest and certain witnesses to it – moderated the verbal excesses that might have been feared, and led many to greater respect and deeper thought. *Veritatem facere cum charitate* [to do the truth with charity] is good Pauline doctrine, and it does honour to everyone (*Utopia*, Ital., p. 301).

This was a large claim. He meant that his courtesy towards the Socialists had already proved effective. They had been changed by his intervention, wooed by his welcome. Roncalli was not imagining things. His judgement was confirmed by Count Giuseppe Dalla Torre, editor of *l'Osservatore Romano*, whom we last met in 1919 (see p. 93 above), who wrote *privately* to congratulate him on 'disarming sectarianism' (*Utopia*, Eng., p. 222). It was by no means, as the right-wing critics charged, an 'opening to the left', but it was a prior condition of any such opening. Many Italians were grateful.

If Roncalli's attitude to the Socialists was a way of responding to the present demands of history and closing the gap between the Church and 'men of good will', the celebration of the 500th anniversary of the death of St Laurence Justinian in 1956 was an attempt to make the past relevant. There had been bishops in Venice since 1178, but Laurence in 1451 was the first to be granted the title of patriarch. Apart from the Bishop of Rome – the 'Patriarch of the West' – the only other Patriarchate in the Latin Church was in Lisbon, established in 1716. The Giustiniani family, to give them their Venetian name, claimed descent from the Roman emperor, Justinian. They were certainly one of the most ancient families in Venice. In the twelfth century all the male members of the family were killed in battle except for one monk who was rapidly released from his vows in order to continue the family line (Morris, p. 55). Roncalli's pastoral letter for Lent 1956 was devoted to 'St Laurence Justinian and the Bible'.

He describes Gentile Bellini's portrait of the saint in the white habit of the canons of San Giorgio in Alga, his clear, lively eyes contemplating the patriarchal cross on his breast, his right hand raised in blessing while the left hand holds a book. It was important for Roncalli that his predecessor the protopatriarch, whose cross he now wore, was not some shadowy, anonymous figure. The

'Complete Works', all 638 pages of them, held the key to the man and his spiritual doctrine. That doctrine was *biblical* through and through. Fifteenth-century Catholics like Laurence Justinian had not yet been made nervous about the Bible by Protestant claims to hold a monopoly of its interpretation. For them it was the book of life. And the two aspects of the Word of God – the Word proclaimed in the Gospel and the Word made present in the Eucharist – were related to each other on the deepest level. As Roncalli put it: 'The voice of Christ resounds in the book; in the chalice the blood of Christ is present as grace, propitiation, our salvation' (Alberigo, p. 226). The book and the chalice correspond to the Word and Sacrament of later discussion. Roncalli states it rather quaintly but effectively: the book is the *alpha*, the beginning, while the chalice is the *omega*, the end; in between come all the letters of the alphabet which stand for, he explains, all the personal, domestic, social and political concerns that make up human life.

Don Giuseppe De Luca, who knew more about the history of Italian spirituality than anyone else (and just failed to be the Henri Bremond of Italy), had helped Roncalli with his pastoral. Together they had no difficulty in proving, texts in hand, that reading the Bible had been encouraged throughout the patristic and mediaeval period. The notion that it was a banned book was a polemical *canard* of the Reformation. Anyway, Italy never had the Holy Inquisition:

> In Italy especially, although there were occasional warnings about strange
> interpretations that could compromise the purity of Catholic faith, the
> freedom to read the Bible was always taken for granted. And here in the
> Veneto the reading of the Bible in the vernacular was so common that
> certain chroniclers tell how they heard gatherings of young women singing
> passages from scripture as they worked the spinning wheel (Alberigo, p. 227).

It is a naïve and touching picture, like a mediaeval illumination. It was shattered by the Reformation which made the Bible itself an object of controversy. The Protestant principles of *Scriptura sola* (Scripture alone) and 'private interpretation' broke the unity of the Church and dissolved the Christian inheritance. Against this, says Roncalli, the Catholic Church sets 'Jesus Christ as its sole founder, and the witnesses to his foundation are Apostolic Tradition and Sacred Scripture. Tradition first, then Scripture and Scripture based on Tradition' (*Ibid.*, p. 228). He adds St Augustine's remark: 'The Christian reads the Bible not according to his talent or fantasy but kneeling alongside the Church, its sure and authentic interpreter'. This was run-of-the mill stuff.

But by the 1950s such oppositions between Protestants and Catholics, though by no means dissipated, no longer looked insurmountable. The work of Yves-Marie Congar and many others had shown that Catholics could acknowledge with joy the primacy of the Word of God, and that Protestants could admit that the Scriptures formed part of the Tradition of the early communities whose faith they recorded. The Pauline formula, 'I have handed on what I have received' – used of both the Eucharist and the Resurrection – offered a scriptural way out of the *impasse*. What was needed was to cleanse the eye of inherited polemics. Then a Bible-based ecumenism could start. Roncalli believed that the Catholic 'biblical movement' was by now well launched after Pius XII's encyclical *Divino Afflante Spiritu* (1943) and the work of the Pontifical Biblical Institute. He was not to know that its Rector, Fr Augustin Bea S.J., the Pope's confessor, had not only drafted Pius' encyclical but would play a key role in his own pontificate.

But at this stage Roncalli's ecumenical interest was still focused on the Orthodox rather than on the Churches of the Reformation. His own experience in the East and the Venetian tradition impelled him in that direction. On September 18, 1957, he was invited to lecture at the 7th Week of Study of the Christian East held at Palermo, Sicily. It was his most important contribution to ecumenism before he became pope. He saw what he called 'the modern renaissance of patristic studies' as opening the way to reconciliation. In the patristic era the differences between East and West did not lead to schism. But he still assumed that the aim of the Catholic ecumenical movement was to encompass the 'return' to the one true fold of those who had strayed from it. In the diocese of the highly conservative Cardinal Ernesto Ruffini, Ottaviani's ally, no other approach was thinkable. In any case he was merely echoing current Catholic orthodoxy, expressed in the Litany invocation *'Ut omnes errantes ad unitatem ecclesiae revocare'* ('That all those who have gone astray may be called back to the unity of the Church'). He reminded his hearers of this prayer. He described Leo XIII's 1896 apostolic letter 'to princes and peoples' as 'a touching appeal for a return to unity' and Pius XII's encyclical *Mystici Corporis* of 1943 (which identified the 'Mystical Body of Christ' and the Roman Catholic Church) as 'a most wonderful document' (Alberigo, p. 241). These were the parameters within which Catholic ecumenists had to work at that date. But an ecumenism of 'return' had little hope of making any progress.

There were other strands in Roncalli's thinking, however, that pointed beyond it. Christ's command 'That all may be one' was clear and imposed a special urgency. Roncalli quoted the impassioned words of Cardinal Bessarione to the Council of Florence:

> What defence will we make before God for being separated from our
> brothers, when it was to unite us and gather us into one flock that Christ
> came down from heaven, became flesh and was crucified? What defence do
> we have before posterity? Venerable Fathers, we will not suffer such shame,
> we will remain far from such counsels, we will not provide so badly for
> those who come after us (Alberigo, pp. 242–3).

But so long as one side was blaming the other for the breach of Christian unity, it could not be healed. Only when they came together in repentance and mutual forgiveness could there be any hope of reconciliation. Roncalli does not spell this out, but he states its premise: 'Is the reponsibility for the split all on the side of our separated brothers? It is partly theirs, but it is also ours to a great extent (*in gran parte è nostra*)' (*Ibid.*, p. 243).

Roncalli wanted 'this splendid movement towards Christian unity' to have a regular place in Catholic teaching, preaching and catechesis. To this end he revived an idea first put to him by Dom Lambert Beauduin in 1926. Beauduin proposed an organised ecumenical movement in the Church on the analogy of Propaganda Fide, the missionary Congregation. That implied working on two levels: a broadly-based movement in the local churches to sensitise Catholics to the problems; and a Rome office within the Curia to co-ordinate and keep the ecumenical cause on the Roman agenda. It was the germ of the idea of the Secretariat for Christian Unity.

Back in Venice Roncalli was immersed in the final preparations for the diocesan Synod. It took place in St Mark's Basilica from November 25 to 27, 1957. It was the culmination of his pastoral plan for Venice. It 'crowned', as he put it, the pastoral visits he had been making to parishes since he arrived. It was prepared for in depth by study commissions and courses at the Seminary in which 'all were able to speak their mind' (Alberigo, p. 247). But it was not a democratic assembly and there was no debate. Roncalli was following the recommendations of canon law and the example of Radini Tedeschi who held a Synod in Bergamo in 1910 (see above, pp. 64–5). He also had St Charles Borromeo in mind and presented the Synod as a typically Tridentine institution which still had life in it and met 'the demands of the modern age'. This ability to pour new wine into old bottles constantly baffled those hasty commentators who wanted to know whether Roncalli was a 'conservative' or a 'liberal'.

It was in the context of the Synod that he first used the term *aggiornamento* which became his slogan and trade-mark. In his October 8 letter to the people of Venice he wrote:

> You've probably heard the word *aggiornamento* repeated so many times.
> Well, Holy Church who is ever youthful wants to be in a position to
> understand the diverse circumstances of life so that she can adapt, correct,
> improve and be filled with fervour. That in brief is the nature of the Synod,
> that is its goal (Alberigo, p. 248).

He would use the same language, adding the notion of 'reform', to describe the purpose of the Council. He saw synods and councils as the 'constitutional' way of renewing the Church's youth.

Roncalli addressed the Venice Synod on each of its three days. His most important contribution was his account of 'episcopal authority'. The bishop is described in the liturgy, he said, as *pastor et dominus*, shepherd and lord. But he preferred to think of the bishop as *pastor et pater*, and had this phrase inscribed over his door (Alberigo, p. 249). He developed the concept of 'spiritual paternity' as it is found in St Paul: 'For though you have many teachers in Christ, you do not have many fathers. For I became your father in Jesus Christ through the Gospel' (1 Corinthians 4.15). In so far as the bishop is constantly providing spiritual nourishment for his family and protecting them from dangers, he may be said to be 'bringing Christ to birth in them' (*Ibid.*, p. 250).

But Roncalli was realistic. He had enough experience of ecclesiastical life to know that the language of spiritual paternity could mask the reality of tyranny and oppression. It was the problem he had thought about often before, notably in Istanbul: as bishop he must be neither bully nor doormat (see p. 183 above). He found a helpful formulation of the problem in the French Archbishop Emile Guerry of Cambrai who denounced both 'authoritarianism' and its twin temptation 'paternalism'. Roncalli understood the terms in this way:

> *Authoritarianism* stifles life and leads to a rigid, external discipline and to complicated, harmful over-organisation. It represses legitimate initiatives, is unable to listen, confuses harshness with firmness, inflexibility with dignity. *Paternalism* is also a caricature of paternity. It keeps people immature in order to maintain its own superior position, behaves liberally towards some, but fails to respect the rights of its subordinates. It speaks protectively, and does not accept true collaboration (Alberigo, p. 252: address of November 25, 1957).

Some might have heard in Roncalli's account of 'paternalistic authoritarianism' a not-so-veiled description of Pius XII who did not require collaboration and was incapable of listening. Robert Leiber S.J., one of his private secretaries, admitted that Pius was 'difficult to approach . . . and remained a solitary. It was hard to penetrate the depths of his soul' (Hoffmann, p. 140). Probably there was nothing further from Roncalli's *conscious* mind than to criticise the Pope. But those looking for an alternative way of exercising papal authority were encouraged to think again about the patriarch of Venice.

A conclave seemed imminent. Pius XII was now 81. He was kept alive by his Swiss gerontologist, Dr Paul Niehans, who had devised what he called 'living cell' therapy – the regular injection of finely ground tissues taken from freshly slaughtered lambs (see Hoffmann, p. 24). It would have seemed very remiss of Curial cardinals not to have thought about the succession in advance. Roncalli would make a welcome contrast with Pius XII. Not only that, but historical analogy worked in his favour. Two generations before, so ran the legend, a simple and holy Patriarch of Venice, Sarto, had become Pope Pius X, now St Pius X.

What had happened before could happen again. But the resemblance between Sarto and Roncalli was very superficial, based on the fact that both were of humble origins, fat and patriarchs of Venice. But while Sarto, who had never travelled outside Italy, was nervous, anxious and fanatical, the much-travelled Roncalli remained serene and used to weary people in Venice, as he admits, with the exhortation of St John the Evangelist in old age – 'Love one another – that is enough – it is the Lord's command, the Lord's command' (Alberigo, p. 255).

There was a sharp contrast between them in spiritual temperament. Yet memories of Pius X were found at every turn in Venice. The third and final day of the Synod was placed under his patronage. Roncalli recalled that his predecessor had addressed the 1898 Synod in the same Basilica, and that his four addresses – on faith, catechetics, penance and the eucharist – adumbrated the policies of his pontificate. He also recalled that 1898 was the year when Don Lorenzo Perosi conducted the oratorios which 'enriched the apostolate of religious instruction' (Alberigo, p. 255). Perosi was undergoing something of a revival in 1957, and helped to balance Igor Stravinsky who produced original works for the Venice Festivals of 1956 and 1958. Roncalli was sometimes seen in animated conversation with Stravinsky (Trevor, p. 239). He was interested in Stravinsky's use of themes from the Russian Orthodox music that he loved. But he preferred Perosi's more predictable sub-Puccini brashness not least because the priest-composer had 'implemented the liturgical reforms of Pius X'. There was no way in which Pius X could be eluded in Venice.

Roncalli theorised about authority to the Venice Synod. It remains to ask how far he managed to live up to his own ideal. Did he achieve 'spiritual paternity' in which he did not 'lord it over his flock, but loved them as sons and brothers' (Alberigo p. 250)? Was he perceived as one who, in his own words, combined 'trust with prudence, firmness with mercy, patience with decisiveness' (*Ibid.*, p. 252)? These are impossible questions. Since they describe an ideal, they belong rather with the postulator of his cause than with a biographer. One cannot say that there was never a disgruntled cleric in the diocese of Venice. All one can say is that his clergy were sorry to see him go but glad that it was to become pope.

His difficulties with the laity came from the special brand of Venetian conservatism expressed in the motto, '*Veneziani, poi Cristiani*' (Venetians first, Christians second). Here is Capovilla on the Venetian 'character': 'The Venetians are marked by their respect for venerable traditions and age-old religious and civic memories. They are courteous but austere and – one could say – isolated and rather odd (*singolare*) . . . They have a smiling indulgence towards the novelties that arise in the course of time, and a readiness to welcome some of them' (*Letture*, p. 32). The very last phrase gives the clue. The Venetians were choosy about change. Some of them believed that Patriarch Roncalli was a dangerous innovator. Evidence is not usually required for such judgements, but when pressed, they could point only to his welcome to the Socialist Party Congress and his fiddling with the altar screen (he wanted people to be able to *see* the altar). Hardly very heinous crimes.

Perhaps Roncalli understood Venice better than Venice understood him. He was immersed but not imprisoned in its history. In a lyrical apostrophe to Venice old and new, Capovilla declares that 'he discovered the beauties of your nature and art with the discerning eye of the scholar; during the night he studied your history – more than most of your sons; and he never tired of contemplating your face, reflected in the bulky volumes of your libraries, your stones and your canals' (*Letture*, p. 32). He certainly loved Venice. To his successor as patriarch, Giovanni Urbani, appointed with remarkable speed, he wrote:

> Ah! the Venetians really do deserve esteem and affection. In the six years of shared spiritual life with them, our whole experience was one of joy and consolation. And they are still in our hearts, all the priests and laypeople, as though we could never be separated from them – perhaps for ever in this life – without hidden tears of deep emotion (*Lettere*, p. 80).

He then lovingly listed all the towns and cities that made up the diocese, the mainland as well as the islands, the working class as well as the 'historic' places, before bequeathing to Urbani 'the mantle of Elijah'. The phrase 'perhaps for ever in this life' was inserted, according to one commentator, to scotch the idea that as pope he was going to return to Venice in triumph (*Corriere della Sera*, January 9, 1959). He never did. But henceforward pilgrims from Venice got as much attention as those from his own native Bergamo.

But that lay in the future – not a very distant future. We are early in 1958. Roncalli's life had always been rhythmed by the liturgy. It was his way of entering into the 'time of the Lord', salvation-history as theologians had begun to call it (*Heilsgeschichte*). This chimed in with Roncalli's long-standing conviction that there were not two sorts of history, one ecclesiastical and the other secular, but only one history in which God is mysteriously at work. So the seasons of Venice were juxtaposed with the liturgical seasons.

In his Ascensionday sermon of 1958 he preached on the meaning of the Paschal Candle which is greeted with the threefold acclamation, *Lumen Christi, Deo Gratias*. It was a simple exposition in three points. *Christ is Light* for individuals, source of grace and truth which bring new energies into everyday life and fashion the human person towards holiness. *Christ is Light* for the Church which still today, 'despite centuries of conflict and hazardous erosion', remains 'the mother of the saints and the image of the heavenly city, the new Jerusalem'. Finally, *Christ is Light* for 'the social order which finds in the Gospel and the teaching of the Church immortal principles leading to progress, prosperity and peace' (Alberigo, pp. 260–1). So Christ is seen as Light for individuals, for the Church, for society (or the 'world'). Behind that simple scheme can be discerned the outline of the Council and the title of its most important document: *Lumen Gentium*.

At the end of his Ascensionday sermon, Roncalli stated in very simple terms the need to be inserted into the mystery of Christ that was the stuff of his prayer and his preaching:

> I greet you. We may see each other within the year as the liturgical feasts succeed each other one by one from season to season. That is Christian life. To follow the episodes of the mortal life of Jesus and let our spirit be penetrated by his spirit, his joys, his sufferings, his sacrifices – and his victory.
>
> So it is year after year and century after century (Alberigo, p. 262).

Does this contain a hint of foreboding that he might not celebrate another Ascensionday in Venice?

Did he have any premonition that six months later he would be elected pope? The curious 'hallucinations' of Gaston Bardet had not been forgotten. The fact that Roncalli was reluctant to talk about the matter at all suggests that he had some inkling of what could very soon happen. Tommaso Gallarati Scotti records an enigmatic conversation with the Patriarch in June, 1958, about a month after the Ascensionday sermon. Gallarati Scotti discussed what might happen in the 'not very far distant conclave' and piously deplored the way it was already being set up in the press as though it would be a straightforward political choice between left and right. Gallarati Scotti concludes his report: 'The Patriarch heard me out, but seemed far above such vain concerns, and in the end he said to me with his usual simplicity, "The ways of God are manifold" ' (*Utopia*, Ital., p. 461). In other words, he was not ruling himself out. But the longer the delay, the less his chances were. He felt he was getting old. In September, 1958, only a month before the conclave, he complains of fading memory and says he 'must be chary of accepting engagements to preach outside my diocese, because I have to write down everything first' (*Journal*, p. 316).

With hindsight the Venice years have inevitably been seen as an apprenticeship for the papacy. The truth is that they were probably the best preparation he could have had. He was dealing with people all the time, of all conditions and cultures. In his waiting room you could meet the art historian Bernard Berenson or Cardinal Stefan Wyszyński or the boys from the Maghera football team. He had played an important and sometimes controversial role in national affairs. He had continued to travel abroad – to the Lebanon, Portugal and France – on Marian business. He had kept his friendships in good repair and made new ones. He had come home after thirty years of exile and shown that he could run an Italian diocese with skill, tact and a style of authority that enabled people to grow. He had worked towards a systematic pastoral plan for his diocese. He had shown a remarkable capacity for work and meeting deadlines. One of his secrets was that he was orderly. 'Most long-lived people', writes Desmond Morris, 'have a sense of self-discipline'. This does not mean driving the self despotically but 'imposing a pattern on the ordinary events of the day'. Roncalli had his Breviary and his afternoon nap in a chair. He also had the other qualities needed, to age well: 'a twinkle in the eye', a sense of humour and impishness, and something to live for (*The Sunday Times Magazine*, November 20, 1983, p. 79).

At seventy-six he did not have the mind-cast of an old man. The prospect of a conclave has been known to rejuvenate cardinals who were otherwise heading for the grave. When Roncalli heard the news of the death of the Pope he noted in his diary: 'Sister death came quickly and swiftly fulfilled her office. Three days were enough. On Sunday, October 9 at 3.52 a.m. Pius XII was in paradise' (*Lettere*, p. 481). But having got Pius safely into heaven he did not look backwards. Instead he looked to the future good of the Church and expressed his hope in a typical image: 'One of my favourite phrases brings me great comfort: we are not on earth as museum-keepers, but to cultivate a flourishing garden of life and to prepare a glorious future. The Pope is dead, long live the Pope!' (*Ibid.*). He left Venice for ever by the 9.40 train on October 12, 1958, seen off by the mayor and other notables.

Chapter 12

1958: the wide-open conclave

In a world filled with frightening violence, it would not be totally strange if
the Lord were pleased to give his Church a poor and humble pontiff,
concerned only with protecting the helpless and dissipating darkness from
people's minds and terror from their hearts. We are weary of too much
learning, too much power, we are weary of greatness, prestige . . . words
(Don Primo Mazzolari in *Adesso*, on hearing of the death of Pius XII).

On Saturday, October 11, 1958, his last full day in Venice, Cardinal Roncalli
watched on live television as the mortal remains of Pope Pius XII were
transported from Castelgandolfo to the Vatican. In his diary he wondered
whether any Roman emperor, on his way to the Campidoglio, had enjoyed such
a triumph. The crowds were paying tribute, he thought, not to evanescent
military might but to 'spiritual majesty and religious dignity'. He was reminded
of Alessandro Manzoni's remark that nothing could surpass the power of charity
(*Vent'Anni*, p. 13).

No doubt that was true enough. But careful editing spared the viewers the
more horrendous incidents along the route. When the cortège arrived at St John
Lateran, it paused for a last tribute to the late pope in his cathedral church. Those
close enough heard a startling noise like a fire-cracker from within the coffin. In
the Roman heat a process of fermentation had begun which burst it open (see
Hoffmann, p. 25). That was bad enough, but then the man responsible for
embalming the body, the papal doctor Riccardo Galeazzi Lisi (he was really an
oculist) worked throughout the night to re-embalm the much abused corpse. He
assured worried Vatican officials next morning that Pius XII could safely be
exhibited in St Peter's. He was wrong. Throughout the day the mourners filed
past the bier on which Pius XII lay in state: gradually his face turned green, then
ashen-coloured, and a foul stench was emitted. Roncalli heard what had happened
when he arrived in Rome that afternoon.

His diary on Monday, October 13, was mostly concerned with what had gone
wrong at the funeral that same day. He could not see why the public needed to be
present when the body was placed in its triple coffin – it was now blotchy and
disfigured. He went on: 'The wretched scaffolding put up before the altar of the
Confession looked like a stand for the guillotine. Once the veil of white silk is
placed on the face of the corpse, it should be seen by very few people. This is what
the cardinals think' (*Vent'Anni*, p. 40). However, the most vivid and precious

memory of the day was his 'last look at the cadaverous face of the Holy Father. Oh, the great lesson of death!' (*Ibid.*). Another observer remarked that it was only in death that Pius XII was seen without his glasses. The result was that he looked 'more human, more friendly, more defenceless'.

Yet the exploding corpse and disastrous incompetence of Galeazzi Lisi were symbolic of the unhealthy atmosphere that prevailed in Rome during the last years of Pius XII. The moment he died, court favourites departed and old scores were settled. The once-powerful Sister Pascalina Lehnert, known as *Virgo Potens* because she controlled access to the Pope, left the Vatican to write her memoirs. Galeazzi Lisi tried to hawk pictures of the papal corpse to the international press. He gave a press conference at which he described in great detail his own specially devised method of taking out the inner organs and embalming the body. The press found it nauseating (Lai, p. 280). Without waiting for the conclave, the cardinals dismissed Galeazzi Lisi from the Vatican service on October 20. Roncalli was well aware of the mood in Rome. The papal nephews had been so important in the pontificate just ended that Roncalli found it necessary to warn his own nephew, Don Battista Roncalli, not to dare come anywhere near Rome. He wrote to his bishop, Giuseppe Battaglia of Faenza, on October 24 in the strongest terms: 'I have already written to him (Don Battista) to say that on no account should he move until he has my approval. The atmosphere here is foul (*viziato*) with verbal malice and the press that the weary old remark is bound to be heard: "Here's the nephew, here come the relatives" ' (Alberigo, p. 490). Though he did not hold Pius XII personally responsible for the unsavoury atmosphere, he recognised that from 1954, date of Pius' grave illness, the pontificate had been dominated by intrigue, nepotism and gossip. He welcomed the conclave as a chance to make a fresh start.

On the day of the funeral Roncalli installed himself along with Don Loris Capovilla and Guido Gussi, at Domus Mariae, a large conference centre on Via Aurelia 481. He later remarked that it would have been a better venue for a conclave than the Vatican where the rooms were either too cramped or too grandiose. Strictly speaking a conclave does not begin until all the cardinals and their assistants are sealed up inside the Vatican, which in this case did not happen until Saturday October 25, 1958. So there were two working weeks devoted to preparing the conclave and celebrating the *novemdiales* or nine days of mourning. Cardinal Aloisi Masella was elected *camerlengo* or chamberlain (Pius having neglected to fill the post). He presided over the daily meetings of cardinals known as 'general congregations'. Their purpose was not to 'fix' the conclave or to pre-empt its decision. It was rather to provide a job-description of the sort of pope the Church needed in 1958. Names were not supposed to be discussed at this stage.

The problem facing the cardinals was one which always occurs after a long pontificate: continuity or change? The atmosphere already evoked after the death of Pius suggested that there would have to be 'change' of some sort. This did not imply any discredit to his memory. There was a consensus for change both on the part of those who regarded the late pope as an unrivalled genius, the like of whom could not be expected to recur, and also by those who felt that the pontificate just ended, despite its splendid facade and the enthusiastic audiences the Pope had gathered, had not altogether met the needs of the contemporary Church.

One of those unmet needs could be grasped simply by looking round the table in the Consistorial Hall where the cardinals met. The full complement of the college of cardinals was seventy. But when Pius died, there were only fifty-three cardinals, and two more died before the conclave could begin. So they were reduced to fifty-one electors. For unfathomed reasons, Pius had held only two consistories in his long reign, in 1946 and in 1953. The result was not only that the college was undermanned and restricted in its choice; it was also an immensely aged body. Twenty-four of them, nearly a half, were actually older than Roncalli. Why Pius neglected his succession is something of a mystery. *'Après moi, le déluge'* he is supposed to have said to the French ambassador. In this geriatric group, it was not surprising that some of the eighty-year olds should have regarded Roncalli as a sprightly youngster.

Though names were not to be mentioned in the general congregations the ban could not be applied to informal meetings and consultations. Lobbying was intense but discreet. There were invitations to lunch, and many phone calls. The lobbying was all, of course, on behalf of someone else. It was not done to push oneself forward, but some cardinals played the role of king-makers. Roncalli was not a king-maker, and he was surprised to find after the first general congregation on October 13 that some of his brother cardinals considered him a serious candidate. Cardinal Maurilio Fossati, archbishop of Turin, told him plainly 'We want you'. Gaetano Cicognani, prefect of the Congregation of Rites and brother of the apostolic delegate in Washington, said 'I could imagine kneeling at his feet'. A few days later Cardinal Elia Dalla Costa, archbishop of Florence, remarked to Roncalli, 'You'd make a good Pope'. 'But I'm seventy-six', he objected. 'That's ten years younger than me', replied the ancient (*Quale Papa?* pp. 151–2). Dalla Costa's support was important: he was the protector of Giorgio La Pira, the radical Christian Democratic mayor of Florence, and he represented the non-curial, reforming wing of Italian Catholicism.

But it would be wrong to conclude from these early hints that Roncalli was already home and dry. He was *papabile,* one candidate among others. On the evening of Pius' funeral he relieved the gloom by having dinner with Giovanni Urbani, bishop of Verona, and Giuseppe Piazza, bishop of Bergamo. These were both good friends to whom he could speak freely about the ghastly events of the day. Some speculation about his chances could hardly have been avoided. But neither man had anything to do with the conclave. They were not in it, and too far away and insignificant to have any influence on its outcome. Much later Roncalli was able to claim that he had accepted the burden of the pontificate 'with the joy of being able to say that I did nothing to obtain it, absolutely nothing'. 'Indeed', he added, 'I was most careful and conscientious to avoid anything that might direct attention to myself' (*Journal*, pp. 348–9). There is no need to impugn Pope John's truthfulness. But his remarks should be applied, as he intended them, only to the conclave itself. In the pre-conclave period he was as active as anyone.

The Italians led the intrigues and the plotting. Some of them had been preparing for years for this moment. At eighteen out of fifty-one, they formed the largest national block by far. They knew each other and they knew the field. The non-Italian cardinals had scarcely met at all; Pius XII never brought them together for consultation. Cardinal Maurice Feltin, archbishop of Paris, said 'Each one of us knew perhaps about three or four of his colleagues or at most about a dozen' (Bergerre, p. 199). What Feltin omitted to say was that all six French cardinals undoubtedly knew Roncalli, and some of them became cardinals on his recommendation. The French and Italians together made up about half the college. They held the key to the conclave. But there was no guarantee, or even likelihood, that they would vote together.

Yet after the second general congregation on Tuesday October 14, Roncalli was a worried man. His candidature was already looking solid enough to make him fear that he might be elected. He prayed, 'on bended knees, that the conclave should not be a disaster for the universal Church' ('*Orandum est, flectis genuis, ut non sit conclave nefastum Ecclesiae universae*', *Vent'Anni*, p. 40). It is worth giving his diary for the day, discreet though it is:

> Second day in Rome. At 10.30 the Congregation of Cardinals in the Consistorial Hall. Everything went well, but it's all confidential. After leaving I visited the substitute, Mgr Dell'Acqua, who is always very kind. His account of the last hours of Pius XII was pretty miserable but also very edifying. He confirmed the continued good will of the Pope for me personally and for what I was doing. The welcome he gave me in March on my return from Lourdes, and the letter he wrote to congratulate me on my September 18 homily at Castelfranco, brought me great consolation. To lunch today I had dear Augusto Gianfrancheschini, Bishop of Cesena, and in the evening a most delightful and valuable conversation with Count Dalla Torre, editor of *l'Osservatore Romano* (*Vent'Anni*, p. 40).

His September 18 homily had been a tribute in Latin on the hundredth anniversary of St Pius X's ordination. Gianfrancheschini had been his auxiliary in Venice and had nothing to do with the conclave. Dell'Acqua and Dalla Torre were not inside the conclave either. But they could give him a good breakdown on the state of opinion within the Roman Curia. As editor of *l'Osservatore*

Romano for nearly thirty years, Dalla Torre knew the scene. It was probably he who advised Roncalli to make a friendly gesture towards Mgr Domenico Tardini. But Dalla Torre didn't know who was going to be elected. His paper prepared twenty-five biographies of *papabili*. In 1939 ten had been considered sufficient, and even that was unnecessary because 'everyone knew' that Pacelli would be elected.

No such predictions could be confidently made in 1958. It was a genuinely open conclave. Lists of contenders appeared from time to time, but they sprang from nowhere and had not the slightest authority. They reflected discussions outside the conclave as much as inside it, but since the same reasoning can give the same results, that was not necessarily discreditable. Roncalli, contrary to some reports, was on almost everyone's list, even if not highly placed. Capovilla recalls that Giacomo Lercaro (Bologna), Ernesto Ruffini (Palermo), and Alfredo Ottaviani (Holy Office) appeared as the leading contenders, closely followed by Aloisi Masella (*camerlengo*), Valerio Valeri (Religious) – Roncalli's predecessor in France – and only then the patriarch of Venice. Capovilla also admits that Roncalli, though by no means unknown, was not regarded by the Roman Curia as a 'first class man' ('*uomo di primo piano*'), and that even his fellow Bergamesques, though they loved and appreciated him, thought of him as an old buffer in carpet slippers who was unlikely to transform the Church or indeed do anything at all (*Vent'Anni*, p. 14).

Nevertheless his candidature continued to gain ground. On Wednesday October 15 he was up early to celebrate Mass for the domestic staff at Domus Mariae and preached on Martha and Mary. His diary hints at what was happening: 'Great butterfly flutterings around my poor self. The odd fleeting encounter which, however, did not disturb my calm' (*Vent'Anni*, p. 41). In other words he was being sounded out. Ottaviani began to support him, arguing for a 'transitional pope' (*Quale Papa?* p. 151). What this meant was well put by a French abbot, who was 'close to' Cardinal Achille Liénart, archbishop of Lille. He was countering the candidature of Cardinal Giuseppe Siri, archbishop of Genoa, who was fifty-two. If elected, he could be pope for forty years. 'What we need', said the abbot, 'is an old man, a transitional pope. He won't introduce any great innovations, and will give us time to pause and reorganise. In that way the real choices that cannot be made now will be postponed'. Of course the consensus that was building up about a caretaker pope did not point inevitably or only to Roncalli. There were other suitable candidates for a do-nothing papacy.

Even though he was not a member of the conclave, Mgr Domenico Tardini was influential from his privileged position in the Secretariat of State. He knew its workings intimately, better than anyone except his old rival, Archbishop Giovanni Battista Montini. Roncalli met Tardini for an hour before lunch on October 15. He found the gruff old bear 'friendly and good' and somewhat pathetically anxious to be invited to lunch at Domus Mariae where he would find more cardinals gathered under one roof than anywhere else (*Vent'Anni*, p. 41). A few days later Roncalli visited Tardini's *élite* orphanage at Villa Nazareth, where working-class boys were given a first-class education, and was delighted by it. So during this pre-conclave period the two men cleared up what ever misunderstandings may have lingered on. This was common prudence on both sides. It was obvious that a future pope, whoever he was, would have to make use of Tardini in some capacity.

However he was not yet won over to supporting Roncalli's candidacy. He was said to be working on behalf of Cardinal Aloisi Masella. But the real threat to Roncalli came not from Masella but from Cardinal Gregory Peter Agagianian. He became aware of this when he visited his friend Cardinal Celso Constantini, formerly prefect of Propaganda and an old China hand, who was awaiting an operation in the Margherita Clinic, via Massimo. Roncalli feared for his life, rightly, for Constantini died the next day, October 16. But with his dying breath he told Roncalli that he thought the time had come for a non-Italian pope and that he would be supporting Agagianian.

Roncalli did not think Agagianian really qualified as a 'non-Italian'. Born in Akhaltzikhe in 1895 he had received the nominal title of 'Patriarch of Cilicia of the Armenians' in 1937. But he had become 'more Roman than the Romans', and was now prefect of Propaganda Fide, sometimes known as the 'red pope' because of his supposed inflence. On the eve of the conclave, Roncalli said to Giulio Andreotti, the Christian Democrat politician:

> The other day I went to see Cardinal Constantini just before he died. He said to me: 'This time, at long last, we'll have an Oriental Pope'. I was amazed that any well-informed man could say such a thing. The 'East' doesn't exist except as a category created by Westerners. Ask a Chinese whether he has anything in common with an Indian or a Turk. It's much easier for an Italian to reconcile the Lebanese and the Egyptians than for a so-called 'Oriental' pope (Andreotti, pp. 72–3).

If Roncalli was prepared to make this point so openly to a layman, it is a fair bet that he argued in the same way with his fellow-cardinals. But of course to oppose Agagianian's candidature did not mean that he was pushing his own.

But he was taking some initiatives, and the notion that he merely waited on events with arms folded can be refuted by inspecting his diary. On October 16 he sought out Cardinal Giuseppe Pizzardo, who rather fancied himself as a *grande elettore*, at his apartment. Pizzardo brought up the matter of Montini. Those who had secured his exile from Rome in 1954 did not want to see him return in 1958 as Secretary of State, the only conceivable post for someone with his background. Had Montini been a cardinal, he would himself have been a strong runner. Even in absence, he hovered over the conclave. Pizzardo sounded Roncalli out about whether he would bring back his friend Montini. According to Zizola, 'the Patriarch calmly replied that he did not and would not seek to be elected pope, and so the question did not arise' (*Quale Papa?* p. 154). So no deal was struck. But Roncalli remembered such conversations after his election, and though he honoured Montini in every way he could think of, there was never any question of him returning to Rome. Later, there was the further consideration that Montini was more useful to the Council outside than inside the Vatican.

A bitterly cold wind, harbinger of winter, blew over Rome on October 16, the day Constantini died. Next day Roncalli dashed off a letter to Mgr Valentino Vecchi, rector of the Patriarchal seminary in Venice. Was he saying farewell? The letter allows us to glimpse part of the case he was putting in the general congregations:

> As for the Pope now dead and taken up into glory, it only remains to
> continue the acclamation, Long live the Pope! and to pray that his successor,
> whoever he may be, may not represent a new departure but rather progress
> in living out the perennial youthfulness of the Church, whose mission is
> always to lead souls towards the divine heights where the Gospel
> sanctification of human life is realised . . . (*Utopia*, Italian, p. 459).

So there was to be no formal repudiation of Pius XII, on the contrary: Roncalli did not think that the Church progressed by turning somersaults. But that the 'continuity' he argued for would be 'continuity with a difference' was hinted at by the use of his favourite image: the Church's perennial youthfulness. But how was it to be expressed by these fifty-one elderly men gathered in Rome?

The second week of general congregations began on Monday, October 20. It was one of Roncalli's busiest days so far. He was assiduous in meeting all the right people. His diary records 'a long conversation with Cardinal Ottaviani at the Holy Office, followed by a visit to Cardinal Masella, *camerlengo*' (*Vent'Anni*, p. 41). The same day Tardini achieved his ambition of lunch at Domus Mariae, and it was after lunch that Roncalli visited his orphanage. That evening a Bergamesque prelate, Mgr Pietro Sigismondi, was invited to dinner. The purpose of their meeting was not to swap stories about Bergamo. Sigismondi was a close collaborator of Agagianian at Propaganda Fide, so he may have come along to mediate between the two candidates who were now beginning to outstrip the rest of the field.

As if this were not enough for one day, Roncalli also went to confession to Mgr Alfredo Cavagna, national chaplain to the Young Catholic Women, and records 'I was very happy with it' (*Vent'Anni*, p. 51). Perhaps we should probe no further. But the text Roncalli quotes immediately afterwards: '*Qui spiritu Dei aguntur, hi sunt filii Dei*' ('Those who are guided by the Spirit are sons of God',

Romans 8.14), seems to echo a conversation in which Cavagna settled a scruple
by assuring him that he would have to follow wherever the Spirit led. That is a
guess. But it is not a guess that as soon as Roncalli became pope, he chose
Cavagna as his regular confessor.

On Tuesday, October 21, the cardinals attended the funeral of Cardinal
Constantini at San Giovanni dei Fiorentini and drew lots for their 'cells' in the
·conclave. They also entrusted Cardinal Antonio Bacci, a celebrated Latinist, with
the task of writing the speech *De eligendo pontifice* to express their common mind
about what kind of pope they were searching for. It seemed to point
unambiguously to Roncalli.

This would explain why the following day, Wednesday, October 22, it looked
almost as though he had resigned himself to becoming pope. He went down into
the crypt of St Peter's where he had said his first Mass in 1904. He prayed that
Peter 'would be the true protector of Christ's Church' ('*ut sit protector ecclesiae
suae*') in the 'great impending event of the conclave'. He entrusted himself to the
great popes of the past, dwelling especially on the memory of Pius XII. He said a
De profundis (Out of the depths have I cried to thee, O Lord) not for the deceased
popes but to beg for their intercession. He was crying to them 'out of the depths'
for help (*Vent'Anni*, p. 42). In 1904 he had imagined 'the marble and bronze
popes . . . giving me courage and confidence' (*Journal*, p. 171). Now in 1958 he
felt they would soon become his 'venerable predecessors'. This was also the first
time he was able to inspect the excavations under the crypt, and he pronounced
himself well pleased. Later, however, the leading archaeologist complained that
he was ignorant of the excavations and that, whenever she tried to talk about the
bones of St Peter, he turned the conversation to St Charles Borromeo (Guarducci,
p. 74). He simply did not share Pius XII's passionate interest in the supposed
apologetic value of the finds.

Meanwhile, he was working quietly on the French connection. Cardinal
Maurice Feltin came to see him at Domus Mariae on October 21, and on
Thursday October 23 he went to the French College, via di Santa Chiara, where
he met the agoraphobic Roques of Rennes and Grente of le Mans who was 'in
good shape despite his age'. 'Both of them', he confided in his diary, 'were very
friendly towards me' (*Vent'Anni*, p. 23).

October 23 was the day when the inescapability of what was going to happen
began to come home to him. Three pieces of evidence all point in the same
direction. He had a conversation with Mgr Dell'Acqua who later reported:

> Cardinal Roncalli, with that simplicity that always marked him, said to me,
> pensive and confused, 'As you've seen, Don Angelo, my name has been
> appearing as *papabile*. What should I do?' I answered, your eminence, leave
> it in the hands of the Lord, and if such is his will, do not refuse. Let him

guide you and help you to face up to the sacrifice involved. You won't lack good aides (ANSA, July 3, 1973).

Yet a letter written the same day to Giuseppe Piazza suggests that he had a fairly shrewd idea what God's will was going to be. He had seen Piazza, bishop of Bergamo, only ten days before, on the day of Pius' funeral. So the letter was designed to let him know how things had moved on since then:

> Just a word as I enter the conclave. Treat it as a request for prayers from the Bishop and the diocese that as a good Bergamesque I hold most dear.
> Thinking of all the lovely images of Mary dotted around the diocese, calling to mind our patron saints, bishops, famous and holy priests, religious men and women of outstanding virtue, my soul finds comfort in the confidence that a new Pentecost can blow through the Church, renewing its head, leading to a new ordering of the ecclesiastical body and bringing fresh vigour in progress towards the victory of truth, goodness and peace. It little matters whether the next pope is from Bergamo or not. Our common prayers will ensure that he will be a prudent and gentle administrator, a saint and a sanctifier. You follow me, your excellency? (*Vent'Anni*, p. 47).

His excellency would have understood perfectly well. Roncalli was paying tribute to the spiritual traditions of the Bergamo diocese that had formed him. Though it didn't strictly matter where the next pope came from, it now seemed likely that he would come from Bergamo, Capovilla heads this letter 'presentiment'. One could just as easily call it 'foreboding'. Roncalli ended the day by going to pray in two of his favourite Roman churches, San Andrea della Valle and the Gesù (*Cronologia*, p. 746). This was what he had always done when he had a problem. He had a problem now.

Friday, October 24 was the eve of the conclave. Roncalli wrote his last letter before becoming pope to Giuseppe Battaglia, bishop of Faenza, to say that he was 'rather worried'. It was the letter already quoted in which he forbade his nephew, Don Battista, to come to Rome for the time being. But this ban only made sense if he expected to become pope; otherwise he would have no patronage to dispense. Once again he turned to the Psalm, his daily prayer for a lifetime, and invited Battaglia to say with him Psalms 77 ('I cry aloud to the Lord') and 86 ('Incline thine ear, O Lord . . . for I am poor and needy'). Towards the end of the letter, Roncalli becomes quite explicit. It is no longer a question of perhaps or maybe:

> When you have heard that I had to surrender to the darts of the Holy Spirit, expressed through the common will of those gathered here, you can let Don Battista come to Rome with your blessing. And then between us you and I can decide what is the best thing to do for him 'in the Lord'. As

for me, would to heaven that this chalice might pass away from me (*ut transeat calix iste*)! Do me the kindness to pray for and with me. I have reached the point at which if the words of Daniel apply to me – 'You have been weighed in the balance and found wanting' (Daniel, 5.27), I would inwardly rejoice and bless the Lord for it. Naturally, not a word to anyone. Affectionately (*Vent'Anni*, p. 49).

He had no illusions about what becoming pope would mean. The 'flourishing garden' he had talked about on the death of Pius XII had now become Gethsemani. To a Venetian visitor he remarked: 'Venice is a bed of roses compared with Rome. Rome will be a bed of thorns' (*Quale Papa?* p. 155). After the letter to Battaglia, even Capovilla, a most cautious witness, conceded that Roncalli now had 'the clear and unambiguous awareness of the probability that he would be elected Pope' (*Letture*, p. 412).

On the evening of October 24 Roncalli summoned Giulio Andreotti to Domus Mariae. It may seem strange that the patriarch should want to see a layman and Christian Democrat politician – he had already been Minister of Defence – at this eleventh hour. But there were both personal and public reasons for a meeting. Andreotti was the nephew by marriage of Mgr Giulio Belvedere, an old Roman seminary friend of Roncalli, who had fought for justice within the Roman Curia and been shabbily treated as a result (Andreotti, pp. 49–51). Again, in 1956 Andreotti had been instrumental in persuading the government to allow the Venice junior seminary, then some distance away at Grappa on the mainland, to return to a listed building next door to the Patriarchal seminary. So Roncalli now wanted to thank him for this good work and make sure that he left 'without any debts'. He trusted his Roman friends to conclude the affair of the junior seminary. From this Andreotti concluded that Roncalli was saying '*addio*' to Venice. He did not expect to return.

Their Venetian business over, Roncalli launched with cheerful indiscretion into the tabu topic of the conclave: 'You haven't mentioned the gossip that's been going the rounds in the last few days. It's true we're all saying 'Not me, Lord, not me', but the Holy Spirit's tongues of fire have to fall on one of us. In these weeks I've twice meditated on the *Spiritual Exercises* of St Ignatius because one has to keep one's feet on the ground' (Andreotti, p. 72). This was most probably an allusion to the 'three degrees of humility' with its preference for 'insults with Christ rather than honours' (see p. 130). Why should Roncalli feel the need to keep his feet on the ground unless he were in imminent danger of being swept off them?

Then he said: 'I received a message of good wishes from General Charles de Gaulle, but that doesn't mean the French cardinals will vote the way he wants them to. I know they would like to elect Montini, and he would certainly be good; but I don't think the tradition of choosing from among the cardinals can be set aside' (Andreotti, p. 72). So Roncalli's cultivation of the French cardinals had not guaranteed him their automatic support. Indeed one of them had set off for the conclave declaring openly: 'The only certain thing is that it won't be Roncalli' (Dreyfus, pp. 139–40). However, one witness, Cardinal Eugène Tisserant, says in his posthumous memoirs that 'the French cardinals were the great electors of Roncalli – he had assured them that he would solve the priest-worker question' (*Quale Papa?* p. 155). But this is not incompatible with Roncalli's eve-of-conclave doubts. The French cardinals – or some of them – might have preferred to vote for the absent Montini. Quite a lot of energy was being expended in scotching the idea that a non-cardinal (i.e. Montini) could be a serious candidate. Benny Lai met Cardinal Siri who had thumped the table with so much vigour at the absurd notion of electing an outsider that he had smashed the ruby in his ring. No one thought of Tardini.

Roncalli's concluding remarks have already been quoted. He rejected the idea of Agagianian who was only spuriously 'non-Italian'. Andreotti deduced from this remarkable interview – Capovilla vouches for its substantial accuracy – that he had been talking to the next pope. The uncertainty was over. So sure was he that he rang *Concretezza,* a magazine he edited, and directed them to prepare just one photograph: that of Angelo Roncalli.

Andreotti got the main thing right. But he is quite mistaken in suggesting that 'in this October 1958, none of the newspapers discussed Roncalli's candidature' (Andreotti, p. 65). Paul Johnson gives another view:

> At the beginning of the conclave Roncalli was quoted at two to one; there were odds of three to one on Cardinals Ottaviani and Agagianian, five to one on Tisserant and Ruffini, and six to one on Siri and the Polish Cardinal Wyszyński . . . Among journalists attending the conclave, Roncalli was judged, on balance, to be the most likely winner; so I reported in the *Reynolds News* immediately before the conclave began (Johnson, p. 110).

Providing this was not written with benefit of hindsight, it indirectly makes an important point about the 1958 conclave. Roncalli's election was not a total surprise. It did not surprise him, and it ought not to have surprised anyone else.

Those looking for clues could have done worse than peruse the speech *De eligendo pontifice* given the next day by Cardinal Antonio Bacci. It was the last public act before the conclave's veil of secrecy descended. Bacci's task was to turn into decent Latin the job-description thrown up by the general congregations. A shy and retiring man, he was rather astonished to be suddenly taken notice of. He explained why in a book entitled *With Latin at the Service of Four Popes:* 'I remember that my address was well received by the press. Some wrote that I had clearly and precisely drawn the portrait of John XXIII. In fact I had simply presented to the cardinals the ideal figure of a pope that the present age demanded. So the merit was not mine' (Bacci, p. 89). Bacci was too modest. Whether by luck or inspiration, he was prophetic:

> We need a pope gifted with great spiritual strength and ardent charity . . . He will need to embrace the Eastern and the Western Church. He will belong to all peoples, and his heart must beat especially for those oppressed by totalitarian persecution and those in great poverty . . . May the new Vicar of Christ form a bridge between all levels of society, between all nations – even those that reject and persecute the Christian religion. Rather than someone who has explored and experienced the subtle principles belonging to the art and discipline of diplomacy, we need a pope who is above all holy, so that he may obtain from God what lies beyond natural gifts . . . He will freely receive and welcome the bishops 'whom the Holy Spirit has chosen to rule over the Church of God' (Acts 20.28). He will be prepared to give them counsel in their doubts, to listen and comfort them in their anxieties, and to encourage their plans.

The whole address was deeply 'revisionist'. It was a point by point description of what Pius XII was not. Bacci voiced the cardinals' desire to have a pope who was accessible to bishops. They wanted someone less aloof, autocratic and remote. Pius was magnificently endowed with 'natural gifts', and his outlook had been shaped (some said deformed) by a lifetime in diplomacy. Bacci said clearly that they wanted someone different. The most remarkable piece of prophecy concerned the hope that the new pope would 'form a bridge . . . even towards those who reject and persecute the Christian religion'. Pius XII had been content to denounce them. When Hungary was invaded in 1956 he expressed his sense of outrage (and impotence) with three encyclicals in as many days. If Bacci were heeded, the conclave would elect a different sort of man with a different style.

Bacci's address was at 2 p.m. on Saturday October 25. By four o'clock the conclave was cut off from the world. The shutters on the windows looking out over the city were sealed (to prevent communication by flash-light or mirror). There was enough food in the kitchens to withstand a minor siege. The good weather had returned. It was sticky and uncomfortable inside the Vatican, especially in the apartments of the Noble Guard where Roncalli was quartered. Eight cardinals, their secretaries and servants (known as *conclavistas*) lived rather on top of each other. But they formed a sympathetic little group – what Capovilla called 'a splendid family' (*'una bella famiglia'*, *Letture*, p. 9). Besides Roncalli, there were four other Italians, all old friends and well-disposed towards him: Ernesto Ruffini (Palermo), Maurilio Fossati (Turin), Gaetano Cicognani (Rites) and Valerio Valeri (Religious). Finally there were Benjamin Arriba y Castro of Tarragona, Spain, and two Latin Americans, Giacomo Luigi Copello of Buenos

Aires, Argentina, and Carlos Maria de la Torre of Quito, Ecuador. Congenial though these companions were, they did not form a pressure group within the conclave; but there is plenty of evidence that they talked things over between ballots. Capovilla had never seen Roncalli 'so engrossed and moved' ('*assorto e commosso*', *Ibid.*).

The secret of the 1958 conclave was well kept. But Roncalli himself set us on the way towards understanding what happened. The very last entry in his *Journal of a Soul* reads: 'As the voting in the Conclave wavered to and fro I rejoiced when I saw the chances of my being elected diminishing and the likelihood of others, in my opinion truly most venerable and worthy persons, being chosen' (*Journal*, p. 349). So the conclave was by no means a foregone conclusion. There was a contest, and a relatively tough one, for Roncalli did not receive the two thirds plus one he needed until the eleventh ballot. There were four inconclusive ballots on Sunday October 26, feast of Christ the King. By the end of the day, according to Zizola, Roncalli had twenty votes and Agagianian eighteen. Lercaro of Bologna, considered the most 'progressive' candidate, had four votes, as had Valeri. Two votes, believed to be French, had gone to Montini as a protest against his absence (*Quale Papa?* p. 157). At the Armenian College three months later, Pope John revealed that the names of Roncalli and Agagianian 'went up and down like two chickpeas in boiling water' (*Vent'Anni*, p. 25). But by lunchtime next day, two ballots later, the conclave was deadlocked. Agagianian was making no progress. The attempt to present him as someone who, in Bacci's words, could 'embrace the Eastern and the Western Church' failed: he had become remote even from his fellow Orientals. Tisserant therefore abandoned Agagianian and fell back on Masella as an alternative. Tisserant, a massive bearded figure, was immensely learned. He thought Roncalli didn't know enough to become pope. At this point, Roncalli may have lost some votes and slumped to about fifteen ('wavering to and fro'). Two more ballots and still the smoke was black. Nothing was resolved.

Two fragments of conversation are recorded from the evening of October 17, second day of the conclave. The first came from Cardinal Fossati. In his preface to Leone Algisi's biography of Pope John he wrote:

> Everyone knows that the cardinals drew lots for the cells. Cardinal Roncalli drew number 15, and I drew 16, next door to him in the apartment of the Noble Guard. So we were neighbours. I'm sure the Holy Father will forgive me if I break the secrecy and say that at a certain moment the friend felt the need to go along to the cell of the other friend, *confortans eum*, to encourage him (Algisi, p. 6).

The context makes it clear that Fossati was comforting him because he was gaining ground, not because he was losing it.

The second conversation that can be assigned to this same evening is less banal. Cardinal Alfredo Ottaviani gave an interview in 1968 in which he said:

> In the last days of the conclave I went to visit the Patriarch in his cell and said: 'Your eminence, we have to think about a council'. Cardinal Ruffini, who was also present, was of the same opinion. Cardinal Roncalli made this idea his own, and was later heard to say, 'I was thinking about a council from the moment I became Pope' (*Epocha,* December 8, 1968).

Ottaviani was of course here claiming credit for having been the first to propose the summoning of a Council. It would be ill-becoming to accuse the pro-prefect of the Holy Office of bare-faced lying. Anyway, the aging and half-blind cardinal repeated it in conversation with Bernard R. Bonnot, an American graduate student, in February 1975. He said that on the night of October 27, 'many cardinals', including himself and Ruffini, visited Roncalli in his cell because they already knew that he was going to be elected. Among the topics they discussed was 'what a beautiful thing (*che bella cosa*) it would be to call a Council' (Bonnot, p. 13). So in the minds of such shrewd operators as Cardinal Ottaviani and Ruffini, the contest was already over. Their minds raced ahead to Roncalli's pontificate. Roncalli's own votes, by now thrown away, went to Valerio Valeri, as a somewhat belated consolation for his humiliation in France. Roncalli stated this publicly, many times (*Dodicesimo anniversario,* p. 62. fn. 2).

But he was still just short of the thirty-five votes he needed. Zizola assigns him thirty-two, as Agagianian's support crumbled and Ottaviani, now firmly on his side, brought over the 'packet' of votes from Masella (*Quale Papa?* p. 159). It took three more ballots on October 28 for him to reach the haven of thirty-eight. He began the day with Mass at 6 a.m. in the Mathilde Chapel. He then served Capovilla's Mass, bringing up the cruets at the offertory and ringing the bell at the *Sanctus* and consecration – a throwback to his time as altar-boy in Sotto il Monte. Cardinal Wyszyński was also present. The Introit Psalm took on a special resonance for Roncalli, 'O Lord, thou hast searched me and known me . . . thou discernest my thoughts from afar' (Psalm 139.1–2). In the Gospel Jesus told his disciples to 'love one another' (John 15.17). After a speedy continental breakfast in the Sala Regia, the cardinals conferred in subdued tones and glided silently about visiting each other singly or in small groups until at 9 a.m. the bell summoned them to the Sistine Chapel for Mass and the *Veni Creator* (*Vent'Anni,* p. 6, for this whole paragraph).

Once more the voting slips were tipped into the waiting chalice for the ninth and tenth ballots. To the intense disappointment of the crowd, at 11.10 a.m. black smoke emerged once more from the Sistine flue. But within the Conclave, there was a growing sense that the *dénouement* was not far off. 'Certain looks and certain allusions' convinced Capovilla that there would be a pope before the day was out. Roncalli went straight from the Sistine Chapel to his cell, sat down on the divan and said he wanted to be alone. Towards one o'clock Capovilla returned to accompany him down to the Sala Regia for lunch. But Roncalli said: 'I'm not coming down. I'll have a bite here. Have something brought. We'll eat together' (*Vent'Anni*, p. 7). The resourceful Guido Gussi had made friends with the sisters in the kitchen. He returned at 1.20 with a meal that Roncalli and Capovilla ate facing each other across rather a rickety table: soup, a slice of meat, a glass of wine, an apple. But neither found it easy to eat or talk. Perhaps a dozen words were exchanged in quarter of an hour. Roncalli dozed for about twenty minutes and then settled down at his desk to jot down some notes towards his acceptance speech: he already knew its majestic and striking opening chord – '*Vocabor Joannes*, I will be called John'. At four o'clock the bell rang to call him back to the Sistine Chapel for the decisive eleventh ballot. At 4.50 p.m. he was elected pope with thirty-eight votes.

Even on this day, of all days, Roncalli remained self-possessed enough to make a few notes for his diary. Becoming pope was not going to alter the methodical habit of a lifetime. What had happened to him had not yet had time to sink in, but his spontaneous response was, 'I'm ready', *Adsum:*

> Third day of the conclave. Feast of the Holy Apostles Sts Simon and Jude.
> Holy Mass in the Mathilde Chapel, with much devotion on my part.
> Invoked with special tenderness my saintly protectors: St Joseph, St Mark,
> St Lawrence Justinian and St Pius XII, asking them to give me calmness and
> courage. I thought it wiser not to eat with the cardinals. I ate in my room.
> At the eleventh ballot I was elected pope (*eccomi eletto papa*). O Jesus, I too
> can say what Pius XII said when he was elected: '*Miserere mei, Deus,
> secundum magnam misericordiam tuam*' (Have mercy on my, Lord, according
> to thy great mercy – Psalm 51). One would say that it is like a dream and
> yet, until I die, it is the most solemn reality of all my life. So I'm ready,
> Lord, '*ad convivendum et ad commoriendum*' (to live and die with you – 2
> Corinthians 7.3). About three hundred thousand people applauded me on
> St Peter's balcony. The arc-lights stopped me from seeing anything other
> than a shapeless, heaving mass (*Vent'Anni*, p. 12).

This text is unique in papal history: a diary entry for 'the day I became Pope'.

Chapter 13

The first ninety days

If anyone expected Roncalli to be a mere caretaker Pope, providing a
transition to the next reign, he destroyed the notion within minutes of his
election . . . He stomped in boldly like the owner of the place, throwing
open windows and moving the furniture around

(*Time Magazine*, November 17, 1958).

The doors to the Sistine Chapel remained firmly locked, but the secretaries and
attendants already knew that a pope had been elected and guessed who he was. By
about five o'clock, most of them had gathered on the so-called Ladies' Balcony
overlooking St Peter's Square: this was the first sign to the waiting crowd and the
television crews that there would soon be 'white smoke'. Don Loris Capovilla
and Guido Gussi were waiting in the deserted Sala Ducale. Tradition had it that
the new Pope's secretary should be the first outsider to enter the Sistine Chapel.
After half an hour or so a door was opened and out came Cardinal Thomas
Tienchensin, Archbishop of Peking, in a wheelchair because of a car accident.
Capovilla looked in and saw Roncalli's empty throne, the third from the end of
the right-hand side. All the canopies except his were folded down (*Letture*, pp.
10–11). So he *was* pope. But where was he? Smiling cardinals told Capovilla, now
catapulted into prominence, that his Holiness was already vesting in the sacristy.

Another *conclavista*, Mgr Jean-François Arrighi, a Corsican who was in the
conclave as Cardinal Tisserant's secretary, described the transformation that had
come over Roncalli during the conclave: 'Before the final vote, the Pope looked
overcome (*accablé*), but when the result was announced, he was completely calm.
I said to myself, "That man has faith" ' (Lawrence, p. 19).

It was Tisserant, as dean of the college of cardinals, who had asked the ritual
question, 'Do you accept?' Until he answered this question, Roncalli was still the
patriarch of Venice. He replied:

> Listening to your voice, *'tremens factus sum et ego, et timeo'* (I tremble and am
> seized by fear). What I know of my poverty and smallness is enough to
> cover me with confusion.
> But seeing the sign of God's will in the votes of my brother cardinals of the
> Holy Roman Church, I accept the decision they have made; I bow my head
> before the cup of bitterness and my shoulders before the yoke of the cross.
> On the feast of Christ the King, we all sang: 'The Lord is our judge, the

Lord is our lawgiver, the Lord is our king: he will save us' (Isaiah 33.22)
(*Vent'Anni*, p. 50).

With these words he became pope.

Tisserant's next ritual question was: 'By what name do you wish to be
known?' The Pope's answer was the first of his many surprises: 'I will be called
John'. Not another Pius, or even a Leo or a Benedict whom he greatly admired:
John. Some explanation was called for. Pope John gave it, prompted by the notes
he had jotted down earlier that afternoon: 'The name John is dear to me because it
was the name of my father, because it is the dedication of the humble parish
church where we were baptised, and because it is the name of innumerable
cathedrals throughout the world, and first of all of the blessed and holy Lateran
Basilica, our own cathedral' (*Vent'Anni*, p. 51). That confident and affectionate
mention of 'our own cathedral' was a first hint that he would take his duties as
'Bishop of Rome' seriously. As the cardinals racked their brains trying to
remember what they could about the long and mostly ignominious line of Johns,
the new Pope helped them out and allowed himself – could it be? – a wry
historian's joke: 'It is the name which has been most used in the long series of
Roman Pontiffs. Indeed there have been twenty-two unquestionably legitimate
supreme pontiffs named John. Nearly all had a brief pontificate' (*Ibid.*). Just the
name for a 'transitional pope'. Pope John did not reveal that for years he had been
studying Pope John XXII, last legitimate pope of the name, who reigned from
1317 to 1334. The archbishop of Avignon later remembered that Roncalli had
visited the former papal city in October 1952 and astonished the local archivists
with his thorough knowledge of the Avignon popes. He told Cardinal Maurice
Feltin that the choice of name was partly a tribute to France (Bergerre, p. 70). But
more profoundly, it was the deliberate retrieval of an *evangelical* name from the
rapscallions who had dishonoured it and the anti-Pope John XXIII who had, so it
was believed, made it unusable: Baldassare Cossa, the last claimant to the name,
was an ex-pirate who had massacred, cheated and perjured his way to the papacy.

Pope John explained very simply that he loved the name John because it had
been borne by the two men in the Gospels who were closest to Jesus: John the
Baptist and John the Evangelist. John the Baptist 'prepared the way of the Lord',
and shed his blood as a witness to the Light. John the Evangelist, favoured by
Jesus and his mother, leaned on his breast at the last supper and derived from this
'a charity which burned with lively flame until extreme old age' (*Vent'Anni*, p.
51). But it was his conclusion that moved even the hard-bitten college of
cardinals. He had called himself John in order to renew the exhortation of the
Apostle John: 'My children, love one another. Love one another because this is the
greatest commandment of the Lord. Venerable brethren, may God in his mercy
grant that we, bearing the same name John, may with the help of divine grace

have his holiness of life and strength of soul, even unto the shedding of blood, if God so wills' (*Ibid.*, pp. 51–2). The message was love, the means sacrifice.

The next hour was aimiably chaotic. Before leaving the Sistine Chapel, Pope John revived an old custom by placing his now redundant red skull cap on the head of Mgr Alberto di Jorio, secretary of the conclave, thus creating him a cardinal. In the sacristy, prelates fussed and pressed around him, congratulating him and asking for a blessing. Capovilla pushed his way through and asked that the first blessing should be for Venice, Bergamo and all the family at Sotto il Monte. 'Yes, gladly' he replied, 'first for those related according to the Spirit and then the relatives according to blood; we'll talk about it later, later'. Pope John subsequently denied that he had given a special blessing for Padre Pio, the Franciscan stigmatic (*Lettere*, p. 159), but that was because adepts of the holy man were claiming that he had predicted John's election. In the crush, it was difficult to know precisely who had been blessed and what had been said.

According to *Time*, a reliable source on such matters, the new Pope weighed 205 lbs (Fox, p. 335). His girth was not stated, but it was enough to embarrass Annibale Gammarelli, the pontifical tailor, for whom popes came in two sizes: thin and fat. The larger of the two white cassocks failed to meet round the front. Gammarelli had to fix it with safety pins, and a surplice concealed his improvisation from the television cameras. At 6.08 p.m., exactly an hour after the 'white smoke', Cardinal Nicola Canali announced to the world the 'great joy' that we had a pope, and at the name of Roncalli, and still more that of John, what Capovilla called 'a wave of enthusiasm' swept over the square (*Letture*, p. 9). Anthony Burgess put it more vividly: 'The crowd gaudiated magnally: old ladies in black wept, teeth gleamed in stubbled faces, strangers shook hands with each other, children jumped as though Mickey Mouse were soon to come, the horns of Roman cars rejoiced plaintively' (*Earthly Powers*, p. 550). At 6.20 Pope John appeared on the central *loggia* of St Peter's and gave his first blessing *urbi et orbi*, on the city and on the world. He did not make a speech: that 'custom' was introduced only later. It is doubtful whether he could have made a speech, so intense was the emotion. But it little mattered. Pope John had passed his first and crucial test: the people of Rome loved him.

He afterwards tried to describe his feelings as he stood up there before the noisy, invisible crowd:

I remembered Jesus' warning: 'Learn of me, for I am meek and humble of heart'. Dazzled by the television lights, I could see nothing but an amorphous, swaying mass. I blessed Rome and the world as though I were a blind man. As I came away I thought of all the cameras and lights that from now on, at every moment, would be directed on me. And I said to myself: if you don't remain a disciple of the gentle and humble Master, you'll understand nothing even of temporal realities. Then you'll be really blind (*Vent'Anni*, p. 21).

Meanwhile, back in the sacristy, there were more scenes of cheerful chaos. Tardini and his staff from the Secretariat of State had come to present their homage. Cardinal Tisserant, now in charge as dean of the sacred college since the office of *camerlengo* lapsed on the election of a pope, thundered that they were all excommunicated. They had broken in before the conclave had been officially declared over. There followed half an hour of comic confusion during which Tisserant strode around with upset dignity, his beard wagging as he alternately excommunicated or cried, 'Don't kill him now you've made him Pope' (*Vent'Anni*, p. 22). The cause of all this uproar gently enquired, 'Where do we go now?'

It was up to him to decide where to spend the night. He preferred not to go back to cell number fifteen, and headed for the almost deserted apartment of the Secretary of State. It had not been lived in for years. The vivas continued to echo round the square below, but since the shutters were still sealed, nothing could be seen. Pope John certainly did not literally 'fling open the windows of the Vatican' on his first night. The telephone was dead. There was no radio. Pope John was completely alone. Guido Gussi was despatched to bring his gear from cell fifteen and Domus Mariae.

At 7.30 p.m. Mgr Dell'Acqua arrived with a Latinist to help draft his radio message for the next day. He dined alone at 9 o'clock in a badly-lit corner of the vast apartment. Capovilla, unsure of the protocol, had already eaten, but he stayed long enough to see an aged manservant, Pio Manzia, totter in with a bottle of champagne. 'Holy Father', he explained, 'it is a tradition that the head of the household should open a bottle of champagne, offer it to his Holiness, and take away what's left for himself' (*Vent'Anni*, p. 23). Pope John took a glass, and let Manzia have most of it. He was not going to deny anyone his perks.

Then he paced up and down in the gallery, saying his rosary. He broke off to say, 'Before lying down I want to see Tardini'. Capovilla objected: 'But you've seen him with all the others in the sacristy'. 'I know', said Pope John, 'but hasty compliments are not enough. He's the most important person around here. Get him along' (*Vent'Anni*, p. 23). Exceptionally, he departed from routine and wrote up his diary the next day:

> From yesterday I gave myself the name John. I spent the night in the Secretariat of State, dozing rather than sleeping . . . Today the entire world writes and talks of nothing except me: the name and the person. O my dear parents, O mother, O my father and grandfather Angelo, O Uncle Zaverio, where are you? What brought this honour upon you? continue to pray for me (*Ibid.*, p. 43).

Why was Tardini summoned late at night on the very day of the election? There is a slight discrepancy in the accounts of what happened. Capovilla asserts that Pope John offered him the post of Pro-secretary of State (pro-secretary because he was not yet a cardinal) there and then at about 10 p.m. Tardini cannilly asked: 'Is this an order in obedience?' Pope John replied:

> Yes. Now the roles are reversed; tonight I can ask obedience of you . . . You've had forty years of service in the immediate entourage of the pope; you've been a faithful servant and priest; you know the problems; you had the confidence of my predecessor; I can't imagine you pensioned off and in retirement. I'll be loyal to you, and you'll be loyal to me. The Lord will guide us (*Lettere*, p. 59).

According to Capovilla, Tardini then fell to his knees, received the Pope's blessing, and was embraced by him. And so to bed.

Giulio Nicolini, Tardini's biographer, says however that this late-night meeting was merely to fix an appointment for the following morning. Pope John lifted the absurd excommunication and said, 'The *first* audience will be for you' (Nicolini, p. 176). According to this version, Tardini divined what was coming and worked through the night on his *scaletta* or list of points to bring up. Next morning, Pope John surprised him by inviting him to sit down – in Pius' time subordinates knelt before the Pope – and asked him to become his Secretary of State. Tardini consulted his notes and stated his objections. He was 'ready to obey'. But he was 'old, tired and ill', and had brought along a medical certificate to prove it. He pointed out that he had already offered his resignation to the college of cardinals during the conclave, but that they had instructed him to carry on with current business until it was over. He made some remarks on immediate problems that had to be dealt with (*Ibid.*).

Then came a rather strange 'precision' about the past, and specifically about the years 1946–52. Tardini said: 'It is not true that Pius XII wanted to keep me out of the limelight. It was I who wanted this' (Nicolini, p. 176). What old war-scar did this reveal? It was well-known that Pius XII had wanted to make Tardini and Montini cardinals, but it had to be *both together*. So Tardini's refusal meant that Montini could not become a cardinal either.

Tardini was manfully trying to clear the air. The 'reconciliation' effected in the pre-conclave period had not entirely erased past memories. Pope John had been a friend of Montini and was puzzled by his Milanese exile. Tardini had not had a high opinion of the new Pope's intelligence and diplomatic skill. On both sides there was material for friction. So Tardini was genuinely surprised at being appointed Secretary of State, and tried to get out of it. His own account (as reported by his former pupil, archbishop, later cardinal, Sebastiano Baggio) is frankest of all, and catches an echo of his gruff, *staccato* style:

He didn't give me any choice. I told the Holy Father that I wouldn't serve under him, because new policies would need new people; and I reminded him that I had frequently (*più di una volta*) disagreed with him in the past; I reminded him that I was tired, whacked out (Tardini used the Roman dialect word, *stufo*) and that my health was getting worse; I told him about my long-cherished ambition of at last giving myself entirely to the orphan boys of Villa Nazareth. It made no difference. The Pope listened to me with kindness and interest, but to every point he replied: 'I understand, but I want you to be my Secretary of State'. Finally I knelt down and offered him my obedience. Such is life (Nicolini, pp. 177–8).

Cardinal Giuseppe Siri confirms that Pope John had to beg Tardini to accept the post. His argument was: 'We're both priests, and have to submit to the will of God' (*Ibid.*, p. 178).

Why should Pope John have to be so determined to appoint as his closest collaborator someone with whom he had disagreed in the past and who was so reluctant to accept the office? The hypothesis of a deal struck during the conclave – votes for Roncalli on condition that Tardini was his Secretary of State – has already been excluded. A two-man ticket was against the spirit and the letter of the conclave rules. But that does not mean that Pope John was insensitive to the feeling in the conclave that a pope inexperienced in the ways of the Curia should be flanked by someone who knew its workings intimately.

Since Pope John's relationship with the Curia is crucial for understanding (or misunderstanding) his pontificate, it will be as well to give here the witness of Mgr Igino Cardinale, soon to become his chief of protocol:

Pope John was not a curial man. He didn't know too much about the Curia, and *what he knew he didn't like*. His relationship when in Bulgaria, Istanbul and elsewhere had not always been very good. So he remained the outsider. He never intentionally over-ruled the Curia, but he felt free to make up his own mind. His attitude was that he would always be respectful towards the Curia, but would not be bound or limited by it (Cardinale, conversation with the author, Brussels, March 30, 1980).

This was common knowledge in the inner circles of the Vatican. Consequently, the immediate appointment of Tardini was a clear signal to the whole Curia. Pope John began his pontificate with a gesture of reconciliation towards the Curia he had inherited. There would be no sackings or abrupt dismissals. He would not employ a new broom.

Though the pope is an absolute monarch, with a power of patronage that would make an American president green with envy, Pope John resisted the temptation to bring in his own team. He did not emulate St Pius X who introduced so many Venetians into Rome that he was said to have 'turned the barque of Peter into a gondola'. Nor did he appoint a close friend like Angelo Dell'Acqua as Secretary of State, for that would have exposed him to the charge of favouritism. He made it clear that he would not attempt to govern the Church against the Curia, and would try to enlist its co-operation for whatever projects he had in mind – and Tardini already sensed that he had something up his sleeve ('New policies would need new people'). Later Pope John would pay a painful price for this kid-gloved handling of the Curia; but as an opening move it was tactically shrewd.

Having secured Tardini's consent, Pope John discussed with him another appointment which in his own eyes, if not those of the world, was almost as important. He wanted a confessor and spiritual director. Tardini explained that the official confessor of the papal household was by tradition a friar. But he was free to choose anyone. Pius XII had a learned Jesuit, Fr Augustin Bea, rector of the Biblical Institute. Pope John's diary records: 'I prayed and reflected about this. I chose without hesitation Mgr Alfredo Cavagna; he is holy, good, learned, prudent; he knows the Roman scene well, and will be able to help me with discretion on many matters' (*Pastore*, p. 11). Cavagna was two years older than Pope John and had a similar background. He had been secretary to a bishop and helped organise a diocesan Synod. He had organised national clergy weeks to bring clergy and laity closer together. He met St Teresa of Avila's criterion for a good confessor: it was no use having a holy man unless he were also learned and prudent. He served Pope John in many other roles, as we shall see. But his most important role was as confessor. Throughout his pontificate, unless prevented by some urgent business, Pope John made his confession to Cavagna at 3 o'clock on Friday afternoon, the day and the hour of Jesus' death. He took his time over it, seeing in confession a way of reviewing his life, week by week, in the light of the demands of the Holy Spirit. This is one of the keys to his pontificate. But it is not accessible to the historian.

On this first crowded day of his pontificate, Pope John was driven up the hill to Vatican Radio to broadcast his first message to the world, *Hac trepida hora* (In this moment of trepidation). It seemed at first hearing a conventional enough discourse taking the form of greetings and thanks to all and sundry in the Church. It was strongly anti-Communist. He had a special message for the bishops and Catholics of those countries 'where the Catholic religion has no freedom, where the sacred rights of the Church are abusively trampled upon, where legitimate pastors are exiled, banished or hindered in the fulfilment of their ministry' (*Vent'Anni*, p. 53). He could hardly have said less with Cardinal Stepinac, whom he'd known since 1938, still in prison and Cardinal Mindszenty immured in the U.S. Embassy in Budapest. He wrote them sympathetic letters the same day (*Lettere*, pp. 34–5). But in his broadcast he departed from Pius XII's thunderous denunciations and adumbrated his opening speech to the Council when he prayed that such 'inhuman persecutions might cease, not only because they threaten the peace and tranquillity of these peoples, but also because they are in *open contrast with modern civilisation and with the rights of man' (Vent'Anni*, p. 53). There was no need to condemn errors that condemned themselves.

This first speech was programmatic. In it Pope John announced the two major themes that would mark his pontificate: *unity* in the life of the Church and *peace* in the secular order. His good wishes embraced the Orthodox Churches and 'All those who are separated from this Apostolic See'. He quoted Jesus' prayer 'that all may be one' (John 17.11); it became the linking thread of his pontificate. He deplored the way the wealth of nations was squandered on the arms race and devoted to preparing 'pernicious instruments of death and destruction', instead of being used 'for all classes of society, especially the least favoured' (*Vent'Anni*, pp. 53–4). This contained the germ of his great social encyclicals. He quoted the *Gloria* which speaks of *pacem in terris omnibus hominibus bonae voluntatis.* How to speak of 'peace on earth to all men of good will' became his abiding question.

This first radio message, it should be noted, picked up many of the themes of Cardinal Bacci's *De eligendo pontifice* address (see above, p. 281). This is important for grasping how he understood his office. He felt that he had received a mandate from the college of cardinals. It was through them that the Holy Spirit had made his will known, not through the Roman Curia. He felt justified in embarking from the outset on a new style of papacy. Not everyone understood this straight-away. Someone who did was the elderly Don Luigi Sturzo, once leader of the Popular Party, who commented on the radio message: 'Peace, justice, liberty, mutual understanding of rights and duties – all in the accents of love' (*Avvenire d'Italia*, November 1, 1958). Pope John meanwhile, his first day as pope over, moved into the papal apartments and noted in his diary, mysteriously, 'emotion and sadness' ('*emozione e mestizia*') (*Vent'Anni*, p. 43.)

By next day he was feeling more cheerful. His diary records:

> October 30, Thursday. The first nominations arouse general approval,
> especially that of the secretary of state. Begin with him the most urgent
> business and appointments. Above all the consistory and the nomination of
> new cardinals. I give him the names beginning with mgr Montini,
> Archbishop of Milan, and mgr Tardini, who headed a litany on which we
> were in perfect agreement. When we reached the total of seventy, old and
> new, we paused for a moment but then, reflecting that at the time of Sixtus
> V the Catholic Church occupied only about a third of its present territory,
> we went on and arrived at a list of 23 new cardinals (*Vent'Anni*,
> pp. 43–4).

Sixtus V (1585–90) had founded the Curia in its modern form and decreed that the number of cardinals should not exceed seventy. Pope John departed from precedent because, in the changed situation, it seemed common sense to do so. He also put right, at a stroke, Pius' neglect of the college of cardinals and began to realise his predecessor's largely unfulfilled ambition of 'internationalising' it. Pope John's consistory included 'first ever' cardinals from the Philippines, Japan, Mexico and Africa. He was particularly pleased with his appointment of the first black cardinal, Laurean Rugambwa, archbishop of Dar-es-Salaam, Tanzania. But with Tardini's approval, he placed Giovanni Battista Montini at the top of his list as a consolation for past injustice and a presage for the future.

However, this did not mean that he intended that his pontificate should be merely 'keeping the chair of Peter warm' for Montini whose eventual return as pope was regarded by the Roman Curia, not without apprehension, as inevitable. He knew that many would continue to think of him as a stop-gap pope whose reign would be characterised by placid inactivity. One 'old prelate' took Capovilla aside and exhorted him: 'Beg the Pope not to dream of writing encyclicals or making too many speeches or canonising too many saints or inventing new festivities for St Peter's Square. Let's have a period of calm' (*Vent'Anni*, pp. 17–18).

The undemanding old prelate would have been delighted that Pope John seemed more interested in reviving lost traditions than starting new ones. He restored the fur bonnet seen in portraits of Renaissance popes, and preferred it to the white skull cap, which kept slipping off. He fussed over his coat of arms. Mgr Bruno Heim, the heraldry expert who had been a colleague in Paris, instructed to include a lion of St Mark's, Venice, depicted the beast rampant, with claws extended. 'Don't you think' asked the Pope, 'that he's too fierce, a little too – er – Germanic?' (Trevor, p. 268). He wanted his lion to be 'more human'.

Pope John's love of tradition came out in the preparations for his coronation, fixed for November 4, feast of St Charles Borromeo, the man to whom he had devoted so much midnight oil. He would have the full ceremonial, complete with the Franciscans burning smoking flax to remind him of mortality ('*Sic transit gloria mundi*' – 'Thus does the world's glory pass away'), the fans of ostrich plumes, the *sedia gestatoria* or portable chair, and the tiara. Albino Luciani, whom Pope John named bishop of Vittorio Veneto a few weeks later and who would succeed him as John Paul I in 1978, swept away all these traditions. Pope John liked them. Nevertheless, the tiara, symbolising regal power and the temporal claims of the papacy that he was happy to abandon, always seemed incongruous on his head. But he enjoyed pomp. His diary for November 4, 1958 reads simply: 'Wednesday. Grand coronation in St Peter's. The event communicated to the whole world' (*Vent'Anni*, p. 44).

There was, however, one simple innovation which turned out to have crucial importance: Pope John decided to preach a homily at his Coronation Mass. This had never been done before. The ceremony was already immensely long, and it was a triumph rather than an occasion for teaching. But Pope John insisted. He went over his prepared text with Mgr Cardinale, who winced over what he thought were certain linguistic 'modernisms'. Formed in the school of Pius XII, Cardinale was accustomed to the curial practice of taking Palazzi's *Dizionario* as the standard authority on usage. He explained this to the Pope, who peered over the top of his spectacles and said: 'Well, if need be, we shall reform *even* Palazzi' (Cardinale). Pope John aimed for a literary style that was simple, direct, unpompous. He had already summoned the evergreen editor of *l'Osservatore Romano*, Count Giuseppe Dalla Torre, now onto his fourth pope, and told him to cease referring to 'the illuminated Holy Father' or 'the most Supreme Pontiff'; and he was to drop phrases like 'as we gathered from the august lips' (Elliott, p. 256). If he meant 'the Pope said' he was to write 'the Pope said'. I shall follow this precept from now on and call him 'the Pope', 'Pope John' or simply 'John'.

As Coronation Day approached, John's worries went beyond questions of style. He felt that since he became pope, he had been neglecting his family. His nephew Don Battista had turned up on his first day as pope, and been gently returned home to Fustigiano (*Vent'Anni*, p. 43). The others mattered more. So on the eve of his Coronation more than thirty brothers and sisters, nephews and nieces, disembarked at Stazione Termini. In sober Sunday suits and black dresses, they fidgeted with their hats as they tried to make conversation with the Vatican officials sent to greet them. They were whisked by bus to Domus Mariae. Then they had their audience. Some of them wept openly. John said: 'Come on now, no crying. After all, what they've done to me is not *so* bad'. He wanted to know how everyone was. Yes, Don Battista had been to see him, had trouble explaining himself to the Swiss Guards, and had got lost. No, he would not be having a job in the Vatican. No, his niece, Sr Angela, would not become his housekeeper. *Sotto voce*: 'One Sr Pascalina was enough'. So, the mayor of Bergamo wanted to honour his brothers with the title of *Cavalieri della Repubblica Italiana* (Knights of the Italian Republic). It would be better to decline. They were to remain the Pope's brothers, the Pope's family. That should be enough. And after the Coronation they went back to their fields.

The Coronation Mass began at 8 a.m. and lasted for five hours. Mgr Enrico Dante, master of ceremonies, saw to it that everything went according to the rubrics. This was no mean feat considering that the last Coronation had been in 1939. But there was something different about *this* coronation. The forms were the same, but John's homily gave them a different meaning.

Cardinal Nicola Canali had placed the tiara on his head with the age-old formula: 'Know that thou art the father of princes and kings, pontiff of the whole world and Vicar of Christ on earth'. But in his homily John had carefully explained that he wanted to be a good shepherd of the flock, after the pattern of

Christ. Because it was so simple, it was revolutionary. Moreover, as John developed his thoughts, he seemed to be contrasting his pontificate, just begun, with that of his predecessor: 'These are those who expect the pontiff to be a statesman, a diplomat, a scholar, the organiser of the collective life of society, or someone whose mind is attuned to every form of modern knowledge' (*Vent'Anni*, p. 56). These expectations had been created by Pius XII, who was often discovered late at night mugging up some new technical subject so that next day he might dazzle his hearers. John would not try to emulate him, partly because he could not but even more because it involved a mistaken idea of the papacy (or in John's orotund Vaticanese, 'betrayed a concept of the Supreme Pontiff that was not fully in conformity with its true ideal'). But what was the alternative? John went on: 'The new Pope, through the events and circumstances of his life, is like the son of Jacob who, meeting with his brothers, burst into tears and said, "I am Joseph, your brother" ' (Genesis 45.4) (*Vent'Anni*, p. 57). Joseph (Giuseppe) was John's second baptismal name. Here he was, as it were, descending from his throne and putting himself on the same level as his brothers. It was a long time since a pope had used such language. It had certainly not been used, and could not be imagined, on the 'august lips' of Pius XII.

Pope John's 'revisionism' continued. He repeated what he had already said: the Pope should be a good shepherd. Then: 'Other human qualities – learning, diplomatic cleverness (*accorgimento*) and skill, organising ability – may embellish and fill out a pontificate, but they cannot be a substitute for being the shepherd of the whole flock' (*Vent'Anni*, p. 58). The word here translated 'cleverness' has a hint of pejorative 'smartness' (as in 'smart alec'). One begins to suspect that Cardinale's objections were not merely those of a linguistic purist: he realised that Pope John's words would inevitably be interpreted as a repudiation of his predecessor. This was not his intention; but it was the effect. He was trying to say that he would not compete with Pius and that Pius should not be admired for the wrong reasons: his true greatness was to be sought not in his genius but rather in the way he had acted as Good Shepherd. But it didn't come out quite like that. He seemed to be emphasising that his pontificate would be very different, for 'every pontificate takes on its character, its face as it were, from the supreme pontiff who embodies it and gives it its special features' (*Ibid.*).

Finally, moving on to less contentious ground, Pope John explained why the Coronation was being held on November 4, a Wednesday, rather than on the traditional Sunday. Some of the diplomats had complained about having their working week disturbed. The explanation was simple. It was the feast of St Charles Borromeo. Thirty-four years before he had received his episcopal ordination in San Carlo allo Corso, 'close to the most precious relic of the saint's heart'. In case anyone did not realise the significance of St Charles Borromeo not only in his personal life but in the life of the Church, he added:

The Lord's Church has had its moments of stagnation and revival (*stasi e ripresi*). In one such period of revival Providence reserved for St Charles Borromeo the lofty task of restoring ecclesiastical order (*riconstituzione dell'ordine ecclesiastico*). The part he played in implementing the reforms of the Council of Trent, and the example he gave in Milan and other dioceses of Italy, earned him the glorious title of teacher of Bishops, and as such he was adviser to popes and a wonderful model of episcopal holiness (*Vent'Anni*, p. 60).

To Pope John this was home ground. To some of his hearers it suggested that he might one day resume the unfinished reforming work of St Charles.

With this homily Pope John stated clearly the kind of Pope he aimed to become. Of course he still had to realise it. But already he had shown that a fresh way of conceiving the 'Petrine ministry' was possible. Whenever theologians subsequently tried to sketch out their 'ideal pope', they returned to this text to give substance to their dreams (see *Infallible?* pp. 198–203, 'Portrait of a Possible Pope'). But the effect of this November 4, 1958 homily was practical as well as theoretical: the idea that a pope should be above all 'pastoral' was used as a yardstick in the 1978 conclaves.

Two days after his Coronation, Pope John met the Roman and international press. This was another 'first'. It was an important meeting, because these were the men and women who would help shape and diffuse his public 'image'. In modern Rome press and pope live in an inevitable symbiosis, but the quality of the *rapport* varies a great deal. John had the press on his side from this first meeting. It is not too much to say that he had them eating out of his hand. Some tough-minded journalists admitted, afterwards and in private, to tears. It was not so much what he had to say as his evident friendliness and warmth that won them over. He had been reading the papers a lot, he told them, 'not out of vanity but because it gives me great pleasure to see the interest which the world had in the papacy and also' – with a broad smile – 'to learn the secrets of the conclave' (Negro, Silvio, in *Corriere della Sera*, November 7, 1958). But his remarks had a sting in the tail: 'It seems that though the efforts of the journalists have been remarkable, the silence of the cardinals has been even more remarkable'. The subtle Silvio Negro, then the reigning prince of Vaticanologists, pointed out that the Pope spoke only of the silence of the *cardinals*, and did not mention the *conclavistas* or attendants who were also inside the conclave.

Negro noted that Pope John looked younger than his seventy-six years – he would be seventy-seven within the month, that his gestures were vigorous, his eyes twinkling and that, far from being overwhelmed by his awesome office, he seemed to relish being pope. He had a quality that can only be called gusto, which was also seen in his liturgical style: he incensed the altar *allegro con brio*. What most struck Negro, however, was the fact that the Pope was improvising and did not have a prepared text. This was a great contrast with Pius XII who always wrote out his speeches in full, and once confessed: 'When I speak, I see only the pages in front of me'. John, when not blinded by television lights, evidently saw the people who were there, not the pages he did not have.

He told the journalists his favourite story about Joseph meeting his brothers and said: 'I am your brother, too, even if before God I am the first of brothers and as pastor have to guide my brothers'. Negro concluded his article: 'His face is constantly illumined by a confident and humorous smile. The listener feels that he is gradually caught up in a family atmosphere and that he is taking part in a conversation' (*Corriere della Sera*, November 7, 1958).

This first favourable impression remained and grew. It is the reason why Pope John had such a good press, especially in the 'honeymoon' period of his pontificate. (Later, the right-wing press would declare him to be politically naïve.) But once again, contrast heightened the effect. After the gravely hieratic and austere Pius XII, a fat and genial 'brother Pope' was astonishing. Moreover, the spontaneity of his approach meant that he was constantly unpredictable, and therefore 'newsworthy'. That the Pope should walk in the Vatican gardens and actually chat with the gardeners – they had been instructed to vanish on the rare occasions that Pius XII went for a walk – seemed like a major event: the papacy had been reclaimed by humanity.

The Roman Curia was less easily impressed than the journalists. Its members read the enthusiastic stories in the press about the 'peasant Pope' who was so poor that he had to carry his shoes to school. They were well aware that a process of mythologisation starts as soon as someone is elected Pope: talent becomes genius, and ordinariness is proof of humanity. Their ingrained professionalism made them sceptical of such romancing, and the 'revisionist' remarks at the Coronation Mass had startled some. Then Pope John took an initiative to get the Curia on his side. The key department, the Secretariat of State, was summoned for an audience on November 17. Some of them, Tardini above all, had given him orders when he was in Turkey and France. John confirmed them all in their posts, said he needed them, emphasised that a 'pastoral' pontificate needed a 'pastoral' Curia, and let them into a secret: he had decided that Tardini and Montini, another product of the Secretariat of State, would be made cardinals along with twenty-one others at a public consistory in St Peter's on the following December 18 (*Vent'Anni*, p. 103). He told them this well ahead of the official announcement in *l'Osservatore Romano*. So they enjoyed the keenest pleasure bureaucrats can experience: a sense of being trusted and in the know. In truth, no great perceptiveness was needed to guess that Tardini and Montini would both have to be made cardinals sooner or later. But it could have been later. And he didn't have to tell the Curia in advance. It was a simple ploy, but it worked.

On Sunday, November 23, Pope John 'took possession' of his cathedral, the Basilica of St John Lateran. In his mind, it was an event almost equal in importance to his Coronation; and it lasted just as long. He describes the day in his diary:

> November 23, Sunday. One of the most wonderful days of my life. Took possession of my cathedral of St John Lateran. Everything beautiful and solemn. My two speeches: one short, and in Latin, at the entrance to the Basilica in answer to the address of welcome of card. Luigi [*sic*] Masella, the archpriest. The other from the throne in the apse, in Italian, the *celebration* itself, and its meaning in the light of the *book* and the *chalice*. It was listened to attentively.
>
> The return from the Lateran to the Vatican: simply triumphal. The homage of the Roman people, all along the route, to their new Bishop of Rome, was moving and unexpected, and therefore all the more precious. On the way there and back arranged to be accompanied by cardinals Tisserant, the dean, and Pizzardo. They wept with emotion. All I could do was remain in a state of humiliation, a sacrificial offering for my people; in abandonment, but with great and confident simplicity (*Vent'Anni*, p. 44).

That the people of Rome gave their new bishop a moving welcome seems hardly worthy of comment; but John had been brought up at a time when Popes could not even leave the Vatican to test the public response. Rome was not just an indifferent backcloth for him. It was alive with memories.

The first part of his Lateran homily was a lengthy meditation on the rite of 'taking possession'. It had begun in the thirteenth century, and mediaeval Popes like John XXI (how he loved to bring him in) had come on horseback from the Vatican to the Lateran along the very route he had followed that morning. What happened at the Lateran was not a formal investiture: he had already become bishop of Rome when he said 'I accept' to Cardinal Tisserant. But there is a 'human aspect' even to the greatest spiritual events. In mediaeval times the cavalcade had progressed with great pomp, preceded by a dozen standard bearers. It had paused before the richly decorated Campidoglio where the Senator of Rome had pledged the homage of the city to the Pope. Pius IX, he recalled, had entered the Lateran on November 8, 1846, at a time of 'collective fever and threatening confusion' (an allusion to the fact that within two years Rome was in revolution and the Pope had fled). So long as the Papal States lasted, the 'taking possession' was an expression of the Pope's temporal power over the city of Rome. After 1870, it became a private affair.

The public ceremony was revived by Pius XII in 1939. But relations with the Fascist authorities were cool and tense, and the people of Rome were not encouraged to cheer the Pope. But now all that was changed. The wheel of history had flicked on once more. Pope John explained:

> The entry of the Pope into his cathedral has lost most of its pomp in the course of time; but how much has it gained in spirituality! One no longer looks at the prince, the ruler, who adorns himself with external signs of splendour and prestige, but at the priest, the father, the shepherd. At the beginning of the century a modern sociologist, a fervent and profound Catholic, troubled by the problems of social order and disorder, expressed the following prayer for the twentieth century: that Christ should return in triumph on the shoulders of the people (*Vent'Anni*, p. 69: the 'sociologist' was Giuseppe Toniolo).

He was not saying that this prayer was now completely realised. But the fact that so many Romans could uninhibitedly share in the Church's joy over a new pope was 'a sure sign of spiritual progress'. It meant that the Vatican and Italy were no longer in sullen competition but could work together harmoniously, their respective spheres of competence clearly distinguished. The reconciliation merely promised and sketched out in 1929 was now achieved. That was why the homage of the people of Rome mattered.

It was precisely this new relationship with the Italian Republic, now firmly wedded to democracy, that allowed Pope John finally to relinquish all temporal claims and present himself as *pastor*. In practice it would mean a disengagement (*disimpegno*) from national politics. That theme will be explored in a later chapter. But withdrawal from the political arena did not imply either silence or abdication. The essential tasks of every priest and bishop in the Church was to teach. 'Go and teach all nations' was the mandate given by Christ. Great Popes who had lived at the Lateran like St Leo and St Gregory had understood this well (*Vent'Anni*, p. 73).

But there are many forms of teaching. Pius XII had been a great didactic Pope, who had exalted his own *magisterium* more than any pope since Pio Nono. Pope John, however, was more concerned with catechesis than with *magisterium*. He wanted a catechesis that would be 'vigorous, resplendent and attractive' (three almost untranslatable adjectives, '*robusta, splendente e fascinatrice*': *Vent'Anni*, p. 72). It was his concern for catechesis that led him to depart from custom and preach this homily. Roman liturgy was often no more than a baroque spectacle. But he wanted the liturgy to teach. Inert and passive presence were not enough. He quoted Bossuet: 'There can be no practice and perfection of Christian life without participation in the eucharistic banquet'. This was to be the basis of the Council's liturgical reform. Those who say Pope John would not have approved of it do not know their man: he always linked together liturgy and catechesis, worship and teaching, the Word proclaimed in the Gospel and the Word shared out in Communion, or, in his language, the *book* and the *chalice*.

This emphasis on catechesis rather than *magisterium* was novel. The difference
in the two approaches can be put this way: while *magisterium* lectures the world
from the outside, catechesis takes people where they are and seeks to ground the
Gospel in the thick of human life. The *Deus nobiscum* (God-with-us) of the
Incarnation makes this possible: 'God is among us as the revealed and
contemplated truth, as perennial grace, educating and sanctifying men and
women, the family and the various forms of human society in the exercise of the
highest virtues' (*Vent'Anni*, p. 74). Pope John was more concerned with
communicability than with orthodoxy. It is fair to add that the distinction (which
should not be hardened into an opposition) between catechesis and *magisterium*
was not used by Pope John to contrast his own pontificate with that of Pius XII.
Indeed, aware by now that his Coronation homily had been interpreted as an
attack on his predecessor, he tried at the Lateran to correct any such impression.
This is often a recipe for making things worse. The new Pope, he roundly
declared, could not forget the twenty volumes of magisterial teaching bequeathed
by Pius XII, and they remained 'perhaps the most notable expression of his
pastoral genius' and 'a source to be consulted by anyone who intends with the help
of God to plough the same furrows'. But didn't that put Pius on the shelf, as a
work of reference? John's metaphors became decidedly mixed as he claimed he
would follow 'the luminous furrows' traced out by Pius XII. He concluded
reassuringly: 'The memory of Pius XII will remain glorious throughout the
centuries. His merit lay in his proclamation in season and out of season of apt and
profound evangelical truth, in the light of which he viewed all the manifestations of human genius' (*Vent'Anni*, p. 72). It was a fine panegyric, and sincerely
meant. But it could not conceal the fact that his papal style would be completely
different.

His visitors noticed the difference. He didn't impose on people. If an audience
with Pius XII was, as Mgr (later Cardinal) Antonio Samorè admitted, 'rather like
undergoing a particularly stiff oral examination', meeting John was more like
chatting with one's favourite grandfather. There was little concern for protocol.
Cardinal Joseph Martin, archbishop of Rouen, told the following story from this
early period: 'I apologised for calling him "your eminence" instead of "your
holiness". But he said there was nothing to apologise for, all the more since he'd
changed his title so many times in the course of his life: don Angelo, monsignore,
your grace, excellency, eminence, holiness. "But now", he said with a smile,
"I'm through with changing titles" ' (*Letture*, p. 390). He brought the same
informality to his meetings with political leaders. His first audience with a head of
state was with the ill-fated Shah of Iran, Mohammed Reza Pahlavi Aryamehr,
then still on the way to the zenith of his power. The Secretariat of State prepared
the usual speech. John said to Capovilla: 'We'll see how the conversation goes. I
can tell him about the time I saw his father in the Piazza Quirinale when I was in

my twenties ... Then I'll read my speech. After all, he's going to be far more worried about making a good impression than I am. Making a good impression is none of my business; but he probably cares about it' (IME, p. 67). His diary was now crammed. He hardly had time to notice his seventy-seventh birthday on November 25. He received Paul Henri Spaak, Secretary-General of NATO, in the afternoon. Next day it was the turn of Igor Stravinsky, the exiled Russian composer, and Cardinal Stefan Wyszyński from Warsaw. At least here he seemed to be emulating Pius XII and behaving as what *Pravda* called 'the Pope of the Atlantic Alliance'. He had been in office for just over a month. He felt the need to retire to Castelgandolfo to rest and take stock.

But before that there was one event that added some more brush strokes to the portrait that was gradually being filled out. He went along to the Lateran Athenaeum, the modern equivalent of the old Roman seminary where he had studied more than fifty years before. It was another informal 'conversation', slightly rambling, full of joky stories about eccentric professors of his day, all done in the school speech-day style of 'as I sat on these benches, I little thought that one day I would become pope'. Cold print could not recapture this tone and, not for the first or last time, *l'Osservatore Romano* provided only an inadequate paraphrase. Capovilla preserved John's own version, and sent it as an end-of-year present to *Sursum Corda*, the Roman seminary magazine (*Lettere*, pp. 85–7). Its conclusion was a revelation of the mind and heart of Angelo Roncalli as he set about the business of being pope:

In the last month, since October 28, when my name and official title were changed, I've had this experience: I hear people talking about the Pope, in indirect or direct speech. For example, 'The Pope should be told this' or 'This will have to be dealt with by the Pope'. When I hear this I still think of the holy father Pope Pius XII, whom I venerated and loved so much, forgetting that the person they are talking about is *me*, who chose to be called John.
Very slowly I'm getting used to the new forms of speech involved in my new ministry. Yes, I am, most unworthily, 'the servant of the servants of God', because the Lord willed it; the Lord, not I. But every time I hear someone address me as 'Your Holiness' or 'Holy Father' you can't imagine how embarrassed and thoughtful it makes me.
Ah! my sons – *saltem vos amici mei* (at least you are my friends) – ask the Lord in prayer that I may be granted the grace of the holiness that is attributed to me. For it is one thing to say it or believe it, and quite another to be holy. The grace of the Lord can raise you much higher than his humble and faithful servant; but nothing counts, nothing has value for history and human life, nothing has any value for the Church and for souls,

unless the Pontiff is holy in deed as well as in title.

My sons, pray for me to the Madonna, Mother of Jesus and our dearest
Mother; pray to the two famous Johns whose cult flourishes in St John
Lateran nearby . . . This is what I wanted to say to you. It comes sincerely
from the heart and is a great consolation for me, and for all of us it is an
encouragement and a joy (*Lettere*, p. 87).

It was entirely characteristic that John should have reserved his most intimate
thoughts on his office for the seminarians who reminded him of his own youthful
hopes. He was the pope who forgot that he was pope. Humility is always a
difficult virtue to evaluate, and its pious counterfeits are legion. But the
seminarians knew enough to distinguish the genuine from the bogus article, and
to understand that the essence of humility does not lie in having a low opinion of
oneself but rather in being at God's disposal, ready for whatever He wills.

This 'conversation' at the Lateran Athenaeum was widely if selectively
reported. But the next day, Friday November 28, there was a private conversation
that remained undisclosed until well after his death. John was walking in the
Vatican Gardens towards sunset, as 'the dome of St Peter's took on fairy-tale hues'
in Capovilla's phrase (*Letture*, p. 352). He was in a mood to sum up his first
month. Still walking briskly, he said to his secretary:

A month has gone by and everything has happened with great naturalness. I
announced a consistory for the creation of twenty-three cardinals, going
beyond the number fixed by Sixtus V. I've provided for Venice, made other
appointments and met all kinds of people. I took possession of the Lateran
and the same day went to San Clemente [the tomb of St Cyril] so that
everyone would know of my love and respect for the Christian East. I've
been to Castelgandolfo. The day after tomorrow I'll be visiting the
Urbanianum, the college of Propaganda Fide. I feel in my heart the
problems of the whole world. But my soul is at peace. If a commission of
cardinals came to tell me that, all things considered, I should return to
Venice, it would not cost me anything to retire (*Letture*, p. 252).

Capovilla interrupted to object rather pedantically that since he had already
appointed Giovanni Urbani as patriarch of Venice, he could not return there.
'Very well', said John, 'I'd happily retire to Sotto il Monte'. But he was not really
thinking of resignation. He continued, more gravely: 'I'm not afraid of
opposition and do not refuse suffering. I think of myself as the last of all, but I
have in mind a programme of work and I'm not fussing about it any more. In
fact, I am pretty well decided' (*Ibid.*). He was talking about the Council, but so
far very few knew about his project. This decision, the most important of his
pontificate, was based on a realistic appraisal of the likely opposition, and was

partly a way of overcoming or circumventing it. The notion that a group of cardinals might recommend his abdication was fanciful, but it had just enough truth to be uncomfortable. He needed to be assured not so much that he had God on his side, but that he was on God's side.

Christmas was coming – another chance to sing again 'Glory to God in the highest and peace on earth to men of good will'. On Christmas Day he went to the Bambin'Gesù children's hospital and the next day to the Regina Coeli prison down by the Tiber. For John there was nothing remarkable about such visits: visiting the sick and consoling prisoners were two of the 'corporal works of mercy' that were so much part of the Counter-Reformation tradition. But this was where his reputation took off and soared. In the otherwise dull Christmas period the world media saw the visits as another manifestation of the approachably human Pope who confessed (though this was censored by *l'Osservatore Romano*) that one of his brothers had been caught poaching, and embraced a murderer who had asked, 'Can there be forgiveness for me?'

John's diary for these two days expresses his genuine surprise at the remarkable effect of his visits to the hospital and prison:

Thursday 25. Nativity of Our Lord Jesus Christ. First Christmas as Pope. Midnight Mass in the Pauline Chapel for the diplomats accredited to the Holy See. About 200 people. Numerous Holy Communions, devout beyond all expectation. Excellent singing directed by Bartolucci. At 11 a.m. Mass in St Peter's: crowd impressive and devout. My third Mass. More suitable music, in the presence of the archpriest, card. Tedeschini. A simple Mass but followed with great participation; it seemed to me to be more alive than in the past.

After Mass gave the solemn benediction to the vast crowd in the square. Appeared in tiara. Good order and great joy and peace. Afterwards went to the Bambin'Gesù hospital for children suffering from polio; then to the S. Spirito Hospital, welcomed by the Prime Minister Fanfani and other dignitaries. Two hours of spiritual joy and, I think, genuinely edifying emotion. *Laus Deo* [Praise be to God]. For lunch I wanted to have with me mgr Angelo Rotta, my predecessor in Istanbul and friend for over forty years. I was alone with him and Don Loris (Capovilla), who wore the robes of a domestic prelate for the first time.

Friday 26. My visit to the Regina Coeli prison. Much calm on my side, but great astonishment in the Roman, Italian and international press. I was hemmed in on all sides: authorities, photographers, prisoners, warders – but the Lord was close. These are the consolations of the Pope: the exercise of the fourteen works of mercy. *Soli Deo honor et gloria* [To God alone be honour and glory]. In the morning a good start to the official diplomatic

visits: Austria, Uruguay, the Lebanon, Panama.
Yesterday afternoon I met a splendid group of handicapped people from Don
Gnocchi and another wonderful group of boys of various ages from card.
Tardini's orphanage whom I'd already met in their own place. The press,
Italian and international, continues to exalt [*magnificare*] my gesture in
visiting the prison yesterday. And for me it was such a simple and natural
thing (*Vent'Anni*, pp. 45–6).

John was often accused of naïveté. As this passage shows, he could be naïve in not
appreciating the workings of the press and its understandable desire for heroes. To
have a hero who was good rather than powerful was a bonus.

Whatever the press was saying, the children kept his feet on the ground. They
had not treated him with exaggerated respect. '*Viene qui, viene qui, Papa*' ('Come
here, come here, Pope/father') they cried, and the old grandfather figure had
waddled over to embrace them. It was the same in the Regina Coeli prison.
Italian prisons are not among the most enlightened or luxurious in Europe. But
here was the Pope in a pell-mell, hugger-mugger riot of prisoners, politicians and
guards assuring them that he was 'Joseph, your brother'. 'Generally edifying
emotion', he noted in his diary. That was an understatement: there was not a dry
eye in the prison. But his actions were inspired by an instinctive sense of what was
right, not by publicity calculations. The long-term importance of these visits was
that they illustrated what he meant by saying that he would be first and foremost
a 'pastor'. In such matters, example counts for more than laborious explanations.
He had found a lived parable of goodness. And the world responded.

Some saw a still deeper meaning in his spontaneous actions. An unnamed
'writer' copied out a text from *Il Santo* (*The Saint*), the novel by Antonio
Fogazzaro that had been placed on the Index of Forbidden Books by St Pius X.
He sent it to Pope John as a thank-you offering. It read:

Vicar of Christ, there is something else that I beg of you. I am a sinner
unworthy to be compared with the saints, but the Spirit can speak even
through the most tainted lips. If a woman (St Catherine of Siena) could
beseech a pope to return to Rome (from Avignon), so I can beseech your
holiness to go out of the Vatican. Go out, Holy Father. But the first time,
at least the first time, go out for one of the works of your ministry. Daily
Lazarus suffers and dies, so go out and meet Lazarus. In every poor
suffering creature Christ cries out for help (*Transizione*, p. 17).

In the early years of the century, such sentiments were absurdly taxed with
'Modernism'. St Pius X did not need jumped-up novelists or pseudo-prophets to
tell him how to behave as pope. Fogazzaro was simply impertinent and was
punished for it. Of course, even as he fulfilled it and 'went out of the Vatican',

John did not have this passage in mind. It was the changed political situation that made such sorties possible. What was impossible for Pius X was easy for him. But that was a charitable interpretation.

So Pope John ended 1958, a year like any other year except that in it he chanced to become pope. He was astonished by the world's response to his simple gestures and deeply grateful to God. His diary simply records: 'Wednesday, 31. The spirit of the day was one of thanksgiving: Holy Mass, breviary, rosary; everything in order and done well. Audiences, audiences, and exchanges of courtesy from 9 till 1 o'clock' (*Vent'Anni*, p. 47). In his first ninety days he had, in famous phrase, 'flung open the windows of the Vatican'. Capovilla, this time behaving like a wet blanket, declares that he never heard Pope John use this expression and that he did not like draughts (*Transizione*, p. 69). Another myth exploded. But Capovilla concedes that it was spiritually true. In a mere three months it was a remarkable achievement. The 'world' was suddenly interested in the papacy again. Simply by being faithful to himself and the spiritual tradition in which he had been brought up, he began to transform the papal office and the way in which it was perceived.

But he had not yet unveiled how he proposed to carry the universal Church along with him in the process of transformation. The means chosen was the summoning of an ecumenical Council. John had been thinking about it in his first three months in office. It was the hidden, unspoken agenda, the inner face of his life as he struggled to discern what the Holy Spirit wanted for his Church.

Chapter 14

The inspiration of the Council

Pius is not the last of the Popes . . . Let us have faith, and a new pope and a reassembled council may trim the boat

(John Henry Newman, writing to Alfred Plummer, April 3, 1871, quoted in *Infallibility in the Church,* Darton, Longman and Todd, London, 1968, p. 77).

After the Christmas visits to hospitals and the Regina Coeli prison, the 'image' of Roncalli as 'good Pope John' was firmly established in the public mind. In the more discriminating world of the Roman Curia he was seen as accessible, unpompous and willing to learn. He restored the audiences *a tabella* – abolished by Pius XII – in which heads of Congregations saw him at regular intervals to discuss routine business. Wherever he could, he delegated authority. The result was that the Curia became more efficient, a fact which the British Minister to the Holy See, Sir Marcus Cheke, grudgingly acknowledged: 'Under Pius XII the Vatican was chaotic; John XXIII made the organisation work' (Lawrence, p. 8). But all this was compatible with the placid, 'transitional' Pope envisaged by some of his cardinal electors. What hardly anyone realised was that Pope John had the idea of summoning a Council right from the start of his pontificate.

We have already seen that Cardinals Ernesto Ruffini and Alfredo Ottaviani claimed to have put the idea to him even earlier. They raised it during the conclave (see p. 283 above). This is not at all unlikely. In 1939 Ruffini, then secretary of the Congregation for Seminaries and Universities, urged the newly elected Pius XII to summon a Council. The problems to be resolved, he averred, 'were as abundant as they were at the Council of Trent' (see Weber, Francis J., 'Pope Pius XII and the Vatican Council', in *The American Benedictine Review,* September, 1970, p. 421). A Council was Ruffini's favourite nostrum for putting the Church to rights. He and Ottaviani were also associated with the 1948 project for a Council. It was not surprising that they should return to the idea ten years later. It was in the air. Capovilla, however, states quite clearly: 'I do not find it hard to believe that Cardinal Ruffini had talked about a council to Pope John, either directly or indirectly. But the fact remains that Pope John always said he made his decision in perfect freedom, and "without anyone having previously talked to him about the matter" ' (Capovilla, letter to the author, April 15, 1981).

John's own subsequent accounts of when and how the idea of the Council came to him have muddled and misled everyone. But Capovilla is emphatic in saying that he first mentioned 'the necessity of holding a council' on October 30, 1958, just two days after his election (*Letture,* p. 746). This was obviously not yet anything so firm as a 'decision', but neither was it merely a vague idea casually thrown out to test the wind. By November 2, we have the first *documented* mention of the idea: in a memo after an audience with Cardinal Ruffini, John noted that they had discussed the possibility of calling a Council (*Lettere,* p. 267). That Ruffini played some part in the genesis of the Council seems undeniable. This same November 2, John said to Capovilla, 'There should be a council' (*Utopia,* Italian, p. 313). So even before his Coronation on November 4, the idea of calling a Council was already beginning to possess him.

It grew naturally out of his conversations with the non-Roman cardinals, his electors, as one by one they came to say farewell. He spent exhausting hours with them as well as with visiting bishops and scholars. The impulse to the Council, if not the idea, came from these early private audiences. In his diary he said that these conversations taught him about 'the expectations of the world and the good impression that the new Pope could make. I listened, noted everything down, and continued to wonder what to do – concretely and immediately' (*Utopia,* Italian, p. 313).

He rotated his immense globe to find out where they all lived. Cardinal Sir Norman Gilroy, archbishop of Sydney, used it to illustrate how Propaganda Fide had devised a perfectly unworkable division of a diocese in Australia. Though the Congregation had a larger staff than any other dicastery (as Curial departments are called), not a single Australian worked there (Capovilla). There were endless variations on this same theme: in pastoral, ecumenical, juridical and Church–state matters the Roman Curia and the local Churches were poles apart. Rome was offering surveillance rather than leadership and collegial support. As he faced this panorama of problems, Pope John began to think about a Council. Becoming pope had not magically endowed him with instant solutions for the universal Church. The best course would be to get all the bishops thinking about these problems together.

Thus the idea of summoning a Council is pushed right back to the first days after Pope John's election. This changes our perspective on both the pontificate and the Council. The Council was not 'accidental' to the pontificate or a kind of afterthought; it was co-terminous with the pontificate as a whole, and acted as its goal, policy, programme and content. John realised that history would judge his pontificate, one way or the other, by what happened at the Council. He admitted as much when he announced it. All eyes were upon him, he said, some friendly, others hostile (*malevole*) or hesitant as they waited for the first decisive move that would 'establish the character of the pontificate which is taking its place, more or less successfully, in history' (Alberigo, p. 275).

But not everyone consulted at this early stage approved of the idea. Capovilla was initially opposed to it, and the fact that he could say so plainly tells us much about their relationship. Capovilla argued very sensibly that for a man of John's age a Council would be a hazardous project entailing a lot of hard work. The safer, more prudent and on balance better course would be to build the pontificate on his strengths, in particular 'the talent or charism of paternity that you undoubtedly possess' (*Utopia*, Italian, p. 314). John went away to think about this in prayer. A few days later after evening rosary with the papal household, he answered Capovilla's objection: 'The trouble is, Don Loris, that you're still not detached enough from self – you're still concerned with having a good reputation. Only when the *ego* has been trampled underfoot can one be fully and truly free. You're not yet free, Don Loris' (*Ibid.*). Capovilla was sometimes accused of acting as Pope John's 'public relations officer' and of 'inventing' his 'image'. This incident shows that it was *against* the advice of Capovilla that he chose to make the Council the main plank of his pontificate. Capovilla's alternative suggestion about 'the charism of paternity' smacked too much of the 'personality cult'.

Once Pope John had fixed his sights on the project, he moved swiftly towards the fateful decision. In early November he spoke about the Council to Giovanni Urbani, his successor as patriarch of Venice, and Girolamo Bortignon, bishop of Padua, Capuchin and secretary of the Triveneto bishops. (It was on Bortignon's recommendation that Albino Luciani, the future John Paul I, became Bishop of Vittorio Veneto.) On November 21 he went to Castelgandolfo accompanied only by his secretary and confessor for a week's rest and retreat. The subject of the Council was discussed again in the car. By November 28, John's mind was almost made up, and he had counted the cost. The conversation reported above (p. 302) can now be referred to the Council: 'I'm not afraid of opposition and do not refuse suffering. I think of myself as the last of all, but I have in mind a programme of work and I'm not fussing about it any more. In fact, I am pretty well decided' (*Letture*, p. 252).

But still the project remained top secret. It was restricted to a few trusted friends. Most significant and surprising of all, Pope John did not confide in Tardini, his Secretary of State. This was not merely because he knew that Tardini would be able to provide, with consummate ease, a dozen reasons why a Council was ill-advised and would not work. Tardini was a brilliant organisation man, and would have a role in the project – later. But at this stage the problem was a spiritual one. What Pope John most wanted to know was whether the idea was 'not some wild fantasy or spectacular improvisation, but an inspiration (*ispirazione*) that bound him, as ever, to submit to the Lord's will' (*Letture*, p. 266). He feared in other words that it might be no more than a temptation, a deceiving will o' the wisp or an indulgent ego-trip. He wanted to know whether it was 'of God', a grace, an inspiration. But how could one tell?

Pope John habitually used the word 'inspiration' to explain how the idea of the council came to him. This led to confusion and misunderstanding. He did not mean that he had a 'private revelation'. He was not claiming to have had some special vision or to have been touched on the shoulder by God ordering him to 'Call a Council'. The school of the *Spiritual Exercises* had taught him to test rigorously the ideas that came to him in prayer, and to be vigilant against the ever-present threat of self-deception. Ideas had to be winnowed and evaluated according to their persistence and the 'consolation' or 'desolation' they brought. St Ignatius called this process 'the discernment of spirits'. The idea of the Council passed this strictest of tests. So John was able to speak of it as 'the second grace' of his pontificate (the 'first' being that he had accepted the office without having sought it):

> To have been able to accept as simple and capable of being put immediately into effect certain ideas which were not in the least complex in themselves, but yet were far-reaching in their effects and full of consequences for the future. I was immediately successful in this, which goes to show one must accept the good inspirations that come from the Lord, simply and confidently (*Journal*, p. 349).

To say 'Let there be an ecumenical council' was indeed very simple; the complexities would come in due time. But the initial decision to set this vast process in motion was an insight tested in prayer and an act of 'trust in the Lord'. The maxim quoted by his confessor, Mgr Cavagna, in the pre-conclave period, 'those who are guided by the Spirit are the sons of God', applied very directly to him now. As pope, his only 'superior' was the Lord. That was awesome, but it was also consoling.

Alongside this activity of spiritual discernment, there was another, humbler form of verification: could the Council be made to work? How would it be organised? Vatican I had been interrupted by war in 1870. But now there were three times as many bishops, and that would create logistical problems. Pope John alaready had a good knowledge of conciliar history, but further studies were done in December, 1958 and January, 1959 to see what could be learned from 'the last time'. He soon became convinced of one thing: six years had elapsed between the announcement of Vatican I and its actual celebration. At seventy-seven, he was too old to contemplate such a leisurely time-scale, and, anyway, modern methods of communication and travel made it unnecessary. A way would have to be found of speeding up the process of consultation and drafting.

The reference to Vatican I also raised the question of the subject-matter of the proposed Council. Vatican I was a truncated Council. It had dealt with the relation of faith and reason and defined the primacy and infallibility of Peter and his successors (whom it nowhere calls 'popes'). It had not had time to consider the role of bishops and how they related to the primacy. This resulted in a lop-sided view of the Church. The balance would have to be adjusted. However, while this was the starting-point, the Church and the world had changed so much in the intervening period that Vatican II would also be a council in its own right, and not simply an appendix to the unfinished Vatican I.

Further research among the archives brought to light two facts that had been unknown outside a small circle of adepts: the idea of calling a Council had already been considered twice in the twentieth century. In 1923 Pius XI asked to see the files on Vatican I – like Roncalli, he was an archivist. But to everyone's embarrassment they could not be found. They were eventually discovered stuffed in an old cupboard under a disused staircase (Negro, Silvio, *Corriere della Sera*, January 26, 1959). Pius XI's notion was that after the holocaust of the Great War, in which Catholics found themselves on opposite sides, a Council would powerfully display and reinforce Catholic unity. But he dropped the idea pending the resolution of 'the Roman Question' (*Letture*, p. 262). Pius XI's 'council' was little more than a fleeting gleam in his eye before he moved on to more interesting matters.

Pius XII's project was much more developed. It began at the initiative of Ruffini, since 1945 archbishop of Palermo, Sicily, and Ottaviani, now assessor at the Holy Office. In February, 1948 they wrote a memo setting out the reasons for calling a council:

> 1) To clarify and define a number of doctrinal points, since a mass of errors are abroad on philosophy, theology and moral and social questions.
> 2) Then there are the great problems posed by Communism and caused by the recent war, not to mention questions that could be raised about the methods and means that could be morally used in any future war.
> 3) The Code of Canon Law needs *aggiornamento* [*sic*] and reform.
> 4) Directives are needed in other areas of ecclesiastical discipline such as culture and Catholic Action etc. . . .
> 5) The Assumption could be defined (Caprile, I, 1, pp. 15–16. Numbering added).

Pius XII was interested. He wanted to define the Assumption anyhow. And in 1948 as in 1923 there were the same reasons for displaying the unity of Catholics after a murderous war had driven them apart. But he hesitated because of the difficulty of lodging so many bishops and the harmful effects of their absence from their dioceses. However, he was sufficiently committed to instruct the Holy Office to set up five secret commissions to make preparatory studies.

Pope John brooded over this material, treasure trove for the archivist. But now it had far more than a mere historical interest for him. It threw light on how his own plan was likely to be received. For Ruffini, the instigator, and Ottaviani, the organiser of the 1948 project, were still very much alive and influential in 1959. Their views carried weight in the Curia. But as he read on, Pope John became despondent as he realised that their idea of a Council was not at all what he had in mind. This can be seen simply by looking at what the two most important commissions wanted to put on the agenda.

The 'Speculative Theology' commission offered to examine:

> False philosophies (idealism, existentialism, new gnosticisms). Relationship of *magisterium* and tradition. Methods of theological research, especially in connection with the dissidents (dogmatic minimalism; convergence of doctrines; treating Catholic and heterodox doctrines as equal). Origins of episcopal jurisdiction. Original sin and polygenism. Errors on the Mystical Body. Inerrancy of Scripture. The literary *genres* of ancient Oriental historiographers. 'Co-redemption' does not seem ready for definition. Mary's Assumption.

The 'Practical theology' commission proposed to study:

> Co-operation with dissidents in religious or mixed social and political affairs. Dignity of virginity and the religious state. Various questions concerning marriage. Onanism, periodic continence, artificial fecundation, sterilisation, psychoanalysis. Validity of baptism administered by a non-Catholic minister who is in error on the nature of the sacrament. The Church and politics. Need for individual states to sacrifice part of their autonomy to constitute a true society of nations. Totalitarianism. Rights of minorities. Organisations of workers and other groups. The just wage. The right of defence against unjust aggression. Wars of aggression. Total war (Caprile, I, 1, p. 17).

In autumn 1948 Pius XII, after consulting Ottaviani, appointed Mgr Francesco Borgongini Duca overall president of the work of preparing the Council. He was an old Roman seminary friend of Roncalli, who regularly visited him at the Nunciature to Italy where he had become a permanent fixture since his nomination in 1929. It is likely that Borgongini Duca kept Roncalli informed at least in general terms of what was happening in the commissions. What was happening was disagreement.

One group argued that a very short Council, say three to four weeks, would be enough to demonstrate Catholic unity and cohesion, and that its main business would be to condemn contemporary errors and define, by acclamation, the Assumption. They believed, probably correctly, that they had Pius XII on their side. Such a Council would not need much preparation and would not leave dioceses orphaned for too long. Their opponents replied that a Council organised in this fashion would be 'untraditional' and could hardly be taken seriously. Meanwhile the sixty-five selected bishops who had already been consulted responded with some enthusiasm and proposed all manner of confusing new topics for inclusion on the agenda. Pius XII began to weary of the whole affair.

He decided that a Council was unnecessary. Anything a Council could do he could do better – and more economically. So in 1950 he defined the Assumption and condemned contemporary errors in his encyclical *Humani Generis*. The work done in the 'Speculative Theology' commission had not been entirely wasted: the errors they had gathered found their way into *Humani Generis*.

This Council-that-never-was contained important lessons for Pope John as he thought about his own project. He did not pay much attention to the horrendous agenda proposed by Ottaviani and his commissioners. It reflected, accurately enough, the defensive-minded and anti-ecumenical attitudes that dominated Roman theology in 1948 and still largely prevailed in 1959. The hints about atomic weapons and the need for a more effective United Nations looked more promising. But the whole approach was wrong. It betrayed an obsession with continuing the battle against 'Modernism'. From the start John determined that his council would be open to wider aspirations and would not just be negative. He expressed this by saying that its purpose was 'pastoral'. This meant it would not be primarily concerned with doctrinal questions but with the new needs of the Church and the world. One feature of this documentation convinced him that he was right: the replies of the sixty-five bishops showed that there was in the Church a genuine hunger for a Council. If a handful of bishops felt that way in 1949, then it was likely that a consultation with all the world's bishops a decade later would evoke an even more enthusiastic response. Thus what led Pius to reject the idea of a Council confirmed John's judgement that it was more than ever necessary.

Pope John's decision to hold a Council crystallised in December 1958 as he discerned the spirits and browsed among the archives. By January he had made up his mind. The actual date of the decision could well have been the night of January 8, 1959. In any event, next morning he met Don Giovanni Rossi who had been secretary to his hero, Cardinal Ferrari, forty years before. John said: 'I want to tell you something marvellous, but you must promise to keep it secret. Last night I had the great idea of holding a council'. Rossi murmured his approval. What can one say in such circumstances? But John's next remark took him by surprise: 'You know, it's not true to say that the Spirit assists the Pope'. Rossi thought he had misheard, but John put his mind at rest when he went on: 'The Holy Spirit doesn't help the Pope. I'm simply his helper. He did everything. The council is his idea' (Rossi, in *Utopia*, Italian, p. 315).

Don Rossi went back to Assisi and recounted this interview, though in vague terms, in an article for his magazine, *La Rocca*. Subscribers to the January 15 issue read this cryptic message:

> The Pope apologised for not having been able to receive me earlier and told me many wonderful things. But most important of all, he confided in me,

as a great secret, an idea of his own. May the Lord give him the joy of carrying it through; it will be in our time one of the most glorious celebrations of the Church and the most memorable event of his pontificate (*Letture*, p. 266).

That almost let the cat out of the bag, ten days before the official announcement. The fact that no one noticed is a measure of how unexpected a Council was. Since the definitions of Vatican I, theologians had come to believe that Councils were redundant.

Pope John had decided to challenge this conventional wisdom. The next step, which was far from easy, was to inform Tardini, his Secretary of State. But before he could do so there was one other matter to be dealt with. On January 25, 1959, John announced not only the convening of the Council but also a synod for the diocese of Rome and the *aggiornamento* of canon law. Many commentators thought it was incongruous to yoke the three items together; they were so clearly disproportionate in importance. Where did the other two ideas come from? Pericle Felici reported:

> As far as the Council is concerned, [Pope John] told me that the idea of summoning it was his. The other two undertakings were suggested to him by others after he had begun talking about the Council. 'They told me', he said, 'that a Synod for the diocese of Rome would be a good preparation for the Council. Fine, I replied, let's hold a Synod. Someone else said to me that it would be a good time to think about revising the Code of Canon Law because it is rather out of date. I said, that's good, let's think about the Code. But in any case, let's make the Council our main concern' (*l'Osservatore Romano*, June 3, 1973, *'Il Primo Incontro con Papa Giovanni'*: the conversation took place on February 10, 1960).

From this we may conclude that the two other projects, though far from trivial, were strictly subordinated in Pope John's mind to the council.

But none of this was clear at the time. At this crucial point – mid-January, 1959 – John did something that was odd but shrewd. He sent his secretary, Mgr Loris Capovilla, to give a lecture at the Giorgio Cini Foundation in Venice. It was odd because no previous papal secretary had lectured on the Pope he was serving; but it was shrewd because it prepared the conservative Venetians – and anyone else who cared to listen – for the shock of the Council. John advised Capovilla to keep his tone simple and conversational, and to tell them that he 'carried Venice and the Venetians in his heart' (*Letture*, p. 18). Capovilla drew a portrait of the 'new Pope' (popes remain 'new' for about a year) that stressed his *sapientia cordis* (wisdom of the heart), his sheer goodness, his peasant origins, and his determination to seek and do the Lord's will in all things. But Capovilla was not telling the Venetians anything they did not already know. In a section alarmingly headed, 'Pius X is back', he congratulated the Venetians on providing the Church with two popes in this century. He reminded them that 'it was well-known in Venice that the patriarch did not like to pose as a reformer, nor did he lash out against the right-wing to teach them a lesson' (*Ibid.*, p. 15). Why was Capovilla propounding such riddles? He was trying to forestall two criticisms that would inevitably be made once the Council was announced – only a week later. He wanted to reassure them that the Pope was still the loveable and rather conservative person they had known and had not gone off his head. And he was explaining in advance why this humble peasant pope was calling a Council when the most learned pope of the century, Pius XII, had not needed to. This message was addressed not merely to Venice; it was also relevant in the Roman Curia.

Capovilla gave his lecture on January 17, 1959, and then hastened back to Rome to be on hand for the decisive meeting with Cardinal Domenico Tardini, fixed for January 20. Tardini's office memo, written that same evening, is couched in his customary laconic style. It does not betray any great emotion or sense of 'history in the making':

> Audience with the Holy Father who told me that yesterday afternoon had been for him a period of meditation and recollection. As the programme of his pontificate, he has thought of three things:
> Roman Synod,
> Ecumenical Council,
> *Aggiornamento* of the Code of Canon Law.
> He will announce these three things to the cardinals after the ceremony at St Paul's next Sunday. I said:
> 1. that these were three splendid initiatives
> 2. that the idea of making the first announcement to the cardinals was very opportune because
>   it is new
>   but it links up with ancient papal traditions
>   and will no doubt be most pleasing to the Sacred College (Nicolini, p. 187).

Though this gives away very little, it is the best starting-point for unravelling the many problems connected with this January 20, 1959, meeting.

Pope John's diary, likewise written that same evening, substantially confirms the Tardini memo:

> In conversation with Tardini, Secretary of State, I wanted to test his reaction to my idea of proposing the project of an Ecumenical Council to the members of the Sacred College when they met at St Paul's on the 25th of

this month for the conclusion to the week of prayer [for Christian Unity]. The Council would meet in due time when everything had been thought through [*omnibus perpensis*]. It would involve all Catholic Bishops of every rite and from every part of the world. I was rather hesitant and uncertain. His immediate response was the most gratifying surprise that I could have expected: 'Oh, that really is an idea, an enlightening and holy idea. It comes straight from heaven, Holy Father. You will have to work on it, develop it and publicise it. It will be a great blessing for the whole world'.

I didn't need anything more. I was happy. I thanked the Lord for my idea which now received its first seal of approval here below – a pledge of that divine blessing which I was humbly confident would not be lacking (*Utopia*, Italian, p. 316).

These two accounts by the participants provide a reasonably clear idea of what happened at their famous meeting. John, unlike Tardini, makes no mention of the Roman Synod or the reform of Canon Law, which confirms that he thought they were secondary compared with the Council. Tardini, for his part, seems to imply – though he is not so naïve as to believe – that the idea had come to the Pope during his 'period of meditation and recollection' the previous afternoon. That may have been what John wanted him to think. But they were both professional enough to know that it could not be true. It was evident to Tardini that Pope John had gone into this meeting with his decision already taken. 'Proposing the project of an Ecumenical Council to the members of the Sacred College' was a euphemism for announcing it. He was not going to ask the cardinals what they thought, any more than he was consulting Tardini in the sense of asking his opinion. Tardini recognises this in confining his comments to the manner of making the announcement rather than to its content (apart from general approval). Nevertheless, John was genuinely 'hesitant and uncertain' because Tardini's response mattered enormously to him: it was the first official reaction by the leading member of the Roman Curia. If Tardini led, others would perforce follow. It was the final stage in determining whether the idea was 'of God'. The test was successfully passed.

To say that Tardini had no real choice in the matter is to underestimate him. He was perfectly capable of telling Pope John that he had taken leave of his senses, as indeed the Roman right-wing magazine, *Lo Svizzero*, later reported (Hales, p. 100). However, his account suggests that he knew he was faced with a *fait accompli*, a decision already taken. He also knew his man, and he may have felt that in the circumstances he might as well endorse what he was unable to prevent. The meeting took place on a Tuesday. The announcement was to be made the following Sunday. The only thing to do was to submit and accept that Pope John, whom he had once regarded as naïve, had the cunning of an old fox. What

Tardini privately thought, we do not yet know. His biographer drops a tantalising hint that there is more to be said about the January 20 meeting than has been recorded. He quotes Tardini's diary account, given above, and then mysteriously goes on: 'This does not mean that his pen stopped here. There is reason to believe that he filled several more pages which await their moment to emerge from the silence of the archives' (Nicolini, p. 188, fn.3). The Vatican Archives have a seventy-five year rule. All will be revealed in the year 2034.

In the meantime, the basic outline of what happened on January 20, 1959, seems beyond dispute. The trouble is that it is flatly contradicted by what Pope John said in 1962. And since these 1962 accounts were the first to be publicly known – the same-day extract from Pope John's diary was not published until 1973 – they have become the authorised version. Yet they are thoroughly misleading. The easy way out is to say simply that Pope John was more likely to have got it right on the day itself than three years later. He was an old man, and his memory sometimes failed him. He was notoriously bad, for example, at getting foreign names right. But that is not an adequate explanation. John misremembered, certainly, but his wholly unconscious editing of his memories throws more light on what he wanted to believe about the Council than on what exactly happened on January 20, 1959.

The first text to pose a problem is an address to Venetian pilgrims on May 8, 1962. Those who had worked with him in Venice were present, and it was delivered in his usual familiar style. To illustrate the maxim that 'a simple and humble disposition enables us to hear the inspirations God always provides', he told them how the Council came about:

> Where did the idea of the Ecumenical Council come from? How did it develop? The truth is that the idea and even more its realisation were so unforeseen as to seem unlikely.
>
> A question was raised in a meeting I had with the Secretary of State, Cardinal Tardini, which led on to a discussion about the way the world was plunged into so many grave anxieties and troubles. One thing we noted was that though everyone said they wanted peace and harmony, unfortunately conflicts grew more acute and threats multiplied. What should the Church do? Should Christ's mystical barque simply drift along, tossed this way and that by the ebb and flow of the tides? Instead of issuing new warnings, shouldn't she stand out as a beacon of light? What could that exemplary light be?
>
> My interlocutor listened with reverence and attention. Suddenly [*a un tratto*] my soul was illumined by a great idea which came precisely at that moment and which I welcomed with ineffable confidence in the divine Teacher. And there sprang to my lips a word that was solemn and

committing. My voice uttered it for the first time: a Council (DMC, IV, p. 258 and *Letture,* pp. 264–5).

Obviously, Pope John cannot really mean that he had never pronounced the word 'Council' until that January 20, 1959, for that would be simply false. He meant that this was an irrevocable statement, self-committing language from which there was no retreat. In that sense his discussion with Tardini acted as a watershed. It was the decisive moment when what had hitherto been discussed only among friends was submitted to the verdict of the Curia through its representative, Tardini.

But there is a trick of memory here. John first telescopes the memory of earlier discussions with Tardini and others about the state of the world and the Church – which gives a fair picture of what impelled him to the idea of a Council. But he gives the impression that it was *there and then* that the 'inspiration' came to him. The memories of the first three months of his pontificate have by May 1962 so fused in his mind that the *most decisive moment* is transformed into the *moment of decision*.

As January 20, 1959, receded even further into the past and as the 'great event' of the Council was almost upon him, Pope John settled even more firmly on the meeting with Tardini as the moment of inspiration. On September 15, 1962, just three weeks before the Council was due to start, he wrote:

> Without having thought of it before, I put forward, in one of my first talks with my Secretary of State, on January 20, 1959, the idea of an ecumenical council, a diocesan synod and the revision of the code of canon law, all this being quite contrary to any previous supposition or idea of my own on this subject. I was the first to be surprised by my proposal, which was entirely my own idea (*Journal,* p. 349).

But by this date, on the eve of the Council, Pope John's mind was concentrated on the future rather than the past. 'After three years of preparation', he added, 'certainly laborious but also joyful and serene, we are now on the slopes of the sacred mountain' (*Ibid.*). Straining at the foot of the mountain, his memory of the past was reduced to its schematic essentials. Typically, he remembers this as 'one of my first talks with my Secretary of State', when in fact he had been seeing Tardini almost daily for the previous three months.

This passage from the *Journal* has embarrassed commentators. 'John's 1962 descriptions', says Bonnot tartly, 'are ingenuous but seem incompatible with the facts' (Bonnot, p. 59). Capovilla resorts to casuistry and explains that in the phrase, 'without having thought of it before', the 'before' (*prima*) refers to the time before he became Pope (*Letture,* p. 266). This is ingenious but misplaced. The January 20, 1959, meeting cannot have happened exactly as he later described it because he himself had already admitted to Felici (see p. 313 above) that the proposals for a Roman Synod and the revision of canon law came to him from others. It would be asking too much to expect that they too suddenly occurred to him during his meeting with Tardini. One can only conclude that John's memory faltered and that his unconscious editing of his reminiscences is designed to emphasise, yet again, that the idea of the Council was an 'inspiration' in the sense defined above. That much was certainly true.

But there remains a problem about his 'surprise' ('I was the first to be surprised by my proposal'). In John's usage, 'surprise' is simply a mark of the presence of grace. 'One must always be ready for the Lord's surprise moves', he noted in December, 1959 (*Journal*, p. 321). After meditating on the Precious Blood in August, 1961 he wrote: 'This inspiration, which has lately taken me by surprise, is like a new impulse, a new spirit in my heart, a voice that imparts great courage and fervour' (*Journal*, p. 329). Here lay the secret of the perpetually renewed youthfulness of this very old man. As bodily infirmities pressed in upon him, his heart and his spirit were fresh, because he was always prepared to be surprised by grace. The idea of the Council was one of God's surprises.

John had told Tardini on Tuesday of the Octave of Prayer for Christian Unity. He still had to tell the world. But he was now bubbling over with enthusiasm and could no longer contain his secret. On Thursday, January 22, 1959, he gave an audience to Giulio Andreotti. In a vain attempt to avoid political interpretations being placed upon the visit, the whole Andreotti family was invited. The two younger children, aged five and seven, bounced about on the gold and damask chairs, while the thirteen- and nine-year-olds looked on with mature scorn. John asked, 'Have you noticed any changes?' Andreotti confessed that he had not. John pointed out that he had had all the doors of the cupboards around the walls removed; whenever he had been in this room as nuncio or patriarch it reminded him of a hat-shop. But this light-hearted opening was only the prelude to more serious matters (Andreotti pp. 77–8). While the younger children were still cavorting about, Pope John revealed his plan: a Council of the universal Church. He said that he thought two years should be enough to prepare it, but Tardini disagreed, quoting the example of Vatican I that needed six years' preparation. At his age, he could not accept such a long time. The Andreotti family – those who had been listening – were sworn to secrecy for another three days. John's familiarity with the archives, the arguments and counter-arguments, confirm that he cannot have thought of the idea just two days before. He had done his homework and could meet objections. Moreover, his remarks suggested that Tardini's alleged enthusiasm had not been unqualified.

Meanwhile the Mass at St Paul's-without-the-walls had already been announced without the slightest hint that anything of significance would take place. Readers of the Saturday, January 24 edition of *l'Osservatore Romano* learned that the Pope would proceed to the Basilica of St Paul's and there recite a prayer he had specially composed for 'the Church of Silence'. In the code-language of the period, to be concerned about 'the Church of Silence' was an expression of the anti-Communism that still prevailed in the Vatican.

The phrase referred to the persecuted Churches of Eastern Europe and China. Other commentators set the scene for the visit to St Paul's in slightly different terms. It would harmoniously complete the round of visits to the four major Roman Basilicas. Pope John had been crowned in St Peter's on November 4, had 'taken possession' of St John Lateran on November 23, and was at St Mary Major on December 8, feast of the Immaculate Conception. So it was 'only natural' that he would go to St Paul's-without-the-walls to complete the circuit of the Roman Basilicas. This accomplished, and his role as bishop of Rome duly brought out, his pontificate would be on its way.

The fact that Sunday, January 25, was the conclusion to the Octave of Prayer for Christian Unity was barely noticed. Roncalli had celebrated it annually since his time in Istanbul. But in Rome it was left to a few specialists and enthusiasts. Nor did anyone intuit that the Basilica dedicated to St Paul, the missionary adventurer, was just the place from which to look outwards towards the 'world'. On the eve of the announcement, John said to Capovilla:

> The world is starving for peace. If the Church responds to its Founder and rediscovers its authentic identity, the world will gain. I have never had any doubts against faith. But one thing causes me consternation. Christ has been there on the cross with his arms out-stretched for two thousand years. Where have we got to in proclaiming the Good News? How can we present his authentic doctrine to our contemporaries? (*Utopia*, Italian, pp. 319–20).

With such questions in mind, he then checked over the draft for the most epoch-making speech of his life. It would 'block the way back'. From now on he could only go forwards.

The next morning John was up before dawn, as usual. He said Mass and attended Capovilla's Mass in his private chapel, remaining there in prayer until 9.30. During breakfast he cast an eye over the newspapers and the reports from the Secretariat of State but said nothing. At 10 o'clock he went down by lift. A car was waiting to take him to St Paul's. On the way he was uncharacteristically silent. Although one eye-witness said he was 'very calm and concentrating intensely' (*Utopia*, Italian, p. 320), the photographs of his arrival at St Paul's show him anxious and tense. He was genuinely apprehensive about how the cardinals would react. Some of them already knew – Tardini had been authorised to inform them – but others would have to wait until after the ceremony in the Basilica. It took longer than anticipated and was not over till 1 o'clock.

Then the seventeen cardinals made their way to the chapter-room of the abbey on the first floor. Since this was technically an 'extraordinary consistory', outsiders – not that there were any – were formally banished by the master of ceremonies, Mgr Enrico Dante. *'Extra omnes'* ('Everybody out') he cried to the empty corridors. Pope John's address began at 1.10 and lasted half an hour. On the somewhat specious grounds of 'respect for cardinals unable to be present', the text of the speech was not made public until the following Easter Sunday; and even then the official version departs notably from John's actual words.

Pope John tried hard to speak in his usual intimate tone. He wanted to open his heart, trusting in their goodness and understanding. He would confine himself to a few points 'suggested by our first three months of contact with the Roman ecclesiastical world'. It was a tactful way of admitting that he was still a newcomer without first-hand experience of the Roman Curia. He went on and on about how the city of Rome had changed since their student days. All this was listened to with impassivity.

But he was universal pastor as well as bishop of Rome. So he moved on logically from the city to the world, from the *urbs* to the *orbs*. But he painted an uncharacteristically gloomy picture of the 'world' using lurid and dualistic colours. He rejoiced that the grace of Christ was still at work, bearing its fruits of 'spiritual elevation, salvation and holiness'. But he was saddened by those who

> abuse and endanger human freedom, reject faith in Christ the Son of God, redeemer of the world and founder of the Church, devoting themselves entirely to so-called terrestrial goods under the inspiration of the one whom the Gospels call the prince of darkness, the prince of this world – as Jesus himself calls him in his Last Supper discourse – who organises the confrontation and struggle against truth and goodness and hardens divisions between what St Augustine called the two cities, ever pursuing his attempts to sow confusion so as to deceive, if that were possible, even the elect, and to encompass their ruin (Alberigo, p. 276).

He was laying it on with a vengeance. No great insight was needed to guess that he was here faithfully echoing the Manichaean interpretation of Communism that was routine under Pius XII. He could have lifted this passage bodily from the speeches of Pizzardo or Ottaviani, to name only two of his hearers. On John's lips it was incongruous. He still seemed to be using borrowed language when he went on to deplore 'the lack of discipline and the loss of the old moral order' which had, he claimed, reduced the Church's capacity to deal with error. In the course of Christian history, he said, these errors – they remained astonishingly vague – had led to 'fatal and unhappy divisions, to spiritual and moral decadence, and to the ruin of nations' (*Ibid.*, pp. 276–7).

This pessimism about the present state of the world – sunk in error and in the grip of Satan – so contradicts Pope John's usual attitudes that some explanation is called for. The simplest explanation is that this address had one precise goal: to win over the cardinals to his project of a Council. To assist this process he reflected the views he knew they held. The borrowed ideas were not, after all, utterly nonsensical. So he was simply following the adage of St Ignatius: going in by their door in order to come out by his own. He was certainly not making a declaration about what kind of Council he had in mind. He never felt obliged to reveal all his intentions at one go. In his *Journal* he sketches a portrait of the prudent man who 'knows how to keep silent about that part of the truth it would be inopportune to declare' and 'knows how to achieve his own good purpose' (*Journal*, p. 332). So his little ruse was not a matter of duplicity but of psychology. It was on a par with the despatch of Capovilla to Venice. It was intended to prepare the cardinals for the shock of his announcement. Not that it worked. There was no visible reaction. The cardinals maintained their *figura di bronzo*, Italian equivalent of the poker-face. Those in the know must have wondered whenever he was going to get to the point.

Pope John maintained the suspense – or drew out the agony – almost until the end of his address. He told them he had reached a decision. It was based on tradition. There were periods of renewal (*rinnovamento*) when the Church sought 'greater clarity in its thinking' (he did not say 'doctrine'), 'a strengthening of the bond of unity, and greater spiritual fervour' (Alberigo, p. 277). Having defined the three aims of the Council, the moment had at last come to use the word: 'Venerable brothers and our beloved sons! Trembling with emotion, and yet with humble resolution, we put before you the proposal of a double celebration: a diocesan synod for Rome and an ecumenical council for the universal Church' (*Ibid.*). That was it. The natural consequence of these two decisions would be the revision of the Code of Canon Law, although that would take time. He was right about that: the New Code of Canon Law was promulgated on January 25, 1983, twenty-four years later to the day.

Pope John added just one thing more. He asked everyone to pray for

> a good start, a successful implementation and a happy outcome for those
> projects that will involve hard work for the enlightenment, the edification
> and the joy of the Christian people, and *a friendly and renewed invitation to our*
> *brothers of the separated Christian Churches to share with us in this banquet of grace*
> *and brotherhood,* to which so many souls in every corner of the world aspire
> (*Utopia*, Italian, p. 322, italics added).

That was what the Cardinals heard Pope John say. But that is not what appeared in the authorised version of the speech. The clause italicised above became 'a renewed invitation to the faithful of separated communities likewise to follow Us, in good will, in this search for unity and grace' (see Hales, p. 98). There are several nuances here. The separated Christians are no longer *brothers*. They are allowed to belong to communities (which is undeniable) but not to *Churches* (which carries a theological load). And instead of 'sharing in the banquet of grace and brotherhood' they are exhorted to *search for* unity and grace as though they had no inkling of them. Though the overall meaning was just about maintained, the edited version was much less friendly in tone and left other Christians perplexed about whether they were being taken seriously and to what they were being invited. The edge of Pope John's ecumenical commitment was blunted by timorous censors. Not for the last time.

The subsequent treatment meted out to Pope John's address helps to explain why it was so badly received. The seventeen cardinals were unresponsive to his dramatic announcement. For all they appeared to care, he might have been reading out his laundry list. He was bitterly disappointed. He said so plainly: 'Humanly speaking, we would have expected that the cardinals, after listening to our address, might have crowded round to express their approval and good wishes' (Caprile, I, 1, p. 51). But they did nothing of the kind. What they felt, if indeed they felt anything, remained locked up inside them. John was puzzled. A spontaneous person himself, he found taciturnity hard to comprehend. He later charitably tried to explain that they had been stunned into silence and needed time to gather their wits. Later still, he contrived to rewrite the whole scene. By the time he addressed the opening session of the Council on October 11, 1962, he believed that the simple words, 'an ecumenical council', had worked a kind of miracle: 'It (the announcement) was completely unexpected and like a flash of heavenly light, shedding sweetness in eyes and hearts. At the same time it gave rise to great fervour throughout the world in the expectation of holding the Council' (Abbott, pp. 711–12). That may have been true of the world-wide response to the Council. But among the cardinals who were actually present on January 25, 1959, no 'flash of heavenly light' was discernible. Instead, as John noted at the time, 'there was a devout and impressive silence' (Rynne, p. 2).

In this impressive and yet disappointing silence Pope John gave his blessing, left the chapter house, descended the staircase, got into his car, registration number VAT 1, and was greeted with applause all the way back to the Vatican. But that happened every time he went out. It said nothing about the Ecumenical Council. Capovilla asked him how he felt. He replied: 'It's not a matter of my personal feelings. We are embarked on the will of the Lord . . . Now I need silence and recollection. I feel tired of everyone, of everything'. '*Nous sommes embarqués*' was an echo of Blaise Pascal's wager: he was now fully committed and there was no going back. He consoled himself with Psalm 84.1, 'How lovely is thy dwelling-place, O Lord'. As the car left St Paul's a solitary voice cried. 'Long live the Ecumenical Council' (*Letture*, p. 268). Either this perceptive individual had been listening to Vatican Radio on his transistor or – much less likely because journalists do not usually participate in events they describe – he was a reporter with access to the wire services.

For despite Pope John's insistence that the cardinals should be the first to know, the news was already out. It had been flashed round the world even before he began to speak. At 10 o'clock that morning, just as John was getting into his lift, the Vatican Press Office received a statement from the Secretariat of State – in effect Tardini – which was to be released at 12.30. It was assumed that by this time the Pope would at least have started his address. But, as we have seen, he did not begin speaking until 1.10. So the regular crew of journalists who haunted the Vatican were the first to know. But they had to read the laconic communiqué very carefully to discover its significance. The key passage read:

> The Holy Father, inspired by the age-old traditions of the Church, announced three events of the greatest importance: a diocesan Synod for Rome, an ecumenical Council for the Universal Church, and the *aggiornamento* of the Code of Canon Law, to be preceded by the promulgation of the Oriental Code.
> As for the celebration of the ecumenical Council, in the mind of the Holy Father it is intended not only for the edification of the Christian people but as an invitation to separated communities to search for the unity to which so many souls in all parts of the world aspire (Caprile, I, 1, p. 51).

That the announcement of the Council should involve a mix-up with the Vatican Press Office was true to form.

The press hand-out was given in *l'Osservatore Romano* the next day. While the page one lead story was about Pope John's anti-Communist speech in the Basilica, the news about the Council was relegated to an inside page. Thus the process of cutting the Council down to size began on the very day it was announced. It was so successful that in New York Cardinal Francis J. Spellman was not even sure that his old buddy the Pope really wanted a Council. He said: 'I do not believe that the Pope wanted to convoke a Council, but he was pushed into it by people who misconstrued what he said' (Elliott, p. 290). It would be difficult to devise a more ludicrous interpretation of Pope John's words; but since no one had yet seen a text of the address, Spellman could perhaps be forgiven. He was firing from the hip. He was very far away.

No such excuses applied to Cardinal Giacomo Lercaro, archbishop of Bologna, usually regarded as the most 'progressive' of the Italian bishops. He was sceptical and withering:

> How dare he summon a council after one hundred years, and only three months after his election? Pope John has been rash and impulsive. His inexperience and lack of culture brought him to this pass, to this paradox.

An event like this will ruin his already shaky health, and make the whole edifice of his supposed moral and theological virtues come tumbling down (Gorresio, quoted by Dreyfus, p. 205).

It was just as well that these remarks were not made public until nine years later. By then Lercaro had made handsome amends. He became the architect of the Council's liturgical reforms and the principal target of right-wing attacks. ('After Martin Luther', wrote Tito Cassani in 1967, 'the most formidable menace to the Church's unity and integrity is Cardinal Lercaro'.) In 1959 Lercaro was not alone in thinking that Pope John was making a grievous mistake in calling a Council. It was the standard opinion in the Roman Curia. It was also the immediate judgement of Giovanni Battista Montini in Milan. On the evening of the day Pope John announced the Council, Montini called his old mentor, the Oratorian Fr Giulio Bevilacqua, and ᵅid: 'This holy old boy doesn't seem to realise what a hornet's nest he's stirring up'. 'Don't worry, Don Battista', replied Bevilacqua, '*lascia fare*, let it be, the Holy Spirit is still awake in the Church' (Fappani–Molinari, p. 171). At least someone had understood what Pope John was trying to do.

Chapter 15

The struggle for the Council

'Where shall I begin, please your majesty', he asked. 'Begin at the
beginning', the King said gravely, 'and go on till you come to the end: then
stop'

(Lewis Carroll, *Alice in Wonderland*).

Pope John's announcement of the Council came as a surprise. It aroused great and
extravagant hopes. The very vagueness of the project in its early stages made it all
things to all men. The far-sighted Cardinal Giovanni Battista Montini soon
overcame his hesitations about the hornet's nest that was being stirred up, and
became an enthusiastic and tireless defender of the Council. But he warned that it
could give rise to 'expectations, dreams, curiosity, utopias, velleities of every kind
and countless fantasies'. This comment seems cold-waterish. But in this same
pastoral letter to the diocese of Milan, Montini put his finger on the essential truth
about Pope John's initiative: 'It seems that he had divined a hidden expectation
not only on the part of the episcopal college but of the entire Catholic world as
well. A flame of enthusiasm swept over the whole Church. He understood
immediately, perhaps by inspiration, that by calling a Council he would release
unparalleled vital forces in the Church' (*Church*, p. 156).

But the enthusiasm and energies generated by the announcement of the Council
still had to be harnessed to the drudgery of preparing it. Yet very little seemed to
be happening between January 25, 1959, and Whitsunday of that year when John
announced that Domenico Tardini would be president of the Ante-preparatory
Commission. Behind the scenes, however, there was an epic struggle that concerned the very nature of the Council. Was it to be a Council of renewal and
reform, as Pope John wanted, or would it be a defensive Council concerned above
all to ward off contemporary errors, like the failed project of 1948–9? The Curia
was prepared to humour the old man's whim and accept a Council, provided it
could keep a firm grip on the preparations. Age-old curial wisdom declared: he
who controls the agenda controls the meeting.

It was difficult to escape the feeling that while Pope John was charming the
crowds with his droll audiences and keeping the press busy with his *bons mots*, the
Curia was getting on with the serious business of running the Church. Cardinals
Ottaviani and Pizzardo, for example, continued to behave as they had in the
previous pontificate, and even intensified their repressive activities. While Pope

John was opening some windows, they were firmly closing others. In December 1958 Pizzardo stopped the Catholic university of the Sacred Heart in Milan from awarding an honorary degree to Jacques Maritain. The distinguished neo-Thomist, who had also served as French ambassador to the Holy See, was deemed 'unsound'. Not to be outdone by the Prefect of the Congregation for Universities and Seminaries, Ottaviani at the Holy Office banned Don Lorenzo Milani's book, *Esperienze pastorali* (*Pastoral Experiments*), despite the fact that it bore an *imprimatur* from the venerated Cardinal Elia Dalla Costa. He censored a 'progressive' review, *Testimonianze*, and hounded its author, Don Ernesto Balducci, out of Florence. In July 1959 Pizzardo ordered the French bishops to put an end to the priest-workers once and for all (see Magister, p. 239 for these three examples). Though the papacy is a monarchy and even, in some sense, an absolute monarchy, these powerful cardinals had great autonomy and behaved like English barons before the signing of Magna Carta. They did not feel beholden to the Pope. After all, they had elected him. Yet John annoyed them. On February 25, 1959, he gave an audience to Don Primo Mazzolari, a remarkably prophetic priest, who had had troubles first with the Fascists and then with the Holy Office. John imprudently called him 'the trumpet of the Holy Spirit in the plain of the River Po' (see Giudici, Marco, '*Il Coraggio della Speranza*', in *Vita e Pensiero*, February, 1980). Ottaviani was very displeased. He reminded everyone that the Holy Office, over which he presided, was 'the *supreme* Congregation'. The quip went the rounds: 'Tardini reigns, Ottaviani governs, John blesses'.

Of course John did have some supporters, but they tended to be younger and members of the papal household rather than the Curia. On February 18, 1959, Mgr Igino Cardinale, chief of protocol, had a long conversation with Sir John Lawrence, an Anglican and editor of *Frontier*. Cardinale was half-American, forty-three, promising, and the nephew of Don Giuseppe De Luca, who was now busily publishing everything by Roncalli that he could lay his hands on. Cardinale's comments reveal what was being discussed by Pope John's closest associates less than a month after the announcement of the Council.

Cardinale thought the Council might begin within two years. This was over-optimistic, but it expressed John's desire to hustle along. Press reactions to the announcement were being studied, and would help in planning the Council. An important decision of principle had already been taken: this would not be a 'doctrinal' council concerned with defining dogmas; instead, it would be a 'disciplinary' Council, by which Cardinale meant that it would deal with practical matters that were not immutable. But what reformable practical matters would figure on the agenda? At this early stage, it was difficult to say. But Cardinale boldly volunteered three examples of possible topics:

1. *Clerical celibacy*. The link between priesthood and celibacy might not be

insisted upon in all situations. The example of the Uniate Churches in communion with Rome proved that celibacy was not absolutely essential to the priesthood. But it might be difficult to make this understood in 'Latin' countries.

2. *Liturgical reform*. Pius XII had already made changes in the Holy Week liturgy, had permitted 'evening' Masses and lightened the rigours of the eucharistic fast. There was much more to be done along these lines. The use of the vernacular and the place of the Bible in worship were bound to come up.

3. *Ecumenical concern*. 'The Holy Father has a great interest in reunion, and considers that some of the divisions of Christendom are based on trivial matters that became important only for historical reasons. In such cases, common sense could do much' (Lawrence, pp. 5–7).

This was the view from within the pontifical household in February 1959. As forecaster, Cardinale scored two out of three. Only clerical celibacy failed to get on the agenda of the Council for reasons we will discover in the next chapter.

One could reasonably conclude that this was going to be a different sort of Council. It was not summoned to deal with particular threats of heresy or schism. Nor was it imposed on the Pope by any outside pressures. As the Oratorian Fr Giulio Bevilacqua, Montini's mentor, put it:

This is something new in the history of the Church. The council that Rome feared for centuries because conciliarists had turned it into an anti-papal weapon, is suddenly convened by the Pope without any pressure from the emperor, the clergy or the nations. Just four centuries ago the Council met at the behest of a powerful emperor more than that of a weak pope. And today the Council comes about through the simple invitation of a meek pope, and is welcomed with joy and universal consent (in *Vita e Pensiero*, 1960, p. 513).

The 'Council that met just four centuries ago' was of course the Council of Trent. The third originality of Vatican II was that although it was not technically a 'council of reunion', in the sense that Florence was, it would have a strong ecumenical dimension.

Just how important the ecumenical dimension would be was a matter for debate. Fr Charles Boyer S.J., professor at the Gregorian University, might be expected to know. For over ten years he had been holding meetings with Anglicans, alternately in England and in Italy, always with permission and discretion. Lawrence described him as 'a little Frenchman with a clever, sensitive, spiritual face'. His fellow Jesuit, Fr Joseph Gill, says he was 'a very saintly man, who knew his way about Catholic Rome' (letter to the author, January 29,

1984). Boyer was rather perplexed. He stressed that the Council was an essentially Catholic event. The word 'ecumenical' used in its official title meant 'general' as contrasted with 'local'; of itself, it said nothing about inter-Church relations. Still, it might be possible, Boyer conceded, to invite 'schismatic' or even non-episcopal Churches to send 'observers'. Boyer thought that the doctrine of the Church would be high up on the agenda, but added: 'Until the Pope speaks, no one really knows what the Council will do' (Lawrence, p. 4). So the ball was thrown back into Pope John's court.

There was, however, another informal ecumenical group that felt its hour had come. Founded in Holland in 1952 by Fr (much later Cardinal) Jan Willebrands and Fr Frans Thyssen, the 'Catholic Conference on Ecumenical Questions', as it was vaguely called, sought to 'follow' the work of the World Council of Churches in Geneva. Willebrands met with many misunderstandings and obstacles. The conventional Catholic view was that the WCC was insufficiently 'theological' in its quest for unity. Willebrands was forbidden to attend the WCC meeting in Chicago in 1953 (Kaiser, p. 32) and rebuffed by Archbishop Cyril Cowderoy of Southwark, England. The participants in the Willebrands group fluctuated, but they included the Jesuit, Augustin Bea, rector of the Biblical Institute, the French Dominican Christophe Dumont and Pierre Dumont, monk of Chevetogne, Jean-François Arrighi, Cardinal Tisserant's secretary, and Mgr Josef Höfer of the diocese of Paderborn, theological advisor to the German ambassador to the Holy See. They were nearly all destined to play an important role later on.

Pope John had known Arrighi in Paris and thought highly of him. Legend has it that he gave Pope John lessons in Protestant theology. What is true is that they had many conversations on ecumenical matters in the run-up to the Council. Arrighi provided a link with French theologians such as Yves-Marie Congar who was still under a cloud. Congar thought the Catholic Church ought to have the decency to recognise that others had been ploughing the ecumenical field for some time. He wrote: 'At the moment when the Holy See emerged from semi-absenteeism, it found the ground tilled and sown and covered with thick-set and high-grown grain' (Congar, *Dialogue between Christians*, p. 41). Arrighi was already urging in February 1959 the setting up of 'a small, high-powered body to handle ecumenical matters' (Lawrence, p. 20). Ecumenism in Rome, he argued, was a spare-time activity for enthusiasts who already had their hands full with other work. Until there was a body set up to deal specifically with inter-Church relations, the case would go by default. A problem is not allowed to exist in Rome unless there is someone to deal with it. But this chrysalis of an idea had not yet developed into a definite proposal.

If Arrighi, although a Corsican, provided the link with French theologians, Höfer knew the German ecumenical scene and had come to Rome at the request of his bishop, Lorenz Jaeger, with the intention of making it better known (Nash, p. 10). Jaeger, archbishop of Paderborn, was the founder and president of the Adam Möhler Institute whose purpose was 'to form specialists in Lutheran and ecumenical questions and to take part in inter-denominational conversations' (*Ibid.*, p. 100). Höfer was familiar with the work of the thirty-year-old Swiss theologian, Hans Küng, who had written a thesis demonstrating that Luther's understanding of 'justification' was not incompatible with that of the Council of Trent (*Rechtfertigung*, 1957). Karl Barth wrote an admiring but somewhat baffled preface to Küng's book, admitting that if Küng were right, the Reformation reposed upon a mistake.

A key-word among all these Catholic ecumenists was 'collegiality'. It meant that the pope was not a solitary Atlas propping up the entire world – as some interpretations of Vatican I suggested. Rather, he was surrounded, sustained and assisted by the bishops of the whole world who shared with him in 'the solicitude of all the churches'. Pope John was known to be for collegiality. In Istanbul he had always tried to act collegially with the bishops of varied rites who shared his ministry.

The act of calling a Council was an extension of the same principle to the universal Church. On a humbler level, collegiality could be seen as an instance of what papal social teaching called 'subsidiarity': never put up to a higher level what can be dealt with on a lower level. John was already practising 'subsidiarity'. On February 23, 1959, Arrighi explained:

John XXIII really applies the collegial system of government, and works with his fellow bishops. Unlike Pius XII, he trusts his subordinates. For example, I have to advise on matrimonial cases which involve the Uniate Churches. I make my recommendations to Cardinal Tisserant, who then puts them before the Pope. He says: 'Have you looked into this? Is it all right?' If the Cardinal says yes, the Pope signs (Lawrence, p. 19).

Arrighi also had some perceptive comments on Pope John's approach to ecumenical matters:

He really cares about unity. His starting point is the Orthodox Church, but 'when you become ecumenical, you have to take in everybody'. He has some experience of Protestantism in France. The Pope has used the phrase *la ricerca della unità* [the search for unity] at a private meeting. This expression was significant, and it seems that he meant it to apply to the Roman Catholic Church too. Recently he called the Congregation for the Oriental Churches together and said: 'I know that humanly speaking my plan is impossible, but God demands unity and we must do something about it' (Lawrence, p. 19).

These comments came from someone who was already enthusiastic about Pope John and did not need to be persuaded of the importance of ecumenism. It was a novel experience for the much-battered breed of Catholic ecumenists, more used to kicks than ha'pence, to have a pope on their side. So they made the most of it. However, nearly all Rome's ecumenists, and all those so far named, were non-Italian. This widened the gap with the watchdogs of orthodoxy in the Roman Curia, and introduced an ugly element of xenophobia into the clash of theological opinions. The foreigners, *questa gente da fuori* (the people from outside), were at it again and would have to be stopped.

Pope John made no immediate moves to reassure his supporters or clarify his intentions. Having announced his Council, he was surprisingly reticent about it. He seemed to lean back and watch things happen. He was discovering, the hard way, the limits of papal authority. 'I'm only the Pope around here' was partly a joke, partly a genuine lament at his impotence. The barons still ruled. On January 31, 1959, he wrote to Don Angelo Pedrinelli, a contemporary at the Bergamo seminary who was now gravely ill. Banned from teaching during the 'Modernist' crisis, he became parish priest at Carvico, the next parish to Sotto il Monte, in 1911. He remained there till his death forty-nine years later. He must have been surprised to get a letter embossed with the Vatican seals, and delighted to discover that the Angelo he used to know had not changed one bit: 'I'm astonished to find myself still the same as ever, that is simple and sincere, above all calm and serene, without illusions, and most humbly ready *ad omnia ut vinctus Christi* ['a prisoner for Christ on behalf of you all': Ephesians 3.1] (*Lettere*, p. 94).

The great event of the Council, now that it was decided upon and announced, did not monopolise his attention or his time. This was partly because he had to wait for the response from the local Churches – that was another aspect of collegiality. But it was also because he had to remain alert on so many other fronts. In the first six months of 1959 he received in audience or state visits General Charles de Gaulle, Queen Elizabeth II, King Paul and Queen Frederika of the Hellenes, King Hussein I of Jordan and the presidents of Turkey, Indonesia and Tunisia, not to mention the Japanese prime minister and Prince Rainier of Monaco with his beautiful consort, Princess Grace (*Cronologia*, pp. 748–50). The whole world – with the exception of the Soviet bloc – appeared to be trooping to the Vatican. Cardinale kept the score. In seventeen years, Pius XII had ten visits from heads of state; John, who had the shortest pontificate of the century so far (apart from the 'flashing meteor' of John Paul I), had thirty-four (Cardinale, pp. 385–6). John was more inclined to talk with such personages about their children than about the Council. In any case, his more immediate concern on the Church front was with the Synod of the Rome diocese rather than the Council of the universal Church. On July 31, 1959, he wrote to Giuseppe Battaglia, bishop of Faenza, as usual about his restless priest-nephew, Don Battista Roncalli, who now wanted to change dioceses. In the final paragraph John casually remarks: 'Here the preparations for the Roman Synod are going so well that I hope it will be celebrated within the year' (*Lettere*, p. 151). Not a word about the Council.

But Pope John had already made a momentous decision. He made Domenico Tardini, Secretary of State, president of the Ante-preparatory Commission which would have the task of sounding out the bishops. Tardini's biographer claims that he was appointed on the advice of Cardinal Pietro Ciriaci who argued that Tardini's vast experience and ability to see the wood for the trees made him the ideal person to organise the work of preparing the Council (Nicolini, p. 191). This is touching but unlikely. John hesitated and canvassed other possibilities before settling on Tardini. In the end he may have felt that it was better to have Tardini involved in preparing the Council than epigrammatically sniping at it from the outside. John announced Tardini's appointment on Whitsunday, 1959. It was the day the serious preparation for the Council was set in motion.

It was not by chance that this announcement was made on Whitsunday. John had noted how Pius IX used December 8, feast of the Immaculate Conception (which he had defined in 1854), to advance the various stages of Vatican I. John was not lacking in Marian piety, but he regarded Pentecost as the feast of the Church. So he tried to link it intimately with the celebration of Vatican II. It made perfect sense: since the Holy Spirit had planted the idea of the Council, the Holy Spirit would take care of its unfolding and conclusion. During the preconclave period he had talked about the need for a 'new Pentecost' (see p. 278 above). He used the same expression in his 'prayer for the Council': 'Renew thy wonders in this day, as by a new Pentecost' (Abbott, p. 793). He said explicitly that 'it is from the spirit and doctrine of Pentecost that the great event of the Ecumenical Council draws its substance and its life' (AAS, 52, p. 517). That was the vision.

Working it out in practice proved more difficult. His first meeting with the Ante-preparatory Commission on June 30, 1959, gave him a chance to say what he hoped the Council would do. Its purpose was, he said, 'to demonstrate the striking diversity of rites together with the unshakeable unity of the Catholic Church'. This was the concept of the Council as 'spectacle' of which John was fond: it would speak to the world simply by meeting, and bring new energy and drive to the whole Church. But this was all rather vague – a bit like declaring that in future everything will be better. Equally vague was the pledge that the Council would both meet modern needs and be faithful to the past:

> Ever faithful to the sacred principles on which it is based and the immutable teaching entrusted to it by the Divine Founder, and always following in the paths of ancient tradition, the Church proposes . . . to reaffirm its cohesion and face up to many modern situations and problems by establishing

effective norms of conduct and activity (*Letture*, p. 146).

What *did* he mean? It was like the rhetoric of Georges Bernanos, of which one critic said: 'It makes you fairly bursting to fight, but it doesn't show you the enemy'. There was, of course, no contradiction between fidelity and meeting the demands of the contemporary world. *Aggiornamento* and renewal would only be of value if they grew out of the authentic tradition. But the emphasis in this June 30, 1959, speech fell on consolidating and preserving the past rather than on responding to the present. What John said was perfectly compatible with the 'defensive' view of the Council represented by Tardini, Ottaviani and Pizzardo.

John's first encyclical, *Ad Petri Cathedram* (To the See of Peter) came out at the same time (June 29, 1959). It had been eagerly awaited: first encyclicals are usually programmatic, and it was expected to shed light on the Council. But this was a compromise, hybrid document whose final revision had been entrusted to Tardini. Pope John's trumpet was distinctly muted. Much of *Ad Petri Cathedram* was lifted from his predecessors. Pope John (or his script-writers) repeated Leo XIII's idea that class divisions are a law of nature. The encyclical was negative in tone, firmly anti-Communist, full of dire warnings about the mass-media, and it demanded obedience from all. It was difficult to square all this with the 'Good Pope John' so assiduously depicted by the very media he was berating. In an attempt to resolve this contradiction, commentators claimed that John had deliberately allowed himself to be influenced by Tardini as a way of soothing the Curia, still shell-shocked from the announcement of the Council. *Ad Petri Cathedram* proved that, despite his 'adventurism', he was a sound traditionalist at heart.

But that was a feeble explanation for *Ad Petri Cathedram*'s treatment of other Christians. Could this really be the voice of Pope John? He took his stand on Pius XI's 1928 encyclical *Mortalium Animos* which had ruled out Catholic participation in the international ecumenical movement and warned of the perils of indifferentism. We know, John editorialised, that among some communities divided from this Apostolic See there has been 'a certain movement of sympathy towards the Catholic Church'. One expected him to grasp this out-stretched hand. But no. He went on: 'Those who call themselves Christians, although separated from us, have held many congresses with the aim of establishing a closer relationship with each other, and to this end they have set up various bodies. These show that they are moved by the desire to reach some sort of unity' (No. 32). This was a rather lofty and apparently disdainful reference to the World Council of Churches. Its rather wishy-washy attempts to achieve unity were contrasted with the Roman Catholic Church which already has 'the unity willed by Christ' and so did not need to seek it. The Catholic Church has unity of faith, unity of government, and unity in worship (Nos. 33–8). Quite evidently this is 'real' unity, the genuine article, and it is very different from the shadowy 'some sort of unity' aimed at by others. *Ad Petri Cathedram* makes the point with elegant triplets: 'Unity, venerable brothers and beloved sons, should not be something evanescent, fleeting and hazardous, but rather something solid, stable and secure' (No. 34). Solidity, stability and security could be found in the Roman Catholic Church, and only there. It was an argument that could have found a place in Bossuet's classic *Histoire des Variations des Eglises Protestantes*.

A conclusion followed, and John did not hesitate to draw it, even though it put in jeopardy the high ecumenical hopes he entertained for his Council: if the papacy was the guardian of the unity willed by Christ for his Church, then the solution to the scandal of Christian divisions was that all should 'return', repentant, to the sheepfold they had abandoned. The use of the word 'return' was almost catastrophic. For Orthodox, Anglican and Protestant alike the term was offensive: it implied that reunion could only come about at the price of submission and surrender to the institutional claims of the bishop of Rome. It also implied that the responsibility for Christian divisions lay on one side only – contrary to what Roncalli had said in Palermo in September 1957 (see p. 264 above). After reading *Ad Petri Cathedram*, it was reasonable to ask: would the real Pope John please stand up? It seemed that with his first encyclical he had perpetrated an ecumenical *gaffe* of some magnitude.

Or had he? A more careful reading of *Ad Petri Cathedram* (together with hindsight) suggests that among the faded flowers of his venerable predecessors Pope John had carefully planted one or two seeds that could bear ecumenical fruit. It was unreasonable to expect that he would abandon the convictions of a lifetime and cease to believe that the Roman Catholic Church was 'the one, true Church' willed by Christ and that the papacy was the focus of its unity. But that did not have to mean that other Christians had to be consigned to outer darkness. John would need Augustin Bea to show him how this could be done and how common faith in Christian baptism could provide the basis for ecumenical work. But in June 1959, Bea was only a name to him and, judging from the man's workrate, John imagined he must be two people. Bea's moment would soon come.

The truth is that *Ad Petri Cathedram* was a duet for two voices. So far we have heard from Tardini. Pope John certainly intended his encyclical to be an ecumenically friendly document, and thought he had succeeded. This is clear even in the famous passage that uses the obnoxious word 'return'. It is specifically directed to the separated brethren: 'Let me address you with ardent desire as brothers and sons. Let us nourish the hope of your loving return [*ritorno*] with all the affection of a father . . . When we lovingly invite you to the unity of the Church, we do not invite you to some strange house but to your own, shared paternal home . . . "I am Joseph, your brother" ' (Nos. 39–40). We have already seen the importance of this text from Genesis 45.44. John uses it to express his readiness to step down from a superior position and place himself alongside and on the same level as his partners in dialogue. The image of 'father', natural enough in a patriarchal figure of seventy-eight, is qualified by that of 'brother'. And both images, father and brother, belong to John's *spiritual* vocabulary. There is nothing juridical about them at all. Hence his intentions were falsified if the story of Joseph were read in such a way as to bring out that he had been previously wronged or that his guilty brothers were embarrassed. John meant something much more simple. He had said it earlier in *Ad Petri Cathedram*: 'All are brothers, and so all questions must be resolved in friendly fashion with mutual brotherly charity'. One of John's endearing features was that he could make such clichés sound credible.

Moreover, he brought some other personal touches to *Ad Petri Cathedram* in the form of favourite quotations. The first was from St Augustine: 'Whether they want it or not, they are our brothers. They will only cease to be our brothers when they have forgotten to say "Our Father" ' (No. 40: *In Psalmos 32, En.* 29). It was a text that Bea would exploit to the full. John's other noteworthy reference was to Enrico Giovanni Newman, whom he calls 'a famous English writer'. He quotes John Henry Newman (for it is he) in *Difficulties of Anglicans* to make the point that disputes among theologians, so long as they are concerned with non-defined matters, do not wreck the unity of the Church, and ought to be encouraged since they lead to a deeper understanding of doctrine (No. 36). He paraphrases Newman and optimistically writes, 'from the clash of discordant opinions there always flows new light'. The relevance of this to the forthcoming Council was obvious. It was vital to insist on freedom of expression and not allow disputes between theological schools to degenerate into squabbles about unorthodoxy. The brief reference to Newman was also his rehabilitation. The anti-Modernist campaign had portrayed him as a 'quasi-Modernist' who disdained scholasticism and whose 'development of doctrine' was no more than an illegitimate 'evolution of doctrine'. John laid those forlorn ghosts quietly to rest, and opted for Newman and development rather than for Bossuet and fixity.

It might be objected that the 'positive' reading of *Ad Petri Cathedram* proposed here is based on hair-splitting subtleties and stretching points. So it is. But in ecumenical matters much depends on nuances and liberating distinctions. And much depends on the tone of voice. *Ad Petri Cathedram* did not dent the image of 'Good Pope John'. But it was evident that he had not yet managed to find a satisfactory way of expressing himself in the literary form of an a encyclical. He was still under the tutelage of Tardini for whom Pius XI represented the master in this very special *genre*.

Yet John and his team were producing encyclicals at a great rate. There were three more before the end of 1959: *Sacerdotii Nostri Primordia* (August 1, 1959, on the hundredth anniversary of the death of the Curé d'Ars, St Jean-Marie

Vianney); *Grata Recordatio* (September 26, 1959, on the Rosary); and *Princeps Pastorum* (November 28, 1959, commemorating the sixtieth anniversary of *Maximum Illud* in which Benedict XV reorganised missionary work). They have been largely forgotten, and it cannot candidly be said that they created much of a stir at the time. They seemed too much like trips down memory lane. They confirmed the impression that John was a man of great piety, very loyal to the enthusiasms and practices of his youth, and with half his mind in the past. This is the sort of Pope he would have been had he not summoned a Council. But he had summoned a Council, though no one would have guessed it from reading these worthy encyclicals.

Tardini, meanwhile, was busily remedying the charismatic vagueness of his chief. He was not over-keen on the notion of the Council as a 'new Pentecost' because it slotted into no known juridical categories. Still brisk, brusque and apparently fit at seventy-one, Tardini made most of the early running. On July 3, 1959, three days after *Ad Petri Cathedram*, he addressed a meeting of rectors of Roman Universities and other theological institutes. Tardini was a stranger to doubt. For him the purpose of the Council was absolutely clear. His telegraphic notes have been preserved:

It is more than likely from what can be seen as of now
(a) that the Council will be more practical than dogmatic, more pastoral than ideological, and that it will provide norms for action rather than new definitions. However,
(b) this does not take away the fact that
(i) we can (or should) recall and reaffirm those points of doctrine that are most important and nowadays most threatened, or,
(ii) that we can (or must) move rapidly from a speedy and solid summary of doctrinal principles to 'practical norms' (Nicolini, p. 193).

In Tardini's first point – he ticked them off on his fingers – one could just about discern the originality of this Council ('more pastoral than dogmatic') as John conceived it; but his second point seemed to transform it into an exercise for canon lawyers ('practical norms') that was hardly likely to interest still less inspire anyone.

Tardini's address, however, was the opening cannonade in the battle for the Council. He was addressing the rectors of Roman Universities because he expected them to provide the bulk of the 'experts' or *periti* who would be needed. The universities already provided most of the 'consultors' for the Roman Congregations. It would save time and money if they worked on the preparations for the Council. Thus – Tardini did not need to spell this out – there would be no need to invite experts from other Catholic universities whether they were in Washington D.C., Louvain or Milan. Tardini was soon to appoint a 'Secretary' for the effective day-to-day control of the operation. Mgr Pericle Felici was forty-eight, professor of Canon Law at the Lateran University, and a member of the Roman Rota – the court that deals with disputed marriage cases. He was well-known, in a restricted milieu, for the elegance of his Latin verses. He later became secretary general of the Council itself. Tardini had carefully selected a man who shared his own juridical approach to the Council. His control, at this stage, was complete.

On October 30, 1959, Tardini summoned a press conference to tell the world what a Council was. This was unheard of: Roman Cardinals were not in the habit of meeting the press and exposing themselves to impertinent questions from the ignorant and the Anglo-Saxon. But Tardini blinded them with science. He held the press conference not in the Vatican but at his orphanage, Villa Nazareth, which ensured he got publicity for the place and showed what a pastorally-minded person he was. There are many accounts of what Tardini said on this occasion. His biographer reports that 'he gave an historico-doctrinal lecture on the nature of ecumenical councils with the dash (*brio*) and humour that are his wont, interspersing his remarks with witty asides (*battute*)' (Nicolini, p. 193). Bernard Wall, an English man of letters, described it rather more vividly:

> Cardinal Tardini came into the room with swift steps. He was a small man, with a thick brush of iron grey hair cut very short and businesslike. His spectacles were thick and gave him a peering look and these, with his mouth, which was not expressive of human sympathy, made him seem like a pedant or a schoolmaster, dried up, almost sour (Wall, p. 197).

Wall also gathered, accurately enough, that Tardini was not interested in ecumenism or Church reform, still less in 'learning from the world'. So what had happened to Pope John's great idea?

> What surely had happened was that Pope John in a flush of universal benevolence after his election, and with his interest in the Orthodox Christians of the East, had a great project for reunion. He had overlooked the detailed difficulties, and the difficulties were first and foremost matters of detail. And of course he had not considered the Vatican offices enough (*Ibid.*, p. 198).

This was a shrewd judgement. It raises a more fundamental question: did Tardini really believe in the Council at all?

Pericle Felici tried to answer it some years later: 'Despite his gruff manner and his pungent Roman wit, Tardini was a man of great faith, and he lived by devotion to the Pope. Whatever exalted the Church and the Pope rejoiced his spirit. The positive response he gave Pope John when he announced the Council was dictated by such feelings' (Felici, p. 120). Though he wraps it up, Felici is here admitting that Tardini had little natural sympathy with the conciliar project as such, did not share Pope John's view of its aims, and obeyed only out of his elevated sense of the papal office. But his view of obedience did not exclude trying to hi-jack the Council preparations and divert them to his own ends. In a way, Tardini was probably the least suitable man to prepare Vatican II; but at least a Tardini-sponsored event could not be suspected of unorthodoxy or novelty.

While Tardini was entertaining the press with his *battute* or quips, Capovilla was giving lectures in Padua and Bergamo ostensibly to mark the first anniversary of Pope John's election. But what he was really doing was trying to put the record straight. Capovilla admitted that it was unusual and delicate to 'speak in public about one's own superior or father'. But he proposed to abandon this custom, without any breach of confidence, for the following reason: 'The good things that are known about others are always the most difficult to put into words. It is easy to speak ill of someone, just as it is easy to sin. But to speak well of a person is already the beginning of virtue' (*Letture*, p. vii). So Capovilla's lectures were a reply to those who had been speaking ill of Pope John. Like the British monarchy, popes are not supposed to answer their critics directly.

But what were the critics saying, and who were they? In curial circles in Rome the objection to Pope John was that he was a dangerous innovator whose actions were an implicit criticism of his predecessors, particularly of the great and learned Pius XII to whom he could not hold a candle. It was also suggested – Tisserant used to go on about this at his exquisite dinner-table – that John was not very bright. So in his first lecture in Bergamo on October 20, 1959, Capovilla shows that, far from being an innovator, Pope John is still the good-hearted and traditionalist Catholic who had been so well-trained in the glorious Bergamo seminary. He was certainly reflecting Pope John's own feelings in this hymn of praise to Bergamo:

> His [Pope John's] Bergamo – as he sees and feels it – is a good, intelligent
> and hospitable city; solid in its faith, unshakeable in its traditions; jealous of
> its religious and civic heritage; sometimes seeming rather set apart in the
> austere beauty of its mountains and valleys, but proud of its natural beauties
> and its monuments. It is a blessed land. Blessed in the story of its martyrs
> and saints, in the wealth of its shrines, the fecundity of its religious and civic
> institutions . . . (*Letture*, p. 57).

And so on. John was certainly sad at not being able to go to Sotto il Monte again; until he became Pope, he had almost always spent the anniversary of his ordination, August 10, at home. In 1959 all he could do was write a moving letter to the parishioners of Sotto il Monte (*Lettere*, pp. 153–4).

But it was not nostalgia that prompted Capovilla's rhetorical flourish. He was really saying that a man who came from and remained loyal to such a background must be sound and trustworthy. Further, Capovilla's Bergamo lecture was structured according to Blaise Pascal's 'three orders': earth, intellect, charity (*Pensées*, Ed. Martin Turnell, No. 585). Pope John was firmly rooted in the Bergamo province; as for his mind, he had received the grace of *sapientia cordis*, wisdom of the heart, which placed him in 'the order of charity' and so transcended the mere intellect (*Letture*, p. 62). That disposed of Tisserant's complaint that Pope John was none too clever. There were other tests of a person besides quickness of mind. Tisserant, the aging would-be *enfant terrible* of the Curia, was greatly bucked by being elected to the *Académie Française* where he could move among his intellectual equals. So much for Bergamo.

In Padua on November 9, 1959, Capovilla emphasised Pope John's continuity with his predecessors. John is presented as the true heir of the popes of his lifetime, and indeed as the synthesis of their virtues. He had picked up traits from all of them: 'The enlightened Christian humanism of Leo XIII; the simple and attractive loveableness of Pius X; the general nobility of Benedict XV; Pius XI's longanimity; and from Pius XII the heart-beat of universal love' (*Letture*, p. 78). These judgements belong to hagiography rather than to history. But in 1959 they made the point that Pope John, far from straying from the paths of his predecessors and launching the Church upon some wild and unpredictable adventure, consciously set himself in the admirable papal tradition of the twentieth century. He was not in the least original or 'revisionist'. He owed everything to the popes who had gone before. This was meant to be reassuring.

But at Padua in November 1959 Capovilla also dealt with a more precise and worrying question. The comparison with Pius XII was still being made, sometimes to John's credit, more often to his discomfiture. He had allegedly told the new bishop of Le Mans who was wondering how he could possibly succeed the remarkably wise, good and learned Cardinal Georges Grente: 'Don't worry. Just do what I do: the opposite of my predecessor'. It doesn't much matter whether John actually made this remark. It was *ben trovato* and it entered the oral tradition. It was also potentially highly damaging to him. So to scotch such stories Capovilla dug out a remark made by Patriarch Roncalli to Pius XII: 'Holy Father, you will leave a difficult heritage for any successor who tries to emulate you in your role as teacher and master of the word (*maestro della parola*)' (*Letture*, p. 37). Translate: John thought Pius XII was incomparable and inimitable. An obscure and pious article written about Pius when Roncalli was still nuncio in Paris was adduced as still further evidence of his unbounded admiration for his immediate predecessor. This needed to be said, for the curial opposition to Pope John came largely from the 'men of Pius XII'. Capovilla also tried to dispel the notion that there was any hint of disagreement between the Pope and Tardini. Gossip travels swiftly by the clerical bush-telegraph. To prove his point, Capovilla quoted Tardini's speech in John's presence on the first anniversary of Pius' death.

'Cardinal Domenico Tardini', he told the Paduans, 'exclaimed in a vibrant and deeply emotional tone: "Holy Father! Popes may die, but the Pope does not!" ' (*Ibid.*, p. 72). But that was a double-edged remark.

So in the end, Capovilla's attempt to establish continuity between the two pontificates miscarried. The more he stressed the similarities, the more one became aware of the differences. His own evidence showed that there was a new spirit in the Vatican, and that Pope John's style was completely different from that of his predecessor. Capovilla quotes two of John's favourite maxims which speak volumes about how he thought of his office. The first is almost untranslatable: '*Fare, saper fare, lasciar fare, dar da fare*' (which is only crudely rendered as, 'To act, to know what to do, to let things happen, to make things happen') (*Letture*, p. 61). This was a key principle in the preparations for the Council: it was essential to know when to intervene, and when not to. In John's mind it was linked with the maxim attributed to St Bernard: '*Omnia videre, multa dissimulare et pauca corrigere*' ('To notice everything, turn a blind eye to much and to correct a few things'). These were not axioms either cherished or practised by Pius XII and Tardini who liked to be omniscient and omnicompetent. The St Bernard principle, Capovilla patiently explains – answering yet another objection – 'is not a sign of weakness or compromise; it involves rather a precise knowledge of situations and the ability to overcome obstacles gradually' (*Ibid.*). In other words 'Good Pope John' was nobody's fool and knew exactly what was being muttered behind his back. He saw it all (*omnia videre*). The signal from Padua to the Roman Curia was clear: John would not be pushed around or manipulated by anyone. He was his own man.

John's journal confirms that Capovilla, when not indulging in rhetorical hyperbole, was faithfully reporting on his attitudes. *Pauca corrigere* (to correct a few things) implied that he would be some sort of reformer. After a year, John judged that he had not made such a bad start: 'The experience of this first year gives me light and strength in my efforts to straighten out, to reform, and tactfully and patiently to make improvements in everything' (*Journal*, p. 321: dated November–December, 1959). In everything? The scope was vast. There was one particular reform he thought urgent. During meals on his retreat John had Capovilla read to him St Bernard's *De Consideratione* which he found 'rewarding reading for a pope at any time'. Why? 'Certain things which did not redound to the honour of the Roman clergy in the twelfth century still survive today. Therefore one must "watch and correct", and bear in patience' (*Ibid.*, p. 320). St Bernard's diatribe was concerned with nepotism – showing favour to one's relatives – and pluralism, the habit of holding several offices or benefices at once. John hated nepotism, as his nephew, Don Battista, had already discovered. Nepotism was not a problem in his pontificate.

Pluralism was. Roman cardinals often held several top posts at the same time.

Pizzardo, for example, was both prefect of the Congregation for Universities and Seminaries and secretary of the Holy Office (*Lettere*, p. 173). Tisserant was Vatican librarian and had been prefect of the Congregation for Oriental Churches since he became a cardinal in 1936; he was sufficiently well dug in to believe himself immoveable. At first Pope John tried dropping gentle hints. At the secret consistory of December 15, 1958, he explained that he was creating so many cardinals so that the burden of work might be shared out more equitably (*Lettere*, p. 173: Letter to Pizzardo, October 12, 1959). Perhaps this was too subtle. Pizzardo and Tisserant remained obstinately at all their posts and showed not the slightest inclination to move. Though it was against his temperament, John had to order them out. They could only be removed by main force. Accustomed to obeying all his life, John found disobedience hard to comprehend.

He wrote an official letter to each of them, published in *l'Osservatore Romano*, thanking them for spontaneously offering to resign. It was a white lie, but it was the usual form. But he was distressed at having to resort to such methods. 'They have refused the Pope', he said in sad disbelief, 'they have refused the Pope' (Trevor, p. 271). Cardinal Montini in Milan was also interested in the reform of the Curia. He was not even a member of the Ante-preparatory Commission, but he wrote to Tardini to say that it would be a good thing 'if the Roman Curia were to abandon certain honorific or ritualistic or merely juridical ways of behaving, so as to set an example of Christian brotherhood and evangelical humility' (Monaco, p. 61). He was already set on curial reform.

Tisserant tried to pour oil on these troubled waters. He was still Vatican librarian and bishop of Ostia, Porto and St Rufino. In the latter capacity he wrote a pastoral letter dated November 4, 1959, the first anniversary of the coronation of *our* Holy Father, John XXIII. 'It was entirely shot through', noted Capovilla wonderingly, 'with sentiments of admiration for both supreme pontiffs' (*Lettere*, p. 191). John thanked Tisserant for his pastoral letter, and gave him the present of a *rocchetto* or surplice (*Ibid.*, p. 190). It was Christmastime and *Pax in terris* broke out on all sides, briefly. Pope John wrote in his journal: 'I feel I am under obedience in all things and have noticed that this disposition, in things great and small, gives me, unworthy as I am, a strength of daring simplicity so wholly evangelical in its nature that it demands and obtains universal respect and edifies many' (*Journal*, p. 321). The 'strength of daring simplicity' so far from diminishing, grew as the pontificate went on. 'The whole world is my family', he noted in his journal (*Ibid.*). Becoming pope had enabled John at last to become fully himself. It upset the usual law by which the old become ever more cautious and staid. In the New Year, 1960, there would be the Synod of the diocese of Rome. He was indeed starting at the beginning, at home and in Rome.

Chapter 16

At home and in Rome

Can Rome be true to itself if it remains merely a national capital? No, for another Rome survives on another level, the Rome of the Catholic faith . . . *Roma patria communis*: no one is a stranger in Rome

(Cardinal Giovanni Battista Montini, speech in the Campidoglio, October 11, 1962, opening day of the Council).

The official Vatican handbook describes the Pope's immediate entourage as belonging to a home (*casa*) and a household or family (*famiglia*). These age-old terms can be contrasted with *curia* which evokes royal courts and consequently courtiers and, indeed, flunkeys. The Pope has both a *casa* and a *curia*.

Like his immediate predecessors, Pope John lived in the Apostolic Palace on the right of St Peter's Square, on the same floor as the Secretariat of State (the so-called *terza loggia*). *Time* was mistaken in imagining that he stomped in and began to move all the furniture about. He tried something more radical: to create a family atmosphere in these lofty, marble-floored salons. Above the altar in his private chapel was a Holy Family by a painter of the school of Paolo Veronese, a gift from the Rome football team, Lazio (Capovilla: letter of January 31, 1984: the picture is reproduced in *Secolo*, facing p. 48). No doubt it reminded him of his own family and the Holy House of Loreto. It was not a very fashionable theme. Pope John took it as a hint about how he should behave. He became the father of the household rather than the monarch sitting on the throne. But there was not much time for chatting. The five sisters from Bergamo looked after the kitchen and the domestic arrangements but, warned by the fate of Sister Pascalina, they stayed in the background, discreet, almost invisible. Giampaolo Gussi came down from Venice to join his brother Guido. They served at table and, after the death of Angelino Stoppa, Pius XII's driver who had been tactfully kept on, took turns at doing the driving (Capovilla, *Ibid.*). They were both married men with children, but they lived in the Vatican, not the Apostolic Palace. One or the other would always be present at Pope John's Mass at 7 a.m.

A member of the papal household described its life to James W. Spain, the man from the CIA:

It is difficult for you Americans to comprehend how the Holy Father thinks of us and we of him. None of us have wives, children or social obligations. Nor do we lead a prescribed communal life like monks. Here in Rome we

341

very often talk, read and listen to music together . . . The Holy Father is our
real father; to him we are literally sons. Sometimes we tell him new things
which interest him and he is proud of us. Sometimes he tells us to stop
talking nonsense and to go away and learn wisdom (Spain, p. 5).

Unfortunately this idyllic picture is, according to Capovilla, not wholly true.
John did have the relationship described to Spain with a number of people on
whom he liked to try out ideas. But they did not form a community of work, and
did not sit around of an evening listening to music. Sometimes John liked to listen
to music during supper, but that was all. Otherwise his only relaxation was a
walk in the Vatican gardens in the afternoon.

This was also the time when, weather permitting, he read or browsed through
books not strictly connected with his immediate work or, more usually, got
Capovilla to read them out to him. The scrupulous secretary then noted down
what had been read. Thus on Nicolas Gogol's *Lettres Spirituelles* he had written: 'I
did a number of readings from this copy for Pope John *in hortis*, for example pp.
76–79 during the winter months of 1962-63' (Letter of January 31, 1984). One
passage made a deep impression on Pope John:

> Intelligence is not the highest faculty. It acts rather as a kind of police force
> of the mind: it has to restore order and put things back in their
> place . . . Reason is incomparably higher, but it is only arrived at through
> constant victories over our passions. Yet reason alone does not permit
> human beings to aspire to eternity (*Letture*, pp. 384–5, quoting *Lettres
> spirituelles et familières*, Grasset, Paris, 1957, p. 76).

John commented: 'A people that has mystical souls like this is not completely
finished'.

Capovilla's annotations permit one to keep track of Pope John's reading. He
remained faithful to the Latin and Italian classics. He copied down a quotation
from Cicero's treatise on old age, *De Senectute*, which expressed what he felt
about his 'family': 'What is more agreeable than to see an old man surrounded by
a throng of young men willing to learn?' The fact that his 'young men' were
mostly in their forties did not alter the material point. He also noted a more
poignant and ambivalent maxim: 'Old age is like the final act of a play – at the end
we take leave of it with relief, especially if we thought it went on too long'
(*Vent'Anni*, p. 64: classical scholars might like to know he used the Garzanti 1952
edition of *De Senectute*). John had been at home with Dante, Petrarch, Tasso and
his favourite Manzoni from adolescence. He would not have quarrelled with Ezra
Pound's view that 'all great writers are contemporaries'. Manzoni's 1822 poem,
La Pentecoste, confirmed his idea of the Council as a 'new Pentecost'. It speaks of
the 'Spirit of renewal' and prays that the Spirit may 'temper the confident talent

of impetuous youth, and adorn the white hairs of those who joyously seek holiness' (*Tutte le Poesie di Alessandro Manzoni*, p. 206). Well, Pope John still had a few white hairs left; and Hans Küng published his *Konzil und Wiedervereinigung* (*The Council and Reunion*) in 1960.

There is evidence that Pope John read at least one contemporary novel, *La Messa dei Villeggianti* by Mario Soldati. But since it concerned himself, that is not so surprising. He was particularly intrigued by the following passage which expresses a very characteristic 'Italian' reaction to his pontificate. It is in the form of a letter to the priest in the country parish where the Soldati went on holiday:

> Many drift away from the Church, or do not draw as close to it as they should, because they get the clergy wrong. But there is an element of truth in their error. Some of our priests want to mark themselves off from the rest of humanity as though they were not ordinary mortals but people possessed of magical powers. But the Lord himself, for love of mankind, became human . . . Then one evening last November we watched on our television screens the coronation of the Pope. Something inside me rebelled against it. I was both fascinated and appalled by what I saw. I wondered anxiously what my rebellion meant, and whether it was well-founded.
>
> After pondering the matter for a long time, I risked a first answer: what offended me, what struck me in these rites . . . was their claim to codify the sacred, to fix and formulate for ever the religious element. Yet the first instinct of all mankind suggests that the religious or the sacred involves the ineffable, the spontaneous, the individual, the spiritual, the momentary embodiment of the spiritual. Doesn't Catholicism try to deny this insight? A few days later, reading Pope John's speech to the pilgrims of Venice and Bergamo, my doubts suddenly began to vanish and my spirit was re-awakened to hope. For the Pope himself showed that he was wearied and oppressed by ritual. The Pope himself good-naturedly joked about the *sedia gestatoria* on which he was carried around: it reminded him of the time he had been carried on his father's shoulders as a little boy. 'We have to let ourselves be carried by the Lord', he said, 'and so carry the Lord to others'. I was moved and won over. John XXIII understood that the first duty of the vicar of the One who became man is to remain human (*Transizione*, pp. 121–2).

It made a change from the usual charge that he was not the equal of Pius XII.

But not everyone in the Roman Curia appreciated Pope John's 'populist' success. The CIA report gives an important clue about how John's household regarded leading members of the Curia. 'Cardinal Ottaviani', said the anonymous informant, 'is not an enemy. To the Holy Father he is an uncle who is often difficult and must be circumvented, but who is still respected' (Spain, p. 6). That gets it about right. John once said of Ottaviani: 'Alfredo is a very dear friend: it's a pity he's half-blind and has jowls that wobble like a Venetian lagune in the sirocco' (Andreotti, p. 70). As for Tardini, John's household knew what to expect: everyone who had worked in the Secretariat of State for the last thirty years had passed through his hands. Nor was Tardini devoid of self-knowledge. He once described his original method of dealing with superiors in this way: 'I would suddenly blurt out a phrase, a question or a witticism that disconcerted, dismayed, embarrassed or sometimes demolished my interlocutor' (Nicolini, p. 229). Clearly Tardini was another difficult uncle who needed careful handling. Like Ottaviani, however, he was not a member of the papal family. He had to knock on the door.

But John still kept a line open to both men. Despite Ottaviani's general conservatism, he was one of the first to declare nuclear weapons immoral. He applied the most traditional theory of 'the just war' and found it no longer fitted. Tardini's obstructionism was a nuisance and his explosions wearing, but at least he knew whole passages from Manzoni's *I Promessi Sposi* by heart (Nicolini, p. 221) which, in John's eyes, redeemed a lot of faults. The latest quips were reported to Pope John. We know that because he noted some of them down. Humour in the Vatican follows the Italian tradition and is not particularly funny: it makes a point economically. One day John noted the remark: '*Angelo regna, Carlo informa, Alfredo sorveglia, Domenico governa, Giovanni benedice*' (*Lettere*, p. 518). It was a more elaborate version of the 'joke' already reported. It means (full names and functions added):

> Angelo (Dell'Acqua, substitute) reigns, Carlo (Confalonieri, secretary of the Congregation for Seminaries and Universities) spies, Alfredo (Ottaviani, pro-prefect of the Holy Office) keeps watch, Domenico (Tardini, Secretary of State) governs, John merely blesses.

Though not exactly scintillating, the fact that it went into the Pope's private notebook suggests that he knew how the balance of forces in his Curia was perceived in Rome.

John tried to bring a personal touch to all his work. Much of it consisted in preparing documents or letters. As in all administrations, a draft was usually provided by someone else. John's commonest marginal comments were 'Redraft' or 'I can't possibly sign this as it stands' or 'I know this prelate personally and it matters a lot to me that you should let this come through' (*Lettere*, p. 23). Of course it was impossible for him to know personally every bishop in the world. But he prayed for them all. This passage from a letter to Cardinal Montini was more than an idle compliment:

> I should write to everyone – bishops, archbishops and cardinals all over the

world – just as I include every single one of them in my humble prayer to
the Lord. But to reach them all I content myself with writing to the
Archbishop of Milan, because through him I carry them all in my heart, just
as he represents them all for me (*Saggio*, p. 126: letter dated April 4, 1961).

This was a remarkable confession: Montini as a representative bishop, summing
up in his person the entire episcopate. Many diverse strands were woven to make
this judgement: the historic importance of the see of St Ambrose and St Charles
Borromeo, a friendship dating back to 1925, the hope that Montini would play an
important role in the Council, the conviction – which later became a certainty –
that Montini would succeed him.

Yet Pope John didn't just write to cardinals and bishops and Montini. He wrote
to all his old friends, even if it was to say they must not expect to hear from him
again. Among his strictly personal correspondence one letter, hitherto
unpublished, stands out. It was to Adelaide Coari whom we last met in 1929 (p.
135 above). There are not many letters from popes to non-royal women:

> Dear Miss Adelaide Coari,
> You won't think too badly of me if the state of life to which Providence has
> brought me does not permit me to say at any great length how fond [*cari*]
> are my memories of your activity half a century ago . . .
> There's a phrase of St Gregory Nazianzen that I love to repeat: *voluntas Dei
> pax nostra* – God's will is our peace. This phrase follows me like the star of
> the Magi. Guided by its light we move towards Christ, with simplicity and
> courage, and reach out towards the certainty of eternal goodness.
> I'm writing this on St Catherine's eve, on the threshold of my 78th year.
> I'm in good health, and ready for anything, ready to serve the Church here
> below or to live on in the Church triumphant with our saints.
> I noticed with edification how faithful you were to the late Don Rebora of
> the Rosminians, and your fidelity to Mgr Radini. *Sancti tui, Domine, nos
> ubique laetificant* [Your saints, Lord, bring us joy on all sides]. They stand by
> us, encourage and protect us, until the day of our final reunion.
> You will continue to pray for me, and I bless you from the heart. Ask Sts
> Peter and Paul never to draw me away from the two Johns who epitomise
> the light brought by the Old and the New Testament, *Lumen et Pax Christi*
> [the Light and Peace of Christ] (Bologna Archives: letter dated November
> 25, 1959).

Don Rebora was a poet whom Adelaide had helped to convert. The seventy-eight
year old lady who received this unexpected and courtly letter in Milan outlived
Pope John by three years. The day of the 'final reunion' came in 1966.

Pope John, then, left the papal apartments much as they were while trying to introduce a new family spirit into them. The only physical change he made in his tiny state was to have restored the Torre San Giovanni (St John's Tower), built in 848 to ward off the marauding Saracens. John turned it into a four-floor apartment with a lift. He wanted somewhere to withdraw to for prayer and reflection. It was his 'desert', though admittedly quite a comfortable one. He had evidently had his eye on it for some time. The story of the tower in his own words is a good example of Pope John's table-talk:

> In the time of Pope Leo the tower that is now used by Vatican Radio was restored. That left the other tower in the southern corner of the gardens. Until 1926 it was used as an observatory. It was part of the fortifications that guarded the so-called Pertusa Gate. Pius XI thought of turning it into a place for retreat and recollection, and Pius XII had the same idea. But the work being done at Castelgandolfo and then the war meant that the project had to be laid aside. The abandoned tower spoiled that part of the gardens. So in 1960 the Commission for Vatican City examined a plan for the re-ordering of the whole area including the ponderous and rather tumble-down Lourdes grotto. The Commission had already set aside the money. I consulted a few people and was happy to give the go-ahead. But when the work began there were whisperings here and there, so I asked Cardinal Tardini what to do. He said: 'The restoration of the Nicholas V tower is a necessity, its conservation a duty, and its use a bonus for which your successors will be grateful'. It was given the name of St John in memory of Sotto il Monte, where I come from, which also has a Torre San Giovanni on the hill of the same name (*Letture*, pp. 470–1).

When future historians ask what difference Pope John's pontificate made to the Vatican and the Church, one can always reply: he turned a ruined, fortified tower into a place of prayer.

But John didn't have much time to linger in his tower. He was the bishop of Rome and took this, the foundation of his grander titles, seriously. But what, in practice, did it mean? The administration of the diocese was entrusted to a cardinal vicar. John inherited from Pius XII the eighty-year-old Clemente Micara, a crusty old gentleman whose age was beginning to show. He did not always see eye to eye with Pope John, perhaps believing that he ought to get on with running the universal Church while leaving Rome to the man of experience, himself (see the hint in Caprile, '*Ancora su Giovanni XXIII*', p. 52). Micara, however, was flanked by a younger and more amenable pro-vicar, Luigi Traglia, who took over more and more of the work and was made a cardinal at the consistory of March 28, 1960.

There was much that needed attention in the diocese of Rome. In the last year of his life, Pius XII intuited that something was badly wrong. All his life he had used the rhetoric of 'eternal Rome', the sacred city, the second Jerusalem, home of the popes, centre of Catholicism, and model for the entire Church. But as he addressed the Lenten preachers for the last time in February 1958, he in effect admitted that Rome was no longer exemplary – it had become merely typical:

> The first step is to look at things as they really are. You are not unaware that many of your parishioners have fallen into a state of spiritual torpor . . . So can it be said that Rome has its shadow areas, its islands in need of evangelisation, and that it is mission territory? For those who, like yourselves, know Rome, who can refuse to admit it? (quoted in Riccordi, Andrea, 'La Chiesa a Roma dalla Seconda Guerra Mondiale al postconcilio', in *Il Regno*, 5, 1982, p. 183).

Rome a *pays de mission* just like Paris? The idea was novel and unthinkable.

Yet it was true, and John knew it. When he announced the Synod for the diocese of Rome on January 25, 1959, he described in his own breezy way the changes that had come over the city since he ceased to live in it in 1925: 'In the suburbs especially houses, houses have been built, in which families, families are piled up on top of each other, families coming from all parts of the peninsula, from the islands and – we can say – from the whole world' (Alberigo, p. 274). It would be preposterous to call this 'sociology': but at least John avoided the moralising approach and tried to look at the facts. The 'historic centre' of Rome was now surrounded on all sides by vast shoe-boxes of apartment blocks. Beyond them lay the shanty-towns, improvised huts for the poorest. In 1939 Rome had only 700,000 inhabitants served by sixty-two parishes. By the time John became Pope the population was over 2 million, the number of parishes had risen to 190, and the building boom showed no sign of slackening. Rome had never lacked priests. There were over 3000: but most of them worked in the Curia or were religious assigned to the Roman universities. Very few were engaged in pastoral work. At the Rome Synod John gave the statistics himself: there were 220 diocesan priests and 370 religious, making 590 priests in all (Alberigo, p. 310). Clearly Rome needed a bishop who would think seriously about its pastoral problems.

Almost exactly a year after Pius XII's belated moment of truth, Pope John was addressing the Lenten preachers who were once more setting off to proclaim the good news to the people of Rome. He gave them some homely advice on preaching. It should be carefully prepared in both study and prayer. It should obey sound pedagogical principles. They should avoid the temptation of showing off with poetic or purple passages – it was a temptation he had not always avoided. 'Simplicity', he declared, 'is the preacher's greatest gift and the purest way to touch hearts and consciences'. He warned them against seeking for applause because it 'impeded the movement of grace in souls'. This reflected his own practice: he detested applause in church and tried, not very successfully, to stop it.

Finally, the proclamation of the truth had to go hand in hand with charity, or it would fail. 'You must remember', he exhorted his priests, 'that you are called to strengthen your brethren not' – pause for effect – 'to terrorise them' (Alberigo, pp. 278–80: this address was on February 10, 1959).

But John did not merely exhort others to preach well. He joined them in the hugger-mugger of the parishes of Rome, beginning in 1959 with the city centre and then gradually moving out towards the mushrooming suburbs. This was one of the causes of his popularity with the people of Rome: they did not have to go to St Peter's Square: the Pope had come to them.

However, his chosen instrument for the renewal of the diocese of Rome was not parish visits but the Synod. Throughout 1959 he devoted more time to the preparation of the Synod than to the preparation of the Council. In fairness one should add that at this stage there was not much he could do about the Council except sit back and wait for the response of the world's bishops. He saw the Synod as a response to the changed situation in Rome, and a way of coping with the fact that these 'new Romans' were often uprooted peasants whose links and relatives were elsewhere. In a letter to Archbishop Traglia, president of the Synod Commission, he said: 'The new spiritual demands (*nuove esigenze spirituali*) resulting from the present urban sprawl and development justify holding the Synod, and make something which in the past might have seemed superfluous now not only legitimate but necessary' (*Lettere*, p. 178: dated October 25, 1959). From which we may safely conclude that some in the Curia were arguing that there was no need for a Synod and – more boldly – that it was a waste of time and effort.

It has been suggested that the Synod was a 'sop' thrown by Pope John to keep the Curia happy while awaiting the Council, the real and decisive 'event of the Spirit'. Giuseppe Alberigo has a more sophisticated version of this argument. He says that the Curia sought to delay the Council by concentrating on the Roman Synod and the revision of the Code of Canon Law. Given the great age of the Pope and the canonical fact that his successor would not be obliged to carry out any of his projects, this delaying tactic could lead to the scrapping of the whole idea (Alberigo, p. 74: he does, however, say 'perhaps', '*forse*').

This is almost exactly the reverse of the truth. Pope John wanted the Synod very much for the reasons already given. It was not imposed on him by anyone. It is true that the Synod was not part of his original 'inspiration'; but once the idea was put to him, he seized upon it eagerly. In his opening address to the Synod on January 24, 1960, he 'revealed' that 'someone' (most probably Angelo Dell'Acqua) had said to him: 'An ecumenical council is a fine idea, but why not first of all think about the immediate needs of Rome and hold a diocesan Synod. In fifty years its population has gone from 400,000 in 1900 to over two million today' (Alberigo, p. 306). This was always the reasoning to which he returned: the needs of the diocese of Rome were urgent and must be met.

But the Synod also appealed to him because it was part of the post-Tridentine tradition. It was the constitutional way to reform a diocese according to Trent and St Charles Borromeo. Experience backed up history. Radini Tedeschi, his bishop, had held a Synod in Bergamo in 1911; he himself had organised a Synod in Venice in 1957. There had been Synods in many Italian dioceses and all over the world; yet Rome lagged behind. He liked the idea of this being the *first* Synod of the diocese of Rome. He was pleased to inaugurate it in the Lateran, as the cathedral of the diocese the proper place, exactly one year after announcing it. It also proved that he could get things moving swiftly.

And that was the link with the Council. The Synod was a practice run. It was designed to answer the question: can pastors and theologians work together harmoniously and at speed? The answer appeared to be 'yes'. The eight sub-commissions had worked well; religious and diocesan priests got on well. John was pleased. On June 18, 1959, he received all the Commission members and greeted them with the words of St Augustine: '*Tales inveni quales desideravi*' ('I've found you to be just the people I wanted') (*Lettere*, p. 182). On July 31, 1959, he wrote to Giuseppe Battaglia, bishop of Faenza: 'The sharing out of the work is proving highly effective, and the good will shown on all sides surpasses my expectations' (*Ibid.*, p. 151). John had precise comments to make on the draft texts, praising the way the *magisterium* sub-commission had dealt with the desirability of reading the Catholic press:

> Between the old tradition that clerics should read only papers or books that contained the pure substance of Catholic doctrine and the habit of reading worldly or risky publications exclusively, the priest must make a conscientious choice, remembering the maxim *nec prope, nec procul* (neither too close nor too far away) (*Lettere*, p. 488).

He had high hopes that the Synod would blaze a trail for the Council.

But nothing of the kind happened. There was a gap between Pope John's optimistic expectations and the actual event. His theology and theory of the Synod were fine, but its achievement was meagre. When the 755 pre-packaged articles that were the conclusions of the Synod were read out, without discussion or debate, the 'good will on all sides' he had detected the previous summer was dissipated. The only function of the Synod members was to applaud what had previously been decided upon. The Synod's detailed provisions, moreover, looked like an attempt to stem the tide of modernity; they did not suggest the rustle of a new Pentecostal springtime.

Roman priests were told to wear the cassock or black soutane at all times. The tonsure or shaven crown was insisted upon. Worldly events such as the opera and the race-meeting were placed out of bounds for clerics. Priests were not to use cars except in case of necessity, and never alone with a woman (*solus cum sola*) in any circumstances. They were warned off faith-healers and psychoanalysts. They were to show great prudence in their dealings with Communists, Freemasons and heretics (*Prima Romana Synodus*, Vatican Polyglot Press, 1960). Those who had hoped that the Council would be a great ecumenical event were mystified and appalled by the Roman Synod. It looked like the dashing of all their hopes. Conversely, those in the Roman Curia who did not like the idea of the Council – it meant foreigners in Rome – rubbed their hands with glee over the Synod. 'If the Council is going to be anything like the Synod', said one of them, 'it will be the most innocuous council in the history of the Church' (see *L'uomo che non divenne papa*, p. 272). There was no longer any need to bother about the Council. The curial critics had been right, and Pope John proved wrong, at least in a juridical sense: it was illogical to have the Synod precede the Council, since all its decrees would have to be rewritten in the light of the Council. In which case, it would be better to wait. The Synodal Decrees, therefore, were obsolescent almost on the day – July 29, 1960 – they were solemnly proclaimed. They were still-born. They were widely ignored.

Was Pope John disappointed by the world-wide hostile reaction to the Roman Synod? He certainly felt it had been misunderstood. In an official letter to Cardinal Micara he thanked the old man for standing aside and allowing him to act as bishop of Rome, an elaborate and unnecessary courtesy. But then he goes on to explain that the Synodal Decrees, though they may seem a little arid or heavy, when read as a whole 'yield up their beauty and inner coherence, with occasional delicate touches that result in an unexpected psalmody, bringing clarity to the mind and savour to the heart' (*Lettere*, pp. 211–12: letter dated June 29, 1960). He also believed the decrees were written in excellent Latin. So he thought highly of his Synod and defended it. In an address to the Roman clergy, he rounded on his critics and dismissed them as so many 'doubting Thomases'. It was an anticipation of the way he would denounce the 'prophets of gloom' (see Abbott, p. 712) in his opening speech to the Council. It also showed his obstinacy or, less pejoratively, his resolution. But he knew it had not been received with universal acclaim. In private he consoled himself with the thought that 'nothing is perfect in this world. If there are inadequacies or futilities my successor can always put that right by celebrating the *second* Roman Synod. It will always be the humble Pope John who celebrated the *first*' (*Lettere*, p. 182: to Capovilla). Pope John was perhaps over-confident that history would vindicate him on the importance of the Roman Synod. But two further points need to be made before the Synod is written off as a total failure.

The most important is that John was well aware of the difference between a Synod and a Council. It was an elementary topic for an undergraduate essay. That there was no debate at the Synod did not seem shocking to Roncalli; in Bergamo in 1911, Radini Tedeschi, his prestige as a canonist assured, had written all the decrees in advance. But it did not follow that the Council would be modelled on the pattern of the Synod. On the contrary. A Synod is not a teaching body. It is a meeting of one diocese and directed towards its disciplinary reform. Only when several dioceses combine is there a local Council, and only when the whole Church meets in Council with the Pope does the Church display the full panoply of its *magisterium* or teaching authority. A Synod does not have to teach; teaching is of the essence of a Council and the only way to get at doctrinal truth is to hammer it out in argument, but always in the context of charity. A Synod, therefore, is a predictable event, and its conclusions are foregone. No one knows what will happen at a Council. Its conclusions cannot be programmed in advance. John knew that Pius IX had tried to manipulate the preparations for Vatican I – and had failed. He did not propose to make that mistake. He, and we, would only discover what the Council was really about when it actually met.

Secondly, one has to note that John's own personal contribution to the Roman Synod, discreet as it was, set it firmly on the path of pastoral charity. He felt very strongly about the way 'ex-priests' (the term is theologically improper, and he avoided it) were treated. The Church said that they should be avoided (*vitandi*) while the Concordat stipulated that they should not be employed in state posts. This excluded teaching, for which they were quite well prepared, and the postal service to which, in desperation, they might be attracted. Contemporaries of John at the Roman seminary had been caught in this trap. The problem was particularly acute in Rome where so many 'ex-priests' had been trained and whither they drifted in hope and anonymity. In this context, decree 35 of the Roman Synod, written personally by Pope John and undemocratically imposed on the Synod (like everything else), represented a dramatic new departure:

> Priests labouring under censure or other penalties, or who have perhaps unhappily left the Church, should never cease to trust in the mercy of the Lord or the humanity and decency of ecclesiastical superiors. Other priests, especially their friends, moved by heavenly charity, should strive to build up this trust. No one is to be denied the friendship of his fellow priests or consolation in his difficulties or even material help should it be needed (*Prima Romana Synodus*, Vatican Polyglot Press, 1960, p. 21).

That 'ex-priests' should be given money was as startling a notion as that Rome was missionary territory.

John practised what he preached within the limits imposed by his office. His confessor, Mgr Alfredo Cavagna, and his secretary, Mgr Loris Capovilla, were bombarded with requests from priests who, impatient with the delaying tactics of the Curia, wanted the Pope to intercede on their behalf. John's instructions were clear: firmness on the principles, gentleness in their execution. His two aides were told that they must assure these men that their requests had reached the Pope, but that the 'proper channels' would have to be respected (*Lettere*, p. 532). Sometimes Pope John annotated these cries for help. Here is one case:

> X is an unhappy man who should not have been ordained. His psychological state justifies a release from priestly duties, and also financial support that will help him to resign without causing either scandal or shock [*admiratio*]. He deserves mercy *coram Deo et hominibus* [before God and men] (*Lettere*, p. 531: May 1, 1962).

So X would have received an 'annulment' of his ordination. Y was less fortunate: 'I have read the memo of the unhappy Y. Evidently this is a pathological case, and I'm sorry that the act of mercy that would save him from despair is not being recommended to the Pope' (*Ibid.*, August 6, 1962). He was 'only the Pope'. He could not bring himself to bend the rules or leap-frog over his subordinates – he was supposed to trust them. But, as he told the Roman Synod, nothing in his pontificate brought him greater suffering than having to listen to 'the groanings of priestly souls which come to me not just from Rome but from all parts of the world' (*Ibid.*, p. 533). John did what he could. But Bonnot paints too rosy a picture when he says that in this pontificate 'marriages were blessed, situations normalised, jobs secured' (Bonnet, p. 77).

For all his compassion, John had not the slightest intention of relaxing the rule of celibacy for the Western Church. We have already seen that in February 1959 Igino Cardinale thought that the abolition of mandatory celibacy might well be on the agenda of the Council. Aware of this opening to the future, an Italian Dominican, Fr Raimondo Spiazzi, published a 'sensational' article in the austere pages of the *Monitor Ecclesiasticus* (vol. no. 84, 1959). His argument was banal but astonishing to the media: the historical evidence for the present discipline of clerical celibacy was extremely shaky. This was a tabu topic. But Spiazzi made out a good case. Even the Fathers of the Council of Trent did not think that clerical celibacy was a matter of 'divine positive law', nor could they since there were validly ordained married priests in communion with Rome. Reporters, unaccustomed to reading the *Monitor Ecclesiasticus*, thrilled to this exciting topic, rushed to their telephones, and told their news editors that Pope John, the radical, was not averse to dropping the rule of celibacy.

They were hasty and wrong. There had been a number of attempts in John's lifetime to bring up the question of clerical celibacy. In 1898 a bogus bull was circulated in which Leo XIII was said to have relaxed the ban on clerical marriage especially for Latin America. The effects were catastrophic, but the fact that this counterfeit won credence proved the idea was not absurd. In 1911 – a bad year for authors – a work by French Abbé J. Claraz, *Le mariage des prêtres*, was rather predictably placed on the Index of Forbidden Books. The author, chagrined, put his book into practice and disappeared from the face of theology. Worse was to follow. In 1920 a group of Czech priests known as *Jednota* campaigned for priestly marriage (Schillebeeckx, *Clerical celibacy*, p. 41). Roncalli knew about *Jednota*. We know this because he kept beside him a quotation from a letter of Benedict XV to Archbishop Frantisek Kordac, Archbishop of Prague: 'The law of ecclesiastical celibacy, as the chief glory of the Catholic priesthood and the well-spring of its best virtues, is to be kept holy and inviolate. At no point in the future would the Holy See wish to abolish or mitigate this law' (*Lettere*, p. 532: the text came from AAS, 1920, pp. 33–4).

All this was in Pope John's mind when he addressed the Roman Synod on January 27, 1960. The row over the Spiazzi articles was an invitation to show his hand. Silence would have been interpreted as weakness, especially since Ottaviani was by now demanding the moral execution of Fr Spiazzi. Others said that Pope John should not have pre-empted the judgement of the Council on so important an issue. But he may have felt that any hesitation on priestly celibacy would have given rise to dangerous expectations. Yet he was also a reformer. In the eleventh century, he claimed, the real reformers were those who *imposed* clerical celibacy after a period of scandalous corruption. So John's conclusion was: 'The law of ecclesiastical celibacy, and the concern to make it prevail, remain a permanent reminder of the heroic age when the Church of Christ had to do battle and succeeded to the extent that it earned the threefold title that is the emblem of its victory: "The Church of Christ, free, chaste, Catholic" ' (*Lettere*, p. 133). Strategically, this was a shrewd argument. It is undeniable that the Gregorian reform 'became the starting-point of one of the most exciting spiritual and mystical movements the West has known' (Schillebeeckx, *Clerical celibacy*, p. 36). But Pope John's appeal to the heroic age could not put a stop to the theological debate.

John's second address to the Synod on November 27, 1960, was concerned with many other aspects of the priestly ministry. He urged his priests to get a proper balance between the 'direct' and the 'indirect' ministry: it was no good spending all one's time editing the parish magazine and counting the collection if these were alibis for not meeting people. This warning was particularly relevant in Rome where members of the Curia could become so immersed in the 'indirect' ministry that they completely lost touch with the 'direct' ministry. In the sixteenth century the hope was that curialists might spend their week-ends ministering to galley-slaves; in the twentieth century one curial archbishop was persuaded that he still had a 'direct' ministry because he preached once a week to sisters. John urged his priests to take the same pastoral approach to their ministry as he did to his. He had received whatever pastoral wisdom he had, he told them, from Gregory the Great's *Regula Pastoralis* (Pastoral Guide) 'which has kept me good company for almost half a century, and brought me untellable joy so many times in my life' (Alberigo, p. 313). All great spiritual writers are contemporaries.

In his Coronation homily Pope John had made it clear that he understood his office in pastoral and spiritual terms. The 'temporal' power of the papacy was gone for good, and he did not feel nostalgic for it. This allowed him to have a new relationship with the city of Rome and its civic authorities. They were no longer in competition. The Rome of Catholicism and the Rome, capital of Italy, could live together in peace, in what John always described by the almost untranslatable word *convivenza* (harmonious living together). People had no difficulty in distinguishing between the different Romes. John wrote in his *Journal*:

> What seems clear and providential is that all these crowds of Italians and still more of 'foreigners' who come to Rome know at once how to distinguish between the sacred and the profane; that is, Rome the capital of Catholicism and seat of the univeral Roman pontiff, and the Rome of ancient ruins and the whirlwind of secular and . . . worldly living which rages even on the banks of the Tiber. All this, however, with mutual respect among the various human elements, and no unfriendliness between Italians and non-Italians (*Journal*, p. 344: dated July–August, 1962).

This text indicates that the 'reconciliation' proclaimed in 1929 had by now become a reality. There was no longer, as in the 1930s, a gradiloquent dispute about which Rome was the true heir of ancient Rome. Nor did John emulate Pius XII in turning every election into a battle for the 'soul' of Rome. So, quite apart from anything else, John believed that the Council would be an opportunity to demonstrate to the world the *convivenza* that now prevailed: 'Government and municipal authorities are now busily co-operating so that the Council may be worthy of Rome as the spiritual centre of the world, and that Rome's arrangements for the accommodation, civic hospitality and the honourable treatment of guests from all over the world may excel all the finest achievements of her past' (*Ibid.*, pp. 344–5). That was one way of putting it.

The story of Pope John's relationship with Rome would be incomplete if a major concern of the last year of his life were overlooked. He did not leave his mark on Rome by new buildings. But he did transfer the diocesan curia of Rome to its proper place in the Lateran Palace alongside his cathedral. John seemed to have stumbled into this decision almost by accident. The minutes of the Commission set up to consider the transfer have been published (*Lettere*, pp. 408–9). Here one can see Pope John at work, cajoling a group of cardinals to do his bidding and – even more – see the point of his decision. John recalled that when he was a seminarian the diocesan offices were housed in a few poky and obscure rooms overlooking the Piazza Sant'Agostino. Later they moved to the somewhat grander Palazzo Marescotti, Piazza della Pigna. But even that proved inadequate for a diocese that had expanded so rapidly – now it counted over 3 million people. John surveyed the room over the top of his spectacles. There was the aged

Cardinal Clemente Micara, vicar of Rome, and Cardinal Luigi Traglia, his deputy. They had been keeping something from him. John said: 'The news has just reached my ears that it has been decided to transfer the diocesan curia to San Callisto and that furniture and equipment have already been moved in' (*Ibid.*, p. 408). It was the familiar complaint: 'I'm only the Pope around here, nobody tells me anything'. The difference was that this time it was his position as bishop of Rome that had been usurped.

The minutes do not tell us why John opposed the move to the Palazzo San Callisto, but it is not difficult to guess. San Callisto is the monumentally huge 1930s neo-baroque barracks in the heart of Trastevere. It would no doubt have been convenient as a site for the diocesan offices. But it would have been symbolically all wrong, for it would have made the offices of the Roman diocese a mere appendage of the Roman Curia. John had his counter-proposal ready: move the diocesan offices to St John Lateran. This would revivify the place and make it what it ought to be, the true and living centre of the diocese of Rome. He had been to St John Lateran on June 24, 1962, feast of St John the Baptist, and spoken at length about his desire, as *Romanae ecclesiae episcopus* (bishop of the Church of Rome), to make his cathedral the heart of diocesan life. 'From today onwards', he declared, 'the Lateran is no longer on the edge of the city, but at its effective centre' (*Lettere*, p. 408). Historical, theological and above all pastoral reasons led John to begin the reanimation of the cathedral and Palazzo of St John Lateran.

So one cannot really say that 'Roncalli was much less preoccupied with Rome' than were his predecessors (Hales, p. 86). But he was preoccupied in a different way and for different reasons. Rome concerned him because he was its bishop. He recognised that others had other responsibilities. As he said to the president of Italy, Antonio Segni, who visited him on July 3, 1962:

> This Rome of ours is certainly a father's house in which there are 'many mansions'; 'many mansions' indeed, clearly distinct by nature and grace.
> But on both descends light from a common source, the light of a loving and divine Providence . . . The tasks of each one are precisely defined: the Pope in the Vatican is one thing, the President in the Quirinale is another.

So from Rome we move outwards to consider Pope John's Italian policies.

Chapter 17

The Italian connection

It came about that Italy took over the role once occupied by the Papal States. But Italy still provided the providential earthly basis of the Holy See and its point of insertion into the world. This is the link between 1848 and today

(Arturo Carlo Jemolo, in *Chiesa e Stato in Italia negli ultimi cento anni*, Turin, 1963, p. 540).

No pope can fail to have an Italian policy. He has to make up his mind how much, or how little, he will involve himself in the affairs of the country he sees from his window. Pope John's originality was that he presented himself from the outset as a spiritual pope, a pastor, who made a clear distinction between the papacy and the republic of Italy. No longer in competition, they could live together in that spirit of harmonious collaboration he called *convivenza*. The result of making this distinction was that John's Italian policy was marked by 'disengagement' (*disimpegno*) and 'reserve' (*riserbo*). These are the terms he spontaneously uses whenever he thinks about the relationship between Church and state. He wanted the Church to withdraw from the immediate party-political battle-ground.

But this did not mean that he was washing his hands of Italian affairs or turning the Torre San Giovanni into an ivory tower. He thought that once the Church was detached from the hurly-burly of everyday politics, it would be better placed to speak about the rights and duties of Christians in the social and political sphere. Thus his 'disengagement' made *Mater et Magistra*, his first great social encyclical, possible. So although this chapter will be largely concerned with Italy, its significance is universal.

However, John's Italian policy soon ran into difficulties and had to be fought for. It was so utterly different from the policy of Pius XII who frankly exploited Catholic Action and the Christian Democrats to keep Italy safe from Communism (see pp. 242–3 above). Yet the 'men of Pius XII' were still at their posts. Ottaviani continued to threaten and bluster at the Holy Office. Ruffini reigned in Sicily. Cardinal Giuseppe Siri, archbishop of Genoa, was in complete control of the Italian bishops. He was president of the episcopal conference (CEI), president of its Catholic Action committee, president of the Italian social weeks, and much else besides. He preferred the precision of commitment to the vagueness of 'disengagement'. He held that through the Christian Democrats, the Vatican and the Church exercised a powerful influence for good on Italian society that it would be manifest folly to renounce. His friends in the Roman Curia were Tardini and Ottaviani.

Another favourite of Pius XII, Fr Riccardo Lombardi, S.J., was still piping the old tunes, unaware that there was a new conductor. His anti-Communism was based on the premise that 'communism forms a whole in which it is impossible to make distinctions between ideology, programmes and tactics' (quoted in Magister, p. 62). In *Pacem in Terris* Pope John was to make the very distinctions that Lombardi had declared impossible. Moreover, Lombardi continued to present the Pope as the lynch-pin of the entire Italian political system. 'Only the Pope', he proclaimed, 'reckons history in centuries, not in years, and so is far removed from the passions of the hour' (*Ibid.*, p. 84). John was perfectly prepared to look at history in the long perspective of the centuries, but for that very reason he was also open to the possibility that something new might just be happening. So by the end of 1960 a strange situation was reached in which Italian churchmen, acting ostensibly in the name of the Pope, continued to propound a policy of which the Pope strongly disapproved. But since Pope John was for the most part silent on such issues, it was understandable that they should carry on as before out of habit, persuaded that nothing had changed.

John's disapproval was patent, but it was at first confined to his household and the pages of his journal. On August 13, 1961, he deplored the way bishops were being diverted from their primary task of preaching the Gospel:

> The impediment may most easily arise from human judgements in the political sphere, which are diverse and contradictory according to various ways of thinking and feeling. The Gospel is far above these opinions and parties, which agitate and disturb social life and all mankind. The Pope reads the Gospel and with his Bishops comments on it; and all, without trying to further any worldly interests, must inhabit that city of peace, undisturbed and blessed, whence descends the divine law which can rule in wisdom over the earthly city and the whole world. This in fact is what wise men [*saggi*] expect from the Church, this and nothing else (*Journal*, p. 338).

As usual in John's lexicon the 'wise men' (*saggi*) were contrasted with the zealots (*zeloti*). His reflection on the role of Bishops in politics may seem banal. But they represented a break with the past and were a *cri de coeur* wrung from him as he observed the behaviour of the Italian Episcopal Conference with its president, Siri, in the van. Siri was beyond doubt a 'zealot'. Precise and very painful events lay just beneath the surface of Pope John's apparently serene retreat reflections in the summer of 1961. The whole story can now be told thanks to the hitherto unpublished material found in Giancarlo Zizola's two articles, 'Rapporti tra Moro e Giovanni XXIII' (*Panorama*, May 10 and May 17, 1982).

On May 18, 1960, *l'Osservatore Romano* published an article under the heading

Punti Fermi (Here we stand). It was unsigned, but Cardinals Tardini, Ottaviani and Siri had worked on it. The article reaffirmed the hierarchy's right and duty to issue commands in the political and social sphere. The bishops, it explained, were alone competent to judge the legitimacy of 'coalitions' or 'alliances'. This was a *moral* judgement that could not be left to the whim of the faithful. *Punti Fermi* recalled that there was 'an insurmountable opposition between Christian dogma and the Marxist system', and forbade Catholics to 'belong to, support or in any way collaborate with those who adopt and follow the Marxist ideology and its applications'. In the pontificate of Pius XII such an article would have been boring in its predictability; in the pontificate of Pope John it seemed disappointing and even faintly shocking. Where was the 'good will towards all men'? One could not both claim to be a 'spiritual pope' and interfere in politics in so blatant a fashion. It wasn't known who wrote the article. But it was assumed that the Pope approved of what appeared in his official newspaper.

Among those disappointed by *Punti Fermi* was Aldo Moro, leader of the Christian Democrats. For some time he had been trying to broaden the basis of his government by forming an alliance with the Socialists (PSI). This was the strategy known as 'the opening to the left' (*apertura a sinistro*). Pope John had already been faced by this problem in Venice (see p. 258 above) and was not unsympathetic towards Moro's case.

What was probably true in 1956 had become self-evident by 1960. Come what may, the Christian Democrats were going to remain in power. Foreigners might scoff at the annual musical chairs of ministers, but in reality Italian political life had great stability. But this stability was threatened. Moro's idea was that by the 'opening to the left' the Christian Democrats would cease to be merely the party of the Church and Confindustria, the employers' organisation, and their drift to the right where the neo-Fascists beckoned would be halted. The Christian Democratic Party would be revivified by being recalled to its origins when, far from being the Italian conservative party, it had been committed to social justice and reform. Italian democracy, still in 1960 a fragile growth, would be greatly strengthened if peaceful and democratic change were shown to be possible. Then the siren voices of totalitarianisms to left and right would lose their alluring charm. Such threats were not imaginary. The head of the Secret Service (SIFAR), General Giovanni De Lorenzo, was already building up his network in Confindustria which led to the abortive *coup* of 1964 (see Richard Collin, *The De Lorenzo Gambit*, or, in more popular vein, Morris West, *The Salamander*). The 'opening to the left', finally, offered a more palpable advantage: it was hoped that in alliance with the Socialists the Christian Democrats might reverse the appalling losses they had suffered in the November 6, 1959, municipal elections when they lost over a million votes.

But such was the power of the Church in Italy that Moro's whole scheme would fail if it were opposed by the bishops. *Punti Fermi* made it clear that they would oppose it, vehemently. It talked about Marxists rather than Communists: this was to make the point that the Socialists were considered to be Marxist fellow-travellers. Also at issue – and indeed the heart of the matter – was the autonomy of the laity in politics. If the Christian Democrats were not to be allowed to make up their own minds about alliances and coalitions, then they would remain tied to the episcopal apron-strings and never attain the kind of political maturity that French or American Catholics considered normal. Where did Pope John stand?

It was quite evident where the official spokesmen of the Italian bishops stood. The local Catholic papers, almost invariably edited from the diocesan curia, attacked Aldo Moro as both heretic and traitor. *Verona Fedele* assured its readers that the Lord had already condemned Moro to hell-fire (an ironical judgement in view of his eventual death, tortured and murdered by the Red Brigades in 1978). Cardinal Siri inspired an article in his own paper, *Il Nuovo Cittadino,* called 'An Open Letter to Moro' that was a litany of insults and abuse. He followed this up with a personal letter, soon published, informing Moro in case he did not know that the Church's attitude to Communism had not changed. It ended: 'What has happened makes one deeply fearful for the future. In the name of God I beg of you to reflect on your responsibility and the consequences of your actions' (*Panorama,* May 10, 1982, p. 251).

But no matter how hard he reflected in his office in the Piazza del Gesù, Moro could be forgiven for feeling that these attacks were directed to the wrong address. He was not, in 1961, proposing an alliance with the Communists. His Christian conscience was clear. As he understood Catholic social doctrine from his old mentor Cardinal Montini, its guiding principle was the common good rather than the defence of sectional interests.

Moreover, the 'alliances' and 'coalitions' denounced by *Punti Fermi* were no longer just a theoretical possibility: they were actually being set up in Milan, Florence, Genoa (Siri's own fief) and forty other large Italian towns. But this merely increased the venom of the attacks on Moro. He desperately needed some ecclesiastical support. In Milan, the curially influenced newspaper, *Italia,* had joined the pack in condemning him. But Cardinal Montini promptly sacked its clerical editor and replaced him with a distinguished lay historian, Giuseppe Lazzati, whose democratic credentials were unimpeachable. That was encouraging. Even more encouraging was the total silence of *l'Osservatore Romano* which feigned not to know that anything at all was happening. It was assumed, correctly, that Pope John was responsible for this diplomatic silence.

But Moro needed more than silent acquiescence. He needed Pope John on his side. His deputy, Giovanni Battista Scaglia, was a Bergamesque and editor of *Studium,* a review for Catholic graduates founded by Cardinal Montini. Scaglia was in touch with Mgr Andrea Spada, since 1938 the editor of *l'Eco di Bergamo,* the only paper Roncalli read every day of his adult life. Spada was a friend of the Pope, who had once toyed with the idea of bringing him to Rome as editor of *l'Osservatore Romano* (*Lettere,* p. 176) but instead had made him president of the newly founded Conference of Catholic Editors. Spada met Moro on January 27, 1961, and suggested that he should state his case in a personal memorandum for the Pope. Moro wrote his report, Spada delivered it to Pope John and told him that in his judgement the Christian Democratic leadership should be trusted and that the unjust attacks on them should cease.

However, Moro's memo and Spada's audience had no immediate or perceptible effects. The project for a coalition (*giunta*) in Sicily brought a thunderous condemnation from Cardinal Ruffini. Siri sent him a telegram of 'heartiest congratulations'. It seemed that an impasse had been reached which Pope John was unable to breach.

But although John did not intervene directly on the 'opening to the left' issue, he was not inactive. He tried to raise the level of debate above sterile polemics. On April 11, 1961, he received the Prime Minister, Amintore Fanfani, and made his clearest statement to date on the relationship between the Church and Italy. The *Risorgimento* which had unified Italy at the expense of abolishing the Papal States, was a providential event. No Pope had dared to say that before:

> The celebration this year of the hundredth anniversary of Italian unification
> is a cause of great joy for Italy, and both of us, on the two banks of the
> Tiber, share the same feeling of gratitude towards Providence who, despite
> vicissitudes and conflicts which enflamed passions, as happens in every age,
> had guided this most favoured part of Europe (*questa porzione elettissima*)
> towards a position of respect and honour in the concert of nations . . .
> If we look serenely at the events of a more or less distant past, the truth
> of the maxim comes home: history conceals and reveals all (DMC, III, p.
> 205).

John recalled Pius XI's achievement in signing the Lateran Treaties and said that they had paved the way for 'the true and perfect unity of race, language and religion that had been the hope of the best Italians'. However, this did not mean, he hastened to add, that there was any confusion between the roles of Church and state:

> The special situation of the Catholic Church and the Italian State – two
> organisms which differ in structure, character, level and aims – presupposes
> a certain reserve [*riserbo*] in the relationship which, based on courtesy and
> respect, makes the occasions on which their representatives do meet from
> time to time all the more agreeable (*Ibid.*).

This speech was a landmark. It became known as 'The Wider Tiber' speech (*Tevere più largo*).

Since Fanfani the prime minister had fully endorsed the line of Moro and Scaglia on the need for an 'opening to the left', Pope John's 'reserve' meant in effect that he did not propose to interfere in political choices which properly belonged to the electors and their chosen representatives. He was abstaining. He would not seek to exercise jurisdiction in political matters. He was repudiating *Punti Fermi*. It followed that Siri and his supporters in the Roman Curia were being dropped, however gently, by the Pope.

This context helps to explain the significance of *Mater et Magistra*. Intended for May 15, 1961, to mark the seventieth anniversary of Leo XIII's *Rerum Novarum*, it did not in fact appear until July 15. This delay suggests an argument behind the scenes about its opportuneness. It also meant that the encyclical appeared just as the Roman Curia was going *ad aquas* (that is, on holiday) so there would be less opportunity of concerted moves. *Mater et Magistra* was eagerly scrutinised by Italian bishops and politicians to see on whose side Pope John had come down. On the whole Moro and his friends felt encouraged while the Siri camp was discomfited.

Mater et Magistra calmly accepts 'the welfare state' as an expression of the 'common good'. That may sound unremarkable, but Pius XII had recoiled from the prospect of 'communal kitchens, free health services and free education' (see Hales, p. 45). John, on the other hand, welcomed the fact that there had been 'an increase in social relationships' and 'a development in man's social life'. He called this process 'socialisation', a term borrowed from Pierre Teilhard de Chardin. Teilhard held that the inter-locking of human destinies through technological developments was a form of spiritual progress since it asserted the Christian value of inter-dependence. The sense of belonging to one world, to spaceship earth, grew. Commentators who wished to stress 'the continuity of Catholic social doctrine' tied themselves into intricate semantic knots as they tried to explain that 'socialisation' did not and could not possibly mean 'socialism', since 'socialism' had been condemned by previous popes. The word 'socialisation' did not even appear in the Latin text which used expressions like *socialium rationum incrementa* or *socialium rerum progressus* (see Campbell-Johnston, p. 382). But it *was* found in the translations.

Whether 'socialisation' implied 'socialism' was largely a matter of definition. But if 'socialism' meant the welfare state, then it was plain that Pope John approved of it: 'It (socialisation) is an effect and a cause of the growing intervention of the state even in matters of such intimate concern to the individual as health and education, the choice of a career, and the care and rehabilitation of the physically and mentally handicapped' (*Mater et Magistra*, No. 48). But doesn't this, Cardinal Siri was soon to ask, subordinate the individual to the amorphous mass, the monstrous Leviathan evoked by Pius XII in his broadcast to Austrian Catholics on September 14, 1952? Had not this great pontiff precisely warned them not to submit to 'an all-embracing socialisation' (*allumfassende Sozialisierung*)? He had (see AAS 44, 1952, p. 792).

Pope John anticipated this objection, and put it in his encyclical: 'Must we then conclude that increased social action necessarily reduces men to the condition of being merely automatons? By no means' (No. 48). The safeguard against the potential evils of state control and excessive bureaucracy were twofold. First, 'a healthy view of the public good must be present and operative in men invested with public authority' (No. 51). Second, 'the numerous intermediate bodies and corporate enterprises' should enjoy real autonomy (No. 52). It was the classic 'liberal' defence against the totalitarian state. The 'numerous intermediate bodies' – political parties, trades unions, the judiciary, the broadcasting services, the press – should be genuinely independent, and through their stimulating inter-play the common good would be served.

But the acceptance of the welfare state was not the only originality of *Mater et Magistra*. Though it is disingenuously presented as merely 'confirming and making more specific the teaching of our predecessors', its whole approach was novel. It is clearly referring to the real world of 1961. Gone is the semi-feudal world evoked by Leo XIII in which 'the simple workman, surrounded by his family, settles down to his frugal but sufficient meal, the just reward of his labour' (Hales, p. 45). John's world is that of colleges of further education, the European Economic Community (which Italy joined from the outset) and the United Nations. He was optimistic about them all. This marked a new tone in 'Catholic social teaching'. John does not scold. He welcomes the good wherever he finds it. In Pius XI and Pius XII one sometimes got the impression that the world was being lectured at and castigated from the outside by an irate headmaster who knew better. 'Catholic social doctrine' in the 1930s and 1940s brought comfort to Latin dictators like Franco in Spain and Salazar in Portugal, both of whom claimed to be implementing its principal of *interclassismo,* the harmonious collaboration of all that was the Catholic response to the Marxist class-war. John did not speak from the outside or adopt a superior tone. The Church was *Mater* (Mother) as well as *Magistra* (Teacher). John eventually revealed that he had got the phrase *Mater et Magistra* from Pope Innocent III's address to the Fourth Lateran Council (Alberigo, p. 348). Few could compete with him in 'thinking in centuries' while keeping an eye on the present.

Mater et Magistra interested the CIA, worried about where the 'opening to the left' might lead. A good researcher would have discovered that the encyclical owed much to the 47th Semaine Sociale which met at Grenoble in July 1960 to discuss '*Socialisation et Personne Humaine*' (Campbell-Johnston, p. 383). So behind *Mater et Magistra* one could descry the Dominicans of *Economie et*

Humanisme and the Jesuits of *Action Populaire*. Though James W. Spain's CIA report comes later, it reflects accurately enough the thinking of John's closest advisors at the time. Fr Roberto Tucci, son of a Neapolitan father and a Scottish Episcopalian mother, was the young editor of *Civiltà Cattolica*. He told Spain: 'You are very interested in what our changes will mean vis-à-vis the Communists. I am even more interested in what they will mean in Spain and Portugal' (Spain, p. 7). Mgr Pietro Pavan, professor of sociology at the Lateran university (John had raised his old college to this dignity on May 17, 1959), brought the conversation back to Italy: 'In the past, when someone was for the Church, he was also for the Christian Democratic Party. But now there are good men who are against Christian Democracy, but that does not mean they have to be against the Church' (*Ibid.*, p. 10). And that, paradoxically, was a proposition which intelligent Christian Democrats like Moro approved of.

So it was in Italy that *Mater et Magistra*, though addressed to the whole Catholic world, had its most immediate application. Not that it settled all the controversies. The human mind is endlessly resourceful in rejecting what it finds uncongenial. Cardinal Siri continued his anti-Moro campaign, but he seemed more and more to be beating the air. In arguing over the letter of *Mater et Magistra* one could so easily miss its spirit.

After this long flash-back, we can now return to Pope John's journal for August 13, 1961 and begin to appreciate its real meaning and richness:

> It is very important to insist that all bishops should act in the same way: may the Pope's example be a lesson and encouragement to them all. The bishops are more exposed to the temptation of meddling immoderately in matters that are not their business, and this is why the Pope must admonish them not to take part in any political or controversial arguments, and not to declare for one faction or section rather than another. They are to preach to all alike, and in general terms, justice, charity, meekness, gentleness and the other evangelical virtues, courteously defending the rights of the Church when these are offended or compromised (*Journal*, p. 331).

From this we may infer that John had 'admonished' the Italian bishops, and no doubt their president, Cardinal Siri, but to little avail. The theocratic habits instilled by Pius XII could not be eradicted so easily. What Pope John described as 'immoderate meddling', Siri considered to be his ordinary, everyday and – he would have added – *sacred* duty. Not much room for compromise there.

Pope John had another objection to the behaviour of the Italian bishops. Their passionate involvement in politics led them not only to wild and intemperate language, but to string-pulling and intrigues:

> At all times and especially just now, the Bishop must apply the balm of

gentleness to the wounds of mankind. He must beware of making any rash judgement or uttering abusive words about anyone, or letting himself be betrayed into flattery by threats, or in any way conniving in evil in the hope that by so doing he may be useful to someone; his manner must be grave, reserved and firm, while in his relations with others he must always be gentle and loving . . . Any effort or intrigue of a purely human nature is worth very little in these matters of worldly interest (*Journal*, p. 331).

'Grave, reserved and firm', but at the same time 'gentle and loving': this epitomised his own attitude. He said as much in his 'Wider Tiber' speech.

So 'disengagement' meant not only steering clear of interference in political matters but also giving up the intrigues, the *combinazioni* and *astuzie*, to which prelates in the land of Niccolò Machiavelli were particularly prone. John had never used such strong language before: 'Conniving in evil in the hope that by so doing he may be useful to someone'. What was he talking about?

One well-established feature of Italian life is '*clientalismo*' by which superiors do favours for friends or friends of friends. Networks of contacts are built up which at the limit become simply criminal: the *mafia* in the south and the *camorra* (underworld) in Naples are the best-known. Clerics enter the system by the use of the '*raccomandazione*'. A Sicilian worker, going to Turin to look for a job, would have to have a 'recommendation' or testimonial from his parish priest; a known Communist wouldn't get one at all. A 'recommendation' from a bishop, still more from a cardinal could smooth the career of a civil servant or a banker or a policeman, who would then do 'good turns' in gratitude. The obvious danger is that the borderline between the legal and the illegal can become blurred. Shady deals and the helping hand of charity went side by side. Cardinal Siri, though personally very austere, was in practice the national chaplain to Confindustria, the employers' organisation, and as such particularly exposed to temptations.

It would be wrong to suggest that the whole Italian Church was sunk in corruption; but it would be equally wrong to imagine that such temptations had not invaded the Vatican itself. John knew what was going on about him as the following story, from an impeccable source, illustrates. Any vagueness in the narrative is deliberate.

At about this time, summer 1961, a certain cardinal of aristocratic origins was on his death-bed. He had been engaged in the financial operations of the Vatican for many years. Pope John suddenly became worried that the aged cardinal might die unshriven, his soul in agony as much as his body. So he sent along a friar (usually described in hagiography as ' a humble friar') to hear the cardinal's last confession. The friar returned, rather crest-fallen, and reported that the relatives were blocking the ante-chambers, and refused to let him through. 'Just as I thought' said Pope John, by now angry, 'find an archbishop, they surely will not refuse an archbishop'. But they did. This was work for a cardinal. A cardinal was found who was able to pull rank, make his way through the relatives and hear the dying man's confession. The point of this puzzling story is that the nephews and nieces of the cardinal feared that if he made a final confession, he might feel obliged in conscience to change his will. John's own will was already carefully drawn up. No relatives would crowd around his death-bed: 'born poor', he wrote, 'I am particularly happy to die poor' (*Journal*, p. 367). 'Disengagement' had moral as well as political implications.

But it did not mean that he was uninterested in the details of practical politics. On the contrary. In February 1962 he called for and studied with great care Aldo Moro's prolix report to the eighth Christian Democratic Congress that had just met in Naples. It put the case for the 'opening to the left'. Andreotti joked that it was Moro's encyclical *Cauti Connubii* (Cautious Marriage) (Magister, p. 275). Pope John found that Moro's report was 'coherent'. In other words, it made sense. But just to make sure, he submitted it to the judgement of experts who concluded that it was 'not only in harmony with revelation but with the social doctrine of the Church from *Rerum Novarum* to *Mater et Magistra*' (*Panorama,* May 17, 1982, p. 246). That was an accolade. Moro was informed of this *nihil obstat*. He wrote to Pope John, thanking him for his 'paternal interest and understanding'. Composed in Moro's customary complex and oblique style (he later invented 'parallel convergences'), his letter defies all attempts at translation into passable English. The gist of it was that Moro pledged his loyalty to the Pope, the hierarchy and the social doctrine of the Church, declared that under his leadership the Christian Democrats would always strive to work for the real good of Italy, and asked for a blessing on himself, his family and his party (*Ibid.*, p. 257). But he did not at this stage crave an audience. That would have been immediately seized upon by his critics. For the time being 'reserve' continued to be the best papal policy. And Moro understood perfectly well why.

Moro wrote his letter to Pope John on February 3, 1962. The same day John published the *motu proprio* fixing the start of the Ecumenical Council for October 11 of that year. This ought to have concentrated the mind of Cardinal Siri on the impending 'event'. Far from it. He soon hurled himself into a fresh political battle. On March 2, 1962, Amintore Fanfani presented his reformist programme to the Italian parliament. This time round he was Prime Minister in a 'centre-left' administration which meant that he was in power thanks to the abstention of the Socialists; they would not vote with him, but neither would they bring him down. Fanfani's main proposal was for the nationalisation of the electricity industry. Siri sniffed the most sinister implications in this measure. He set down his worries in a memorandum which landed on Pope John's desk in June, 1962.

It was a passionate document. Siri denounced nationalisation in general as immoral because it set limits on freedom and opened the door to tyranny and dictatorship. These evils would inevitably follow if political and economic power were concentrated in the same hands. The Leviathan loomed once more. Siri accused Moro of betraying 'Catholic social teaching' by preferring one social class to another. This was the sin of '*filoclassismo*' and it was contrasted with the sound doctrine of '*interclassismo*' whose meaning we have already seen (see p. 362 above). It was not altogether clear why nationalising electricity should be deemed to have such devastating effects, but it was now too late to halt Siri in his tracks. Insofar as the Christian Democratic Party had abandoned Catholic social doctrine, it had forfeited the right to the title 'Christian'. This was a barely veiled threat to split the Christian Democrats by setting up some right-wing alternative to which good Catholics could in conscience adhere. In practice that meant joining the neo-Fascists. Two other factors made Siri's stand still more menacing. He was clearly reflecting the views of *Confindustria,* and they were a power in the land, if not an occult power and an alternative government. And the controversy was yet another episode in the long-running comparison of Pius XII and Pope John. Pius XII, one was left to understand, would never have allowed the Christian Democrats to get away with this effrontery.

John wondered what to do about Siri's memorandum and, as usual, called for a second opinion. This time he consulted Mgr Agostino Ferrari Toniolo who had worked on *Mater et Magistra* and Mgr Pietro Pavan who – though this was still to come – would help draft *Pacem in Terris*. The two experts flatly rejected Siri's arguments: 'There can be no doubt that electrical energy is one of the economic resources that reasons of the common good may suggest or even require should be nationalised'. They failed to see how nationalising electricity would impair freedom, and counter-attacked by pointing out that a privately-owned monopoly prevented the govenment from realising the common good. As for the alleged unfaithfulness of the Christian Democratic leadership to Catholic social doctrine, Toniolo and Pavan replied that 'a party respects its Christian inspiration not merely by embracing various social categories, but by ensuring that its political options are based on a constant concern for the good of the whole country and not merely of a sectional interest' (*Panorama,* May 17, 1982, p. 256). Pope John agreed with this verdict, and in his meeting with President Antonio Segni on July 3, 1962, he repeated his remarks on the specific differences between Church and state: 'The Pope in the Vatican and the Lateran is one thing; the president of the Republic in the Quirinale is another' (see above, p. 355). It helps to know that the Quirinale in the heart of Rome had been the papal summer palace, and that many conclaves had been held there.

But Siri was not yet finished. Chagrined at not being able to convince the Pope himself, he tried an indirect approach. On July 7, 1962, Capovilla received a letter from the President of *Confindustria,* Furio Cicogna, requesting an audience for himself and his deputy, Angelo Costa. They were both Venetians, which was one reason for approaching Capovilla, who was an honorary Venetian as well as the Pope's secretary. They did not need to say why they wanted an audience: it was too obvious that they were going to protest about the electricity nationalisation bill. Pope John refused them an audience. On July 9, 1962, he typed out a note which Capovilla was to commmunicate to Cicogna. It is a classic – and hitherto unpublished – statement of Pope John's political 'reserve':

> The Holy Father wishes to remain outside conflicts of a politico–social nature between sons whom he respects and loves with an equal measure of comprehension. It is the Lord who searches out all our hearts. So you will understand the Pope's silence in the discussions that have been going on in the last few months, discussions between brothers whom the father holds equally dear . . .
> In the four years that Pope John has exercised his ministry he has never once had, sought or exploited any meeting with government ministers, trades unionists or any other concerned party to emerge from his reserve [*per uscire dal su riserbo*]. In this he follows the example of the patriarch Jacob who, in the midst of his quarrelling sons, confined himself to watching, suffering and keeping silent.
> These explanations are also a request that the president and vice-president of *Confindustria* may dispense the Pope from an audience that could not remain confidential and could not fail to give rise to various speculations (*Panorama*, May 17, 1982, pp. 256–7).

John remained unfailingly courteous, even when he had to say no.

Jacob, the Old Testament patriarch, was a figure with whom he increasingly identified. It was an idea he had long been familiar with. He had quoted Genesis 37.11, about the 'silent father' to remind himself to remain neutral in wartime Turkey (see p. 175). Now in July, 1962 he believed that he had managed to 'hold himself aloof from questions of a political nature', and he returned to the same Genesis text:

> The biblical words about the reserved attitude of the old patriarch Jacob, caught between his sons on the left and the right, had a good effect: *Pater autem rem tacitus considerabat* (But the father pondered the matter in silence). Everyone has learned to stick to his own role. It was against all forecasts that the president of the Republic, Segni, should be a daily communicant, and that the mayor of Rome, La Porta, should have been one of the best students of the Jesuits at the Massimo College (*Giornale*, p. 354: in the English translation the first part of this passage is mistranslated, and the second unaccountably omitted. See *Journal*, pp. 244–5).

John was thinking of the early years of the century when the 'Roman Question' still raged, and when a pious president was as unimaginable as a Jesuit-educated mayor of Rome (whose name, Glauco Della Porta, he characteristically gets wrong). These were signs of the 'spiritual progress' he had talked about when he first went to the Lateran.

Yet the patriarchal pope was not quite so neutral as he appeared. On August 3, 1962, he gave to Aldo Moro the audience that he had refused to the chiefs of industry only a month before. It was a meeting that both men had long desired. It took place at Castelgandolfo, which was more discreet and less supervised by the media, and lasted about an hour. There were no speeches and protocol was at a minimum. In a note written later the same day Pope John described Moro as 'an excellent Catholic, a statesman, a man of great social concern' (Capovilla, letter to the author, May 13, 1983). This meeting on the eve of the Council with someone who was still being publicly attacked by Siri spoke for itself. It did not need elaborate commentary. 'It was', remarked Giancarlo Zizola, 'a metaphor for the Pope's recognition of the political liberty of Italian Catholics' (*Panorama*, May 17, 1982, p. 259). It may also be described as the patriarch Jacob at last recognising his son, Joseph. They were able to meet again more openly on October 17, 1962, after the Council had begun.

Meantime, what had Cardinal Siri been up to? To borrow the expressive word from Carlo Falconi, Siri had been 'limbo-ised', consigned to limbo, where he could neither suffer nor inflict harm (*L'Uomo che non divenne Papa*, p. 249). This was achieved by the simple device of rewriting the statutes of the Italian Episcopal Conference (CEI). From now on they would have an elected and not a Vatican-appointed president. Other responsibilities would be shared out equitably. Siri's monopoly of power was broken. Little wonder that he was heard to complain that Pope John's pontificate was 'the greatest disaster in recent ecclesiastical history', explaining that by 'recent' he meant in the last five hundred years. (In his evidence to the beatification process of Pope John, Siri withdrew this judgement and said that he had been wrong.)

John's reform of the Italian episcopacy was not the least of his achievements. In essence, the Italian bishops were brought into line with other episcopal conferences who did not enjoy a 'special relationship' with the Vatican. Naturally, since the Holy See was in Italy, the relationship would still be unique; but the umbilical cord had been cut, and the Italian bishops could thrive and grow up. E. E. Y. Hales' conclusion about Pope John's approach to Italian politics is entirely justified: 'He was largely free from the Renaissance habit of using politics to strengthen the papal position in Italy, and from the mediaeval habit of using politics to build a papal ascendency over Europe' (Hales, p. 63). This had evident implications for the rest of the world. What *Gaudium et Spes* has to say about politics reflects Pope John's practice as much as his theory. Clerics are not omnicompetent (No. 43), lay persons have 'freedom of enquiry and thought'

(No. 62), the Church is prepared to renounce 'privileges' once sanctioned by concordats (No. 76), and it is in the profoundest sense 'the Church of the poor' (No. 1). The Council could have arrived at these conclusions unaided; but it was helpful to have the example of Pope John to prove that such attitudes were found at the highest level of the Church. In that sense, Pope John's example was more immediately influential than his encyclical *Mater et Magistra*.

But it is time to pick up the threads of the Council. It was being assiduously prepared. Many of the same actors who have already been met in this chapter were involved, but others were new.

Chapter 18

Enter Augustin Bea

The first opinion of a ruler's intelligence is formed on the quality of the men he has around him

(Niccolò Machiavelli, *The Prince*, Penguin Classics, 1961, p. 124).

Getting the Council under way was like cranking up some enormous machine. The Ante-preparatory Commission had been set up at Pentecost 1959. Out of 2,821 prelates or institutions (like Catholic universities) consulted, 2,150 replied. This was 76.4 per cent – a good 'market response'. Their replies will be invaluable to future historians who want a graph of Catholic leadership mentalities in 1960. A sampling suggests that they had not yet grasped the possibilities put within their reach by the Council. They confined themselves to minor reforms: the Holy See should concede more 'faculties' to the local bishops, and a surprising number of Italians wanted to abolish or curb religious 'exemption' (Rouquette, I, p. 88). One English bishop shared his ambitions for the Council with his people. He assured them that 'there were great hopes of new definitions' such as that of Our Lady as 'Mediatrix of All Graces' (Pawley, p. 430). It was difficult to be more wrong than that. All these suggestions and requests, known as *voti*, were later published by the Vatican Press in fifteen massive volumes (*Acta et Documenta Concilio Oecumenico Vaticano Secundo apparando*). But since at the time all this material was confidential, no one knew what the bishops had been saying. Yet this formed the basis of the first draft texts, and helps to explain their poverty. They contained no hint of the 'new Pentecost'.

Although John chose the eve of Whitsunday, June 5, 1960, to announce the setting up of the Preparatory Commissions proper, they did not set to work until November 13, 1960. There was a suspicion that Cardinal Domenico Tardini was deliberately spinning out the preparations for whatever reasons; if he thought that John might not last much longer, he fell victim to a divine irony, dying himself on July 30, 1961, almost two years before the Pope. Even for an institution which 'thinks in centuries', the delay was disquieting with so many old men around. Still more disquieting was that the Central Theological Commission and its ten sub-commissions were largely under curial control.

This was the result of a decision taken by Pope John himself. He decided that the president of each sub-commission would be the prefect of the corresponding Roman Congregation (or dicastery). So Cardinal Gaetano Cicognani, of the

Congregation of Rites, was responsible for liturgy while Cardinal Marcello Mimmi from the Consistorial Congregation dealt with episcopal matters – crucially important if Vatican I were to be 'completed' and 'collegiality' asserted. Cardinal Alfredo Ottaviani presided over the Theological Commission, and held that it had a right of veto over everyone else because the Congregation to which it corresponded, the Holy Office, was traditionally known as 'the *supreme* Congregation'. (Ottaviani was strictly its 'pro-prefect' because the Pope himself was its 'prefect': but this was a distinction without a difference.) The effect of these arrangements was that the control of the preparations for the Council was firmly vested in the hands of the Roman Curia.

This became perfectly clear when the names of the members of the preparatory commissions were unveiled. There were over 800 of them. Generalisations about so vast a group are not easy, but critics were soon claiming that in the main they represented the 'Roman school' for which theology was the exposition and defence of known truth rather than an exploration on the frontiers of knowledge. However, there were plenty of individual exceptions. Cardinal Giovanni Battista Montini managed to smuggle his mentor, Oratorian Fr Giulio Bevilacqua, onto the Liturgy Commission (for which he composed a Montini-like paper on 'the mystery of the sacred liturgy and its relationship with the whole life of the Church') (Bugnini, p. 27). But Montini himself was still excluded at this stage. John had his own official link to the Central Preparatory Commission through his confessor, Mgr Alfredo Cavagna (Bonnot, p. 76). But the names of those not summoned to serve formed a roll-call of 'the great and the good' of the period: uninvited were the Jesuits John Courtney Murray and John L. McKenzie from the United States, the brothers Karl and Hugo Rahner from Bavaria, and Frenchmen Henri de Lubac and Jean Daniélou; also absent were the French Dominicans Yves-Marie Congar and Marie-Dominique Chenu. In short anyone touched even lightly by the fall-out from *Humani Generis* or who had otherwise had problems with the Holy Office was rigorously excluded.

Moreover, John's instructions provided only a mild incentive to seek outside help. The fact that the Curia is responsible for the organisation of the Council, he explained on June 5, 1960, 'does not exclude from time to time (*volta a volta*) the co-operation of enlightened wisdom from ecclesiastics invited in view of their acknowledged personal competence'. Note the absence of laymen and women. It is assumed that male ecclesiastics hold a monopoly of 'enlightened wisdom'. It would be easy but unjust to make Tardini alone the scapegoat for these arrangements. Pope John bore his share of responsibility. The upshot was that many feared the Council would be a packed assembly, lacking the best available scholarship and the essential attribute of freedom.

Had John made a bad mistake? Should he have foreseen what would happen? It seems that he half-foresaw it, tried to forestall its worst effects, but persisted for

372 *Enter Augustin Bea*

reasons he believed good. The July 5, 1960 address contains this further clue:

> The Ecumenical Council has its own structures and organisation, and should not be confused with the ordinary and characteristic functions of the various dicasteries and congregations of the Roman Curia. These will carry on with their routine tasks throughout the pre-conciliar period . . . There is thus a precise distinction: the ordinary government of the Church is one thing, the Council is another (*Letture*, p. 147).

The curialists, in other words, were being invited to wear two hats. In this way Pope John hoped they would be involved in the work of the Council and so committed to it. It would not suddenly burst upon them as a threat to be resisted or a foreign invasion to be repulsed. This part of John's plan did not altogether miscarry. Mgr Dell'Acqua claimed that there was a new spirit in the Curia:

> In the Secretariat of State no one any longer feels they have to go out and do pastoral work to keep themselves sane. They realise that their work in the Secretariat of State is itself pastoral. Pope John had changed the outlook of the Church's central administration, while its juridical position remained unchanged (*L'Uomo che non divenne Papa*, p. 265).

Well and good. But it seems rather odd that working on the preparations for a would-be 'pastoral' Council should lead one to abandon pastoral work outside; and what Dell'Acqua said was only patchily true. Bureaucracies have their own in-built inertia and resistance to change.

Yet one reason why Pope John was not particularly worried at this stage was that alongside the laborious official preparation for the Council, so tightly controlled by the Curia, there was another form of preparation that was free, unofficial, independent, and above all public. Unlike the official preparations that were secret and therefore invisible, the books, articles and television interviews about the Council carried the discussion to everyone in the Church and beyond. This media activity created expectations, gave rise to arguments about the purpose of the Council, and reflected in however crude a manner the *sensus fidelium*, that instinctive sense of what is right doctrine lodged in the hearts of all the faithful. From this vast output, two contrasting works may be selected because in different ways they directly influenced the Council. They also illustrated the truth of Pope John's maxim, *historia magistra veritatis* (history is the teacher of truth).

Lorenz Jaeger, archbishop of Paderborn, has already been mentioned (p. 329 above) as the founder of the Adam Möhler Institute. As soon as the Council was announced on January 25, 1959, he embarked on an historical study of the Council, called in English translation *The Ecumenical Council, The Church and Christendom*. It was as though Pope John's announcement had been long awaited if not expected in Paderborn. Jaeger's solid and dependable book had a considerable influence. It clarified the questions and changed some perceptions. He pointed out that there was no fixed or prescribed historical 'model' for a Council. They had all been time-conditioned events dependent on all manner of external factors such as, for example, the role of the emperor. Another variable in a Council was the Church's own self-understanding at the time; for there could not be a council at all without some implicit ecclesiology or doctrine of the Church.

This was dynamite. For the way the Council was actually being organised, apparently at the behest of Pope John, reflected a centralising, authoritarian, clerical, juridical, un- or anti-ecumenical and world-defying understanding of the Church that could have the most appalling consequences. There would be no point at all in meeting merely to repeat the Syllabus of Errors. Vatican I, Jaeger went on, had been a monarchically run Council reflecting the autocratic spirit of the age, and it reacted against all contemporary movements. Vatican II would have to reflect the more 'democratic' or – if that word were alarming and improper – 'collegial' temper of the mid-twentieth century. It followed that there would have to be 'free and close discussion of all objections and difficulties' (Jaeger, p. 86) This was aimed at Cardinal Ottaviani who held that controversial matters should not be discussed at the Council lest the faithful be disedified; and quite evidently ecclesiastical linen should not be washed in the *aula* or council hall. Jaeger also argued that there should be some kind of 'lay participation' in the Council as a reminder that, in the last analysis, the teaching of the Church reposed upon the *sensus fidelium*. Jaeger, in short, tried to define the features that would make this Council *different*, and he invited Pope John to supply the vision and organisational savvy to make it happen. He was not required to dictate in advance what it should do – that would be to repeat the mistake of Pius IX; but he would have to see that it got under way in the right spirit. John might ruefully complain, 'I'm only the Pope around here'. But there were some things that only the Pope could do.

Another German-speaking theologian, Swiss-born Hans Küng, responded with equal alacrity to the announcement of the Council. The German edition of *Konzil und Wiedervereinigung. Erneuerung als Ruf in die Einheit* appeared in 1960 (translated in England as *The Council and Reunion* and in the United States as *The Council, Reform and Reunion*). That same year Küng was appointed professor of Theology at Tübingen at the remarkably early age of thirty-two. Unlike Jaeger's rather heavy tome, Küng's book was lively and readable. Moreover, he ventured to set out an agenda for the Council. Needless to say, it was not quite the programme the Roman Curia had in mind – and his book had to wait until 1965 for an Italian translation. For Küng the plain purpose of the Council was the reform of the Church. If this reform were properly done, it would lead to reunion on equal terms with the 'separated brethren'. Küng catalogued the steps that would have to be taken to meet the *valid* demands of the Protestant Reformation: some appreciation of the Reformation as a *religious* event (not reducible to political or psychological factors like Luther's libido); growing esteem for and use of the Bible in theology and worship; the development of a 'people's liturgy', naturally in the vernacular; an understanding of the 'universal priesthood' of all the faithful; dialogue between the Church and other cultures; the liberation of the papacy from political entanglements; the reform of the Roman Curia and the abolition of the Index of Forbidden Books. Küng proved an accurate and far-sighted prophet: all of his seven demands were embodied, even if in modified form, in the final documents of the Council.

Moreover, Küng skilfully appealed to Pope John who, he assumed somewhat gratuitously, would share his enthusiasm for all these causes. He overlooked that John's experience of ecumenism had been largely with the Orthodox. But it didn't matter. 'Always have the Pope on your side' is a sound rule for a Catholic theologian. Küng contrasted the wide-awake Pope with slumbering Christendom:

> Schism is a scandal. But it is perhaps an even greater scandal that the majority of Christians, in all communities, even today, and including theologians and pastors, are profoundly indifferent to this scandal; that they feel the division of Christendom at most as a deplorable imperfection, not as an immeasurably crippling wound which absolutely must be healed; that they are deeply concerned over a thousand religious trivialities, but not over Our Lord's desire that 'all may be one'. Will the words and actions of the Pope be enough to waken these sleepers? (*Council and Reunion*, p. 57).

It was, in every sense of the term, rousing stuff. Especially when repeated to crowded audiences across Europe and the United States.

Shrewd, too, and well calculated to appeal to Pope John, was Küng's presentation of the sixteenth century Council of Trent as essentially a *reforming* Council. He did not make the mistake of those who used Trent as a bogey and blamed everything corrupt on its bigoted narrowness. Küng explained that it had some good effects: 'It hardly needs stressing that for all their limitations, these acts of restoration were productive of immeasurable good. It is thanks to them that the Church of the Baroque period displays a purity and a strength that are very different from the Church of the Renaissance' (*Council and Reunion*, p. 120). This was exactly the thesis of Roncalli in his edition of the *Acta* of St Charles Borromeo. True, Küng went on to say that after Paul IV, the polemical atmosphere and political manoeuvrings led to an inquisitorial repression of error that was less admirable. But John as historian could not quarrel with that either.

He never made any public comment on Küng. There was no reason why he should. But already what may be termed the 'first battle of Küng' was being waged. The Curia was furious at the way this jumped-up young man was denouncing the Holy Office and waving his personal programme for the forthcoming Council in the press and on television while sound theologians and serious-minded persons like themselves were exchanging decent Latin memos on the limits of religious 'exemption'. It was intolerable. (To tell the truth, there were some in the Curia who were delighted at the thought that Ottaviani had at last met his match.) But Küng had a lot of support. Cardinal Franz König, archbishop of Vienna, a scholar with whom few in the college of cardinals could compete, introduced the German edition and called the book 'an happy omen'. In his introduction, Cardinal Achille Liénart of Lille stressed its ecumenical importance (see Nowell, p. 82). It was reasonable to conclude that whatever the Preparatory Commission might be doing, Küng had provided the real agenda for the Council, and drawn up the battle lines for its first session. Never again would an individual theologian have such influence.

There did not seem to be any easy way in which the various streams of preparation could merge. Yet if they did not, the Council would fail to live up to the expectations aroused by theologians like Jaeger and Küng. Was there anyone in Rome who knew German theology and knew his way about the Vatican? There was Fr Augustin Bea S.J., rector of the Biblicum. But he was six months older than Pope John, and already looked so frail that it seemed a puff of wind would blow him over. He was stooped and his tortoise-like face was deeply lined. As a Jesuit he would have to refuse a cardinal's hat at first, but if Pope John insisted in obedience, then he would accept without enthusiasm or demur. Bea was created cardinal on January 28, 1960, though his precise role was not yet clear. He did not look like a man who would launch the Church on a radically new course. Yet without Bea, it is unlikely that Pope John would have got the Council he wanted.

The idea of a 'small, high-powered body dealing exclusively with ecumenical questions' had been canvassed early on (see p. 328 above). But it was Jaeger who drew up the detailed plan which Cardinal Bea presented to the Pope in a letter dated March 11, 1960. John annotated the letter:

> Heard the views of the cardinal secretary of state [Tardini] and of cardinal Bea (12 and 13 March). The project is approved. Cardinal Bea will be president of the proposed Pont. Comm. Answer and reach an agreement with the Bishop of Paderborn [Jaeger].
>
> Prepare everything but wait till after Easter for the official publication: this will bring it into line with the other commissions which will be named on various other matters. *Ita. Die XIV Martii*, 1960 (*Lettere*, pp. 495–6).

Ita, wrote John, yes, so be it. Did he realise that he had just made the most important appointment of his pontificate? He seems to have taken it in his stride as one of his 'silent inspirations from the Lord'. Though he entrusted the future to the Lord and refused to be 'curious and anxious about the shape of things to come' (*Journal*, p. 336), he was perfectly capable of thinking and planning ahead. His *motu proprio, Superno Dei Nutu*, which set up the Secretariat for Christian Unity, defined its purpose in clear and ungrudging tones:

> In order to show in a special manner our love and good will towards those who bear the name of Christ, but are separated from this Apostolic See, and in order that they may be able to follow the work of the Council and find more readily the way to attain that unity for which Jesus besought his heavenly Father, we have established this special Office or Secretariat (*Unity of Christians*, p. 166).

It was the hoisting of a signal. It let the separated brethren know that they too were officially invited to take part in what Karl Barth was soon to call 'the event' (of the Spirit). John's original annotation spoke of a pontifical commission: to call it a 'secretariat' was to put it on the same level as the ineffectual body devoted to the mass media and so to downgrade it – and this interpretation was sometimes put about by the Curia. It was 'only' a secretariat and therefore insignificant. Bea, however, with Pope John's backing, did not fuss about titles and maintained that 'no difference in status is implied, merely a difference in organisation' (*Ibid.*, p. 162). This was Bea's typically disarming way of saying that the Secretariat for Christian Unity was something totally new. For, as he went on in another whopping understatement: 'Our many and varied contacts with Non-Catholic Christians introduce an element not found in the other preparatory commissions' (*Ibid.*).

He could say that again. No other commission had the slightest interest in what other Christians thought. So Bea's Secretariat had a new method from the start, and it needed new men. Bea scoured the Catholic universities and seminaries for members and consultants chosen for their biblical, ecumenical or patristic competence. Some, like Fr Maurice Bévenot S.J., of Heythrop College, England, had led a blameless life entirely dedicated to the study of the transmission of the St Cyprian manuscripts. Others were too young to have incurred Holy Office displeasure. Bea spotted for example the thirty-seven year old Canadian Augustinian, Gregory Baum, whose Fribourg, Switzerland 1956 thesis, *That all may be One*, had been followed by work on the anti-semitism of the Gospels. Thus the organisation, method of work, personnel and spirit of the Secretariat for Christian Unity were something utterly foreign to the Roman Curia. They even talked different languages, preferring German, English and French to Italian. This was not out of anti-Italian prejudice but simply because few native Italian-speakers had much experience of ecumenism. The rare Italian Protestants, mostly Waldensians, remained aloof and jealously guarded their identity.

So this ecumenical 'cuckoo in the nest' was unwelcome to the Roman Curia. With it Pope John had out-flanked and by-passed the Curia that was supposed to be preparing the Council. He had introduced a wholly new criterion into the pre-conciliar discussions: what will other Christians think? This would give a programme much closer to Hans Küng than to Cardinal Ottaviani, and both of them knew it: conformity to the Gospel was to be the first norm of faith. The curial monopoly on the preparations for the Council had been broken. John's original 'mistake' had been adjusted. For the first time the Council preparations were on course and heading in the direction Pope John had hoped for from the start.

The purpose of the Council came into clearer focus. John had always known that Vatican II would not be a 'council of reunion' in the sense that Lyons in the thirteenth and Florence in the fifteenth century had attempted to be. No doubt that would come at some future date. But the time was not yet ripe. But this did not mean that it had no ecumenical dimension at all. On the contrary. In one of his countless interviews, Cardinal Bea stated very clearly what Pope John had in mind:

> The Holy Father hopes that the forthcoming Council may be a kind of invitation to our separated brethren, by letting them see, in its day-to-day proceedings, the sincerity, love and concord which prevail in the Catholic Church. So we may say, rather, that the Council should make an indirect contribution to union, breaking the ground in a long-term policy of preparation for unity (*Unity of Christians*, p. 158: originally *Katholische Nachrichten Agentur*, January 22, 1961).

Those whom Tardini only nine months earlier had described as 'dissidents' were transmuted into 'separated brothers'. Instead of being kept at barge-pole length with condemnations, they were invited to 'Come and see' (John 1.39). Even if they might not find the idyll imagined by Bea, they could still learn. And their responses and expectations would help to shape not only the nature and extent of their own participation but the agenda itself. Bea and his secretary, Mgr Jan Willebrands, embarked on a vast programme of correspondence and travel to discover the answers to these questions and build up their team. Bea was rejuvenated. There were many stories of old men being transformed and throwing away their sticks on becoming cardinals. It released an extraordinary energy in Augustin Bea. 'SEE THE WORLD WITH BEA' was a Roman joke of the time (BEA being the current acronym for British European Airways).

But coming from the stay-at-home Curia of Pius XII such jokes left rather a sour taste in the mouth. All this gadding about was unnecessary and had not happened before. In the midst of the consultations that led to the setting up of the Secretariat for Christian Unity, Cardinal Francis J. Spellman, archbishop of New

York, military vicar, showed that his sense of timing had gone awry. He petitioned Pope John to start the historical investigation that might eventually lead to the beatification and canonisation of Pope Pius XII (*Lettere*, p. 499). John tried to reply, but found it difficult. 'The feelings of devoted esteem and admiration', he bravely began, 'that so many in the Church have for Pius XII, are well-known'. But there he laid down his pen. He left the matter to his successor. He did not think that canonising popes was of much help to the mass of Christians. On this occasion he could not find a formula to say 'no' to Spellman without letting him down badly. But the petition had a pharisaic aspect. The comparison between John and his predecessor continued to be made. It was made even more sharply after the creation of the Secretariat for Christian Unity and Bea's appointment as its first President. For by this act – it was whispered – the ecumenical rules laid down in his instruction *Ecclesia Catholica* (December 20, 1949), were being manifestly flouted. And this was Pope John's doing. He was responsible. However, since it was not good form to attack the Pope directly, Bea became the target.

But Bea, despite his frail shoulders, was a tough man to bring down. He had lived in Rome since 1924 and knew the ropes. It was particularly difficult to drive a wedge between him and Pius XII since he had been the Pope's confessor. Indeed, this is what alarmed some ecumenists when they heard of his appointment as president of the Secretariat for Christian Unity: he seemed to be too much a 'man of Pius XII', another venerable survivor from the *ancien régime*. This was one reason why he could be useful to Pope John. Bea formed a bridge between the two pontificates. He had the right to assert continuity even when, one might reasonably think, there was a new development. Bea, the Jesuit, was jesuitical.

He can be seen at work in an interview given in February, 1961, to Giorgio Berlutti, whose admiration for Pius XII was boundless. Again we enter the realm of understatement and nuance. Bea never said anything even remotely critical of Pius: coming from his confessor, that would have been unseemly. Indeed, he leaned the other way and claimed Pius as a pioneer of the ecumenical movement, saying 'in his encyclical on the Mystical Body (*Mystici Corporis*), Pius XII expressed such tender love of our separated brethren as may surprise us, coming from a jurist' (*Unity of Christians*, p. 182). Bea's 'surprise' is understandable, since it was precisely the encyclical *Mystici Corporis* (1943) that identified the Roman Catholic Church with the Mystical Body, thus setting up a mighty ecumenical barrier. But perhaps Bea meant to stress the word 'jurist': the surprise was that ecumenical sentiments should come from a canon lawyer. Bea was a master at the diplomatic game which consisted in using nuances to create an area of freedom.

Berlutti, a persistant interviewer, did not let Bea off the hook so easily. 'Do not the twenty volumes of Pope Pius XII', he innocently enquired, 'make a valid contribution towards solving the problems that will be examined at the Council?'

(*Unity of Christians*, p. 182). This was a truly pharisaical question. For if Bea said 'yes' he was accepting the curial view that the Council would be simply the application of Pius' twenty volumes to the contemporary situation; if he said 'no', he would appear to be repudiating this great Pope and his magisterial teaching. Bea firmly replied:

> Undoubtedly. But I do not mean that the Council ought or will follow mechanically the whole programme set out by Pius XII. Every pontificate has its own character which corresponds to the personality of the Pope, to the needs of the time and, above all, to the mysterious plans and intentions of the Holy Spirit, who always animates and guides the Church. The last, most eminent Pope left twenty volumes containing a wealth of valuable doctrinal material. Among these writings will be found, in general terms at least, solutions to many modern problems that no one concerned with the renewal of the Church can possibly ignore (*Ibid.*).

Bea kept a straight face throughout this interview. He was a very serious man. So too was Cardinal Giuseppe Siri who many years later 'revealed' that Pope John had said to him: 'In his pontificate Pius XII completed a veritable theological encyclopaedia' (Siri, address to Synod, October 8, 1983). Siri was completely insensitive to the ironic possibilities of this remark: encyclopaedias, however worthy, tend to gather dust on the shelves, and are only consulted in emergencies. They are not daily fare. But Bea did not have a strong sense of irony either. In his spiritual journal he notes that he once asked his famous penitent, Pius XII, why he devoted so much time to preparing his addresses and homilies. Pius grandly replied, 'Because it is always the Pope who speaks' (*è sempre il Papa che parla*) (*Spiritual Profile*, p. 66).

No one, then, could fault Bea on loyalty to Pius XII. He would therefore have to be attacked on other grounds. Ottaviani emerged as his principal opponent. Not very scrupulous when it came to in-fighting, Ottaviani probed for weaknesses and throughout the next three years varied the point of attack as occasions arose. Bea was deemed unsound because he had contributed to if not drafted the Pius XII encyclical, *Divino Afflante Spiritu* (1943) which conceded that the study of ancient literary *genres* could help in the understanding of the Bible: this innocuous proposition was believed to 'give in to form-criticism' as practised by Rudolf Bultmann. Bea's second weakness was that he was supposed to be unfaithful to the 1949 instruction of the Holy Office, *Ecclesia Catholica*, already mentioned, which stressed the need for great caution in ecumenical contexts (known humorously at the time as 'mixed bathing'), and the peril of taking actions which might 'compromise the revealed doctrine of the Church'. Since *Ecclesia Catholica* had not been rescinded, it was assumed with impeccable logic that it was still in force. Nuncios and Apostolic Delegates were on the look-out for rash or indiscriminate bathers in ecumenical waters. These two charges against Bea will recur with tedious repetitiveness. Of course the main objection was simply that he was an outsider brought in to manage a wholly new enterprise with a completely different way of going about its work.

Bea was subjected to continual pinpricks of harrassment. For example in autumn 1960 he asked Pope John for permission to speak at Gazzada, where the Catholic Conference on Ecumenical Questions was due to meet from 19 to 23 September. It seems extraordinary that Ottaviani – for it was he – should have claimed the right to interfere in the speaking arrangements of a fellow cardinal. But he did, on grounds of fidelity to *Ecclesia Catholica*. Pope John's memo to Bea on the matter, though it granted permission, was not particularly encouraging:

> It is good that your eminence should speak at Gazzada, even if briefly. A problem arises about the dimensions the Secretariat could take on compared with the Central Commission, given the concern manifested by the separated brethren to move swiftly and their desire to have contacts that could distract the Fathers of the Council and create disarray or delay in their own characteristic work. As for permission for Catholics to attend meetings with non-Catholics, consult the HO (*Lettere*, p. 504: dated September 14, 1960).

The HO was the Holy Office. At this stage, Pope John was closer to Ottaviani at the Holy Office than to Bea at the Secretariat for Christian Unity. He seems to have swallowed both Holy Office arguments against the Secretariat: that it was getting to rival the Central Commission in size and importance, and that excessive attention to the separated brethren would jeopardise the Council as an inner-Catholic event. John made no attempt to curb Ottaviani. But he encouraged Bea to reply in a reasoned manner to criticisms. So Bea gave endless interviews and wrote articles, notably in *Civiltà Cattolica*.

This estimable Jesuit fortnightly had been founded to defend the Ultramontane case and the Syllabus of Errors. In the nineteenth century it had carried edifying novels in serial form. In the twentieth century it had become, as it were, the adult version of *l'Osservatore Romano*. It had the rule that no non-Jesuit could write in it, and it was censored by the Secretariat of State. John wanted to stop the censorship. He told Roberto Tucci, its new editor, that each of them should get on with his own work: he as Pope, Tucci as editor of *Civiltà Cattolica*.

At the start of 1961 Bea published an article called 'The Catholic Attitude to the Problem of Christian Unity' (*Civiltà Cattolica*, I, 1961, pp. 113–29: *Unity of Christians*, pp. 19–46). It was an apologia for the Secretariat and, by the same token, for the pontificate of Pope John. Yet it was a boring and rather conventional article that did not yield up its meaning straightaway. It began from St Augustine's recommendation that one should hate error but love those who err

(*Odisse errorem, diligere errantes*). This became one of the key points in *Pacem in Terris*. Bea proceded dialectically.

First, one should hate error, firmly and unequivocally. The New Testament, he pointed out, shows great 'severity' towards heresy and schism. He quotes a cluster of fierce Pauline texts to illustrate what happened to the incestuous Corinthian (he was 'handed over to Satan': I Corinthians 5.4–5) and those who have 'made shipwreck of their faith' (I Timothy 1.19–20). Bea blandly remarks that 'whatever the interpretation of this "handing over to Satan", there can be no doubt that it meant a punishment of extreme severity' (*Unity of Christians*, p. 22). Moral evil and deviations from faith are equally harshly dealt with in St Paul. And in both cases the authority of the Church is engaged, as is clear from the 'ecclesiastical chapter' of St Matthews's Gospel which says of the recalcitrant: 'If he will not listen to the Church, then count him all one with the heathen and the publican' (Matthew 18.17).

It is easy to imagine Ottaviani reading this passage and suspecting a catch somewhere. Perhaps it came in the notoriously obscure St Paul. Ottaviani is reliably reported to have joked that St Paul, although undoubtedly inspired, was so confused that his works would not have got through the Holy Office censorship. That Bea should be doing Ottaviani's work for him and praising the severity of the New Testament was suspicious-making. So it was. This was only the first part of the dialectic, the thesis to be followed by the antithesis.

Once again St Augustine helped the transition. In *Ad Petri Cathedram* Pope John had quoted his remarks on the separated brothers: 'Whether they like it or not, they are our brothers. They will only cease to be our brothers when they have forgotten to say "Our Father" ' (see p. 334 above). Moreover, Bea went on, the New Testament severity that he had so vividly illustrated applies *only* to those who have individually and deliberately withdrawn from the true faith. Severity, therefore, is not the right attitude towards 'the great majority who inherit their faith from their fore-fathers'. The old adage, so important in Germany, *cuius regio eius religio* (your religion depends on where you live), suggested to Bea the following conclusion: 'As it is no merit of ours to have been born and brought up in a family belonging to the Catholic Church, so it is no fault of theirs that they are children of parents separated from our Church. Accepting in good the faith the inheritance handed on by their parents, these non-Catholics can sincerely believe that they are on the right path' (*Unity of Christians*, p. 27). The remainder of Bea's article was concerned with the common faith in which all Christians shared. The basis of ecumenism was baptism: 'Non-Catholic Christians must not, therefore, be put on the same plane as the non-baptised; for they always bear, not only the name of Christ on their foreheads, but his actual image in their souls, deeply and indelibly imprinted there by baptism' (*Ibid.*, p. 32). More than twenty years later, these are banalities, blunted by endless repetition. In the early 1960s they were liberating discoveries, enlightening truths. They showed what could happen when divided Christians abandoned the defensive mentality of Ottaviaini's Holy Office and looked upon each other with the eye of love.

But Ottaviani was not yet finished. He still had two cards to play. The first was *Ecclesia Catholica*, the 1949 Holy Office decree. Bea treats it with the greatest respect, knowing that Ottaviani worked on it and was proud of it. Bea shrewdly draws attention to the sentence in *Ecclesia Catholica* which notes that growing desire for union 'may be attributed under the Holy Spirit, to external factors and the changing attitudes of men's minds, but above all to the united prayers of the faithful' (*Unity of Christians*, p. 28). If the accent were put on the right words, this could be taken to mean that the Holy Spirit was the great inspirer of the ecumenical movement, which is the Christian way of saying that it is a Good Thing. And one should not 'resist the Spirit' – indeed it is futile to try. This trick went to Bea.

But Ottaviani still had the card of the passage in Pius XII's encyclical *Mystici Corporis* which seemed to call into question the value of heretical and schismatic baptism:

> Only those are to be accounted really members of the Church who have been regenerated in the waters of baptism and profess the true faith, and have not cut themselves off from the structures of the Body by their own unhappy act or been severed therefrom for very grave crimes, by the legitimate authority . . . It follows that those who are divided from one another in faith and government cannot be living in the one Body so described, and by its one divine Spirit (*Mystici Corporis*, No. 21, Catholic Truth Society, London, translation).

This doctrine, Bea observes with hardly a flicker of those hooded eyes, recalls the severity of the New Testament, and emphasises 'what a terrible thing is the separation caused by heresy and schism' (*Unity of Christians*, p. 31).

But having made this concession, he denies that the passage has the consequences often drawn from it. Once more he insists on the distinction between those responsible for heresy and schism, and those who merely inherit them. Then he quoted Pope John's address to the preparatory Commission on November 13, 1960: 'One great point to be held by every baptised person is that the Church remains for ever his Mystical Body. He is the Head, to it each of us believers is related, to it we belong' (*Unity of Christians*, pp. 32–3). The syntax was tortured but the meaning clear: this was a decisive move from an ecclesiology that excluded other Christians to one that embraced them; it was based on an older tradition that regarded baptism as the common bond between all who invoked the name of Christ; it by-passed *Mystici Corporis* and left it stranded in the pages of Denzinger, a curious historical monument from 1943.

Within two weeks of making this liberating statement, Pope John received Dr Geoffrey Fisher at the Vatican. It was on December 2, 1960, that a pope and an archbishop of Canterbury met for the first time since the Reformation. It was also the first-fruits of Bea's indefatigable letter-writing and the first response to Pope John's invitation to 'Come and see'. The Curia was hostile to this hob-nobbing with 'dissidents'. Tardini scarcely bothered to conceal his hostility and did everything he could to cut the visit down to size. Bea was not even allowed to see the archbishop, still less to be present at the audience. Tardini sent along a relatively junior member of his staff, Mgr Antonio Samorè, to keep an eye on Pope John and report back. No ecclesiastical title was accorded to Fisher who was addressed throughout as *Dottore*, as though he were some kind of university professor (all these details from Col. Robert Hornby, in a letter to the author, February 23, 1982: he was Dr Fisher's press officer). As Peter Nichols put it: 'The visit was treated like a guilty secret. No photograph was permitted, and every effort made for the event to pass off as unobtrusively as possible' (*Politics*, p. 314). 'Behind those walls', a frustrated television commentator was reduced to saying, 'history is being made'.

If there was official coolness on the Roman side – Pope John excepted – Archbishop Fisher displayed a certain amount of Anglican truculence. Geoffrey Fisher was, in the judgement of John Carmel Heenan, then archbishop of Liverpool, a complex character: 'In no way devious, his approach was often a combination of affection and censure' (*Crown of Thorns*, p. 262). That was certainly his approach on this occasion. He pointedly included the visit to Rome in a journey that led him to Istanbul to see the ecumenical patriarch. Having arrived in Rome, he then preached a sermon in the Anglican Church in which he contrasted the 'Anglican' concept of 'collegiality' with the 'Roman' idea of papal monarchy. Collegiality, he declared, was admirably reflected in the unity and diversity found in the British Commonwealth, while the papal monarchy, if unchecked, could lead straight to dictatorship. Moreover, Fisher fully intended to lecture Pope John on the ineptitude of the 'Return-to-Rome' theory enshrined in *Ad Petri Cathedram* of the previous summer. He told Pope John that this was an out-of-date idea, and that 'the two Churches are running in parallel – maybe they are two straight lines that will merge in eternity' (Hornby, as above). Pope John told Giuseppe De Luca that they talked of St Gregory the Great and of St Augustine's mission to Canterbury (*Lettere*, p. 165). That was predictable enough.

Cardinal Bea shrugged off his humiliations as all part of the ecumenical cross, and rejoiced that the visit had taken place at all. It was officially described as a 'courtesy visit' and no 'negotiations' had taken place. After four centuries, the ice was broken and contact was re-established. It was Bea's first major success – but there were to be no more visits until after Tardini's death. In *Civiltà Cattolica* Bea interpreted the meaning of the 'living parable': 'When we are dealing with a meeting between the heads of Christian communions, one inspired not only by friendship or purely human charity but, more than that, by an essentially Christian spirit, that is, loyalty to the person of Christ, we must realise that we are treading on the most holy ground' (*Unity of Christians*, p. 69).

For Dr Fisher, too, the visit was an undoubted success. He was charmed by Pope John's evident goodness, but he had stuck to his Anglican principles and protected his flanks. He was able to return home and resign, as he had already decided to, on a high note. A six-hour debate in the House of Lords showed that the majority of Anglican peers were strongly in favour of the ecumenical cause as they perceived it, and wished to banish bigotry. The visit did a great deal to establish the Anglican Communion as an original body, distinct both from the Orthodox and the Protestants. To drive home this point, the archbishops of Canterbury and York appointed Canon Bernard Pawley to be their 'personal representative' to the Vatican. He was received by Pope John on July 12, 1961. No other Church or Communion had the wit to have its own ambassador in Rome.

The Fisher–Roncalli meeting had another sequel: an anecdote. On January 4, 1961, Evelyn Waugh, the master novelist, wrote to Elizabeth Pakenham (now Lady Longford): 'Did you know that Archbishop Roberts had an audience with the Pope a week after Dr Fisher had gone charging in crying: "Your Holiness, we are making history"? The Pope said to Roberts: "There was another Archbishop from your country here the other day. Now who was he?" ' (*Letters*, p. 558; also, less elaborated, *Diaries*, p. 777). Anyone who knew Thomas d'Esterre Roberts, the sometime archbishop of Bombay, would realise that inventing such a story would have given him as much puckish pleasure as Waugh derived from repeating it. But the story is *ben trovato*. Roberts did in fact have an hourlong audience with Pope John on December 6, 1960, just four days after the Fisher visit. He wished to complain that the apostolic delegate in London, Archbishop Gerald P. O'Hara, had defamed him on a number of occasions. They conversed in French. The report Roberts presented to the Pope concluded with a reference to his work with the peace movement Pax Christi: 'On the issue of war, my measures of self-defence in Rome will, I hope, clear me of any suspicion of soft pacifism in resisting tyranny from any quarter'. Quite evidently, Pope John found the whole encounter puzzling and could not quite understand what Roberts was protesting about. Roberts' account of the audience concludes: 'At the end of the interview Pope John, rather typically, added a promise to send me a signed photograph of himself as soon as the affair should be concluded. He died two and a half years later – without giving either enquiry or photograph' (Hurn, p. 107). There was no mention of the archbishop of Canterbury.

In the Evelyn Waugh fiction, however, can be seen the beginnings of the conservative myth that presents Pope John as an aimiable but bumbling old boy who could not remember from one day to the next who he had been talking to. From that it is only a step to saying that he was being manipulated by Capovilla or Bea for their nefarious schemes. All the evidence is to the contrary. John was perfectly lucid and alert on these big occasions. He was certainly not the puppet of Bea or Capovilla or of anyone else. Conversely Bea, while knowing perfectly well the role that only he could play in this pontificate, never tried to up-stage the Pope. As the CIA man was informed: 'Bea is the learned cousin who must always be listened to' (Spain, p. 6). But John had his own life to live and his own pontificate to complete. He was approaching eighty, four score, and that makes anyone pensive.

Chapter 19

Getting on for eighty

A conservative in all but essentials

(A. J. Balfour on Mr William E. Gladstone, quoted by Paul Johnson in *Pope John XXIII*, p. 53).

The summer of 1961 marked the turning-point in Pope John's pontificate. He had grown in confidence and sureness of touch, and he had a fresh Secretary of State in Amleto Cigognani. The 'new tone' struck in *Mater et Magistra* had been a success. He had found his own voice. In June 1961 he addressed the first session of the Central Commission, and so launched the immediate preparations for the Council. In July he sent a message to Pax Christi that was a first signal to the Soviet Union, made all the more necessary in that relations between Nikita Khrushchev and the new American president, John F. Kennedy, were increasingly fraught. The rhetoric of Kennedy's inauguration had been followed by the Bay of Pigs disaster. While John spent his summer at Castelgandolfo reflecting on his pontificate, Berlin was in turmoil, thousands were crossing daily to the West, and on August 13 rubble and barbed wire were unloaded in the deserted streets of East Berlin. Four days later the 'Berlin Wall' was complete. From now on international events counter-pointed the pontificate.

The meeting of the Central Commission in June 1961 marked the beginning of the final stage in the preparation of the Council. In his address on June 20, John listed the practical matters that would have to be solved before it could start: the choice of theologians and canonists to serve as experts; the rules of debate; the voting procedures. One question was already settled: 'It is obvious that Latin should be the official language of the Council; but on occasions, and where necessary, the use of modern languages will be permissible in speech' (DMC, 3, pp. 574–5). He meant that *documents* would have to be in Latin. The idea that Latin was 'the official and ordinary language of the Church' had been put forward in *l'Osservatore Romano* almost as soon as the Council was announced. Cardinal Antonio Bacci, the Latinist, was making a pre-emptive strike against those monoglot Anglo-Saxons who would undoubtedly demand simultaneous translation facilities. Later, Cardinal Richard J. Cushing, Archbishop of Boston, offered to pay for them. 'In Latin', he is supposed to have said, 'I represent the Church of silence'. Mgr Alfredo Cavagna, Pope John's confessor, argued for the use of modern languages, but he was outvoted in the Central Commission (Alberigo, p. 85; also Rynne, p. 101).

The great interest that the world was taking in the Council, John went on, meant that the media would come to Rome in force to report it. What was to be done about the press and the electronic media? Vatican I offered no helpful precedents: in 1870 the best that happened was that a well-connected reporter might dine with a bishop or corner a *monsignore* in the fire-engine room of the Apostolic Palace. John stated a simple principle that, had it been generously interpreted, would have averted much frustration: 'Nothing which helps souls should be hidden. But in dealing with grave and serious matters, we have the duty to present them with prudence and simplicity, neither flattering vague curiosity nor indulging in the temptation of polemics' (*Ibid.*). The trouble was that the maxim 'Nothing which helps souls should be hidden' was ambivalent: who was to decide what was edifying and what not? How did one know one was dealing with 'vague curiosity'? There were already those who thought that the best way the press could help souls was by shutting up.

More important than these practical questions was John's clear statement that the purpose of the Council was the *aggiornamento* or bringing up to date of the Roman Catholic Church. This of itself would set up ecumenical vibrations. He reminded the Central Commission that 'the Council is not a speculative assembly, but a living and vibrant organism which embraces everyone in the light and love of Christ' (DMC, 3, p. 575). It was not a Council *of* reunion, but it could be called a Council *for* reunion leading to 'the recomposition of the whole mystical flock of Christ'. He freely admitted that to achieve this great goal would involve 'a change in mentalities, ways of thinking and prejudices, all of which have a long history'. So he anticipated that some would feel threatened and disturbed. Finally, he hinted at a principle of the utmost importance: 'The language we use in the Council should be serene and tranquil; it should throw light on and remove misunderstandings; and it should *dissipate errors by the force of truth*' (*Ibid.*: my italics). It would need more than that to persuade Cardinal Alfredo Ottaviani, president of the Central Commission, that this gentle and non-judgemental approach was the right way to deal with 'errors'.

But having learned this principle in an ecumenical context, John now extended it to the whole world. Addressing Pax Christi, the Catholic peace movement, in French on July 26, 1961, and with one eye on the worsening situation in Berlin, he said:

Too often news reaches us of tensions between men, of threats and – alas – of conflicts. The worries of fathers and mothers find an echo in our heart. For our part, we remain resolutely faithful to the peaceful teaching of Our Lord; and we try to be a man of peace in the deepest meaning of the word.

And while we suffer from what is happening, we prefer to stress what unites and to walk along the road with anyone as far as possible, without compromising either justice or truth (*Lettere*, pp. 335–6).

That was precisely what was lacking in the summer of 1961. Bridges were being destroyed and walls built. Shouted slogans replaced dialogue.

At this point Cardinal Domenico Tardini, Secretary of State and the principal link with the previous pontificate, was struck down by a massive heart attack. He died on July 30, 1961, and was buried in the Carmel at Vetralla. The death of Cardinal Nicola Canali, for so long the financial wizard of the Vatican, on August 3, 1961, heightened the feeling that an era had come to an end. Nor was it entirely a matter for regret. John remembered the time early in 1960 when Tardini had tried to get rid of Mgr Angelo Dell'Acqua by 'promoting' him to the Paris nunciature. Having failed, Tardini called a press conference in his flat to announce that either Dell'Acqua went or he would. 'When one understands that one is no longer useful', said Tardini in his usual blunt fashion, 'one goes away' (*Magister*, p. 254: the date was March 16, 1960). Well, now Tardini had finally 'gone away'. John went to both funerals, but they did not fill him with thoughts of mortality. In fact he complains to Cavagna, his confessor, that they nearly spoiled the retreat he wanted to make in preparation for his eightieth birthday: 'Alas, even on this occasion, circumstances have not allowed us to realise our common desire and intention to have absolute and tranquil solitude. The departure to the highest sphere of two cardinals, both most distinguished servants of the Holy See, has caused me many grave preoccupations' (*Journal*, p. 341). He makes it sound as though the two cardinals had gone up to some celestial House of Lords.

The business of appointing a new Secretary of State could not long be delayed; yet it was a distraction, and John wanted to get it over with swiftly. Here is one reliable account of how Amleto Cicognani got the post:

> On the evening of the day Cardinal Tardini was buried, August 2, the Pope's secretary telephoned Cardinal Amleto Cicognani, asking him to call on the Pope. The cardinal was not happy at having to turn out at that late hour (John often kept late hours) but, given the circumstances, could hardly do otherwise. John explained that as the members of the sacred college gathered for the late cardinal's funeral, he had looked at each of them to see which might be Tardini's successor. And he had decided on Cicognani. The latter demurred, pointing out that he was old, not in the best of health, and would like some time to think about it. John apparently talked on about other subjects (he could always fill in the time talking when the situation demanded it, sometimes amusingly, sometimes to no great point). He then pointed out that the cardinal had had time to think and, of course, would be accepting the post. And that was what Cicognani did (*Politics*, pp. 117–8).

Peter Nichols uses this story to illustrate Pope John's apparent nonchalance and lack of foresight: 'He had not thought about the problem of a Secretary of State until Tardini was literally in his grave'. Certainly the decision was based on a hunch.

It would be going too far to say that Cicognani's appointment was, in any sense of the word, 'inspired'. John chose him because he wanted someone whose hands were clean of the clinging mud of Italian politics. Like Pope John a country boy from a north Italian village, Amleto Cicognani was two years younger. Their paths crossed in 1928–33 when Cicognani worked in the Congregation for the Oriental Churches and sometimes dealt with tangled Bulgarian and Uniate affairs. In 1933 Cicognani became apostolic delegate in Washington where he remained for a wholly unprecedented twenty-five years. Roncalli understood the problem of being 'the forgotten man' of the Vatican diplomatic service, and no doubt heard the rumours that Pius XII was displeased with Cicognani. At any rate his career seemed definitively blocked in 1953 when his brother Gaetano was made a cardinal. According to canon law, that ruled out a red hat for Amleto. In 1958 Pope John cheerfully disregarded this anti-nepotism rule and made Amleto a cardinal in his first consistory. As soon as the formidable Tisserant could be dislodged, Amleto Cicognani was put in charge of the Congregation for the Oriental Churches. His wheel had come full circle. Though not a brilliant man, and by now past his best, Cicognani was loyal, was believed to know English, the United States and even the Kennedy family and, having fewer ideas of his own, was much more comfortable to work with than Tardini. The CIA report says he was regarded as 'an old friend of great experience who has become one of the family, like a trusted doctor' (Spain, p. 6).

A new Secretary of State meant the chance of a new departure. Another reason why August 1961 marked a turning-point was that John was at last able to do some spiritual stock-taking. He is still turning to the future, and can now comment ruefully on the theory that he would be a 'stop-gap' Pope:

> When on October 28, 1958, the cardinals of the Holy Roman Church chose me to assume the supreme responsibility of ruling the universal flock of Jesus Christ, at seventy-seven years of age, the idea was abroad that I would be a provisional and transitional pope. Yet here I am, already on the eve of the fourth year of my pontificate, with an immense programme of work ahead of me to be carried out before the eyes of the whole world, which is watching and waiting (*Journal*, p. 325. Translation modified. Dorothy White translates: 'Everyone was convinced that I would be a provisional and transitional pope'. This is too sweeping. John wrote: '*La convinzione si diffuse che sarei stato un papa di provvisoria transizione*').

He was happy, too, with the style of his pontificate. Whatever gossips might think, he was not even trying to compete with the grand manner of Pius XII: 'It is commonly believed and considered fitting that the everyday language of the pope should be full of mystery and awe. But the example of Jesus is most closely followed in the most appealing simplicity' (*Ibid.*, p. 331). However, 'simplicity' was not to be confused with naïveté: 'Simplicity contains nothing that is contrary to prudence. Simplicity is love; prudence is thought. Love prays, the intelligence keeps watch' (*Ibid.*, p. 332).

But John's satisfaction with his pontifical style did not slip over into self-congratulation and complacency. He could always do more and do better. His meditation on the Gospels gave him a still deeper sense of what has to be called 'a spirituality of the papal office'. He had always had the spirituality appropriate to his state of life, first as a seminarian, later as priest and bishop. He recalls Aquinas' teaching that 'Christ is the source of all priesthood', and of course priesthood and episcopacy are enfolded in the papal office. But now he has the added title, 'Vicar of Christ', a term he never uses without fear and trembling. However, for John, it does not mean the blasphemy that he substitutes himself for the absent Christ, but rather that he has to be ever more obedient to Christ in love: 'The Vicar of Christ knows what Christ wants from him, and does not have to come before him to offer advice or insist on his own plans' (*Journal*, p. 336). Now he sees the New Testament references to Peter not as 'proof-texts' confirming the teaching of Vatican I, but as a call to greater love:

> When I ponder this mystery of intimate love between Jesus and his Vicar I think what an honour and a joy it is for me, but at the same time what a reason for shame at my own littleness and worthlessness. My life must be filled with the love of Jesus, and also with a great outpouring of goodness and sacrifice for individual souls and for the whole world. From the Gospel passage which proclaims the Pope's love for Jesus, it is but a short step to the law of sacrifice (*Ibid.*, p. 340).

The reference is to John 21.15–19, where Peter's protestations of love are followed by the prediction of his death. The 'law of sacrifice' now has a very precise meaning for him. He is seventy-nine, and though not yet 'entered upon helpless old age', knows that 'the great tribulation' of dying cannot be far off (*Ibid.*, p. 335).

So Jesus' words to Peter came home to him now with special force: ' "When you are old, another will gird you and carry you where you do not wish to go" ... O Jesus, I am ready to stretch out my hands, now weak with suffering, and allow others to dress me and support me along the way' (*Journal*, p. 340). To be 'Vicar of Christ' does not mean power and domination but closer identification with the life-bringing Passion of Christ. In old age, John's spirituality was simplified. He returns to the bold, but traditional, sense of God as

Mother. Psalm 130, he notes, 'has always made a great impression on me'. It concludes: 'But I have always calmed and quieted my soul, like a child quieted at its mother's breast' (*Ibid.*, p. 335).

But John's spiritual stock-taking did not rule out perceptiveness about the world around him. It was during this retreat that he sketched his portrait of 'the prudent man' who 'in every question knows how to distinguish the substance from the accidents' (*Journal*, p. 332). And here too he rejected Cardinal Siri's position on the political role of bishops (see p. 363 above). He interrupted his retreat on August 15 because of 'some anxieties about the problem of preserving world peace'. He said Mass in the parish church of Castelgandolfo and urged everyone to join him in prayer to Mary, 'the Queen of peace and peacemaker of the whole world' (*Journal*, p. 337).

As Pope John sat in the shade of the Castelgandolfo cedars, he 'rediscovered' Antonio Rosmini, the great nineteenth-century prophet of a renewed Catholicism. He transcribed passages from Rosmini's ascetical writings, but was even more interested, as a historian, in a letter written by Rosmini from Rome on November 23, 1848, on the eve of Pius IX's flight from revolution. Unable to maintain his position in the Papal States, of which he was both temporal and spiritual sovereign, Pius took refuge in Gaeta in the Kingdom of Naples. Though there was not a lot in common between 1848 and 1961, John was glad to find in Rosmini the judgement, utterly unconventional for the period, that 'good religious education' would do more for Italy than all the Papal Zouaves (*Journal*, p. 331). The principle had not changed: in 1961 'good religious education' was more important for Italy than making sure the Christian Democrats won the next election. The return to Rosmini was another return to his youth and the reforming tradition of north Italian Catholicism. John also knew that Rosmini had been put on the Index of Forbidden Books as a result of Jesuit intrigues. He dismissed this dead and otiose controversy with the remark that Rosmini's ideas on sacrifice 'are in line with all the ascetical teaching of the *Spiritual Exercises* of St Ignatius, whose admirable book Rosmini always kept beside him' (*Ibid.*, p. 329). So he 'rehabilitated' Rosmini long before the Holy Office formally got round to it.

One last feature of Pope John's Castelgandolfo retreat in August 1961 needs to be noted. Never before had his retreat reflections been so extensive and wide-ranging, occupying eighteen pages in the English translation. (Manuscript comparison does not help, since the pages are of irregular sizes.) Before then his longest retreat notes had been: Roman seminary, 1902, fourteen; Istanbul, 1942, five; Algiers, 1950, five. Mere length doesn't signify. Nor was it that Pope John was becoming garrulous in old age and couldn't stop. His prolixity, better, his expansiveness, is part of his attempt, as he moves towards his eightieth birthday, to see his past life and his present ministry in the light of the divine vocation by which he is absorbed. After 'half a century of living with pen in hand', he realised that he might not get another chance to set it all down. His stock-taking had an aspect of leave-taking.

He also sketched out an understanding of the Petrine ministry that would prove to have great ecumenical importance. He probably did not intend this consciously: as far as he was concerned, he was merely reflecting on his own experience. But his own experience provided a unique picture of the papal ministry seen from the inside – it turned out to be a profoundly Christian ministry that no 'Evangelical' Christian could blush for. This retreat summed up the simplification that had gone on in his spiritual life; it was also a synthesis of his entire ministry:

> What is important is to co-operate with God for the salvation of souls and of the whole world. This is our true mission, which reaches its highest expression in the pope.
>
> 'In all things look to the end' (*in omnibus respice finem*). I am not here thinking of death, but of the purpose and divine vocation to which the pope has been summoned by a mysterious decree of divine Providence. This vocation is shown in a threefold splendour: the personal holiness of the pope, which gives its own glory to his life; the love which the universal Church bears him, in the measure of that heavenly grace which alone can inspire him and assure his glory; finally, his obedience to the will of Jesus Christ, who alone rules, through the pope, and governs acording to his own pleasure, for the sake of that glory which is supreme on earth as it is in heaven. The humble pope's most sacred duty is to purify all his own intentions in the light of this glory, and to live according to the teaching and the grace of Christ (*Journal*, p. 333).

Glory: the word occurs four times in this passage. It refers not to the sound of heavenly trumpets or hosannahs, but to God himself in the splendour of his presence and the energy of his light. In the New Testament, it belongs to the Risen Christ in whose flesh 'dwells the glory of the only Son of God' (John 1.14, 18). Glory is the 'epiphany' or manifestation of God. If Pope John is to be called a 'mystic' – a term he avoided as presumptuous – it was because he had begun to dwell habitually in God's glory, of which grace is a foretaste and an inkling. How to live *Ad majorem Dei Gloriam*, to the greater glory of God, was the first lesson of his seminary; it was the final key to his life. In being brought closer to death, he was brought closer to glory.

He stayed on at Castelgandolfo until the end of September 1961. From there on September 10 he despatched a message of peace and good will to the Conference of Non-aligned Nations, then meeting in Belgrade, Yugoslavia. He reminded the world leaders of their 'dreadful responsibility before history, and, more importantly, before God's judgement' (Stehle, p. 302). This message evoked interest in Moscow, so much so that on September 21, 1961, *Pravda* published an interview with Khrushchev who said:

> John XXIII pays tribute to reason. From all parts of the world there rises up a desire for peace that we can only approve of . . . It is not that we fear God's judgement, in which as an atheist I do not believe, but we welcome the appeal to negotiate no matter where it comes from. Will ardent Catholics like John F. Kennedy, Konrad Adenauer and others heed the Pope's warning? (*Ibid.*).

There was a blatant element of propaganda in the contrast between the 'peace-loving' Pope and the 'war-mongering' lay Catholics (who were a little less 'ardent' than Khrushchev imagined). But it was an historic statement: for the first time since the Revolution a Russian leader had brought himself to say something good about the Pope. *Pravda* had dismissed Pius XII as 'the Pope of the Atlantic Alliance' and Stalin scornfully enquired how many divisions he could deploy. Khrushchev's interview had a more general international importance: it was a sign that for all his bluster, he was not prepared to push the world to the brink of nuclear war for the sake of getting the Allies out of Berlin. On October 17, 1961, he told the Communist Party Congress that 'the Western powers are showing some understanding of the situation' and so he would not insist on December 31 as the deadline for their departure from Berlin. That was a major concession.

The art of diplomacy consists in profiting from the slightest change in the wind. John took a discreet initiative. He knew that Palmiro Togliatti, secretary of the Italian Communist Party, was due to go to Moscow. He authorised Don Giuseppe De Luca to meet Togliatti in secret at the flat of Franco Rodano who maintained till the end of his days (July 21, 1983) that he was a Communist and a Catholic. De Luca's mission was to discuss how Moscow–Vatican relations could be improved. He suggested, and Togliatti agreed, that a telegram of congratulations on John's eightieth birthday would be an effective and non-committal sign. It would be well received in the Vatican, and need not be compromising for Khrushchev: to reach eighty and still be active was a remarkable human and non-ideological achievement (Magister, p. 272). However, De Luca was 'torn apart' by a dilemma: he had to choose between his long-standing friendship with Ottaviani who strongly disapproved of such overtures, and loyalty to Pope John, who trusted him and gave him his *juvenilia* to publish. He chose Pope John, but it killed him within the year (Guarnieri, pp. 82–3).

Khrushchev's telegram, therefore, was not a bolt from the blue – though that is what the world was allowed to think. It duly arrived, in Russian with an unofficial Italian translation, at 1.30 p.m. on Pope John's eightieth birthday, November 25, 1961. The Soviet Ambassador to the Republic delivered it to the papal nuncio to Italy who brought it along to the Secretariat of State. This

punctilious respect for protocol was typical of Soviet diplomacy when faced by a
novel situation. 'Well, it's better than a slap in the face', said John to Capovilla, as
he went off to pray. Later he said: 'There is something going on in the
world . . . Today we have received a sign from Providence' (Stehle, pp. 300–2:
confirmed by Capovilla). No doubt Khrushchev would have been surprised,
indignant even, to be considered an anonymous agent of Providence. But that is
what Pope John believed. His telegrammed reply to Khrushchev read: 'His
Holiness Pope John XXIII thanks you for your good wishes, and for his part
sends to the whole Russian people cordial wishes for the increase and
strengthening of universal peace by means of understanding based on human
brotherhood: to this end he prays fervently' (*Lettere*, p. 336). It went by the
reverse route to Khrushchev's telegram, and was in Italian, with a Russian
translation.

Pope John's diary for this November 25, 1961, provides a fascinating glimpse
into his state of mind. Khrushchev's telegram does not even rate a mention:

> Exactly eighty years: 1881–1961. *Deo Gratias* [thanks be to God]. Day of
> serenity and grace. In the morning office of St Catherine in the chapel as far
> as Nones. H[oly] Mass at eight in the chapel of Propaganda Fide with a few
> words from card. Agagianian and me: memories and edification. Followed
> the visit to the new upper storey of the vast building with a magnificent
> view all round. In the morning audience with card. Confalonieri on the
> affairs of the Consistorial [that is, the Congregation that appointed
> bishops]. In the Clementine Hall a magnificent audience with Austrian
> pilgrims and card. König: our dialogue much appreciated; among those
> present were twelve Scalabrini priests about to set off for the missions.
> Lunch with Mgr Loris. In the afternoon a good nap to restore myself, as
> usual in the armchair. At 4 o'clock a short walk in the garden. From 6 to 8
> continuation of the arduous business with card. Confalonieri. Then Rosary
> and *Te Deum* with Benediction of the Bl. Sacrament in the chapel. Supper.
> Listened to a moving radio programme commemorating the Pope and his
> LXXX years. Final prayers in the chapel: in prolonged and confident
> abandonment *in Domino, et in sinu Matris Jesu, et matris mei dulcissimae* [in the
> Lord, and on the breast of Jesus' mother, my most sweet mother] (*Gran
> Sacerdote*, p. 83: capitals and abbreviations as in *mss*, N 6/a, Capovilla
> Archives).

So Pope John spent his eightieth birthday routinely nominating bishops.

The same spirit of gratitude comes through in the official letter he wrote the
next day to Cicognani, thanking everyone for the birthday greetings he had
received. He recalled what he said 'with such trepidation' on the day he took
possession of his cathedral:

The Christian is commanded to bless the Lord 'all the days of his life'. But there are particularly solemn circumstances in which the act of blessing the Lord takes on a vaster meaning.

The wide-ranging nature of the birthday greetings we have received permits us to embrace, in a single gesture of affection, the beloved sons of the Catholic Church and the entire human family, and to call down on everyone the longed-for gifts of peace, serene and constructive prosperity, mutual understanding and collaboration, in the abundance of the Lord's unfailing blessing (*Lettere*, p. 335).

But not all the 'beloved sons of the Catholic Church' were prepared to join in the *Te Deum*. Ottaviani was fuming. This was what was bound to happen now that Tardini was no longer there and Dell'Acqua was effectively in charge. If the Pope himself could so cavalierly converse with top Communist leaders, what hope was there of holding the anti-Communist line in Poland, or, more to the point, in Italy? Ottaviani was not alone. *L'Osservatore Romano* feigned to ignore the exchange of telegrams until December 17 – three weeks late.

Pope John knew what was being said. He made a brief note in his diary: 'Lengthy commentaries in the press in all directions on this unexpected novelty. Naturally the zealots seize the chance to distinguish themselves' (*Gran Sacerdote*, p. 84). Unable to reply to his critics directly, he prompted an article in *l'Eco di Bergamo*. It was signed *Gladius*, a rather obvious pen-name for his old friend Mgr Andrea Spada. It was rambling and long-winded and it contained the extraordinary and inaccurate piece of information that until the time of Pope John, 'Anglicans' had burned an effigy of the pope on November 5. Spada made some serious points: Khrushchev's telegram was the 'moral recognition' of a 'spiritual authority' not based on military strength; it was an act of courtesy and good manners, and as such should be accepted as a new factor in international relations; and that whatever Khrushchev's 'ulterior motives' – no naïveté there – it was to be welcomed (*Lettere*, p. 337: *l'Eco di Bergamo* article was on December 2, 1961). Spada was such a faithful interpreter of his mind, that John thought yet again of bringing him to Rome to edit *l'Osservatore Romano*. But that would cause further upset in the Curia. He let things be, and went into a brief Advent retreat with the Capuchin Fr Ilario de Milano whom he found 'difficult to follow' (*Gran Sacerdote*, p. 83).

None of his short notes reflect any excitement about what had just been happening. He reread his summer reflections with profit. For the first time he confesses that he is beginning to feel his age: 'I notice in my body the beginning of some trouble that must be natural for an old man. I bear it with resignation, even if it is sometimes rather tiresome and also makes me afraid it will get worse. It is not pleasant to think about this; but once again, I feel ready for anything' (*Journal*, p. 342). Was he already being affected by stomach cancer? Despite these worries about his health, he resolved to do some reading 'in order that what I say may not be superficial but substantial'. Moreover, 'In recent months I have felt very much at home with St Leo the Great and with Innocent III. It is a pity so few ecclesiastics study these writers, who abound in theological and pastoral doctrine. I shall never tire of drawing from these sources, so rich in sacred learning and sublime and delightful poetry' (*Ibid.*, pp. 342–3). Why poetry? In John's vocabulary, 'poetry' refers to any passage of prose or verse which he finds eloquent and memorable (see, for example, 'What is my poor life of fifty years of priesthood? A faint reflection of this poem, "My merit – God's mercy" ': *Journal*, p. 307).

But why Leo the Great and Innocent III? Popes notoriously exaggerate the importance of their own office: '*Il croit trop à la papauté*' (He believes too much in the papacy) said a witty Frenchman of Paul VI; and if like John they have a sense of history, they are naturally drawn to their predecessors . . . and equals. John treated the popes of the past not as dead butterflies trapped in the pages of a book but as living voices that sprang up from the page and witnessed to the continuity of the Petrine office. It is worth asking why John should reach back beyond the Renaissance and even the mediaeval Popes to someone from the patristic era who exercised his ministry from 440 to 461. We are not bereft of an answer, for John wrote one of his minor encyclicals, *Aeterna Dei*, for the fifteenth hundred anniversary, to the day, of Leo's death, November 11, 1961.

Pope John explains that the true greatness of Leo does not lie in his dramatic confrontation with Attila the Hun on the banks of the River Po in the summer of 452. (This used to be a set-piece essay for Italian historians.) Leo turned Attila back by sheer force of personality or spirituality. It is not known what he said to the barbarian. John does not stress this episode because it would have been all too easy for Ottaviani to contrast his irresolution before Khrushchev with Leo's firmness before Attila. John's interest in Leo is that he was pope at a time when the division between the Eastern and the Western Church still lay six centuries ahead. Moreover, his teaching authority was accepted in the whole, undivided Church. His *Tomos* was accepted in Constantinople in 449 and influenced the Council of Chalcedon two years later. When the Anglican Roman Catholic International Commission sought an example of how the bishop of Rome as 'universal primate' helped to preserve the Church from error, it resorted to this incident at Chalcedon: 'Peter has spoken through Leo' (ARCIC, p. 94). So Pope John's intuition of the importance of Leo was ecumenically perceptive.

It is less easy to explain what he hoped to learn from Innocent III. Innocent reigned from 1198 to 1216. He used every spiritual weapon in the papal armoury. He excommunicated the Venetians for not getting on with their crusade against the Saracens, placed England under an interdict, declared *Magna Carta* invalid, and launched a terrifying campaign to root out the Cathars from southern France. None of these actions offered a precedent for anything John wanted to do.

Innocent was also the first pope to be called 'Vicar of Christ', this novelty gradually displacing the more traditional 'Vicar of Peter' (see Tillard, p. 100). This was not very promising. Innocent interested John for other reasons. In 1215 he called the Fourth Lateran Council in Rome which was attended by 2,283 representatives of the Catholic world. That was not much below the number who would be assembling for John's own Council. But Innocent's Council members were much more diverse and less clerical than those John expected to meet in 1962. Innocent, too, had provided at least two famous phrases. He supplied the title *Mater et Magistra* (Mother and Teacher) and spoke of 'the five wounds of the Church'.

So Pope John's browsings among 'the old popes' were not merely the self-indulgence of an historian; they added a dimension to the preparation for the Council and they helped to define what a pope was. It was the Council that now took up most of his time. On December 2, 1961, he notes laconically:

A great deal of my work is in preparation for the Second Vatican Council. There begins to take shape in my mind the desire of gathering around me in my daily prayer the prayers of all the clergy, secular and religious, and of all the women's religious congregations, in some official and world-wide form. I shall await a happy inspiration to invite . . . (*Journal*, p. 343).

The sentence breaks off there. His opening remark is the understatement of his life: the programme of work he had before him was immense and would have daunted a lesser man in his prime. It was astonishing that an eighty-year-old could get through it at all. But John's methodical habits paid off: one thing at a time, and in order, saw him through.

And his request for prayers was extended to the whole Catholic and indeed Christian world in *Humanae Salutis*, the solemn apostolic constitution which convoked Vatican II. It appeared on Christmas Day 1961. He was working on *Humanae Salutis* early in December 1961. There is evidence of at least three drafts in his own handwriting: the fortunes of a single sentence can be studied in *Lettere* (p. 522). The most important feature of *Humanae Salutis* is the way it emphasises, more clearly than ever before, the idea that the Council will be *at the service of the world*. It will not be a navel-gazing inner-churchy event, but an attempt to speak to 'the crisis that is under way in society' (Abbott, p. 704). This concern for the world's problems – summed up in technical progress without spiritual progress and bloody wars – commands the structure of *Humanae Salutis*. It deals first of all with the 'world' and only then with the Church which, says John, 'always living and always young, feels the rhythm of the times' (*Ibid.*, p. 706).

Fine as rhetoric, but what does it mean? It is here that Pope John, in a single sentence, provided his Council with a method and commentators with material for a lifetime. He spoke of the need to 'discern the signs of the times': 'We should make our own Jesus' advice that we should know how to discern 'the signs of the times' (Matthew 16.4), and we seem to see now, in the midst of so much darkness, a few hints which augur well for the fate of the Church and humanity' (Abbott, p. 704). In the Matthew text and its parallels, Jesus quotes proverbs about weather-forecasting. They were the equivalent of the English proverb: 'Red sky at night is the shepherd's delight; red sky in the morning is the shepherd's warning'. Jesus then says to the multitudes: 'You know how to interpret the appearance of earth and sky; but why do you not know how to interpret the present time?' (Luke 12.56). Most exegetes think that 'the times' means the new Messianic age inaugurated by Jesus, and that the 'signs' are his miracles. Pope John gave this an accommodated meaning to express his confidence that the Spirit was still at work in the world. He acts through the men and women, the trends and the movements of the present age. Salvation is always in the present tense.

Pope John did not deny the negative factors. There was enough gloom and darkness in the world of late 1961 to make anyone pessimistic: the Berlin crisis was not resolved, nuclear weapons were being tested, and sites for them were already being prepared in Cuba. Jürgen Moltmann accused Pope John and Marie-Dominique Chenu O.P., who influenced him, of ignoring the apocalyptic signs of disaster and concentrating on those that could be given a more optimistic reading (*Church in the Power of the Spirit*, p. 368, fn. 64.) It is true that John was not very interested in the signs that the end was nigh: there wasn't much he or anyone else could do in the face of the world's end. In the meantime, he was concerned with what the Holy Spirit was saying to the Churches.

This also involved a different way of stating the relationship between the Church and the 'world'. John broke down the false dichotomies between the Church (holy) and the world (sinful), between grace and nature, between eternal salvation and temporal commitment. One may distinguish between them, but they are different aspects of one reality. He was explicit on this point:

> Though not having directly temporal ends, the Church in its mission cannot fail to concern itself with the problems and worries of here below. It knows how helpful for the good of souls are those means which tend to make the individual people in need of salvation more human. It knows that by vivifying the temporal order with the light of Christ it reveals men to themselves; so it leads them to discover in themselves their own true nature, dignity and purpose (*Abbott*, p. 707).

That anticipated the spirit and the language of *Gaudium et Spes*. Pope John's Christmas message for 1961 was that 'glory to God in the highest' was the surest path to 'peace on earth'.

Humanae Salutis marked a victory for Cardinal Bea. Pope John no longer prayed for the return of the separated brethren to Roman obedience, but for 'the return of unity and peace, according to the prayer of Christ to the Father'. That left the *how* of unity in God's hands. Again, John noted that other Christian Churches had welcomed the Council 'and hope to send representatives of their communities to follow its work at close quarters (*da vicino*)' (Abbott, p. 709). This was the first discreet yet official recognition of the fact that there would be non-Catholic 'observers' at the Council. Bea had come a long way in a short time. Only a year earlier his first meeting with Willem Visser't Hooft, secretary general of the World Council of Churches, took place in secret and in a cloak-and-dagger atmosphere (Nash, p. 108). With Tardini gone, the need for such precautions was removed, and five Roman Catholic 'observers' were able to attend the Third General Assembly of the WCC in New Delhi. The welcome they received and the access they were given to documents and debates, encouraged Bea to make comparable arrangements for the Council.

The only matter *Humanae Salutis* failed to clear up was the date of the Council. It was going to be vaguely 'some time in 1962'. But John, now past eighty, was nearly there. 'Three years have passed', he wrote, 'during which we have seen, day by day, the little seed develop and become, with the blessing of God, a mighty tree' (Abbott, p. 707). It was a mighty tree, and it had some pretty tangled branches.

Chapter 20

The dress rehearsal

The meetings of the Central Preparatory Commission of the Council will
be more important than the sessions of the Council itself, since greater
frankness and sincerity may be expected in them

(Cardinal Bernard Alfrink, Archbishop of Utrecht, in *Herder-Korrespondenz*, XVI, 2,
1962).

Few could have known at the time how heart-felt were Cardinal Alfrink's words
early in 1962. For the meetings of the Central Commission were held behind
well-locked doors. They were so impenetrably secret that the reports on them in
l'Osservatore Romano were written in advance so that nothing untoward might
leak out. They had a feature shared by many Vatican press office hand-outs then
and later: they were strong on insignificant detail. The Central Commission, the
world learned, was made up of 102 members and 29 consultors; among them
were 60 cardinals, 5 patriarchs, 27 archbishops, 6 bishops and 4 general superiors
of religious orders. They came from 59 countries (the complete list followed). The
Hall of Congregations in which the Central Commission forgathered had been
redecorated. It was described in detail from the chandelier, a gift of the Murano glass-
blowers of Venice to Pius IX in 1877, to the central tapestry which, measuring 9 by
5.30 metres, depicted the Last Supper: it was here because Pius VI had washed the feet
of the poor in this hall on Maundy Thursday (Caprile, I, 2, p. 225).

But that was in 1780. *L'Osservatore Romano's* reports in 1961 and 1962 were less
exhaustive. They presented a picture of the meetings of the Central Commission
in which all was sleep-inducing sweetness and light. Needless to say, this was
nonsense. To those who took part in them, the meetings of the Central
Commission acted as a kind of 'little Council' and were a dress rehearsal for the
real thing. In 1965 Cardinal Giacomo Lercaro declared that the time had come for
a thorough historical study of the preparations for the Council: he believed it
would bring out the contrast between what Pope John intended and what the
Curial preparations actually achieved (*Linee*, p. 20). Ten years later, Philippe
Levillain, relying on unnamed 'unpublished sources', began to answer Lercaro's
desideratum. But since he wrote from a narrowly 'French' point of view, his work
will have to be filled out from other, equally anonymous sources.

That the Central Commission would have such an important role had not been
anticipated. Busy cardinals with full diaries thought they could dispense
themselves from attending. But they were 'chased up' (as one of them said) by

Pericle Felici, secretary general of the council, who revealed himself as a highly efficient man who kept the paper – or rather the thick, red-bound volumes – moving. Its members were soon disabused of the notion that the Central Commission was a kind of Honorary Committee of notables which left all the hard work of drafting to the sub-commissions. This complacent theory was wrecked first because Cardinal Alfredo Ottaviani, who since the death of Cardinal Domenico Tardini had assumed the mantle of leader of the conservatives, claimed for the Central Commission the right of veto over the work of all the other commissions. It had the same function in the Council preparations as the Supreme Congregation of the Holy Office had in the Curia generally.

Moreover, the main immediate task of the Central Commission was to judge whether the in-put from the other commissions was 'worthy of a Council'. It was not an easy criterion to apply. At one point they found themselves discussing the draft of a decree on diocesan archives and seminary libraries (Caprile, I, 2, p. 234), a matter that was close to Pope John's heart. At another time they earnestly debated whether the cassock or a grey suit, light or dark, was fitting garb for a priest. The meetings got longer and longer. They began at 9.30 a.m., and often lasted well beyond one o'clock. At the May session, Cardinal Pietro Ciriaci, who looked remarkably like the French comedian Fernandel, broke up the meeting at 1.50 by noisily gathering up his papers and saying to the acting chairman, Pizzardo: 'It is time. Lunch. No more today'. If Roman cardinals found the pace hard to bear, those who were jetting back and forth across the Atlantic or the Pacific almost once a month found it even more taxing.

The 'foreigners' grumbled when they noticed that Curial cardinals only came to meetings when the matter in hand concerned them. This prepared the ground for the dramatic clash in November, 1961. The question, what is the Council for? had still not been given a full answer. As late as September, 1961 Felici still thought that the function of the Council might be 'to condemn the gravest errors of our time and reaffirm the principal points of Catholic doctrine' (Rouquette, I, p. 104). Felici, however, conceded that 'others' (and that included Pope John) wanted the Council to be 'pastoral'. Unfortunately, he did not offer much clue as to what this slippery concept might entail except that the Council would 'bring back those who are distant from the Church, gather in those who are scattered, and call to life those who are dead to grace' (*Ibid.*). There was not a lot to choose between Felici's condemnations and a twitch of his pastoral staff. Yet Felici was secretary general of the Council. He ought to have known what it was for.

Felici's concept of the Council was echoed, thunderingly, in a proposal that Ottaviani laid before the November, 1961 meeting of the Central Commission. With a naïveté far out-stripping that alleged to have been displayed by Pope John, he proposed a new 'Profession of Faith' for the forthcoming Council that would repeat the anti-Modernist oath, repudiate the errors condemned by *Humani*

Generis as well as those subsequently circulating about Mary's virginity, solemnly affirm that there was an essential difference (and not merely a difference of degree) between the hierarchical priesthood and the general priesthood of all the faithful and, finally, denounce those who spoke 'with exaggerated emphasis about the Church's guilt and sinfulness *etc*' (Caprile, I, 2, p. 229). Ottaviani had simply dusted down his old files from 1948 (see p. 311 above).

Ottaviani succeeded in uniting against him a majority of the diocesan cardinals and bishops. It was not so much that anyone disagreed with what he was saying; they just could not see the point of saying it all over again in a Council that was supposed to be dedicated to 'renewal' and *aggiornamento*. Whatever these notions might be stretched to mean, Ottaviani's proposal could not be considered as a glowing instance of them. Ottaviani, accustomed to speak in the name of the Holy Father for over fifteen years, had the disagreeable experience of being attacked. Moreover, whereas he habitually spoke as one who had authority, he was now treated as an equal, one member of the college. Cardinal Bernard Alfrink of Utrecht, the Netherlands, led the attack. He was quickly backed up by the Germans and Cardinal Franz König of Vienna; the French bided their time; the Americans who took it in turns to come, found it hard to follow the Latin debates and tended to trust Cardinal William Godfrey, of Westminster, by now a very sick man, who was an excellent Latinist. Suspicious of all things new or strange, he tended to take Ottaviani's side on disputed questions.

There were so many disputed questions at this November, 1961 meeting. Cardinal Augustin Bea presented his scheme for having non-Catholic observers at the Council (Caprile, I, 2. p. 229). The response to the announcement of the Council had been so welcoming, he maintained, that it would be folly not to profit from the evident good will it had aroused. Ottaviani tried to ensure that these 'observers', supposing they came, should know as little as possible about what was going on. The Council was an essentially *Catholic* event. *Per se* it did not concern anyone else. But since, anyway, decisions of the Central Commission by a two-thirds majority were merely 'consultative', in the end it all depended on what the Pope decided. On the issue of 'observers', John was on Bea's side. It was at this November, 1961 session that Ottaviani also launched the first version of his ill-fated *schema* (or draft text) on 'The Two Sources of Revelation'. A year later it would suffer a terrible battering at the Council and be withdrawn, along with most of the other prepared texts. The Council was to confirm what the meetings of the Central Commission had already suggested: the Roman Curia could no longer impose its will on the Church as a whole. The dress rehearsal took place in private, but the characters already had their allotted roles; a year later they played them out before the eyes of the world.

Had Pope John already guessed what would happen at the Council? Mgr Alfredo Cavagna kept him informed about the disputes in the Central

Commission. But there is no evidence that he expected, still less hoped, that the Curia's draft texts would be rejected when the Council met. Yet this is what the liberal or 'progressive' myth presupposes. It assumes that Pope John, with his peasant shrewdness, out-manoeuvred the Curia, artfully leaving it the illusion of control while knowing full well that it would shortly be routed. All the evidence goes the other way. No wedge can be driven between Pope John's preparations for the Council and the Curial preparations. They went hand in hand at every stage. He saw the secretary general, Felici, certainly weekly and sometimes more often (Caprile, '*Ancora su Giovanni XXIII*', in *Civiltà Cattolica*, April 5, 1980, p. 54). He never complained of Felici's approach – though there might have been grounds for complaint. Nor did he ever show any deep dissatisfaction with the way the work was going. He read all the draft texts personally, and annotated them. His notes are usually on minor points or else record simply that he had read them attentively and, sometimes, with joy: '*Lectum maxima cum attentione*' and '*lectum attente et laetanter*' to quote two (see Carbone, Vincenzo, '*Genesi e criteri della pubblicazione degli Atti del Concilio Vaticano II*', in *Lateranum* XLIV, 1978, pp. 579–5). These are not the comments of a man who thought the draft texts were on a wrong track or were likely to lead the Council up the garden path.

Moreover, Pope John made a point of thanking the Central Commission each time it met. On January 23, 1962, he praised the draft texts rather lavishly. At their last meeting on June 20, 1962, he was even more fulsome: 'Three years of magnificent, edifying and most devoted hard work'. If the progressive myth were true, all this was a Machiavellian feint. True, it would have been bad public relations to tell them that they had been wasting their time. But was he really capable of saying one thing while thinking another? The word for that is hypocrisy.

The problem is deepened if we consider the unexpected bombshell of *Veterum Sapientia* (The Wisdom of the Ancients) which burst upon an astonished world on February 22, 1962. It was a eulogy of the Latin language which was said to be *the* language of the Church. It was therefore imposed or re-imposed as the teaching medium of philosophy and theology in seminaries. It was surely the most ineffectual document ever published by Pope John. For the rest of that academic year – rarely longer – tongue-tied Anglo-Saxon professors exercised their rusty Latin on bewildered and sometimes uncomprehending students. This was all in the name of 'good Pope John' who despite his liberal image was now engaged in 'putting the clock back'. His admirers had a hard time making sense of it. Some claimed it had been imposed on him by the Roman Curia – a fact Pope John vigorously denied whenever he got the chance; others used it to illustrate the difference between 'Roman' and 'Anglo-Saxon' attitudes to law – the authors of the document did not expect it to be taken literally, while those who received it did (Trevor, p. 295).

Certainly *Veterum Sapientia* was a triumph for Cardinal Antonio Bacci, the celebrated Latinist, whose hobby was devising Latin neologisms for terms such as 'jet-plane' and 'transistor radio'. He wrote it for Cardinal Pizzardo, prefect of the Congregation for Seminaries. Pope John's interest in Latin was more because it was the language of the 'old fathers' among whom he loved to browse to avoid 'superficiality' (*Journal*, p. 342). Moreover, since it had been decided that Latin would be the language of the Council, he thought it not unreasonable that priests and bishops of the future ought at least to be able to read it fluently. He himself did not find conversing in Latin at all easy or natural, and as the Council approached practised twice a day with Fr Luigi Ciappi O.P., the gaunt Master of the Sacred Palace, and Mgr Alfredo Cavagna, his confessor (*Journal*, p. 345 and p. 348).

The timing of *Veterum Sapientia* makes more sense if we relate it to an inner-curial battle over liturgy. The Liturgy Commission was much better organised and broadly-based than any of the other commissions. It escaped from curial control and generated a measure of reforming enthusiasm in its members. As Mgr Annibale Bugnini remarked after their spring, 1961, meeting: 'One felt the contribution of different cultures and experiences; local situations coloured and refined our thinking and our way of expressing ourselves. We formed a true family in which the "sense of the Church" was vividly alive' (Bugnini, p. 29). Bugnini was not making this up: in the Liturgy Commission they had the true experience of 'the Council before the Council' and their draft text was the only one – of seventy – to survive. But their proposals for a modest use of the vernacular were already causing alarm in the Curia.

The real drama came on January 22, 1962, when the aged Cardinal Gaetano Cicognani, president of the Liturgy Commission because Prefect of the Congregation of Rites, was presented with the text that would be laid before the Council. 'He welcomed it', said Bugnini, who was Secretary of the Commission, 'with joy and apprehension' – joy because the work was complete, apprehension because whenever he had to commit himself, he became nervous, hesitant and timorous, and wanted more time to re-read and consult. But he took the plunge, signed on February 1, 1962, and died four days later on February 5. Bugnini concludes his account: 'If Cardinal Cicognani had not signed this document, humanly speaking it would have been a disaster, for everything would have been thrown into the melting pot yet again. But who knows the ways of the Lord?' (Bugnini p. 37). Bugnini's question has a note of personal pathos. Regarded by the Curia as a dangerous iconoclast, within the year he was disgraced and forbidden to teach (Rouquette, I, p. 234). Paul VI rehabilitated him in 1967 by making him Secretary of the Council for the implementation of the liturgical reforms.

As soon as Gaetano Cicognani had appended his last and most fateful signature on February 1, the way was open for the release of the *motu proprio*, *Consilium Dei*

Nostra, which fixed the start of the Council for next October 11. Twenty days later, *Veterum Sapientia* appeared. It was therefore a concession made to those powerful curial forces who regarded the work of the Liturgy Commission as highly dangerous. Pope John was doing the balancing act that he would do so often once the Council began. Not that he needed to be insincere in this: he genuinely valued Latin. But he always preferred to bend rather than to break.

On another level, however, the argument over *Veterum Sapientia* was not about Latin at all: it was about who would control the Council. The use of Latin gave the Curia a built-in advantage that it did not propose to throw away. Felici, the secretary general, was perfectly at ease in Latin, could dazzle and make jokes that at least his cronies appreciated. Conversely, Cardinal William Godfrey of Westmister, having struggled to get out the phrase '*Debemus levare Latinam*' (by which he meant raise its status) was astonished to read in *Il Tempo* the next day that he had called for Latin to be abolished (*levare* in Italian means to take away: see Rynne, p. 101).

On a still deeper level, *Veterum Sapientia* was about the relationship of language to faith. It praised Latin as an 'immutable' language, not subject to the hazardous lability of modern languages where words shift and slide. Precisely because Latin is a dead language, *Veterum Sapientia* claims, it is 'fixed and invariable' (No. 8). In short it is the perfect language for a scholastic theology preserved – so it believes – from the ravages of time and history. But this was not Pope John's last word on the subject. In his opening address to the Council he said that 'the substance of the ancient deposit of faith is one thing and the way it is presented is another'. Without actually contradicting *Veterum Sapientia,* this statement is hard to reconcile with it. John's mind could accommodate such puzzling incompatibilities: the important thing is to know what he says when it really matters, when the crunch comes.

Pope John's thinking about the Council moved on many levels – spiritual, personal and political – and was never the realisation of a clear-cut and well-formulated blue-print. His essential role was to be an enabler and an improviser. He was happy to accept the curial plans – until something better came along. When something better came along, he pounced upon it and made it his own and sometimes claimed – with perfect truth – that it was what he had wanted all along. Bea's work at the Secretariat for Christian Unity is an obvious example: Bea helped Pope John to become himself and realise his vision. The meetings with Church leaders were an education in themselves, but they were also a hint of what would happen at the Council: it was more difficult (though not impossible) to attack caricatures or straw-men if representatives of the straw-men were listening to you.

Thus Pope John was led to range well beyond the curial preparations for the Council which in his more sanguine moments he found satisfactory. That he was an improviser is proved if we consider how eagerly he seized upon and adopted ideas put forward by Cardinals Wyszyński of Warsaw, Suenens of Malines-Brussels, Bengsch of Berlin and – last, not least – Montini of Milan. What they brought to him will be the subject of the rest of this chapter.

There were two main problems. Was it the task of the Council to condemn contemporary errors? And how could the sheer daunting mass of material – seventy *schemata* or drafts were being prepared – be reduced to manageable scale while still realising the goals of the Council?

On February 17, 1962, on the eve of *Veterum Sapientia,* John gave an audience to Cardinal Wyszyński and discussed with him what could be done abut Mgr Josef Slipyi, major archbishop of the Ukrainians, who had vanished into a Soviet labour camp after the enforced destruction of his Church in 1948. John had noticed that it was Slipyi's seventieth birthday. Over supper he said to his secretary, Mgr Loris Capovilla:

> The Council is approaching. I've been thinking of the bishops who are in prison or in exile and who can't come. We have to try to do something for them . . . Of course we must defend truth, freedom and justice, and not flinch before the men of power; but over and above that there has to be paternal and fraternal tenderness towards those who may be tempted to feel abandoned or think they have been forgotten.
> The exchange of greetings on November 25, 1961, my eightieth birthday, should not lead sensible people to fantastic conclusions; but it was a step towards prudent contact. We should let the East Europeans know this: they have shown respect for the pope as the head of the Catholic family, and for the first time they have paid tribute to his work for peace. The response was swift and sincere, and brought a twinge of nostalgia to the former Vatican diplomat who remembers his cordial relations with the Slav peoples.
> So without using protocol and strict diplomatic forms, it would be good to let them know the pope's sorrow at being unable to welcome the bishops from certain countries; and they should also realise that this is why it is difficult for the pope to make some of these prelates cardinals (IME, p. 170).

So he proposed to use the prospect of a red hat as a bait. This piece of table-talk did not appear until 1983. Published earlier, it would have cleared up some of the mis-understandings about Pope John's *Ostpolitik,* a term, incidentally, he never used.

But who should be approached informally? And through whom? There were no ordinary diplomatic relations between the Vatican and any communist country. Pope John realised that Khrushchev held the key to the religious policy of the entire Eastern bloc. His Secretary of State, Amleto Cicognani, reminded him of Mgr Francesco Ladrone, who had been professor at the Catholic university of Washington and confessor to the Apostolic Delegation at 3339 Massachusetts Avenue. Originally from Piedmont in northern Italy, Ladrone was now in Pope John's old post in Istanbul. It had been raised to the status of a pro-nunciature and was still a good window on the East. A straightforward man, now aged seventy-six, Ladrone had an unusual background for a diplomat. When invited to take a holiday in Rome in February, 1962 he replied that he had work to do in Ankara and didn't need a holiday. A 'phone call told him that he was needed urgently. He arrived lackadaisically in mid-March. A few precious weeks had been lost.

Pope John surprised Ladrone by receiving him not in his library but in the Vatican gardens. It was easier to talk there. As they strolled, Pope John said, 'For me you are the top diplomat of the Holy See' (*Utopia*, Italian p. 249). Then Ladrone discovered his mission: working through the Soviet ambassador to Turkey, he was to try and find out whether there was any hope that bishops from Eastern Europe would be allowed to come to the Council. This walk in the Vatican gardens did not go unremarked in the Secretariat of State which, suspecting that something was afoot, chose precisely this moment to offer Ladrone the prestigious post of nuncio to Brussels. Pope John told him to decline the offer. He had something else in mind (*Ibid.*, pp. 247–8).

Back home in Turkey, Ladrone got in touch with the Soviet ambassador Nikita Ryjov who was affable and within a week reported that he had an answer from Moscow: agreed. Ladrone then handed over the official invitations to the Catholic bishops of the Soviet Union who were mostly in the Baltic republics. The ambassador took them personally to Moscow – to avoid losing them in the post, he explained, possibly humorously. Emboldened by this success, Ladrone presented his respects to the other ambassadors of the Soviet bloc and invited their bishops to come to the Council. They all agreed to pass on the Pope's request. Khrushchev's example was the determining factor.

On June 2, 1962, Ladrone was back in Rome to report on the apparent success of his mission. Although the audience had been fixed for the next day, John received his 'top diplomat' immediately and explained: 'This time you've taken the place of the Princess Maria Gabriella. This is how it came about. While I was shaving I heard on the news this morning that today is Italy's national feast, and I thought it wouldn't be proper to receive a princess of the house of Savoy on the feast of the Republic' (*Utopia*, Italian, p. 248). This is an example of Bergamesque humour: dry, but with a twinkle in the eye. But the main point of the whole Ladrone episode is that Pope John was not only prepared but was delighted to depart from official channels – in this case the Secretariat of State – when it suited him. He had a certain conspiratorial pleasure in outwitting his officials.

He was equally open to the unofficial when it came to preparing the Council. If a bishop's pastoral letter seemed to him to sum up the spirit of the Council, he wrote to him immediately to ask for advice. This happened twice. The first

pastoral letter to catch his eye was written by Cardinal Léon-Joseph Suenens of
Malines, Belgium. He liked it so much that he asked Suenens to pen a memo on
how the work of the Council should be organised (De Riedmatten, p. 53). This
was becoming an urgent question. Unless something were done and done soon,
the Council would be enmeshed in the overlapping and endlessly proliferating
branches of the giant tree. Suenens promptly obliged with a lucid document in
two parts: (i) what the Council should not attempt to do; (ii) what the Council
should do. Suenens argued that a Council that appeared obsessed with inner-
Church matters would disappoint the expectations of the world. It would have to
face up honestly to questions of war and peace, the morality of nuclear war, birth-
control and 'the population explosion'. Suenens did not mean that questions like
collegiality and ecumenism were not important. But he wanted to distinguish and
keep in balance the inner life of the Church (*ad intra*) and the Church seen in
relation to the world and its problems (*ad extra*). This put neatly what Pope John
had tried to say in *Humanae Salutis* (see p. 398 above), and it affected all later
statements. From now on Suenens became one of Pope John's confidants. And
the fact that he was backed up by the Catholic university of Louvain, of which he
had been vice-rector, brought into consideration a new set of experts to balance
those who were predominantly Roman-trained. The small commission of six, three
priests and three medical doctors, discreetly set up later to consider 'population
problems' had three Belgians and no Italians on it (St John-Stevas, p. 106).

Cardinal Montini's Lenten pastoral, written from Rome, was an epistle to the
Milanese. It was called *Pensiamo al Concilio,* Let us think about the Council.
Though he modestly described it as 'a simple pastoral', it had the sweep and scope
of an encyclical. He had evidently read and assimilated all the literature and, like
Suenens, was backed up by a Catholic university, the Sacred Heart university of
Milan. He set himself the task of answering a simple question: 'What are the
Pope's intentions concerning the forthcoming Council?' Though he did not
claim any inside knowledge, it was obvious to all that he knew Pope John's mind
and emphasised what he wanted emphasising. He said that the central theme of
the Council would be the mystery of the Church. This was not in the least trite,
since it meant that the Church would not be seen as it was in the prepared
documents as a juridical institution; and it meant that the criterion for retaining or
discarding a text would be whether it was Christo-centric or not. 'It is the whole
Church that expresses itself in the Council', said Montini, explaining why the
Milanese were involved in it, 'and we are the Church'.

Though he had spent most of his life in Rome, as he reminds them, Montini
understood why the Catholic world felt resentful about the centralising
tendencies of the Curia. Of course, Rome is the centre and what it says is received
with joy. But then, almost concealed beneath the verbiage, comes the rapier
thrust:

The Church throughout the world received orders and instructions which it obeyed willingly enough, though it sometimes regretted that there were no arrangements for dialogue and that it had not been invited to collaborate; the result was unity had to be lived out in passive acceptance rather than celebrated in fraternity (*Pensiamo al Concilio*, No. 9).

The Council would have to put that imbalance right.

Where Felici had been uncertain about the purpose of the Council, Montini is crystal-clear. He says bluntly that 'the Council is not likely to define any new dogma as part of revelation' (*Pensiamo al Concilio*, No. 46). Its main business will be renewal and *aggiornamento*. Like Suenens, he wanted the Council to speak to the world but as 'sister and mother'. It should 'enter into a dialogue with history' (*Ibid.*, No. 54). He found a metaphor for *aggiornamento* which in a way summed up what Pope John's pontificate had already achieved: 'The Church will divest itself, if need be, of whatever royal cloak still remains upon its sovereign shoulders, so that it may put on the simpler forms modern taste demands' (*Ibid.*, No. 55).

Montini was clear, finally, on the vexed question of how to deal with errors. He wrote: 'We shall have a Council of positive rather than punitive reforms, and of exhortation rather than anathemas' (*Pensiamo al Concilio*, No. 37). Moreover, he linked this positive attitude to Pope John's 'optimism' which, he claimed, 'has spread throughout the whole Church, deepening our sensibility' (*Ibid.*, No. 39). Pope John's optimism was infectious. But Montini sees it, correctly, not as a form of naïveté but as a heightened sensitivity to the action of the Holy Spirit in the world. So there was a profound link between Pope John's denunciation of the 'prophets of gloom' and his preference for 'the medicine of mercy' rather than condemnations. He had every reason to feel that Montini had understood him, perhaps more profoundly than Suenens. Montini – but this was incidental – had also staked out his claim to succeed Pope John, when that question arose. Both Montini and Suenens would play a discreet yet decisive role when the Council met in six months' time.

Optimism in the sense just defined, sensitivity to the Spirit, was gaining ground in the ecumenical sphere. With Tardini out of the way, Bea could arrange audiences for any Church leader who cared to come. The complete list of ecumenical meetings before the Council is as follows: Dr Arthur Lichtenberger, president of the American Episcopalian Church (November 15, 1961); Dr Joseph Jackson, president of the National Baptist Convention of the United States (December 20, 1961); Dr Archibald C. Craig, moderator of the General Assembly of the Church of Scotland (March 28, 1962); Dr Mervyn Stockwood, Anglican bishop of Southwark, London (April 7, 1962); Professor Edmund Schlink, of Heidelberg University, representing the Council of the German

Evangelical Church (April 27, 1962); Dr Arthur Morris, Anglican bishop of St
Edmundsbury and Ipswich (May 10, 1962); Metropolitan Damaskinos, of Volos,
Greece (May 17, 1962); and Dr Joost de Blank, Anglican archbishop of Cape
Town, South Africa (June 20, 1962) (listed in *Natale, 1975*, pp. 51–3).

Bea's secretary at the time, Jan Willebrands, explained why these meetings were
important. They suited John's style. He preferred people to books, and radiated
goodness and friendliness. He has sometimes been presented as anti-intellectual
and mistrustful of the subtleties of theologians. But that judgement was based on
the false premise that he was a shrewd but ignorant old peasant. What is true is
that he thought theological dialogue alone was insufficient. He needed this
personal contact with Church leaders to begin to understand the historical context
in which they had emerged and their present positions. History held the key to
understanding. From his previous experience, Pope John knew a great deal about
the Orthodox Churches; but now he was learning fast about Canterbury,
Geneva, Moscow, Cairo and so many other places.

One might conclude from all this that Bea was riding high. He was educating
the Pope and shaping the course of the Council. Precisely for that reason, the
curial attacks on Bea redoubled. One episode, tedious enough in itself, is worth
recalling to show how the battle-lines were drawn up. Pope John had made his
own college, the Lateran, into a University directed by secular priests. This mark
of favour impelled some of them to get even with the Jesuits, who had been
particularly influential in the pontificate of Pius XII. In December, 1960 *Divinitas*,
the learned journal produced by the staff of the Lateran, launched an intemperate
attack on the Biblical Institute (the 'Biblicum') and hinted that disciplinary
measures would shortly be taken against two of its professors, Frs Stanislaus
Lyonnet and Maximilian Zerwick. They were accused of exalting scripture over
tradition. They were reproached for holding that 'the study of the literary forms
of ancient Oriental literature' was essential to understanding both the Old and the
New Testaments. In this way they challenged those 'dogmatic theologians' who
for centuries had expounded the meaning of scripture without having the
slightest knowledge of ancient literary forms. It would be easy to guy this
position. But its exponents provide their own caricatures. Here, for example, is
Cardinal Ernesto Ruffini, former scripture professor, 'friend' of Pope John,
writing in *l'Osservatore Romano* in June, 1961:

> How can one suppose that the Church has presented the Divine Book to its
> children for nineteen centuries without knowing the literary genre in which
> it was composed, and yet this is said to be the key to exact interpretation?
> Such an assertion becomes all the more absurd when one takes into account
> that these superior-minded critics . . . and so on (Rynne, p. 55).

One rubs one's eyes and asks what this has to do with scholarship or understanding the scriptures. The truth is that Ruffini and Mgr Antonio Romeo, author of the article in *Divinitas,* behaved more like inquisitors than scripture scholars. It was highly unusual and against all the conventions for a would-be 'learned journal' to be predicting and advocating 'disciplinary measures'. Yet Romeo clearly knew what he was doing. He had advance information – not surprisingly, for he was the secretary of the Congregation for Seminaries and Catholic Universities. Romeo would not have written such an article without the approval of his chief, Cardinal Giuseppe Pizzardo. So the plot was rumbled. The attack was inspired by Pizzardo and, although ostensibly directed at the two luckless Jesuits from the Biblicum, was really aimed at Bea, for so long its Rector, and behind him against Pope John who was foolish enough to listen to such misguided counsellors. *Odium theologicum* (detestation of other theological views) has not been much studied. It has something to do with celibacy, which permits a single-minded concentration on a vendetta, undistracted by family cares. Pizzardo, like Bea, his chosen foe, was over eighty.

Pope John only found out about the anti-Bea, anti-Biblicum campaign by accident. All 400 Italian bishops – except the bishop of Rome – had been sent a copy of Mgr Antonio Romeo's famous article exposing the iniquities of the Biblicum. One of the bishops chanced to mention the article in an audience with Pope John. Scripture scholars were undermining faith, he explained, as though stating some obvious truth. So the whole story came tumbling out. Pope John was very angry. He told Capovilla to 'phone the Rector of the Biblicum at once and assure him that 'the Pope has complete confidence in the orthodoxy of the Biblicum'. Then John ordered Pizzardo to write a letter of apology to Bea, disclaiming any fore-knowledge of Romeo's article. Pizzardo complied, but it made no difference to his behaviour. The principal instrument of the 'fundamentalists' was the Biblical Commission presided over by Cardinal Eugène Tisserant. Although Bea was one of the twelve cardinal members, the dominant tone was set by the trio of Pizzardo, Ruffini and Ottaviani, who had just been joined by the former Dominican Master-General, Michael Browne, a self-confessed Irish conservative and proud of it.

On May 21, 1962, Pope John decided that enough was enough. He would have a showdown with the Biblical Commission. He wrote a memo to Cicognani, Secretary of State, that bristles with impatience: 'The time has come to put a stop to this nonsense. Either the Biblical Commission will bestir itself, do some proper work and by its suggestions to the Holy Father make a useful contribution to the needs of the present time, or it would be better to abolish it and let the Supreme Authority replace it in the Lord by something else' (*Lettere,* p. 536). This was the toughest language ever used by Pope John, and the only time he uttered a threat. An unreformed Biblical Commission was worse than useless. Its intolerance was creating needless anxieties, uncertainties and absurdities. Though he preferred to be an enabler, he would have to intervene. 'Reforms have to begin from above', he noted on Maundy Thursday 1962 (Alberigo, p. 87). Moreover, the ecumenical dimension of the Council, which was becoming more and more apparent, required that the best Catholic biblical scholarship should be available. Otherwise, the Protestants would not be able to take the Council seriously. The fierce memo went on:

> Those who have the charge – better, the honour – of promoting the Bible as the most sacred treasure of the Church, alongside and after the apostolic Tradition, should take care not to fail in their vocation.
> It would be very consoling for the humble servant of the servants of God if in preparation for the Council there was a Biblical Commission of such reputation and integrity that it would be a resource which our separated brethren could rely on and respect (*Ibid.*, p. 537).

Pope John's own use of scripture was devotional rather than critical. He never posed as a scripture scholar. But he could see how harmful these polemics were both to individuals and to the prospects for the Council.

Pope John carried out his threat. The Biblical Commission was provided in July, 1962 with a new secretary and 'consultors' as eminent as Rudolf Schnackenburg, Bernard Rigaux and Xavier Léon-Dufour. But the 'battle of the Biblicum' was still not finally won. Its climax would come during the first session of the Council.

Getting the Council on the road was hard work. Scrapping the prepared texts at this late stage would have meant abandoning the Council. Pope John could not brook the further delay that would be involved in rewriting drafts. He did not want to miss his own Council. Nor was he dissatisfied with the work done. On May 23, 1962, he decided to make Mgr Pericle Felici secretary general of the Council. As secretary of the Preparatory Commission he had given 'ample proof of wisdom and discretion' (*Lettere*, p. 538).

At the same time Pope John ordered that the *schemata* (drafts) should be circulated to all the members of the Council not in September, as had been originally foreseen, but in July and August. This would give the bishops more time to do their homework during the summer holidays. But John had another motive. Some bishops complained that they were being kept in the dark and would arrive at the Council in ignorance. Others had the impression that the Central Commission – made up when all were present of 102 members and 29 consultors – had decided everything in advance, and that the Council would have nothing to do except rubber-stamp what was laid before it. That could be a matter for praise or blame. The good-hearted Cardinal Sir Norman Gilroy of Sydney, Australia, declared that the men in the Curia were so experienced in preparing documents that he was happy to leave the work to them.

The more sophisticated Cardinal Montini went so far as to say that 'never has a Council been so thoroughly and carefully prepared' (*Pensiamo al Concilio*, No. 32). A brief comparison with Vatican I showed how true this was. The preparation of Vatican I had been entrusted to nine curial cardinals and eight consultors from Roman universities. So Pope John had every reason to feel pleased with the wide-ranging international consultation that would make his Council so different. That is why he wanted to share these good things with the bishops: 'It would be good to let them know as soon as possible that they will be receiving this material earlier. This will put a stop to certain reactions that have been noticed here and there. It will prevent unprofitable, wearisome and harmful chatter that merely results in wasted time and wasted energies' (*Lettere*, p. 536: May 20, 1962). Those were not the words of a man who expected still less hoped that the bishops would turn down the draft texts when they saw them.

On the contrary, at the end of the fifth session of the Central Commission in April, 1962 Pope John remarked that 'the consent of the Bishops will not be difficult to obtain and their approval will be unanimous' (Rouquette, I, p. 114). This confidence raised another problem. It had all along been assumed that the Council would complete its work in a single session from October 11, feast of the Maternity of Our Lady, to December 8, feast of her Immaculate Conception. Yet the *schemata* were piling up: the feat of discussing, amending and re-writing seventy of them in two months made pouring a quart into a pint pot look easy by comparison. It simply could not be done. There were hints that a further session might be needed. *La Croix* reported that during his Lenten station visit to Santa Maria in Traspontina Pope John had made this remark himself; but *l'Osservatore Romano* had edited it out. The Curia wanted a short, sharp Council, after which the foreigners (*questa gente da fuori*) would depart and normality would return. Pope John, however, always encouraged those from outside Rome and urged them not to miss the regular meetings of the Central Commission, even though some of them had to travel half way round the world every six weeks. They were to 'hang on' and not let the Curia run everything. Cardinal Franz König, of Vienna, thought that 'several sessions' would be needed. He was proved right. But for Pope John personally, there was a dilemma: however much he wanted to see the Council through, the Council was sovereign and had to be free to take its time, even if that meant he might not see its end.

But general satisfaction with the preparatory work certainly did not exclude the desire to improve the drafts. Pope John was particularly impressed by a confidential document, dated May 4, 1962, drawn up by Cardinal Alfred Bengsch who lived in East Berlin. It was a devastating critique of *De Animarum Cura in Particulari* (On the Pastoral Care of Special Groups). Bengsch addressed himself to the section on 'the pastoral care of those afflicted by communism' (*de cura pro Christianis communismo infectis*). He thought its tone and approach were disastrous.

He offered a lexicon of terms to be avoided in conciliar documents. They should not speak of 'fear of Soviet power', 'the free world', 'hatred of communism' or the 'iron curtain' (Stehle, p. 444, where Bengsch's full text was published for the first time). He also rejected the use of the key-term, 'the Church of silence', for the simple reason that it was not true. The best way to help the Christians of Eastern Europe, he remarked in an epigram that sounded better in Latin, would be 'to keep silent about the Church of silence' (*Ibid.*). Stehle claims that since Bengsch's post was censored, this document 'which conveyed an impression of changes in Catholic anti-communism, landed in Moscow, deliberately launched through East German channels' (Stehle, p. 304). This is to attribute Machiavellian cunning to Pope John.

It is much more likely that they were the unprompted reflections of Bengsch on a document that had annoyed him, and that Pope John subsequently realised that this was one way of 'sending a signal to Moscow'. But Bengsch's remarks were directed first of all to the Central Commission. He could not be suspected of being 'soft on communism' and therefore his words had greater weight. They were based on the common sense view that if the decisions of the Council were to be applied in Eastern Europe, it would be better not to begin by alienating and insulting its rulers. But that was what one did every time one spoke of 'the free world' for example. It was a matter of tact, not a philosophic discussion on different kinds of freedom.

Moreover, a more general principle was involved of the utmost importance for the Council: it would be impossible to 'enter into a dialogue with history' if one began with condemnations. In so far as the preliminary drafts had made condemnations their main theme, then they probably would have to be discarded. This criterion would also have the advantage of whittling down the number of draft texts to more manageable proportions. This was where Pope John really did begin to diverge from some of the preliminary drafts. One day, he measured a page with his ruler and said: 'Seven inches of condemnations and one of praise: is that the way to talk to the modern world?' It was Cardinal Montini who was given the task of making this point at the decisive final meeting of the Central Commission in June, 1962. Anathemas and condemnations, said Montini, were not the answer to contemporary errors. In the modern world the remedies for errors were mercy, charity, and the witness of Christian life. It was after this speech that Cardinal Ottaviani was heard to murmur: 'I pray to God that I may die before the end of the Council – in that way I can die a Catholic' (*Panorama*, p. 257). That shows that Ottaviani realised Montini had been speaking with the authority of Pope John.

Then it was time to go on holiday (*ad aquas* in Vatican language) once more. Pope John couldn't get away until July 31, feast of St Ignatius. Before going to Castelgandolfo which is in the Alban Hills to the south of Rome, he struck north to Vetralla to pray at the tomb of Domenico Tardini on the first anniversary of his death. Two episodes from this period reveal his state of mind two months before the start of the Council.

On July 30, 1962, he received Shizuka Matsubara, superior of the Shintoist Temple at Kyoto, Japan, together with members of his family. Superficially it was another of those incongruous exotic scenes that make life in the Vatican so diverting. John saw it differently. The whole world was now his family. He noted in his diary:

It gave me great pleasure to receive a visit that was well and courteously done. I managed to share with him, tiring though it was waiting for the translation, my good wishes for his family, whom he introduced to me: his good mother, his beloved daughter with her baby and his son-in-law. I was also pleased to evoke the sympathy that I had in my youth for Japan, and recalled the memory of General Nobunaga Oda who was the great patron of Christians in sixteenth-century Japan. And I expressed the desire that these ancient virtues of friendship might continue and develop more and more, bringing light, prosperity and peace under the gaze and grace of the omnipotent God.

The Pope loves to be united with all honest and upright souls, wherever they are, to whatever nation they belong, in a spirit of respect, understanding and peace. He asks the Lord to bless their good will so that each one may come to serve him, know him and love him in the quest for universal brotherhood and the expectation of eternal life.

Finally, I thanked him for the precious robe of bright scarlet that will be kept in the Vatican as a memento of this visit (IME, p. 188).

It was this universalist impulse and perspective that led him to write *Pacem in Terris*.

Cardinal Suenens is the source for the following story. Pope John had spent the day in the garden at Castelgandolfo, pen in hand, studying the draft texts for the Council. It was the task he had imposed on the bishops; he had to give them a lead. Suenens met him, and Pope John tried out some of his marginal comments on him. But then John suddenly stopped and said: 'Oh, I know what my personal part in the preparation of the Council will be . . . '. After a pause, he added: 'It will be suffering' (Novak, p. 19: from Suenens' tribute to Pope John in St Peter's, October 28, 1963).

As usual, Pope John under-rated himself. It is time to go *ad aquas*.

Chapter 21

On the slopes of the sacred mountain

After three years of preparation, certainly laborious but also joyful and serene, we are now on the slopes of the sacred mountain

(Pope John, *Journal of a Soul*, p. 349, September, 1962).

Despite all Pope John's urgings, only seven draft texts were ready to be sent to the bishops in August 1962. Four came from Cardinal Alfredo Ottaviani's Theological Commission: The Sources of Revelation, The Moral Order, The Deposit of Faith and The Family: all would be rejected by the Council. The Liturgy Commission had worked well, and though its draft annoyed the devotees of Latin, it cunningly presented its proposals as in continuity with the liturgical reforms begun by St Pius X and Pius XII. There remained a derisory draft on 'the means of social communication' presented by the Secretariat of that name, and a draft on The Unity of the Church prepared, some thought eccentrically, by the Oriental Churches Commission.

Pope John spent his summer at Castelgandolfo. But it was not much of a holiday. He was still working through the prepared texts; and even at this eleventh hour, he had to defend the Council against Cardinal Joseph Frings of Cologne and Cardinal Julius Döpfner of Munich who begged him to postpone it. But John was not going to be deprived of his Council at this late stage. The 'suffering' that he had talked about to Cardinal Suenens was a premonition of the illness that would kill him. He had already revised his last will and testament the previous summer. 'I await the arrival of Sister Death', he had written, 'and will welcome her simply and joyfully in whatever circumstances it will please the Lord to send her' (*Journal*, p. 369: September 12, 1961). On August 2, 1962, he completed the preparations for his death by drafting a *motu proprio* to deal with the *sede vacante* period, when the chair of Peter would be empty. Its chief concern was to avoid any repetition of the grisly scenes that followed upon the death of Pius XII. Its main provisions were that no photographs should be taken of the Pope on his deathbed, that only those strictly needed should be allowed into the crypt for the burial, and that no one at all should live in the papal apartments at this time (*Lettere*, pp. 549–50). All three points were embodied in the *motu proprio, Summi Pontificis Electio* (The Election of a Supreme Pontiff) of September 5, 1962 (AAS,

56, n.11, pp. 632–640) and were retained in Paul VI's *motu proprio* of October 1, 1975, *Romani Pontificis Eligendo* (On Electing the Roman Pontiff).

But although Pope John accepted the prospect of suffering and death, this did not mean that he was inactive. On the contrary, he 'took charge' of the final preparations for the Council in the most effective way open to him: he worked hard on the two speeches that would give it impetus and direction. He knew that his address on October 11 would be the most important of his life. As he went into retreat in his beloved Torre San Giovanni, he explained why this would be no ordinary retreat: 'This time, everything is with the intention of preparing the Pope's soul for the Council; everything, including the preparation of the opening speech which the whole world gathered in Rome awaits' (*Journal*, p. 346). But with the international situation so menacing, it was difficult to concentrate. Attention had moved from Berlin to Cuba where, according to refugees, Soviet offensive missiles were already in position or would shortly be. Pope John had a first-hand report from Vice-president Lyndon B. Johnson who had an audience on September 7, 1962.

It wasn't much of a holiday for Cardinal Bea who was ploughing the ecumenical furrow at Heythrop College, then a pastoral retreat some twenty miles from Oxford, on the road to Stratford-upon-Avon. Cardinal Gustavo Testa, now prefect of the Congregation for the Oriental Churches, and his predecessor, Cardinal Eugène Tisserant, were engaged in secret negotiations with the Russian Orthodox Church on the vexed question of 'observers'. The Curia, meanwhile, was not slothful either but it had different priorities. In June 1962 Cardinal Giuseppe Pizzardo secured the suspension from teaching of the Biblicum Jesuits, Stanislaus Lyonnet and Maximilian Zerwick (see p. 410 above). In August Cardinal Alfredo Ottaviani bagged an even bigger prize for the Holy Office: he published a *monitum* or warning that reading the works of the late Pierre Teilhard de Chardin S.J. could prove damaging to Catholic minds (AAS, 54, 1962, p. 526). The net result of these summer manoeuvres was probably an honourable draw. But a clear distinction was emerging between those who represented the 'wave of the future' and those busily fighting the wrong battle in the last ditch. So we'll leave Pope John in the garden at Castelgandolfo for a moment and see what his allies and opponents were up to.

It was Cardinal Bea's first visit to England. He came at the invitation of John Carmel Heenan, then archbishop of Liverpool, who had made himself responsible for unity work in England and Wales. Cardinal William Godfrey, archbishop of Westminster, was a sick man and 'frankly suspicious of the whole ecumenical movement' (*Crown of Thorns*, p. 324). He felt unable to receive Bea at Archbishop's House. He was upset because Bea had first gone to see Dr Michael Ramsey, then archbishop of Canterbury, at Lambeth Palace. The story was later put about that Ramsey, who had just returned from Moscow, had acted as intermediary between Cardinal Bea and Patriarch Alexis (see Rouquette, I, p. 214, reporting *Herder-Korrespondenz*). Asked about this, Lord Ramsey replied: 'As to my visit to the Patriarch in July 1962 I have no recollection of acting as an intermediary for Cardinal Bea and it is most unlikely that I did. Evidence? I did not know Cardinal Bea at the time. Cardinal Bea was eager to see me when he came to England because of his longing for relationships with the Anglican Church' (letter to the author, February 25, 1984).

That was the simple and real reason why Bea was *persona non grata* to most English bishops. Heenan patronised Bea, declaring him ignorant of the English situation ('Like most foreigners he had a picture of the typical Anglican which applied only to high churchmen': *Crown of Thorns*, p. 325) and ignorant of the language ('His English was scarcely intelligible': *Ibid.*, p. 329). Bea did not mind being chaffed about his English. His Heythrop lecture on the carefully chosen theme of 'The Priest, Minister of Unity', began with what might have been considered, had anyone understood it, rather a good joke: 'It was announced that this conference would be in Latin, but I thought it would be easier to express this modern matter in a modern language. I only hope that my English is not too offensive to your ears' (*Unity of Christians*, p. 73). It was only six months since *Veterum Sapientia* had re-imposed Latin as a teaching language.

Representative priests from each diocese and religious order had been brought to Heythrop to learn about the new attitudes. As Heenan noted, with characteristic litotes, 'they were not all enthusiastic ecumenists' (*Crown of Thorns*, p. 328). Bea knew this, and knew that he had to win them over. He confined himself to a few simple points. Divisions between Christian theologians are accentuated by the fact that while Catholics worked broadly from the base of 'the perennial philosophy', Protestants were in dialogue with modern philosophers. Next, theological positions on all sides have 'evolved': 'The mentality of our separated brethren at the present time is not simply that of the sixteenth century, nor even of the nineteenth century' (*Unity of Christians*, p. 77). Finally, where Catholics once saw only 'adversaries' to be demolished, the 'priestly view will reveal to us brothers in Christ, errant brothers indeed, but still brothers' (*Ibid.*, p. 77). Bea said nothing that would have been unfamiliar to anyone who had been following the literature on ecumenism. But to many in his audience, what he said had the ring of novelty. One participant described Bea's impact:

> We'd all been explaining in radio interviews and so on that the word 'ecumenical' in the title of the Council meant simply 'general' as opposed to 'local' or 'provincial', and therefore as such it had nothing to do with inter-Church relations. Now here was Cardinal Bea telling us that we were wrong and that, on this matter, the Anglicans had been right all along (Archbishop Derek Worlock, conversation, April 29, 1983).

What happened at Heythrop College early in August 1962 was important because it was emblematic of what was happening elsewhere on the eve of the Council: 'liberal' or 'progressive' causes were accepted in obedience because that was what Pope John was thought to want. Thus Heenan remarks that Cardinal Godfrey, who had grave misgivings about ecumenism, was also 'passionately loyal to the Holy See' and 'determined to follow Pope John's ecumenical lead' (*Crown of Thorns*, p. 324). It may be doubted whether obedience without understanding really helped the cause of ecumenism. But Bea was taking no chances. He arrived at Heythrop with a letter from Cardinal Cicognani, Secretary of State, which conveyed the Pope's blessing on the conference (text *Ibid.*, p. 329). 'If Pope John were with us', Heenan smugly concluded, 'all would be well' (*Ibid.*, p. 328). Moreover, something of Pope John's charismatic authority seemed to have rubbed off on Bea and his holiness impressed Heenan: 'Cardinal Bea resembled Pope John in the serenity of soul shining in his face' (*Ibid.*, p. 330). So if Archbishop Heenan knew about the attacks on Bea in Rome, he kept quiet about them and did not allow a wedge to be driven between Pope John and Bea. That was reassuring.

But less reassuring, indeed positively alarming, was the 'image' which Heenan constructed of Pope John. It seems reasonable to assume that cardinals who meet the Pope face to face should have some insight into his character and outlook not available to outsiders. Cardinal Heenan's judgement shatters such confident expectations:

> Pope John's idea of ecumenism was rudimentary. He has been given the reputation of being a liberal if not a radical prelate, a rollocking Nonconformist, an ecclesiastical Khrushchev. Historians who will be guided by his words and actions will present a very different picture of good Pope John. Ecumenism in his view meant being kind and loving to separated Christians thus facilitating their return to Mother Church (*Crown of Thorns*, p. 323).

In his eagerness to refute journalistic myths, Heenan goes to the opposite extreme and portrays Pope John as an ignorant if holy traditionalist and simpleton:

> Pope John was the old-fashioned 'Garden-of-the-Soul' type of Catholic . . . He was not an original thinker. It was Pius XII, not Pope John, who allowed married men to become priests, revised the rules for the eucharistic fast and introduced Evening Mass. Pope John was no innovator . . . The Pope I knew was not in the least like this mythical John. My Pope John was more like a benevolent parish priest. I doubt if he had read many of the books of contemporary theologians (Hales, p. 3: originally in *Westminster Cathedral Chronicle*, July, 1964).

Note the unfavourable comparison with Pius XII who was, presumably, 'an original thinker' and an 'innovator'. True, but he did not call a Council.

While Bea was trying to convert the English and Welsh to ecumenism, his colleagues were engaged in secret negotiations designed to permit 'observers' from the Russian Orthodox Church to attend the Council. This was what Pope John wanted more than anything else. Since the Russian Orthodox Church was subservient to the Soviet state, the presence of Russian Orthodox observers would be a sign not only of the improved ecumenical climate but of East–West *détente* – and it might get Slipyi out of his labour camp in Siberia. The United States and the USSR were already scowling at each other over Cuba. If there were observers present, the Council would at least be one forum in which East and West were still conversing. If it would help, Pope John was ready to meet Khrushchev himself. Capovilla remembers a conversation about Pius XI and Hitler. Although it was true that Pius had left for Castelgandolfo rather than be in Rome at the same time as the obnoxious German dictator (see p. 155 above), this did not mean that he would have refused a meeting with him. Pius, John recalled, always acted on the principle that he would 'eat with the devil if the good of souls demanded it'. So, provided he had a long enough spoon, Pope John was prepared to meet Khrushchev: 'If this good fellow [*bravo signore*] came to Rome and asked to see me, why should I refuse? I would listen to him and then, calmly and politely, give him my thoughts on the Church's claims at the present time: we don't want protection or privileges, but we simply want freedom to preach the Gospel' (IME, p. 68). This text was published in 1983. If it had appeared earlier it would have cleared up misunderstandings about Pope John's alleged 'kow-towing' to Khrushchev.

Still, if he couldn't meet Khrushchev, he could at least try to entice some Russian Orthodox observers to Rome. The *Journal of the Moscow Patriarchate* had already rejected the idea on the grounds that the Council was merely another instance of Roman Catholic imperialism. John, the old diplomat, regarded this as a predictable opening gambit. Cardinal Gustavo Testa and Bea's number two, Mgr Jan Willebrands, were instructed to try anything they could think of to re-open the question. Testa was a shrewd choice: he was an old and trusted friend of Pope John, and like him was both fat and Bergamesque. His episcopal motto was *Sola gratia tua* (By your grace alone) which he used to interpret, with a twinkle in his eye, as meaning that without Pope John's favour (*gratia*), he would never have become a cardinal. That was probably true. Cardinal Eugène Tisserant, his earlier clinging to power now forgiven, was brought in to help because of his immense experience of the East. He began to enter into the spirit of the pontificate with some zest. The Secretariat of State was by-passed.

Nothing happened for many weeks. Then in August Metropolitan Nikodim of Leningrad, who was officially responsible for the 'foreign relations' of the

Russian Orthodox Church, let it be known that he would like a confidential meeting with top Vatican officials. Willebrands met him in Paris, and Tisserant in Metz: meetings in France escaped the prying eyes of the Roman press. The gist of Nikodim's message was that the Russian Orthodox Church would consider sending observers to the Council provided an assurance was given in advance that it would be a strictly apolitical event (that is, that it would not condemn atheistic Communism). Since the principle of 'no condemnations' had already been established as one of the ground-rules of the Council, this assurance could be given. Nikodim would deliver the invitations himself.

But Pope John had a scruple about this. He did not need the wily Tisserant to point out that invitations to *all* Orthodox Churches ought to be sent through the Ecumenical patriarch in Constantinople, Athenagoras. There was a grave danger of getting embroiled in an inner-Orthodox dispute. Late in September he sent Willebrands to Moscow. His mission was to inform Patriarch Alexis and the Holy Synod that the Council had no political objectives and would issue no anathemas (*Utopia*, Italian, p. 184). Willebrands set off on September 28, but his journey was kept secret. So it was that on October 8, just three days before the start of the Council, having received no word from Moscow, Athenagoras announced that the Orthodox Church would not be sending observers to the Vatican Council. Athenagoras was very sad about this. He was the man who had greeted Cardinal Gustavo Testa with the words: 'There is a man, sent from God, whose name is John'. But although he had the primacy of honour over the Orthodox Churches, he also had to defer to the Russian Orthodox Church as 'the largest and the least free' (to borrow Stehle's excellent phrase: p. 303). So on the eve of the Council, it looked as though all these strenuous efforts had come to nothing.

Still, there was some sort of communication with the Russians. To Pope John's intense disappointment China, the other great Communist power, proved totally impenetrable. Yet the 'Chinese Catholics' – there were 2 million of them in 1949 – had presented him with an altar on the first anniversary of his election. He had it set up in the new chapel in the Torre San Giovanni. He called it 'my Chinese altar' and said 'it will always remind me of the missionary activity to which the Pope is called' (*Journal*, p. 347: September 10, 1962). The altar was also a reminder of how little he could do for the Catholics of China. In 1962 little was known about them.

Most of the twenty or so Bishops who were alive when Mao took over in 1949 had vanished. In 1956–7, at the time of the 'hundred flowers' campaign ('Let a hundred flowers blossom', declared Mao, 'and let a hundred schools of thought contend'), forty-two 'patriotic' bishops were appointed with government approval. Pius XII promptly pronounced them to be in schism. At first Pope John echoed this usage, causing distress in China and delight in Taiwan. Then he had a meeting on February 26, 1960, with Charles Joseph van Melckebeke, who had been bishop of Ning-sia in Outer Mongolia. After the revolution he had distributed church property and gone to work on a farm. He told Pope John that the term 'schism' was not strictly applicable to the Chinese bishops, since they had not *volenter et pertinaciter* (deliberately and obstinately) broken with the Church of Rome. And they had been condemned unheard. They were never given a chance to explain their position and the pressures they were under (*Utopia*, English, p. 191). After this conversation, Pope John never again used the term 'schism' in speaking of China. But this was not enough to allow Mao's government to let Chinese bishops go to the Council. They knew it was happening (see Caprile, Giovanni, in *Civiltà Cattolica*, February 16, 1974, reviewing *Utopia*, p. 366). But none came. Instead, ten bishops from Taiwan and the *diaspora* arrived at the last minute on October 11. Pope John did not solve the 'two Chinas' problem.

Pope John's thinking and prayer extended to embrace the whole world. From time to time he was made aware of some squalid manoeuvre happening beneath his very eyes. He followed St Bernard's principle quoted above: 'To notice everything, turn a blind eye to much and to correct a few things'. His trust in subordinates meant that he could not undo the suspension of Frs Lyonnet and Zerwick. But he found a diplomatic solution by allowing Lyonnet to continue acting as vice-dean of the Biblicum and encouraging Zerwick to carry on teaching biblical Greek (which was his speciality). But he had never read Teilhard de Chardin and so could not judge whether the Holy Office *monitum* was justified or not. But strangely enough 'Teilhardian' phrases began to enter the speeches he was working on at this time. The optimism of his inaugural address to the Council, his fascination with space travel which allowed the world to be seen as 'one planet', and his reference to 'a new order of human relationships' (Abbott, p. 712) all echoed Teilhardian themes.

On September 11, 1962, exactly a month before the Council was due to start, he broadcast a speech on Vatican Radio in which he at last indicated the direction he wanted the Council to take. According to the progressive myth, this was the moment when he cast aside the mask and rejected all the preparatory work. This judgement is surprising in view of Pope John's opening remark:

> In the course of three years of preparatory work, a host of distinguished minds chosen from every nation and language, united in affection and determination, has brought together a superabundant wealth of doctrinal and pastoral material worthy to be offered to the Bishops of the whole world who, gathered beneath the vault of St Peter's, will find grounds for the wisest applications of Christ's evangelical *magisterium* which for twenty centuries has enlightened the humanity redeemed by his blood (Alberigo, p. 354).

It is true that this encomium on the preparatory work is studiously vague. No examples of this 'wealth of doctrinal and pastoral material' are given. He damns with faint praise. But it would not have been proper to anticipate the Council on particular controversial points, and Pope John had a keen sense of what was proper.

However, the 'progressives' were right to see in this speech a view of the Council that had not so far been articulated in the draft texts. It took up the Cardinal Suenens distinction between the Church *ad intra* and the Church *ad extra*, the Church in itself and in relation to the world's problems. Suenens had called for a balance to be kept between the two. Yet of the 70 *schemata* still being worked upon, only 2 had anything to do with the world's problems. In response to a specific request from Pope John, Ottaviani's Theological Commission was trying to complete *De Ordine Morali et Sociali* (On the Moral and Social Order) and *De Communitate Gentium* (On the Community of Nations) (De Riedmatten, p. 49). But a score of 68–2 was not a balance.

It is a pity that the September 11 broadcast did not become known by its opening words: *Lumen Christi Ecclesia Christi* (The Church of Christ is the Light of Christ). Pope John saw the Council as a way in which the whole Church would acclaim the Paschal Candle or Christ as Light (see Chapter 11 above for the same theme on Ascension Day in Venice). 'Has there ever been an ecumenical council', he asks, 'which was not a way of self-renewal through an encounter with the Risen Jesus, the glorious and immortal king, whose light illumines the whole Church for the salvation, the joy and the glory of all peoples?' (Alberigo, p. 355). The question was rhetorical. It put the Council in the right spiritual perspective. It was another way of saying that there would be no condemnations, for 'illumination' in John's vocabulary became synonymous with 'helpful'. Thus it will be illuminating, he says, to present the Church 'in the under-developed countries as the Church of all, and especially of the poor' (*Ibid.*, p. 357). The 'Church of the poor' was not a theme that any of the draft texts, composed almost entirely by 'first world' theologians, had even alluded to.

Also illuminating in the sense of helpful was the thought that this Council, meeting seventeen years after the end of the Second World War, was the most diverse, broadly-based, 'universal' and therefore truly 'Catholic' Council that had ever met. 'From every people', said Pope John, 'we expect a contribution based on intelligence and experience that will help to heal the *scars* of the two World Wars that have so profoundly changed the face of all our countries' (Alberigo, p. 357: italics in the original). Just as mothers and fathers detest war, he went on, so 'the Church, the Mother of all without exception, will once more repeat the proclamation that echoes down the centuries from Bethlehem, *pacem in terris*, peace on earth' (*Ibid.*, p. 358). And peace was inseparable from justice.

Finally Pope John reflected on the experience of preparing the Council. He did not see it as negative at all. In fact he was starry-eyed about it. The bonds of love which had held the Church together in Europe and the known world in the first centuries had been subsequently weakened or even broken. But the project of the Council had brought almost everyone together in fraternal recognition in the arms of their common mother, *sancta et universalis Mater Ecclesia* (Alberigo, p. 359). The theme of the Church *ad intra* and *ad extra* was vividly summed up in the contrast between St Peter, concerned with order and stability, and St Paul, concerned with missionary endeavour and reaching out towards 'those who had not yet received the Gospel' (*Ibid.*). The Council would have to be both Petrine and Pauline.

But did Pope John write this speech himself? This question was sometimes asked by his curial 'opponents' who wanted to hint that he was incapable of having such ideas unaided and must therefore have delivered himself uncritically into the unsafe hands of 'outsiders' like Cardinal Suenens. But it was also posed by 'friends' who wanted to show his 'openness' to new ideas wherever they came from. Henri de Riedmatten O.P., known to his brethren as 'Henry the Navigator' for his skill in negotiating choppy Vatican waters, said bluntly in 1967: 'It is no longer indiscreet to say that the September 11, 1962, speech was very largely inspired (*s'inspirait largement*) by the second of Cardinal Suenens' memoranda, so much so that the very next day Pope John gave Cardinal Suenens a gift of his works as a pledge of his agreement and gratitude' (De Riedmatten, p. 53). All attempts to get Cardinal Suenens to comment on this passage having failed, one must assume that it is true. (If it were false, he would have instantly denied it.)

But 'very largely inspired by' does not mean that Pope John simply copied down a Suenens text: as was his practice with a draft that he liked, he thought it through, made it his own, and added personal touches. One effect of this collaboration was that from now on Cardinal Suenens became still closer to Pope John. There was even a project for setting up a Secretariat for the Church *ad extra*, that is for dealing with the Church in relationship to world problems, based on the successful model of Bea's Secretariat for Christian Unity. Among those who discussed this idea were Cardinals Suenens, Montini and Siri (see Caprile II, 1, p. 264).

Pope John's retreat in the Torre San Giovanni in the Vatican garden came to an end on September 23, feast of St Nicodemus. He complained, mildly: 'I have not been able to use the retreat as I wished, entirely for the purpose I set myself' (*Journal*, p. 348). But he had cut out most business distractions and made 'a more intense effort to find union with the Lord in prayer, thought and calm and determined will' (*Ibid.*). He was ready for the Council, and was not going to panic if it took an unforeseen turn.

He needed all the calm he could muster for during the following week he underwent a battery of x-rays and medical tests at the hands of specialists and his doctors. Their report was ready by the following Sunday, September 23. It has never been made public. In his Chronology, published in 1970, Capovilla tersely noted under September 23, 1962: 'The first revelation of the serious illness that threatened his health' (*Cronologia*, p. 760). In a letter to the author, Capovilla spoke of 'the unexpected and disconcerting news of the illness that threatened the life of the Pope' (Capovilla: letter of February 2, 1983). So the threat was not merely to John's health but to his life. Capovilla goes on: 'The Pope appeared calm when he asked for explanations about the x-rays and the gastric pains that troubled him'. That same Sunday, Pope John went down to the crypt of St Peter's to pray at the tombs of his immediate predecessors, now knowing that within six months or a year he would be joining them. However, it was decided to say nothing publicly about his state of health, since that would trigger off pre-conclave speculations and be a distraction from the Council. Pope John would behave 'as if' nothing were wrong.

Pope John's remark that his contribution to the Council would be suffering took on a deeper and more poignant meaning. From now on he would be living on borrowed time. He had said of Pius XII that 'Sister Death came to him swiftly'. That would not be his experience. He was approaching eighty-one, and in old age stomach cancer is slow to develop, painful and ineluctable. He now knew what his sisters Ancilla and Maria had undergone in the 1950s. His death sentence meant that every day he lived was experienced as a gift from the Lord, a grace that was granted for a purpose. This brought an added edge of urgency to all his projects. It also gave him the freedom that came from knowing that, humanly speaking, he had nothing more to lose. Pride, self-will, even vanity no longer meant much.

Fortified by his new knowledge, he decided to go on pilgrimage to Loreto and Assisi on October 4, 1962. Apart from visits to his own property at Castelgandolfo, it was the first time a pope had left Rome officially since 1870. He boarded the presidential train at 6.30 a.m. at the Vatican's neo-baroque station. Normally it has no passengers. He was joined at the Trastevere Station by Amintore Fanfani, the prime minister. It was raining steadily. President Antonio Segni was waiting to greet him in Loreto. So the event had a political significance within Italy: it was the final seal set on the reconciliation of 1929. At every halt along the route – at Orte, Narni, Terni, Spoleto, Foligno, Fabriano, Iesi, Falconara and Ancona – enthusiastic crowds greeted Pope John with vivas. There were tears in his eyes. 'This conversation without intermediaries between a father and his children revealed that Italian attitudes had indeed changed for the better' (Capovilla: letter to author, February 2, 1983).

But that was not what Pope John's pilgrimage meant to non-Italians. That he should go to Assisi to pray for the coming Council was understandable. If the Council was going to stress the 'Church of the poor', as he had suggested in his September 11 broadcast, then St Francis, the poor man of Assisi, was a fitting patron. Moreover, in his Assisi sermon John linked poverty and peace: only when 'the good and beautiful things that Providence has placed in this world' were equitably shared out could there be true peace. Few could quarrel with that. And everyone loved St Francis.

But Loreto was a different matter. The dubious story of the holy house of Nazareth being transported by angelic removal men to a rocky eminence over-looking the Adriatic gave the sceptics a chance to scoff. Some of the 'observers', already in Rome, thought it a tactless blunder to be emphasising mariology on the eve of a Council which had such high ecumenical hopes.

It would, however, have been insensitive to deny to an old man – no one knew he was dying – the right to return to a place he had first visited sixty years before on September 22, 1900. And anyone who actually read or, better, listened to what he said would have discovered that he made no mention of the alleged miracle on which Loreto is based. Far from encouraging mariological excesses, he talked very simply and directly on three points: the Incarnation, the family and work. Everything he said was directed towards the Council. The Angelus prayer, he said, invites us to reflect on 'the coming together of earth and heaven that is the purpose of the Incarnation and Redemption'. But that 'coming together of earth and heaven' is precisely the goal of the Council, which will bring 'health and light to all forms of social life'. This reminded him of the 'social aspirations' of Leo XIII, Pope of his first twenty-two years. So he had an easy transition to the themes of family life and the dignity of daily work, both of which were illustrated by memories of his own family at Sotto il Monte.

Finally, his prayer for the Council was that it would be 'a joyful proclamation of the Gospel, leading to brotherly harmony (*convivenza*) between all peoples and ever more generous justice, so that the light of God's mercy may shine on everyone' (*Rosario*, p. 141). Even the most rigid Protestant could not object to that – except, perhaps, to the fact that it was being said at Loreto. But John's personal reasons for going there were not fully appreciated, and could not be at the time.

Bishops were by now pouring into Rome. There were about 217 from the United States who mostly installed themselves in grand hotels on the Via Veneto. The Rome Hilton was not yet built. According to Robert Kaiser, of *Time* magazine, they were accompanied by 'two or three clerical buddies, whom they called "theologians" ' (Kaiser, p. 76). The 531 Latin Americans economised by staying at their own colleges. The Europeans were still the largest group: over 400 Italians who scarcely knew each other scattered round the city, except for Cardinal Montini who, it was noticed, was given a room in the Apostolic Palace;

159 French who claimed to know Pope John at first-hand; 95 from Spain, still wondering what *Mater et Magistra* meant for the Franco dictatorship; 68 Germans aware of their responsibility to theology and learning (*Wissenschaft*); 42 from England and Wales who felt they were back at the Venerable English College again; 33 from Catholic Ireland; 27 from Portugal living with apparent contentment under Salazar and Our Lady of Fatima (dissident bishops were exiled to the Azores).

There were many surprises. Although the Netherlands had only 9 bishops, the total list of Dutch bishops, once the missionaries were counted in, came to 76. They had worked hard on the preparatory documents, and had commissioned Edward Schillebeeckx O.P. to write a theological commentary on them. His *Animadversiones*, a manuscript of 47 pages, were devastating; the only draft for which he had a good word was that on liturgy. Again, though Belgium itself had only 15 bishops, the full list of Belgians had 59 names. All in all the number of missionary bishops came to over 800 out of an official total of 2,449. If the North European bishops supplied the intellectual input to the Council, the missionaries were to act as its conscience.

There were 296 bishops from Africa, 93 from the Philippines, Japan and Indonesia, and 84 from India who left a country at peace and returned to find it at war with China. Additional colour was provided by the Uniates: Maronites from the Lebanon led by their Patriarch Meouchi of Antioch, proud of their 700-year-long resistance to Turks and Arabs; their neighbours the Melkites headed by 84-year-old Patriarch Maximos IV Saigh who refused to speak Latin on the grounds that Arabic was the language of his Church – he spoke French instead; and the bearded representatives of the Malankars, the Copts, the Chaldeans and Armenians – all seeming exotic to the Latins and yet familiar to Pope John from his time in the East. Before a single word had been spoken, the gathering said something about the true nature of Catholicity: it could not be reduced to the monochrome uniformity demanded by the Curia.

But one element in the spectrum of Catholicism was still missing. Where were the East Europeans? On Sunday October 7 Pope John regretted the absence of Stefan Cyril Kurtev, whom he had appointed forty years before and who was still exarch of the Bulgarians, and of another Bulgarian bishop whom he misremembered as Popov (in fact Simeon Kokov) (*Lettere*, p. 352). John was reminded of these old friends by ex-King Simeon of Bulgaria, whom we last met at the age of six in 1943 (see p. 189 above), who now wanted a ticket for the inaugural Mass. Of course he should be admitted, John noted, provided he does not remind everyone of his former title.

The next day, October 8, Cardinal Wyszyński arrived with thirteen Polish bishops, among them Karol Wojtyla from Kraków. Nine more were to arrive later. Pope John was delighted to see them. His *Ostpolitik* was beginning to pay off. In a speech that was not made public at the time, but which was relayed to Moscow, Pope John mentioned almost casually 'the Polish Western territories recovered after centuries', which was code-language for recognising the post-war frontiers of Poland and Germany (Stehle, p. 304). The next day three Hungarians and two Yugoslavs arrived and, even more remarkably, on Wednesday, October 10, Pope John was able to embrace three Czech bishops and Petras Mazelis, Apostolic Administrator of Telsiai, Lithuania, now a republic of the Soviet Union. These were all signs of the improving relations with the Communist bloc. On the other hand, Willebrands had returned from Moscow, apparently empty-handed, on October 4.

So now by October 10, 1962, the eve of the Council, most of the cast had been assembled. Not all of them were sure what for. Archbishop Aston Chichester S.J., always known as 'Chick', an Englishman who had spent most of his life in what was then Southern Rhodesia (now Zimbabwe) and who at eighty-three was not only older than Pope John but fatter, was seen wandering round the Jesuit Curia enquiring: 'Just who is this bloke Otto . . . Ottoviani?' (Kaiser, p. 76: amended by oral tradition). He didn't have much time to find out, for he died as he entered St Peter's on October 24, and was thus spared a Council he might have found hard to comprehend.

It was drizzling on the morning of October 11, 1962, the first day of the Council. Someone recalled the violent thunderstorm that had marked the end of Vatican I. Yet October 11 became the date which summed up the elusive 'spirit of the Council'. Italians use dates as code-language and name streets after them. Peter Nichols quotes a not untypical political statement: 'While far from expecting an April 18, but in the spirit of September 22, renewed by April 25, we offer progress without adventure' (*Italia, Italia*, p. 240). Pope John's opening address to the Council made October 11 the date to remember it by. It acted as a criterion or yard-stick: this or that is to be rejected because it is not in accord with the spirit of October 11. Archbishop Thomas Roberts once said: 'Whenever I get depressed during the Council, I reread Pope John's opening address, and have my spirits lifted'. In this speech Pope John, having toiled to the upper slopes of the sacred mountain, pointed to the promised land beyond.

But Pope John's speech came only at the end of a long ceremony that began at 8 a.m. Until he began to speak, October 11 meant simply a baroque endurance test. Cardinal William Godfrey's train-bearer sets the scene:

> The contrast between the grand ceremonial of the past and new demands of the Council was evident as the procession of Bishops entered St Peter's. The entire length of the basilica up to the papal altar under the cupola had been transformed into a mighty council chamber with tiers of seating raised high on either side, and with tribunes aloft for religious superiors and *periti*. This

constituted an unforeseen practical difficulty: where to put the cardinals' secretaries and train-bearers who could no longer occupy their privileged position sitting on the floor at the feet of their masters. For there was no more floor.

As we arrived at the doors of the basilica, papal masters of ceremonies tucked scarlet silk trains over cardinalatial arms, and then clapped their hands at us in the vain hope that we might vanish. We were driven hastily round the back of the tiered seating and up into the tribunes from which we were swiftly evicted by the self-righteous *periti*. Next we were tucked into a corner near the diplomatic corps and ecumenical observers, who were having a splendid time with their cameras . . . Then Mgr Willebrands came along, shook my hand, and called out to the Swiss Guard: 'They cannot remain here'. Thus cardinals' train-bearers were significantly the first victims of renewal and ecumenism . . . We joined the attendant members of the papal household, and for the next few hours stood unseeing, close at hand (Worlock, Archbishop Derek, 'The Sharing Church', in *The Tablet*, October 9, 1982, pp. 1005–6).

History in the making always tends to be uncomfortable. The less stout-hearted could always watch on television as Pope John, having arrived at the door of the Basilica, descended from his undulating *sedia gestatoria*, and *walked* up the main aisle, casting a glance towards the statue of St Peter on the right.

After the *Veni Creator*, Cardinal Eugène Tisserant said the Mass. Some of it was in Greek. The Sistine Choir sang Palestrina's *Missa Papae Marcelli* with its customary *vibrato*: the Counter-Reformation at its best. The bishops neither participated nor communicated at the Mass: liturgy as spectacle. Mass over, the cardinals made their obeisance to the Pope: splendid pageantry, but not exactly a scene of evangelical simplicity. Then Pope John read out, as canon law demanded, the fierce and formidable profession of faith of Pius IV. It dated from 1564 and breathed the polemical atmosphere of that period. 'I confess and hold the Catholic faith', Pope John solemnly swore, 'outside of which no one can be saved'. In 1887 Pius IX had added the acknowledgement of 'the primacy and infallible *magisterium* of the Roman Pontiff' about which Trent had been lamentably silent (text in ASCV, I, 1, p. 158). Mgr Pericle Felici then recited the oath in the name of all the Council Fathers. It was said that the 'observers' were profoundly shocked by this oath; but more often than not, it was Catholic theologians and reporters who were shocked on their behalf. The children of the household could be more blunt in speaking the truth. Anyway, it didn't matter, for Pope John's speech dissipated whatever bad impression had been made.

Or did it? Here again, hindsight plays tricks with memory. The speech came at the end of a very long morning. It lasted thirty-seven minutes. It was in Latin.

Not everyone grasped its meaning straightaway. It made its real impact only when it was translated and published in the press. But for those who could understand, it was a remarkable achievement, a *tour de force*. With his 'robust and harmonious voice' (Falconi), Pope John seemed to shed his years and obesity and become a youthful prophet launching the Church on a great adventure of the Spirit.

But – the question recurs – was it all his own work? Capovilla assures us that it was. He quotes Pope John saying: 'I would like the first Italian draft of this speech to be published, not because I want to be praised for it but because I want to take responsibility for it; it should be known that it belongs to me from the first to the last word' (*Letture*, p. 197). One could hardly be more emphatic than that. So the idea that Bea or Suenens wrote it is nonsense. For 'technical reasons' (that is, to make sure it contained neither heresy nor political folly) it was checked over by the gaunt Fr Luigi Ciappi O.P., papal theologian, and Mgr Angelo Dell'Acqua, substitute. But that was routine. Pope John wrote it himself and was rather hurt by the suggestion that he did not (Capovilla, conversation, April 23, 1981). But even if we did not have this external evidence, internal evidence confirms that it was Pope John's own work. The ideas it contains had long been familiar to him. It was deeply embedded in his own experience of life and history. Since this speech summed up his entire life, most of this book can be considered as an implicit commentary on it. For that reason, we can be relatively brief about it now (see Alberigo, Giuseppe, *'Dal bastone alla misericordia'*, in *Cristianesimo nella storia*, October 1981, pp. 487–521, for the best study of its importance and originality).

The October 11 speech contained four main themes which lifted it above banality and shaped the future course of the Council: the idea of a council as the celebration of faith ever-old, ever-new; an optimism in the Spirit which involved a denunciation of the 'prophets of misfortune' (usually translated indiscriminately as 'prophets of gloom' or 'of doom'); a clear statement on what the Council was for and what not; and a novel approach to 'errors'.

The Council was to be a celebration of Catholic faith. Once again one may regret that this speech was never known by its magnificent opening chord, *Gaudet Mater Ecclesia*, Mother Church rejoices. The Council celebrated Catholic faith simply by assembling; and it renewed this celebration of faith in its daily liturgies which reflected the fact that Catholicism was 'reconciled diversity' rather than bland uniformity. This would have to be remembered throughout the rough and tumble of harsh debate. Catholic faith and Christian faith were not distinct in their object: but Christian faith expressed a fidelity to the Gospel, while Catholic faith drew attention to continuity with the past ('tradition'). So they were not in contrast still less in contradiction with each other. This made possible both the renewal of the Catholic Church and a spirit of ecumenical openness. It sounded more like a 'one source' view of revelation than a 'two source' view (in which scripture and tradition were separate).

Pope John's hearers, however, only began to wake up when he spoke directly of the Roman Curia. This retranslation of his Italian text is designed to bring out its vigour and freshness:

> In the everyday exercise of our pastoral ministry, greatly to our sorrow, we sometimes have to listen to those who although consumed with zeal do not have very much judgement [*discrezione*] or balance. To them the modern world is nothing but betrayal and ruination. They claim that this age is far worse than previous ages, and they go on as though they had learned nothing at all from history – and yet history is the great teacher of life [*maestra di vita*]. They behave as though the first five centuries saw a complete vindication of the Christian idea and the Christian cause, and as though religious liberty was never put in jeopardy in the past. We feel bound to disagree with these prophets of misfortune [*sventura*] who are for ever forecasting calamity – as though the end of the world were imminent. And yet today Providence is guiding us towards a new order of human relationships which, thanks to human effort and yet far surpassing its hopes, will bring us to the realisation of still higher and undreamed of expectations; in this way even human oppositions can lead to the good of the Church (*Lettere*, p. 426: see Abbott, p. 712 for the familiar translation).

Pope John's 'sense of history', however, was not merely a strategy for dealing with embattled misanthropes who sought security by returning to the past and denigrating the present. It also made him see the importance of responding to the Spirit *now*. This defined the purpose of the Council, negatively and positively:

> Our task is not merely to hoard this precious treasure, as though obsessed with the past, but to give ourselves eagerly and without fear to the task that the present age demands of us – and in so doing we will be faithful to what the Church has done in the last twenty centuries. So the main point of this Council will not be to debate this or that article of basic Church doctrine that has been repeatedly taught by the Fathers and theologians old and new and which we can take as read. You do not need a Council to do that. But starting from a renewed, serene and calm acceptance of the whole teaching of the Church in all its scope and detail as it is found in Trent and Vatican I, Christians and Catholics of apostolic spirit all the world over expect a leap [*balzo*] forwards in doctrinal insight [*penetrazione*] and the education of consciences [*la formazione delle conscienze*] in ever greater fidelity to authentic teaching. But this authentic doctrine has to be studied and expounded in the light of the research methods and the language

[*formulazione letteraria*] of modern thought. For the substance of the ancient deposit of faith is one thing, and the way in which it is presented is another (*Altra è la sostanza dell'antica dottrina del* depositum fidei, *ed altra è la formulazione del suo rivestimento*) (*Lettere*, p. 427: see Abbott, p. 715 for comparison).

The last sentence became, understandably, an object of controversy. Those who held an 'immobilist' view of language regarded it as pernicious neo-modernism; those on the other hand who thought that history was a necessary dimension of all theology found it liberating.

There can be no doubt about what Pope John said and meant. The above translation is based on the Latin transcript provided by Vatican Radio, and can be checked in its archives. Yet when the Latin version of the inaugural speech appeared in *Acta Apostolicae Sedis*, the official collection of papal documents, the text had been tampered with and censored. The idea of the 'substance' of faith vanished, and cautious qualifications were introduced. They are italicized in the following text and in the translation which immediately follows:

> Est enim aliud depositum fidei, *seu veritates, quae veneranda doctrina nostra continentur,* aliud modus quo eadem enunciantur, *eodem tamen sensu eademque sententia* (AAS, November 26, 1962, pp. 786–95 for the whole speech; ASCV, I, 1, p. 172, for this sentence).
> For the . . . deposit of faith itself, *or the truths which are contained in our venerable doctrine,* is one thing, and the way in which they are expressed is another, *retaining however the same sense and meaning.*

The last clause, not by chance, comes from the anti-Modernist oath of 1910 which also speaks of holding fast to 'the absolute and immutable truth' (Daly, pp. 235–6). So the censoring of Pope John can be safely attributed to the authors of *Veterum Sapientia* who were still trying to preserve language in aspic and deny history.

This was not the only sentence of Pope John that was bowdlerised and distorted. The previous sentence was given the same treatment. In the Latin version of his speech, there is no 'leap forwards', and indeed no movement of any kind. Once again, the additions are indicated by italics, but this time the omissions are graver still: 'Oportet ut haec doctrina *certa et immutabilis, cui fidele obsequium praestandum est,* ea ratione pervestigetur, quem tempora nostra postulant.' 'This *certain and immutable doctrine, to which faithful obedience is due,* should be investigated in the way our age demands.' What happened to 'the research methods and the language of modern thought'? When Pope John discovered these outrageous changes in late November 1962, he was too canny to sack the editor of *Acta Apostolicae Sedis*. He simply quoted himself, in the original non-edited version, in important speeches. (*Time* magazine for October 5, 1962, quoted an anonymous editor on *l'Osservatore Romano* who frankly admitted that he 'changed the Pope's words, whenever he said something which caused raised eyebrows'. No doubt that was true. But as Robert Rouquette remarks, it is totally improbable that any Roman would make such a confession, least of all to *Time*: Rouquette, I, p. 218.)

If curial theologians were alarmed by the apparent 'relativism' of Pope John's remarks on language and faith, his comments on how to deal with errors sent shivers down the spine of the more politically inclined. No resourceful editing could alter the fact that in refraining from condemnations he had broken with a tradition at least four centuries old. Yet Pope John did it with great tact and skill. He did not deny that errors existed in the contemporary world; indeed, they positively abounded. In a characteristic image he said that 'errors often vanish as swiftly as they arise, like mist before the sun'. It was an experience he had often had as he sat on his balcony at Sotto il Monte. There was a wry humour in the suggestion that the perspiring heresy-hunters arrive on the scene of error just as their quarry departs. So the Council was not being summoned to condemn errors: 'Today the Spouse of Christ prefers to use the medicine of mercy rather than severity. She considers that she meets the needs of the present age by showing the validity of her teaching rather than by condemnations' (Abbott, p. 716: retranslated). Pope John modestly described this new attitude as a 'preference'. But he knew perfectly well that if one looked at the history of the papal *magisterium* in the last 150 years, it was little short of 'revolutionary'.

John knew that he was turning things upside down. In a laconic aside he noted that 'the Church has frequently condemned these errors with the greatest severity'. In 1832 Pope Gregory XVI – incidentally the last professional theologian to become pope – had defended the need for 'severity' in his encyclical *Mirari Vos* (We are surprised at you). The times were bad, said Gregory (like the prophets of misfortune). Europe had just emerged from the French Revolution, 'that great conspiracy of the wicked'. Gregory uses an ironical text of Paul to justify his principled severity: 'Am I to come to you with a stick in my hand, or in love and a spirit of gentleness?' (I Corinthians 4.21). Gregory wielded the stick vigorously, Pius IX – whom there was wild talk of beatifying – followed his example, and the pontificate of St Pius X was single-mindedly dedicated to theologian-bashing. Pope John laid aside the rod.

The results would be seen very shortly. The new approach meant that the nineteenth-century thesis, still defended *mordicus* (to the hilt) by Cardinal Alfredo Ottaviani, that error has no rights, would have to be revised. Catholics could be tolerant without compromise. As for what the laying aside of the rod would mean for the Communist world, time would tell. But the treatment of error in *Gaudet Mater Ecclesia* is sufficient proof that Pope John really wrote this speech himself. And he could use the words Sir Edward Elgar wrote on the completed score of *The Dream of Gerontius*: 'This is the best of me'.

Two events, very disparate in nature, sum up the 'spirit of October 11'. Train-bearer Derek Worlock went in search of his cardinal and found him standing beneath the statue of St Peter with its well-worn toe. Also present was Cardinal Pietro Ciriaci. 'When this Council is over', announced Cardinal Godfrey, who like Pope John was dying of cancer, 'Peter will still be there, serene and true'. 'Yes' replied Ciriaci, prefect of the ominously named Congregation for the Discipline of the Clergy and the Faithful, 'but we are not all made of bronze'. The next day two observers from the Russian Orthodox Church, Archimandrite Vladimir Kotliarov and Vitalij Borovoi of Leningrad, arrived in Rome. This time the overworked word was justified: it was 'sensational' news. It meant that Pope John's olive branch had been picked up. The Council was now ready to begin.

Chapter 22

Sixty days to change the Church

> When the Fathers of Trent met in Council, under the guidance of the Holy
> Ghost, they did not quash their differences or silence objections, but let
> each opinion assert itself manfully, and even rudely, in what may be justly
> called a trial of strength
>
> (Lord Acton, *Essays on Church and State*, p. 170, written in 1863).

Everything – nearly everything – that was publicly said and done at what came to
be known as the 'first session' of Vatican II can be found in the four massive
volumes of the *Acta Synodalia Concilii Vaticani II* (ASCV from now on) or in
Giovanni Caprile's *Il Concilio Vaticano II, Primo Periodo* (Caprile II).

The most delightful item is the conversation – to call it a speech would be
pompously misleading – Pope John had with the crowd gathered in St Peter's
Square on the night of October 11, 1962, the date the Council began. The police
estimated that half a million people were present. The youths of Catholic Action,
bearing torches, formed a huge cross around the central obelisk. There was much
chanting and singing. The object of the exercise was to get Pope John to appear at
his window on this the greatest day of his life. It worked. John appeared at his
window and cried: 'Dear children, dear children, I hear your voices'. In the
simplest language, he told them about his hopes for the Council. He pointed out
that the moon, up there, was observing the spectacle. 'My voice is an isolated
one', he said, 'but it echoes the voice of the whole world. Here, in effect, the
whole world is represented'. He concluded: 'Now go back home and give your
little children a kiss – tell them it is from Pope John' (ASCV, I, 1, p. 202). One
could almost touch the emotion. The 'patriarch' gave and generated love with all
his being.

With the Romans on his side, Pope John turned his attention next day to the
diplomats who had come to Rome for the opening of the Council. Seventy-nine
nations were represented in one form or another. He told them that although the
Council was a religious event, he hoped that it would contribute towards world
peace, 'peace based on growing respect for the human person and so leading to
freedom of religion and worship'. The previous day he had talked about 'a new
order of human relationships'. Now he explained what it involved:

> love for one another, brotherhood, the ending of strife between people of
> different races and different mentalities. The help which developing

countries need so urgently in their quest for well-being would thus be provided more quickly, but 'without any attempt to gain power over them'. It is time something decisive was done . . . For all men are brothers and, we say it from a full heart, all are sons of the same Father (Caprile, II, p. 10).

The quotation was from *Mater et Magistra*; but the speech as a whole was a sketch for *Pacem in Terris*. Perhaps only the U.S. Ambassador, G. Frederick Reinhardt, knew or suspected that within a week the Cuban missile crisis would bring the world to the edge of doom.

Next day, October 13, Pope John met the 'observers' in the Consistorial Hall and the journalists – so that the awesome responsibility might strike home – in the Sistine Chapel. Between them, observers and journalists were to ensure that this Council would be different and known about.

All these speeches were in French, the language John invariably used on 'international' occasions. *Chers messieurs* (dear sirs), he began his address to the observers. It was an oddly cold introduction to a speech of great warmth: '*Portat onera nostra Deus* – God bears our burdens. He carries us along. He carries us as we are and with what we have: with his riches and with our poverty . . . As for me, I don't like to claim any special inspiration. I hold to the sound doctrine: everything comes from God' (*tout vient de Dieu*, ASCV I, 1, p. 197). That, incidentally, confirms the view of inspiration argued for in Chapter 14. It also suggested that spirituality could form common ground between separated brothers. Then John talked about his feelings on the morning of October 11: 'My duty was to be recollected, to pray and to thank the Lord. Yet from time to time I couldn't help looking round at so many sons and brothers. And when my eyes fell on your group, and on each of you, I felt comforted by your presence' (*Ibid.*).

The observers were captivated. Dr Joseph Jackson, president of the National Baptist Convention Inc, of Chicago, a black minister who was there because Pope John, having met him, invited him along, detected 'good will on both sides'. Dr John Moorman, Anglican bishop of Ripon, said, 'We had the feeling of being members of one family'. Max Thurian, from Taizé, remarked on John's 'simplicity and cordiality – as he said these things, he spoke like a priest' (Caprile, II, p. 15). Asked for their impressions, the Russian Orthodox observers sweetly replied – as they did in answer to most enquiries – 'Nothing'.

Marshalled and chaperoned by Cardinal Bea's men, the observers soon got the hang of things and picked up the jargon about the *aula* (the Council chamber) and the *schemata* (the draft texts). They sometimes had the painful experience of being misrepresented in the *schemata* and abused in the *aula*. Cardinal William Godfrey, for example, argued against the use of the vernacular on the grounds that the Anglicans had tried it and, despite the beauty of their worship, 'their churches are empty while ours are full' (ASCV, I, 1, p. 374: October 23, 1962). Trying to recover lost ground, he explained on December 4 that it was quite false to say that English Catholics were 'cold and lacking in sympathy towards their separated brethren'. They loved them greatly, but didn't want to deceive them. It would be 'false irenicism' if it were put about that 'all non-Catholic believers are close to us in faith' (ASCV, I, 4, p. 221). Frankly, it would have been better if Godfrey, who was terminally ill, had stayed at home. As his eventual successor, Archbishop John Carmel Heenan observed in his diary: 'The cardinal is still suffering from the effects of an operation last year, and it is hard to put a point that he can grasp clearly or quickly' (*Crown of Thorns*, p. 347). Bea's men consoled the observers with the thought that things had been much worse at Vatican I: when Bishop Joseph Strossmayer of Bosnia said that there were many Protestants who 'erred in good faith', he was shouted down with cries of 'Shame: heretic: get down from the pulpit! *Anathema sit!*' (McGregor, p. 36). So matters had improved. The observers believed that they had Pope John on their side and knew that through Bea and Bishop Emile Josef de Smedt of Bruges they could make their views known in the *aula* itself. Their title, observers, suggested a passivity that did not accurately describe their real role. It developed enormously in subsequent sessions.

Then came the journalists! Over 1,200 were accredited for the opening session, but only about 200 stuck it out for the whole period. Even for someone who had a theological education, it was a difficult event to report; for the theologically untrained, it was utterly bewildering. There was – at first – a great gulf between those in the know, who were vowed to silence, and those wanting to know. The eager seekers after truth had to content themselves with 'sources' who often turned out to be the man on the next desk or the chestnut vendor outside the Holy Office.

Pope John addressed this motley and restless crew on October 13. 'You can make it understood', he said, 'that there are no political machinations here' (ASCV, I, 1, p. 201). This was true in the sense he meant it; but even Pope John could not exclude the political element involved in any large international gathering. 'You can bear witness', he continued with a smile, 'that the Church has nothing to hide'. That remark, remembered later, caused raised eyebrows. If there was nothing to hide, why was it that speeches at the Council were baldly summarised and never attributed? 'The following opinions were expressed' was the discouraging formula adopted in the official hand-outs. And why was it that everything remotely interesting was covered by something called 'the pontifical secret', which was a super-secret secret. Thus Fr Sebastian Tromp S.J., a Dutchman and Cardinal Ottaviani's favourite theologian, when asked about the relationship between the Holy Office and the Secretariat for Christian Unity, replied with horror: 'This is a very delicate matter; I thought it was supposed to be secret' (*De Gelderlander Pers*, December 18, 1962).

Some reporters took a high and mighty tone about the obstacles placed in their path. Here, for example, is the witness of the eminently respectable Christopher Hollis, former member of parliament, man of letters, son of an Anglican bishop, brother of a chief of the British secret service later alleged to be a Soviet 'mole':

> The press relations of the Council were in the hands of Curial officials. It would perhaps be a discourteous exaggeration to say that this is as if one were to ask the prisoner in the dock to report on his own trial, but it is certainly true that this first session of the Council revealed . . . the existence of a vast mass of dissatisfaction with the lack of knowledge and imagination of the bureaucracy which has in its hands the management of the administrative affairs of the Church. The strength of this dissatisfaction came as a total surprise to most of the officials. They cannot understand it, and are not the best people to interpret what they cannot understand (*The Critic*, Chicago, February–March 1963).

Resourceful reporters solved their problems in characteristic ways. Patrick O'Donovan, of *The Observer*, London, eschewed theology and wrote divinely. He surveyed the bishops as they went into St Peter's and saw 'executive faces and kindly faces and imperious faces and ascetic faces, and faces that have known good tables' – including his own, no doubt. Others knew they had a book in the making. Bob Kaiser, from *Time*, made friends with Archbishop 'Tommy' Roberts who left confidential documents strewn about his flat. Antoine Wenger, a French Assumptionist priest and editor of *La Croix* was actually inside the Council as an expert on communications. This led him into agonised hair-splitting about what he could and could not say. The general rule was that if some Italian had said it, even incorrectly, Wenger thought he could tell the truth as he saw it.

The odd thing was that the rule of secrecy did not seem to apply, or at any rate was not respected, in the case of the Italian press. The professional *Vaticanisti* or Vaticanologists had sources not available to anyone else. At the same time most of them were ideologically committed to an alarming degree. Writing in *Il Tempo*, Cambridge-educated Prince Guglielmo ('Bill') Rospigliosi saw Pope John as moving disastrously to the left, and rang the alarm bells. Mario Tedeschi, editor of the scurrilous *Il Borghese*, was given tips by right-wing curialists who thought the Council was unnecessary. Cardinal Bea was the chief object of this right-wing fury: he was said to be willing to shake hands with Protestants, Orthodox, Jews, Freemasons and even Moslems, while being incapable of establishing concord within the Church (see Kaiser, pp. 77–8). The only reliable Italian source was *Civiltà Cattolica*, the Jesuit fortnightly. The Jesuits knew everything, and sometimes shared their knowledge. They were firmly on the side of Bea and Pope John.

Among those who made light of the journalistic problems was the mysterious 'Xavier Rynne' who wrote copiously in *The New Yorker*. With admirable candour, 'Rynne' claimed no inside knowledge and confessed that his eventual book was based 'on sources available to the general public' (Rynne, p. xi). Fr Francis Xavier Murphy C.SS.R., who with a twinkle in his eye denies that he was 'Xavier Rynne', wrote in 1984: 'Any journalist incapable of cracking a Vatican secret after diligently reading the Italian press, scrutinising *l'Osservatore Romano*, and attending an embassy reception or two, should change his profession' (Murphy, F.X., 'Vaticanology: separating fact and fiction', in *National Catholic Reporter*, February 24, 1984, p. 7). This is perfectly true. But it completes the identification of Murphy with 'Rynne'. For Murphy has been recycling 'Rynne' material for two decades. For example, in 1984 he asked: 'Why conciliar secrecy? Answer: because secrets travel faster'. This joke was first used in 1963. So either Murphy has plagiarised 'Rynne' or they are one and the same person.

All these writers recounted the dramatic events of October 14, the first working day of the Council. The Council asserted itself by deciding to elect its own Commission members rather than meekly accepting the 180 names provided by the Curia. Cardinals Achille Liénart of Lille and Joseph Frings of Cologne delivered this double blow to Cardinal Alfredo Ottaviani. He was visibly shaken, as could be seen on television news, which had pictures without sound (Wenger, p. 59). The politically-minded said the Council had made a bid for independence; theologians preferred to say that it illustrated the meaning of 'collegiality' and was, anyway, an obvious move. It was certainly fun. The mood of almost schoolboy exhilaration was caught in Heenan's diary:

> The rest of the day was spent lobbying. Bishop de Smedt of Bruges was on the 'phone and came round for the second time. His story was that when Liénart asked to speak, the chairman, Cardinal Tisserant, refused . . . Cardinal Liénart asked again after Mass. Once more leave was refused. He therefore just took the microphone and spoke. His example was followed by Cardinal Frings. Collapse of some Italian cardinals: *Scandalo! Che spettacolo davanti del mondo!* Scandalous! What a sight before the whole world! (*Crown of Thorns*, p. 349).

This makes one regret that Heenan's diary dries up at this point. But there was so much else to do. It did not occur to Heenan to wonder whether Liénart's intervention had been long-planned or was on the spur of the moment. It was in fact neither. During the summer holiday, the archbishop of Toulouse, Gabriel-Marie Garrone, carefully studied the *regolamento* or rules of procedure for the Council. He quickly realised that the make-up of conciliar commissions was a matter of the utmost importance. For if the draft texts were to be referred back – and there was every likelihood of that happening – there was not much point in sending them back to the same people. As Yves-Marie Congar drily remarked: 'An apple tree produces apples, a cherry tree cherries'. On arrival in Rome Garrone tried out his theory on his contacts: some assured him there was nothing to worry about; Cardinal Paul Emil Léger, of Montréal, felt 'ill and pessimistic' about the whole thing (Levillain, p. 190). Finally, it was a chance meeting with Liénart that enabled Garrone to make his point and have it grasped. So the intervention was written on the eve of the decisive session, and Liénart learned it by heart in the car on the way to St Peter's that very morning (*Ibid.*). Philippe Levillain's account is, admittedly, rather Gallo-centric, and the Germans seem to play no role in it. Liénart himself reported that on emerging from the Basilica, he met Fr C. Balič, the Croatian mariologist, who sarcastically remarked: 'You French! *Allons enfants de la patrie, le jour de gloire est arrivé'*(*Ibid.*, p. 191). On this same October 14, Pope John was neither lobbying nor phoning. He was busily writing a letter to the provost of Bergamo Cathedral, Mgr Guglielmo Scattini, about Don Battista Roncalli, his restless nephew, who had returned to his native diocese in 1961 with his uncle's blessing (*Lettere*, p. 151). John thanked the provost for informing him of Bergamo's reponse to the opening of the Council which had been 'echoed throughout the whole world'. Then he went on:

> Let us thank the Lord that the most unworthy Bishop of Rome has received
> so much light and strength, but a blessed cross (*una buona croce*) both for
> him and those about him cannot be avoided, a cross that the ecumenical
> Council will certainly have to learn to carry so that it may emerge as an *opus
> perfectum* (a perfect achievement) (*Lettere*, p. 424).

What did he have in mind? Had Ottaviani been in to complain about the rudeness of the foreigners? Had Pope John sensed already what was going to happen? Capovilla comments that this remark excludes any 'superficial optimism' (*Ibid.*, p. 425). True enough. But the 'good cross' also implies that the Council for him would be lived through as a spiritual experience. It could be very painful. But it was in the hands of the Lord. It will turn out well in the end. His Council was happening in another dimension.

At the second General Congregation (so the sessions were called) on October 16, Cardinal Ottaviani tried to recover lost ground. His motto was *Semper idem* (Always the same) and a volume of his collected speeches was published under the title, *Il Baluardo*, the bastion or bulwark. So he willingly accepted the role of leader of the conservatives. But now he was behaving reasonably. He spoke at some length on an apparently trivial procedural point. For an election to be valid (for example, a papal conclave) canon law usually required a two-thirds majority. He proposed that in the election for the Council Commissions, a simple majority should suffice. This would 'save time' and prevent protracted 'electoral joustings' (*ludi electorales*). It would also avoid dragging out the Curia's embarrassment, as Ottaviani realised that his men were bound to be defeated in an open contest. He presented himself to the Council as someone who wanted to get on with the job in hand as soon as possible. He used a little blackmail or – shall we say? – moral pressure. He reminded the bishops that the longer they were away from their dioceses, the greater the harm to the faithful. Moreover, the cost of living in Rome for too long might bankrupt a poor diocese. This solicitude was not wholly disinterested. It was the last flicker of the 'lightning council' envisaged in 1948 (see p. 311 above) on which Ottaviani had worked. The longer the Council lasted, the more it would be able to take charge of its own agenda, commissions, procedure, and documents. Ottaviani wanted a short, sharp Council.

But then his old friend and colleague, Cardinal Ernesto Ruffini, got up to insist that the rules must be obeyed: they had to ballot on and on until everyone had the necessary two-thirds majority. This was not the last time the self-confessed conservatives showed a lack of co-ordination. A ruling was needed. Who was supposed to give it? The question was referred to Pope John who took four days – until October 20 – to waive the requirement of canon law and accept the first-past-the-post method, without the need for a second ballot.

This episode raised the question: who was really organising the Council? In theory its day-to-day management was in the hands of the supposedly prestigious 'Council of Presidents'. All were cardinals. Four of them we have already met: Tisserant, Ruffini, Liénart and Frings. The others were Francis Spellman of New York, Sir Norman Gilroy of Sydney, Enrique Pla y Deniel of Toledo, Spain (ill and absent for most of the session) and Bernard Alfrink of Utrecht in Holland, a biblical scholar and former student of Ruffini. As far as can be discovered, the only decision of any importance taken by the Council of Presidents was that the first *schema* to be examined was that on liturgy. As Liénart explained: '*We* decided to begin with liturgy. We ought really to have started with a doctrinal *schema*, but we thought that an easier *schema* would allow us to play ourselves in' ('*roder*') (Grootaers, Jan, '*L'attitude de l'Archevêque Montini au cours de la première période du concile*', a paper given at the Paul VI colloquy in Milan, September 23–5, 1983). The idea was that everyone, however obtuse, would have something to say about worship.

But the Council of Presidents was an ineffectual and largely notional body. It held no regular meetings. It met 'on an *ad hoc* basis, when a question had to be dealt with' (Grootaers, p. 3, quoting Liénart). There was little in common between its members, and they had no plan. Although very few were aware even of its existence, authority at the Council was vested in the seven cardinals who sat on the Secretariat for Extraordinary Affairs. Article 7 of the Council rules said that its function was 'to examine the new questions posed by the Fathers and, if need be, to submit them to the Holy Father'. But in a novel situation, everything was a new question. In theory the Secretariat was important because it was the hourglass connecting Pope and Council. Its existence was not totally unknown. In 1963 Wenger noted that Amleto Cicognani, Secretary of State, was its president, and confidently declared that 'the directives of this body expressed the will or the feelings of the sovereign pontiff' (Wenger, p. 74). We already know three of its seven members: Montini, Suenens and Wyszyński. The others were Carlo Confalonieri, a curialist who prided himself on his independence of mind, Albert Meyer of Chicago, a scripture scholar who won the esteem of Fr Andrew Greeley, Julius Döpfner of Munich who balanced Giuseppe Siri of Genoa, later described as 'the arch-conservatives' conservative'. But there is not much evidence that this body met very often or decided anything of consequence. Much more influential was an unofficial group headed by Montini and Suenens that had no name. If it has to be labelled, it could be called the 'friends of Pope John'.

They were worried right from the start of the Council because it seemed aimless and without a plan. On October 18, 1962, Montini put his worries in writing in the form of a letter addressed to Cicognani. That was what protocol demanded, but it was meant for Pope John's eyes. He appended Suenens' attempt, based on the distinction between the Church in itself and in its mission, to synthesise the draft texts. He was critical of the Council of Presidents. 'The choice of the liturgy as the first topic for discussion', Montini wrote, 'although it was not placed first in the volumes distributed to us and although there was no need for it to come first, confirms the fear that there is no pre-established plan' (*l'Osservatore Romano*, January 26, 1984). It was a question that had long preoccupied him. One could not discuss the prayer of the Church without knowing what the Church was. So the Church was the only logical starting-point. He had made this point with some heat ('*vivamente*') to Felici after a meeting of the preparatory commission (Caprile, II, p. 251). The quarrel between the Curia and the foreigners might divert the groundlings of the press, but it left intact the serious question: what was the Council actually going to do?

For the Council, Montini averred, should not be 'a mere heap of disparate building blocks, but a thoughtfully constructed monument'. It was another way of saying that most of the preparatory work was useless. Debating the liturgy for a month might mask this fact, but it would soon have to be faced. It followed that the hope of completing the Council in a single session was illusory and would have to be abandoned. Montini thought that *three* sessions would be needed to bring order into chaos. This was bad news for Pope John. He already knew that he was dying. But he had to admit that Montini's plan, which was backed by Suenens, made sense. And *there was no other*.

Montini's programme for the Council as outlined in his October 18, 1962 letter may be summarised as follows:

1. The Council should focus on one theme: the nature of the Church. Why? Because it was the completion of Vatican I which had half-dealt with ecclesioiogical questions, and because in the twentieth century there had

been a renewal in the Church's self-understanding, illustrated by the encyclical *Mystici Corporis*.

2. But while dealing with the Church, the Council should not be introspective. 'Christ the Lord is the principle of the Church, which is an emanation and continuation of Christ. The image of Christ, like the Pantocrator in the ancient basilicas, should rule over the Church which gathers around him and in his name'.

3. The Council should recognise the 'acquired certainty' about the primacy of Peter and his successors. 'After the definition of papal primacy and infallibility, there were some departures' [he means the Old Catholics under Johann Döllinger] 'and some hesitations, but now there is docile acquiescence'. Since in order to 'complete' Vatican I they had to discuss collegiality and the role of bishops, why not say 'briefly, clearly, solemnly and in heartfelt fashion' that the papal office was not being called into question?

4. Then the Council should concentrate on the 'mystery of the Church'. It would have to deal with different tasks or roles in the light of the renewed self-understanding of the Church: bishops, priests, religious, lay people. The point was to arrive at a vision of the Church that was not merely juridical – seeing the Church as a 'perfect society' – but to see it rather as 'humanity living in faith and love, animated by the Holy Spirit as the Spouse of Christ, one and Catholic, holy and making holy. It seems to me that this was the original intention of the Pope when he called the Council'.

5. The *second session* should consider the mission of the Church, or what the Church does. '*Operatio sequitur esse*: action depends on nature'. Montini suggests that this would be the right place to deal with liturgy (the Church at prayer) or the 'young Churches' (the Church as mission).

6. Finally a *third session* would be needed to deal with the Church's relationships with other human groups. This would include:

(i) 'relationships with the separated brethren – to try to deal with this at the start of the Council seems to me to make any solution impossible'.

(ii) relations with civil society (peace and war, relations with states etc).

(iii) relations with the world of culture, the arts and sciences.

(iv) relations with the world of work, economics etc.

(v) relations with the Church's enemies etc.

At this point Montini added that the texts for the 'third session' he envisaged would have to be written in a different style. They would have to be more like 'prophetic messages addressed to our contemporaries, whether they were believers or not' (*l'Osservatore Romano*, January 26, 1984: letter dated October 18, 1962).

Montini's letter is the single most important document for understanding not only the first session but the whole Vatican Council. The fact that it was virtually unknown until September 1983 – when Suenens gave his copy to the Paul VI archives in Brescia – means that hitherto historians have lacked the key that would have unlocked the Council. It was to go more or less the way Montini proposed only a week after it started. True, it needed four sessions rather than the three he thought needed – but that was a trifling error since Pope John and the majority of Council Fathers optimistically believed that the Council would be over by the following Christmas. The letter was designed to fill the 'leadership vacuum'. Suenens recalled a conversation with Pope John the previous March. 'Who is organising the Council?' Suenens asked. '*Nessuno* (nobody)', replied John. Freedom was no doubt a good thing, but unrestrained freedom led to confusion. Pope John grasped this in late November when he asked Montini and Suenens to say in the *aula* what they had said privately in October. They duly obliged. Pope John could not have drawn up such a plan himself. He had not the scholarship. But he could recognise and appreciate lucidity in others. His own, more modest role, was not in doubt. He told Cardinal Gabriel-Marie Garrone, in a metaphor that would have delighted Archbishop Roberts, that his task was that of launching this big and heavy ship. 'Another', he said sadly and prophetically, 'will have the task of taking it out to sea' (*l'Osservatore Romano*, English edition, February 1, 1982).

Thus by October 18, 1962, just one week after Pope John's opening address, there were two scenarios for the Council. Ottaviani imagined a quick, one-session Council that would ratify all the prepared texts after making minor adjustments to them. Montini and Suenens foresaw a long-haul Council, requiring at least three sessions and involving, no doubt, some blood-letting (John's 'good cross'). One question a session gave them their plan: what is the Church? what should it do? what about its relationships? No one else saw the issues with so much clarity at the time. Not much imagination was needed to grasp that Montini was Pope John's preferred successor. He was the pilot who would get the big ship out to sea.

Two days later, there was further evidence of inept planning when the Council of Presidents acting 'in the name of the Holy Father' invited the Council to endorse a 'Message to the World'. It seemed rather presumptuous to be addressing the whole world before they had actually done any work. Archbishop John Carmel Heenan was briskly dismissive: 'I believe it is not yet time to be sending a message to all men, and it makes me sad to see a first message that is so vapid and long-winded. I am quite sure the press will pay very little attention to it' (ASCV, I, 1, p. 237). Heenan was right. The message left no mark on history and quickly passed into merited oblivion. The debate on it consisted of speaker after speaker regretting the absence of his pet topic, be it Our Lady, the 'Church of silence' or relations with the Orthodox.

But the damp squib of a message acquired importance for accidental reasons. The original idea for a message to the world came from Yves-Marie Congar and Marie Dominique Chenu, two French Dominicans who were still under a minor cloud (see Chapter 10 above). Off their own bat they produced a text addressed to all men and presented it to six well-disposed cardinals. They liked it, but thought that in a laudable desire to speak to all men it overlooked the Gospel and relied only on 'the natural law'. This would never do for a Council which required a 'Christian' text. So four French bishops, Liénart, Garrone, Emile Guerry of Cambrai and Alfred Ancel, auxiliary of Lyons, set to work to devise a document that began with God's love and his saving plan (details in Rouquette, I, p. 232, quoting Guerry, who wrote a pastoral letter about it). Thus the importance of the message was that it began the tacit rehabilitation of Congar and Chenu, and lodged in Pope John's mind the dream of a text that would be addressed not just to Catholics but to all men.

Such a text was urgently needed. For the world had suddenly become notably unsafe. On October 15 reconnaissance photographs proved beyond doubt that Soviet missiles were in Cuba, within easy reach of the United States (Schlesinger, p. 506). On October 20, the day the Council debated its ineffectual 'message', President John F. Kennedy announced a quarantine or blockade on the Soviet ships that were known to be heading for Cuba. There followed a hectic week in which it seemed quite likely that a nuclear war might engulf the world. Families of politicians were evacuated from Washington. In Rio de Janeiro, Dr Billy Graham announced the end of the world, prematurely as it turned out, but not unreasonably.

Pope John played an important pacifying and reconciling role in this fateful week. Khrushchev acknowledged this later. 'What the Pope has done for peace', he told Norman Cousins, editor of the *Saturday Review*, on December 13, 1962, 'will go down in history' (Stehle, p. 306). But what Pope John did has not gone down in the history of the Kennedy era. One searches in vain for any mention of Pope John in the biographies of John F. Kennedy or the accounts of the Cuban missile crisis. One can only speculate that having their first ever Catholic president made American historians reluctant to admit that the Pope might have had some influence on him. At the other end of the spectrum, *Vaticanisti* exaggerate Pope John's role. They present him as a last-resort mediator when all other diplomatic channels had broken down. But to inflate his role is just as bad as to underestimate it.

The key day in the story was October 23, 1962. Having made his strong stand and imposed the blockade, John F. Kennedy tried gentleness. His brother Robert had built up a friendly relationship with the Russian ambassador in Washington, Anatoly Dobrynin. The president sent his brother along to explain how he read Khrushchev's intentions. No threats were uttered. Robert pointed out that John F. was far less hawkish than others in the administration, and that although he and

Khrushchev did not agree on many issues, 'there was now a measure of mutual trust and confidence between them on which he could rely' (Schlesinger, p. 514). That same day the president, pulling out all the stops for peace, called Norman Cousins and said he wanted to make contact with the Vatican. Why Cousins? Why the Vatican? Cousins was well known. In 1945 he had published a book called *Modern Man is Obsolete* in which he argued that the invention of the atomic bomb had changed the course of human conflict. He had tried to stay in touch with the Russians. He had also argued that the only 'third force' in a bi-polar world was the papacy. Moreover, at this very moment, Cousins was engaged in dialogue with Soviet writers and scientists in Andover, Massachusetts. Also present at Andover was the enigmatic Belgian Dominican, Fr Félix Morlion who had been thrown out of Rome by Cardinal Pizzardo in February 1960. He was widely believed to be a CIA agent (Magister, p. 252). But now his contacts in the Vatican proved useful. He eventually got through on the evening (Rome time) of October 23 and talked to Mgr Igino Cardinale, chief of protocol, who assured him that Pope John would be willing and anxious to help in any way he could.

The Russians at Andover were apprehensive and wanted to go home. Cousins persuaded them to talk to Morlion. Talking to a priest was a new experience for them. They knew Khrushchev personally and transmitted portions of a coded telegram: 'We really believe that you are a friend of peace and do not want the death of millions'. In the Vatican, meanwhile, Pope John had received Morlion's request for intervention. With Dell'Acqua he worked throughout the night on a message to be broadcast the following day. From time to time he went off to his private chapel to pray. He knew exactly what was expected of him. What was it he had said on the night of October 11? 'My voice is an isolated one, but it echoes the voice of the whole world'. Some public sign of papal esteem would help Khrushchev persuade the Kremlin hawks that peace was the wiser course. John's previous discretion now stood him in good stead. He had stopped talking about 'the Church of silence'; he had welcomed the Cuban ambassador to Italy, Amado Blanco; he had made it clear that the Council would not issue condemnations. In other words, he had earned the right to be listened to.

The following day, Wednesday October 24, there was the usual weekly audience. At the end of his address, Pope John added a loosely linked sentence on the good will of statesmen: 'The Pope always speaks well of those statesmen, on whatever side, who strive to come together to avoid war and bring peace to humanity'. Banal enough, but it was a first signal to Khrushchev. The second signal was Pope John's message which was delivered to the Soviet Embassy in Rome for transmission to Moscow. It read:

> I beg heads of state not to remain insensitive to the cry of humanity, peace, peace. Let them do all that is in their power to save peace; in this way they

will avoid the horrors of a war, the appalling consequences of which no one could predict. Let them continue to negotiate. History will see this loyal and open attitude as a witness to conscience. To promote, encourage, and accept negotiations, always and on every level, is a rule of wisdom that draws down both heavenly and earthly blessings (DMC, pp. 614–15).

John broadcast his message on Vatican Radio that afternoon. By Friday October 26, it made page one of *Pravda* under the banner headline: 'We beg all rulers not to be deaf to the cry of humanity'. This was unheard of. It meant that Khrushchev was preparing his retreat. Pope John's intervention helped to let him off the hook. He could appear as a lover of peace. 'The Pope's message', he told Cousins later, 'was the only gleam of hope' (Stehle, p. 305).

On Sunday October 28 Khrushchev replied to Kennedy. He declared that work on the missile bases would be suspended, that the weapons would be sent back to the Soviet Union, and that he would begin negotiations within the framework of the United Nations. The Soviet ships had already turned back. In his private chapel, Pope John celebrated a Mass for peace. Soon after, Dell'Acqua, substitute at the Secretariat of State, brought him a message that had just arrived from President Kennedy. He thanked Pope John for his help. Not only was the immediate crisis resolved, but Khrushchev wanted further contacts to discuss disarmament and *détente* (*Utopia*, English, p. 9). It was the fourth anniversary of John's election and the feast of Christ the King.

The Rome newspapers that Sunday morning had not got the latest news and were still alarmist. So Pope John's words to an anxious crowd at the Angelus brought news as well as hope:

There have been four years of prayer and service, of meetings and conversations, of joy but also some suffering; but every day has been lived with a readiness to do the divine will, and in the confidence that all things work together for the edification of all.

On today's feast of Christ the King, I feel deeply moved and my spirit is led to serenity and calm. The word of the Gospel has not changed; but it rings out to the ends of the earth and finds its way into human hearts. Dangers and sufferings, human prudence and wisdom – all these should issue into a canticle of love, and a renewed plea, addressed to all men, to seek and restore the Kingdom of Christ . . . A new spirit is beginning to enter the minds of politicians and economists, scientists and men of letters (AAS, 54, 1962, p. 860).

Capovilla dates the origin of *Pacem in Terris* to October 25, 1962, when Pope John was working on his message (IME, p. 180). The Council was wondering how to address modern man. John would talk about what most concerned people

– war and peace. So the encyclical was conceived at the height of the Cuban missile crisis. His 'readiness to do the divine will' led him to this at a time when illness and preoccupation with the Council ought to have dispensed him from extra effort.

No one would have blamed him if he had not written *Pacem in Terris*. He had quite enough to do as it was. But he wanted, before it was too late, to deliver his last will and testament. His old diplomatic habits began to operate once more: when you sense an opening, hasten to exploit it. Khrushchev and Kennedy, the two most powerful men in the world, were well-disposed toward him and even, relatively, towards each other. So keep up the pressure for peace. There was a sense in which this work was more important than the Council. Its debates on the liturgy were dragging on repetitively and interminably. Cardinal William Godfrey produced the 'argument from lipstick' (*labia tincta rubri coloris*) against conceding the chalice to the laity. The 'argument from tourism' against the use of the vernacular plodded its weary way. There had already been some furious clashes in the *aula*. This was an additional reason for working on *Pacem in Terris*: it would be a hint to the Council that the Church existed, not to contemplate its navel, but to serve the world. So Pope John did not find it necessary to follow everything that was being said in St Peter's. He kept his closed-circuit television on all the time, of course, but he only switched up the sound when someone who interested him appeared.

But Pope John's physical absence from the *aula* did not mean that he was uninfluential in it. During the debate on the liturgy, his October 11 speech was quoted time and time again by those who wanted freedom, adaptation and changes. His key-terms and attitudes were echoed repeatedly: renewal and optimism, pastoral and ecumenical. This was what Pope John had taught the bishops. Those opposed to change, on the other hand, were unable to quote the October 11 speech. Cardinal James F. McIntyre, of Los Angeles, went directly against it when he claimed that 'the attack on the Latin language in the liturgy is indirectly, but no less truly, an attack on the fixity of sacred dogmas' (ASCV, I, 1, p. 370). This was not the majority view among the United States bishops. Cardinal Joseph Ritter of St Louis went so far as to say that 'once one has accepted the necessity and usefulness of renewal, then nothing can be *a priori* excluded from scrutiny, except the essence of the Mystical Body and its divine origin . . . and for that reason the Council cannot be indifferent to the reform and renewal of the liturgy' (ASCV, I, 1, p. 351). The difference between the two American cardinals was that while McIntyre appealed to Pius XII, the 'liberals' appealed to Pope John. In a sense it was a continuation of the debate that went on during the first year of his pontificate: was he worthy to be compared with the truly phenomenal and magisterial Pius XII? But now the issue was being debated not in private ante-chambers but in the full glare of publicity.

The reformers, however, were neither crude nor foolish. Their strategy was to claim that they were merely continuing the liturgical reforms that had started with St Pius X and been further extended under Pius XII. The argument had the merit of being largely true. But it led Ottaviani to protest about the way the authority of Pius XII was being misused. He granted that Pius XII was liberal and generous in admitting adaptations and the use of the vernacular in certain sacraments. But those who quote him in favour of the vernacular must have forgotten what Pius XII told the liturgical congress held at Assisi in 1956. Ottaviani was in full spate: 'Pope Pius XII said: "The Church has serious reasons for maintaining firmly and unconditionally" – note those words "firmly and unconditionally" – "the use of the Latin language in the Latin rite." So if you want to use the authority of Pius XII, use it not just when it agrees with you. Use it honestly' (ASCV, I, 2, p. 20). Ottaviani saw himself as the faithful guardian of Pius XII's memory. He made a tactical blunder, however, in this same speech when he said that priests would soon lose their enthusiasm for this 'new-fangled concelebration', when they learned it would mean forfeiting their Mass stipends. At this point he was stopped by Cardinal Bernard Alfrink not because he had made a petty and stupid remark but because he had run over the allotted fifteen minutes. '*Iam finivi, iam finivi!*' he cried as he departed, jowls quaking and leaving his hearers uncertain whether he meant he had had his say or had enough. He was not seen in the *aula* for another two weeks. Though Alfrink was merely doing his duty, the fact that a Dutch cardinal should have halted Ottaviani in his tracks provided a symbolic vignette of how much the Church was changing. This happened on October 30, 1962.

Deprived of the presumed approval of the *reigning* Pope – the conservatives were at a loss what to do next. They clumsily put the ball in their own net. Cardinal Antonio Bacci, who had seemed so impressive at a distance as the much-trumpeted Latinist, now revealed that he was almost incapable of grasping a rational argument. Antonio Rosmini, he said, had asserted in *The Five Wounds of the Church* that 'the use of Latin set up a barrier between priest and people'. An interesting idea, worth examining. But, said Bacci, 'Rosmini's book was rejected by the Church!' No first-year student would have been allowed to get away with such a slip-shod argument. Bacci also alleged that some passages in scripture, such as the story of the chaste Susannah and the libidinous old men, not to mention the Canticle of Canticles, were best left in the decent obscurity of the Latin (ASCV, I, 1, p. 408).

Bacci was closely followed by Archbishop Pio Parente, secretary of the Holy Office. Strictly speaking he should not have spoken at all, since Pope John had ruled that Vatican diplomats and secretaries of Roman dicasteries should not address the Council (Wenger, p. 97). This was intended to preserve their 'objectivity' in controversial matters. Parente may have come to regret disobeying this wise rule. His entire speech was a tearful apologia for the Holy Office, whose staff toiled away like stakhanovites and got no thanks for it:

> We are true martyrs at the Holy Office. We know how much patience, how much work, how much prudence is needed to prepare *monita* (warnings), decrees etc. It's very hard work. You've no idea. And all this work is done in Latin, and a good thing too. All you innovators should learn from the Holy Office which rightly holds fast to tradition and embarks on new ways only with the greatest prudence, a serene heart and calm nerves (*pacatis nervis*). So to attack the Latin language would be a very serious matter, for it would risk splitting the unity of the Christian family at least in the greater part of the world (ASCV, I, 1, p. 425).

This outburst had the merit of spontaneity. It revealed some pretty raw wounds. But it failed to impress hard-bitten missionaries and others who simply refused to believe that bureaucrats led such a hard life. Parente was clearly one of the 'prophets of misfortune' mentioned by Pope John in his inaugural speech. Like his master Ottaviani, he accepted the diagnosis which said that the trouble with the Church was 'the itch for novelties', known in Latin as the *pruritus innovationum*, which made it sound like a particularly repugnant disease, highly contagious, found most commonly in the Netherlands, and spread by contact with the works of Edward Schillebeeckx O.P., whose critique of the draft texts had been devastating and was resented.

So everyone inside the Council had to react, positively or negatively, to the aims which Pope John had fixed for his Council. However, on the details of the debates that were engaging the Fathers in the *aula*, Pope John made no public comment. Nor did he make any in private. Meeting the French bishops on November 19, the most critical and controversial moment of the session, he described himself once more as the Patriarch Jacob who refused to be drawn into taking sides between his quarrelling sons. *Pater autem rem tacitus considerabat*, he quoted, 'the father considered the matter in silence'. These almost daily meetings with groups of bishops were his means of sharing in the work of the Council. Archbishop Franjo Seper, of Zagreb, Yugoslavia, described them in the *aula* as 'intimate and familiar conversations' (Caprile, II, p. 246). John had just completed the first round of audiences, and was about to begin the second – starting with the East Europeans – when illness forced him to stop. They were, essentially, morale-boosting sessions. They were very informal. John used them to sound out opinion on, for example, whether and when there should be a second session. Typical was the meeting with the French bishops – he knew as many of them as of his Italian colleagues – to whom he said: 'Yes, there's an argument going on. That's all right. It must happen. But it should be done in a brotherly spirit. It will all work out. *Moi, je suis optimiste*' (Wenger, p. 114).

So Pope John was 'present' to the Council even though he was not in St Peter's. And although his views on liturgy in the vernacular or communion under both kinds were officially 'unknown', everyone knew that the Patriarch Jacob had some favourite sons. Montini or Joseph reminded the Council on October 22 why liturgical changes were being proposed: it was so that the prayer of the Church might be more pastorally effective. This was the golden rule. Montini steered a middle course – as he did in his pontificate – between 'arbitrary innovations' and simply doing nothing. He had a criterion of innovation. He aptly quoted St Augustine: 'It is better that we should be blamed by literary critics than that we should not be understood by the people' (ASCV, I, 1, pp. 314–15). Having said this on October 22, Montini who – it must not be forgotten, thought liturgy the wrong starting point – fell silent in the *aula* until December 5.

Even for a patriarch, it was difficult to turn Augustin Bea into a 'son'. They had both been born in 1881. But on October 30, 1962, the day Ottaviani stalked out in a huff, one began to understand why Pope John so valued Bea. John had said that 'history is the teacher of life'. Now Bea illustrated the point perfectly. Ruffini had gone back to the condemnation of Martin Luther in 1520 to prove that communion under both kinds was ruled out for Catholics. Bea put the historical record straight. Trent's treatment of this topic, he pointed out, was presented as a *disciplinary* rather than a *doctrinal* matter. So (but he didn't bother to spell this out) there was nothing absolute about it. Moreover, the two legates of the Pope at Trent, entrusted with the task of expressing his mind (*mens*), had voted in favour of conceding the chalice to laypeople. Furthermore, Pius IV himself, only two years after the Council of Trent, conceded that in certain German dioceses the chalice might be given to the laity. As a parting-shot, Bea showed how narrow the vote had been at Trent: 79 in favour of the chalice: 87 against (ASCV, I, 2, pp. 23–4). He forbore to say that, in current canon law, such a majority would have been insufficient. He just raised his aged eyebrows. It was a relief to have some information instead of passion and polemics.

And it pleased Pope John. He did not like the Council of Trent to be turned into a byword for obscurantism. Apart from his work on St Charles Borromeo, he had researched the life of Gerolamo Raggazoni who was nuncio to France before becoming bishop of Bergamo (two excellent reasons why Roncalli should be interested in him). In the middle of the Council, Pope John, overcome by scruples, returned to the library of the Bergamo seminary a book about Raggazoni he had 'borrowed' in 1921 (*Lettere*, p. 556: note dated November 7, 1962). Why Raggazoni mattered was that he had given the closing address at the Council of Trent, and it was full of the ecumenical spirit. He actually said: 'We came to Trent in order to be closer to the Protestants. Here we got rid of a certain defensiveness; we trusted the Protestants and looked longingly towards them' (*Letture*, p. 195: Capovilla quotes an 1854 edition of the Canons and Decrees of

Trent). This was a rather different version from the Trent being presented in the press (Ottaviani to taxi-driver: 'Take me to the Council'. The taxi-driver takes him to Trent). So it was not utterly absurd of Pope John to think that the four hundredth anniversary of the conclusion of the Council of Trent, which would fall in 1963, was a happy omen for his own Council, Vatican II.

There was yet another way in which Pope John could influence the Council: by dropping hints. The broadest hint was dropped on November 4, 1962, feast of St Charles Borromeo and fourth anniversary of his coronation. It conveniently fell on a Sunday. Mass was celebrated in the ancient Ambrosian rite of Milan by Cardinal Giovanni Battista Montini. But Pope John himself preached the homily. He lavished praise on the Ambrosian rite as an instance of that liturgical diversity which greatly enriched the Church. He quoted the Latin tag *ars una, species mille* – which means that though the creative impulse is one, it produces manifold forms. He spoke with authority of St Charles Borromeo who 'contributed to the renewal of Church life through the celebration of provincial councils and diocesan synods . . . and this, thanks be to God, gives us hope for the future' (DMC, V, p. 13). By this time it must have been evident to all but the most dull-witted Council father that Pope John was saying he was in favour of moderate liturgical change. He used the example of the Ambrosian rite to put the case for diversity and so reject the uniformity being demanded by the Curia. Similarly, his decision to add the name of St Joseph to the list of saints in the canon of the Mass, announced on November 13, though most often seen as a simple act of piety towards his patron, was also a signal that the liturgy was not immutable.

Pope John's homily on the feast of St Charles Borromeo was his most important intervention on the debate actually going on in the *aula*. The Ambrosian rite, he claimed, was closest to the original Roman rite, and so it was fitting that it should be celebrated in the Council along with all the other rites. But the Copts and the Chaldeans had said Mass without the presence of the Pope. (On hearing drum-beats one day in St Peter's, someone asked what was going on. Reply: 'I don't know, but I think they're getting ready to boil a cardinal'.) Moreover, Pope John explained that Rome had learned from Milan: the washing of the feet on Maundy Thursday was not originally a Roman custom; it came from Milan, as St Ambrose testifies in his *De Sacramentis* (*On the Sacraments*, 3,1,5: DMC, V, p. 10). To say that Rome had learned from somewhere else shattered curial complacency. It was 'history as teacher of life' once again. Finally, by his presence and warm words about 'the first cardinal whom we created', Pope John seemed almost to be designating Montini as his successor. He knew that he had no right to do so. But given his cancer, it was natural that the two questions, how the Council should be continued and who should succeed him, would fuse in his mind. For Montini had a plan. Yet he was silent in the *aula*.

Montini was waiting for the crisis to mature. The debate on the liturgy had exposed contrasting positions. A clear majority was emerging in favour of change. The debate on the two sources of revelation was likely to be even more acrimonious, and it was already clear that Ottaviani's draft was probably doomed. Montini kept his diocese informed by articles in the Milan newspaper, *l'Italia*. On the eve of the debate, he made it clear that the crunch had been arrived at: 'Only those who are familiar with the development of theology, the progress that has been made in biblical studies, and the controversial heat generated by these questions, both within and without the Church, can appreciate the apprehensions, hopes and fears which this new topic brings to the Council' (after Kaiser, p. 157).

The debate on the 'two sources' began on November 14 and lasted a week. At its centre was the question: is the revelation made in Christ contained in Scripture or Tradition or partly in both? The draft text picked up the idea of *Humani Generis* and claimed that the *magisterium* was the *proxima norma veritatis* (the nearest criterion of truth) and therefore subordinated both Scripture and Tradition to it. Most theologians thought this was a mistaken approach, that it was ecumenically disastrous and was, anyway, the wrong way to set up the problem. But many other themes could be worked into the debate on revelation. The 'progressives' attacked the view that revelation was embodied in propositions rather than in the person of Jesus. The 'conservatives' launched a vicious attack on scripture scholars who were thought to be tearing the heart out of the Gospel; in the background loomed the Lateran's quarrel with the Biblicum and Bea.

Ottaviani, back in the Council after his two weeks' furlough – so much work to do – was defensive from the start. He knew what was going to happen. The draft would be rejected. The conservatives were fighting a rear-guard action. The loquacious Ruffini – he spoke twice as often as anyone else in this first session – defended the *schema* on the grounds that it had been prepared by very capable theologians. It could not be rejected because there was nothing to put in its place. 'It would be', he declared in a revealing metaphor, 'as though a calamitous storm suddenly swept away the foundations of a great building' (ASCV, I, 3, p. 37). A few days later Cardinal Valerian Gracias of Bombay, just back from India and war, replied that it was often more economical to demolish an old house and build a completely new one than to patch up the old. Architectural considerations apart, the argument that 'you-have-nothing-to-put-in-its-place' was risky since there were dozens of theologians in Rome at that time who could produce an alternative text at the drop of a biretta. Without waiting for an invitation Karl Rahner had already done so. Before coming on to 'the presence of God revealed in the Church's preaching', it had a characteristic section on 'the hidden presence of God in the history of mankind', which anticipated his theory of 'anonymous Christians'. A furious Ottaviani harangued the Theological Commission about 'unauthorised documents that were against the rules and only caused trouble'

(Wenger, p. 106). It was just as well that burning dissidents had gone out of fashion.

The only remaining defence of the draft text was the argument from authority. To reject it would be an insult to the Preparatory Commission, which had laboured so hard, and an insult to the Holy Father, who had approved it. It was tragic to see Giuseppe Battaglia, bishop of Faenza, and an old confidant of Pope John, get everything so wrong. He claimed a privileged insight into the mind of Pope John. From his vantage point he explained that 'the task of the ecumenical Council is . . . to warn the faithful of errors and dangers to their faith' (ASCV, I, p. 98). Battaglia – Pope John had written to him on the eve of his election (see p. 278) – knew his remarks would be unpopular. He said he felt like Daniel in the lions' den. He showed courage. But he still claimed to be speaking in the name of Pope John as he warded off the charges that the draft was too scholastic, too anti-ecumenical, and insufficiently pastoral. But neither he nor his friends seriously faced the question: would the rejection of this *schema* really be an insult to the Pope?

There is no evidence that Pope John saw it that way. Rejection would be a disappointment, certainly, but not the end of the world. The Council would have to make up its own mind. The papal role was not to take sides in the dispute but to find some way of resolving it without splitting the Council. When Ruffini, Ottaviani and Bacci went to him with their grumbles about the allegedly monstrous behaviour of the 'progressives', he consoled them with history. Things had been far worse at Trent, where an irate Latin bishop tore the beard off a Greek. And Vatican I offered a precedent for rejection. On the first day of its debates a *schema* prepared by Fr Franzelin S.J. was described as 'too long, too vague, and too academic' (Butler, I, p. 160). His students at the Gregorian were delighted to have their own spontaneous judgement confirmed by a Council. Franzelin's schema was rejected. So there was no need to get upset. Pope John would not use his authority to save the *schema* from defeat; but he would use it to spare its authors from humiliation.

Yet there was still a lot of gloom in the Council. On November 12 it was announced that there would be a second session in 1963 from May 12 to June 29. It seemed likely that the first session would end in chaos, with nothing to show. Alfred Ancel, auxiliary of Lyons and a former priest-worker, summed up the pessimistic mood on November 19: 'As I listen to what is being said, I am filled with anxiety. I don't see how we can move forwards. I can see no way out at all' (ASCV, I, 3, p. 203). The same note was struck by Bishop James H. Griffiths, an auxiliary of New York: 'Lord we have laboured all night and caught nothing, but in your name we will let down our nets' (*Ibid.*, p. 181). He evidently didn't expect to find anything in the nets. Yet this was the day on which Pope John was saying to the French bishops, Ancel among them, *'Je suis optimiste'*.

John's optimism was not just a Micawber-like disposition to hope that something would turn up. On November 14 Suenens made a speech entirely devoted to procedural matters. He drew out the implications of the decision to hold a second session: they might indeed go home after December 8 with very little to show, but they would not have wasted their time, provided they issued clear instructions about what should happen in the inter-session period. Suenens had other suggestions for speeding things up and avoiding repetitions. But his most important suggestion was to introduce a closure motion: after views had been sufficiently aired on a given *schema*, it should be put to the vote to discover whether it was generally acceptable as a basis for future work. If yes, the debate went on; if not, the *schema* would be scrapped.

Suenens' guillotine unexpectedly fell on the 'two sources' schema on November 20 (so it may have explained Pope John's 'optimism' the day before). Felici put the question in Latin, and it was then translated into five other languages, including Arabic. Mgr John J. Krol, under-secretary, read out in English: 'Should the discussion on *De Fontibus Revelationis* (On the Sources of Revelation) be discontinued, terminated?' This was very odd. For in the usual terminology of the Councila *placet* vote meant that you were in favour of a text, while a *non placet* vote meant you were against it. (There had been a proposal to have a green light for *placet*, a red light for *non placet*, and an amber light for *placet iuxta modum* – approved with amendments – at each desk.) But here this sensible way of asking questions was stood on its head. There was great confusion, and sheer weariness impelled some to vote to stop the discussion. Amid uproar Ruffini grabbed the microphone and attempted to explain what was at stake. It takes several readings, even today, to discover what he was really saying. 'Interrupted', said Ruffini, 'really means "renewed"'. If you vote *placet*, that means there will be no further mention of this *schema*'. Eleven minutes elapsed while this riddle was interpreted, during which keen Council Fathers milled around the secretary's desk and demanded an explanation. It must have been in a comparable session at Trent that the Greek lost his beard.

Who had devised this curious formula? Was there a plot? If so, what was it supposed to achieve? Bishop Wilhelm Kempf, the German-language under-secretary, reports a telephone conversation between Ruffini and Frings on the eve of November 20. Ruffini devised the question, and Frings noted it down. But next day Frings, whose eyesight was not good, omitted the explanation that those who voted *placet* were voting 'to interrupt the debate, *so that a new draft might be prepared (ut novum schema praeparetur)*' (Caprile, II, p. 176). It's a pity no one said this at the time.

When Felici eventually came back to the microphone with his usual cry of '*Audiant omnes* (Listen, all of you)', he conceded that many Fathers were still puzzled, which was an understatement. But he hardly did more than repeat the question, in its original form, adding however the vital clue that 'to interrupt the debate' meant not just to stop it for the time being but 'for ever' (if that was what *sine die* really meant, and it did). There must have been many Fathers who felt spun round like tops. But then, even more astonishingly, while the votes were being laboriously counted by students from Propaganda Fide, the now doomed debate continued, except that Bishop Antonio Quarracino of San Domingo, Argentina, who was due next, could not be found. It was that sort of day. Eleven speeches later and after some complaints about the delay, with another *Audiant omnes*, Felici announced the result: present and voting, 2209; *placet*, 1368; *non placet*, 822; null 19. The cheers of the 'progressives' turned to groans as Felici explained that since the required two-thirds majority had not been reached – it would have been 1437 – the discussion would continue.

It did indeed continue the next day when the forty-two-year-old Bishop of Kraków, Karol Wojtyla, made his maiden speech. He pointed out that a fresh-water spring was a 'source' in the strict sense, and that wells and cisterns were only improperly and analogously called 'sources'. In this way he sought to abolish the problem the Council had been debating. The only true and proper 'source' was God speaking. Tradition and Scripture were not 'sources' in the strict sense. Therefore if the document were to be retained, its title would have to be changed (ASCV I, 3, p. 294). It cannot truly be said that on hearing this Barthian mini-lecture, the Fathers of the Council nudged one another and said: 'One day Kraków will be Pope'. But at least they were able to distinguish him from his Polish colleague, the auxiliary of Gniezno, who wanted to change the creed to 'I believe in the Holy, Catholic and *Petrine* Church' (Caprile II, p. 240).

But the real action of the Council was now taking place in private. For the most part it eluded inspection. But there was one meeting on the night of November 20 that we do know about. Cardinal Paul-Emile Léger of Montréal was highly esteemed by Pope John who had known him from his Paris days. On November 21 John wrote: 'I have thought about our meeting last night, and of your kindly letter* and the intimate conversation that followed it' (*Lettere*, p. 434. *Capovilla is uncertain whether to read *lettere* or *letture*, letter or lecture). Then he evoked the memory of the Madonna della Salute in Venice where there was a traditional pilgrimage on November 20. He concluded: 'And in this serenity how much joy and peace! So that there should remain some memento of our meeting and of my affection for you, dear Cardinal, I make you a present of this episcopal cross' (*Ibid.*, pp. 434–5). Why should this meeting have made such an impression on Pope John? Heenan thought Léger 'mercurial' (*Crown of Thorns*, p. 257). He was mercurial enough to depart for a leper colony in Africa in 1967.

Over twenty years later, Léger still remembered this meeting. He was summoned by Pope John, late at night. The Swiss Guards would not let him in through the Bronze Door. Eventually Capovilla was phoned and came scurrying down to lead him to the papal apartments (interview in Montréal, May 14, 1984). For some hint as to the details of Léger's 'intimate conversation' with Pope John, we have to turn to an earlier television interview:

> I remember, in the early stages of the Council, the tragic vote on *Revelation* when the fathers formed two opposing factions. That very evening, during an audience with Pope John, I unburdened my heart to him. I told him that I thought that piercing thorns were tormenting my soul, but he replied, 'Go forward. Do what your heart tells you' (Bonisteel, Roy, *Man Alive: the Human Journey*, p. 180).

Three days later, emboldened by John's words, Léger opened his heart to the Council. On November 24, eve of Pope John's eighty-first birthday, Léger intervened on the mass media. Though it was a mediocre debate on a mediocre text, Léger's words applied to the Council as a whole and the spirit in which it should be conducted. He thought the *schema* expressed the Church's mission in too juridical a way, that it should convey pastoral solicitude rather than assert rights, and that the Church ought to be more like a mother proposing doctrine in charity rather than an institution uttering threats (ASCV, I, 3, p. 465). This was what Pope John wanted to hear. Without being an emissary of Suenens and Montini, Léger was in close touch with them. With the help of this group John now took some decisions of crucial importance for the future.

First, the vote on the 'two sources' would be taken as a rejection of the *schema*: though it did not have the necessary two-thirds majority, it was clearly not a text that could win unanimous assent. Second, the topic of revelation would be entrusted to a 'mixed commission'. This was announced in *l'Osservatore Romano* on November 24. Its co-presidents were Bea and Ottaviani, its co-vice-presidents were Liénart and Cardinal Michael Browne, and its co-secretaries were Fr Sebastian Tromp, S.J. and Mgr Jan Willebrands. This symmetry was maintained all down the list. This, says Heenan in his free-booting style, 'was Pope John's way of banging our heads together: he shrewdly judged that men who made flaming and intransigent speeches in the *aula* might behave more reasonably in private' (*Crown of Thorns*, p. 356). But nothing Bea had so far said or would subsequently say could be called 'flaming or intransigent'. Perhaps Heenan knew that on the night of November 25, Ottaviani had declined to meet Bea to discuss the fusing of the three rival *schemata* on the nature of the Church (Caprile, II, pp. 203–4). The real point of Pope John's decision was that the monopoly of the Holy Office was broken. Respect for other schools of thought and concern for what the separated brothers valued would from now on have to be built into the texts, not tacked on afterwards as an inconsequential post-script.

The final two weeks of the session confirmed the need and the wisdom of enhancing the role of the Secretariat for Christian Unity. First the *schema* produced by the Oriental Churches Commission, *Ut Omnes Unum Sint* (That all may be one), was referred back, despite the fact that John persuaded Amleto Cicognani, his Secretary of State, to present it. Then Ottaviani's *De Ecclesia* was rejected. From Pope John's point of view, the snag was that all this reworking would take time; and yet there was not much time between December 8 and May 12 when the second session was due to begin. Pope John consulted nearly everyone on this. At his meeting with the English and Welsh bishops, Cardinal Godfrey told the Pope that he personally wanted the session to begin 'as soon as possible', but that was because he did not expect to live long – and in fact died on January 22, 1963. Godfrey had been in the Vatican diplomatic service. This led Heenan to remark: 'The good diplomat is anonymous and Cardinal Godfrey never had the slightest difficulty in keeping silent' (*Crown of Thorns*, p. 359). But Pope John preferred diplomats to smart alecs and, what's more, discovered that he shared with Godfrey not only the same illness but the same devotion to the Precious Blood. Godfrey's secretary guesses that they spent more time discussing these topics than the Council (Worlock, conversation, April 29, 1983). Archbishop Heenan, however, favoured a September 1963 start: 'To return home for only a few weeks seemed futile. Bishops would hardly have resumed their pastoral programme before it was time to return. Many of us therefore let the Pope know that we thought it unsatisfactory to return to our dioceses only for Christmas and Easter' (*Crown of Thorns*, p. 373).

The Heenan view prevailed, though not necessarily for his reasons. On November 27 Felici announced that 'many Bishops have asked, on pastoral grounds, that the second session should not begin in May but in September. So the Holy Father in an audience with the Secretary of State yesterday has deigned to accept this request, and has fixed the feast of the nativity of Our Lady, Sunday, September 8, 1963, for the start of the second session'. This announcement was greeted with volleys of applause – despite the fact that Ruffini had tried to ban all applause on November 10, on the grounds that if expressions of approval were allowed, one could not rule out expressions of dissent (boos? catcalls? whistles?), which would be inappropriate in the august *aula*.

Though it won the approval of the Council, this decision must have cost Pope John a great deal. It meant that he was virtually certain not to see the second session. It was precisely at this moment that *l'Osservatore Romano* for the first time admitted that Pope John's health was giving trouble. It could not be concealed any longer. On November 29 the Vatican paper disclosed that on medical advice Pope John had been obliged to cancel audiences because 'the symptoms of gastric disturbance were getting worse; for some time the Holy Father has been on a diet and undergoing medical treatment that have led to rather severe anaemia'. This was seriously incomplete. It avoided the dreaded word 'cancer'. The truth was that on November 16, John's doctor, Pietro Valdoni, introduced him to a new doctor, Pietro Mazzoni, who recommended cobalt-ray treatment, then the latest thing. But anaemia was one of its side-effects. 'From the doctors' words', wrote Giancarlo Zizola, 'Pope John could grasp that inoperable cancer left him with less than a year to live' (*Utopia*, English, p. 11). The remarkable result was that John became more than ever determined to write the encyclical about peace, conceived on October 25. If he were going to miss the second session of the Council, he could at least finish *Pacem in Terris*. It did not yet have this name.

No sooner had Pope John's illness been announced than it was said to be going away. He would struggle to appear at his window for the Angelus on December 2. Those who saw him were not reassured. Ottaviani, meanwhile, was presenting his last *schema*, significantly entitled *De Ecclesiae Militantis Natura* (On the nature of the Church Militant) which had ferocious chapters on authority and the absolute necessity of the Roman Church for salvation. But this was a different man from the confident and assured Ottaviani who had first spoken on October 14. He was now chastened and sad. It was difficult and unchristian not to feel some sympathy for him. Already half-blind, the butt of the cruellest lampoons, defending a concept of the Church he believed to be the only orthodox one, the baker's son from Trastevere knew that he was beaten. Pope John had persuaded him not to resign and would persuade him to work with Bea, but that was the limit of the concessions he was prepared to make. Ottaviani determined to go down in style. Introducing his hopeless *schema*, he said:

> I expect to hear the usual litanies from you all: it's not ecumenical and it's too scholastic, it's not pastoral and it's too negative, and similar charges. This time I will make a confession to you: those who are accustomed to say 'Take it away and replace it' [*tolle, tolle, substitue illud*] are already poised for battle. And I will reveal something to you: even before this *schema* was distributed, an alternative *schema* was already prepared.
> So all that remains for me is to fall silent for, as scripture says, where no one is listening, there's no point in speaking [*Ubi non est auditus, noli effundere sermonem*] (ASCV, I, 4, p. 9. Cardinal Laurence Shehan, of Baltimore, thought Ottaviani had said 'Take him away! Take him away! Down with him: *Tolle, tolle, subicite eum*': *Blessing of Years*, p. 148).

Ottaviani left the microphone beaming, amid general hilarity.

But his smile cannot have lasted very long. For that same morning his *schema* was demolished in a single speech which connoisseurs considered the most effective of the first session, if not of the Council. It was given by Bishop de Smedt of Bruges, but he was speaking in the name of the Secretariat for Christian Unity, which gave him added punch. De Smedt denounced three sinful attitudes: 'triumphalism' (the feeling as H. V. Morton said of the Saints on the façade of St Peter's that 'We have it in the bag'); 'clericalism' (the idea of the Church as a pyramid with the Pope at the apex), to which de Smedt opposed the Church as the people of God, filled with the gifts of the Holy Spirit and radically equal in grace; and 'juridicism' or the legalistic spirit. 'No mother ever spoke in this way', he said, echoing Léger (ASCV, I, 4, p. 142). These defects would have been banished, de Smedt intimated, had the Secretariat for Christian Unity been allowed to work on the text.

Then, by one of those ironies in which conciliar history abounds, the next speaker after de Smedt was Archbishop Marcel Lefebvre, at the time superior general of the Holy Ghost Fathers, but by 1975 head of a dissident sect of traditionalists with headquarters at Ecône in Switzerland. His main point in December 1962 was that the Council risked incoherence by pursuing too many goals:

> At one and the same time we have to propound true doctrine, extirpate errors, encourage ecumenism, and manifest the truth to all men. We are pastors, and we know perfectly well that we don't use the same language with those who know theology and with the laity. So how can we, in one and the same document, define doctrine so that contemporary errors are refuted and yet expound the faith intelligibly to everyone, even those who have no grasp of theological sciences (ASCV, I, 4, pp. 144–5).

What Lefebvre in 1962 regarded as a confused method, became by 1975 a diatribe against the 'neo-modernist and neo-Protestant tendencies that manifested themselves in the Second Vatican Council' ('Profession of Faith', in Congar, *Challenge to the Church*, p. 77). As Aquinas says, a small error at the start leads to a big error in the conclusions.

Though few regarded Lefebvre as a prophet, he had put his finger on a real problem: how does one speak simultaneously to the faithful and to 'all men of good will'? Emile Guerry, archbishop of Cambrai, another friend of Pope John's, tried to tackle it on December 4. Guerry argued that it would be lethal to oppose dogmatic and pastoral theology. 'The first duty of our pastoral office', he said, 'is to teach our people integral and pure doctrine, but in such a way that they can hear the Word of God, accept it in faith, and carry it into every corner (*spatium*) of their lives'. Then he made a distinction about 'adaptation' or *aggiornamento*. If it means compromise with the spirit of the age and glossing over whatever modern man does not like, then it is a betrayal of the pastoral office. What really needs adaptation, he went on, is not the doctrine but the way in which it is presented. We need a deep study of the past so that familiar truths may shine out with fresh clarity and so prove enlightening, life-enhancing and attractive, disclosing God's immense love (ASCV, I, 3, p. 101). This was a typical French attempt to stake out the common ground between pastors and doctors in the Church. Pope John listened to it on his television set and liked it so much that the same afternoon he sent the three volumes of his Venice writings to Guerry, marking the page where he had quoted the archbishop of Cambrai on 'paternalism' and 'authoritarianism' (Caprile, II, p. 249: see p. 265 above).

So the Council was not ending in total failure. On December 2, Montini, still mute in the *aula*, wrote in *l'Italia*: 'A vast amount of excellent material has been brought together, but it is too disparate and uneven . . . a central and controlling idea is needed to co-ordinate this immense material' (Grootaers, p. 25). Everything Montini said in his December 2 article looked back to his letter to Cicognani of October 18, and looked forwards to his speech in the *aula* three days later:

> Some are afraid that the conciliar discussion will be endless and that instead of bringing people together it will divide them even more. But that will not happen. The first session has been a running-in period. The second will progress much more swiftly, and there is already talk of concentrating the material in briefer drafts (*schemata*), and of laying before the Council only matters which are justified by today's pastoral needs and of general interest (Grootaers, p. 26).

Armed with that principle, one could cut a broad swathe through much of the conciliar material, and throw it to one side. Montini concluded: 'Thus the Council arrives, filled with the breath of the Spirit, at its central theme: the Church' (*Ibid.*). But this was what Montini had believed all along. It was hard to say which was the more influential: an article in a newspaper or a speech in the *aula*, the appeal to public opinion or the appeal to the peer-group. Montini worked on all levels. The effect of his moves was that he appeared as the natural successor of Pope John. He was not merely *papabile*, he was *the papabile*. He showed leadership. He fixed the agenda for the rest of the Council.

Montini, of course, was not acting alone. The 'talk about concentrating all the material in briefer drafts' was going on in meetings towards the end of November, 1962. Jan Grootaers described one of them at the Belgian College vouched for by the Rector: 'The principal purpose of this meeting, organised with Pope John's blessing, was to replan the Council's agenda. Besides Montini, Cardinals Lercaro, Döpfner, Léger and Suenens were also present' (Grootaers, p. 25). But one couldn't expect to replan the Council in a single evening. Giovanni Caprile speaks of more meetings and gives Pope John a more active role than merely blessing them all. He says Pope John *asked* Suenens to discuss privately with Montini and other colleagues the idea of a Secretariat for the Church's activity *ad extra*. This referred to all the questions which arose where the Church and the 'world' intersected. There were 'a few meetings' at which Suenens' re-ordering of all seventy *schemata* was accepted. This was the overall plan, the *plan d'ensemble*, which Suenens submitted to Pope John 'some days before December 4'. John, still convalescent, made some marginal comments with the help of

Dell'Acqua. He suggested that Suenens should find some way of 'bringing in' Pius XII, and suggested that it would be better to avoid talking of a Secretariat *ad extra* but rather of a sub-commission, so as to keep all the options open and not alarm people unduly. Thus, concludes Caprile, from whom these details come, when Suenens spoke in the *aula* on December 4, he knew that he had the support of the Pope, and of Cardinal Montini and his friends (Caprile, II, p. 264).

It should by now be clear that the first session of the Council was organised, more and more, not by the Council of Presidents, but by a loosely co-ordinated group centred on Suenens and Montini. But nothing happened behind Pope John's back. He was still ultimately responsible, intervening with suggestions and decisions as they were required. Perhaps his most important single decision was to make the unofficial official. To avoid a repetition of the free-for-all in the preparations before the Council, a Co-ordinating Commission was set up to oversee its continuation into 1963. Presided over by Cicognani, Pope John's trusty lieutenant, its members were Liénart, Spellman, Urbani, Confalonieri, Döpfner and Suenens (Caprile II, p. 259). But this was not announced until December 17, when most of the Fathers had gone home. The obvious 'conservatives' like Spellman of New York and Urbani, Pope John's successor in Venice, were there so that they could tug along their huge episcopal conferences. Confalonieri, we have already seen, was a curialist with an open mind. France, Germany and Belgium in the persons of Liénart, Doepfner and Suenens, would organise the Council. It was the 'golden triangle' of Lille, Brussels and Munich. Montini was not there because he was going to be pope. Ottaviani and Ruffini had completely lost control. Nothing had been heard from Pizzardo, still in charge at the Congregation for Seminaries and Universities. Asked on Bavarian Radio what his hopes for the future of the Council were, Ottaviani replied: 'This question is too delicate' (Caprile, II, p. 292).

It is difficult to say exactly how much of this was known at the time. There were moments when secrecy was blown sky-high. In a homily at a journalists' Mass on November 25 Dom Helder Pessôa Câmara, then auxiliary of Rio de Janeiro, remarked that 'unofficial meetings at which Bishops from all the continents meet fraternally and talk' were just as important as the formal proceedings in St Peter's. He went on:

> You certainly know that one result of such meetings had been the idea of setting up a body to implement *Mater et Magistra*. It has been suggested that there should be a special commission with the task of studying the problems raised by the modern world, especially world peace and the relationship between the industrialised and under-developed countries (De Riedmatten, pp. 60–1).

This was obviously Suenens' Secretariat *ad extra*. Câmara was optimistic if he thought everyone already knew about this gleam in the eye, which was variously named the commission for charity, for peace or for the poor. Just over four years later it was actually set up on January 6, 1967, as the Justice and Peace Commission. It was another instance of the way the Council set up its own organisation and set its own agenda.

Helder Câmara belonged to another unofficial group presided over by Cardinal Pierre-Marie Gerlier of Lyons. They were concerned with 'the Church of the poor' (see Congar, *Power and Poverty in the Church*, p. 12). They took heart from, and constantly quoted, Pope John's September 11 broadcast in which he had said: 'Faced with the developing countries, the Church presents herself as she is and as she wishes to be, as the Church of all and especially the Church of the poor' (Alberigo, p. 357). This had theological implications for the exercise of authority in the Church. They were drawn out by Yves-Marie Congar in a lecture on 'The Historical Development of Authority' (*Power and Poverty*, pp. 40–79). So while in the morning session of the Council, the conservatives were beating the Counter-Reformation drum, in the afternoon Congar was telling those who wished to hear that all authority in the Church was for service. Although still not officially *periti* at the Council, Congar and Chenu were working their way back and made their presence felt. After an enforced absence of ten years, Congar's first lecture to his Dominican brothers at Le Saulchoir near Paris was in January 1963. It was on the first session of the Council.

It remained only to publish from the conciliar house-tops (that is, in the *aula*) what had already been whispered in private. It was a well-coordinated campaign which left the conservatives flummoxed. On December 4 Suenens gave the speech previously vetted by Pope John. He revived the distinction between the Church *ad intra* and the Church *ad extra*. He listed four topics that clamoured for attention under the second *ad extra* heading: everything concerned with human dignity – and that included 'the population explosion'; social justice; the Church of the poor; war and peace. The proper treatment of these subjects, Suenens went on, 'involves us in a threefold dialogue: with the faithful, with our separated brothers; and with the world'. 'In this programme', Suenens concluded to immense applause, 'there is nothing that was not already contained in the speech already mentioned' (Caprile, II, p. 247). This was a slight slip of the tongue. He had referred only to the September 11 broadcast, to which he had contributed importantly. But it didn't matter. He was understood to be referring also to the October 11 address. The applause meant that the vast majority of Council Fathers accepted Suenens' analysis of events at this first session: thanks to Pope John's opening speeches, it began well; then it meandered into frustration and deadlock; it was being saved at the last gasp by a return to Pope John's original intentions. Suenens heeded John's advice and said that he was merely 'continuing the brilliant magisterium' (*magisterium fulgens*) of Pius XII. But he continued to advocate setting up 'a *Secretariat* for the problems of the contemporary world' (ASCV, I, 4, p. 224). That dealt with the Church *ad extra*.

Next day, December 5, Montini dealt with the Church *ad intra*. There is no need to quote it: it simply took up material from his letter of October 18 and various articles in *l'Italia*. The concerted moves continued on December 6 with Lercaro who had been assigned 'the Church of the poor'. He took his cue from Pope John's October 11 speech, in which he had quoted St Peter in Acts: 'Silver and gold I have not, but what I have I give you'. Lercaro, who had turned his episcopal palace in Bologna into an home for orphans, exhorted the whole Church to follow Christ who 'though rich, became poor for us' (ASCV, I, 4, p. 330).

On December 5, Pope John struggled to his window at noon – the Council ended early so the bishops could see him – and put a brave front on things: 'As you see, my children, Providence is with us. There's progress from one day to the next, *piano, piano* (gently, gently). Sickness, then convalescence. Now we are convalescing'. Seeing the crowd made him feel better, and in a few faltering words he summed up the gist of what was later to be called his 'revolution': 'What a spectacle we see here today – the whole Church in all its fullness: behold its bishops! behold its priests! behold its Christian people! A whole family here present, the family of Christ'.

Pope John had compared the Council to a mighty ship. Now it was cruising into port – or rather dry-dock, for John insisted in his final address on December 8 that the nine months between then and September 1963 were not a holiday from the Council: its work would continue and modern means of communication (telephones and jet-planes) would keep them in touch. The first session, he said, 'had been like a slow and solemn introduction to the Council – a generous willingness to enter into the heart and substance of the divine plan' (Caprile, II, p. 270). This was John's answer to those who said the first session was a failure. In the work of God 'quantitative judgements do not apply', and the Beatitudes over-turn the usual criteria of success and failure. What God wanted had to be sought in patience.

The laborious start had been an exercise in group dynamics:

> Brothers gathered from afar took time to get to know each other; they needed to look each other in the eyes in order to understand each other's heart; they needed time to describe their own experiences which reflected differences in the apostolate in most varied situations; they needed time to have thoughtful and useful exchanges on pastoral matters (Caprile, II, p. 270).

Pope John did not foolishly try to cover up the clash of ideas at the Council. He thought the 'sharply divergent views' that had been put forward illustrated 'the holy liberty that the children of God enjoy in the Church'. Archbishop Roberts said the same thing more picturesquely: the children of God were able to slide down the banisters in the house of the Lord. So Pope John's judgement on the first session was positive. It may not have turned out as he had expected, but they were all in the hands of the Lord and would have to reckon on the surprises of the Holy Spirit.

Yet despite this spiritual optimism, the atmosphere at this closing meeting of the first session was oppressive, 'almost penitential'. What Pope John was saying was overshadowed by anxieties about his health. This was not the man who had so confidently walked, well, waddled, up the aisle of St Peter's on October 11. John was now a sick man. His face was sunken, his skin livid, his eyes looked under sedation. Many thought they were seeing him at the Council for the last time. 'What was intended as an *au revoir* turned into a *adieu*', said Karol Wojtyla when, as Pope John Paul II, he visited John's birthplace. There was sadness.

Yet this final speech had one very important function: it was designed to console those who were feeling hurt and defeated. Pope John did not rejoice over anyone's discomfiture, and he knew that Ottaviani and Ruffini, among his oldest friends, were feeling badly bruised. He offered them a healing olive-branch with several quite unnecessary references to Pius IX who had not only defined the Immaculate Conception, the day's feast, but opened the First Vatican Council on this very day in 1869. Moreover, his Council would finish in 1963, another significant co-incidence because it was the four hundredth anniversary of the conclusion to the Council of Trent. He even went so far as to quote Pius IX who had said at Vatican I: 'See, brethren, what a blessed and joyful thing it is to go forward in harmony in the house of God . . . As Our Lord Jesus Christ gave peace to his apostles, so I too, his unworthy vicar, give you peace in his name. Peace, as you know, casts out fear; peace shuts its ears to what is said without real knowledge' (Caprile, II, p. 272). Pope John was too ill, and the occasion too grave, for irony. But he must have known that there was not much 'holy liberty of the children of God' at Vatican I, and that the phrase about shutting ears 'to what is said without real knowledge' meant rejecting whatever the Pope disagreed with. The truth is that Pius IX, who was seventy-eight when Vatican I began, was often an embarrassment and was regarded by some of the Fathers of Vatican I as gaga.

What could it all mean? Was Pope John, in Gregory Baum's phrase, 'smiling in two directions' (Kaiser, p. 70)? Did he take seriously the project of beatifying and eventually canonising Pius IX? A society existed in the Roman Curia to promote this goal. According to Capovilla, Pope John used to ward off their demands for immediate action by saying: 'Tell me what the objections to concluding the cause are, and whether they can be overcome' (Capovilla, archives). Those in the Curia who wanted to re-do Pius IX's Syllabus of Errors, might just have found that encouraging. But despite such poultices for the bruised, Pope John continued to speak of Vatican II as a 'new Pentecost' and his deep-down optimism was undimmed. His last word on December 8 was that it seemed as though, in the Council, 'the heavens are opened above our heads, and the splendour of the heavenly court shines down upon us' (Caprile, II, p. 272). It was the vision of the *Spiritual Exercises*. Its principal meditations are set in 'the heavenly court', that is, the communion of saints.

Archbishop Heenan expressed astonishment that Pope John did not mention ecumenism or say farewell to the 'observers' at this final meeting (*Crown of Thorns*, p. 378). That puzzle is resolved once we grasp he was speaking to the defeated conservatives. In any case he had planned to meet the forty-six observers that same afternoon. At the last minute, he was forced to telephone and apologise for his absence. Cardinal Cicognani deputised for him. There was no discourtesy. Everyone understands illness. Lukas Vischer, observing on behalf of the World Council of Churches, made a speech in which he thanked the unavoidably absent Pope John for his welcome. 'From the very first day of the Council', he said, 'we realised the importance the Holy Father gave to the presence of observers from the Churches separated from Rome' (Caprile, II, p. 34). Nothing had been hidden from them. They had felt free to comment on everything. They had done some sliding down the banisters. They had formed friendships that would last a lifetime. Difficulties remained – every ecumenical speech has to recall this truism – but they could now be seen in different perspective.

That was not the least result of the first session of Vatican II. Astonishingly, it had lasted only sixty days. Everything happened so swiftly, Karl Rahner said afterwards, that it was difficult to remember who said what, or where a particular idea came from. Difficult, but not impossible. Pope John had only another six months to live.

Chapter 23

Last will and testament

I never dared be radical when young.
For fear it would make me conservative when old

(Robert Frost, *Precaution*, in *Complete Poems*, p. 337).

Convalescence, Christmas and a message from Khrushchev came at about the same time.

In the excitement of the Council, Pope John had not forgotten about Metropolitan Josef Slipyi, still in a Soviet forced labour camp. The problem was to find some way of communicating with Khrushchev. The Russian Orthodox observers at the Council finally broke silence on November 20, 1962. Vitalij Borovoi told a Soviet news agency that Pope John and the Secretariat for Christian Unity 'have a love for our Church and our Patriarch, and also respect and friendship for our people in its struggle for peace' (Novosti: Caprile, II, p. 343). That was encouraging if cliché-ridden. But the observers were not well prepared to risk their necks for Slipyi. The Italian Communist leader, Palmiro Togliatti, promised to bring the case to Khrushchev's attention, but got nowhere. It was Norman Cousins who made the breakthrough. As the first session of the Council drew to a close, he met Dell'Acqua and Cardinale with the news that he had a rendezvous fixed with Khrushchev for 11.30 a.m. on December 13. They told Cousins that Pope John would regard Slipyi's release as a clear sign of good will.

Within a few days Cousins' twenty-page report on his conversation was on Pope John's desk. Khrushchev, who was also from the Ukraine, told Cousins that he knew of Slipyi and had been present at the funeral of his predecessor who, he hinted, had been murdered. He didn't know where Slipyi was now. But he said: 'I will have the case examined and if there are assurances that it will not be turned into a political case, I will not rule out liberation. I've had other enemies, and one more at large doesn't alarm me' (*Utopia*, English, p. 140). Khrushchev appeared genuinely grateful for Pope John's intervention in the Cuban missile crisis, and essayed a folksy comparison between himself and the Pope: 'We both come from humble origins and worked on the land in our youth'. The new element to emerge was that Khrushchev wanted regular though private contacts with the Vatican; the Cuban emergency had shown how necessary this was. There was to be give and take in this new relationship: the Vatican should recognise the separation of Church and state, and the Soviet Union should recognise that the

Catholic Church wishes to serve all men. Cousins put the final point of agreement as follows: 'Khrushchev recognises that it was very courageous of the Pope to act as he did, given that he has problems within the Church, just as Khrushchev has in the Soviet Union' (*Ibid.*, p. 139).

On December 19 the indefatigable Cousins had a forty-minute audience with Pope John. He delivered a personal message from Khrushchev:

> To His Holiness Pope John XXIII. On the occasion of the holy season of Christmas, I beg you to accept good wishes for your health and energy to pursue efforts in favour of peace, well-being and prosperity for all humanity. N. Khrushchev (*Lettere*, p. 439).

John said to Cousins:

> I get many messages these days from people who are praying that my illness may be without pain. But pain is not my enemy. I have memories, so many marvellous memories. These memories being me great joy, and fill up my life so that there is no room for pain. When I was young I was apostolic delegate to Bulgaria. I came to understand and love the Slav peoples. I tried to study Slavonic languages, including Russian. Do you know Russian?

Cousins did not know Russian. John went on:

> A pity. You should learn it. You are much younger than I. It wouldn't take you too long. It is a very important language. The Russian people are a wonderful people. We must not condemn them because we don't like their political system. They have a deep spiritual inheritance which they have not lost. We can talk with them. We must always try to speak to the goodness that is in people. Nothing is lost in the attempt. Everything may be lost if men do not find a way to work together to save peace (*Utopia*, English, pp. 141–2: quoting Cousins, Norman, 'The Improbable Triumvirate', in *The Saturday Review*, October 30, 1971).

Cousins also delivered a message from President John F. Kennedy, thus demonstrating – if it were not already evident – that he was not merely a free-lance intermediary but had an intelligence role. He was a dove for *détente*.

Back in New York Cousins saw to it that Pope John became *Time*'s 'man of the year'. A tasteful drawing by Pietro Annigoni adorned the cover, and the fulsome article proclaimed: 'To the entire world Pope John has given what neither diplomacy nor science could give: a sense of the unity of the human family' (*Time*, December 31, 1962). Robert Kaiser, *Time*'s man in Rome during the first session, was writing a book to explain it all and exalt the Pope (*Lettere*, p. 569: alas, Capovilla calls him Robert B. Piser). In February *Time–Life* invited Pope John to a spectacular summit lunch in New York, where the other guests would include Kennedy, Khrushchev, de Gaulle, Adenauer, Karl Barth and Pablo Picasso. It was to be most exclusive: only those who had made the cover of *Time* were asked. John didn't reject the idea out of hand, but thought it needed time to 'mature' (*Lettere, Ibid.*). And a visit of Kennedy to the Vatican in that same month of May was also tentatively arranged. If Norman Cousins and *Time* cannot be said to have 'created' Pope John's American image, they certainly did their best to make it widely known.

Meanwhile, Pope John was wondering how to reply to Khrushchev's message. Rejecting the icy, anodyne draft proposed by the Secretariat of State, he typed out the message himself:

> Cordial thanks for the courteous message of good wishes. We return them from the heart in words that come from on high: Peace on earth to men of good will.
>
> We bring to your attention two Christmas documents from this year which call for the consolidation of a just peace between peoples.
>
> May the good Lord hear and respond to the ardour and sincerity of our efforts and prayers. *Fiat pax in virtute tua, et abundantia in turribus tuis* ['Peace within your walls, and security within your towers': Psalm 122.7].
>
> Joyful good wishes for the prosperity of the Russian people and all the peoples of the world (*Lettere*, p. 438).

He enclosed his Christmas broadcast to be given the next day, December 22, and his address to the diplomatic corps. The Secretariat of State thought it was a mistake to use such a warm tone and to be quoting scripture – in Latin – when addressing an atheist dictator. So Pope John had to use Cardinal Bea's secretary, Fr Stjepan Schmidt S.J., to deliver his package to the Soviet ambassador. John sealed it with a picture of Our Lady by Tiepolo and the prayer *'Ave, mundi spes, Maria; ave mitis, ave pia; ave Dei amore plena, virgo dulcis et serena'* ('Hail, Mary, hope of the world; hail, holy and meek Virgin, filled with God's love, gentle and serene'). Khrushchev was not to know that this prayer, attributed to Pope Innocent III, rhythmic as a mantra, had been used by John since his seminary days (*Rosario*, pp. 5–6). Khrushchev was being assaulted by prayer.

On December 22 Pope John broadcast the Christmas message he had just sent to Khrushchev. It was on the theme of *Gloria in excelsis Deo* (Glory be to God on high). These words, he said, had been sung at the Council in so many different languages – Greek and Slavonic, Armenian, Coptic, Syrian, Latin – and this diversity in unity summed up the experience of the Council (*Caprile*, II, p. 273). How wonderful it was, he went on, to hear over 2,000 episcopal throats singing the *Gloria* at the final Mass on December 8. He did not mean that it was an impressive musical performance: but after the opening Mass on October 11 when the bishops had listened passively to Palestrina, to be singing the *Missa de Angelis* was a step towards that 'active participation' the liturgical *schema* said was so important. Death was never far from his thoughts these days. 'At the day of judgement', he declared, 'we won't be asked whether we realised unity, but whether we prayed, worked and suffered for it' (*Ibid.*, p. 274). Then the 'glory of God' led him naturally to 'peace on earth' (*pacem in terris*). From now on John saw concluding the Council and working for peace as two complementary tasks. Which was uppermost at any given moment would depend partly on events. He wanted to be free to respond to the Spirit.

The critics in the Secretariat of State, increasingly irritated by Pope John's naïveté, were right in this: the presence of a Latin quotation from scripture in the message to Khrushchev was incongruous. But it is easily explained. When Pope John decided to write an encyclical on peace, he jotted down an anthology of biblical texts on the subject of peace. So he had notes on 'lasting peace' (Ecclesiasticus 50.23–4) and on the 'holy city' that was at peace because its inhabitants obeyed the laws (2 Macchabees 3.1–3). The Latin Bible was alive for John. Giacomo Manzù, who spent many hours sculpting him, says that John would declaim poetic passages from the Old Testament. When Manzù pointed out that he did not know Latin and – more diffidently – that he was a Communist, John would translate into Italian with equal gusto. There was no reason why Manzù, or Khruschchev for that matter, should not enjoy poetry.

The work on *Pacem in Terris* was going well. John had set up a small editorial team headed by Mgr Pietro Pavan, professor of social doctrine at the Lateran. Now fifty-eight, Pavan was the son of a Venetian shopkeeper and anti-Fascist. His 1952 book on *Christianity and Democracy* followed Jacques Maritain in showing the affinities between the two – an unusual position for an Italian cleric. To set Pavan on his way, John had typed out a passage from St Augustine's *The City of God*:

> Peace is tranquillity in the order of things,
> ordered obedience in fidelity to the eternal law.
> Order is giving each thing its place.
> The peace of mankind is ordered harmony in the home, in the city, in man.
> Wretched, therefore, is the people that is alienated from God
> (*Utopia*, English, p. 12: the reference to St Augustine is too vague to be checked; John probably conflated several texts).

Right from the start, John insisted that there should be no condemnations in his projected encyclical. 'I can't attribute ill-will to one side or the other', he told Pavan, 'if I do, there will be no dialogue, and all doors will be closed' (*Ibid.*, p. 26). Pavan emerged from the papal library and said to Capovilla: 'What marvellous limpidity of mind he has'. At the same time Pavan realised that Pope John's 'optimism' radically transformed the theology of *The City of God*: no longer would the 'heavenly city' be set over against the 'earthly city', and John would be unable to dismiss the barbarian hordes hammering at the gates as a *massa damnata*, a condemned heap.

However, none of this meant that Pope John was being complaisant with error or 'blurring the difference between right and wrong' or 'naïvely falling into Khrushchev's trap' – to quote the commonest charges made against him. If John's critics could have read his diary for St Stephen's day, 1962, they would have been surprised to find him as concerned about 'the conversion of Russia' as Piux XII:

> December 26. A calm St Stephen's day. The liturgy made a great impression on me. My spirit continues to be concerned with whatever it is the Lord is mysteriously doing. Is not this Kroucheff – or Nikita Khrushchev as he signs himself – preparing some surprises for us? After a long meditation last night, and after reading the introduction to Ettore Lo Gallo's *Russian Grammar* that Mgr Capovilla gave me as a Christmas present, I got out of bed and then, kneeling before the crucified Lord, I consecrated my life and the final sacrifice of my whole being for my part in this great undertaking, the conversion of Russia to the Catholic Church. I repeated it in the same spirit at holy Mass. At noon during the general audience in the Sala Clementina, still under the same inspiration, I put great fervour of heart and lips into the words, *Domine, tu scis quia amo te* (Lord, you know that I love you. John 21. 17) (*Lettere*, pp. 453–4).

This 'inspiration' or grace remained with him till his death.

But at the turn of the year, his immediate concern was with the Council. On January 1, 1963, he was up at 4 a.m. 'as usual' and working on his letter to 'the Bishops of the Council' (Caprile, II, p. 300). He was rather pleased with this new and collegial title, 'Bishops of the Council'. On January 4 he noted that he found composing rather laborious. When the letter was finished and sent, he reflected that it had 'cost me quite a bit. But I wanted it to come wholly from the personal thought, the heart and the pen of the Pope, and I thank the Lord I managed it' (*Ibid.*). The purpose of the letter was to remind bishops that although they were now having a rest from the Council, it was not over and they would soon have some documents to ponder. Working on the Council documents should take priority over all other work. It should be 'the apple of your eye'. Even the plea of 'urgent pastoral work' would not be accepted as an excuse for not answering swiftly requests for comments on draft texts. After a shaky start, the Council had now found its feet. It now had a good *modus operandi*, a method. He described the role of the Co-ordinating Commission; it was to be the dynamo of the Council. He recalled that although conciliar decisions needed papal approval to be valid, until that final stage had been reached the bishops should not sit around waiting for the Pope to give them a lead. 'It is up to the Bishops', he wrote, 'to supervise, according to the rules, the free development of the Council' (*Lettere*, p. 443). He did not need to explain that in this way they would forestall any attempt by the Roman Curia to wrest back lost control. He recommended them to meditate on Acts, Chapter 15, which describes the Council of Jerusalem: 'In this simple narrative', he wrote, 'twenty centuries old, is the perfect model for a Council' (*Ibid.*). As can be seen, the letter came from the heart.

John's conclusion was very characteristic: the interest the Council had aroused among the Catholic people had exceeded all expectations. But thanks to the observers – 'a very rare occurrence in conciliar history' he says, knowing it to be unique – the interest of the separated brothers had been equally engaged. Finally, the Council was reaching out to 'all men' who by now were not an anonymous mass (though he did not say this) but individuals with names like Kroucheff (he always had difficulty with the transliteration). He made the point by quoting St John Chrysostom: 'Remember, brothers, that you will have to give an account not only of your life, but of everyone's' (*Lettere*, p. 448: Fifteenth Homily on St Matthew). His own reckoning was coming closer. The Letter to the bishops of the Council was published on January 6, the Epiphany, feast of Christ as the Light of Nations, *Lumen Gentium*. It is bathed in light and common sense. It was not written by a man who was weary of the Council or disillusioned by it.

Pavan had been working fast. He delivered the first draft of *Pacem in Terris* on January 7, 1963. John annotated it: 'Important applications of a pastoral nature' (*Utopia*, Italian, p. 30). That was more perceptive than it may seem. Pope John realised that the theoretical sections of the encyclical, even though they notably extended the range and number of 'human rights' and were structured – as he wished – on a reading of three new 'signs of the times', would probably pass his censors without too much difficulty. It was the fifth and final section concerned with how to deal with unbelievers (euphemism for Communists) that would rock the foundations. John wanted to keep open the possibility of 'prudent co-operation' with those of different views (*Pacem in Terris*, No. 100).

A recent experience of Cardinal Augustin Bea brought home to Pope John just how difficult it would be to make this acceptable. On January 13, 1963, Bea presided at an *agape* or love feast organised by Pro Deo (Félix Morlion's foundation and therefore not unrelated to the work of Norman Cousins). Over seventy countries and twenty-one religions were represented. Bea was in cracking form. The theme of his lecture was 'Truth in Charity'. It was an eloquent plea for mutual tolerance and religious liberty. He condemned religious wars as evil. He explained that the maxim, 'Error has no rights', so glibly used in the nineteenth century, was manifest nonsense, since 'error' as such is an abstraction incapable of having, or not having, rights. Only persons can have rights, and these rights do not vanish simply because they are in error (Caprile, II, pp. 367-70; also Rynne, p. 248).

The right-wing was furious. That 'error has no rights' was not just a museum-maxim from the nineteeth century: it was still being defended by Cardinal Ottaviani at the Holy Office. *L'Osservatore Romano* pretended the lecture had never happened. It was left to *Il Tempo* to attack Bea on the grounds that he had 'sacrificed truth to charity' and was tolerant to the point of indifferentism. *Il Tempo* also intimated that its judgement was shared by the Holy Office. It was.

Bea replied to these accusations in a 'note':

> It should be obvious that in speaking of the freedom to follow one's conscience, Cardinal Bea did not propose to undermine God's sovereignty or assert complete human autonomy. He was not speaking of any kind of freedom but of the freedom to follow one's own *conscience*. The word conscience, properly understood, also includes the moral law that God has placed in the hearts of all men and without which liberty becomes licence. It follows that man has the duty to *strive to know this law* and to study to form his conscience (Caprile, II, p. 368).

Though there was still a long and rocky road ahead, this was the germ of the Council's declaration *On Religious Liberty (Dignitatis Humanae)*. The same principles also prompted the passage in *Pacem in Terris*, written personally by Pope John (*Utopia*, Italian, p. 35), which distinguishes between the 'error', always to be repudiated, and 'the person who falls into error', always to be respected. It was one of the most direct and forceful passages of the encyclical: 'A man who has fallen into error does not cease to be a man. He never forfeits his personal dignity; and that is something that must always be taken into account' (*Pacem in Terris*, No. 158). This idea was essential if the ecumenical goals of the Council were to be achieved, and if his work for peace were to be effective. Once again, completing the Council and making the world a more peaceful planet were two panels in the same diptych.

That is why Pope John attached so much importance to the first meeting of the Co-ordinating Commission, 21–27 January, 1963. It would prove whether or not a new and effective method had been found for guiding the future work of the Council and concluding it – this was still John's hope – by the following Christmas. By applying Occam's razor (*schemata non multiplicanda praeter necessitatem* – drafts should not be unnecessarily multiplied) and Cartesian logic, Cardinal Suenens had succeeded in reducing the number of drafts from seventy to twenty. He ordered those which remained according to the principles stated by Cardinal Montini and his own distinction between the Church *ad extra* and the Church *ad intra*. In particular he proposed that the old *schema* on The Community of Nations should be incorporated in a wide-ranging draft dealing with 1) the human person in society; 2) marriage, the family and demographic problems; 3) culture; 4) the economic order and social justice; 5) the community of nations and peace (Caprile, II, p. 329). Suenens did not revive his project for a Secretariat for the Problems of the Contemporary World. But he proposed that genuine experts, including laymen, should be involved in the work. Some of the *periti* at the first session had been bogus. Cardinal Spellman's chauffeur was included on the grounds that 'Jack couldn't be left waiting outside'. Suenens' proposal was accepted. It was the genesis of the pastoral constitution, *Gaudium et Spes*. There was a slight overlap with what Pope John was proposing to do in *Pacem in Terris*, but that was of no consequence: the ordinary *magisterium* of the Pope and the extraordinary *magisterium* of the Council would reinforce each other. John had explained this in his opening speech to the Council on October 11, 1962. The Pope had not abdicated simply because the Council was in session.

That same day, January 28, Pope John wrote a letter to his secretary, Loris Capovilla. The reason why he should be writing to someone he saw almost hourly is obvious: he was entrusting Capovilla with a mission, and there had to be written proof of it:

> Dear Monsignor,
> At four this morning I was awake and looking over conciliar material when it struck me that it would be good to think of a future 'historian' of the great event that is under way, and that he will have to be chosen with care.
> I think that the obvious witness and faithful exponent of 'Vatican II' is really you, dear monsignor: and in so far as a *mandate* can come from me – Pope of the Council, alive or dead – you should be authorised to accept this task as the Lord's will, and do honour to it, which would also be an honour for holy Church, a pledge of blessings and a special reward for you on earth and in heaven (*Lettere*, p. 453).

In a cryptic footnote, Capovilla says that 'this is not the place to reveal how this letter came to be written' (*Ibid.*). But he then gives the game away by setting the letter in the context of Pope John's international preoccupations. It is not difficult to deduce that John wanted Capovilla to present his side of the argument over *Pacem in Terris* and the new-found good relationship with Khrushchev. Though not a professional historian, Capovilla may be said to have carried out his 'mandate', though without writing a history of the Council.

The Soviet Union was on his mind at this particular moment, for Mgr Jan Willebrands was on his way to Moscow to negotiate the release of Metropolitan Slipyi. That involved accepting that his liberation would not be exploited for anti-Soviet propaganda. The right-wing would inevitably regard this as another instance of Pope John's 'weakness'. He lay down before Communism as the lamb before the lion. Moreover, it was clear that the political right-wing in Italy was allied with the 'opposition' within his own Curia. They were talking about him as though he were already dead, and thinking about the succession. John knew perfectly well what was being said behind his back, and talked about it frankly with Roberto Tucci, S.J., editor of *Civiltà Cattolica*, on February 9, 1963: 'Look, dear father, I know that I don't have very long to live. I must therefore be extremely careful in everything I do to prevent the conclave after my death being a conclave "against me", because then it might make a choice that would destroy everything I have started to achieve' (Magister, p. 294). In this light, the letter to Capovilla can be seen as part of John's tidying up in preparation for his death. John's diary for the day simply records: 'February 9, Saturday. Thank God only two visitors, Mgr Bafile, Nuncio to Germany and Fr Roberto Tucci, editor of *Civiltà Cattolica*, a review that seems younger as it grows older. It was founded in 1849, and so is in its 114th year' (Caprile, II, p. 424). Whatever was happening in the Curia, John knew that he could count on *Civiltà Cattolica* for intelligent support. Tucci's colleague, Giovanni Caprile, became the semi-official historian of the Council.

Pope John concluded another piece of unfinished business the next day, February 10, when he officially opened the process intended to lead to the beatification of Cardinal Andrea Carlo Ferrari, archbishop of Milan. He had left it late. But recent historical research in Milan – in no way discouraged by Montini – made it quite clear that Ferrari had been scurvily treated by the Roman Curia and St Pius X. So by starting the process John was partly honouring his old friend and mentor, but also righting an injustice suffered by the diocese of Milan. John spoke with unusual frankness. It had taken forty-two years for the process to be introduced: 'But every saint has to go his own way; and this way seems long only to those who do not realise the secret designs of the Lord who often permits bitter situations to arise – those responsible were gravely wrong – which have nothing to do with the personal merits of the saints themselves' (*Dodicesimo anniversario*, p. 114). This was said in the presence of Cardinal Giovanni Battista Montini, who had also known 'bitter situations'. But the most remarkable feature of this return to his past is that, unlike the historical *Disquisitio* on Pius X that he read through with care in 1959, he does not gloss over the fact that 'those responsible were gravely wrong'.

Ferrari had died in 1921 on the eve of the Purification, as the Angelus rang out. But at least he died a cardinal. Ernesto Buonaiuti, unfrocked, excommunicated three times, victim of the Fascists, lay on his deathbed on Easter Saturday, April 26, 1946, and asked for the windows to be opened so that he could hear the Easter bells. Pope John noted down all these details, including the precise time of death, 1.15 p.m. Buonaiuti had been beside him at his first Mass fifty-nine years ago. Pope John's last words on his old colleague are compassionate, affectionate even:

So he died at 65, *sine luce et sine cruce* [without candles or crucifix]. His admirers have written that he was a deeply and intensely religious spirit, adhering to Christianity with every fibre of his being, bound by unbreakable bonds to his beloved Catholic Church. Naturally no priest was there to bless his body; and no church welcomed him for his funeral. Words from his spiritual testament between March 18 and 19, 1946: 'I may have made mistakes. But in the substance of my teaching I can find nothing to retract or disavow'. *Dominus parcat illi* [may the Lord spare him] (*Dodicesimo anniversario*, p. 121: non-dated).

John always gave Buonaiuti his priestly title: he remained *Don* Ernesto. Catholic scholars were already rewriting the history of Modernism, and it would soon become possible to present Buonaiuti as a 'prophet of renewal' (see Bedeschi, Lorenzo, *Buonaiuti, il Concordato e la Chiesa*, 1970). John would have welcomed this trend. His last words on Buonaiuti were an absolution.

Metropolitan Slipyi had been ordained priest in September 1917, on the eve of the Russian Revolution. Now in February 1963 he was suddenly and without explanation hauled out of his prison camp and sent under guard to Moscow. On arrival he was taken to the Hotel Moscow where he was astonished to discover Mgr Willebrands who told him that he was being freed. But Slipyi's feelings of relief turned to horror when he realised that there were conditions. He would not be allowed to return to his beloved Lviv in the Ukraine, and would have to spend the rest of his days in exile. Negotiations dragged on, punctuated by awkward silences. Slipyi had the choice: permanent exile or back to the labour camp. He held the fate of Pope John's *Ostpolitik* in his hands. Eventually, Slipyi fell to his knees and gave in. 'Good', said Willebrands, 'we'll go to the airport tomorrow'. Slipyi hated planes, so they boarded a train and came back via Vienna and Venice. The final knife-twist was that Slipyi's request to take a train that passed through Lviv was refused (Lomax, Benedict, 'Pope John's Ostopolitik', in *The Month*, September 1974, pp. 691–6).

To avoid the press, it was arranged that the Alpen Express should stop at Orte, fifty miles north of Rome. Cardinale, chief of protocol, and Capovilla, bearing the gift of a pectoral cross, formed the reception committee. Due in at 21.40, the train did not arrive till 22.15. Slipyi was greeted and driven off to the nearby Abbey of Grottaferrata, accompanied by Cardinale, while Capovilla hastened back to Rome to tell Pope John. His light was out, so Capovilla hastily scribbled a note and slipped it under the door:

> Holy Father! I got back at midnight. Metropolitan Slipyi arrived safely. He is very grateful to your Holiness. He admired your gifts. He said: 'If Pope John in his goodness hadn't brought this off, I wouldn't have lived much longer. Cancer was getting the better of me'. He gives the impression of being a wise man, strong and gentle at the same time. He's at ease in

Italian. As they passed through Venice, they stopped to pray for you in the basilica – before the relics of St Mark and the Nicopeia Madonna. Don Loris (IME, p. 172).

Capovilla telephoned the deputy editor of *l'Osservatore Romano*, Cesidio Lolli, with the great news. Through him it appeared in the papers the following day. But no one guessed where Slipyi had arrived.

That morning John blessed a foundation stone for the new Lombardy College. Montini was present. At the end of his prepared speech about Cardinal Ferrari, he added some improvised remarks. This day, February 10, was the anniversary of the death of Pius XI, 'the father of my episcopacy' and a great Milanese. It was Pius XI who had sent him 'to the East'. That was the transition he needed:

> From Eastern Europe there came last night a moving and consoling grace
> for which I humbly thank the Lord, an event which in the secret designs of
> God can help the Church and all honest people grow in sincere faith and the
> apostolate of peace.
> Let us not wreck the mysterious plan which God invites everyone to
> collaborate with, bringing into unity the threads of a cloth woven by his
> grace and the readiness of innocent, humble and generous souls to serve him
> (DMC, V, p. 123).

So John saw Slipyi's liberation as something momentous: it was an answer to prayer, a sign of the times, an epiphany.

They met that same evening. John advanced with arms out-stretched to embrace him, but Slipyi fell to his knees and insisted on kissing the papal feet. John lifted him up and gave him the kiss of peace. 'Thank you, holy Father', said Slipyi, 'for all you have done to pull me out of the well'. What is there to say when one has been suddenly transported from a log-cabin in Siberia to the Vatican? They went to John's private chapel and recited the *Magnificat* together. Truly, it seemed, 'he that is mighty has done great things'. Then they had a conversation lasting an hour and twenty minutes. John wanted to know about the labour camps – Slipyi had brought along his prison uniform – and about other priests and bishops to be found there. Slipyi gave him a map of the Soviet Union with all the camps marked – a guide to what Alexander Solzhenitsyn was soon to call 'the Gulag Archipelago'. John kept it beside him till he died. He wrote in the margin: 'The heart is closer to those who are further away; prayer hastens to seek out those who have the greatest need to feel understood and loved' (IME, p. 173).

The release of Metropolitan Slipyi came just as the work on *Pacem in Terris* had reached a crucial stage. It seemed to confirm the analysis that under Khrushchev the Soviet Union really was changing. The CIA report of May, 1963, says that the Pope and his friends thought that Marxism was declining in the Soviet Union and that religious feelings, far from being extirpated, were reviving. Mgr Pietro Pavan explained that the Vatican wanted to strengthen the Russian Orthodox Church because 'for a long time it will be in a better position to serve these feelings than we are' (Spain, p. 13). Khrushchev was seen as an agent of liberalisation. He had defied the hawks around him by allowing Solzhenitsyn's *A Day in the Life of Ivan Denisovich* to be published and in releasing Slipyi. The CIA man reported:

> Much is made of the alleged fact that Khrushchev in defending Slipyi's release insisted that this must be done, not because of its propaganda or political value, but because the Soviet state is civilised and moral.
> Khrushchev is said to have taken the position that Slipyi was a criminal, but the USSR did not simply kill him as Hitler would have done. It made him work out his debt to the state in labour camps. The debt is now paid, Khrushchev insisted, and Slipyi has a right to go. The Pope was said to have privately described Khrushchev's act as one of 'the greatest political heroism' (Spain, pp. 13–14).

John had said that.

This interpretation of what was happening in the Soviet Union left its traces in *Pacem in Terris*. The encyclical declares that 'there exists in man's very nature an undying capacity to break through the barriers of error, and to seek the road to truth' (No. 158). This fundamental conviction was the reason why *Pacem in Terris* could presume to address 'all men and women', whoever they might be, in the name of the 'natural law' inscribed in their hearts (see Romans 2. 15). After making a distinction between a false philosophy, and the economic, social, cultural or political programme based on it, *Pacem in Terris* evoked the analysis of the Soviet Union described above:

> True, the philosophic formulation does not change once it has been set down in precise terms, but the programme clearly cannot help being influenced to some extent by the changing conditions in which it has to be worked out. What is more, who can deny the possible existence of good and commendable elements in these programmes, elements which do indeed conform to the dictates of right reason and are an expression of legitimate human aspirations? (No. 159).

But those who 'received' the encyclical knowing nothing of its background were puzzled to know what these 'good and commendable elements' might be. Or they regarded the changes in the Soviet Union under Khrushchev as merely cosmetic. John was disappointed to find that this was the judgement of Dr Eugen Gerstenmeier, speaker of the West German Bundestag, who was reflecting the view of his chancellor, Konrad Adenauer.

But *Pacem in Terris* was not allowed to monopolise his attention or his time. On February 25, 1963, John received Pastor Roger Schutz, founder and prior of Taizé in Burgundy. Not only had Schutz been an observer at the first session, but he brought along members of his community to pray for the Council. Their modest flat at via del Plebiscito 107 became an unofficial ecumenical centre in which the Latin Americans, who were interested in 'the Church of the poor', were particularly welcome (Caprile, II, p. 340). It may have been this background which led Schutz to surprise Pope John by saying that 'evangelically-minded people' were frankly shocked by the pomp and pageantry of the Vatican. He claimed that these apparently minor problems of sensitivity were more important than dogmatic differences. John was put out: 'Ah! *monsieur le pasteur,* just think to whom you are speaking. Our family is a poor family. Do you imagine that I don't suffer here in the Vatican? But reform takes a long time, and I can't change everything in a few years' (Guitton, p. 16). But by the end of the audience John had completely forgotten that he was talking to a Protestant and treated Schutz as one of his own priests, urging him to pray to Our Lady. Not that Schutz minded.

Two days later Pope John began the celebration of Lent by going to Santa Sabina, home of the Dominican master-general, for Ash Wednesday. Though increasingly breathless, he insisted on his usual round of parish visits throughout Lent. They were cheerful, chaotic affairs, more like a farewell party than anything else. The old *nonno* or grandfather was visiting his people. They loved him. Everyone wanted to catch a glimpse of 'good Pope John' before it was too late. By the time he came to visit Ostia, Borgata di San Basilio and Quarto Miglio, the general election campaign was well under way. But all political parties agreed to remove their posters and cancel meetings when Pope John came among them. It was as though his mere presence was enough to produce a truce, a moment of *convivenza,* of harmonious being together. In this way he touched 'all men of good will'.

But it was easier to do that on the streets and squares of Rome than within the Vatican, as John was about to discover. On March 1, 1963, it was announced that he had been awarded the Balzan Prize for, said the citation, 'his activity in favour of brotherhood between all men and all peoples, and his appeals for peace and good will in his recent diplomatic intervention' (*Lettere,* p. 456). The last phrase referred to his role in the Cuban missile crisis. Some in the Secretariat of State disapproved most strongly of Pope John accepting the award. Many years later, Mgr Igino Cardinale explained why:

> They thought the Balzan prize was rather obscure and not very significant. They held it was undignified for a pope to be receiving a prize at all – he should move on another plane and not be in competition with anyone. Anyway, in working for peace, he was merely doing his duty. There was

also the danger of a 'personality cult' developing. And in the background was the threat of various financial scandals (Cardinale, March 30, 1980, at the Brussels Nunciature).

It should be said that Cardinale, though he rejected these arguments, also saw their force.

But then another factor complicated and envenomed the whole affair: Khrushchev's son-in-law, Alexis Adzhubei, thirty-eight-year-old editor of *Izvestia*, arrived in Rome with his wife Rada on February 28. He let it be known that he had a gift for Pope John from his father-in-law and would like an audience to hand it over. Pope John, distressed at the way the Secretariat of State was refusing to help him but still anxious to go through the 'proper channels', consulted Cardinal Alfredo Ottaviani at the Holy Office on the wisdom of receiving Adzhubei. Ottaviani's answer was an unhesitating 'no'. In his judgement, the request was a propaganda move: it would suggest that agreements were being negotiated, would give rise to endless conjectures and arouse unrealisable hopes. Ottaviani opined that honour would be satisfied if Adzhubei were received by Augustin Bea at the Secretariat for Christian Unity or Gustavo Testa at Oriental Churches. Since Adzhubei was plainly not a Christian, this seemed a rather quixotic idea, and Pope John was not satisfied with it. Then Adzhubei helped him out. In a press conference he said: 'I haven't come to Rome to establish diplomatic relations with the Vatican'. Why had he come? 'I will visit St Peter's: I hear it is a great work of art'. Adzhubei also adroitly stressed that though he would like to meet Pope John – as a journalist one met all sorts – he wouldn't put any pressure on the Pope and was used to biding his time (*Utopia*, English, p. 152).

Adzhubei was evidently the Soviet counterpart of Norman Cousins. Was it guesswork or a leak that made him so aware of Curial objections? His wholly correct behaviour allowed Pope John time to devise a formula. John wrote a memo:

> I would be breaking my word and condemning all my previous behaviour if I refused to see someone who has courteously and sincerely asked to see me in order to bring a message and a gift. It should be recalled that, without any initiative on my part, three times the Russians have made courteous gestures towards the Pope: on his eightieth birthday, last Christmas, and on his nomination for the Balzan peace prize (a prize that I accepted to please Cardinal Montini) (*Utopia*, English, p. 154).

So he was now consulting Montini more than the Secretariat of State. The diplomatic solution devised was that Adzhubei, who was after all the editor of an important newspaper, could be present among the reporters at the Balzan peace prize announcement and would meet the Pope privately afterwards. But this decision was not made known until March 6, the day before the ceremony.

At this point some members of the Secretariat of State started to abandon all restraint. The daily press survey recorded story after story designed to prove that the Soviet Union was still the ghastly hell-on-earth it had been under Stalin, that there had been a new wave of persecution against Catholics in Lithuania, and above all that if Khrushchev wanted better relations with the Holy See, this was for propaganda, political and economic reasons. The release of Slipyi was privately pooh-poohed: it merely drew attention to the millions who were still unjustly held in the slave labour camps (*Utopia*, English, p. 155). Pope John, in other words, was foolishly walking into a carefully prepared trap. He was misled by goodness, betrayed by his political naïveté.

On the morning of March 7, 1963, the blond, chain-smoking Alexis Adzhubei was mobbed by photographers as he crossed St Peter's Square and entered the Vatican by the Bronze Gate. In the throne room he met Fr Alexander Koulic S.J., from the Oriental College, who was to act as interpreter. Adzhubei asked the meaning of the motto embroidered on the papal throne: '*Ubi Petrus, ibi ecclesia*'. Koulic explained that it meant 'Where Peter is, there is the Church'. Adzhubei, in the second row of scarlet armchairs, listened carefully to Koulic's murmured translation of Pope John's words about 'active neutrality', and bowed solemnly for the papal blessing at the end. Then the other journalists were presented to the Pope, while Adzhubei and his wife waited patiently. Pope John greeted Giancarlo Zizola, condemned by the alphabet to be last, and chatted aimiably about *l'Eco di Bergamo*, his favourite paper, and then said: 'I'd like to talk to you at greater length, but I have another audience coming up'. He waved a blessing and added ironically: 'That's how much freedom and sovereignty the Pope has' (*Utopia*, English, p. 157). He vanished into his private library where the Russian couple were waiting for him. The doors closed. As far as press and public were concerned, that was that. Nothing would be reported. Naturally the effect was that speculation about what had been said ran riot.

The secrecy was totally unnecessary: Pope John had given Capovilla, his 'historian', a full account of the audience, intending that it should appear in *l'Osservatore Romano*. But the Vatican newspaper did not see fit to publish it. Yet its substantial accuracy was confirmed by Fr Koulic's report submitted to the Secretariat of State the next day, March 8, 1963. Putting the two together, one can form a clear enough idea of what happened.

Rada Khrushchevska made a low bow; her husband bent his head over the Pope's hand, touching it with his brow, but not quite managing the homage of a kiss. Rada understood French, so John rattled on in French and explained the paintings and tapestries that decorated his library. He then sat them down on either side of him. With the ice broken, Alexis Adzhubei sketched a parallel between his father-in-law Khrushchev, considered a reformer in the Communist

world, and Pope John, an innovator in the Catholic world (Koulic in *Utopia*,
English, p. 159; Capovilla omits this detail). Khrushchev wanted (according to
Capovilla) to have direct contact for solving problems as they arose or (according
to Koulic) wondered whether it would be a good idea to establish diplomatic
relations, a very different matter. Whatever the question was, both sources agree
on Pope John's answer:

> You are a journalist, and as such you know the Bible and the story of
> creation. The Bible says that God created the world and on the first day he
> created light. Then creation went on for another six days. But the days of
> the Bible, as you know, are whole epochs, and these epochs last a very long
> time. We are looking into each other's eyes and we see the light there.
> Today is the first day of creation, the day of light, the day of *fiat lux*. It all
> takes time. Let me say it again: the light is in my eyes and in your eyes. If
> the Lord so wills it, he will show us the way to go (*Utopia*, English, p.
> 158).

That is Capovilla. Koulic adds the remark: 'We must go gently, gradually in these
matters, preparing minds. At present such a move would be inopportune' (*Ibid.*,
p. 159).

Then the conversation became more familiar. John talked about Bulgaria, the
beauty of Slav music, and the 'spiritual riches' of Russia. He explained that the
Pope saw all as brothers without distinction of race, nationality or colour (*Lettere*,
p. 455). He talked about life in his own village of Sotto il Monte, with the large
and united family, not much given to displays of emotion (*effusioni esteriori*). Rada
ventured in French: 'We come from a peasant family too. In Russia it is said that
you are a countryman. You have hands that have been hardened by toil, like my
father' (*Lettere*, p. 456). Had she been coached?

Finally came the exchange of gifts. John said that non-Catholic lady visitors
usually had coins or stamps or books. But he preferred to give her a rosary
'because it reminds me of peace in the home and of my mother who used to say it
by the fireside when I was a child and while preparing supper. Oh! it wasn't much
of a supper'. Rada kept on nodding her head. John went on in French, dispensing
with Fr Koulic: 'Madame, I know that you have three children, and I know their
names. But I would like *you* to tell me their names, because when a mother speaks
the names of her children, something very special happens'. Rada said faintly and
tremblingly: 'Nikita, Alexei, Ivan'. John had planned this and prepared his little
speech. In the West Nikita was called Nicephorus and he was specially honoured
in Venice. Alexei was Alexander to whom so many churches were dedicated in
Bulgaria. Ivan, of course, is simply John 'the name of my grandfather, my father,
the name I chose for my pontificate, the name of the hill above my birthplace, the
name of the basilica of which I am bishop'. He concluded 'When you get home,

madame, give all your children a hug, but give Ivan a very special one – the others won't mind' (*Utopia*, English, p. 158). There were also stamps for the boys, coins for Alexis, and for the 'grandfather' Khrushchev medals struck by Giacomo Manzù, 'one of the most famous Italian sculptors'. (It was the medal for the opening of the Council, and bore the words *Una, Sancta, Catholica, Apostolica* – One, Holy, Catholic and Apostolic.) He did not reveal that Manzù was a Communist; but they would have known that anyway. He showed them Murano's painting of the Nativity. Koulic adds that Adzhubei asked Pope John if he could publish something, if only a couple of lines, about their meeting. John said 'no'. When the press gets involved, things become too complicated.

But when nothing is revealed, speculation and guesswork fill the vacuum. What was said during the Adzhubei visit remained a mystery until the following August, by which time Pope John was dead. This was not his intention. He wanted Capovilla's article and Koulic's memorandum published to clear his name. But the 'first section' of the Secretariat of State would not hear of it. John's remark to Zizola – 'That's how much freedom and sovereignty the Pope has' – was now cruelly verified. His orders were simply not being obeyed.

On March 20, 1963, John wrote a note 'for history'. It makes it clear that disobedience at this level was incomprehensible to him:

> The absolute clarity of my language, first in public and then in my private
> library, deserves to be known and not withheld on some pretext. It should
> be clearly said that the Pope has no need to defend himself. I have told
> Dell'Acqua and Samorè repeatedly that the note written by Fr Koulic, the
> sole witness to my meeting with Rada and Alexis Adzhubei, should be
> published. But the first section [of the Secretariat of State] does not agree,
> and I'm unhappy about that [*me ne dispiace*]. A desire of the Pope ... When
> I was Nuncio or Patriarch ... When it is known what I said, and what he
> said, I think people will bless the name of Pope John. Everything should be
> carefully noted down. I deplore and pity those who in these last few days
> have lent themselves to unspeakable manoeuvres [*giochi innomabili*]. *Ignosco et*
> *dimitto* [I forgive and put it from my mind] (*Utopia*, Italian, pp. 222–3;
> English, pp. 162–3).

Ignosco et dimitto came in a prayer used by a bishop while vesting for Mass. The 'unspeakable manoeuvres' included forbidding *l'Osservatore Romano* and Vatican Radio from mentioning that Adzhubei had received any special treatment; and forbidding Caprile at *Civiltà Cattolica* from reporting the meeting at all or even including Adzhubei's name on the list of journalists present.

Pope John's 'note' – disabused in tone, even though it ended with forgiveness – was written just three days before *Pacem in Terris* was sent to the printers. Even the first section of the Secretariat of State could not suppress an encyclical. John was in a hurry. He wanted *Pacem in Terris* to appear on Maundy Thursday not only for good symbolic reasons – it was the night Jesus announced that he was to die for all and interpreted the meaning of his Passion – but because he had to make sure it was published. On the death of a Pope all his projects are halted. A Pope has no authority beyond the tomb. Some of John's opponents wished he were already there.

John's opponents were not stupid or wicked men. Historians still argue about how far Khrushchev really changed Russian society and foreign policy. Roy Medvedev believes that Khrushchev 'destroyed not only the Stalin myth but also the myth of the infallibility of the Party and its leaders'. The fact that he used authoritarian methods to push his changes through was inevitable, and confirmed that change could only come from the top. On the other hand, Khrushchev's foreign policy adventures and visits abroad eventually proved his undoing: they put more power in the hands of those he left minding the shop (Medvedev, Roy, *Khrushchev*, 1983). But this is the sophisticated judgement of an insider using hindsight. For the curialists who opposed Pope John the issue was much simpler: the Italian general election was due on April 28. If 'good Pope John' was seen talking in friendly fashion with a Communist leader like Adzhubei, then it would be impossible to prevent Italian Catholics from voting Communist. For Pope John had taught them that Communists could be 'men of good will'.

One cannot blame the Secretariat of State for its interpretation of events. But John was deeply hurt. They were thinking of short-term political consequences; he was thinking in epochs, centuries . . . They were calculating; he was imagining things, dreaming of Utopia . . . But utopia, though its name means nowhere, is not just an illusion: it stretches the imagination, makes people aware of possibilities they hardly dared think of. This was why *Pacem in Terris* made such a powerful impact on public opinion. It was what Pope John had been trying to say all along. It was the resumé of his long life. The misunderstandings of those who should have been his collaborators and his physical sufferings – all the time this lump in the gut was growing – made it more than ever necessary to speak before it was too late. So *Pacem in Terris* became his last will and testament.

Pope John was bubbling over and announced it on March 31, 1963. He signed the first five copies of *Pacem in Terris* in his private library before the television lights on the Tuesday of Holy Week. He wore a stole to indicate that this was a religious event. The press had the text the next day and it was officially dated, as John had wished, Maundy Thursday, April 11, 1963. This is not the place to write a commentary on *Pacem in Terris*. We have already seen some of its key passages. It remains to ask what inheritance John bequeathed to the Church and the world, and how it affected the future.

Pacem in Terris completes and carries further the process begun in *Mater et Magistra* (see p. 362 above). Now that the restraining hand of Tardini was no longer there to curb him, Pope John felt free to take the modern world seriously and to appraise it positively. Even though he builds his encyclical on the contrast between the 'order' willed by God and the 'disorder' that is sin, he finds much to praise in the contemporary world. He starts, for example, with a confession of faith in science that is worthy of Teilhard de Chardin: 'That a marvellous order prevails in the world of living beings and in the forces of nature is the clear lesson to emerge from progressive modern scientific research' (No. 2).

Then, in the section called 'Order among human persons' (Nos. 8–38) John develops the idea that respect for the dignity of the human person provides the norm of morality. The person has rights and corresponding duties. What helps the human person to grow is good; what trammels or destroys human growth is bad. *Pacem in Terris* illustrates the difference between the simple and the *simpliste*. Pope John is as stylistically direct and simple as can be, because he wants to communicate; but he has the simplicity of what is basic, fundamental. When tested, his ideas are found to be load-bearing.

That the dignity of the human person should be respected had been a principle of Catholic social doctrine at least since *Rerum Novarum* in 1891. John's originality lay in the range and number of rights he deduced from it. When John declared that 'every human being has the right to worship God in accordance with the rights of his own conscience, and to profess his religion both in private and in public' (No. 14), he was saying something *new*: in the nineteenth century Protestants were conceded no such liberty. When he defended the right of developing nations to determine their own future, he was again saying something *new*: in the nineteenth century both Catholic Poland and Ireland were ordered by the papacy to be obedient to legitimate authority, however foreign or unpleasant it might be. *Pacem in Terris* also has a preference for democracy that was novel: persons have a right to take an active part in public life (No. 73).

John's originality can be put this way. Whereas in the nineteenth century the Church defended its own institutional rights against a state perceived to be hostile, *Pacem in Terris* gives the priority to the rights of individual human persons, whoever they may be. It therefore speaks up on behalf of minorities (Nos. 95–7) and refugees (Nos. 103–8). Again, while the nineteenth century was suspicious of the language of 'human rights' as the slogan of the French Revolution ('Only God has rights', as Archbishop Marcel Lefebvre reminds us), John saw human rights as fundamental to the preaching of the Gospel. For the act of faith is free. And while the nineteenth century *magisterium* thought Catholicism should unashamedly use the state to maintain its dominance where it could, John envisaged a pluralist society in which Church and state are distinct, and therefore could be well-disposed towards each other. But to start from the dignity of the human person was not to introduce a new element into 'Catholic social doctrine'; the novelty lay in the way it was applied.

The real originality of *Pacem in Terris* and its true starting point are to be found in Nos. 39–45. It begins, unarrestingly: 'There are three things which characterise our modern age'. In previous encyclicals this would have been a prelude to the denunciation of three evils (like laicism, materialism and scientism). John's three features, however, are all positive. First he noticed 'a progressive improvement in the economic and social conditions of working men' who insist on being treated as human beings (No. 40). Next 'the part that women are now playing in political life is everywhere evident' and 'women are gaining an increasing awareness of their natural dignity' (No. 41). Thirdly 'imperialism is rapidly becoming an anachronism' since 'all people have either attained political independence or are on the point of obtaining it' (No. 42). All these were instances of emancipation or liberation.

But it was not enough merely to register what was going on. John gave a positive evaluation of these three features of the modern age because he believed them to be 'signs of the times' (see p. 398 above). The Holy Spirit has to be discerned at work in the trends and tendencies of the age. It would be idle to pretend that the Church had single-handedly promoted the social advance of the working class or feminine emancipation or decolonisation. So the Church had to admit that sometimes the 'world' was ahead and could teach the Church lessons. The Vatican II pastoral constitution, *Gaudium et Spes*, adopted Pope John's 'signs of the times' approach explicitly: 'With the help of the Holy Spirit, it is the task of the entire people of God, especially pastors and theologians, to hear, distinguish and interpret the many voices of our age, and to judge them in the light of the divine word' (*Gaudium et Spes*, 44). *Pacem in Terris* taught the Council how to approach the problems of the contemporary world, for which Cardinal Suenens had wanted a special Secretariat. It also showed how one could respect tradition while being open to the action of the Holy Spirit in the now of history. This was John's bequest.

Two further points need mentioning. *Pacem in Terris* was not presented as a casuistical document solving moral conundrums. But on one major question it advanced further than previous papal teaching. Pius XII had talked a great deal about peace. As Graham Greene remarked '*Pax, pacem, pacis, pace* – the comforting word, in all its declensions, tolled like a bell throughout his long pontificate' ('Pius XII', in *The Month*, December 1951, p. 329). But following the Augustinian tradition, Pius had always insisted that there could be 'no peace without justice'; and since he believed that the Yalta agreement and the post-war settlement in Europe were deeply unjust, he sometimes seemed to be legitimating 'wars of liberation from Communism'. He denounced the Soviet invasion of Hungary in 1956, was upset that the West did not intervene, and railed against 'co-existence'.

This is the background to understanding Pope John's remarks about nuclear weapons: 'In this age which boasts of its atomic power, it no longer makes sense to maintain that war is a fit instrument with which to repair the violation of justice' (No. 127). The phrase 'it no longer makes sense . . .' is a better translation than the Italian version which said 'It is almost impossible to think that war could be used . . .' Pope John was not saying that an atomic war was hard to imagine: he said it was *'alienum a ratione'*, that is, irrational or even insane. Of course, Pope John was no less convinced than his predecessor that peace had to be based on justice, and he quotes St Augustine on this very point: 'Take away justice, and what are kingdoms but mighty bands of robbers?' (No. 92). But he believed that the robbers could be domesticated, brought within the range of civilised discourse, reminded of their humanity. In the nuclear age, the choice was between dialogue or catastrophe or permanent international tension.

One last objection to *Pacem in Terris* from the ultra-right is that it is not a 'Christian' document. By taking his stand on 'natural law' in the laudable but impossible desire to speak to everyone at once, Pope John fails to deploy the full force of the Christian case. This is a half-truth. There is a self-denying ordinance at work in *Pacem in Terris*. However, it remains a deeply Christian text because it is concerned with the way God is at work in today's world ('signs of the times'). Moreover, in the final section of the encyclical John speaks of peace as the free gift or grace of Christ, 'the Prince of peace' (No. 167). Peace is not attainable by human efforts alone, however essential they are. John knew the maxim attributed to St Ignatius: 'Do everything as though it depended on you, knowing that it depends on God'. *Pacem in Terris*, moreover, is 'Christian' in its challenge to conventional wisdom. That the 'balance of terror' was the only way to keep the peace between the super-powers was already widely accepted in 1963. They were becoming mirror-images of each other. Each side projected onto the other its own aggression and suspicions. To this Hobbesian idea that man is naturally a wolf to man (*'Homo homini lupus'*), John opposes the Gospel which invites Christians to go out 'as sheep among wolves' (Matthew 10. 16). If someone asked him to go one mile, he went two miles (Matthew 5. 41). *Pacem in Terris* caught the world's imagination because it came from someone who had no power in the conventional sense. So whatever authority it had come from the cogency of what it said and the hope it inspired. It remains the only encyclical that has been set to music – by French composer Darius Milhaud.

For Pope John *Pacem in Terris* was a supreme effort. It cost him a lot. On Maundy Thursday he talked about the encyclical to the diplomatic corps, and had to struggle to conceal the torment he was in. Through the pain, the passion, his words reached a new level of simplicity:

I'm glad that the encyclical has been published today, the day on which the lips of Christ pronounced the words, 'Love one another' [John 13. 14]. For what I wanted to do above all was to issue an appeal to love for the people of this time. Let us recognise the common origin that makes us brothers, and come together! (DMC, V, p. 196).

The long ceremonies of Holy Week were a torture. On Good Friday the doctors stood by in St Peter's during the veneration of the cross, fully expecting him to collapse at any moment (IME, p. 194). But somehow he came through. He was consoled by a letter from Josef Beran, archbishop of Prague, and sent a telegram of condolences to President Kennedy for the loss, with all its crew, of the atomic submarine *Thresher*.

On Holy Saturday at noon, John gave an audience to Giacomo Manzù. The sculptor felt reasonably satisfied with four of his bronzes – those he disliked he destroyed – and they were set out like soldiers on parade for John to inspect them. 'So many Pope Johns', said the subject of the bronzes, 'isn't one enough?' But where was the one he really liked, the one in which he could see the face of his mother? Manzù hadn't the heart to tell him that it was now a hundred pieces of plaster somewhere on a Roman rubbish dump. But John liked the bronzes and said: 'You've done more than give me a portrait – you've chronicled my pontificate in bronze'. They laughed. But Manzù, with his sculptor's eye for physical detail, was appalled and broken-hearted. The face he had tried to recapture was no more. 'Most of it had fallen, except the big hooked nose and the immense ears which were left to ride above all else like an alarming sentinel, gaunt towers of a crumbling castle' (Pepper, pp. 212–13). It was that ravaged face that was seen on the balcony of St Peter's the next morning, Easter Sunday, blessing the city and the world.

Chapter 24

Eastertide

On the natural level the death of a man is an absurd phenomenon,
something that denies all the promise man bears within himself in his
earthly life and shatters all his inmost hopes

(Edward Schillebeeckx O.P. 'The Death of a Christian' in *Vatican II, a Struggle for
Minds*, p. 65).

April 14, Easter Sunday. Mass at 7 a.m. A bad morning. Very fatigued. Struggles
to his window at noon, and says: 'The Easter message is full of light – not death
but life, not conflict but peace, not lies but truth, not whatever depresses and casts
down but the triumph of light, purity, mutual respect' (DMC, V, pp. 212–13).
He looks at the children and says: 'Here is tomorrow's Rome! I stretch out my
arms to embrace you, but my words can scarcely express what my heart feels'. In
the afternoon sees John Casserly's television film about the Vatican. No comment.
He writes in his diary:

> I came through Easter well enough, though with considerable pain . . . A
> peaceful Mass at home, then abandonment to God. St Peter's Square was
> simply triumphal, as is usual on special occasions . . . Final greetings in
> twenty-six languages: peace and joy spread visibly through the crowd. The
> encyclical *Pacem in Terra* [sic] acclaimed more than ever . . . Unbroken pain
> that makes me seriously wonder about my chances (IME, p. 195).

April 16, Tuesday. Mass at 7 a.m. Receives Cardinals Bea and Cicognani. Feels
that he is in the garden of Gethsemani (IME, p. 196).

April 19, Friday. Anna Frank's father has an audience and gives him a copy of
his daughter's Diary and her children's stories, which he loves.

April 20, Saturday. Exhausted. Audiences start at 10 a.m., and he finds it
impossible to stick to the allotted ten minutes each. Doesn't finish till 1.45 p.m.
At 5 the annual concert of the RAI orchestra. What ought to be a pleasure
becomes 'seventy-five minutes of pain'. But Rimsky-Korsakoff's *Russian Easter*
reminded him of the church music he had heard in Bulgaria in the 1920s. He goes
straight to bed as soon as it is over.

April 22, Monday. Feeling much better. In the afternoon retires to the Torre
San Giovanni in the Vatican gardens. Browses through *Jadis, avant la première
guerre mondiale*, the memoirs of Edouard Herriot, former mayor of Lyons and
president of the National Assembly. Stays in the French mood by correcting the

proofs of his own *Souvenirs d'un Nonce* (Englished as *Mission to France*). Health definitely improving.

April 25, Thursday. Mass at 7 a.m. Recites, on his knees, the litany of the saints. Works on the new draft documents prepared for the second session of the Council with the help of his confessor, Mgr Alfredo Cavagna. Appears at his window at noon for the Angelus and to greet the *Bersaglieri*, the sympathetic regiment who wear feathers in their hats and trot where others march. 'I didn't make such a bad sergeant', he tells them.

April 26, Friday. A flash of anger as he rejects the proposal to hold the Balzan Peace Prize award in St Peter's. 'I will not go down to St Peter's', he says firmly, 'it isn't right to honour a pope on the tomb of the crucified St Peter' (*Utopia*, English, p. 112).

April 28, Good Shepherd Sunday and election day. Wakes at 2 a.m. and prays till 6.30 a.m. Meets Cardinal Gustavo Testa and Metropolitan Slipyi. There seems to be a faint hope of rescuing Cardinal József Mindszenty from the U.S. Embassy in Budapest, where he has been immured since 1956. Gives an audience to Pericle Felici, secretary of the Council, who later described this last meeting:

> He wanted to make me a gift of his book on Radini Tedeschi, and read out extracts from it. He said: 'My Bishop, Radini Tedeschi, would have made a very good secretary of the ecumenical council'. Then with tears in his eyes, he evoked the death of 'My Bishop'. It was an anticipated account of his own death little more than a month later . . . When I looked at the dedication, I was moved to see that he had written: *Ubi patientia, ibi laetitia* [Where there is patience, there is joy] (Felici, p. 61).

He also bequeathed to Felici his well-thumbed edition of the catechism of the Council of Trent (Caprile, II, p. 374).

April 30, Tuesday. The election results show that, compared with five years ago, the Communists have gained over a million votes. They now have a respectable 7,700,000 votes which makes it difficult to disregard them completely. The wildest theories circulate to explain these figures. The right-wing says that Aldo Moro's Christian Democrats are being punished by the electorate for their 'opening to the left'. But according to some papers, the real culprit is Pope John and his encyclical. An evening paper in Milan changed its title to *Falcem in Terris* ('The Sickle on Earth'). In Germany *Die Welt* published an open letter from a German Catholic who apostrophises the pope with the charge: 'You have misused the Chair of Peter'. There is much more in the same vein. Cardinale and Roberto Tucci console him with the thought that the trend against the Christian Democrats had already set in, long before *Pacem in Terris*. John confines himself to noting the voting figures for Sotto il Monte in 1958 and 1963 (IME, p. 199). Tomorrow, he has an audience with John McCone, director of the CIA and

Knight of Malta. As though to steel himself against what he knows is going to happen, he writes on a scrap of paper: '*Cum enim infirmor, tunc potens sum* ["For when I am weak, then I am strong": 2 Corinthians 12.10]. Would to heaven that these words might crown my physical and spiritual sufferings with the gift of spiritual fruits for my ministry, and for the good of holy Church at such a hazardous time' (IME, pp. 199–200).

May 1, Wednesday. Loses his place during Mass. Memory going. Mgr John O'Connor, rector of the North American College, interprets for John McCone, top spy. There is no meeting of minds. McCone tries to warn him against Khrushchev who is not to be trusted. The success of the Communists in the Italian elections is grist to his mill (and the reason why he is here). Afterwards John, incorrigible, remarks: 'I'm not going to put off my stroke by the unseemly fuss that some people try to impress churchmen with. I bless all peoples, and withhold my confidence from none' (IME, p. 200).

May 2, Thursday. Mass at 8 a.m. An unwonted burst of fresh energy sees him through the new conciliar texts. Cavagna is always by his side. The liturgical commission is in session: it started on April 28 and will go on till May 10. John approves of its democratic methods and appeal to a wide range of genuine experts (Caprile, II, p. 406). But twelve other *schemata* are sufficiently far advanced to be sent out to the bishops in mid-May. This includes the three tricky ones involving Bea and Ottaviani: Revelation, the Church, and Ecumenism. The battles of last November now seem light-years away. John notes: 'All these *schemata* have been *personally* gone through with great attention by the holy Father, who reserves the right to see them again before they are definitively approved' (*Lettere*, p. 575). When Cicognani sent them out a few days later, he quoted this comment. It is evident that Pope John wants very much to be able to conclude his Council. The notion that he became disenchanted with it is a baseless right-wing piece of wish-fulfilment. Twenty years after the event, Malachi Martin will state it in classical form: 'Roncalli changed his mind before the end. Already in the spring of 1963, when an inoperable cancer was slowly killing him, he came to the conviction that it had all been a mistake' (Malachi Martin, p. 243). John did not change his mind about the Council. It took him down unexpected paths, but that is another question.

May 5, Sunday. Mass at 8.30 a.m. Spends the afternoon in the tower and welcomes the Venetian architect, Lorenzo Barbato, and his wife, who bring along their ten-month-old son, Luca, Luke. John jokes: '*Lucas, medicus charissimus*' ('Luke, the beloved physician': Colossians 4.14). 'Do you want him to be a doctor? or a lawyer? or . . . an evangelist?' (IME, p. 201).

May 6, Monday. James W. Spain, after an intensive three days in Rome, flies to Frankfurt for a meeting of CIA European and Middle Eastern experts. He arrives late, and slips into the last available chair – next to John McCone, director of the whole operation. McCone alludes to his meeting with Pope John, but in 'neutral' tones. As the meeting breaks up, Spain tells his chief something of what he has learned in Rome, and how Pope John's policies now appear to him in a new light. McCone says: 'That will interest the president – write a report'. Spain agrees. We know that Spain's report got through to the president, for he annotated it in his own hand (Letter of Spain to the author, April 8, 1984). So the CIA report was the result of the private initiative of a Chicago Catholic who was supplied with Roman addresses by Mgr George Higgins, whom Spain knew in Washington.

May 7, Tuesday. Hurt by what the Italian and international press is saying about the April 28 elections. Finds it hard to understand why Catholics cannot accept the pastoral instructions in Part V of *Pacem in Terris*. Still more pained by the way the encyclical and the Adzhubei visit are being yoked together to explain the increase in the Communist vote. When Capovilla asks whether it would have been better to have delayed publication of *Pacem in Terris* until after the election, John replies:

> The doctrine expounded in the encyclical is in accord with the Lord's
> Gospel and in harmony with the papal *magisterium* of the last sixty years.
> The meeting with Adjoubei fitted in with the overall line of my ministry.
> I've said it clearly enough, several times already, that one could publish the
> text of our conversation in perfect tranquillity (IME, p. 202).

May 9, Thursday. Mass at 7 a.m. At 8 consultation with Professor Antonio Gasbarrini, a specialist from Bologna. Receives François Marty, archbishop of Rheims, to whom he says:

> Many people were surprised by the Adjoubei visit; and some were upset by
> it. Why? I have to welcome everyone who knocks on my door. I saw
> them, and we talked about the children . . . one should always talk about
> children . . . I saw that Madame Adjoubei had tears in her eyes. I gave her a
> rosary, explaining that she probably didn't know how to use it and that,
> obviously, I wasn't asking her to. I told her that looking at it would remind
> her that there once existed a perfect mother (*Gran Sacerdote*, p. 117).

From 5 p.m. to 6.45 talks with Cardinal Stefan Wyszyński in the Torre San Giovanni. The Polish bishops have proposed that qualified lay people should take part in the Council as *socii Concilii* (companions of the Council). In the event, they were known as *auditores* (listeners) (Caprile, II, p. 413). Discusses the welcome given to *Pacem in Terris* in Eastern Europe. In playful mood, John thinks up some recondite Latin names for his tower, '*oppidulum, casula, tugurium, gurgustium* [roughly village, cottage, shack, hovel]' (IME, p. 203).

May 10, Friday. Balzan Peace Prize. At John's insistence, he receives the award 'privately' in the *sala regia*, the throne room. In this way the honour paid to him will be sharply distinguished from the religious ceremony in St Peter's which comes later and will, in principle, be devoted to paying for peace.

In his speech in the throne room, John does all he can to direct attention away from himself, claiming that the award is as much to his predecessors as to himself. The five Popes of his lifetime, from Leo XIII to Pius XII, were all 'true friends of humanity, wise and courageous peace-makers, who worked untiringly to maintain, develop and consolidate peace among men' (IME, p. 203). True enough, but that is not what was always perceived. With a glance at the frescoes by Vasari and Salviati that adorn the walls, he reminds the Italian president, Antonio Segni, that in this very room kings and emperors had once prostrated themselves at the feet of the pope. But then with the loss of the papacy's temporal power, it was the workers, not the great of the world, who began to come here. Cheap rail travel made it possible in the pontificate of Leo XIII. 'So', concludes John, 'the sons of the people found their way back to the Vatican, and the desire for a just peace has entered the minds and hearts of all without distinction but more markedly, it seems, those of the working classes'.

Then it was to St Peter's for the silver trumpets and *Tu es Petrus* and a procession of chamberlains and Noble Guards in crimson jackets and horsemane helmets. Among the thirty cardinals the white headdress of Metropolitan Slipyi stands out – it is his first public appearance since emerging from the Gulag Archipelago. Sergei Romanowski, representing the Soviet Union, scrutinises Michelangelo's ceilings. John delivers another optimistic speech. He is convinced that in the years to come 'a fair and objective evaluation of what the Church has to say about peace will mean that the doctrine she offers will grow in authority by its very clarity'. It will increase the number of peace-makers in the world. He climbs onto the *sedia gestatoria* and puts his head in his hands, oblivious to the waves of applause that break around him as he is carried out, gently swaying.

In the Torre that afternoon he produces a clipping from an Italian newspaper which quotes *The Baltimore Sun*. Citing 'a Vatican staffer well placed to know', the American paper said that 'recently the Pope has been waking up during the night and asking for sedatives'. This is false. John has neither asked for nor used sedatives. He wonders who this Vatican 'staffer' is or whether he exists. He isn't angry that his stoicism is not being recognised. 'File it away', he says with a smile, 'every detail helps to document situations and the movement of minds' (IME, p. 202). Actors in history never know what is going to be important.

May 11, Saturday. John spends two hours on his knees in the afternoon. He says: 'An exceptional event is going to take place – we must pray'. The 'exceptional event' is his visit to President Segni at the Quirinale Palace fixed for 5.30 p.m. His illness dispenses him from the obligation of a return visit, but John insists on this final act of respect towards Italy. The whole event is deeply symbolic. The Quirinale had been the pope's summer palace. Conclaves had been held there. Then what Pius IX always called 'the usurpers' took it over and it became the royal palace and finally the residence of the president of the Republic. Pius XII, a monarchist at heart, could not have brought himself to meet with a mere president in the Quirinale.

John is in great pain in the car. He tells Capovilla that he is going 'as an act of deference towards my country, because I owe so much not only to Bergamo but to Italy'. Passing the tomb of the Unknown Soldier in the Piazza Venezia, he raises a hand in salute to the men he had helped to die well more than forty years ago. President Segni greets him, and tactfully steers him first to the Pauline Chapel. Then they go out onto the balcony, from which the dome of St Peter's can be seen. John greets his fellow prize-winners who include the composer Paul Hindemith, whose music was banned by the Nazis, the Russian mathematician Andrej Kolmogorov, and the American historian Samuel Eliot Morison (IME, p. 204). John sits there, slumped in a chair, while President Segni greets him, with what observers take for a strange smile on his lips: in fact he is trying to dominate the pain. He makes a simple speech in reply, rejoicing at the way he has been welcomed 'in this historic place', a welcome that 'is but the echo of public opinion'. Segni is deeply moved and falls to his knees. John raises him to his feet and embraces him saying: 'For you and for Italy' (*'A lei e all'Italia'*). With this embrace, the reconciliation of the Holy See and Italy was finally sealed.

On the way back he feels drained of all strength. He has pushed himself to the limit. Back in the Vatican, he recovers enough to watch himself on television. He remarks on the contrast: 'A few hours ago I was being fêted and complimented, and now I'm here alone with my pain. But that's all right: the first duty of a pope is to pray and suffer' (IME, p. 205). He is in great pain and keeps coming back to this contrast, obsessively: 'Out there the world exalts me, while here the Lord rivets me to this bed'.

May 12, Sunday. *Regina Coeli* at noon from his window: Rejoice, queen of heaven. Walks in the garden in the afternoon. Face paler than ever. A new form of pain attacks him: inflammation of the gums. Yet he writes notes on the conciliar *schemata* and discusses them with Cavagna (*Lettere*, p. 575).

May 13, Monday. A busy morning. It is the eleven hundredth anniversary of the mission of Sts Cyril and Methodius. John greets the Orientals living in Rome, and blesses the foundation stone for the new Slav College being built on the Via Cassia. He recalls what he had written in 1927 to an ecumenical gathering at Velehrad:

> I hope that my stay in Bulgaria will not only help towards the revival of Catholicism in this region but also, since we are midway between Rome and Constantinople, that it may help prepare some consoling surprises and so lead to a renewal of brotherhood among the Churches and unity around the Prince of the Apostles (Caprile, II, p. 400).

Away in New York, Cardinal Suenens is handing a copy of *Pacem in Terris* to
U Thant, secretary general of the United Nations. He addresses a thronged
assembly for over an hour. He calls the encyclical 'an open letter to the world'. He
summarises it economically: its theme is peace, and peace needs truth as its
foundation, justice as its norm, love as its driving force, and freedom as its setting.
Suenens quotes Antoine de Saint-Exupéry: 'If respect for the person dwells within
our hearts, we can devise a social, political and economic system that will enshrine
respect'. More boldly still, he says that, like Beethoven's Ninth, *Pacem in Terris*
may be called 'a symphony for peace'. Suenens is asked the obvious question:
'Does Pope John bless Communism?' He replies with the distinctions made in the
encyclical: as a doctrine Communism is wrong, but 'persons are always deserving
of respect and have a value far above the views they hold. Pope John would be
happy to bless any sincere human being' (Hamilton, Elizabeth, *Cardinal Suenens, a
Portrait*, pp. 90–2).

By an interesting co-incidence, today is the day James W. Spain hands in his
memorandum 27–63 to the CIA. We have seen most of it already. Relevant here
is an unattributed comment on the election results: 'While many of the clergy
were deeply disturbed by the increase of the Communist vote, others shrugged it
off. According to one: "Even if it had been twice as great we would not worry.
We are on the offensive now. If we give men true Christian teaching and social
justice, in a decade there will not be a Communist vote in Italy" ' (Spain, pp.
10–11). Roberto Tucci made a similar point: 'You are interested in what our
changes mean vis-à-vis the Communists. I am even more interested in what they
will mean for Spain and Portugal' (*Ibid.*, p. 7). Tucci was the better prophet.

May 14, Tuesday. Mass at 7 a.m. As he is putting on the amice, he winces and
grows pale. Capovilla askes how he feels. 'Like St Laurence on the grid-iron', he
says. But he is a little better after Mass. He listens to the Bamberg Philharmonic
play Beethoven's Sixth Symphony in the Sala Clementina. He talks at length with
Emile-Joseph de Smedt, bishop of Bruges, whose speech against 'triumphalism'
swung the first session round.

May 15, Wednesday. Was up most of the night reading the 'Diary of Vatican I'
kept by Giulio Arrigoni, bishop of Lucca. The manuscript has just been discovered, lying unheeded and uncatalogued in the seminary library. Arrigoni was
from Bergamo, a point in his favour; but it was his vivid style and his insights that
led John to order its publication. (It was published, edited by Michele Maccarone,
president of the Pontifical Committee for Historical Sciences, on the third
anniversary of Pope John's death: Caprile, II, p. 403.) This was his last effective
decision.

May 16, Thursday. His newly married niece, Maria, and her bridegroom, Luigi
Gotti, are present at Mass. Receives the directors of the Pontifical Missionary
Society, for which he had worked from 1921 to 1925. Cardinal Agagianian gives

the address of homage. In his reply, John divides his life into two periods: first at the service of the Bergamo diocese, and then 'forty years at the service of Propaganda Fide' (IME, p. 207). He was claiming that he had always been a 'missionary' at heart. He was glad that the Italian Missionary Society built its new seminary at Sotto il Monte: his birth-place is in its garden.

In the evening has a two-hour long conversation with Mgr Agostino Casaroli, under-secretary at the Secretariat of State, just back from Hungary and Czechoslovakia. Much later Casaroli said of this journey:

> One thing struck me in my meetings in Prague and Budapest: it was quite evident that these Communist leaders were convinced that the Pope was sincere, trustworthy and loved them as well. These feelings of warmth and affection melted the miles of ice-floes that had kept us apart for so long. Their judgement on Pope John was always positive (Casaroli in *Famiglia Cristiana*, April 4, 1971).

After listening to Casaroli, John says: 'Monsignor, the Church may have many enemies but she is no one's enemy' (IME, p. 207). As a commentary on this conversation, he notes down the phrase attributed by St Augustine to John the Baptist: '*Tam infirmi sumus, per lucernam quaerimus diem*' ('We are so weak that we seek daylight in a lamp' (Migne P.L. IV, 198). It was an appropriate comment on his *Ostpolitik*, and shows that he could be self-critical and recognise limitations.

May 17, Friday. At 7.30 a.m. John says his last Mass, and knows that it is his last Mass. Receives Thomas Ryan, the lanky Irishman who was his secretary in Istanbul 1943–4. Says: 'I never managed to speak English as I wanted to in those distant days when you gave me my first lessons; but you enabled me to read and understand the language. I hope that my efforts will be remembered as an act of reverence towards all the English-speaking peoples' (IME, p. 208). They will.

May 18, Saturday. A very disturbed night. Vomiting. Stays in bed and from now on Mgr Capovilla will say Mass for him and give him Communion in the room next door; it has the 'window of the Angelus'. Flicks through the Secretariat of State press review. The attacks on him as a naïve dupe of the Communists continue, adding moral suffering to his already intense physical sufferings. But he won't condemn the authors of what he considers a calumny. *Ignosco et dimitto*, he repeats, I forgive and put it out of my mind. However, he is greatly consoled by a message from President John F. Kennedy. Through Cardinal Richard J. Cushing, archbishop of Boston, Kennedy says: 'The Pope should know that the US administration deplores and regards as unfounded the insinuations made in the press and in certain political circles'. The Spain report is annotated by the president himself.

May 19, Sunday. Slept well through the night. Reviews the proofs of his apostolic exhortation, *Novem per dies*, in which he invites the whole Church to a

Novena of prayer for the Council in the days before Pentecost. The doctors are puzzled by his desire to withdraw tomorrow to the Torre San Giovanni. They say it can't be done. He appears at his window for the Angelus, and blows paternal kisses to the crowd below (*'porta la destra alle labbra e fa scendere il suo bacio paterno sui diletti fedeli'*: Capovilla, IME, p. 209).

May 20, Monday. Exhausted. In the diary is an audience for Wyszyński and four Polish bishops. Dell'Acqua says: 'You could perfectly well receive them in your bedroom – they would be honoured by this mark of confidence'. John replies: 'We're not that far gone yet. Anyway, if I died during the audience, what a wonderful way to go' (IME, p. 209). He insists on getting up and receiving his old friend in the library on the floor below. He has prepared a broadcast for the workers of Poland to be transmitted during their annual pilgrimage to Piekary on May 26. Wyszyński admires his vision and sense of history. It is John's last audience. 'Good-bye until September', says Wyszyński. John is not fooled. 'In September you'll find me or . . . someone else. It only takes a month, you know: the funeral of one and the elevation of another . . . If it weren't for this blessed protocol, I'd come down with you to the bronze door' (*Ibid.*, p. 210).

Minor haemorrhages in the afternoon, but he responds to treatment and in the evening makes plans for the future. Says: 'If the Lord grants me life, after the Council I want to visit all the parishes of Rome – and all the municipal offices as well' (IME, p. 210). 'After the Council' is his horizon, his mirage. It is the feast of St Bernardine of Siena, whom he has thought of making a doctor of the Church. That probably won't be possible now, so he writes a note addressed to St Bernardine:

> Along with the sweetness of remembering you came indications of a great physical pain that simply won't leave me. It makes me think and suffer. This morning, for the third time, I had to be content with holy Communion in bed, instead of enjoying celebrating Mass myself: patience, patience. But I couldn't fail to see Cardinal Wyszyński who was going home with four of his fellow bishops. The rest of the day was spent in bed with renewed spasms of even more intense pain. My household is looking after me with great charity . . . (IME, p. 210).

May 21, Tuesday. A restless night. Communion at 6 a.m., after which he says:

> I'm ready to go. I've said all my breviary and the whole rosary. I've prayed for the children, for the sick, for sinners . . . Will things be done differently when I'm gone? That's none of my business. I feel joy in the contemplation of truth and in duty done. I'm glad I was able to correspond to every impulse of grace . . . It's all happened without excessive effort: audiences, journeys, the revival of penitential services and pastoral visits in Rome, the synod, the council (IME, p. 210).

Yet Dr Pietro Valdoni doesn't think the end is near. He even believes there could be a partial recovery.

May 22, Wednesday. Audiences cancelled.

May 23, Ascension Thursday. A much better night. Gets up to receive his nephew Flavio Roncalli. The red of his cape heightens the pallor of his face. At noon he intones the *Regina Coeli* from his window in a voice that is still musical and strong. The applause of the crowd almost prevents him giving his blessing. This is the day he had planned to go to the Benedictine Abbey of Montecassino. Of course the idea had to be abandoned, but not without a struggle. 'You can't go', Capovilla argued, 'what would you do if you had a haemorrhage?' John said: 'I'd go to bed. I'd go to a cell in the Abbey. Think of it: to die at Montecassino, the cradle of monasticism!' (Pepper, p. 223). At 6.30 p.m. he receives Cardinal Gustavo Testa, who had been 'entrusted' to him in 1905 at the age of nineteen. Seeing John's condition, Testa begins to blubber uncontrollably, like a child. John says:

> Dear Don Gustavo, we have to take things as they are. I've had a long life and served the Church and left some sort of mark on history. By God's grace I haven't behaved badly: so, not a day more. If the Lord wants me to remain a little longer, well and good, otherwise – we're off (IME, p. 212).

But the rack of pain is screwed up another notch. 'I wish I could say Mass', he says to the Augustinian friar, Frederico Belotti from near Sotto il Monte, who is acting as night-nurse. 'But this bed is your altar', says Brother Frederico (who remembers the incident very well: letter of Fr Thomas A. Hunt O.S.A., June 19, 1983). John liked this:

> Dear Brother Frederico! On the threshold of my priestly life a Passionist lay-brother inspired me by his example to generous self-giving [see *Journal* for August 1–10, 1904]; now, at the end of my long life another lay-brother brings the phrase I was waiting for from the Lord. You are right: this bed is an altar, an altar needs a victim, and I'm ready. I wouldn't mind going tonight on the feast of the Ascension (IME, p. 212).

May 24, Friday. Feels his strength ebbing away. Yet in the presence of Cardinal Amleto Cigognani and Mgr Angelo Dell'Acqua, he draws himself up in bed to deliver the message which sums up his entire life:

> Today more than ever, certainly more than in previous centuries, we are called to serve man as such, and not merely Catholics; to defend above all and everywhere the rights of the human person, and not merely those of the Catholic Church. Today's world, the needs made plain in the last fifty years, and a deeper understanding of doctrine have brought us to a new situation,

as I said in my opening speech to the Council. It is not that the Gospel has changed: it is that we have begun to understand it better. Those who have lived as long as I have were faced with new tasks in the social order at the start of the century; those who, like me, were twenty years in the East and eight in France, were enabled to compare different cultures and traditions, and know that the moment has come to discern the signs of the times, to seize the opportunity and to look far ahead (IME, p. 212).

These are not the words of a defeated or disappointed man. In the endless conflict between the 'realists' and the 'prophets', John, on his death-bed, comes down on the side of the prophets. He wagers on utopia.

May 25, Saturday. A bad day. Great pain between 10 a.m. and 5 p.m. Then he picks up again and gets Capovilla to read *The Imitation of Christ*, Book Three, Chapter 48: 'O merciful Jesus, when shall I behold you? when shall I contemplate the glory of your kingdom? when will you be all in all for me?' John comments:

> The Lord knows that I am ill. The ship continues to plough steadily
> through the waves. That's the proof that the invisible helmsman is
> Christ . . . And all these demonstrations of affection around a dying old
> man, aren't they perhaps a *sign of the times*? At the beginning of the century
> official Rome ignored the death-agony of Leo XIII. As a young seminarian
> on my way to the Vatican to get news of the Pope, I can remember hearing
> disrespectful and insulting remarks on the streets . . . Times have changed for
> the better (IME, p. 213).

May 26, Sunday. Still more haemorrhages. But he gets up. The doctors forbid him to appear at the window, and the *Regina Coeli* of the Ascension is broadcast instead. The medical bulletin goes on about 'gastric troubles'. But few believe it. Antoine Wenger writes an emotional editorial in *La Croix* headed '*Notre Prière*'. His prayer is that God may preserve our father a long time yet. John is touched by the students of the Centre Richelieu in Paris, who are praying for him. He had met them on Holy Saturday, with their chaplain Jean-Marie Lustiger, who twenty years later will become archbishop of Paris. Of Polish Jewish origin, his parents perished in concentration camps. But everyone is praying for Pope John, including, according to *Time*, Paul Tillich.

May 27, Monday. Insomnia but calm. In the afternoon his nephew, now Monsignor Giovanni Battista Roncalli, arrives. John wants him to assure all the family that his love for them is unchanged. Battista's other duty will be to tell them about John's final dispositions and his will: 'I was born poor, I have always been poor, and I want to die poor' (IME, p. 215). He had thought a good deal about his will. Various versions of it are given in the *Journal of a Soul* (pp. 365–80). His possessions are to be given away as mementos. But he has not yet given up hope and tells Battista: 'So you come here and find me in bed . . . But let's hope I'll get over it soon and be able to get back to work on the Council' (Caprile, II, p. 419).

May 28, Tuesday. A night of torment. The internal pains are worse than ever. John's condition causes alarm to his household, but the doctors think he may still pull through the crisis. By 10 a.m. he is feeling much better, and chats familiarly with Cavagna and Dell'Acqua as they read him a selection of the countless get-well messages he has received. They come from the famous and the anonymous. Cicognani arrives at 12.15 and John, still a public figure, dictates a reply to his well-wishers:

> Since everyone is praying for the sick pope, it's only natural they should have an intention: if God wants the sacrifice of my life, let it be of some use in calling down copious blessings on the ecumenical Council, the Church and on humanity that so longs for peace; but if it pleases the Lord to prolong my pontifical ministry, then let it be for the sanctification of my soul and of all those who work and suffer with me to extend the kingdom of Our Lord (IME, p. 216).

These words will appear in *l'Osservatore Romano* this evening. If they seem a little too pat for spontaneous remarks on a death-bed, the explanation may be that they were edited. Not for the first time.

May 29, Wednesday. Slept well. After Mass has blood transfusions. In the afternoon doesn't want to be left alone, and doesn't want to talk either. Absorbed in prayer. Tries to joke with the doctors. The phials with plasma become 'my silent church bells'; on being administered a medicine, he remarks '*liquida non frangunt*' (liquids don't break), a maxim that probably came from his junior seminary. He dictates some more edifying words for *l'Osservatore Romano*. He gets Capovilla to telephone Clemente Micara, cardinal vicar of Rome and not his favourite person, to thank the Roman people for their prayers. To the end he retains his respect for the 'proper channels'.

May 30, Thursday. A good night at last, the 'peaceful night and quiet ending' that he had so often invoked at Compline. Night and death. Dawn and light. He had once sent Don Giuseppe De Luca – who died much younger than himself – a postcard of 'the window of the Angelus'. On the back he wrote two texts: '*Donec dies elucescat*' (2 Peter 1.19) and Dante's '*pur che l'alba nasca*' (III, V, 76). He had just discovered that Dante was quoting St Peter, and wanted to make the phrase his motto: 'Until the day dawns' – and Peter goes on – 'and the morning star rises in your hearts'. John is reminded of this because he is reading De Luca's Gospel commentary. And the 'Angelus window' is there, tantalizingly out of reach.

These ruminations are interrupted because at 11.30 a.m. he is wracked by a violent abdominal pain. Dr Piero Mazzoni thinks that there could be a perforation of the tumour, in which case an operation will be impossible. John's days are counted. He is given sedatives. Ironically enough, none of this gets into the 1 p.m. medical bulletin which asserts that the Pope is responding to treatment. Antonio Gasbarrini, the specialist from Bologna, is so confident that his task is over that he goes home. Throughout the night the newspapers follow the optimistic lead of the medical bulletin.

May 31, Friday. The doctors confer. There is nothing more they can do. As has been agreed in advance, Capovilla has the task of breaking the news. 'Holy Father', he begins solemnly, fighting back the tears, 'I'm keeping my promise: I have to do for you what you did for Mgr Radini at the end of his life. The time has come. The Lord calls you'. John, not in the least put out, reflects for a moment and says: 'It would be good to have the doctors' verdict'.

'Their verdict, holy Father, is that it's the end. The tumour has done its work'.

'So, as with mgr Radini . . . there will be an operation?'.

'It's too late. The cancer has at last overcome your long resistance'. Capovilla falls to his knees, weeping, and buries his face in the bed-covers while John calmly gives instructions about his last hours. If the phrase were not open to misunderstanding, one could say that he stage-managed his death. The directions were found in the *Caerimoniale Episcoporum*. He says simply: 'Help me to die as a bishop or a pope should' (IME, p. 218). On the day he was elected he had thought of 'all the cameras and lights that from now on, at every moment, would be directed on me' (p. 287 above).

At 11 a.m. in the presence of Cicognani, Dell'Acqua and Samorè (representing the Secretariat of State), the pontifical household, the doctors, the nurses, and the five Bergamo sisters who had been his housekeepers, he receives the Viaticum, food for the final journey, from Mgr Alfredo Cavagna. John is sitting up, in a white shirt and a white stole. The papal sacristan, Bishop Peter Canisius Van Lierde O.S.A., is about to anoint his five senses when John speaks:

The secret of my ministry is in that crucifix you see opposite my bed. It's there so that I can see it in my first waking moment and before going to sleep. It's there, also, so that I can talk to it during the long evening hours. Look at it, see it as I see it. Those open arms have been the programme of my pontificate: they say that Christ died for all, for all. No one is excluded from his love, from his forgiveness.

What did Christ leave to his Church? He left us *'ut omnes unum sint'* ['that all may be one': John 10.16] . . .

I had the great grace to be born into a Christian family, modest and poor but with the fear of the Lord. I had the grace to be called by God as a child: I never thought of anything else, I never had any other ambition. Along the way I've met holy priests and good superiors. Oh! Don Francesco

Rebuzzini, monsignor Radini, cardinal Ferrari . . . all helped me and loved me. I had lots of encouragement.

For my part, I'm not aware of having offended anyone, but if I have, I beg their forgiveness; and if you know anyone who has not been edified by my attitudes or actions, ask them to have compassion on me and to forgive me. In this last hour I feel calm and sure that my Lord, in his mercy, will not reject me. Unworthy though I am, I wanted to serve him, and I've done my best to pay homage to truth, justice, charity, and the *cor mitis et humilis* [the meek and humble heart] of the Gospel.

My time on earth is drawing to a close. But Christ lives on and the Church continues his work. Souls, souls. *Ut unum sint! ut unum sint!* (Synthesised from many witnesses, including IME, pp. 218–19; Pepper, pp. 228–9).

Van Lierde then anoints his eyes, ears, nose, mouth, hands and feet. Overcome by emotion, he forgets the right order. John helps him out.

After that John has a personal word for all the by-standers. There are about twenty of them. Some are weeping. He shares a memory with each one, as though reviewing his whole life for the last time. From 4.30 p.m. Roman cardinals and members of the Curia begin to troop through his room, and the farewell audiences continue in the same style. He briefly alludes to the forthcoming conclave: 'I'm sure the sacred college will provide for the succession without any difficulty, and I'm sure the Bishops will bring the Council to a happy conclusion' (IME, p. 220). So the conclave would not be 'against him' as he had feared in February. It would be a conclave of continuity. But he also made a more precise prediction: 'In my opinion my successor will be Montini. The votes of the sacred college will converge on him' (*Ibid.*).

Montini has been summoned, but has not yet arrived from Milan. At 6 p.m. the second series of audiences is concluded. He says to Capovilla his secretary for the last ten years: 'We've worked together and served the Church without stopping to pick up and throw back the stones that have sometimes blocked our path. You've put up with my defects, and I've put up with yours. We'll always be friends . . . We have many friends: and now, you'll see, we'll have some more . . . I'll protect you from heaven' (IME, p. 221). John knows that the secretary of a deceased Pope has no further role in the Vatican. He entrusts his family at Sotto il Monte to Capovilla. 'When this is all over', he advises, 'get some rest and go and see your mother'. Outside in St Peter's Square a huge crowd is quietly praying.

At 7 p.m. more spasms of pain. He is put under sedation and is asleep when Montini ushers in John's brothers, Zaverio, Alfredo, Giuseppe and his sister Assunta. They kneel at his bedside, watching and praying.

June 1, Saturday. Just after midnight, Capovilla celebrates Mass for the

Roncalli family. At 3 a.m. John wakes up and imagines he is in France. He starts talking in French, as though to his Paris doctor. Then he pulls himself together and greets his family. He sits up, drinks a cup of coffee, is revived. 'I'm still here', he says cheerfully, 'when yesterday I thought I was gone . . . I don't know what's going to happen. I could get better. We're made to live . . . If I get worse, what a disappointment for you'. Then, in a different tone, he comments on Jesus' question to Martha, 'Do you believe that I am the resurrection and the life?' [John 11.25–6]. He dozes off again. At 3.45 he wakes up and there are more brief encounters with the bishop and the mayor of Bergamo and Andrea Spada, editor of *l'Eco di Bergamo*; and then with the parish priest and mayor of Sotto il Monte. The cycle of his life is complete. Though his own world is narrowing down, messages of good will are pouring in from the five continents. There is one from Khrushchev. There is one from Plovdiv in Bulgaria from someone who remembered him from the earthquake of 1928. But he has drifted off into unconsciousness again. From two American children: 'Dear Pope John, we love you'. From Anglicans: 'Our Australian hearts are more than ever with you'. From a Buddhist: 'May God love you'. From an atheist: 'In so far as an atheist can pray, I'm praying for you' (IME, p. 222).

June 2, Whitsunday. The Novena of prayer for the Council has become a Novena of prayer for 'the Pope of the Council', as he liked to define himself. Throughout the night 20,000 young people are praying in the cathedral of Milan. Cardinal Montini is among them. He speaks in sadness and affection. We need, says Montini, to 'gather up his inheritance and his final message of peace'. 'Perhaps never before in our time', says Montini, 'has a human word – the word of a master, a leader, a prophet, a pope – rung out so loudly and won such affection throughout the whole world' (IME, p. 225). No one thinks this is an exaggeration. He needn't have used that cautious 'perhaps'.

The prophet is sleeping. By 10 a.m. his temperature has risen alarmingly. 'What time is it?' he asks on the dot of noon, time of the Angelus. John glances at the window, his window on the world, at which he will never appear again. To his nephew, Zaverio, who is standing at the foot of the bed, he says gently: 'Out of the way, you're hiding the crucifix from me'. Time hangs heavily. At 8 p.m. he takes a turn for the worse, but medication brings him some relief. At 9 p.m., Cardinal Fernando Cento, grand penitentiary, starts the prayers for the dying, the liturgy of death. But John is tough or – as the official bulletin puts it – 'has exceptional physical strength'. It sees him through another day, another night, to another dawn, his last.

June 3, Whitmonday. John wakes up at 3 a.m. and says twice, with great emphasis, 'Lord, you know that I love you'. Capovilla says Mass at 5 a.m. Then John drowses off again, fitfully waking up and making the sign of the cross. At 1 p.m. a new crisis. It is overcome by 3. His breathing is regular. At 5 p.m. a vast crowd begins to fill St Peter's Square. Cardinal Luigi Traglia, pro-vicar of Rome, is saying the Mass *'pro infirmo'*, for the sick bishop of Rome. At John's bedside are the members of his family, Cicognani, Cavagna, Capovilla, the doctors, the Gussi brothers, Brother Frederico, the Bergamo nuns. They say the prayers for the dying while the Mass proceeds in the square. Towards 7.45 the Mass is over. In the Pope's bedroom, the words of dismissal, *Ite Missa Est*, can be clearly heard over the microphone. Pope John gives a last shudder. His breathing becomes faint and, after a barely audible death-rattle, stops. The doctors bow reverently and shrug. It is 7.49 p.m.

Those present knelt and recited the *In paradisum* from the office of the dead: 'The angels lead you into paradise'. Then they said the great hymns of Christian thanksgiving, the *Magnificat* and the *Te Deum*. John's brow was ritually tapped to make sure he was really dead. The 'window of the Angelus' was suddenly illumined, and the crowd knew the truth. Giacomo Manzù, hastily summoned, took a plaster cast of John's face and right hand, the blessing hand. Next day, contrary to custom John's body was carried through the grieving crowd in the square and then into St Peter's to await burial in the crypt.

He had lived eighty-one and a half years, been a priest for fifty-eight years, a bishop for thirty-eight years, and pope for less than five years – the shortest pontificate of the century so far. Yet in him the Church and the world were prodigiously blessed.

Bibliography and Sources

AAS = *Acta Apostolicae Sedis* (the official collection of papal and curial documents).

Abbott, Walter J., S.J., Ed *The Documents of Vatican II*, Geoffrey Chapman, London, 1966.

Actes et documents = *Actes et documents du Saint-Siège*, Eds Pierre Blet S.J., Robert A. Graham S.J., Angelo Martini S.J. and Burkhart Schneider S.J., Libreria Editrice Vaticana. Eleven volumes. The following are relevant for Roncalli:

> vol. 4: *Le Saint-Siège et la situation religieuse en Pologne et dans les pays Baltes 1939–1945*, part II (1967).

> vol. 6: *Le Saint-Siège et les victimes de la guerre, mars 1939–décembre 1940* (1972).

> vol. 7: *Le Saint-Siège et la guerre mondiale, novembre 1942–décembre 1943* (1973).

> vol. 8: *Le Saint-Siège et les victimes de la guerre, janvier 1941–décembre 1943* (1981).

> vol. 9: *Le Saint-Siège et les victimes de la guerre, janvier–décembre 1944* (1975).

> vol. 10: *Le Saint-Siège et les victimes de la guerre, janvier 1944–juillet 1945* (1980).

> vol. 11: *Le Saint-Siège et la guerre mondiale* (1981).

Acton, Lord, *Essays on Church and State*, Ed Douglas Woodruff, Hollis and Carter, London, 1952 (Acton learned history in the house of Ignaz Döllinger in Munich, and survived the experience to become Regius Professor in Cambridge).

ADAP = *Akten zur Deutschen Auswärtigen Politik 1918–1945*, Vandenhoeck and Ruprecht, Göttingen, series E, volume 7 (1979).

Aimé-Azam, Denise, *l'Extraordinaire Ambassadeur*, La Table Ronde, Paris, 1967 (splendidly anecdotal account by a Jewish convert of Roncalli's time in Paris).

Alberigo = *Giovanni XXIII, Profezia nella fedeltà*, by Giuseppe and Angelina Alberigo, Queriniana, Brescia, 1978 (after a long, 100-page introduction, an extensive anthology of Roncalli's writings from all periods of his long life: for Italian readers the best possible introduction to Pope John).

Alberigo, Giuseppe, 'Dal bastone al misericordia', in *Cristianesimo nella Storia*, October 1981, pp. 487–521 ('From the rod to Mercy' shows how the exercise of authority changed between Gregory XVI and John XXIII).

Alexander, Stella, *Church and State in Yugoslavia since 1945*, Cambridge University Press, 1979 (a ground-breaking work that has no competitors).

Algisi, Leone, *Giovanni XXIII*, Marietti, Turin, 1959 (was checked for accuracy by Pope John himself: but he found it too flattering).

Andreotti, Giulio, *A Ogni Morte di Papa – I Papi che ho conosciuto*, Rizzoli, Milan, 1980
    (a peculiarly Italian form: Andreotti, back again as Foreign Minister in 1984,
    knew all the Popes from Pius XI and had some important conversations with
    Pope John).
ANSA = the Italian news agency.
ARCIC = The Anglican Roman Catholic International Commission, *The Final Report*,
    SPCK and CTS, London, 1982.
ASCV = *Acta Synodalia Concilii Vaticani II*, Vatican Polyglot Press, 4 vols. 1970–1 (the
    'Hansard' of the first session: even if the 'real' Council was happening somewhere
    else, the indispensable record against which immediate journalistic accounts have to
    be checked).
Gli Atti della visita apostolica di S. Carlo Borromeo a Bergamo (1575), Ed by Angelo
    Giuseppe Roncalli and Pietro Forno, Leo. S. Olschki, Florence, in two parts and
    five volumes, 1936, 1937, 1938, 1946 and 1957 (Roncalli's life-work, begun in 1906
    when Achille Ratti – the future Pius XI – photocopied the material for him;
    completed just before he became pope).
Avvenire d'Italia. Italian Catholic daily. Its pale ghost survives in *Avvenire*.

Bacci, Antonio, *Con il Latino a servizio di quattro papi*, Studium, Rome, 1964 (memoirs
    of a Latinist, once defined as 'someone who doesn't know enough Greek to be a
    classical scholar': unfair to Bacci).
Baltimore Sun, The (one of the world's oldest newspapers: in the eighteenth century it
    announced that it would appear weekly – or more often 'if there were a glut of
    occurrences').
Baronio = *Il cardinale Cesare Baronio*, by Angelo Giuseppe Roncalli, Storia e letteratura,
    Rome, 1961 (Roncalli's 1907 lecture republished).
Battaglia, Giuseppe, 'Francesco Pitocchi', a paper read at the Istituto per le scienze
    religiose in Bologna, November 14, 1981.
Bedeschi, Lorenzo, *Buonaiuti, il Concordato e la Chiesa*, Il Saggiatore, Milan, 1970
    (much unpublished material which reveals Buonaiuti, hitherto the arch Italian
    'Modernist', to have been a prophetic figure).
Bedeschi, Lorenzo, *Modernismo a Milano*, Pan, Milan, 1974 (more *inédits* throwing light
    on renewal movements in Milan under Cardinal Ferrari).
Bell, George K., *The Kingship of Christ, The Story of the World Council of Churches*,
    Penguin, Harmondsworth, 1954 (the Anglican Bishop of Chichester reflects on the
    international ecumenical movement that had brought him into contact, *inter alios*,
    with Roncalli's Bulgarian Orthodox Christians and Dietrich Bonhoeffer).
Bergerre, Max, *Six Papes, un journaliste*, Téqui, Paris, 1979 (the unpretentious memoirs
    of the *doyen* of the Vatican press corps).
Bertoli, Bruno, *La Questione Romana negli Scritti di Papa Giovanni*, Morcelliana, Brescia,
    1970 (a short – 42 pp. – study of Roncalli and the Lateran Pacts).
Bertrand, Dominique, S.J., gave information about Fr Alfred de Soras S.J., who
    'preached' the retreat made by Roncalli at Clamart, a suburb of Paris, December
    8–13, 1947. Roncalli wrote of de Soras: 'Good doctrine, expounded in an

interesting way, but quite modern in construction, language and imagery' (*Journal*, p. 288). Bertrand scotched the notion that this might have been a 'directed' retreat.

Bevilacqua, Giulio, 'Il Concilio', in *Vita e Pensiero*, 1960, p. 513 and following (important article by the Brescia anti-Fascist Oratorian who was Montini's mentor: became a cardinal under Paul VI).

Binchy, D. A., *Church and State in Fascist Italy*, Oxford University Press, 1941 (the best book on its subject, written by an Irish diplomat turned academic: the 1970 edition has a new preface).

Bishops and Writers, Ed Adrian Hastings, Anthony Clarke, Wheathampton, 1977 (a *Festschrift* for and worthy of Mgr Garrett Sweeney, historian of Vatican I: includes outstanding essay by Professor Nicholas Lash on 'Modernism').

Blessing of Years, A, The Memoirs of Lawrence Cardinal Shehan, Notre Dame Press, Notre Dame and London, 1982 (relatively frank confessions of a tiny and bewildered US bishop who, however, later redeemed himself with good interventions on religious liberty).

Bologna Archives: this refers to the material gathered at the Istituto per le scienze religiose in the University of Bologna. Thanks are due to its director, Giuseppe Alberigo.

Bonisteel, Roy, *Man Alive: The Human Journey*, Collins, Toronto, 1983 (a CBC TV interviewer for over twenty years who persuaded Cardinal Paul-Emile Léger, former archbishop of Montréal, to talk about Pope John).

Bonnot, Bernard R., *Pope John XXIII, an Astute Pastoral Leader*, Alba House, New York, 1979 (grew out of a thesis: a careful and largely unappreciated study of the pontificate).

Borghese, Il, right-wing scurrilous magazine, edited in the relevant period by Mario Tedeschi (its regular feature, 'Through the Bronze door', picks up and embroiders Curial gossip).

Boudens, Robrecht, of Leuven University, Belgium, provided information on the relationship between Cardinal Mercier and the Vatican, most of it drawn from his book, *Karl Mercier en de vlaamse beweging*, 1970. In 1913 Mercier sprang to the defence of the Bollandists, the Jesuit Church historians, who were being threatened with the Index. Mercier pleaded: 'At least consult the Belgian Bishops first'. Though the scare turned out to be a false alarm, Merry del Val, Secretary of State, assured Mercier that 'the Pope did not feel obliged to consult anyone when dealing with false teachings against which half-measures achieve nothing'. Roncalli admired both the Bollandists and Mercier.

Bugnini, Annibale, *La Riforma Liturgica 1948–1975*, Edizioni Liturgiche, Rome, 1983 (this enormous volume traces the continuity in liturgical reform from Pius XII onwards; attacked as a 'termite' gnawing away at tradition, Bugnini had the misfortune to become Apostolic Delegate in Teheran where he was abused by student partisans of Ayatollah Khomenei; this hastened his death).

Burgess, Anthony, see *Earthly Powers*.

Butler, Cuthbert, OSB, *The Vatican Council*, two vols., Longmans, Green & Co, London, 1930 (classic English account of Vatican I – it was not so numbered when the book was written – that relies on the letters and diaries of Archbishop William Ullathorne, Yorkshireman, Benedictine and apostle of Australia).

Campbell-Johnston, Michael, S.J., 'The Social Teaching of the Church', in *Thought*, autumn, 1964 (shows the 'French' and *Semaines Sociales* background to *Mater et Magistra*).

Caprile, Giovanni, S.J., *Il Concilio Vaticano II*, Civiltà Cattolica, Rome:
vol I, part 1: *Annunzio e preparazione 1959–1960* (1966);
vol I, part 2: *Annunzio e preparazione 1961–1962* (1966);
vol II, *Primo Periodo* (1968) (no one interested in the Council can do without this veritable mine of information; even his omissions are interesting).

Caprile, Giovanni, 'Pio XII e un nuovo projetto di Concilio Ecumenico', in *Civiltà Cattolica*, August 6, 1966, pp. 209–27 (the first article on the-Council-that-never-was).

Caprile, Giovanni, reviews *L'Utopia di Giovanni XXIII*, by Giancarlo Zizola, *Civiltà Cattolica*, February 16, 1974.

Caprile, Giovanni, 'Ancora su Giovanni XXIII', in *Civiltà Cattolica*, April 5, 1980, pp. 50–4.

Carbone, Vincenzo, 'Genesi e criteri della pubblicazione degli Atti del Concilio Vaticano II', in *Lateranum*, XLIV, 1978, pp. 579–95.

Cardinale, Igino, *The Holy See and the International Order*, Colin Smythe, Gerrards Cross, 1976 (the standard work on Vatican diplomacy).

Cardinale, Igino. In a long meeting at the Brussels Nunciature on March 30, 1980, Archbishop Cardinale answered with frankness every question that I put to him about Pope John. May he rest in peace.

Cartier, Raymond, *La Seconde Guerre Mondiale*, vol 5, juin 1944–février 1945, Presses Pocket, Paris, 1976.

Chiesa e Stato nell'Ottocento, Miscellanea in onore di Pietro Pirri, 2 vols, Antenore, Padua, 1962 (*Festschrift* for a Jesuit historian: much light on nineteenth-century Church problems).

Chronicle = *The Chronicle of the Worker-Priests*, preface by André Latreille, translated and edited by Stan Windass, The Merlin Press, London, 1966 (though Emile Poulat says that it is 'chock-full of errors' – *fourmille d'inexactitudes* – a useful compilation if checked against other sources).

Church = *The Church*, by Giovanni Battista Montini, Palm Publishers, Montréal, 1964 (lectures and pastoral letters on the Council while Pope John was still reigning).

Church in the Power of the Spirit, The, by Jürgen Moltmann, SCM Press, London, 1977 (the rediscoverer of 'the theology of hope' finds Pope John's treatment of 'signs of the times' too optimistic).

Ciano's Diary 1939–1943, edited with an introduction by Malcolm Muggeridge, foreword by Sumner Welles, Heinemann, London, 1947 (Mussolini's son-in-law and foreign minister, opposed Italian participation in the war, was executed by his father-in-law).

Civiltà Cattolica, Rome, the fortnightly review of the Rome Jesuits founded in 1849: it became the prototype of other Jesuit reviews – *Etudes, Stimmen der Zeit, Razón y Fe, The Month* etc.; but while they went their own way, *Civiltà* allowed only Jesuits to write in its pages and was censored by the Secretariat of State.

Collin, Richard, *The De Lorenzo Gambit: the Italian Coup Manqué of 1964*, Sage Research Papers in the Social Sciences, Beverly Hills/London, 1976 (though General De Lorenzo did not attempt his coup till 1964, he was preparing it from long before as head of the Secret Service – SIFAR).

Combat pour la liberté, Lettres inédites de Georges Bernanos, 2 vols, Plon, Paris, 1971.

Congar, Yves-Marie, O.P., *Challenge to the Church*, Collins, London, 1977 (translation of a 1976 pamphlet, *La Crise dans l'Eglise et Mgr Lefebvre*, Cerf).

Congar, Yves-Marie, *Dialogue between Christians*, Geoffrey Chapman, London, 1966.

Congar, Yves Marie, *Power and Poverty in the Church*, Geoffrey Chapman, London, 1964 (Jennifer Nicholson's translation of *Pour une Eglise servante et pauvre*, Cerf, 1964, Paris: most of the book grew out of lectures given in Rome during the Council).

Corriere della Sera, influential Milan paper that for good or ill has reflected Italian life faithfully for over a century.

Council and Reunion, by Hans Küng, Sheed and Ward, London, 1961 (English translation of *Konzil und Wiedervereinigung. Erneuerung als Ruf in die Einheit*. The Americans – Doubleday, 1965 – called it *The Council, Reform and Reunion*).

Cousins, Norman, 'The Improbable Trumvirate', *The Saturday Review*, October 30, 1971 (the trio was Kennedy, Khrushchev and Pope John).

Cristianesimo nella storia. The journal of the Istituto per le scienze religiose, Bologna. Edited by Giuseppe Alberigo.

Critic, The, Chicago.

Croix, La, Paris. During the Council edited by Antoine Wenger A.A.

Cronologia = pp. 515–765 of *Giovanni XXIII, Quindici Letture*, by Loris Capovilla, Storia e Letteratura, 1970 (indispensable starting point for any biographer: expanded and corrected in later works).

Crown of Thorns, A, An Autobiography 1951–1963, by John Carmel Heenan, Hodder & Stoughton, London, 1974 (a sequel to the earlier volume, *Not the Whole Truth*: in the *New Statesman*, the review was headlined: 'Too Clever by a Quarter').

Cugini, Davide, *Papa Giovanni nei suoi primi passi a Sotto il Monte*, Istituto Italiano d'Arti Grafiche, Bergamo, 1965 (an art-historian friend of Roncalli on his childhood and time in Venice).

Daly, Gabriel, O.S.A., *Transcendence and Immanence. A Study in Catholic Modernism and Integralism*, Clarendon Press, Oxford, 1980 (the most thorough and 'revisionist' Catholic study of 'Modernism').

De Gasperi, Alcide, *Lettere sul Concordato*, Morcelliana, Brescia, 1970, with an introduction by Maria Romana De Gasperi and a long essay by Giacomo Martina S.J. on the background and the consequences of the Lateran Pacts (also contains family snaps of De Gasperi and a photograph of the desk he sat at in the catalogue room of the Vatican Library).

De Gaulle, Charles, *Mémoires de Guerre*, vol 2, Plon, Paris, 1954.

De la Bedoyère, Michael, *The Life of Baron von Hügel*, Dent, London, 1951 (courageously broke new ground: dedicated to the Duke Gallarati Scotti, then Ambassador at the court of St James, London, and a friend of Roncalli).

De Luca, Giuseppe, *Altar, Gift and Gospel*, St Paul Publications, London, 1967 (with an important introduction by Mgr Igino Cardinale, De Luca's nephew, who compares him to Mgr Ronald Knox).

De Luca, Giuseppe, *Il Cardinale Bonaventura Cerretti*, Istituto Grafico Tiberino, Rome 1939.

De Riedmatten, Henri, O.P., 'Histoire de la Constitution Pastorale', in *L'Eglise dans le Monde de ce Temps, Schema XIII, Commentaires*, Mame, Paris, 1967 (along with Roberto Tucci's booklet, essential reading on the origins of *Gaudium et Spes*).

Decimo anniversario = *X anniversario della morte di Papa Giovanni*, by Loris Capovilla, Storia e Letteratura, 1973 (unpublished letters on the charge of 'Modernism').

Disquisitio, Vatican Polyglot Press, 1950 (the historical study for the beatification of Pius X: while defending Pius, it throws a flood of light on his methods: Pope John read it through in 1959 and corrected a few misprints: Giancarlo Zizola now possesses this copy, gift of Loris Capovilla).

DMC = *Discorsi, messagi, colloqui del Santo Padre Giovanni XXIII, 1958–1963*, five volumes plus index, Vatican Polyglot Press 1960–7 (the official collection of all Pope John's public utterances: not entirely reliable, since he was frequently over-edited).

Documenti Segreti della Diplomazia Vaticana, Società Cooperativa Operaia, Lugano, 1948 (a fraud: but thanks to Roland Hill for lending it, and to Emil Poulat who pointed out that forgeries could be more interesting and revealing about 'what was perceived' than authentic texts).

Dodicesimo anniversario = *XII anniversario della morte di Papa Giovanni* (essential reading for Roncalli's relationship with Cardinal Ferrari and Ernesto Buonaiuti).

Dreyfus, Paul, *Jean XXIII*, Fayard, Paris, 1979 (fast-moving French biography with seventy pages of learned appendices and yet, strangely, no references in the text).

D–S = *Enchiridion Symbolorum, Definitionum et Declarationum de rebus fidei et morum*, by H. Denzinger and A. Schönmetzer, Freiburg im Breisgau, 1965.

Earthly Powers, by Anthony Burgess, Penguin, Harmondsworth, 1981 (like myself an old boy of the Xaverian College, Victoria Park, Manchester, Burgess was kind enough to imagine that I was in Rome during the 1958 conclave and wrote a book about it, *Rebirth of a Church*, p. 548).

Elliott, Lawrence, *I will be called John*, Reader's Digest Press, New York, 1973, and Collins, London, 1974 ('It began on a day when the summer had slipped almost imperceptibly into golden autumn. It began in the olive hills southeast of Rome... There, Pius XII died... exhausted by the burdens of holy office in a world of skepticism and rage' *etc*).

Epocha, Rome, Italian weekly.

Erikson, Erik, *Identity, Youth and Crisis*, Faber and Faber, London, W. W. Norton, New York, 1968 (breviary of the 1960s).

Exercises = *The Spiritual Exercises of St Ignatius*, edited by Louis J. Puhl S.J. Loyola University Press, Chicago, 1951.

Falconi, Carlo, see *Popes of the Twentieth Century*.

Famiglia Cristiana. Italy's most widely diffused Catholic magazine.

Familiari = *Giovanni XXIII, Lettere ai familiari*, two vols, edited by Loris Capovilla, Storia e Letteratura, Rome, 1968 (727 letters from Roncalli to his family at Sotto il Monte: he kept carbon copies).

Fappani-Molinari = *Gianbattista Montini Giovane*, by Antonio Fappani and Franco Molinari, Marietti, Turin, 1979 (essential documentation on the 'young' Montini; the authors, serious historians, still regard him as young at 47; full of surprises).

Felici, Pericle, *Il Lungo Cammino del Concilio*, Ancora, Milan, 1967 (the former Secretary General of the Council tells his story).

Fonzi, Fausto, *I Cattolici e la Società Italiana dopo l'Unità*, Studium, Rome, 1977 (surveys the Vatican and Italian politics from Roncalli's childhood and youth to 1929).

Fox, Matthew, O.P., *Religion U.S.A.*, Listening Press, Dubuque, Iowa, 1971 (originally a doctoral thesis on the way 'religion' is presented in *Time*: a joyous romp through a delicious field).

Frost, Robert, *Complete Poems*, Jonathan Cape, London 1967.

Gill, Joseph, S.J., historian of the Council of Florence, was Rector of the Oriental Institute in Rome when the Council was announced. He supplied precisions about the Roman ecumenical scene in 1959–60.

Giornale dell'Anima, see *Journal*.

Giudici, Marco, 'Il Coraggio della Speranza', in *Vita e Pensiero*, February 1980 (a report on the 'prophetic' figure, Don Primo Mazzolari).

Gogol, Nicolas, *Lettres spirituelles et familières*, Grasset, Paris, 1957.

Gorresio, Vittorio, *La Nuova Missione*, Rizzoli, Milan, 1968 (useful for Cardinal Giacomo Lercaro's early misjudgement of Pope John).

Graham, Robert A., S.J., 'Quale pace cercava Pio XII?, in *Civiltà Cattolica*, May 1, 1982, pp. 218–33 (particularly interesting because the author had written in *America*, June 24, 1944, on the same theme: 'What peace does the Pope want?' How journalism becomes history).

Gran Sacerdote = *Papa Giovanni XXIII, Gran Sacerdote, come lo ricordo*, by Loris Capovilla, Storia e Letteratura, Rome, 1977 (includes unpublished diaries from the pontificate and a selection of letters: useful for Roncalli's time at Propaganda).

Greene, Graham, 'Pius XII', in *The Month*, December 1951, pp. 327–39 (the editor, Fr Philip Caraman, was reprimanded by the Vatican for this allegedly 'disrespectful' but actually blameless article. Writes Greene: 'It is a long time since a Pope has awoken even in those of other faiths such a sense of closeness' – p. 338).

Grootaers, Jan, 'L'Attitude de l'Archevêque Montini au cours de la première période du Concile', a paper given at the Paul VI Conference, Milan, September 23–25, 1983. MS.

Guarducci, Margherita, *Saint Pierre Retrouvé*, Editions Saint-Paul, Paris, 1974 (complains that Pope John was not interested in the excavations).

Guarnieri, R., *Don Giuseppe De Luca tra cronica e storia*, Bologna, 1974 (a biography of this enigmatic priest, the Orvietan Giuseppe De Luca: his nephew, Mgr Igino Cardinale, called him 'the Mgr Ronald Knox of Italian Catholicism' – but that overlooks his 'Fascist' phase and his secret dealings with Communists later).

Guitton, Jean, *Paul VI secret*, Desclée de Brouwer, Paris, 1979 (memories of the only Catholic layman present at the first session of the Council: says key word for John was *rajeunir* while Paul's key word was *approfondir*).

Hales, E. E. Y., *Pope John and his Revolution*, Eyre and Spottiswoode, London, 1965 (far and away the best study in English of the pontificate of Pope John, and especially of his 'social teaching').

Hamilton, Elizabeth, *Cardinal Suenens, a Portrait*, Hodder and Stoughton, London, 1975 (hagiography).

Helmreich, Ernst Christian, *The German Churches under Hitler*, Wayne State University Press, Detroit, 1979 (shows that Hitler's policy towards the Catholic Church *varied*).

Heppel, Dr Muriel, checked up on my Bulgarian history.

Hill, Michael, *The Religious Order*, Heinemann, London 1973 (discusses how the 'institutional personality' is formed in prisons and seminaries).

Hoffmann, Paul, *O Vatican! A Slightly Wicked View of the Holy See*, Congden and Weed Inc., New York, 1984 (somewhat better than its title would suggest).

Holmes, J. Derek, *The Papacy in the Modern World*, Burns and Oates, London, 1981 (a solid and dependable survey).

Hornby, Col. Robert, formerly press officer to the Archbishop of Canterbury, supplied material on Dr Geoffrey Fisher's visit to Pope John on December 2, 1960.

Hurn, David Abner, *Archbishop Roberts S.J., His Life and Writings*, Darton, Longman and Todd, London, 1966 (the bizarre *nom de plume* conceals Margaret Rowland of *The Universe*).

IME see *Ite Missa Est*.

Infallibile? by Hans Küng, Collins, London 1971 (a provocative work that is less 'controversial' for those who know any Church history: makes Pope John a hero).

Irénikon, an ecumenical review founded by Dom Lambert Beauduin O.S.B. in 1926: published from Amay-sur-Meuse and, from 1939, the Abbey of Chevetogne in Belgium.

l'Italia, the Milan newspaper to which Cardinal Montini contributed during the first session of the Council.

Ite Missa Est, by Loris Capovilla, Messagero, Padua and Grafica e Arte, Bergamo, 1983 (invaluable documentation on Roncalli's childhood, his time in Venice, and certain key episodes in the pontificate; with a reworked account of the last two months; sumptuously illustrated).

Jaeger, Lorenz, *The Ecumenical Council, the Church and Christendom*, Geoffrey Chapman, London, 1961 (discussed in Chapter 18).

Jemolo, Arturo Carlo, *Chiesa e Stato in Italia negli ultimi cento anni*, Marietti, Turin, 1963 (classic work by the *doyen* of Italian Church historians).

Johnson, Paul, *Pope John XXIII*, Hutchinson, London, 1975 (the author's last book before swinging, vigorously, to the right).

Journal = Journal of a Soul, Pope John XXIII, introduced by Loris Capovilla, translated by Dorothy White, Geoffrey Chapman, London, revised edition 1980 (this edition has been referred to throughout: to find passages in other editions, consult the dates; the White translation has been revised where necessary, and her omissions have been remedied with reference to the *Giornale dell'Anima*, Storia e Letteratura, Rome, fifth edition, 1967).

Kaiser, Robert B., *Pope, Council and World, the Story of Vatican II*, Macmillan, New York, 1963; and Burns and Oates, London, 1963 (one of the first books to 'open the windows of the Vatican' by the *Time* magazine correspondent).

Keneally, Thomas, *Schindler's Ark*, Hodder and Stoughton, London, 1982.

Kerr, Fergus, O.P., provided information on how *Humani Generis* affected French Dominicans.

KNA = Katholische Nachrichten Agentur, the German Catholic News Agency, which used to have a special interest in the Vatican's *Ostpolitik*.

Küng, Hans, see *Council and Reunion* and *Infallible?*

Lai, Benny, *Les Secrets du Vatican*, Hachette, Paris, 1983 (supersedes the author's previous books such as *Vaticano sotto voce*, Longanesi, Milan, 1961, and retells the old stories. The 'prelate' who smashed his episcopal ring as he thumped the table on hearing that some wanted Montini to be elected in 1958 is revealed as Cardinal Giovanni Siri, p. 60).

Larkin, Maurice, *Church and State after the Dreyfus Affair*, Macmillan, London, 1974.

Latreille, André, *De Gaulle, la libération et l'Eglise Catholique*, Cerf, Paris, 1978 (gives balance to the much mythologised story of Roncalli and the French bishops).

Lawrence, Sir John, Roman Diary, February–March 1959 (unpublished: offers a unique insight into the atmosphere in Rome in the weeks after the announcement of the Council).

Lettere = Giovanni XXIII, Lettere 1958-1963, Ed Loris Capovilla, Storia e Letteratura, Rome, 1978 (217 letters, private and public, written by Pope John during his pontificate followed by 131 'notes' and memoranda: fully annotated by Mgr Capovilla, this volume is essential to the understanding of the pontificate).

Letture = Giovanni XXIII, Quindici Letture, by Loris Capovilla, Storia e Letteratura, Rome, 1970 (fifteen lectures on Pope John, the first given on January 17, 1959 and the last on June 3, 1967; with appendices on the *Journal of a Soul*, the last days of Pope John and the 'Chronology' of his life; a monumental work that becomes part of the story it has to tell; much unpublished material).

Levi, Primo, *If this is a Man*, Penguin Modern Classics, Harmondsworth, 1979 (*Se questo è un uomo* appeared in 1958; Levi survived Auschwitz and came home via Russia and Poland).

Levillain, Philippe, *La mécanique politique de Vatican II, Majorité et l'unanimité dans un concile*, Beauchesne, coll. *Théologie Historique*, Paris, 1975 (applies the categories of political science to the Council, with interesting results; based on the notes of Henri de Lubac, S.J.).

Linee = Giovanni XXIII, Linee per una ricerca storica, by Giacomo Lercaro; with an appendix by Gabriele De Rosa on *Angelo Roncalli e Radini Tedeschi*, Storia e Letteratura, Rome, 1965 (the first plea for a serious historical study of Pope John).

Loisy, Alfred, *Mémoires pour servir à l'histoire religieuse de notre temps*, 2 vols, Paris, 1931.

Lomax, Benedict, 'Pope John's Ostpolitik', in *The Month*, September, 1974, pp. 691–6 (I can now reveal that Benedict Lomax was a *nom de guerre* for Peter Hebblethwaite).

McGregor, Geddes, *The Vatican Revolution*, Macmillan, London, 1958 (an assault on Vatican I from the point of view of a Scottish theologian: there was a 'revolution' because the definition of infallibility represented a departure from tradition; anticipates Bernard Hasler and Hans Küng).

Machiavelli, Niccolò, *The Prince*, translated by George Bull, Penguin Classics Harmondsworth, 1961 ('Old Nick', as he was sometimes known in England in Shakespeare's time, was never the cynical monster he was presented as; alas no ruler ever availed himself of his political wisdom).

Mack Smith, Denis, *Mussolini*, Weidenfeld and Nicolson, London, 1981 (comfortably the best biography of Mussolini who 'having been once praised to excess, was now being blamed for doing more harm to Italy than anyone had ever done').

Magister, Sandro, *La Politica Vaticana e l'Italia 1943–1978*, Editori Riuniti, Rome, 1979 (excellent study of a period that is more complex than it looks).

Manzoni, Alessandro, *I Promessi Sposi*, Mursia, Milan, 1966 (Roncalli's favourite novel, quoted by him more often than any other literary work).

Manzoni, Alessandro, Tutte le Poesie di, Ed Giovanni Titta Rosa, Ceschina, Milan, 1966 (Manzoni's *inni sacri* – sacred hymns – contain a poem on Pentecost which is dated 1817–1822).

Marrou, Henri-Irenée, *Crise de notre temps et réflexion chrétienne (de 1930 à 1975)*, Beauchesne, Paris, 1978 (collected pieces of a historian whose concern with St Augustine and the collapse of the Roman Empire did not blind him to the iniquities of French colonialism; also, under the pseudonym Henri Davenson, music critic for *Esprit* while Roncalli was in Paris).

Martin, Bryan, *John Henry Newman*, Chatto and Windus, London, 1982.

Martin, David, *The Religious and the Secular*, Routledge and Kegan Paul, London, 1969 (this most literate of sociologists writes two rather unexpected chapters on Bulgaria).

Martin, Malachi, *The Decline and Fall of the Roman Church*, G. P. Putnam's Sons, New York, 1981 (in which the author eats his earlier informed judgements and now alleges that Pope John 'created the circumstances in which the authority and unity of his Church were destroyed'; tells us more about Malachi Martin than Pope John).

Medvedev, Roy, *Khrushchev*, translated by Brian Pearce, Basil Blackwell, Oxford, 1983

(accepts that there was some 'change' in Khrushchev's Soviet Union, but also
shows that in the closing down of churches and contemptuous treatment of
Christians, the later Khrushchev years were *more* authoritarian than the post-war
Stalin period).

Memorie = *Giovanni XXIII, Memorie e Appunti 1919*, in *Humanitas*, Number 6, June,
1973, pp. 428–87, with an introduction by Loris Capovilla (substantial extracts from
Roncalli's diary and notebooks for the year 1919).

Merry del Val, Rafael, *Memoirs of Pius X*, Newman Press, Westminster, Maryland,
1951 (very brief and self-justifying: at the age of thirty-seven, Merry del Val became
Pius X's Secretary of State; after the death of Pius in 1914, his faithful henchman
drifted into an ineffectual limbo).

Mission = *Mission to France 1944–1953*, by Angelo Giuseppe Roncalli, Geoffrey
Chapman, London, 1966 (English trans of *Souvenirs d'un Nonce 1944–1953*, Storia e
Letteratura, Rome, 1963: a collection of letters, homilies and addresses during
Roncalli's French period).

Moignt, Joseph, S.J., invited me to give a paper at his conference on the *Magisterium*,
Chantilly, June, 1982: it appeared as 'Le discours de Jean XXIII à l'ouverture de
Vatican II' in *Recherches de Sciences Religieuses*, avril–juin, 1983, pp. 203–12.

Momigliano, Arnaldo, *Terza contributo alla storia degli studi classici*, Storia e Letteratura,
Rome, 1966 (Polyglot Jewish scholar from Turin who found a haven in Oxford:
keenly interested in Italian historiography and therefore in Roncalli on Baronius and
Charles Borromeo).

Monaco, Franco, 'Montini a Milano', in *Vita e Pensiero*, Milan, November, 1983, p. 61
and following (a report on the second meeting of the Paul VI Institute held in
Milan 23–5 September, 1983: argues that Milan 'explains' Montini).

Mondrone, Domenico, S.J., 'L'Episcopato del Card. Andrea C. Ferrari in uno studio
di Carlo Snider', in *Civiltà Cattolica*, July 18, 1981, pp. 154–61 (admits that a study
of the relationship between Ferrari and Pius X will show 'how far a well-
orchestrated campaign of calumny can win over the mind and discernment of a
saint': which seems to let Pius X off the hook).

Month, The, review of the English – now British – Jesuits.

Morris, James, *Venice*, Faber and Faber, London, 1960 (the author later claimed a sex-
change and became Jan Morris: the prose remained as vivid as ever).

My Bishop = *My Bishop, a Portrait of Mgr Giacomo Maria Radini Tedeschi*, by Angelo
Giuseppe Roncalli, English trans by Dorothy White, Geoffrey Chapman, London,
1969; a much abbreviated version of *In Memoria di Monsignore Giacomo Radini
Tedeschi, Vescovo di Bergamo*, San Alessandro, Bergamo, 1916; second edition, Storia
e Letteratura, Rome, 1963 (only comes to life when one has seen what questions
were being asked by Italian Catholics before the first world war).

Nash, Margaret, *The Ecumenical Movement in the 1960s*, Ravan Press, Johannesburg,
South Africa, 1975 (a useful work by an Anglican, no doubt neglected because of its
place of publication; in his preface Dr W. A. Visser't Hooft calls it 'a significant
contribution'; has forgivable errors).

Natale 1970, Capodanno 1971, ed Loris Capovilla (in effect Mgr Capovilla's Christmas and New Year greetings: contains correspondence relating to Roncalli's move to Rome in 1921, and also a photograph of his study when Pope).

Natale 1975, Capodanno 1976, ed Loris Capovilla (devoted to Pope John's thoughts on ecumenism, with a complete list of his ecumenical encounters).

The National Catholic Reporter, Kansas City, Missouri (I declare an interest: I first wrote in NCR in 1967 and have been its 'Vatican Affairs Writer' since September 1979; its successive editors, Arthur Jones and Thomas C. Fox, encouraged this book and in effect subsidised it; may they be blessed).

Negro, Silvio, the leading Vaticanologist of his day; worked for *Corriere della Sera*, Milan.

Newman, John Henry, *Sermons, chiefly on the theory of religious belief*, Oxford, 1843.

Nicolini, Giulio, *Il Cardinale Domenico Tardini*, Messagero, Padua, 1980 (insider's book by young – fifty-four – curialist who knows more than he lets on and reveals more than he intends).

Novak, Michael, *The Open Church*, Darton, Longman and Todd, London, 1964 (based on articles in *The New Republic* etc, tried to do for the second session what Robert B. Kaiser had done for the first; denounced 'non-historical orthodoxy'; changed his tune twenty years later).

Nowell, Robert, *A Passion for Truth, Hans Küng, a Biography*, Collins, London, 1981 (believes that Küng is more sinned against than sinning).

Observer, The. Though its news editor once assured me that '*The Observer* is a humanist newspaper', it employed Patrick O'Donovan, the great, the good, to report on the Council.

Orga, Irfan and Margarete, *Atatürk*, Michael Joseph, London, 1962.

Orient Express, by John Dos Passos, Jonathan Cape, London, 1928 (vivid description of a journey on the famous train at the time when Roncalli began to use it regularly).

l'Osservatore Romano, Vatican daily. Indispensable. 'Compared with it', *The Economist* once wrote, '*Pravda* positively bristles with gossip'.

Owen, Wilfrid, 'Anthem for Doomed Youth', in *Poems since 1900*, Ed Colin Falck, Macdonald and Jane's, London, 1975, p. 69).

Panorama, 'Rapporti tra Moro e Giovanni XXIII', by Giancarlo Zizola, in two parts, May 10 and May 17 1982 (essential reading on Pope John and his relationship with Aldo Moro, then Secretary of the Christian Democrats; with unpublished documents provided by Capovilla).

Pasqua, 1976 = Pasqua di Risurrezione, Ed Loris Capovilla (Roncalli on the strike at Ranica in 1909 and his sermon, in the presence of the Fascists, in 1924 on the tenth anniversary of the death of Radini Tedeschi).

Pasqua, 1978 = Pasqua di risurrezione con Papa Giovanni XXIII, Ed Loris Capovilla (detailed chronicle and diary extracts from November 1952 to April 1953, from Paris to Venice).

Pastore = Giovanni XXIII, il Pastore, Ed by Giambattista Busetti, Messagero, Padua,

1980 (a revelation: Roncalli's correspondence from 1911 to 1963 with the diocesan religious congregation to which he belonged, the Priests of the Sacred Heart).

Pawley, Bernard and Margaret, *Rome and Canterbury through Four Centuries*, Mowbray, London, 1974 (the first 'personal representative of the Archbishop of Canterbury' at the Vatican joins with his Russian Orthodox wife to record his candid impressions).

Péguy, Charles, *Oeuvres Poétiques complètes*, Pléiade, Paris, 1948 (to understand the importance of Péguy in John's circle, here is a passage from Don Giuseppe De Luca in a letter to Mgr Loris Capovilla, January 29, 1962: 'Read Péguy. He is the greatest poet of socialism and then of Catholicism – but not the Catholicism of the "*curés*". You follow? The wife he loved was an unbeliever and wouldn't agree to a religious marriage, so he couldn't frequent the sacraments. But he used to walk around Paris saying his rosary, and made three pilgrimages on foot to Chartres. What a poet, monsignore, what a poet! . . . I send you a copy of his *Un nouveau théologien, M. Fernand Laudet*: it is the most ferocious and passionate Christian polemic of the last few centuries – perhaps since Dante'. In *Pur che l'alba nasca*, Ed Loris Capovilla, Grafica e Arte, Bergamo, 1983, pp. 4–5).

Pensiamo al Concilio, a Pastoral letter for Lent, 1962, by Cardinal Gianbattista Montini. Published by the Archdiocesan Press, Milan, 1962 (a bad English trans. is found in *The Church*, Palm Publishers, Montréal, 1964, pp. 149–92).

Pepper, Curtis Bill, *An Artist and the Pope, based upon the personal recollections of Giacomo Manzù*, Peter Davies, London, 1969 (the Communist sculptor from Bergamo was introduced to Pope John by Don Giuseppe De Luca; Manzù's memorial is seen in the new doors of St Peter's; *Newsweek's* contribution to the Pope John saga; it sure is vivid).

Per Crucem ad Lucem, Lettres Pastorales etc, by Cardinal Mercier, Bloud et Gay, Paris, no date but on internal evidence probably 1916 (though it was the Christmas 1914 pastoral, 'Patriotisme et endurance' that made Mercier the spokesman for 'gallant little Belgium', his Lent 1915 pastoral, called simply 'Pius X and Benedict XV' is a masterpiece of litotes in which, properly read, Pius X is largely demolished).

Politics = *The Politics of the Vatican*, by Peter Nichols, Frederick A. Praeger, New York, 1968 (the Rome correspondent of *The Times*, of London, presents the Vatican with his usual charm and perspicacity).

Pollard, John, *From the* Conciliazione *to the* Reconciliazione: *the Church and the Fascist Regime in Italy, 1929–1932* (PhD thesis in the University of Reading; due to be published by the Cambridge University Press; shows that the signing of the Lateran Pacts, far from making peace between Church and State, intensified the conflict).

Popes of the Twentieth Century, by Carlo Falconi, Weidenfeld and Nicolson, London, 1967 (Falconi, a priest who resigned from his ministry, retained the friendship of some of his peers; a witty, engaging, and often penetrating view of the Vatican in this century; officially frowned upon).

Poulat, Emile, *Catholicisme, Démocratie et Socialisme*, Casterman, Paris, 1977 (many unpublished documents and psychological analysis of Umberto Benigni, Roncalli's professor of Church History, who ran the anti-modernist spy ring).

Poulat, Emile, *Intégrisme et Catholicisme intégrale*, Casterman, Paris, 1969 (discusses, among other things, whether the historical study prepared for the beatification of Pius X was fairly conducted; concludes that it was not).

Poulat, Emile, *Naissance des Prêtres Ouvriers*, Casterman, Tournai, Belgium, 1965 (magisterial).

Poulat, Emile, appears again as a friend who has constantly encouraged this book which has aimed to match his high standards of evidence and argument.

Pravda, Soviet Party newspaper. Pope John made the page one headline on October 26, 1962. See p. 447 above.

Prima Synodus Romana, Vatican Polyglot Press, Rome, 1960 (a deservedly rare work containing the 755 decrees of what Pope John called, correctly, the First Roman Synod).

I Promessi Sposi, The Betrothed, see Manzoni, Alessandro.

Quale Papa? by Giancarlo Zizola, Borla, Rome, 1977 (apart from asking 'what kind of Pope is needed in what kind of Church in what kind of world' just before the death of Pope Paul VI, provides the best account of what happened in recent conclaves).

Quindicesimo anniversario = XV anniversario della morte di Papa Giovanni, Ed Loris Capovilla, Storia e Letteratura, 1978 (includes 33 unpublished letters 1918–57).

Ragionieri, Ernesto, *Storia d'Italia*, vol 4, *Dall'Unità a oggi*, tomo terzo, Giulio Einaudi, Turin, 1976 (the standard history of Italy for Italians; the accompanying volume of photographs is a revelation).

Ramsey, Archbishop Michael, made some interesting remarks about Cardinal Bea in a letter dated February 25, 1984.

Repubblica, La, Rome daily (except Monday) post-war, left-leaning.

Riccordi, Andrea, 'La Chiesa a Roma dalla Seconda Guerra Mondiale al Postconcilio', in *Il Regno*, Bologna, No. 5, 1982 (from 'sacred' city to secular city).

Righi, Vittore Ugo, *Papa Giovanni sulle rive del Bosforo*, Messagero, Padua, 1971, with preface by Loris Capovilla (detailed account of Roncalli's work in wartime Turkey and Greece; some unpublished texts; useful despite its persistently 'edifying' tone).

Rocca, La, magazine edited from Assisi by Don Giovanni Rossi.

Rosario = Il rosario con Papa Giovanni, Ed Loris Capovilla, Storia e Letteratura, Rome, 1979 (texts by Roncalli on mariological themes from his student days to the pontificate).

Rotundi, Virgilio, 'Padre Lombardi', in *Civiltà Cattolica*, February 2, 1980.

Rouquette, Robert, S.J., *Vatican II, la fin d'une Chrétienté*, 2 vols, Cerf, Paris, 1968 ('*chroniques*' republished from *Etudes* with afterthoughts; volume I is relevant to Pope John, and includes the famous essay '*Le Mystère Roncalli*' in which he attacked the 'personality cult' growing up around Pope John and denounced the danger of 'dreaming of a Church of angels presided over by angelic men').

Rynne – *Letters from Vatican City*, by Xavier Rynne, Farrar, Straus & Co, New York, and Faber and Faber, London, 1963 (based on his *New Yorker* articles, Rynne 'took the lid off' the Vatican; Fr Francis Xavier Murphy has never admitted to writing the book, but – with help – he did; his mother's maiden name was Rynne).

Saggio = *Giovanni e Paolo, due Papi, Saggio di Corrispondenza (1925–1962)*, Ed Loris Capovilla, published for the Istituto Paolo VI, Brescia by Studium, Rome, 1982 (91 items – letters, telegrams – exchanged between Roncalli and Montini; they had great respect for each other; it is highly unlikely that Pope John ever spoke about Montini's 'Hamletism').

Saturday Review, The.

Schillebeeckx, Edward, O.P., *Vatican II, a Struggle of Minds and other Essays*, Gill and trans of *Het ambts-celibaat in de branding*, Nelissen, Bilthoven, 1966 (not really vintage Schillebeeckx, but a good attempt to trawl the tradition).

Schillebeeckx, Edward, O.P., *Vatican II, a Struggle of Minds and other Essays*, Gill and Son, Dublin, 1964.

Schlesinger, Arthur M., jr, *Robert Kennedy and his Times*, Deutsch, London, 1978 (as the latest of the many Schlesinger books on the Kennedys one expected some mention of Pope John's role in the Cuban missile crisis: in vain).

SD = *Scritti e discorsi*, by Cardinal Angelo Giuseppe Roncalli, Edizioni Paoline, Rome, 1959–62 (the speeches and writings of Patriarch Roncalli in his Venice period; would probably have escaped publication had he not become Pope; the best of them are in Alberigo).

Secolo = *Papa Giovanni, un secolo*, by Loris Capovilla, Grafica e Arte, Bergamo, 1981 (a good reconstitution of Pope John's childhood on the hundredth anniversary of his birth; colour pictures of Sotto il Monte).

Seton-Watson, Christopher, *Italy from Liberalism to Fascism*, Methuen and Co, London, Barnes and Noble Inc., U.S.A., 1967 (the incomparable work on Italian political life between 1870 and 1925).

Siri, Cardinal Giuseppe, address to the Roman Synod on the 25th anniversary of the death of Pope Pius XII, October 9, 1983 (Vatican Press Office).

Snider, Carlo, *L'episcopato del cardinale Andrea Carlo Ferrari*, vol. I, Neri Pozza, Vicenza, 1981 (the first volume of an immense and learned work which will restore Ferrari to his historical context and rehabilitate him; Roncalli should appear in volume II).

Soldati, *La Messa dei Villeggianti*, Mondadori, Milan, 1959.

Spain = Central Intelligence Agency (CIA) staff memorandum No. 27–63, 'Change in the Church', by James W. Spain, May 13, 1963. Declassified March 9, 1978 (Spain wrote to the author on April 8, 1984, and explained how he came to write his report; he was an academic rather than a 'spy', and in any case he soon moved to the State Department).

Spiritual Profile, Ed by Stjepan Schmidt, S.J., Geoffrey Chapman, London, 1971 (notes from Cardinal Augustin Bea's spiritual diary; a labour of love from his former secretary).

St John-Stevas, Norman, *The Agonising Choice, Birth Control, Religion and the Law*, Eyre and Spottiswoode, London, 1971 (correctly traces the origins of the 'birth-control commission' to Pope John's pontificate though it was, so to speak, Cardinal Suenens' baby).

Stehle, *Eastern Politics of the Vatican 1917–1978*, Ohio University Press, Athens, Ohio, 1981; trans with additional material of *Die Ostpolitik des Vatikans*, Piper, Munich,

1975 (a scrupulous and solid work, with much original material, from a reporter who was in Warsaw before going to Rome; not well served by his translator, who ominously gets the title wrong: it should be *policy*).

Tempo, Il, right-wing Roman daily.

Tillard, Jean, O.P., *The Bishop of Rome*, SPCK, London, 1983 (documents the various 'titles' of the pope, and confirms from history the rightness of many of Pope John's intuitions).

Time, New York.

Tomlin, E. W. F., shared his memories of war-time Istanbul.

Tramontin, Silvio, *Un secolo di storia della Chiesa*, 2 vols, Studium, Rome, 1980 (a calm and balanced survey of the last century of Catholic Church history; Italy-centred, but not obsessively so).

Transizione = *Giovanni XXIII, Papa di Transizione*, Ed Loris Capovilla, Storia e Letteratura, Rome, 1979 (Capovilla reflects on the irony of the sobriquet, 'transitional Pope', and in an interview comments on some of the problems posed by John's pontificate; then texts on Pope John from, among others, Albino Luciani – the future Pope John Paul I, Paul VI, Marie-Dominique Chenu and the novelist Mario Soldati).

Trevor, Meriol, *Pope John*, Macmillan, London, 1967 (on the basis of the material available at that time, the best biography in English).

Tucci, Roberto, S.J., my first *maestro* in Vaticanology now – in 1984 – director of Vatican Radio; would have been embarrassed if this book had been dedicated to him – as it ought to have been.

Unity of Christians = *The Unity of Christians*, by Cardinal Augustin Bea, Ed Bernard Leeming S.J., introduced by Archbishop Gerald P. O'Hara, Apostolic Delegate in Great Britain, Geoffrey Chapman, May 1963 (the publication of this book just before Pope John died was an important event, intended to make ecumenism acceptable in the English-speaking world; Bea never wrote a proper book, and these occasional pieces, lectures, radio and TV interviews gain enormously in interest when read in historical context; the original *Civiltà Cattolica* edition bore the title, *L'Unione dei Cristiani*, which is subtly different).

L'Uomo che non divenne Papa, by Carlo Falconi (this *roman à clef* is a useful complement to the same author's *Popes of the Twentieth Century*).

Utopia = *L'Utopia di Papa Giovanni*, by Giancarlo Zizola, Cittadella Editrice, Assisi, 1973, second edition; trans *The Utopia of Pope John XXIII*, translated by Helen Barolini, Orbis Books, New York, 1978 (persuaded me that with help from Mgr Loris Capovilla, a biography of Pope John was perfectly feasible; it is a splendid, passionate and somewhat disorderly book; unfortunately the English translation is so bad as to be unreadable and unusable; so whichever edition is referred to, I have always retranslated).

Vent'Anni = *Vent'Anni dalla Elezione di Giovanni XXIII*, Ed Loris Capovilla, Storia e Letteratura, Rome, 1978 (the conclave and the first three months of John's pontificate, illumined through his private diaries).

Villain, Maurice, *Introduction a l'Oecuménisme*, Casterman, Paris, 1961 (veteran
    ecumenist who wrote the life of the abbé Paul Couturier, founder of ecumenism in
    France, and translated Lancelot Andrewes into French).
Vito e Pensiero, monthly review of the Catholic University of the Sacred Heart, Milan.

Wall, Bernard, *A City and a World, a Roman Sketchbook*, Weidenfeld and Nicolson,
    London, 1962 (observations of an English man of letters with good portrait of
    Cardinal Domenico Tardini).
Walsh, Michael, librarian at Heythrop College, London, chased up every
    bibliographical enquiry and offered me space in which to work.
Wasserstein, Bernard, *Britain and the Jews of Europe 1939–1945*, Clarendon Press,
    Oxford, 1980 (punctures British self-esteem).
Weber, Francis J., 'Pope Pius XII and the Vatican Council', in *The American
    Benedictine Review*, September 1970 (has a useful bibliography: its chief interest,
    however, is that it provides a remarkable illustration of the arch-conservative thesis
    that Vatican II was 'really' the dream-child of Pius XII: thanks to Dom Alberic
    Stacpoole O.S.B. for drawing my attention to it).
Wenger, Antoine, A. A., *Vatican II, Chronique de la première session*, Centurion, Paris,
    1963 (best account of the first session in any language, which was hardly surprising
    since the author, the Editor of *La Croix*, was the only journalist inside St Peter's; he
    also chanced to be a scholar with a good knowledge of Orthodoxy).
West, Morris, *The Salamander*, Heinemann, London, 1973 (a fictional account of the
    failed *coup* of General De Lorenzo in 1964; see Collin, Richard).
Willebrands, Cardinal Jan, '*Papa Giovanni e l'ecumenismo*', lecture at the Lateran
    University, Rome, November 10, 1981, MS (quotes and gives evidence for Dr
    Visser 't Hooft's statement: 'I am convinced that Pope John will go down in
    history as the pope who made dialogue possible').
Williams, George Huntston, *The Mind and Heart of Pope John Paul II*, Seabury Press,
    New York, 1981 (a gallant attempt to understand Karol Wojtyla with much useful
    material on inter-war Poland).
Woodhouse, C. M., *Modern Greece, a Short History*, Faber, London, 1968.
Worlock, Archbishop Derek, 'The Sharing Church', in *The Tablet*, October 9, 1982,
    pp. 1005–6 (a short, amusing, and ill-titled article); also '*Aggiornamento* in Embryo,
    Vatican II to date', in *The Wiseman Review* (formerly *The Dublin Review*), Winter,
    1963–4, pp. 316–34 (Archbishop Worlock has also consulted his memories and
    answered my questions on the Council and its preparation; but he prefers his
    presence to be like that of 'the Scarlet Pimpernel').

Zizola, Giancarlo, see *Panorama* and *Utopia*. In *Oggi*, April 13, 1983, he reported on
    the present state of the beatification cause (historical work completed; miracles
    abounding in Italy). It is fitting that the alphabet permits me to end with thanks to
    Zizola who not only completed my education in Vaticanology but gave me the run
    of his Rome apartment and his remarkable collection of books.

The Roman Curia at the start of the Council, October 1962

Pope John XXIII, 81

Papal Household
Mgr Igino Cardinale, 47, Chief of protocol
Mgr Loris F. Capovilla, 48, private secretary

Curial Departments (Dicasteries)	Conciliar Commissions etc.
Seminaries and Universities Card. Giuseppe Pizzardo, 86 Sec. Abp Dino Staffa, 57	*Seminary Studies and Catholic Education,*[1] Pizzardo Sec. Fr Augustin Meyer OSB
Rites (= Liturgy) Card. Arcadio Larroana, 76 Sec. Abp Enrico Dante, 79	*Liturgy,* Larroana[2] Sec. Fr Ferdinando Antonelli OFM
Religious Card. Valerio Valeri, 80	*Religious,* Valeri Sec. Fr Giuseppe Rousseau OMI
Discipline of the Sacraments (dispensations etc.) Card. Benedetto Masella, 84	*Sacraments,* Masella Sec. Fr Raimondo Bidagor SJ
Oriental Churches (i.e. Uniates) Card. Gustavo Testa, 77	*Oriental Churches*[3] Pres. Card. Amleto Cicognani (made up mostly of Oriental patriarchs)
Consistorial Congregation (selected bishops) Card. Carlo Confalonieri, 70	*Bishops and Dioceses* Pres. Card. Paolo Marella, 68
Secretariat of State[4] Card. Amleto Cicognani, 80 Sec. Abp Antonio Samorè, 58 Under Sec. Abp Agostino Casaroli, 49 Substitute Abp Angelo Dell'Acqua, 60	

The Holy Office
Card. Alfredo Ottaviani, 73
Sec. Abp Pietro Parente, 72

Congregation of the Council
(i.e. Trent: deals with priests and
catechisms)
Card. Pietro Ciriaci, 78
Sec. Abp Pietro Palazzini, 51

Propaganda Fide
(i.e. missionary work)
Card. Pietro Agagianian, 68
Abp Pietro Sigismondi, 55

On the Doctrine of Faith and Morals[5]
Pres. Ottaviani
Vice-pres. Card. Michael Browne OP, 68

*On the Discipline of the Clergy and the
Christian people*
Pres. Ciriaci
Sec. Fr Alvaro del Portillo, Opus Dei

Missions, Pres. Agagianian[6]
Sec. Mgr Saverio Paventi

Secretariat for Christian Unity[7]
Pres. Card. Augustin Bea SJ, 81
Sec. Mgr Jan Willibrands, 54
also Mgr Jean-François Arrighi
Fr Tom Stransky CSP

Commission 'For the Lay Apostolate'[8]
Pres. Card. Fernando Cento, 80
Sec. Mgr Achille Glorieux

Secretariat of the Council[9]
Abp Pericle Felici, 52

Secretariat for Extraordinary Affairs[10]
(Cardinals Siri, Wyszynski, Montini,
Confalonieri, Döpfner, Meyer and
Suenens)

Notes

1. Produced *Veterum Sapientia*: theology to be taught in Latin.
2. Drew up only draft to survive first session.
3. Produced draft on Church unity – heavily criticised, hastily withdrawn.
4. Not formally involved in the Council, but Cicognani, Secretary of State, was President of the co-ordinating work and in overall charge of the Council.
5. Produced 4 draft texts – all rejected. 'Two Sources of Revelation' treated with great severity. Yet claimed a veto over all texts.
6. Concentrated on logistic and financial problems of housing some 800 Missionary Bps.
7. Decisive in shaping the Council. After struggle, attains parity with Holy Office – works on Church and the relationship to other Christians, hosts the 'Observers'.
8. Timidly considers lay participation (by 1963); controls dealings with the media.
9. Brings order out of chaos and keeps the paper moving.
10. This body rather than the Council of Presidents took the vital decisions in consultation with Pope John.

Index

Acton, Lord, 'look at the process', 38; on clashes at Trent, 435

Ad Beatissimi (first encyclical of Benedict XV), 78

Adenauer, Chancellor Konrad, *Time* lunch, 469; mistrusts Khrushchev, 478

Ad Petri Cathedram (J.'s first encyclical), 332–4, 381

Adzhubei, Alexis (Khrushchev's son-in-law), visit to Rome and Pope, 480–3; in line with J.'s ministry, 492

Aeterni Dei (J.'s encyclical on St Leo the Great), 396

Agagianian, Card. Pietro, R.'s rival in conclave, 275; 'went up and down like two chickpeas', 282; on J.'s 80th birthday, 394; last homage, 495–6

Agostini, Carlo, Patriarch of Venice, 232

Aimé-Azam, Denise, on R.'s preaching, 204; 213, 219

Alberigo, Giuseppe, on Rome Synod as 'sop' to Curia, 348; best study of opening address to Council, 430

Alexander VI, Pope, 198

Alexis, Moscow Patriarch, 418

Alfrink, Card. Bernard (Utrecht), 'heartfelt words', 400; leads attack on Ottaviani, 402; on 'Council of Presidents', 441

Algisi, Leone, 282

Aloysius Gonzaga, St, 23, 40

Alphonsus Liguori, St, on suppression of Jesuits, 67

Ambrose, St, baptises Augustine, 20; 198; *mandatum* comes from Milan, 452

Ancel, Bp Alfred (auxiliary of Lyons), works on 'message for the world', 445; pessimistic, 454

Andreotti, Giulio, panegyric of Borgongini Duca, 252; summoned by R. on eve of conclave, 279–80; informed in advance about Council, 318–19; jokes about Moro, 365

Annigoni, Pietro, J.'s portrait, 468

Anthony, St, teeth intact at 105, 256

Anthony Arida, Maronite Patriarch, 92 years old, 252

Arendt, Hannah, the 'banality' of evil, 194

Arriba y Castro, Card. Benjamin (Tarragona), 281

Arrighi, Mgr Jean-François, 'that man has faith', 285; link with French theologians, 328–9; first moots idea of Secretariat for Unity, 328; J. practises collegiality, 329

Arrigoni, Bp Giulio (Lucca), diary of Vatican I, 495

Atatürk (Mustafa Kemal), 140; modernises, secularises Turkey, 145–6; death, 153, 157; made Ankara capital, 171

Athenagoras, Ecumenical Patriarch, Paul VI's visit to him pre-figured, 158; 'a man, sent from God, his name is John', 421

Augustine of Hippo, St, baptised in Milan, 20; *City of God*, 57; R. resolves to reread, 184; on reading Bible, 262; on Christian brothers, 334; quoted, 349, 381; on Scripture, 451; on peace and order, 470; *City of God* transformed, 470–1; peace based on justice, 487; on John the Baptist and the dawn, 496

525